die Familie (-n)

die Mutter
der Vater
die Eltern
das Kind (Kinder)
die Tochter (Töchter)
der Sohn (Söhne)
die Schwester (Schwestern)
der Bruder (Brüder)
der Onkel
die Tante

Groß- = grand-

Ur- = great-

Schwieger- + _____ = _____ -.

(or use der/die X von
{
mein _____
dein _____
sein _____
etc.
} Y)

cousin: der Vetter (-n), die Kusine (-n)
grandchild: das Enkelkind (der Enkel, die Enkelin)
relative: der Verwandte, die Verwandte plural: die Verwandten
die Angehörigen (kin)

ledig (noch nicht verheiratet) verheiratet   geschieden (nicht mehr verheiratet)

der Körper

der Kopf
das Haar (Haare)
das Auge (Augen)
  die Brille
  die Kontaktlinse(n)
das Ohr (Ohren)
die Nase
der Mund   die Lippe (-n)
der Zahn (Zähne)
das Kinn
der Hals

die Schulter (Schultern)
die Brust (Brüste)
der Arm (Arme)
die Hand (Hände)
der Finger (-)
stomach: der Bauch (external)
der Magen (internal organ)
die Rippe (-n)
das Gesäß, der Po, der Hintern
das Bein (Beine)
der Fuß (Füße)
die Zehe (-n)

das ____ bein = ____ bone
organs: das Herz   die Lunge   die Leber

For other parts: Use the official medical term,
but with German pronunciation.

How to keep a conversation going

Wie, bitte?
Echo statements in a questioning tone.
Und?   Und dann?   Und was ist dann passiert?
Aber + expectant pause.
Wie?
Warum (nicht)?
. . . zum Beispiel?
Ich verstehe das/Sie/dich nicht.
Könn(t)en Sie das bitte erklären/beschreiben?
Wie meinen Sie das?
Was glauben Sie?
Aber wenn . . .

die Kleidung, die Kleider

der Hut (Hüte)
der Mantel (Mäntel)
die Jacke (-n)
der Pullover (-)
die Krawatte (-en)
das Hemd (-en)
die Bluse (-n)
  button: der Knopf (Knöpfe)
die Hose or die Hosen
  belt: der Gürtel (-)
dress: das Kleid (-er)
skirt: der Rock (Röcke)
der Strumpf (Strümpfe); die Socke (-n)
der Schuh (-e)
suit: men's—der Anzug (Anzüge)
  women's—das Kostüm (-e)
diaper: cloth—die Windel (-n)
  disposable—Wegwerfwindel (-n),
    das Höschen (-)

Tag und Datum

der Tag (-e)

Sonntag	So	das Wochenende der Wochentag weekday
Montag	Mo	der Werktag workday (includes Samstag!)
Dienstag	Di	
Mittwoch	Mi	What? Heute ist der _____ (s)te (month).
Donnerstag	Do	When? Ich bin am _____ (s)ten (month) geboren.
Freitag	Fr	Since when? Ich wohne seit _____ Jahr(en) in (city).
Samstag	Sa	

Write dates numerically as day. month. year (4.7 = July 4)

die Farbe (-n)

weiß ————→ rosa ←———— rot

hell   orange   purpurn
grau   braun
      dunkel   gelb   blau
schwarz
                    grün

Wie, bitte?

„Ich zahle mit POSTCHEQUE"

BITTE
nicht füttern

50 DDR
LEIPZIGER FRÜHJAHRSMESSE 1986

FREIWILLIG
80/100
DEM WALD ZULIEBE

Gleis 4   Karlsplatz

KÖLNER DOM
Turmbesteigung
Eintritt 1,-- DM
Waren Sie schon in der
Domschatzkammer?
Röbla, Gütersloh
02272

ANNOTATED
INSTRUCTOR'S EDITION

Wie, bitte?

INTRODUCTORY GERMAN
FOR PROFICIENCY

William B. Fischer
Portland State University

Peter N. Richardson
Linfield College

WILEY

JOHN WILEY & SONS
New York   Chichester   Brisbane   Toronto   Singapore

ISBN 0-471-84922-7

Printed in the United States of America

10 9 8 7 6 5 4 3 2 1

Instructor's Guide Contents

Overview

Sprache ist Verhalten in einer Situation. Spielend löst man
sich aus der Situation.

HARALD WEINRICH,
Tempus: besprochene und erzählte Welt

Wie, bitte? has but one purpose: the promotion of proficiency and practical competence in elementary German. To our minds, there is nothing more important in our field than the teaching of introductory German, and we have found – as we hope you, our colleagues, will also find – that there is nothing more challenging or rewarding.

Wie, bitte? seeks to promote proficiency. The modern notion of proficiency is reflected not only in its theoretical orientation, but also in its major structural features, its smallest details, and in the conception of the teaching techniques that we consider appropriate to the package. Oral proficiency is emphasized, in part because oral proficiency is vital to communication in most realistic situations, and in part because a talking classroom is a happy and productive classroom. But the *Wie, bitte?* package also carefully seeks to nurture skill in reading and listening, those skills often termed "passive" or "recognition." The collection of visual and aural realia is rich, and the material is actively employed. As for writing proficiency, we have tried to encourage the notion that writing in a foreign language means far more than using a pen or pencil to perform grammar, vocabulary, and dictation exercises, or to write intellectual essays.

The *Wie, bitte?* package is tightly integrated. The various linguistic skills or modalities are not merely cultivated individually but also developed jointly. Nor is the cultural aspect of language neglected; we have striven to provide the student with an insight into many features of German culture – with "culture" understood in the broadest sense of the word, and yet with a concentration on material of lasting importance rather than ephemeral popularity. Above all, we have sought to show how closely language and culture are interrelated.

SUMMARY OF MATERIALS

Wie, bitte? comprises the following resources:

1. The Class Text is a medium-length book intended for intensive use in the proficiency-oriented classroom. Model dialogs and contextual communication tasks are prominent. Grammar is presented by pattern and brief comment rather than by analytic exposition. Vocabulary is presented in highly visual, thematic displays; there is also a German-English glossary. A section of "recyclable" realia provides resources for situation exercises and texts for reading practice. The end papers offer ready reference materials.

2. The Study Text is a workbook intended for individual use primarily outside the classroom, but also useful in it. The volume contains: 1) an orientation, with advice on study methods; 2) chapter-by-chapter exercises in the various proficiency modalities and in analytic grammar; 3) English renditions of the Class Text dialogs; 4) chapter vocabulary lists; 5) a reference grammar, to whose various sections the student is directed by marginal annotations in the brief grammar presentations in the Class Text; and (6) a collection of recyclable realia which parallels that in the Class Text.

The Study Text is an integral part of the package. It contains many resources that are ordinarily found in the main "textbooks" of conventional packages.

3. The tape set is divided into two parts: 1) renditions and expansions of the textbook dialogs; 2) aural realia and cultural offerings, organized by theme and linguistic structure; these items are the material for homework exercises, for some listening tests, and for cultural enrichment.

The development of listening comprehension with taped materials is an integral part of the package. The student must use the tapes when working with the Study Text, and the model syllabus envisions the use of tapes (or live renditions of the dialogs) in class.

4. The Test Bank contains: 1) materials for proficiency-oriented speaking, listening, reading, and writing tests; 2) answer keys or guidelines for those tests and for selected Study Text exercises; 3) a set of recyclable realia that parallel those in the Class Text and Study Text and are therefore suitable for use in the tests provided in the manual; they can also be used in exercises and tests that the teacher devises. The construction of proficiency-oriented tests requires considerable effort, and it would be inadvisable to teach from *Wie, bitte?* while still intending to rely primarily on conventional tests of grammar-transformation ability and vocabulary memorization.

5. The computer software includes: 1) contextualized listening, reading, and writing exercises; 2) computerized versions of tests in the testing manual; 3) administrative software intended to aid the teacher in record-keeping, test administration, and development of auxiliary materials. Supported computers are the IBM PC and compatibles, Apple IIe/c/gs, and the Macintosh; for the last there is special courseware with natural speech recorded digitally on the disks.

Pedagogical Orientation

Wie, bitte? can be used by teachers espousing many different teaching methods. Its subtitle, however, makes clear our commitment and debt to the ideas of language proficiency developed by colleagues formally or informally associated with the U.S. Government Interagency Language Roundtable (ILR), the American Council on the Teaching of Foreign Languages (ACTFL), and the Educational Testing Service (ETS). The ILR/ACTFL/ETS concepts of linguistic competence and methods of evaluating it, though they were decades in development, began to invigorate our profession so much just a few years ago. Here we can only summarize that work, particularly as it applies to our first-year German package; the interested reader is referred to the publications listed in the bibliography below.

Central to the ILR/ACTFL/ETS notion of proficiency is practical knowledge of the language, the ability, that is, to use it effectively for communication. That notion of competence does not at all deny the usefulness of analytic knowledge of the language, or grammar in the traditional sense. But it does suggest that in language instruction such knowledge should not be an end, as it has often been made in our classes and our textbooks, but rather a means. Here we might note that, whatever language teachers have done in the classroom, this concept of proficiency lies close to our hearts, and to those of our students. We all want to be able to use the language.

It is, or at least has been, far easier to test and to attempt to teach analytic knowledge of a foreign language than it is to teach and test for genuine proficiency. A worthy achievement in itself has been the evolution of the proficiency guidelines now widely familiar to our profession. Their chief feature is the careful description of proficiency by profiles that take into account function, context, and accuracy. Equally beneficial has been the evolution of corresponding testing methods, particularly for oral proficiency, but lately also for listening, reading, and writing. Thus the "oral proficiency interview" is a widely known register of language proficiency, though still not commonly part of mass instruction programs – and for good reason, since such oral testing is extremely labor-intensive.

A more controversial aspect of the ILR/ACTFL/ETS work in language proficiency has been the transformation of standards of measurement into descriptions of and prescriptions for language acquisition. In other words, do the proficiency guidelines constitute a syllabus for language instruction, rather than just a methodologically neutral description of performance? In offering *Wie, bitte?* we share the view of those who have declared that the proficiency guidelines can indeed be a learning syllabus, and that there is nothing wrong with "teaching for the test," if the test and the teaching are both proficiency-oriented.

Our fundamental attitude, then, is this: We share the sentiments of language teachers who preach the gospel of competence. We prize students who say, "When I go there I want to understand them and I want them to understand me." We regret that all too many students recall their study of foreign languages by saying, "I had four years of it, and I can't now and never could say anything." To put it another way: The fundamental premise of *Wie, bitte?* is that if we are going to preach language competence, then we must teach it; if we are going to teach it, then we must test it; and if we are going to preach and teach and test it, then we must grade for it. But we need not regard that prospect as depressing. Instead, it permits us to entertain the notion that we might actually do what we want to do, and that is to teach, in the truest sense of the word.

What are the general implications of the ILR/ ACTFL/ETS work for *Wie, bitte?*

1. It has become evident that the traditional first-year text, which attempts to offer in one year "all" (whatever that means) of German grammar, envisions an inordinately high level of grammatical competence. Typically, such texts culminate well in the ACTFL/ ETS Superior level (= ILR 4). Although it is possible to lead some students through carefully targeted exercises with such features as the special subjunctive or the past perfect passive, in a genuine proficiency test even an excellent first-year German student, taught under favorable circumstances, is unlikely to rate higher than Intermediate-High (= ILR 1+) in speaking or writing. The magnitude of the discrepancy is enormous, since the progression between proficiency levels is described by an ever-steepening curve. One notes that Advanced-Plus/ILR 2+ in speaking has been proposed as a target level for graduating language majors and prospective high school teachers.

Consequently, in *Wie, bitte?* we have lowered the target level considerably. For the speaking modality, the aim of the text is to produce from the best students a proficiency performance of Intermediate-High. Since that level in turn requires rich but not constant demonstration of Advanced performance, the grammatical material intended for occasional production – but *not* mastery – culminates low in the ACTFL/ETS Superior (= ILR 3) level, with heavy concentration at the Advanced (= ILR 2) level. The communicative functions and contexts of *Wie, bitte?* are consonant with its grammatical level. Indeed, we outlined the package in terms of function and context, and then wrote many of its nuclear dialogs, before they determined the details of its grammatical syllabus.

The *Proficiency Guidelines* also lead one to conclude that the traditional first-year package, whatever its ultimate target level, may well neglect the student's development at the very lowest proficiency levels, levels that would seem to be vital way-stations in the quest for higher proficiency. It is our impression that there is too little active work with simple echoing, transcription, list-making, and note-taking; that survival vocabulary, phrases, and everyday cultural knowledge are neglected; and that emphasis on generation of complex grammatical patterns has suppressed instruction in practical discourse strategy and the use of intelligence, common sense, and real-world knowledge.

The lowering of target level and increased attention to the lowest levels of proficiency should not be regarded as implying a lowering of standards. The change represents, instead, a shift from discrete-point instruction of analytic knowledge to teaching and testing of genuine proficiency. We believe that proficiency-oriented instruction and testing can remove some of the major frustrations of our profession. The results of proficiency-oriented theory and research impel us toward a revision of target levels, but they also open to us the prospect of enforcing our standards more rigorously.

2. Very important in the idea of proficiency are the concepts of *function* and *context:* what communicative task the language user undertakes to do and under what circumstances. The third ingredient, *accuracy* – or grammar, in the expanded sense of "structural competence" – completes the description. According to the *Guidelines,* the Advanced or ILR 2 speaker of German, for example, is "able to satisfy routine social demands and limited school or work requirements. Can handle with confidence but not with facility most social and general conversations. Can narrate, describe and explain in past, present, and future time." Thus it is not sufficient merely to set standards in purely grammatical terms, to introduce and demand, say, "the past tense." One must specify, rather, what genuinely communicative act the student/user/speaker is to be taught and expected to perform with the past tense, and under which conditions, and with what degree of precision. Thus the Advanced or ILR 2 speaker of German can, among other things, reliably express facts (past, present, or future) about concrete topics in a manner understandable to native speakers not used to dealing with foreigners. Still more specifically, in an oral proficiency interview such a speaker will exhibit a rich stock of past participles, with choice of *haben* or *sein* correct most of the time, and also produce many regular and irregular verbs in the imperfect, and among the latter of course the modals especially.

The adoption of a proficiency-oriented curriculum has immense implications for testing. The traditional grammar-translation test cannot remain the mainstay of evaluation, though it may still have some value as a preparatory exercise, as a check of analytic and monitoring skills, and even as a nose-to-the-grindstone prod. Instead, at least some testing, and certainly the ultimate evaluation of proficiency, must be conducted in a way that indeed measures the ability to carry out useful communicative tasks in the several modalities. Here volumes could be written, and indeed have been (see the Bibliography). Sample tests are provided below, and the optional test bank and software contain a basic stock of tests for the entire course.

The principles that govern proficiency testing are clear. The test should gauge functional ability, not analytic or intellectual knowledge; thus one poses a task like "Tell me about that great weekend in Köln," rather than demanding, item by item, the conjugation of various verbs in the past tense, the replacement of nouns with pronouns, or the translation of English sentences into German sentences. A corollary is that it may often be advantageous to pose tasks in English, rather than German, to hinder translation attempts and to avoid revealing target structures and vocabulary. Second, the German that students encounter in tests should be quite realistic, though of course selected to fit the anticipated proficiency level. In oral tests the examiner should maintain normal intonation and pace, and reading and listening tests should incorporate *realia* as soon as possible. Third, error evaluation should consider the actual communicative effect of the error and should seek to ascertain the level of consistent performance, rather than fix on idiosyncratic highs or lows in production over a short period. Fourth, if the tests have been designed to mimic "real-world" conditions, one should have no qualms about "teaching to the test" or, of course, testing what has been taught, with regard to either the manner or the content of the test. Students who have several times energetically practiced negotiating for a hotel room or talking about their special interests deserve tests that give them the opportunity to demonstrate their proficiency in carrying out such practical tasks as negotiating for a hotel room or talking about their special interests. As concerns the actual format of tests and their relation to the *Wie, bitte?* exercise materials, we have

sought to make the tests and the exercises very similar; thus the Class Text *Situationen* bear a close resemblance to the situation cards used in the standard oral proficiency interview.

3. Explicit reference to the "four skills" of speaking, listening, reading, and writing has been common for years. But often speaking became a matter of pattern-parroting, writing was exercised in the form of sentence transformation or else high-level essayistic composition, and the so-called "passive" modalities of listening and reading were neglected or trivialized into exercises with vapid synthetic language. The ILR/ACTFL/ETS proficiency concept, with its emphasis on context and its detailed guidelines for each modality, transforms listening and reading into active skills, with the further demand that the student be evaluated according to performance with genuine language materials. Writing skill is viewed as the ability to communicate effectively when performing realistic tasks, such as filling out a hotel registration form (Novice-High/ILR 0 +), writing a simple postcard (Intermediate-Low/ILR 1), or composing a short personal letter (Advanced/ILR 2). The evaluation of speaking skill through the conversational oral proficiency interview is, of course, a widely familiar feature of proficiency evaluation and needs no further discussion at this point.

But a fifth ingredient or "modality" should indeed be mentioned – "culture," or the evidence of knowledge of the society as it appears in the use of the language. Here the most important effects of the proficiency concept are, first, the broadening of the notion of "culture" from the very restricted "highbrow" notion of *Kultur* still present in many German programs, and, second, the suggestion of a hierarchy of cultural-linguistic proficiency that is described in terms of function, context/content, and accuracy, and whose levels parallel those of the other modalities. Thus the Intermediate language user, for example, has among other similar skills a survival-level stock of greeting and leave-taking utterances, knows how to provide addresses in German form, knows where to buy basic consumer items, and understands the *Sie/du* distinction; the Advanced student demonstrates, for example, guest etiquette, ability to apologize, and basic use of telephone; near-native competence is typified by detailed use of geographical and historical knowledge, perception of allusions and paralinguistic clues, and flexibility of speech register.

4. A distinctive feature of the modern concept of proficiency is the perception that many linguistic phenomena treated as single topics in the traditional grammatical syllabus are in fact complex congeries of functional and contextual competences that are distributed over a considerable range in the proficiency scale. Thus the past tense, for example, is not a discrete entity that can or should be "done" (= analytically processed) in some neatly bounded section of a textbook. Instead, elements of a past tense may be learned lexically quite early, followed perhaps by a systematic and generally effective, if flawed, notion of morphology and usage, and then a more sophisticated analytical comprehension and practical management of the tense. The graphical analog of language acquisition, then, is not a neat curve but rather a spiral; the learner climbs higher, but at the same time always dips back down for refreshment, expansion, and refinement of skill in linguistic behaviors that the proficiency-oriented pedagogue understands to be disparate functional and contextual phenomena. Those same phenomena the analytic grammarians, and with them the conventional language textbooks, lumped together into a single decontextualized, function-blind intellectual mass, one that foreign language students have indeed found hard to swallow.

The overriding structural principle of *Wie, bitte?* is not sequential presentation of discrete, conceptually neat blocks of grammar-oriented material (e.g., "Chapter 4: dative case," or "Chapter 17: the present perfect"). Instead, the program employs the "spiral syllabus." Communicative *function* has priority over grammatical *form*. The student gets what is needed for the communicative task, and care is taken both to encourage review and to introduce, at first tacitly, features that will later be presented more analytically. Thus a given grammatical feature, such as the dative pronouns, may be addressed in several distinctly separated chapters, first as a gently insinuated "lexical" item or element of a stock phrase ("*Bitte, bringen Sie uns . . .*"), then in the overt presentation of high-frequency dative pronouns, then in the comprehensive presentation of the full system of dative pronouns. The treatment of dative pronouns will overlap as well with the use of other elements that involve dative case, for example articles and prepositions. Similarly, work with the reading or listening materials might expose the student quite early to structures that, like the preterite, are dealt with systematically only in the later chapters of the text.

It will be noted that the grammatical content or level for a given chapter is not neutral with regard to modality. That is, it is not assumed that the student will encounter and work with similar structures in all the modalities at the same time. Instead, we pose listening and reading tasks that are aimed at higher levels of proficiency than the speaking and writing tasks. Thus the grammatical content or target level of a given chapter should be understood to be the grammar that is presented for emulation in the "active" or "production" modalities of speaking, primarily, but also writing. It may be expected that the student will long since have encountered listening and reading realia that include those same structures. Correspondingly, the *Struktur* pages with their associated Reference Grammar sections are keyed largely to the target level for speaking and writing, though the exposition in the Reference Grammar will often expand the current topic with higher-level material. We consider that policy legitimate for two reasons: 1) The student is thereby exposed in a preliminary and as it were "passive" way to structures that will later be presented for "active" use. 2) Genuine comprehension of authentic reading or listening materials is not based on discrete-point management or translation of vocabulary or grammar, but rather on the parallel and recursive processing of interrelated linguistic materials that constitute the bits and pieces of a larger whole. Thus the reader may functionally "understand" a segment of language as having a past sense, not necessarily by recognizing its past tense(s), but rather by noting time phrases, or even numerical data, that seem to point toward past time. It should go without saying that, in constructing exercises with such material, nowhere do we demand performance that can be achieved only with knowledge of structures that have not yet been presented for use in the "active" modalities.

5. With regard to teaching technique, the orthodox formulation of the proficiency notion claims to be methodologically neutral. And indeed, as testing tools the *Guidelines* and the associated techniques used to elicit language samples for evaluation do not pass judgment on how the examinee has acquired any proficiency that is demonstrated, other than to suggest rather pointedly but also rather generally that, for example, a student who has not been accorded much opportunity to speak will likely do poorly on an oral proficiency test. But the *Guidelines*, and those persons who have been associated with them, do not ordinarily state a positive preference for, say, the Total Physical Response method, as opposed to the Silent Way. Yet it is not too difficult to perceive that the notion of proficiency is hostile to certain individual techniques encountered frequently in our classrooms and exhibited rather prominently in the popular image of foreign-language teaching. Such techniques include, for example, presentation of detailed analytic grammar in the target language, rote pattern drills, and stringent error correction regardless of the functional importance of the error. Consequently, later in the Introduction we present a detailed discussion of teaching techniques we consider appropriate to the *Wie, bitte?* package.

Such principles have determined the overall structure and content of the *Wie, bitte?* package. We turn now to its more specific features.

The Materials and Their Use

We again remark that the *Wie, bitte?* package does *not* consist of a main text supported by more or less optional workbook, tapes, and so on. The Class Text, considerably shorter than most first-year books, has two main functions: 1) it is a handbook and resource center for the proficiency-oriented classroom, in which active use of language, particularly in speaking, is paramount; 2) the terse *Struktur* or grammar pages demonstrate, always with provision for immediate communicative practice, the chief grammatical targets of the chapter, with reference codes directing the student to study the expositions of grammar *outside* the classroom. Thus the Class Text does *not* focus on the elaboration or exercise of grammar in the traditional sense, though the Class Text and the *Wie, bitte?* package as a whole indeed do demand and further competence in grammar.

The Study Text has complementary functions, and in fact the student working outside the classroom will often find it convenient to have the two books open side by side. Where the Class Text will always be used intensively in the classroom, with the Study Text as an occasional resource, the Study Text is intended to be used intensively in study outside the classroom, with the Class Text as a secondary resource. Thus the Study Text has many functions: 1) It conducts the student through listening, reading, and writing exercises. 2) It prepares the student for speaking in the classroom. 3) Its Reference Grammar, accessed by codes on the Class Text *Struktur* pages, presents analytic grammar and could indeed serve as a concise survey of German grammar throughout the student's study of the language. 4) It offers contextualized analytic grammar exercises. 5) It provides extra realia and "props" for use both in and outside the classroom. 6) It includes renditions of the Class Text dialogs and chapter-by-chapter German-English vocabulary lists.

As for its thematic structure or "plot," *Wie, bitte?* is organized around a fairly typical trip to Germany, with entrance from the northwest, a stopover in Aachen, a short stay in Köln, a trip down the Rhine to Freiburg, a lengthier or even indefinite stay in München, and then sidetrips elsewhere within countries where German is spoken. We chose that framework not because we wished to write a "German for Travelers" text (though for some users *Wie, bitte?* might well have such a *vade mecum* use, with our blessing), nor simply because that pattern, augmented with a rich assortment of materials from East Germany, Austria, and Switzerland, does indeed conduct the student-traveler on a grand tour of the realm in which German is spoken.

Instead, we considered the needs and likely behavior of one who enters, survives, and then begins to thrive in the foreign language and culture, on its own terms. Short-term survival needs are satisfied first, in brief interchanges intelligible to the native speaker used to dealing with foreigners; active communication is accomplished largely in memorized utterances or brief sentences (= Novice High). The text and the student then progress to longer-term but still everyday, concrete matters, with encouragement of some linguistic creativity in interchanges involving speakers relatively accustomed to dealing with foreigners (= Intermediate Low/Mid). The final part of the package encourages the learner to communicate relatively freely about somewhat larger but still typically concrete and immediate topics with conversants who are generally congenial but cannot be expected to understand or leniently tolerate foreigners struggling with the language (= Intermediate High). Within the final chapters are topics and structures that probe somewhat higher in the proficiency scale, mostly within the Advanced to Advanced-Plus range, so that the better student can indeed aim at the frequent exhibition of Advanced behavior that characterizes Intermediate-High performance in speaking.

In accord with our own and others' investigations

of language proficiency, we have de-emphasized or even eliminated certain grammatical features that are commonly presented – though seldom really learned – in traditional first-year German courses. The future tense, distinctly beyond the Intermediate level and commonly replaced by the present tense in native speech anyway, is not presented for use in the spoken language, nor are – for similar reasons – the genitive prepositions, Konjunktiv I, the adverbial superlative, or daunting verb combinations like the past passive modal subjunctive. Certain of those features, however, are addressed in the Study Text Reference Grammar, which does present the "complete" grammar contained in traditional classroom texts.

But we do not regard the grammar offered in the Class Text as incomplete. It provides all the structures even an excellent student can be expected to learn to handle proficiently when faced with speaking tasks characteristic of the Intermediate-High level. Field-testing has confirmed the appropriateness of the grammar level and has reinforced our confidence in the principle of letting function lead form. Frequently when our students confidently undertake an oral task, they discover that, though they may be able to perform the function passably with available resources, they need some more sophisticated grammatical feature to do the task well. They will indeed ask for it – often enough just a few classroom hours before it is scheduled for presentation.

The Class Text

The Class Text is intended to be the main everyday resource in a proficiency-oriented classroom, one in which there is much communicative use of language but little analytic discussion of it. We have excluded from the Class Text those elements that, while they may have a purpose in language study, do not have a place in a classroom where demonstration, simulation, and emulation of genuine communication are emphasized.

The Class Text material divides into two parts: the chapters and the resources. The chapters – two preliminary units and 26 regular units – are of course intended for sequential study. Since they are organized on the principle of the spiral syllabus, however, individual functions, contexts, and grammatical topics are covered not once but several times, and there is also careful provision for review. A special chapter, *Feste und Feiertage,* is intended for use as appropriate to the season and contains material keyed to many different levels.

The main section of the Class Text consists of the two preliminary chapters and the 26 regular units. The preliminary units consist largely of brief dialogs intended for memorization and intensive contextual exercise. Their chief purpose is to boost the student as quickly as possible to the ACTFL/ETS Novice-Mid level in speaking. There is no presentation of grammatical features, because at such a level the speaker has effectively no grammar – or rather, what appears to be structural competence is actually lexical achievement. Nor are there any formally posed situation exercises of the kind offered in the main chapters; the student cannot yet be expected to create at any length with the language.

Far more complex are the 26 regular units. In a proficiency-oriented course the classroom text must serve as a departure point for exercise in communication rather than as an object for contemplative examination and cautious precision drill. Thus the *Wie, bitte?* Class Text chapters are always of the same length, and, for each location, their chief features always appear from chapter to chapter not merely in the same sequence, but in precisely the same place and on the same page within the chapter. Care was taken to lay out the pages so that there was no overflow from page to page in the presentation of dialogs, grammar, and exercises. The guiding principle was that the student and teacher involved in energetic use of the book should not have to struggle to find needed materials. The same principle determined the typographical policy – we wanted a text whose vital sections could be read at a glance while the ears, eyes, mouth – and even the rest of the body as well – were engaged in communicative exercise. Typographical emphasis is used frequently, and explanation is kept to a minimum. Photos and realia are included, not as pretty pictures or supposedly intriguing documentary tidbits, but rather as integral parts of the language-learning process.

The *first* page (page # = chapter # + 0) always presents visual material that suggests the themes of the chapter's two basic contexts, and then itemizes in everyday language the aims of the chapter in terms of the "functional trisection" of function, context/content, and accuracy. The facing page (page # = chapter # + 1) presents dialogs (*Gespräche 1*) that explore the chapter's first theme; there follow a page of relevant structural paradigms and exposition (*Struktur 1*) and a page of oral exercises (*Situationen 1*). The second theme of each chapter is presented in a similar way. Between the two thematic sections is a two-page spread, *Strategie – Kultur und Sprache*, which fits the chapter's main linguistic and cultural features into a wider context, shows how to exploit communicative resources, and offers enrichment vocabulary.

The second half or theme of each chapter definitely presupposes knowledge of the first. But the pages of each chapter need not be presented and studied in precisely their given order. Although we recommend that the dialogs, or *Gespräche,* be undertaken before the corresponding *Struktur* sections are presented, some teachers may prefer the reverse order. The *Strategie – Kultur und Sprache* page can be introduced anywhere (or left largely for home study), and certainly the *Situationen* can and should be undertaken over the course of the chapter or sub-section, rather than just at the end.

Several controversial points must be addressed here. In terms of verisimilitude and *Stilfibel* correctness, the *Gespräche* present a spoken German which aims above all at being comprehensible to and functionally reproducible by the first-year student. Though we sought to give the language real flavor, we did not overload it with notorious flavor words (stressed/unstressed *doch*), ephemeral slang, studiously cultivated casual contractions (*'nen* for *einen*), or other warts and wrinkles that would impede the acquisition of functional competence. On the other hand, we did not offer speech that demanded that the student metamorphose into a model *Abiturient;* thus *bekommen* is allowed to do the duty of *erhalten,* as it often does in real conversation, and "*Wann ist der nächste Zug?*" is promoted in early chapters instead of the above level "*Wann fährt der nächste Zug (ab)?*" In general the authors, both non-native speakers of German, can attest that the German of *Wie, bitte?* was conceived in fond recollection of many an actual conversation, that it was passed cautiously through an effective affective filter, and that it was then judged carefully by two and sometimes three or more well-educated native speakers of German – who often differed on what constitutes correct or even natural German.

The presentation of grammar through model language, paradigm, and very brief exposition on the two *Struktur* pages in the Class Text chapters, and the location of the Reference Grammar in the Study Text, are intended to discourage any tendency to turn the class into a lecture on linguistics, when it should be instead a vigorous exercise in communicative skills, with the teacher as model and coach. The an-alytic Reference Grammar is intended for study outside of class; the *Struktur* pages should be used in class to demonstrate the functional nature of grammar. The instructor should show how acquisition of new structures can make communication more efficient. Thus proficiency in handling attributive adjectives enables one to express in one sentence ("*Ich habe einen braunen Regenmantel gekauft.*") what otherwise would require two sentences with attendant labor of conjugation, tense selection, and attention to word order ("*Ich habe einen Regenmantel gekauft.*" "*Er ist braun.*"). In general, it is also beneficial to point out the compensatory relationship between grammar and vocabulary: strength in one can offset weakness in the other.

The two *Situationen* pages in each chapter, and the corresponding preparatory exercises in the Study Text, exemplify the target activity of *Wie, bitte?*, the use of language for communication – and particularly, in the classroom, oral communication. That is indeed the purpose of the *Gespräche* and the *Struktur* pages. The *Situationen* are posed largely in English, which may initially disconcert some teachers who prize the notion of a "German only"-classroom. Colleagues familiar with the standard oral proficiency interview (OPI) will perceive our inspiration and anticipate our argument. For several reasons, proficiency interview situations are usually offered in English, at least at the levels with which we are concerned here. If the situation is posed in German, and the interviewee does not perform well, one cannot be sure that one is measuring *oral* proficiency, since the deficiency may lie in listening comprehension. In fact, posing in German a situation of sufficient complexity to yield good interview data may be quite difficult; in any case, one risks giving away target structures and vocabulary.

The *Situationen* are phrased in relatively low-level, idiomatic English that should be readily comprehensible to most students. It is more important that the idiomatic formulation seeks pointedly to thwart attempts at translation, and that quite often the situations solicit the expression of emotions and the performance of gestures. The student must learn that it is futile or at least extremely dangerous to attempt word-for-word or structure-for-structure transformations, and that language does not exist in an emotional and physical vacuum. Instead, one should establish and reinforce the ability to convert concepts into language, and constantly demand emulation of emotion, gesture, and other paralinguistic phenomena. There are collateral benefits to that effort and to the periphrastic formulation of situations: the students can be led to the confidence that they can find a common means to handle tasks expressed in a variety of formulations, and that what appear to be complex ideas can be divided into several more easily managed concepts. Our goal is that the student who seeks to express a notion like "agree" will resist the urge to consult the dictionary, only to become lost in a web of words – **"übereinstimmen? sich einigen? zustimmen? übereinkommen zu** (*inf*)? (*affect one's health*) **bekommen** (*dat*)?" – and will instead realize that direct agreement can be expressed simply by saying *Ja* and that it can be discussed – indeed fluently! – by combining *ja* and *sagen* or *glauben* and *auch*.

Our own classroom experience with printed situations posed in English argues strongly that students in a proficiency-oriented classroom will not revert more than occasionally to English discussion of the situations rather than German performance of them. Of course, we cannot prevent them from thinking in English – nor can one in a "German only" classroom; and even there, unless the text is in German only, the student will in any case be reading some English. The chief goal, of course, is that the student encounter and produce a lot of German. In a proficiency-oriented classroom that will be the case whether or not one adopts the "German only" policy.

Similar considerations apply to the *Strategie – Kultur und Sprache* sections, which are almost entirely in English, except for the associated realia. They are not intended as *Lesestücke*. We wanted the students to absorb the content of the *Strategie* pages, not struggle with artificial German texts. When reading was the explicit target skill, we wanted everything the student read to be an authentic text. Quite likely the *Wie, bitte?* package, with its extensive realia scattered throughout the Class Text, and its large *Drucksachen* collections in both Class Text and Study Text, exposes the student to considerably more German than other first-year books. That exposure is intensified by the Study Text reading exercises and the test-bank reading tests, which lead the student through a vast range of realia and vigorously promote the active processing of large amounts of language. The same can be said of aural realia in the package.

The Class Text resources, like the spiral-syllabus grammatical features in the chapters, are intended for repeated use or recycling throughout the program. They include materials of a kind found in many texts and of course assumed to be recyclable, such as a glossary. Other resources are not so traditional.

The *Afterword* of the Class Text contains a detailed yet plan-language discussion of linguistic proficiency. Though students may not be able to appreciate the intricacies of either our profession's methodology or of proficiency-oriented instruction, most of them are curious about how they are progressing. At strategic points in the course you may wish to discuss pedagogical matters briefly. The rest of the *Afterword* provides information about further study and travel. Such material can be integrated into the course at many points, especially if at least a few students intend to travel or study abroad, or have already done so.

The *Glossary* serves two overall purposes. It enables the teacher to ascertain when and where which words have been "officially" introduced, and it provides the student with a core dictionary of words we consider important. Both points deserve explanation, and once again we emphasize that *Wie, bitte?* aims to promote *functional* skill rather than memorization of word lists or intellectual mastery of rules. The glossary is proficiency-oriented, in several senses. It is *not* intended as a translation help for the student who wants to look up every word. Most important of all, it does not and could not contain each of the many thousands of German words that the student might encounter – but not necessarily have to understand overtly! – in the various *Wie, bitte?* materials. Instead, it is built around the chapter *Gespräche*, in which the basic structures and vocabulary of each unit are presented. A few incidental words in the *Gespräche* are glossed in page margins, and thus may not appear in the glossary; many obvious cognates are simply ignored. Similarly, compound nouns that are not quite transparent but whose parts should already be familiar are glossed in the text with indications of divison; they may not be listed in the glossary.

The *Glossary* is intended to promote the skills of skimming, scanning, and risk-taking. And, in conjunction with the *Bildwörterbuch* and the recommended conventional paperback dictionary, it takes into account differences in language modalities. The glossary is not a single alphabetical list. Rather, it is divided functionally, and in a manner consonant with the development of proficiency at the Novice-High to Intermediate-High levels. We would hope that the student earnestly working with the *Gespräche* would use the dictionary as a secondary resource, and instead would rely primarily on contextual guessing, recursion, and other practical strategies to comprehend not only the basic meaning of a word but also its subsidiary characteristics (e.g., gender, tense).

Students who wish to look up words in the *Glossary* will have to commit themselves linguistically; that is, they will have to take some risks that are consonant with progress at the Novice-High to Intermediate-High level. Their first decision will be a gross classification: Is the word a noun or "something else?" Then, if the word is a noun, the student must venture a guess about its gender, for the nouns are listed alphabetically *by gender*, with prominent reminders about their articles. The process is not as laborious in practice as it is in description, since the pages of the glossary have been designed to reduce page-thumbing to a minimum.

There is no English-German lexicon. Our intent is to discourage dependence on translation and to encourage students to make do with whatever they have readily available, especially when the linguistic task involves realistic conditions in which use of a dictionary would be inappropriate or impossible. In speaking situations that are truly impromptu or permit only short preparation, the ordinary listener – even the well-disposed native speaker used to dealing with foreigners – will not often wait long enough for the struggling speaker to look up a word. Second, wrong-headed ventures at one-for-one translation can be disastrous or inadvertently comical, in the manner of the "What watch, treasure?" exchange in the film *Casablanca*, or of Thomas Mann's British tourists who render "Look at that!" as *"Besichtigen Sie jenes!"*

Therefore in rapidly paced speaking situations the student should be encouraged to use fluently a smaller but handier stock of words (and grammatical structures). Where time allows for reference to an actual lexicon, in whatever form it is presented, we would hope the student would learn to manage vocabulary thematically; that is, would come to perceive and conceive of words in contexts. One tactic might be recourse to the *Gespräche* themselves, since the dialogs are indeed conceived thematically and ordered according to the functions appropriate to the various proficiency levels. Even more important is the *Bildwörterbuch* with its extensive stock of words arranged contextually. Lastly, you may well recommend that your students acquire a paperback German-English/English-German dictionary. You should remind them, however, that dependence on a dictionary can be dangerous, and that, even in the listening and reading exercises, where they will encounter many unfamiliar words, they will not be asked to undertake anything that cannot be accomplished without the resources they have been given.

The overall principles of vocabulary management in a proficiency-oriented environment might be summed up thus: When it comes to acquiring and applying vocabulary, virtually anything is fair; students should learn to obtain words wherever they can. Second, such complaints as "But this word isn't in the glossary," or "We haven't had this word yet," are not valid objections to linguistic tasks posed in exercises or tests – as long, of course, as completion of the tasks does not hinge directly on comprehension or production of such words in total isolation.

More important than the glossary are two other sections, the *Bildwörterbuch* and the reading materials, or *Drucksachen*. The former, already mentioned, consists of a set of pictorial vocabulary presentations organized by context (e.g., transportation, family) and rough order of proficiency level (e.g., first vital subjects like food and basic environment, then such complexities as landscape and personal interests). Our guiding principles in designing and offering the *Bildwörterbuch* are: 1) we should encourage our students to learn vocabulary in context, and without the easy access to English equivalents that encourages the dangerous assumption of a one-to-one correlation between languages; and 2) although many other textbooks carefully restrict vocabulary but then present grammatical content that is inordinately high in level, a proficiency orientation, at least at the ACTFL/ETS Intermediate level, may favor the opposite – namely, solid command of a modest range of structures, with confident recourse to available lexicons. The student should feel free to consult the *Bildwörterbuch* displays, and the Class Text and Study Text direct attention to them. The teacher should also make systematic use of them in class – not by preaching the vocabulary, but rather by setting appropriate communicative tasks.

The Class Text reading materials – they are actually much more than that – consist of a rich collection of realia that is intended to be useful rather than ornamental. It should be noted first that neither the main chapters of the Class Text nor the corresponding sections of the Study Text include any *Lesestücke* in the customary sense. That is, there are no set pieces which, whether they are drawn from genuine sources or, as is more often the case, are composed especially for the text and are intended, whatever their actual effect, to be a cultural enrichment and a carefully targeted linguistic exercise.

Instead, the reading materials for *Wie, bitte?* were chosen and organized according to other principles. First, every text that the student approaches as material for work in reading, whether as a primary or secondary skill, is a genuine piece of German, something created by speakers of German for the ordinary use of other speakers of German. All texts are presented in essentially their original typographical format, so that the student will immediately feel their genuineness and will also not be deprived of the visual clues and cues so important to proficiency-oriented reading. We have exercised our function as editors or language "input filters" not in the creation of the materials, but rather in their selection and pedagogical transformation. All of the print realia in *Wie, bitte?*, and indeed even many of the incidental photos that contain samples of language, were carefully collected and selected by the authors. Nothing is there simply because a space had to be filled by something visually cute or vaguely apropos in theme.

Second, we intended, as much as possible, to integrate the act of reading into other communicative acts. Thus the *Drucksachen* are eminently suited to use in communicative tasks involving speaking, listening, or writing, and indeed the *Wie, bitte?* program offers many such exercises. But lastly, we wished to follow and reinforce the notion of the spiral syllabus in yet another way. Much of the recyclable realia is archetypal, in several senses. The topics it addresses – food, transactions, transportation, serious personal interests, social issues – are those of lasting import, not just to the native of a culture but also to someone who is visiting it, and particularly to someone who is seeking eventually to function on the levels of proficiency at which *Wie, bitte?* aims. The items themselves have been carefully selected to be accessible to some significant degree at even the lowest levels, and yet to continue to offer challenges when the student returns to them later in the course. The result will be a sort of extended, even months-long version of the kind of exercise that seems so valuable in even a single session: repeat skimming, scanning, and inference-making, with emphasis on recursion, comprehension of context, guessing strategy, and risk-taking, and with care to present language that is constantly challenging but does not unduly raise the student's "affective filter." Indeed, the students' confidence should be enhanced by repeated exposure to such mature realia, even in early chapters.

Many textbooks offer realia, but quite often such materials are offered simply as visual accents, without serious followup, in the sense of including them in communicative tasks. Class testing of *Wie, bitte?* indicates that students very much like to work with realia, even such supposedly dreary things as maps and timetables, provided the realia are introduced in a functional way – that is, as integral parts of communicative tasks. Moreover, sometimes even the most mundane of cultural artifacts – the guidebook to the BMW Museum or a tourist brochure summarizing the history of Freiburg – can open wide vistas into the culture and history of the German-speaking countries, even for the student who is struggling with the language already and who – like most of our students these days – cannot be expected to survive long enough to enroll in our third-year language, culture, or survey of literature courses.

Study Text

The Study Text is *not* an optional part of the *Wie, bitte?* package. Instead, it assumes many of the functions of conventional "main" textbooks and provides certain of the materials ordinarily found in them. The chief principle of separation and inclusion was that the Class Text should provide the materials needed in the communication-oriented classroom, while the Study Text would contain those suitable for study outside of class, whether such study were the rather contemplative examination of analytic grammar, the exercise of listening, reading, and writing skills, or the preparation of spoken material for the classroom. The overall assignments that direct the student's study are also given not in the Class Text, but rather in the Study Text, though the teacher should of course be sure to clarify assignments in other ways.

It should be noted, however, that certain Study Text materials, like the realia and other "props," may well be of use in class, and that the *Gespräche* and *Struktur* pages in the Class Text must be consulted outside the classroom as the student studies them more reflectively. The purpose is twofold. The Study Text contains rich realia resources that would have made the Class Text unwieldy. Some of them are eminently suitable as "props" that might be torn out of the Study Text for more effective situational work, and some are printed forms that might be filled out and handed in. Second, the arrangement obviates annoying book-thumbing; in many activities students will have their books open side-by-side, with one book directing them to study part of another.

The Study Text contains the following major sections:
a) study guide, with advice about language-learning in general, and cultivation of the several modalities in particular;
b) chapter-by-chapter listening, speaking, reading and writing exercises, and worksheets with contextualized exercises of analytical grammar;
c) translations, or rather, somewhat liberal renditions of the Class Text dialogs;
d) chapter-by-chapter German-English vocabulary lists;
e) the Reference Grammar, accessed from the Class Text *Struktur* pages but suitable for study section by section; and
f) a set of *Drucksachen,* or recyclable realia, parallel to that in the Class Text.

Tapes

The tapes consist of:

a) A set of cassettes containing renditions of the Class Text dialogs and performances of the conversations for the Study Text listening exercises. Most likely students will use these materials linearly; that is, they will study them as they work on the successive chapters, and then not need them again. The speech on the tapes is natural or virtually natural in intonation and pace, though free of gratuitous sloppiness or background noise, even though such interference is encountered under real circumstances. The recorded conversations serve two purposes: 1) the Class Text *Gespräche* provide models for student speech production, though we do not recommend slavish memorization; 2) the *Gespräche* and the expanded dialogs used with the Study Text reinforce listening comprehension, so that the student does not become dependent on a single voice – the teacher's – and thereby fail to learn how to understand other speakers, as may happen to an alarming extent in some cases.

b) Two cassettes with aural realia, intended primarily for listening comprehension exercises of a more flexible nature, but also for cultural enrichment. Use of these materials will *not* be linear, but rather anticipatory and recursive. Thus early in the book a

student might be asked to audit a news segment or weather report, listening only for city names and numbers. Later on the same items might be audited again, perhaps even several times, but each time for content higher on the proficiency scale.

c) For the instructor only, a separate cassette with materials suitable for testing.

The exercises and tests conducted with the *Wie, bitte?* tapes are always proficiency-oriented. They consist not of pronunciation and grammar-transformation exercises, but rather of an inital encouragement to reproduce or respond orally to speech models, followed by listening exercises which involve information searches, checks for structural competence, drawing of inferences, and risk-taking. An important stage in the student's use of the tapes is the transition from auditing (without printed script) the rather tame elaborations on the Class Text *Gespräche,* to confronting the aural realia, whose speech segments are genuine and, internally, unedited, though by no means haphazardly selected.

If your program is in a position to take advantage of the publisher's permission to duplicate the tapes, you might suggest that your students purchase three cassettes. Two, used unchanged throughout the course, would store the aural realia ("b" above). The third would provide revolving storage of the current chapter materials ("a" above). Some students, of course, will want to include one or more previous or upcoming cassettes.

The chapter tapes are recorded at fairly natural pace and intonation, as is – of course – the speech on the aural realia tapes. Some students will require careful tutoring in listening techniques and acclimatization to the notion that word-by-word comprehension or imitation is not being demanded of them.

A tape manual contains scripts for the Study Text listening exercises dialogs, selected transcripts of aural realia, and keys for some of the listening exercises that are not open-ended. It appears in the Test Bank.

Test Bank

a) Materials for speaking, listening, reading, and writing tests at intervals of approximately 2 chapters;
b) Test keys and, for speaking and writing tests, descriptive standards and samples of student performances; and
c) Transcripts of selected taped materials.

Software

The larger part of the supplementary computer software for *Wie, bitte?* runs on Macintosh, Apple IIe/gs, and IBM-PC compatibles in common configurations. It consists of:

a) Sets of multiple-choice contextualized reading exercises and tests, many of them using the *Wie, bitte?* realia;

b) Similar listening exercises and tests using the *Wie, bitte?* aural realia;

c) contextualized writing tutorials;

d) listening comprehension exercises using on-disk digitized speech (for Macintosh only);

e) for the teacher, a test curver intended to make bookkeeping simpler and thus help meet the likely need for more time devoted to oral testing.

The courseware aims to be as proficiency-oriented as the rest of the *Wie, bitte?* package. That is, there are neither mechanical drills nor childish games. The student is asked to carry out communicative tasks, such as reading a museum guide, listening to a weather report, or rewriting a social note. Instruction and error correction emphasize the functional learning of language, though analytic grammar is not shirked. Although the courseware can serve as a useful adjunct to the Study Text exercises, and provide a bridge to actual tests, the computer and software are not intended to replace either formally administered tests or classroom instruction. But they may help the teacher and student to use the classroom more efficiently, as a place where human beings rehearse and refine communicative skills.

Classroom Management

Instruction Paradigm

How, then, should the *Wie, bitte?* materials be used? Activity in the classroom must focus on the communicative use of German, whether or not the teacher chooses to limit severely or even virtually eliminate the use of English. Extremely effective, we think, are partner and small-group exercises, primarily in speaking. But other exercises, and most likely tests, will also be regular parts of the class time. Grammatical structures should be presented in class, though briefly and tied to communicative exercises; dialog imitation and guided speaking exercises will be useful preliminaries to speaking situations; and contextual reading, listening, and writing exercises should be undertaken, though the majority of such work should be left to study with the Study Text outside of class.

In our view, the teacher's primary functions should be: 1) demonstration or modeling of language; 2) provision of functional exercises and challenges; and 3) cautious, generally indirect error correction suitable to the student's current level of proficiency. Those functions are addressed at length in subsequent sections of this Introduction; annotations throughout the Instructor's Edition, as well as additional page-by-page comments below, offer detailed aid.

The student's activity in class should consist, correspondingly, of energetic language production and management rather than deliberative analytic study and disquisition. The virtues of stamina, risk-taking, and desire for effective communication should be cultivated. You may want to establish the notion that a proficiency-oriented language class is much like a class in music performance or physical education. Field-testing with ordinary rather than exceptional students suggests that more students will be more productive – and happier – when the chief (but not the only) goal is communication rather than analysis, since all can participate with some degree of accomplishment. Some students, though, whether because of their intellectual proclivities or previous conventional language study, may seek to turn the class into a sort of linguistics seminar. In general, for a proficiency-oriented classroom resolutely resist that impulse – in them and yourself, but there is nothing wrong with an occasional disquisition on language, and indeed *Wie, bitte?* offers historical and grammatical stimuli for such discussion.

Many students will need some guidance in how to study, if not because they have poor study habits, then at least because *Wie, bitte?* is not a conventional textbook package. One aspect of proper outside-class study has to do with simple logistics, another with proficiency modalities, and a third – one common to all communication-oriented language study – with philosophical or psychological attitudes. First, introduce your students to the notion that the Class Text and Study Text complement each other and should be studied – quite literally – side by side. Remind them to alternate modalities in their study and to use the "stage" indications to challenge themselves steadily but not immoderately.

Second, explain that oral proficiency, though it is the focus of classroom activity, is not the only skill. The other modalities are also of considerable importance, and indeed the Study Text assumes the major share of their instruction. You should make it clear as well that, although a proficiency orientation places less emphasis on knowledge of analytic grammar in isolation, they must indeed develop structural competence. *Wie, bitte?* is not a tourist's phrase book, and we do not advocate broken German ("Where hotel?" "Food good.").

Lastly, students have to be convinced that they must indeed work outside class, that steady study is vital, and that their work outside class – like that in class – must involve active exercise of German for communication, rather than just absorption of vocabulary and concentration on abstract structural principles. While your students should be told – and shown! – that there is no substitute for the proficiency-oriented classroom, they should also learn that work outside class, and the Study Text itself, are not simply supplements or extras. We recommend that the serious student who has average aptitude budget two hours of preparation for each class hour. In order to prevent anxious, unproductive assaults on large, undifferentiated blocks of material we have divided the Study Text chapters into modules of varying modality and reasonable length. The individual exercises have been set up in such a way that virtually any student can achieve something with them.

The best advice you can give is to tell your students to talk when they study – not merely because oral proficiency is important in itself, but also because such active iteration of language helps to impress it upon the mind.

Before the details of instruction are addressed, we must deal with several controversial issues that are made all the more sensitive because people – teachers and students both – leave neither their egos nor their preconceptions about language learning behind them when they enter the foreign-language classroom. Here the teacher will find ample evidence that successful proficiency-oriented teaching is both a skill and an art. Our remarks here are addressed not only to novice teachers but also to veterans – including those who teach teachers.

Wie, bitte? is designed for the classrooms in which people talk German rather than talk about German. The student-centered structure of *Wie, bitte?* reduces the role of the instructor as an authority or source of principles of grammar and lists of vocabulary. Put more positively, *Wie, bitte?* aims to encourage instruction in which German is learned and used as students who see value in learning a language for communication interact closely and humanely with teachers who believe in teaching a language for communication.

Proficiency-oriented instruction virtually demands teachers who are – or can seem to be – exuberant, supportive, and oriented toward function rather than form. In such a classroom you must be ready to leave behind the spotlight of the podium and become an apparently unobtrusive rover in the classroom, perhaps even spending much of the hour conversing on your knees, squatting on your heels, or just occupying a vacant desk, in order to close quarters with and yet not appear too foreboding to students who are struggling to use German with some level of proficiency but are still unnerved that someone is actually insisting that they do so.

Most students will affirm that they want to learn how to use the language, but many will evidence serious discomfort or even panic when you ask them to take that first step: actually speaking the language and dealing with authentic reading and, particularly, listening materials. Compassion is definitely in order, but you should immediately establish – by vigorous exercise, exposure to realia, and even reference to testing and grading criteria – the attitude that language students "of course" do such things as negotiate for transportation, scan schedules of cultural events, listen to weather reports, and write quick messages. The first few attempts at such exercises may be upsetting, and the anxiety will recur each time you push your students to higher levels by posing more complex tasks or demanding more accurate management of features already presented. Our class testing, however, showed that students soon develop a calm acceptance of such activities, an attitude that can border on fearlessness. Years of experience in oral testing and commensurate teaching have led us to think in terms of a sort of pedagogical magic charm. We notice a distinct and rather sudden increase in proficiency in students who gain the insight that it is better to attempt to use the language and to register the consequent achievement than to attempt not to use it for fear of being penalized for each error – which should be a false fear in a classroom claiming a proficiency orientation. Whether or not they actually learn some new linguistic material at that crucial time, they seem to register the effect of a verbal release or permission to use what they know. Whatever the case, during the early part of the course you should do all you can to allay your students' fears, particularly about speaking and listening.

In our own courses we have found it beneficial to make the first oral test a serious but non-counting experience. Moreover, to reinforce the emphasis on oral proficiency – students so often think that the only real test is a paper test – we make that test the first major test of the course. The student is assigned a grade, and is told to take it to heart, but the first "counting" oral test comes only after the student has had a chance to find out what an oral interview is like. The policy has the added benefit of partly neutralizing the advantages of students who have previous exposure to German, whether from classes, family, or travel. If they get a high grade from their inherited proficiency, it does not count; if they are not as good as they think they are, we try to put a bug in their ear – but it is indeed saddening how a low degree of proficiency previously acquired can impede further progress by giving a false sense of ability and encouraging lax study habits.

Listening comprehension exercises, especially those conducted with authentic materials, are also stressful occasions. The students, accustomed as they are in our culture to the notion that to study is to use printed materials, are troubled that they cannot depart from essentially linear assimilation of language directed at them, as they can when they read, since there they usually may have direct, repeated recourse to the entire text in any sequence. The students' frustration is compounded by their impression that those speaking German at normal speed are "babbling," or that the sound fidelity of recorded materials is low. The phenomenon can be explained in one way by observing that, to the low-level language learner, even carefully selected speech offers such a richness of sounds that it is extremely challenging to map them against a grammar and lexicon, particularly if the grammar and lexicon have been acquired analytically and visually. An equivalent explanation would be that the students need practice in listening rather than just seeing, and that they must develop the ability to increase their comprehension of linear linguistic input by acquiring sheer stamina, the strategies of inference, and the confidence that the message will contain adequate so-called "redundant" information. In short, they need lots of listening practice.

Still another form of anxiety or misconceived expectation may emerge, whether because the class includes students who have studied German in more traditional ways, or because Americans have certain general preconceptions about foreign-language study. Whatever their stated reasons for learning a foreign language, and whatever their rational understanding of the process, under the pressure of instruction – and particularly in the face of an upcoming test – many students will fall back on the stereotype. They will clutch to their bosoms the notion of rule-memorization and vocabulary-list drill, and will be preoccupied with mastering the small segments of pronunciation (e.g., how most properly to say *ich*) that supposedly constitute a "native" accent. We have found, in contrast, that students in a proficiency-oriented classroom learn vocabulary better in context, and that grammatical "monitoring" is best encouraged by showing how structural competence contributes to superior function. Moreover, we offer no pronunciation exercises of the "*Staat/ Stadt*" type, because in our classes we find that stu-

dents who are encouraged to speak the language for proficiency readily produce speech whose pronunciation satisfies the criteria for comprehensibility at the target level. They do this not by magic. Practice makes (sufficiently) perfect is the trick, and strategic error correction is the key. The student who speaks a lot of German and who hears native or near-native models will make progress in accent and intonation. Progress is facilitated by the teacher who evaluates pronunciation errors in accord with their effect on communication, and corrects accordingly, rather than insisting on precise *Bühnenaussprache*.

Students whose prior knowledge of German comes not from "street" or "osmotic" learning experiences, but rather from traditional grammar-translation study, will be anxious in another way. They may want to know, for example, why the *du*-form is not introduced at the beginning. More serious will be their tendency to desire lengthy grammatical explanations and what they consider coherent presentation of structures. In their production of German they will be hesitant, expecting frequent correction or even confirmation of even the smallest segments of language; in their reading and listening they will cling to linear translation. The best of such learners, however, can become excellent proficiency-oriented students.

The issues of grammar presentation and error correction, and the emphasis on partner and small-group work – not, of course, unique to *Wie, bitte?* – raise yet another question. Will students who work together reinforce each other's errors? We think not. Students doing the *Situationen* and similar exercises together are not proceeding in grammar-translation lockstep, but rather concentrating on function and individual expression; they do not recite vocabulary lists and patterns in unison. Instruction in both music and athletics often includes partner and small-group exercise – and not merely because one teacher must teach many students and because diligent practice improves skills. Important also is exercise in context; a discrete-point element or form (a musical technique, a karate move, a past tense) is made functional by being integrated into a context. It becomes part of a larger individual performance, and it is brought into relation to other people.

A final advantage of partner and small-group work is serendipitous or simply secondary. It increases the students' aural tolerance, in that they must become accustomed to hearing someone other than the teacher – and in a good classroom they will also learn to tolerate background noise like that encountered in real settings. Of course such aural tolerance should not be induced solely by such imperfect means; instead, the *Wie, bitte?* aural realia should be used. The broad principles are that the student should not be allowed to become dependent on the instructor's voice, and that there should be constant exposure to speech which is natural – in pace, intonation, and vocabulary. "Caretaker" speech, which is characterized by a distinctly unnatural slowness of pace, exaggeration of intonation, and restriction of lexicon, should clearly be avoided.

Class-time Budget

The notion of "year" as a useful measure of foreign-language study is becoming ever more questionable, not just because proficiency, rather than mere "seat-time," would seem to be a better gauge, but also because the number of hours of instruction in a "year" varies greatly, commonly from 3 to 5 per week (with or without an outside language lab session). The following recommended class-time allocations presume a 4-hour week. Obviously, they can serve as gauges of proportions for classes meeting more or less often. We cannot say too emphatically, however, that "finishing the book" – *Wie, bitte?* or any other – is not a virtue if the students do not survive the process.

Of course, *Wie, bitte?* offers more material than any student can assimilate perfectly, but, in contrast to other texts, we hope it shows understanding of what should be demanded and can be learned for true proficiency. Good students in a well-run program ought to be able to progress comfortably through *Wie, bitte?* in one year; note that when a book is organized according to the "spiral syllabus," absolute mastery of one unit is not required before the subsequent unit can be undertaken. You may decide that *Wie, bitte?* is not a "first-year" book, but rather a "zero to Intermediate-High" book. You might then "cover" up to, say, chapter 20 or 21 in the first year, quickly review that material and "finish" the book in the first quarter or semester of second year, and then continue with a congenial package that promotes proficiency at the Intermediate-High or Advanced levels.

We suggest the following allocation of classroom time for the various language modalities and sections of the *Wie, bitte?* package in a two-semester or three-quarter sequence. The outline assumes a target level of Intermediate-Mid in speaking for good students, but it does not demand that the "A" student attain Intermediate-High.

(1 week = 4 nominal classroom hours)

Class Text *Gespräche*	1/2 hour
Class Text *Struktur* sections with exercises	1/2 hour
Class Text *Situationen*	1 1/2 hours
listening, reading, writing exercises (practice or test)	1 hour
warm-ups and overt review (recent or old material)	1/2 hour

The chart below presents a reasonably equivalent budgeting of day-by-day class time for a course that meets for 4 hours (or 50-minute periods) a week. Nominal minutes recommended are in ( ); "a" and "b" refer to the first and second halves of chapters; "integrative" refers to activities that involve two or more of the modalities (e.g., use a map while giving oral directions); "Q&A" indicates "safety-valve" time allocated to management of students' inquiries. Specific teaching strategies appropriate to the various segments are discussed further below.

	DAY 1	DAY 2	DAY 3	DAY 4
(2)	warm-up	warm-up	warm-up	warm-up
(15)	(a) *Gespräche und Strukturen*		(b) *Gespräche und Strukturen*	
(15)	(a) Stage 1 Ex/Sit	(a) Stage 2 Ex/Sit	(b) Stage 1 Ex/Sit	(b) Stage 2 Ex/Sit
(15)	reading	listening	reading	writing/integrative
(3)	review/Q&A/enrichment		review/Q&A/enrichment	

Quarter/Semester Schedule

QUARTERS	SEMESTERS
1: Prelim–9	1: prelim–13
2: 10–18	2: 14–26
3: 19–26	

Programs on quarter schedule may have to do slightly more than one unit per week in first quarter.

The pace at which chapters are covered lessens later on in the course, in order to provide time for review.

Teaching Techniques

Discussion here will focus shortly on classroom exercise of oral skills, especially in partner/small-group work. Teaching of listening, reading, and writing is mentioned further below, but exercise of those skills can emulate the items in the Study Text, and in any case does not require the careful management of students that is necessary in oral work. See the Bibliography for further discussion and advice.

Despite the emphasis on partner and small-group work, other techniques will be of value in the development of speaking skills in the classroom. Nothing in *Wie, bitte?* discourages choral repetition of phrases, rapid-fire drills in which students are called on singly, or memorization of dialogs. Certainly repetition and individual checking are appropriate to introduction of the material on the *Struktur* pages. Another technique, one valuable in itself and useful as preparation for other activities in any of the modalities, is fast-paced vocabulary refreshment by association. A single word serves as a departure point for the listing of others words that might plausibly have to do with it, either because they fit the context it suggests (*Restaurant – essen, trinken, Suppe*), or because they also share some structural affinity, such as speech part (*Wir essen im Restaurant – Wir . . . bestellen, trinken, fragen, zahlen*). While the communicative use of German is the goal, there may well be reason to conduct exercises that target structure or grammar rather than just context. Examples are quick checks of noun plurals, *ein/kein* negation, or participles. And quite likely some students will need intensive instruction in pronunciation.

Here we must address two sensitive issues: error correction and pronunciation. By both many teachers and the public, error correction is generally taken to mean vigorous attack on any and all errors in grammar, and acquiring "correct" pronunciation is generally assumed to be a high priority and to require sedulous exercise.

Long-suffering students have learned to say that their chief problem is "grammar," and even novice learners are preoccupied with sounding like native speakers in their pronunciation of single words. Some teachers quickly intervene at the slightest error, and many students – often those intellectually most ambitious – laboriously construct their utterances by rapid vocabulary conversion and mental rule application while constantly looking to their teachers for careful correction – and then sound absolutely mechanical, or are simply nonfunctional, because they cannot communicate their message in a reasonable time. Seldom is the concept of error correction extended to overall sentence intonation or to discourse strategy, and far too often students get preoccupied with the intricacies of pronunciation. They demand from themselves in the rendition of single words an accuracy that they cannot presently achieve and, for communicative purposes at their level, need not achieve. They thereby ignore – and thus prevent themselves from acquiring – a sense of overall intonation that actually contributes more to proficiency than does precise mastery of single sounds.

It is our view, then, that error correction should be conservative, indirect, and sensitive to proficiency level. Our emphasis on encouraging the effort to communicate goes hand in hand with a conviction that fossilization of uncorrected error-patterns is not a great danger, at least when the errors that one lets pass have to do with structures that are distinctly above the student's current level. The student should not be corrected in the midst of speech, error by halting error; instead, the willingness to produce utterances of larger size should be encouraged, even if grievously erroneous speech must later be dissected and corrected quite rigorously. Rich though distinctly flawed speech is better than virtually uncommunicative but formally accurate language. Learn when to leave well enough alone, to see that the glass is not half empty but rather half full, and to elicit more language by praising what has been produced.

Some errors are the result of completely false assumptions and therefore have no compensatory value ("*Was machen Sie da?*" "**Mich? Ich bin schreiben ein Buchstaben.*"). Other errors show a laudably diligent if incorrect extension of a principle, such as happens when the student industriously learns the concept and morphology of noun case and then fails to realize that verbs may be followed not only by direct (accusative) objects but also by (nominative) predicates ("**Das ist einen Regenmantel.*"). But, as we have observed in class testing, cautious error correction and the consequent encouragement of risk-taking may have surprisingly beneficial results, beyond the simple but gratifying tendency of students to use the language without much inhibition. Thus when one has introduced in Chapter 9 the "*-te-*" preterite pattern for *haben* and the modals, one may well find students producing, by fortunate analogy, *sagte-, hörte-*, etc. Such serendipitous accomplishments should be encouraged, even at the expense of tolerating – but only for a while – **trinkte* and **gehte*. Since *Wie, bitte?* is not oriented primarily to a grammatical syllabus, there is nothing wrong with tacitly countering such tendencies by offering speech in which the forms are correct, even before the relevant morphology is introduced explicitly. And of course the *Wie, bitte?* realia will be exposing the student to many such structures along the way.

Often error correction, if it is deemed necessary, can be applied indirectly and in a manner that imitates genuine communication so well that students will claim that the teacher seldom corrects them, or even complain that they do not get sufficient coaching in grammar or accent. Quite often it is sufficient to echo the student's speech, but in correct form, with slight emphasis on the specific correction ("*So. Sie möchten eine Fahrkarte nach Freiburg.*"). In so doing one reinforces the discourse strategy of echoing that is emphasized throughout *Wie, bitte?* and is so much a part of genuine conversation.

Sometimes indirect correction poses more of a problem, particularly when pronouns and differences in perspective are involved. Student: "*Das ist *mein Schwester.*" Teacher: "*So. Das ist Ihre Schwester.*" Student: "*Oh, oops. Ja, das ist *Ihr* [instead of the desired *meine*] Schwester.*" There are many ways to clear up such misunderstandings or insufficiencies without abandoning the friendly communicative persona and resorting to analytic grammar. Thus one might turn to a more proficient student nearby and perform the same exercise, with emphasis on the problematic feature, and then turn to the less proficient student for a reprise.

Above all, error correction should take into account the current and target levels of performance. Here it is important to note that many linguistic features that are treated as unitary concepts in traditional works are presented in *Wie, bitte?* by gradual steps. A gross distinction concerns the difference between incidental use of some word or structure, intended only for current lexical knowledge, and the later inclusion of that same item in an overt presentation of structure. Thus *wenn* and even *wenn Sie aussteigen* occur quite early in *Wie, bitte?*, but they are intended for lexical absorption only, and thus there is no explanation of verb-last syntax or separable prefixes. At *this* stage you should simply look the other way when the earnest student indeed uses *wenn*, though without the verb last, or produces *"*Aussteigen Sie dort!*" as the imperative. Similarly, in Chapter 12, where the chief point concerns establishing the basic concept and morphology of participles, hypercorrection of *"*Ich habe gereist.*" or even *"*Ich haben

gereist." would be stiflingly inappropriate. Much the same can be said for the treatment a few units later of *"*Ich bin gefährt.*" Be thankful for the *bin*, the solid participial structure, and the relic of stem-vowel transformation in the main verb.

Small-group work

If the goal of instruction is proficiency, the means is intensive practice augmented by strategic demonstration and correction. Most reasonably mature students, whether they have elected language study freely or under the duress of curriculum requirements, greet quite amicably the prospect of learning a foreign language for genuine communication. That favorable theoretical disposition will likely remain, even in the poorer learners, and in any case the early part of the course – of any course conducted reasonably well – will likely be a sort of honeymoon in which the student revels in being able to do so many things heretofore unimagined or considered impossible. Over the long haul, though, the teacher must be able to motivate the class and to further the learning process day by day. It is of no small advantage that the proficiency-oriented teacher can blithely "teach to the test"; if there is to be an oral test, then students can be encouraged to realize that they should practice talking in class and even at home. But one must teach, not simply exhort or threaten. And, since in the ordinary classroom there are many students and only one teacher, ways must be found to encourage the student to assume much of the responsibility for using and exercising the foreign language. A mainstay of such exercise in the *Wie, bitte?* program is partner or small-group work, primarily though not exclusively in speaking.

Small-group exercise in *Wie, bitte?* includes many types. The *Gespräche* may be rehearsed thus, though we do not recommend extensive memorization and performance. The practical application of the *Struktur* principles and paradigms is important. Vital, however, is the ability to use German in context. In accord with the teacher's preferences, instruction in that ability will include varying amounts of attention to the Class Text *Struktur* or *Situationen* pages, to the Study Text speaking exercises, and to the several other resources, such as the *Drucksachen* and *Bildwörterbuch*.

Use of the *Situationen*, which are modeled on elements of the standard oral proficiency interview, involves several principles. Most are in English, so that the student does not need to wade through (too) high-level German in order to be prepared to speak, and so that target vocabulary and structures are not revealed. Moreover, the English is periphrastic, so that wrong-headed inclinations to translate may be hindered. Early in the course you may have to explain such features.

While the "Stage 1" exercises, with their "walk-through" scripting, can be rather easy, the "Stage 2" and *Versuchen Sie doch* sections offer a freedom of imagination and expression that may seem daunting to some students. Throughout you will have to aid the student who is called upon to assume the role of the native speaker. You may do that by having the class work up "generic" native-speaker utterances likely in the given situation, by supplying useful utterances on a cue card, etc. Here the material on the *Strategie* pages can be useful, as can a familiarity with discourse theory. Occasionally you yourself should play the native speaker role in a demonstration situation, which can serve not only as a speech model but as an impromptu exercise in listening comprehension. Perhaps you may wish explicitly to assign certain situation exercises for preparation outside class.

We list now a number of "generic" techniques useful in partner and small-group work.

• Refresh vocabulary with quick group exercises in contextual association and list-making. Later in the course you may, in German or English, pose questions like *Was tut/braucht man, wenn man* [target activity]? Earlier on, you might simply list target vocabulary on the board, perhaps divided by part of speech, gender, etc. The "ham" teacher might imitate a psychoanalyst and encourage students to generate vocabulary lists by association. Whatever the technique, the goal is just as much to get the class warmed up as it is to produce useful vocabulary lists; virtually any word should be accepted and, if offered by poorer students, generously praised. All students should feel that they can accomplish something and thus can indeed speak German. The technique can be combined with other strategies; noun lists, for example, can be incorporated into case-oriented pattern exercises, or verbs can be checked for tense formation.

• Get the class up and moving, and emphasize the communicative value of gesture and emotion. Students tend to cling to accustomed seat locations and

partners, with the poorer students joining their companions in misery at the back of the room. Be sure to get to the back of the room yourself to exercise those who need it most. But also be sure to break up other comfy pairs and get everyone up and moving, as befits the notion of proficiency as the ability to communicate with a wide variety of interlocutors. Students can be encouraged to "meet" a certain number of classmates within a specified period of time, remembering certain vital statistics (majors, interests, family members, native countries) in a "cocktail party" atmosphere. Three minutes of *Stehparty* can yield a lengthy time of active and enthusiastic recall once students have returned to their seats. This activity can take place far into the year, including subordinate clauses (*Als X sieben Jahre alt war, wohnte seine/ihre Familie in Y*), if-clauses (*Wenn A Zeit hätte, würde er/sie B machen*), etc. Breaking the pattern of nestling in the customary classroom desk will have several other positive effects: 1) it will reinforce use of the "gambits" that are so important in real communication (*Entschuldigung. Eine Frage, bitte.*); 2) it will increase aural tolerance; 3) it will get the students' noses out of their books and into real communication, which will have – eventually if not immediately – a salutory effect on intonation, accent, and gesture; 4) it will give you as the teacher some breathing space to adjust the further course of the hour; if you are doing the job right you will feel rather superfluous for a minute or two. Note here how effective the introduction of realia can be, including the use of props such as menus and money.

• The teaching of function and form can be alternated. You may wish to introduce group or situation work with a short demonstration of target structures (e.g., prepositions and cases). Or you may pose a function-oriented exercise ("Tell/Find out what is where in X's room."), halt conversation after a few minutes to spotlight the target structures, and then redo the exercise, to show how advantageous it is to learn new skills.

• Situation work (and indeed other communicative exercises) can be livened up by adding more players or kibitzers to the conversation. The kibitzers might tactfully be selected from the better students while the poorer students bear the main responsibility for communication. These nattering supernumeraries can be given two functions: 1) they may echo, in part or whole, what the main participants say, and thus provide another perspective (*Er sagt, es kostet zuviel?*)

or even help the instructor carry out indirect error correction (*Ja. Es kostet zuviel.*); 2) they may keep the conversation active and challenging by parodying the companion who speaks no German but always has some special wish ("Ask him if the shower costs extra." "Tell her I need to know whether I'll be charged for the pictures that don't turn out OK."

• Whether you are presenting grammatical patterns from the *Struktur* pages, seeking to establish good warm-up patterns, or simply encouraging the general exercise of speaking in small groups, you can use the blackboard, overhead projector, or cue cards to set up in schematic form communicative activities that can yield each time many minutes of targeted conversation. Columnar (vertical) rather than paragraph (horizontal) outlining of conversational elements seems better, since it permits clearer outlining of stages and makes convenient extension of the conversation once the basic material has been exercised and a foundation thus laid for the "situation with complication" that is so characteristic of the Intermediate level of oral proficiency. The respective advantages and disadvantages of German and English as the language of presentation are clear. More important are terseness of formulation and awareness of the proper mix of prompts that outline a function (*Erklärt warum.*) and paradigms or samples that model the language (*Sie haben > Ich habe, ein/kein, . . . weil ich kein- X habe*). Obviously, as students progress through *Wie, bitte?* they acquire greater communicative ability and thus need less guidance in performing tasks that are now comfortably within their level. Therefore a brief task description ("Negotiates shelter for family.") can replace the detailed cues needed to lead the student through the same task in earlier chapters.

Here are classroom-tested examples from various chapters:

– third hour of course (Preliminary Chapter 1)
groups of 3 students
blackboard cues for target questions: *Name, wie alt, nationality, who that?*

STUDENT 1	STUDENT 2	STUDENT 3
Q [= a question]	A [= an answer]	echo Q or A
Sind Sie Kanadier?	*Nein, Amerikaner.*	*Oh, Sie sind Amerikaner.*

– fifth hour of course (Preliminary Chapter 2)

groups of 3 students, with #1 and #3 directed to use Class Text country maps or *Zugbegleiter* in the *Drucksachen* collection

STUDENT 1	STUDENT 2 (NO MAP)	STUDENT 3
[city name]	[ventures guess about country]	[echo, kibitz, show]
Zürich	[*Das ist*] *in* ____ .	*In* ____ ? *Ja/Nein . . .*

– during Chapter 5

groups of 3 students, using urban transit maps, deciding themselves what time it is and maybe inventing own timetables

STUDENT 1	STUDENT 2	STUDENT 3
Wann kommt der nächste Bus nach [*Endstation X, etc.*]?	*Um X Uhr V und dann um . . .*	*Also alle Z Minuten*

– during Chapter 12 (targets: review earlier accusative structure, but with recent vocabulary; review *zum/zur* + noun; simple use of *wenn*)

STUDENT 1	STUDENT 2
Ich brauche/habe kein ____ X	*Sie müssen zum/zur V, wenn Sie ein* ____ X *brauchen.*

– during Chapter 13 (targets: body parts, causation, *seit*)

STUDENT 1	STUDENT 2
pain/*X tut mir weh/*____ *Schmerzen*	echo (*dir/Ihnen*); sympathy; *tut leid*
why/how long/*Seit . . .*	advice/*zu viel, sollen*

– during Chapter 17 (target: nationalities, with humbling review of earliest chapters of book)

STUDENT 1	STUDENT 2	STUDENT 3
Ist X ____ ?	*Nein. Kommt aus* ____	*Also, er/sie ist* ____

– also during Chapter 17 (targets: *jemand/niemand*, review of tenses, cases, and prepositions)

STUDENT 1	STUDENT 2	STUDENT 3
Wo ist mein ____ X	*Nein, niemand hat . . .*	*Dein* ____ X *ist* [*in, auf . . .*]
Jemand hat mein ____ X		

Such schematic exercises can be expanded in several dimensions by the addition of new tasks, vocabulary, or participants. Very important is the notion of repetition with variation – not mindless recitation of grammar–oriented substitution exercises, but instead structured yet creative manipulation within a meaningful context. Useful here are parallel lists of elements to be combined and recombined (e.g., column 1 – people; column 2 – activities; column 3 – companions; column 4 – buildings; column 5 – reasons). More students can be involved in the same conversation by assigning them roving functions appropriate throughout many kinds of conversation (echoing, asking *Warum?*), or by making them "resource" persons who provide vocabulary or essential "facts" in the simulated context. Thus in chapter 9 or so, the resource student might "spin the dial" to select the day and time, and thus determine the rest of the conversation:

STUDENT 1	STUDENT 2
Heute ist Sonntag, und es ist 11 Uhr.	[building] *ist geschlossen, aber wir können zum/zur* [building] *gehen.*

An exercise of *schon/noch nicht* with present and past tenses (chapter 19) might be set up similarly:

STUDENT 1	STUDENT 2	STUDENT 3
Ich möchte essen, etc.	*Es ist 23 Uhr.*	*Du hast noch nicht gegessen?*

Lastly, the basic pattern and situation can be expanded by posing, on repetition, a complication or need for elaboration. An example from chapter 13:

	STUDENT 1	STUDENT 2
(stage 1)	[body part] hurts	[echo and sympathize]
(stage 2)	[same as above] *Nur wenn . . .*	[same as above] + *Wann?* [Then don't . . .]

There are several expansion techniques that can be regarded as virtually generic, at least after the structures and vocabulary they involve have been introduced. One that may be used the very first day of class is echoing, the consciously undertaken version of a tactic that we employ unconsciously in our native language. Repetition of part or all of another's utterance both fixes the linguistic pattern and helps maintain conversation. Very soon the echoing can include alteration of perspective (Student #1: *Ich bin Amerikaner.* Student #2: *So. Sie sind Amerikaner.*). Somewhat later on the roving student or teacher can apply prompts like *Wie, bitte?* or *Was sagt er/sie?* to elicit the echo, with or without introductory *Er/sie sagt (, daß).* The same effect can be attained with an "information pass" built into the exercise (Student #2: [reports to #3 about #1]). The unfortunate confusion of the pronouns *Sie* 'you,' *sie* 'she/her,' and *sie* 'they/them,' and of *er* 'he,' *ihr* 'her/you/their,' and *Ihr* 'your,' guarantees trouble – trouble that will emerge in speaking even when the student has apparently acquired the analytical grammar information. The feature should be checked over and over, and review late in the course will likely show serious deficiencies that fully justify information-checking and passing of information as regular tasks.

Much the same can be said for reformulation of situations from present to past. The student groups are led through present-tense utterances that establish vocabulary and overall structure, as in the chapter 13 example above (*Ich habe Kopfschmerzen, aber nur wenn ich lese.*). The past tense version would be something like:

STUDENT 1	STUDENT 2
[has recovered; lists symptoms]	[had it too]
[Wonder what #2 did to get better]	[Describes treatment]

The transformation of present into past can be introduced even as early as Preliminary Chapter 2. After present-tense conversation the teacher may simply wave a sweeping hand and declare, "*Aber das war alles gestern,*" and then model the reformulation. The encouragement of past-tense practice, both early on and recurrently throughout the course, is a prime example of "spiral syllabus" instruction and should become second nature in the classroom, especially since improvement of communication in past time is a prime part of the transition from Intermediate to Advanced. In general, systematic review is vital, and *Wie, bitte?* has been designed to further it.

Three other strategies have to do less with the details of teaching speaking skills and more with establishing the overall function and atmosphere. Sometimes it is useful to give each member of the group information that the partner or the rest of the group either lacks or does not need. Perhaps one wishes to introduce an unexpected complication, or else to conceal target vocabulary from one speaker and provide it to the other, who is perhaps charged with emulating the friendly native. That may be done impromptu by a whispered or partly concealed written message, or even by having one partner in each group face away from the blackboard. By preparing in advance one may provide cues to one or more of the partners by writing them on different parts of a single (duplicated) sheet of paper, partially separating the sections, and then letting the partners choose their own roles much in the same manner that people pull wishbones.

At some point it becomes necessary to progress beyond the simple pattern of prescribed stimulus and predictable response that characterizes the Class Text Stage 1 situations and similar exercises. Moreover, students doing any kind of frequent oral exercise may fall into the natural but pedagogically harmful patterns of communicating in sentence fragments or, if they are producing creative sentences, of just wanting to convey information with their current facilities rather than focusing on newly introduced resources. The Stage 2 *Situationen* should be used in a manner that encourages or even demands the production of longer utterances or groups of sentences. And indeed that is good preparation for oral tests, where the examiner may well offer such situations as special items, and throughout the test may often offer not questions that invite replies, but rather declarative comments followed by loud pauses to be ended by the student (*Es scheint, Sie müssen viel arbeiten.*). Our overall advice is this: habitually engage your students in vibrant conversation, but know when you should back off and let them deliberate as they seek to work their way through the *Situationen*. In a well-run classroom there should be enough noise that occasionally silence will be golden. Pauses are productive.

Two functions, circumlocution and description, can be regarded as broadly generic; those functions are tied neither to a particular exercise type like small-group work, nor to a proficiency modality, though they are manifestly important in speaking. Circumlocution and description are vital to proficiency at and beyond the Intermediate-High level. The two skills should be practiced constantly, with ever greater demand for management of complexity and an occasional view down from the heights to show how much better one can perform an earlier task, or how the current task could have been performed earlier, though not with as much facility.

There are many ways to prompt the student for circumlocution and description. One may simply offer a list of imaginative and challenging items, either for the class as a whole to work out, or secretly to one partner, who must then communicate the idea in verbal charade form to others in the group, who in turn offer useful questions. Examples suitable to Chapter 18 would be: antacid, dandruff, lens-cleaning kit, flexible watchband, earphones, dental floss, appendix. Similarly, with an eye to structural circumlocution, one can point out the compensatory relationship between grammar and vocabulary, and also urge students to cross the boundaries that tradition-

ally isolate from each other the various parts of speech and structural categories. The language of the *Situationen* is intended to further such conceptual habits. Thus after modal verbs have been introduced the student can be encouraged to realize that communicating the informational content of a pattern such as "It is necessry for X to [verb]" does not require one to know or look up the word "necessary"; employing the simple modal pattern "X + *müssen* + verb" will do. Similarly, the past subjunctive with modal (*Du hättest nicht so viel trinken sollen.*) can often be expressed by an indicative past formulation (*Schade, daß du so viel getrunken hast.*). Part of the battle is won when the student is convinced, negatively, that translation is often unfruitful, and, positively, that it is all right to use any available resources, whether from knowledge already acquired or else information available by reference. Among the latter resources is the *Bildwörterbuch* – not only its various contextual vocabularies, but particularly the final "Categories/ Kategorien" spread (pp. 308–09).

While the terms *beschreiben* and *erklären* are valuable words and are thus featured prominently in chapters 12 and 18, the functions themselves are introduced very early in the book. Correspondingly, description, circumlocution, explanation, and elaboration can be elicited by German prompts much earlier on, without the use of *beschreiben*, *erklären*, etc. One may use, for example, leading yes/no questions (*Hat Ihr Vater auch braune Augen?*) to initiate the elicitation or help out a struggling student; the latter, particularly after a lapse into English, will often benefit from a hint to classify and differentiate (*X? Oh, das ist ein ___ Y, aber . . .*), contextualize (*Wo findet man das?*), or describe function (*Was tut man mit dies___ X?*). Often the simple charm-phrase, *Das können Sie mit anderen Worten sagen*, will promote relief and progress. The elicitation may be integrated into a situation, which then specifies not only the function, but also the context/content and standards of accuracy (*Ich kenne Ihren Vater nicht, aber ich muß ihn am Bahnhof abholen. Es sind viele Leute da. Wie kann ich wissen, wer Ihr Vater ist?*). Similar tasks can be posed in writing exercises or tests.

The other modalities in the classroom

Although acquisition of oral proficiency should be the main goal of classroom activity, the other modalities should not and cannot be totally ignored. In class it is pragmatically useful to undertake frequent if brief checks of the students' progress in skills that they are – supposedly! – pursuing largely through the Study Text; help with study skills and habits will be necessary periodically. Secondly, the idea of simulating actual communicative contexts strongly implies that the modalities cannot be kept in strict isolation from each other. People who are deciding what they want to order in restaurants generally have menus to read; often they listen to the waiter or waitress; and sometimes they even write out their food and beverage orders. But lastly, exercise in speaking is an intense activity. Students deserve a change of pace, and they will also benefit from the introduction of the rich selection of *Wie, bitte?* print and sound realia.

The Bibliography includes discussions of what can be treated only briefly here. In proficiency-oriented instruction, learning by doing is vital. In classroom treatment of reading, listening, and writing you will likely want to take your cue – and even your exercises – from the Study Text. The skills that the student is offered there should be reinforced in class, whether you actually carry out or just emulate the Study Text items.

Here we offer some reminders about general principles and a few remarks about technique. Chief among them is an admonition to discourage the urge to translate, not just in speaking but also in writing, reading and listening. If cautious and indirect error correction is important in encouraging oral proficiency at the Novice and Intermediate levels, it would seem appropriate also in the teaching of writing. Beyond that notion as it pertains to the so-called "production" modalities of speaking and writing is the formulation of its equivalent with regard to the so-called "reception" modalities of reading and listening: the student must be encouraged or even laboriously taught to exercise the techniques of skimming, scanning, inferring, and risk-taking. With some hope one can remark that those are skills that most students know how to apply when they listen or read *outside* the classroom, i.e., when they are listening or reading for everyday proficiency – not for academic achievement – in their native language. With some sadness it must be said that many students instead regard academic study in general, and foreign-language study in particular, as a matter of precise analysis, rote learning, and avoidance of risk.

But be that as it may. The common problem in the foreign-language classroom is how to convince students that they can jump right into what *Wie, bitte?* offers. Since the very first few hours of a course

may well determine its overall tone, the habit of resolutely facing mature realia should be established immediately. It is thus very important that realia be introduced in class and that the Study Text exercises for the preliminary units be taken seriously. After much experience we are convinced that, to a significant extent, proficient is as proficient does. Language teachers can find a lesson in *The Music Man*.

More specifically, the exercise of reading and listening must not be allowed chronically to degenerate into translation exercises and the tedious, analytic processing of language. In psychological terms, the student must expand the "catch as catch can" comprehension skill to accompany the common tendency to work word by word. In terms of pedagogical theory, it would seem that reading and listening comprehension at or around the Intermediate level is founded less in detailed application of grammar than in efficient application of lexicon and skillful inference from structural information acquired by bits and pieces throughout the passage. In the quite practical terms of classroom activity, the teacher should emphasize rapid processing of natural language and industrious listing. Here one should note the prominent mention of note-taking skills in descriptions of listening and reading proficiency. Teach your students to underline or jot down apparently useful information. Repeated, structured effort at comprehension is very useful. Initially the teacher sets a very few global comprehension points, and perhaps one or two more difficult comprehension points, as targets of the first encounter with the reading or listening sample. In subsequent stages of the same exercise, or even later on in the course, the student is encouraged to build on previous knowledge. The desire for such repeated encounters was a major factor in the organization of the *Drucksachen* and the audio realia.

As for proficiency-oriented writing, which should not be confused with writing out analytic grammar exercises, the instructor will likely want to assign and collect regularly at least some of the Study Text writing tasks. It would not be a waste of class time to devote some minutes each week to discussion of such exercises; attention should be given both to form (vocabulary and grammar) and to function (organization, efficiency, phrasing, cultural aspects). Also beneficial will be an occasional writing exercise in class, perhaps as small-group work, with the instructor as roving commentator and resource person. Such exercises can grow organically out of exercises in other modalities. Thus in Chapter 15 or so one might use a listing of hotels in scenic areas to elicit first a low-level review of reading and speaking skills (kinds of room and their prices, etc.). Then might come deliberation about alternatives, with planning of a week's stay (comparative, dates, modals). As a third stage the class might draft letters to the proprietors of the hotels, including details about preferences and contingencies (*wenn, weil*, adjectives). Thereafter, the several small groups might be directed to assume that they are in the midst of their stay and that – now up on their feet and strolling through the classroom! – they are to discuss their experiences during chance encounters with other travelers (past tense, *seit* + present tense, prepositions, reportage and expression of opinion with *daß*). A last stage might comprise the composition of a thank-you note or postcard – if time allows; the previous stages could easily occupy an entire class hour. Field-testing argues strongly that the hours spent in such activities are neither unpleasant nor unproductive.

We conclude the discussion of teaching strategy with two points and a paradigm. 1) In the proficiency-oriented classroom work and play (*Formtrieb* and *Spieltrieb*?) may often overlap, and so often it becomes apparent that language and culture are inseparable. The *Wie, bitte?* package gives prominent place to listening activities, and throughout the text we have mentioned music that is appropriate in theme, grammar, and vocabulary. We encourage you to let your students listen and sing. 2) *Wie, bitte?* is filled with print realia that can do much to further communication and convey atmosphere. We urge you to use it.

Alice Omaggio and Judith A. Muyskens, writing in the classic volume *Teaching for Proficiency: The Organizing Principle* (ed. Theodore V. Higgs), offer language teachers the best advice we have encountered. Omaggio (p.51) proposes five hypotheses about the proficiency-oriented classroom. Muyskens (p.189) complements those hypotheses with practical advice.

- *Hypothesis 1:* Opportunities must be provided for students to practice using the language in a range of contexts likely to be encountered in the target culture.
  Corollary 1: Students should be encouraged to express their own meaning as early as possible in the course of instruction.
  Corollary 2: A proficiency-oriented approach pro-

motes active communicative interaction among students.
Corollary 3: Creative language practice (as opposed to exclusively manipulative or convergent practice) must be encouraged.
Corollary 4: Authentic language should be used in instruction wherever and whenever possible.

- *Hypothesis 2:* Opportunities should be provided for students to carry out a range of functions (task universals) likely to be necessary for interacting in the target language and culture.

- *Hypothesis 3:* There should be concern for the development of linguistic accuracy from the beginning of instruction.

- *Hypothesis 4:* Proficiency-oriented approaches respond to the affective as well as the cognitive needs of students.

- *Hypothesis 5:* Cultural understanding must be promoted in various ways so that students are prepared to understand, accept, and live harmoniously in the target-language community.

Checklist for daily progress toward proficiency

1. Did I include a warm-up activity which asked students to perform a function or a contextualized or personalized activity?
2. Was most classroom interaction in the target language?
3. If I presented vocabulary or grammar, did I do so in context?
4. Were any exercises I did contextualized or meaningful?
5. Did I include some speaking practice which required students to interact or be creative with the language?
6. Was small-group work included in the class hour?
7. Did the students participate in some type of role-playing activity?
8. Did I include sufficient listening practice to help my students understand utterances in situations?
9. Did I include or assign writing practice which gave students practice in writing on topics of interest to them?
10. Did I provide a context for culture and an opportunity for students to express a culturally appropriate act?
11. Did I correct students in a way that was helpful to them?

Chapter Notes

Chapter P1

p. 3 (More Personal Information): Lists of academic subjects are provided in the *Bildwörterbuch* (p. 291). We suggest you simplify terms for majors or courses wherever possible, and that you teach students the same strategy. Example: linear algebra = *Mathematik*; weight training = *Sport*. Teach similarly the knack of enumeration as a general technique; present situation: if you don't know the word for the major, but do know the names of individual subjects or courses, then list those – that, too, is an appropriate response to the question, *"Was studieren Sie?"*

Chapter 2

p. 23 (*Situationen* 1): Enliven the situations and underscore the concept of systematic review by setting up situations that are actually two or more simultaneous conversations (like some of the Stage 1 exercises, but not outlined in detail). Example: groups of three students; A and B carry out conversation based on a Chapter 2 situation; C interrupts with questions to A involving material from earlier units (e.g., in the midst of ordering a meal, the student playing guest has to field curious questions about nationality, residence, etc.).

p. 28 (Rather than translating, illustrate the meanings of the new expressions by citing examples from the dialogs): Example: *"Ein Doppelzimmer mit Bad kostet hundert Mark. Möchten Sie das?" "Nein." "Warum nicht?" "Das ist ein bißchen zu teuer."* Encourage similar exploration of the dialogs as archetypal situations that can be elaborated to illustrate the basic points of the chapter and to exercise structures and vocabulary introduced earlier.

p. 28 (*Struktur 2, #2*): Exercise (use menus for props): Rapid-fire orders to waiter, who replies with confirming echo (*"Bringen Sie uns X." "Ja, also X."*), or advice to other diners about which item to eat or not to eat, with similar echoing as reply. Focus correction on the imperative and the negation, not on any flawed attempts at accusative.

We suggest that you not correct the written form **Sein Sie*, at least not *overtly*, and that you readily accept in spoken form anything in the range *"sein/seien"* (cf. Austrian forms). Save correction for the logical but distinctly incorrect and non-native error **Sind Sie!*

Chapter 4

p. 43 (*Situationen* 1, Stage 1, #2): *In general:* You can turn small situations into virtual "crowd" scenes by instructing other students to play the role of nosy bystanders and echo the central characters' words – to the point of mirth, which a good class will read readily. Beneath the fun, of course, is a lot of practice. Covertly, you can use the better students to help you model, coach, and monitor, without turning them into self-conscious lecturers. As bystanders they help poorer students through the main roles. In a similar way, you can have students – poorer or better ones—serve as covert prompters by getting them to assume the role of English-speaking "prompters" – companions who ostensibly speak no German and constantly prod A and B to say things for them ("Tell him what time it is." "No, he didn't understand it. Tell him that 21 o'clock means 9 o'clock.").

p. 43 (*Situationen* 1, Stage 2): Perhaps your students can handle the "native speaker" role without help. One way to make sure things go smoothly is to hand each "native speaker" partner a prompt card with useful utterances on it. Another is to have the partners shift position so that the "native speaker" faces the blackboard and the "victim" cannot see it. You can then write on the board key phrases for the native speaker to use, or directions about how the "plot" of the situation is to progress ("No. The seats are taken." "Ask her how far she's going." "Say you don't know. Someone was there earlier.").

p. 43 (*VSd*): Encourage past tense of *sein* for statements like "We were there on Monday." But note that here many likely utterances can be "tenseless," in the sense that the present tense will cover the past, the present, and the future. Thus the hotel room that cost an outrageous amount like still costs and will continue to cost too much. Note the wording of the task: "Offer some advice drawn from your own experiences" is essentially tenseless and therefore does not lead the translation-oriented person into thinking that the past tense is necessary.

p. 48 (*Struktur 2, #1*): Note the distinction between *tense* and *time*, and the importance of *modality* (speaking vs. writing, listening vs. reading). Grammar-oriented speakers of English tend to overuse the German future tense, especially in speaking. For this reason, and because of the confusion that can be caused by the triple function of *werden*, the Class Text intentionally omits the future *tense* for oral production, but encourages attention to expression of future *sense*. The

Reference Grammar does present the future tense. See ACTFL/ETS *Proficiency Guidelines* for German, speaking and writing modalities, Intermediate to Advanced levels.

Reinforce with an exercise in which time phrases (e.g., months), even those for distant time, are used with present tense for future tense. Can also reinforce verb location if the sentences are set up to begin with the time phrase.

Chapter 6

p. 62 (*Struktur 1, #3*): Exercise: Give city-landmark directions using *suchen, finden, sehen*; encourage production of lists of landmarks, and also echoing strategy; or use a map. Targets: *"Was suchen Sie?" "Ich suche den X." "Den X sehen Sie hier."* Or without map: chain of landmarks (*"und dann sehen Sie X. Gehen Sie 200m weiter, dann finden Sie . . ."*) Now is the time for direct correction of errors in the accusative; be sure any grammatical explanation is accompanied by intense production drill, with plenty of modeling and echoing.

Chapter 7

p. 72 (*Struktur 1, #2*): The presentation of "two-way" prepositions is designed to spread over several units (see Chapter 15), so that the student is not faced with a supposedly momentous case distinction while still learning the prepositions themselves, and while still not at all solid in the notion of case. *Therefore do not try to teach the accusative/dative distinction here.* Note that the exposition does not claim that *in, an,* and *vor* require (much less "govern") the dative case, but rather that they can be used to describe location – and that the dative case is used for that purpose. You need not fear fossilization (i.e., that the student will forever group such prepositions with the dative-only ones). The decision to present the dative usage before accusative was based on the likely predominance of location vs. motion descriptions in common speech, and on the pressing need to present early basic prepositions like *von, aus, mit,* and *nach*. Note also the discussion of preposition and case control in the ACTFL/ETS *Proficiency Guidelines* for

the Intermediate High and Advanced levels.

After modeling the basic patterns, try a couple of rapid-fire, who's-on-first exercises based on the question *"Wo ist X?"* 1) Student A: *"Vor dem/der X;"* Student B: *"Nein, in dem/der* (same noun and thus same case signal)." 2) Student A: *"In dem/der X;"* Student B: *"Nein, in dem/der Y* (different noun, same case, but maybe different case signal)." Use obvious realia. Note the interference of *an* with English 'on,' but don't harp on it.

p. 78 (*Struktur 2, #1*): Exercise Discussion of what to do on arrival; use verbs *ankommen, anrufen, aussteigen, umsteigen*. Aim for plenty of echoing (*"OK, Kantstraße. Ich steige dort aus. Und dann . . ."*) and structural variation (*"Sie müssen mich anrufen . . . Ja, rufen Sie mich an;" "Sie müssen dort umsteigen . . . Dort müssen Sie umsteigen"*). The same exercise can readily be converted to a writing task, and in fact serves as a good review of much of the course up to now (e.g., prepositions, cases).

p. 78 (*Struktur 2, #2*): The book contains many exercises that encourage *production* of time phrases. Be sure to check for listening comprehension – not just of *Viertel* and *um*, but also of *vor, nach,* etc. Most students will still have some difficulty managing such information if it is densely packed (*"Weitere Züge um 91.0, 10.20 und 11.30"*), or if the surrounding language contains distractions.

Chapter 10

p. 108 (*Struktur 2, #2*): You might want to postpone *gern haben*, since it doesn't fit the model "liking to do something." It also tends to be overused by American students. *Gefallen* is introduced in Chapter 14; we suggest you avoid teaching "like" until then. An easy equivalent can be *"ich finde X schön/interessant."* See the *Bildwörterbuch* pages of activities and sports (302–05) for class exercises using *gern: "Sehen Sie gern fern?" "Nein, aber ich lese gern"* etc. At the very *end* of your exercise, when you think the use of *gern* is solid, remind the class about *möchte* and drill that. Then intersperse the two in a single

drill. *"Fahren Sie gern schi?" "Ja, ich fahre gern schi – und ich möchte jetzt schifahren."*

Chapter 11

p. 112 (*Struktur 1, #1*): Drill the *du/Sie* distinction relentlessly. Possibilities: Address a question to the student in *Sie* form; student reformulates the question to a neighbor, changing to *du* as appropriate; the neighbor responds. Example: Teacher: *"Geht er heute abend ins Kino?"* Student A (to neighbor): *"Gehst du heute abend ins Kino?"* Student B: *"Ja, ich gehe heute abend ins Kino."* Stay with the nominative case for now.

Use *du* in genuine student interaction in the classroom, in situations in which they would naturally use it in the target culture. Insist, however, that students continue to use *Sie* where it is appropriate in the role-play situations.

Do not introduce *ihr* yet; wait until Chapter 13.

p. 112 (*Struktur 1, #2*): These four verbs are handy in talking about situations in the zoo. You will find it helpful to use them extensively in describing one person's zoo activities: *"Liesel geht zum Imbiß und ißt dort Eiskrem. Aber sie vergißt ihre Tasche beim Imbiß und muß sie wieder finden. Endlich nimmt sie die Tasche und geht zum Affenhaus. Dort sieht sie ihren Bruder Alfred."* Setup: *Liesel gehen Imbiß essen Eiskrem. Aber vergessen Tasche und müssen finden. Endlich nehmen sie Tasche und gehen Affenhaus. Dort sehen sie Bruder Alfred.* (Present this vocabulary in columns if you wish to avoid the appearance of communication via pidgin.)

p. 118 (*Struktur 2, #1*): Opportunity for review of comparison functions without comparative forms: *kälter = nicht so warm; schöner im Sommer = nicht so schön im Winter* etc. (See Chapter 2 grammar for details.)

Exercises: Refer to *Bildwörterbuch* section "Body Parts/*Körperteile*" (294–295) for clothing vocabulary. Compare clothing of class members: 1) Johns Hose ist schön, aber Leroys Hose ist *schöner*. 2) Leroys Hose ist *schöner als* Johns Hose. 3) Johns Hose ist nicht *so schön wie* Leroys Hose.

p. 118 (*Struktur 2, #3*): Reciprocal exercises: Teacher: *"Ich sehe dich, und du siehst . . ."* Student: *". . . mich."* (After the pattern is established, the teacher stops at *dich: "Ich sehe dich . . ."* Student: *". . . und du siehst mich."* Extend to other subjects and include other accusative forms as review: *"Du siehst Hans . . ." ". . . und er sieht dich." "Monika sieht dich . . ." ". . . und du siehst sie."*

Similar exercise with *du – dein: "Ich habe meinen Hut . . ." ". . . und du has deinen Hut."* Include similar review of other possessive adjectives.

Chapter 14

p. 147 (*Gespräche 2, #1*): Call attention to correct pronunciation: *Jens-chen*, not *Jenschen*. Mention that the suffix says something about Jens's age.

p. 147 (*Gespräche 2, #5*): Call attention to the use of the title instead of *"Professor Lenzen."*

Show students that German has an equivalent to *". . . you know, . . ."* Mention *"Weißt du"* as well.

Call attention to the use of the definite article to refer to a part of the body, but don't talk yet about reflexive constructions using this feature (*sich die Hände waschen*, etc.). Perhaps mention that English makes limited use here of the definite article rather than the possessive; thus a parent preparing a child for bed, or a nurse treating a patient, may say, "Well, now, let's wash the hands, shall we?"

Chapter 15

p. 152 (*Struktur 1, #2*): Provide a change in context, and an opportunity for review, by comparison of people (size, age, etc.). To encourage production of gradations of comparison, and to avoid embarrassing anyone, you might draw or project a chart showing biographical data about a large and colorful family; thus *"Trudi ist weit älter als ihr Bruder."* Note that good management of comparative can often substitute for the much more difficult superlative; thus *"noch billiger,"* for example, can be used when three or more entities are being compared.

Chapter 16

p. 162 (*Struktur 1, #1*): Model the difference carefully and make attention to it part of situation work. If necessary, force the point by encouraging exaggeration of the difference. The final message, though, should not be that the use of the subjunctive is prissy, but rather that it is a powerful resource for those who want to do well at the highest levels of human interaction, whatever the language. Remark that the more expensive the restaurant, or the more important the negotiations, the likelier it is that the subjunctive will be called for; e.g., "Could you bring us the check?" rather than "How much do I owe you?"

p. 163 (*Situationen 1, #3*): Students can use various materials that list opticians and addresses (e.g., Freiburg list used in preliminary units), or can make up addresses suitable to the map being used, or can work around the problem with real-world knowledge and common sense (e.g., C: Go to the center of town and look for the pedestrian zone; there's bound to be one there.)

p. 163. "Asks C to orient them:" low-level = *"Ist das die X-straße?"* or *"Wo sind wir?"*; higher-level = *"Können Sie uns zeigen/sagen, wo . . . ?"*

"Worried about distances:" low-level = *"Ist das weit?"*; higher level = *"Aber wir wissen nicht, wie weit ist," "Das könnte aber sehr weit von hier sein/ liegen."*

p. 168 (*Struktur 2, #1*): The basic pattern was established lexically in Chapter 8: *Opernkasse* (*am* + date, *in der ___en Reihe*). By now there should be no end of possibilities for contextual exercises, since the student should be able to fill the pattern "noun + preposition + article + adjective + noun" in many situations. For contrastive exercise of cases, set up something like the following. Student A: *Ich möchte ein X*. Student B: *Brauchen Sie auch ein Y?* A: *Ja, haben Sie ein X mit einem/r* (*adjective*) *Y?*; or, A: *Ich möchte ein X*. B: *Wir haben Xs mit* (*adjective*) *Ys und Xs mit* (*other adjective*) *Ys*. A: *Ich möchte ein X mit einem/r* (*adjective*) *Y*.

p. 168 (*Struktur 2, #3*): Similar is the alternation of close equivalents of the single common word *freundlich*; the Anglo-Saxon "friendly" is the everyday word, but we also have "amiable" and "amicable" from French and Latin. Students who pooh-pooh the latter two as "bookworm" words should be reminded that the phrase "amicable divorce" is widely used and likely to appear in any supermarket tabloid newspaper.

Chapter 17

p. 172 (*Struktur 1, #1*): There is no way to satisfy everybody about the terms here, and in any case the first-year German student cannot be expected to follow every nuance of geography and ideology. Obviously, our practice conforms most closely to usage in the FRG, which is where most American visitors will spend most of their time. You might point out how the linguistic and political complication of *westdeutsch*, etc., is often avoided by use of "BRD" and "DDR" as quasi-adjectives in compound nouns ("DDR-Hotels") or in noun qualifiers ("die Hotels in der DDR," "die Grenzen der DDR").

p. 175 (*Strategie – man*): Some students may want to discuss how linguistic gender, biological gender, and social issues are related. You might point out that gender is a major feature of German, as it is of many other European languages, and also that over the centuries there have been various overt attempts – successful or not – to reform the language, for reasons aesthetic (Gottsched) or ideological (Goebbels). More comprehensible might be a discussion of changing fashions in courtesy terms or professional titles (*Frau Dipl. Kaufmann, Direktor[in]*). Note too the use of feminine *Person . . . sie/die* as the individual by indefinite "person" of either sex (*die Person, die wir für diese Stelle suchen, . . .*). Mention dangers in the use of *Volk*, tainted by National Socialism ("Ein Reich! Ein Volk! Ein Führer!").

p. 178 (*Struktur 2, #1*): In this chapter, at least, go easy on the challenging topic of reflexive verbs, and instead encourage the student to regard the concept of reflexivity as something rather ordinary. That is, the concept of dative or accusative objects has been introduced earlier, *without* exclusion of reflexive conditions. In ordinary situations the many possible recipients of an action or object might just include the speaker, and indeed some students may on their own successfully produce reflexives in the first or second person. Teach and exercise accordingly. Review dative and accusative case with a whole list of objects possible in a context, and matter-of-factly include the speaker among them. Example: Tell about the people and things on your souvenir (or Christmas gift) list. You've been good, so reward yourself when you go shopping. Similarly in third person form. Demonstrate emphatically – by pointing, etc. – how *ihn/sie/es* and *ihm/ihr/ihnen* are insufficient. Contrast English system (-self) and its special problems (tendency to create *hisself by analogy to myself, yourself, etc.). Perhaps mention the English dialectal reflexives that closely parallel German ("I'm gonna buy me [not 'myself'] a gun." Note that the German verbs used in this initial presentation all have close parallels in English. Expect and deal leniently with confusion of accusative and dative cases, but perhaps point out the ridiculousness of *"Ich kaufe mich. . . ."*

p. 178 (*Struktur 2, #3*): Possibilities for exercises: for *aber:* You are reluctantly going to do X (buy the gift, etc.); discuss your reservations; for *sondern:* Your friend always wants special treatment in restaurants; tell about how he/she tries to substitute menu items. Note, however, that such exercises do not demand *aber* or *sondern,* but rather only create circumstances where the speaker – native or otherwise – might use those resources. You might point out – and not just with the present topic – how lack of ability to use a new feature, though it may not be crippling, may impose a high cost in repetition and circumlocution, though of course one should be able to work one's way around such deficiencies. Thus *"Wir möchten nicht Montag abfahren, sondern Dienstag,"* can be expressed – but laboriously and rather childishly – by *"Wir möchten nicht Montag abfahren.*

Wir möchten Dienstag abfahren." The overall point, long since a part of proficiency notions, is that grammar and vocabulary are mutually compensatory.

Chapter 18

p. 182 (*Struktur 1, #1*): Check again the distinction of *möchte, gern* + verb, and *gefallen*. Don't expect students to produce *gefallen* in any conjugation but the present. In general, go lightly on the dative verbs. Establish the verb itself in the student's vocabulary, and then reinforce the core phrase (e.g., *Das gefällt mir*) as lexical rather than structural knowledge.

p. 185 (Description in detail): The present section may seem verbose and trivial, but remember that the student is now earnestly attempting ACTFL/ETS Advanced tasks in speaking and writing; there the ability to narrate and describe is vital. The skills discussed here seem to come naturally in one's native language, for they are learned very early and exercised often in real life; consequently, they are seldom taught systematically in schools, and are therefore not part of the ordinary foreign language program. Nevertheless, many students do not take these discourse skills with them into the new language. A few sessions of five or ten minutes, in which you work carefully through a description, will not be wasted. The overall skill, of course, is circumlocution, coupled with the confidence that one can get the job done if one keeps trying. By this chapter the serious student should be able and willing to try to describe almost any everyday object and even some abstracts. Here you will find the *Bilwörterbuch* displays useful – not so much those that provide specialized vocabulary, but those that present actions, qualities, and categories.

p. 188 (*Struktur 2, #2*): Exercises: 1) Student A poses a straightforward question, perhaps from an early chapter (*"Wo ist das Hotel Krone?"*); B reacts in surprise or annoyance (*"Wie, bitte?"*); C (A's companion) rephrases the question more

effectively, *"Wissen Sie, wo . . . ?"* 2) The class devises a newsworthy event (store robbery, accident on the street, visit by a dignitary, etc.), then thinks of as many questions as possible that could shed light on the event. (*"Wer war der Mann?"*) Then a police officer interviews bystanders: *"Wissen Sie, wer der Mann war?"* *"Wissen Sie, was er dort machen wollte?"* The present tense can be used to facilitate description in the absence of the simple past, but push the use of *war, hatte,* and past of modals.

Chapter 19

p. 191 (*Gespräche 1, #3*): *Aufstieg* presents a good occasion for work with word roots: *Abstieg, Umstieg, Einstieg* with their verbs *auf-, ab-, um-, einsteigen; Steigung* 'incline,' also the town *Gaislingen an der Steige* south of Stuttgart.

Present *aus-* and *einwandern* with nouns *Aus-, Einwanderer, Aus-, Einwanderung, wandern* with compounds *Wanderschuhe, -möglichkeiten, -lust.*

p. 192 (*Struktur 1, #1*): See how many sentences the class can devise that being with *"Es ist immer gut, . . ."* or *"Es wäre nicht schön, . . ."* Put a list of contextually related infinitives on the board to facilitate creativity. Students work in pairs; the pair with the most legitimate sentences wins something. Perhaps add another level: mutual conversion of formulations using *zu* + infinitive and *wenn* + subject + verb.

p. 195 (Giants of German Music): The list does not aim to be comprehensive. It ignores significant older works that are *"nur für Kenner und Liebhaber,"* and also important recent composers whose works are not widely known. The intent is to raise the student from virtual ignorance to passing familiarity with renowned figures, many of whom have had some effect on American popular culture. How you use the material will depend on the linguistic ability and cultural sophistication of your students – and also their religious background. Thus some teachers will feel it appropriate to mention Moses Mendelssohn. Some, too, may find it appropriate to add to the list of composers Martin Luther, since many students indeed known "Away in a Manger." We suspect that few students will be impressed by a discussion of "Mack the Knife." *Sic transit,* or at least *O tempore!* Above all, carry on the good work of promoting the humanities without making those who know or care little about classical music feel humiliated. Don't hesitate to exploit the cultural eclecticism of the liberals or the cupidity of the Philistines. If the visitor to a truly exotic culture will readily grant the importance of the specialized areas of knowledge it emphasizes, then give Germans their due too. Mention, too, that – all else being equal – the American businessperson who shows awareness of German culture may well enjoy a negotiating advantage in dealing with German firms.

Use the biographies to review ordinal numbers and expressions for years and centuries. Use names of composers and their works to fine-tune pronunciation.

Point out to your students that if one deals seriously with the German-speaking cultures, one will likely find it useful to have a working knowledge of the main classical figures and their works – or at the very least the ability to recognize and pronounce their names. If acquiring such knowledge seems "foreign" to your students, they're right. It may be some consolation to remember that those who grow up in the German-speaking countries ought to know more about classical music than they do. The language of many of the great classical works is their own native tongue, and all around them they can see the traces of the famous composers – monuments, relics, and the actual places in which the musicians were born, lived, performed, and died.

The German musical tradition extends back more than 1000 years. The very first work of German literature, the *Hildebrandslied,* a heroic song of the 8th century, was likely sung or at least chanted. The 13th century saw the peak of *Minnesang,* or courtly love song, verses and melodies composed in honor of idealized love by poets associated with the various royal courts.

Chapter 20

p. 201 (*Gespräche* 1, #1): Do so not by quizzing the information in isolation, but rather by making it part of a communicative context. Examples: 1) In a listening test the student is asked to judge whether pairs of utterances are logically compatible with each other. Logical: *"Eine Oper von Wagner. Möchtest du mit?"* + *"Wie lange dauert die Aufführung?"* Illogical: *"Das ist eine große Messe!"* + *"Wo ist denn der Staubsauger?"* A writing test might direct the student to consult one of the calendars of cultural events and then to write a note telling a friend who likes a certain kind of music (e.g., German sacred music) what days would be best for a visit.

p. 201 (*Gespräche* 1, #4): The dative with *wegen* is intentional. It fits the context – both immediate (taxi driver) and general (prevalence of dative case in casual conversation, even among the educated). Elsewhere *wegen* appears with feminine nouns, which do not raise the issue of genitive vs. dative case. In *Wie, bitte?* the genitive case – *as a target for production* – is presented late, and only in its function of expressing possession. Note, though, that the genitive case may be encountered quite early in the reading and listening materials, where comprehension of it is not a matter of consequence, since meaning is likely fathomed through other and stronger signals. Most first-year students (i.e., most Intermediate-Low or Intermediate-Mid language users) function essentially without consistent respect to case. When the "production" skills of speaking and writing are targeted, most students – and not just those in the first year! – will be so occupied with handling the other three cases, including their complex prepositional distributions, that they cannot cope communicatively with yet another case presented in its entirety. Consider carefully the concept of *modality* and the idea of context/content in the special proficiency-oriented sense. In higher-level communication, and certainly in writing, sophisticated users of German will often seek – sedulously!

– to employ the genitive case, though well-educated speakers may indeed produce the dative with *wegen* even in serious professional discourse. But in situations corresponding to the ACTFL/ETS Intermediate level, assiduous use of the genitive case, particularly in speaking, will likely be regarded as *Stilbruch,* as an indicator of stiltedness, or – when non-native speakers are involved – as a confirmation of foreignness and a sign that the speaker is not comfortable with the language and is preoccupied rather with textbook grammar. The writing done at the Intermediate level is also of a kind in which the genitive might easily be overused. Such considerations – not just the appealing simplicity of an essentially "three-case" grammatical system – determined the authors' management of the genitive case itself, and of the "officially" genitive prepositions as well. The same can be said – though with pangs of conscience – of the treatment of the future tense in *Wie, bitte?* The Intermediate-High speaker does not need it, though it might be argued that the Intermediate-Mid writer should be able to construct it.

Emphasize *vergleichen,* like *beschreiben,* as words and functions important to the concept of proficiency. Offer appropriate exercises, for example, quick descriptions of concrete objects; this is a good opportunity to review Chapter 18.

p. 202 (*Struktur* 1, #1): *Da*-compounds are extremely difficult to elicit in a proficiency-oriented context. Try exercising them as part of exchanges which emphasize echoing strategies (A: *Sind Sie für oder gegen X?* B: *Ich bin für X.* A: *Sie sind also dafür. Nächste Frage: . . .*). Or emphasize their pronominal function by a chain exercise: A: *Ich sehe ein X . . .* B: *. . . und dahinter ein Y.* Note the importance of visual cues in such exercises; try to introduce rich contexts, whether from the realia, the *Bildwörterbuch,* or your own materials. When testing, offer questions that include long but largely comprehensible strings of prepositional phrases (*"Sind Sie für oder gegen finanzielle Hilfe für Sport an* *dieser Universität, auch wenn die Studenten mehr bezahlen müßten?"*). Conceivably some students could repeat much of the string; those who can handle *da*-compounds will likely produce them.

We suggest you not discuss *wo*-compounds, but rather encourage the ability to produce combinations like *an was* and *mit wem*.

p. 202 (*Struktur 1, #2*): The topic is introduced largely as a simple foundation for coursework in the second year and beyond, since proficiency in it is a feature of the ACTFL/ETS Superior level. Specialized (or "abstract" or "idiomatic") use of prepositions should therefore not be belabored, at least by analytic discussion. Important are the high-frequency combinations illustrated here. Intensive context-oriented exercise is probably best, and of course certain formulations will be mastered lexically rather than analytically (e.g., *"Ich interessiere mich für . . . ,"* but not the same pattern with other subjects or tenses). Bear in mind that students at the Intermediate level are still not solid in either the very choice of preposition or, given success in that, the management of case.

Here might be the place to point out – at least to the better students likely to continue study of German – the virtues of careful dictionary use, since all but the briefest of dictionaries address preposition selection in their entries on verbs. Do retain a proficiency-oriented perspective, though. In genuine communicative contexts one seldom has the luxury of time to consult a dictionary for such sophisticated information. Of course one such context is written communication composed at some leisure (e.g., a letter of inquiry about foreign-study programs). If you conduct such tasks as exercises or tests, you might permit use of dictionaries, and then check to see who exploited the opportunity.

p. 202 (*Struktur 1, #2*): If you teach in an area where "wait *for*" is expressed colloquially as "wait *on*" (in the sense of "await," not that of "take meal orders"), concede the

variation, and then maybe turn the point to advantage by mentioning the country-western song, "That Girl Who Waits on Tables Used to Wait for Me at Home" (Ronnie Milsap), which demonstrates that the distinction is understood even in those areas that often blur it in casual speech. Even if the linguistic point of the allusion is not grasped entirely, the idiosyncratic cultural excursus will affect your image in the classroom.

p. 202 (*Struktur 1, #3*) Expect – and to some extent tolerate – serious confusion of dative and accusative cases, especially in lower-frequency patterns (e.g., *ihr* or *sie* ["they"] forms), or when the need to generate tense forms adds a distraction. Like the verb/preposition combinations discussed above, systematically produced reflexives are difficult to elicit in a proficiency-oriented context, though you can focus attention on them and still maintain some situational realism. Example: provide student A with a basic utterance that involves the reflexive (*"Wo kann ich mir etwas zu essen kaufen?"*); student B listens, then asks C what A said; C: *"Wo kann sie sich etwas zu essen kaufen?"* etc. The same "information-pass" technique can be used – *without* sacrificing communicational verisimilitude – in almost any instance where you wish to conduct intense exercises with an entire grammatical system without totally sacrificing the impression of realistic communication.

p. 202 (*Struktur 1, #3*): A useful lower-level exercise might feature elicitation of single shorter comments, followed by a summary that involves structural transformation (e.g., A: *X zieht sich vor dem Essen um, und ich ziehe mich vor dem Essen um.* B: *Was macht ihr?* A: *"Wir . . ."*

We suggest you resist any urge to contrast *sich* (acc.) *anziehen* and similar patterns with *sich* (dat.) *etwas* (acc.) *anziehen*. Though the scintillating alternation of grammatical cases is natural to the native speaker of German, and offers the advanced non-native speaker a chance to show off, the demand for such manipulation from Intermediate

users of German constitutes something akin to pedagogical abuse.

p. 208 (*Struktur 2, #2*): Intermediate speakers do not readily produce infinitive phrases, though they may wander into such structures on their own because English has a structure that seems parallel (sometimes misleadingly so – **Ich wolle zu gehen* for "I want to go"). Thus the feature is difficult to exercise contextually, and also to target for proficiency testing. Quite often a good student will carry out the equivalent function with *wenn* + subject/verb (*um . . . zu* = *weil* + subject + modal verb phrase). Such performance should not be penalized overtly, though the student who can produce both structures is superior. You might try to exercise and elicit the structure by setting up stylized conversations that proceed from simple fact statements (*"Wir gehen in die Stadt"*), through discussion of causes (*"Warum?" "Wir wollen die Karten abholen"*), to the combination of action and reason in a single sentence, with encouragement to reformulate *wenn/weil* clauses into *um/um . . . zu* phrases – *wherever possible;* remember that the infinitive phrases are possible only where the same subject is involved throughout the sentence. Thus *"Meine Frau geht in die Stadt, weil ich Briefmarken brauche"* cannot directly be transformed into a statement with *um . . . zu*, though of course one – though not many first-year German students – might produce *". . . um Briefmarken für mich zu kaufen."* We suggest you limit the treatment to a few carefully structured exercises in which you heartily encourage decent management of *wenn/weil* – still difficult for Intermediate speakers – and joyfully greet infinitive phrases, without suggesting that one is better than the other. Perhaps make two columns on the board, one headed *Was tut X?* and the other *Warum?*, and then list possibilities in telegram style (*geht in die Stadt + braucht Briefmarken"* OR *in die Stadt gehen + Briefmarken brauchen*, the latter to encourage the infinitive). Above all, don't lose what you have won by harshly criticizing the student who discusses facts with their causes and conditions in fluent sequences of separate sentences. Let students find out largely for themselves the advantages of being able to manage several structures rather than only one. You might illustrate, though, how the same infinitive phrases can be combined with clauses involving any tense or grammatical subject, without the need for producing the tense again or fitting a verb and a subject together.

If your students are still having great difficulty merely combining clauses with *wenn* or *weil*, you might nearly eliminate presentation and discussion of this item; where infinitive phrases are encountered in reading or listening, they (or at least *zu*-phrases if not *um . . . zu*-phrases) can often be managed intuitively.

p. 209 (*Situationen* 2, Stage 1, #3 – "gives detail, reasons"): Preparation: listing of appropriate adjectives (*süß, trocken, preiswert*). You might also try soliciting expression of some fancy wine terms with first-year German vocabulary and structures. Thus: "This wine keeps well" = "*Sie können diesen Wein auch nach 10 Jahren trinken*," "*Nach 10 Jahren schmeckt dieser Wein immer noch gut*," or even – to emphasize grammatical targets of the chapter – "*Diesen Wein müssen Sie nicht sofort trinken*" or "*Sie brauchen diesen Wein nicht sofort zu trinken*." By all means have fun burlesquing the fancy language of wine connoisseurs and bringing it down to earth: thus "may appeal to the naïve palate" = "*Wenn man nicht weiß, was gut ist, dann trinkt man diesen Wein gern*."

p. 209 (*VSd* #2): Aside from any ethical function, the item is intended primarily as a reinforcement of modal verbs, particularly *dürfen*. Note, too, how sternly the DDR attempts to deal with drinking and driving. Should you wish to pursue the point, either in class or as a situation in an oral test, pose this task, noting how important the subjunctive might be as mollification: "A friend of yours has drunk too much. Tactfully convince him or her to stop, and to get home some other way than by driving."

Chapter 21
p. 214 (*Die "Deutsche Frage"*): Students in the U.S. may well have

difficulty understanding the deep divisions and ambivalent ideas of cultural unity discussed here, though Canadian students may benefit from their knowledge of Québec's much-debated status, as well as from the larger issue of French vs. British culture. Point out that Americans do not ordinarily say they speak "American," but rather "English," just as Austrians do not speak "*Österreichisch*," but rather *Deutsch*. Offer this larger cultural image: suppose that the Civil War had ended in a Southern victory and a bitter geographical division of the country, with citizens of both countries sharing the adjective "American" and a sense of origin and culture, but divided physically by an armed border stretching westward from the Mason-Dixon Line, with barbed wire separating the White House from the Capitol, and the northern remnant of the United States having its capital in Springfield, IL, home of Abraham Lincoln. You might mention as well that while some Germans will describe themselves proudly as "*deutsch*," not many West Germans identify themselves with emotion as *citizens* of the Federal Republic with the same passion (and sometimes arrogance) that many American will proclaim their citizenship.

Some nastier features: the widespread restriction of the term "*deutsch*" to ethnic Germans, excluding even native-born citizens or residents of other descent; sarcastic comment *echt deutsch* applied to a child whose mother was ethnic German but father apparently Middle-Eastern; Nazi slogans like "*Ein Reich, ein Volk, ein Führer!*"

p. 214 (*Die "Deutsche Frange"*): Mention the terms *Hochdeutsch* and *Schwyzerdütsch,* and note our English word "*Dutch*" and the American habit of calling German-Americans "Dutch" – not just the Pennsylvania Germans, but also application of the word as a nickname ("Dutch" Schulz the gangster, baseball player Honus ["The Flying Dutchman"] Wagner, etc.); if you can, demonstrate a few distinct dialect differences, or bring in appropriate audio materials.

p. 218 (*Struktur* 2, #3): Good chance for a combination of review of present perfect (other verbs) with exercise of these preterite forms: foreground narration (presentation of facts) might well be in present perfect (e.g., *hat . . . geschrieben*), while background commentary is provided in preterite (*sagte, wußte*). But the point should not be harped on; even the Intermediate-High speaker will be limited largely to the very common preterites (*sein, haben,* modals), and will by no means handle the present perfect confidently and accurately. There is much to be said in favor of tacit – but rich! – exposure to the preterite as it appears in print; for that, use the many realia items that, like the city histories, distinctly focus on the past. A caveat: at this stage, the student's actual comprehension of authentic texts whose time-frame is the past may well depend less on recognition of verb forms than on perception of other cues (time phrases, even numerical dates). If ability to deal with genuine language is a sign of proficiency, then perhaps that mode of comprehension can suffice here.

p. 218 (*Struktur* 2, #3): Why the mixture of tenses? Remember the basic principles of German verb placement: (1) in statements, the conjugated verb appears in second position, early in the sentence; (2) the present perfect consists of an initial form of *haben* or *sein*, with the participle at the end of the clause. The past tense is more difficult to form or recollect, where creation of the present perfect requires only an initial use of *haben* or *sein*, after which there may be quite some time before the rest of the verb must be produced. There present perfect can be used "on the fly." But past forms of high-frequency verbs will be learned and reinforced through frequent use. Note the contrast to English: the present perfect does not help one buy time to recollect a verb form, since the participle appears soon after the auxiliary. Therefore the preterite, which involves only a single word and therefore no syntactical complexity, has a relatively greater appeal against the present perfect.

Chapter 22

p. 221 (zerstört): Note the passive construction minus the auxiliary. You might seek to introduce other such elliptical phrases as preparation for the systematic introduction of the passive in upcoming chapters.

p. 224 (Major Political Figures): Earlier in Wie, bitte? there were lists of important historical facts (Chapter 10) and composers (Chapter 19), with details provided. You might now try to encourage your students to seek their own information, whether they use reference works in German or English. It's a chance to push the study of German as part of a liberal education. A great English writer once remarked, "Knowledge is of two kinds: we know a subject ourselves, or we know where we can find information upon it." Your students may well not pursue the matter – no doubt few will actually look up information about the figures listed here. And yet knowledge of major "culture heroes" is commensurate with the student's likely current level of linguistic proficiency. You might reinforce that point generally, reward the dedicated few who actually did some extra reading, and also exercise or test such lower-level or review features as dates by including historical items in listening practice or tests. You might ascertain, minimally, who indeed merely read this section and could recall the names. To emphasize the proficiency context you might pose such content as an excerpt from a guide's speech; much the same could be done to check reading knowledge. If students see little point in such knowledge, remind them how pervasive historical names can be in their own culture (names of streets, counties, even cars).

Chapter 23

p. 238 (Struktur 2, #2): Remark why an infinitive is called an infinitive: it has no ending. Point out that in German, unlike English with its foreign-rooted words, syllable stress does not change radically with expansion or modulation of roots: ver*steh*en > ver*ständ*lich > un*ständ*lich (*ständ* now with secondary stress) > Unver*ständ*lichkeit, vs. compre*hend*,

compre*hens*ible, incompre*hens*ible, incomprehensi*bil*ity. If the class shows more interest in word formation, offer *fliehen* (flee)/*Flucht* (flight)/*Flüchtling* (refugee) from the chapter dialog.

p. 239 (Stage 2, #1): Beim Besuch in einem Altersheim in Saarbrücken treffen Sie einen Mann, der sehr verbittert ist: er lebt von seiner Heimat und seiner Familie getrennt, so wie es auch im Krieg war – nur ist er kein Soldat mehr, sondern ein Problem für seine Familie. Finden Sie heraus, wie sein Leben heute wäre, wenn es keinen Krieg gegeben hätte. (Stage 2, #2): Sie unterhalten sich mit einem Schweizer Rentner über die Kriegsjahre in der Schweiz. Lernen Sie möglichst viel über
a) die Schweizer Neutralität;
b) den Zusammehang zwischen Neutralität und Wohlstand in der heutigen Schweiz.
(Stage 2, #3): Sie besuchen ein pensioniertes Ehepaar, Freunde Ihrer Eltern aus der Tübinger Studienzeit. Sprechen Sie mit ihnen über
a) ihr damaliges Verhältnis mit Ihren Eltern;
b) ihr Verhältnis seit dieser Zeit mit ihren Kindern;
c) ihr Leben als Rentner in einer jugendorienterten Konsumgesellschaft.
If you use the German version, perhaps compare it to the English one, pointing out the specific German terms for some complex concepts like "youth- and consumer-oriented society." Do this *after* you have the students prove to themselves that they can express those concepts adequately without the specialized vocabulary, perhaps with English paraphrases as an intermediary stage. Example: Rephrase "youth-oriented society" as "Today young people get (or are given) everything they want," then elicit a German equivalent.

Chapter 24

p. 242 (Struktur 1, #3): Lower-level exercise: Student A offers – juxtaposed, without any overt connectors – two statements about activities that might take place in association with each other (e.g., *Ich trinke eine Tasse Kaffee. Ich nehme den*

Bus zur Universität.). One or more other students push for the connectors that make explicit the sequence implied (but not mandated) by the temporal order of the original statements. Thus *Du trinkst eine Tasse Kaffee. Und dann fährst du zur Universität* (easy paratactic connection); *Trinkst due eine Tasse Kaffee, bevor du zur Uni fährst?* (hypotactic connection with subordinate-clause word order, but no other alterations); *Also, bevor du zur Uni fährst, trinkst du eine Tasse Kaffee* (hypotactic construction with initial subordinate clause requiring special attention to show how *vorher* can replace an entire clause: *Bevor ich zur Uni fahre = Vorher*).

Higher-level exercise: Refer to the historical table in Chapter 10 or to the city chronicles in the realia and talk about the relative chronology of events. Student A: *Wann hat Bismarck gelebt?* B: *Vor dem ersten Weltkrieg.* C: *Bevor der erste Weltkrieg begonnen hat.* D: *Ist Bismarck im ersten weltkrieg gestorben?* E: *Nein, schon vorher.* Change the focus of the exercise to students' family histories: "*Wann sind deine Vorfahren nach Amerika gekommen? Vor 1900?*" "*Ja, vor 1900 – bevor mein Großvater geboren wurde.*"

p. 249 (Situationen 2): This section contains no A + B + C "walk-through" exercises. By now the student should be experimenting more with larger situation setups. In any case the A + B + C form is too restrictive here, since the topics are very personal.

Additional task: Ask students to look at the various product wrappers and price tags provided throughout the book and then to compare the prices with those in their own country.

p. 249 (Stage 1, #2): Explain the differences between Texas and New York. You can be fairly forthright about geographical matters, but do be careful about sweeping generalizations when you describe the people.

Chapter 25

p. 251 (Gespräche 1 chapter note): In-class activities: 1) Students interview each other and prepare oral or written reports on process. 2) One student describes a process, omitting any direct reference to the product; other students try to guess the product. Progression of in-class activity: First use present perfect (*Zuerst habe ich X, dann habe ich Y*), then change to passive, showing relationship between the two in use of past participle; juxtapose with *man* constructions; vary tenses for practice.

p. 253 (Stage 2, #2): A Turkish couple with several children asks for your help in understanding the operating instructions on a washing machine. a) Explain what must be done (and where), how much it costs, and how laundry is sorted for different machines. b) The children want to wash the baby's diapers in a separate machine. Explain to them simply and clearly how this is done.

p. 253 (*VSd*): Sie haben Ihren Anzug von der Reinigung abgeholt und sind zum Hotel zurückgekehrt, wo Sie sich vor einem wichtigen Jobinterview umziehen wollen. Beim Anziehen der Jacke haben Sie aber einen großen Fleck an der Tasche bemerkt. Jetzt sind Sie wieder bei der Reinigung und sind auch aus verständlichen Gründen aufgeregt. Vor dem interview, das in einer Stunde beginnen soll, müssen Sie unbedingt die Jacke wiederhaben. Überzeugen Sie die Angestellten, den Reinigungsfehler wiedergutzumachen.

p. 259 (Stage 2, #1): Ihr Flug fliegt in 3 Stunden ab, aber Sie sind um die Sicherheitsmaßnahmen mit Röntgengeräten am Flugsteig besorgt und möchten Ihre Fotos entwickeln lassen, bevor Sie zum Flughafen fahren. Sie treten also in einen Laden ("Sofortentwicklung") ein, um das Geschäft abzuwickeln. Der Angestellte muß wissen, daß die Sache dringt.

p. 259 (Stage 2, #2): You have just returned from Berlin, where you took lots of pictures of people and things. Explain to the interested photo shop owner what makes your five favorite pictures so special, and tell her something of the circumstances under which you took them.

p. 259 (*VSd*): Sie haben vor, etwas Wichtiges zu fotografieren. Als einziges Familienmitglied, dem eine Reise in die alte Heimat möglich ist wurden Sie damit beauftragt, Fotos von Familienurkunden in den Kirchen und Rathäusern in der Leipziger Umgebung zu machen. Sie beginnen in Ost-Berlin, wo Sie sich nach der nötigen Ausrüstung für Fotos von hoher Qualität bei manchmal schlechten Lichtverhältnissen erkundigen. Erklären Sie Ihre technischen Bedürfnisse und suchen Sie Rat darüber, wie man Dokumente fotografiert, die – wie Sie annehmen – von politischer Bedeutung sein könnten: Militärdiensturkunden usw.

Chapter 26

p. 261 (*Gespräche* 1): The statements in these sections are not necessarily presented in the hierarchy of mood from polite to desperate, although you will notice a general progression of that kind. The other principle of organization was an increase in linguistic complexity, at least until the final snappy retorts in some sets. With the class divided into several groups, see whether they can establish a reasonable progression. Make special note of the use of *du* under desperate circumstances. Be sure students understand the items are nuclei of conversations rather than part of a continuous conversation.

You will note in some of the *Gespräche* a change of format, from dialog to single-person utterance. Reasons: 1) the wish to offer a broad range of utterances; 2) a desire to avoid offering the offensive utterances that might elicit the responses printed here. If you emphasize role-playing you might very cautiously encourage students to act the part of instigators, just as some participants in self-defense classes assume the role of attackers. But avoid suggesting that many interchanges with actual speakers of German will be unpleasant.

These snippets of speech are not intended to exemplify a European attitude toward Americans, but simply to show how difficult questions can be dealt with in a variety of ways. If there is an agenda expressed here, it is that of the self-preservation and self-respect of a foreigner in the face of inevitable linguistic superiority on the part of a native speaker. The message is the functions, not the opinions. In any case, we have sought to offer a wide range of political views.

p. 262 (*Struktur 1*, #2): Note the following use of *dürfen: Das hättest du einfach nicht tun dürfen* = not "you shouldn't have been permitted to do that," but "you shouldn't have permitted yourself to do that" in the sense of "you went out of your way to please me, and I'm very grateful." The phrase is often said when one receives an extravagant present: "Oh, you shouldn't have!"

p. 263 (*Situationen* 1). Use your own judgment about how realistically such situations should be acted out. Convey the idea, too, that gross unpleasantness is not a frequent occurrence in German-speaking society, but that one should be prepared to handle it – as well as the other extreme. Without sounding sexist, you might suggest that the women in class study these items carefully. The "*Unhöflichkeit*" sections are due in large part to one of the authors' experiences directing a summer program in Vienna. Women participants were sometimes hassled on the streets or in public transportation, and complained that their language training had not prepared them to respond both effectively and with dignity. That is, lack of a range of linguistic techniques left them with the unsatisfactory options of passivity or inappropriate overreaction, including physical violence as a response where it was not really warranted.

p. 263 (Stage 1, #1): Mention the East German "*null pro Mille*" driving laws, which declare an absolute ban on drinking and driving; then repeat the situation.

Ein(e) Bekannte(r) von Ihnen hat zu viel getrunken und meint dennoch, daß er/sie fahren könne. Sagen Sie diplomatisch aber streng, was nötig ist. Versuchen Sie, attraktive Alternativen vorzuschlagen.

p. 263 (Stage 2, #1): Added complication: You've been there all the time – in fact, you were there before the other two people, who apparently didn't realize you were waiting for the clerk to wait on you.

Zwei andere Kunden argumentieren darüber, wer zuerst in der Schlange war. Der Verkäufer bittet um Ihre Meinung. Sie waren schon die ganze Zeit da und meinen zu wissen, wer recht hat. Jedoch haben Sie nicht jede Minute genau aufgepaßt.

p. 263 (Stage 2, #3): Ein(e) Bekannte(r) hat Sie vor einiger Zeit abends eingeladen, und Sie haben die Zeit mit ihm/ihr sehr genossen. Jetzt möchten Sie noch einen Abend mit ihm/ihr zusammen verbringen. Erinnern Sie ihn/sie an den Spaß damals, aber diesmal sind Sie an der Reihe, ihn/sie einzuladen. Beschreiben Sie möglichst genau Ihre Vorschläge – wobei Sie nicht alles wissen, was ihm/ihr gefällt oder mißfällt. Vielleicht wollen Sie sogar einiges offen lassen.

p. 263 (*VSd*): The item does not need to be high-level politics; it could also be "Frankfurt Drug Bust Nets 4 GIs, 2 Germans."

If conversation lags, systematically review and apply the strategies for eliciting amplification, expressing opinion, and disagreeing. Expansion: same circumstances, except: "The comment was of the tone, *Naja, das ist alles nicht so furchtbar schlimm*" – and you, by contrast, *do* think whatever is being reported is indeed pretty bad."

The content of the situation may be controversial, and people do have different viewpoints. The subject of German-American relations and of American politics and society should be dealt with evenhandedly. Note, too, that a higher-level proficiency skill concerns the ability to represent (not simply attack or lightly quote) the opinions of others.

Suchen Sie in einer guten Zeitung nach Berichten von den USA und der Bundesrepublik. Sie sollten fast täglich etwas finden können. Stellen Sie sich nun vo,r daß ein Westdeutscher, der Amerikaner und ihre Außenpolitik nicht besonders schätzt, einen Zeitungsbericht gelesen und Ihnen seine Meinung dazu geäußert hat. Seine Bemerkung war etwa: "Na, so sind ja die

Amerikaner . . ." Ob Sie einverstanden sind oder nicht: können Sie Ihre Seite der Diskussion eine ganze Minute lang aufrechterhalten?

p. 265 (*Strategie*): Consider the many and varied common terms for actions that violate, to a greater or lesser degree, the norms of proper conduct: *Rohheit, Ausschweifung, Gemeinheit, Zudringlichkeit, Frechheit.*

p. 265 (*Strategie*): "Were you born in a barn?" might be considered an equivalent, but the remark is usually only a joke.

If the level of discussion warrants, you might point out that the best-known German proverbial reference to civic behavior is probably "*Ruhe ist die erste Bürgerpflicht,*" which emphasizes duty rather than rights. Note the prominence of "*Ruhe*" in *Gespräche* 1. Here the word would be difficult to translate: "keeping the peace" or "maintaining public order," but probably not "keeping silent." You might point out that such jealously defended prerogatives of rugged individualism as gun control and selection of schoolbooks are not controversial issues in Europe. Nor is there much sign of a tax revolt.

p. 265 (*Strategie*): Note, however, the necessity in German-speaking countries for diplomas certifying one's ability to conduct certain business – even in cases where no such certificate of competence is required in the more freewheeling (but risk-taking) United States. The pride in earning the diploma is reflected in the frequent use of even seemingly insignificant titles as badges of identification and honor: *Familie Straßenmeister Gerhard Braun.*

p. 269 (Stage 2, #2): Ihre Mietfrau hat geweigert, den Überfluß von Ihrem monatlichen Heizungszuschlag der letzten Monatsmiete anzurechnen, weil sie angenommen hat, daß Sie als Ausländer es nicht bemerken oder nicht daran denken würden, so nahe am Abreisedatum die Stadtbehörde darüber zu informieren. Sie haben aber schon mit einem Rechtsanwalt gesprochen und eine gerechte Summe bei ihm für die letzte monatliche Mietzahlung

zurückgelassen. Nun fahren Sie zum Flughafen. Verabschieden Sie sich von der erstaunten Mietfrau, indem Sie höflich aber entschlossen Ihr Handeln rechtfertigen.

Glossary

p. 350 The Glossary includes all words that appear in the Class Text dialogs (*Gespräche*), except for articles, personal pronouns, and numbers (though distinctly irregular ordinals are listed); easily recognized comparative and superlative forms of adjectives; some readily deciphered or trivial compounds; and proper nouns, except for geographical terms that are not cognate and those whose gender is important at this level. The listing includes as well the few additional words that are introduced in the Class Text *Struktur* sections and important words from the *Strategie: Kultur und Sprache* pages. Lastly, a few words were added as having been introduced by implication, inasmuch as the *Gespräche* contain closely related terms from the same evident category and the associated exercises virtually demand that the student learn the larger set (e.g., names for members of the immediate family, chapter 4). In part for the use of teachers who construct their own tests, entries for words in this core vocabulary contain numbers showing the chapter in which they were "officially" introduced. A few words were added from the Class Text *Situationen*, so that the student may indeed translate the text word for word, though we do not encourage the practice. Entries for those words lack chapter references, and they should not be direct targets on tests.

p. 350 (3rd paragraph): You may wish to point out other ways to learn vocabulary systematically in conjunction with ordinary consultation of the Glossary. Example: each time a word is looked up, make a check mark next to it; later on study carefully those words that have the most checks.

If pressed for detail, discuss suffixes and point the student toward relevant sections of the Class Text (p. 238) and Reference Grammar (Nouns §6).

p. 350 (Plurals): The rough-and-ready principles of pluralization offered here are not intended to supplant careful learning of plural forms, but rather to provide recourse when the plural has been forgotten or the noun not yet introduced, and to push the students toward confident application of structures.

Students who claim that English is easier because it has just one basic pluralization pattern – "Just add *s*." – can be shown that the pattern is not at all simple in orthography or pronunciation, the latter involving great complexities in voicing and syllabification. [Orthographically, plural formation may involve interpolating an *e* ('bus'/'buses,' with attendant confusion of 'buss'/'busses'), or even the conversion of syllabic *y* to *i* ('story'/'stories') – but not of non-syllabic *y* ('play'/'plays'). In speaking, the same letter may have far-reaching but not visually evident effects on pronunciation (examples: plays/acts, house/houses).] Here, as elsewhere, you will achieve a larger pedagogical goal by doing what you can to show that one's native language and culture are not nearly as supremely logical and natural as might be supposed.

p. 351 (Verb irregularity): As used here, "irregularity" applies to strong and mixed verbs and to those requiring linking -*e*. Participles of modals are not given, because the distinction between the independent participle and the double infinitive, both relatively infrequent, is too far above the target proficiency level.

Target Proficiency Levels throughout the Course

Though language proficiency in itself, and the ILR/ACTFL/ETS standards in particular, are now hailed widely, debate rages about the theoretical and practical application of proficiency standards to actual courses. Above all, we still do not know, even roughly, how many "years" of college foreign-language study might correspond to which proficiency levels. One would hope that, eventually, "seat time" would correspond to proficiency, in that we would finally teach, test, and grade for proficiency. But it is generally agreed now that one cannot simplistically map the proficiency levels onto either an ABCDF grading spectrum within a single year of instruction, or onto a sequence of "years of study" within an entire college curriculum or major. Certainly the proficiency gradations are not linear; heaven knows what equation defines the scale of proficiency represented by which grading system for which year of study at which institution – and with language learners of what natural ability. Moreover, the discussion must be conducted in quadruplicate, in that not one but at least four modalities are involved: speaking, listening, reading, and writing.

Under those circumstances it is difficult indeed to set proficiency-oriented standards for any language student, whatever the instructional package the student has used. Nevertheless, with regard at least to oral proficiency – the traditional and current "benchmark" of the field – the following observations might be ventured about students of reasonable aptitude and preparation who attend institutions of reasonable quality:

1) Only the very best students will attain Intermediate-High oral proficiency, at least without previous significant exposure to German; typically, the "A" student will be either a facile oral Intermediate-High with notable deficiencies in other modalities, or else a solid Intermediate-Mid in speaking, with abundant proficiency in other modalities, especially writing.

2) At the end of a year with *Wie, bitte?*, the student who is not Novice-High in speaking has indeed failed to acquire satisfactory oral proficiency.

3) Analytical or academically measurable intelligence may be less of a factor in the acquisition of proficiency than it is in programs based on other principles, and thus the customary gap between students at traditionally prestigious institutions and those at less renowned colleges or universities may be less evident, just as it is in the measurement of other skills in other areas, such as athletics or music. To put it another way, proficiency-oriented language instruction gives more students a greater crack at attaining a satisfactory level of achievement.

With those reservations in mind, we offer the following estimate of likely exit levels of proficiency for several grades of students using *Wie, bitte?* in programs where instruction is indeed oriented toward proficiency. The estimate is based on groups of students who have learned German with *Wie, bitte?* under the less than ideal condition of field-testing.

The *best* students will rate at least Intermediate-Mid in both speaking and writing, with Intermediate-High in one of the two and Advanced level in both listening and reading.

The *adequate* students – those who keep up well enough that they are not always severely frustrated when new material is introduced – will likely rate Intermediate-Low in both speaking and writing, though with notable strength in one of those modalities. Listening and reading skills will be somewhat higher, but not likely Advanced, even in one of those modalities.

Students who are *struggling* will likely finish the year at the strong Novice-High level in speaking and writing, with Intermediate-Low in one of the two and Intermediate-Mid level in both listening and reading.

Tests
and Testing

The Test Bank contains proficiency-oriented or "prochievement" tests for all four modalities, spaced at intervals of about two chapters. The tests are appropriate to *Wie, bitte?* in both their content (selection and sequence of vocabulary and grammar) and the style in which the material is presented. We urge you to use the tests or, if you design your own, at least to maintain the principles of proficiency-oriented teaching and testing. To that end we provide sample tests below. The Test Bank also includes a discussion of testing principles and samples of actual student performance.

Most instructors will likely test less frequently than every two chapters. Since the distinction between teaching and testing should be slight in a proficiency-oriented course, the tests not used as tests could then be used as practice tests. In form they would resemble the real tests, but would lack the psychological pressure. In the latter feature they would resemble the Class Text and Study Text exercises in the corresponding modalities, but would be more formally organized.

ORAL TEST FOR CHAPTER 1

Topics: Greetings, name, age, major, days of week, time, polite expressions, *Kontrolle/Imbiß* situation

Note: Somewhere in the test elicit *Wie, bitte?* competence. Say or ask something the student can't be expected to comprehend, but which you can rephrase in German so far presented. Examples: *"Ich wollte zuerst nach Ihrem Familiennamen fragen;" "Darf ich die Fahrausweise sehen?"*

1. Greet. *Wie ist der Familienname?* (check spelling carefully)? *Und der Vorname? Wie alt sind Sie, und was studieren Sie?*
   [check spelling by obvious gesture or by beginning to spell the name; maybe make a mistake; for poorer students offer a YES/NO or EITHER/OR prompt (e.g., for Hanson: *"Ist das S-E-N oder S-O-N?"*)]

2. Days and times? *Ist heute Freitag? Wie spät ist es?*

3. Major situations (do one – present to student on card)

   Fahrkarten und Pässe, bitte!
   You are traveling by train from one German-speaking country to another. You think you are nearing a border, and want to have your documents ready. Gain the attention of a passenger in your compartment and find out:
   a) whether you already crossed the border;
   b) when passports will be checked;
   c) which country that city over there is in;
   d) what nationality she or he is;
   e) whether there is a time-zone change.
   Don't forget to be polite.

   Imbiß
   It's late afternoon. Enter an *Imbiß* and
   a) get the attention of an employee;
   b) order a large snack (with beverage);
   c) pay for the snack with a large banknote;
   d) politely take your leave.

4. Minor situation (for very good or very poor students). Explain in English:

   You have fetched a snack for yourself and someone else, who will pay you back now. The other person's purchases amounted to DM 7,25. He or she offers you a DM 50,-banknote. Count back the change.

5. Thanks and goodbye.

ORAL TEST FOR CHAPTER 19

Targets: description and narration; breadth of vocabulary; past tense, subordinate clauses, present subjunctive, time phrases (*seit, schon, noch*), reflexives and direct/indirect objects.

1. Warm-up: current activities and plans (probe with *wann, wo, mit wem, warum, Datum*); look for basic subject-verb agreement, genders, etc. *Welche Tests haben/ hatten (haben gehabt) Sie, und wann? Haben Sie einen Job für (Sommer, nächstes Jahr) gefunden? Wie?*

2. *Was machen Sie in der Freizeit?/Was haben Sie am Wochenende in der Freizeit gemacht? Haben Sie Hobbys? (wann? wie oft? mit wem? allein? was braucht man, wenn . . . ?) Warum finden Sie das interessant?* What don't you like about (same/ different) hobby? Why is this hobby good/bad for children/old people? Other people's hobbies?

3. Major situations – do one if student is not struggling hopelessly.
   a) Suggest to me some ways we might spend a rainy afternoon together in a German city.
   b) I am the desk clerk in your hotel. On your trip to Germany you've lost an expensive item or set of items (ex: camera equipment) sometime and somewhere during a big day of tourist activities. Tell me about what you lost and how it happened, and discuss with me how I can help you.
   c) Your trip – what do/did you take along (which of similar items?)? How do/did you pack it, and where? (If lots of items, how will you stay below 20 kg baggage limit and still have room for souvenirs?). *Wo würden Sie (lieber) übernachten (und wann) . . . ?* At end of trip: what do/did you (need to) do, and why and for whom?

4. Wind-down: plans for rest of day, next week/year.

Extras: *Sind Sie vergeßlich/Vergessen Sie viel? z.B., auf einer Reise.*

LISTENING TEST FOR CHAPTER 2

Section 1. You will hear – ONCE only – numbers, some by themselves and some within larger utterances. Write the DIGITS of the numbers you hear.

    1. _____   2. _____   3. _____   4. _____   5. _____

Section 2. You will hear – TWICE – statements about prices. On the left write the numbers given in the price. In the middle circle the word that best describes the item. On the right indicate – in English or German – the country whose currency is being used.

1. _____   food beverage shelter transportation _____

2. _____   food beverage shelter transportation _____

3. _____   food beverage shelter transportation _____

4. _____   food beverage shelter transportation _____

Section 3. You will hear information about two restaurants – TWICE for the first one, ONCE for the second one. Some of the information will be spelled out. Fill in the blanks below.

	RESTAURANT #1	RESTAURANT #2
Name	_____	_____
Proprietor	_____	_____
Address	_____	_____
	_____	_____
Telephone	_____	_____

Section 4. Here are the prices for accommodations in the Hotel Krone:

    single without bath, DM55   single with bath, DM75
    double without bath, DM70   double with bath, DM95

You will hear – ONCE ONLY – three customers request accommodations. In each case, write down what the guest will pay the hotel in room charges for his/her ENTIRE stay, IF ANY, at that hotel.

    1. _____   2. _____   3. _____

Section 5. You will hear – ONCE ONLY – a segment from a radio broadcast.

At what time does the broadcast begin? _____

List any names of cities and countries that you hear.

List any prices, monetary terms or other quantities you hear.

List any names of people you hear.

Section 6. You will hear – ONCE – statements or conversations about days of the week. In each instance, write down in English or German what day of the week (NOT WHAT DATE) *TODAY* is.

1. Today is _____ 2. Today is _____ 3. Today is _____

SCRIPT FOR LISTENING TEST

Section 1. READ ONCE ONLY

1. 13   2. Das kostet 2 Mark.   3. Um 20 Uhr   4. Ich bin 50.
5. Die Vorwahl ist 089.

Section 2. TWICE

1. 2 Dollar? In Anchorage kostet ein Glas Bier 2 Dollar?
2. So. Das war einmal Currywurst mit Pommes frites? 22 Schilling, bitte.
3. Eine Fahrkarte erster Klasse nach Venedig – 145 Franken, bitte.
4. In München war das? Für ein Doppelzimmer *ohne* Bad habt ihr 180 Mark ausgegeben!

Section 3. Use items from the *Gaststättenverzeichnis* on Class Text page 322. Do one item twice, the other once. Do not spell out extremely common words like *Straße*.

Section 4. ONCE ONLY

1. Haben Sie bitte ein Doppelzimmer für 2 Nächte?
    Nur mit Dusche.
   Wieviel kostet das?
    DM 95 pro Nacht.
   Schön.

2. Ich möchte bitte ein Einzelzimmer ohne Bad.
    Für wieviele Nächte, bitte?
   Drei.
    Ist gut. Und ist das Ihr Gepäck?

3. Ein Doppelzimmer mit Bad kostet 175 Franken.
    Ich glaube, das ist zu teuer.
   Wie Sie meinen.
    Aber danke schön. Auf Wiedersehen.
   Auf Wiedersehen.

Section 5. ONCE ONLY. Use one of the news broadcasts in the taped realia.

Section 6. ONCE ONLY

1. Heute ist Samstag.

2. Moment. Sonntag war der 15te. Das war der Geburtstag von meiner Mutter. Heute ist also der 17te.

3. Morgen ist also Donnerstag.

Use Part 2 of your SCAN-TRON form. Time: about 30 minutes.

On your SCAN-TRON, in a blank space near your name, write the numbers and names you hear. Some of the names will be spelled out. The easy ones won't. Each item will be spoken ONCE.

Section I. Items 51–60. You will hear – ONCE only – utterances which refer to quantities.

Mark "A" if the utterance refers to ONLY ONE person or thing.
Mark "B" if the utterance refers to TWO OR MORE persons or things.
Mark "C" if it is impossible to tell whether "A" or "B".

English examples:
    That guy there – **A**; These children – **B**; The sheep over there – **C**

Section II. Items 61–70. You will hear – TWICE – sets of two utterances.

Mark "A" if the two utterances MAKE SENSE as parts of a conversation.
Mark "B" if the two utterances DON'T MAKE SENSE together.

Section III. Items 71–75. You will hear – ONCE only – utterances which contain quantities.

Mark "A" if the quantity is unreasonably LARGE under the circumstances.
Mark "B" if the quantity is unreasonably SMALL under the circumstances.
Mark "C" if the quantity is REASONABLE under the circumstances.

English examples:
    I'd like 400 pounds of hamburger. The kids are hungry. – **A**
    The star basketball player is 22 inches tall. – **B**
    I drank about a pint of cola. – **C**

Section IV. Items 76–80. You will hear – TWICE – utterances about things and places. Mark the letter of the word or phrase that completes the utterance correctly, in both meaning and form.

English examples: Where can I buy oranges? In a . . .
                    A) store   B) stores   C) single room   D) Seattle   **A**

SCRIPT FOR LISTENING TEST

Dictation (do in space near name on SCAN-TRON); say ONCE; spell only those noted for spelling.

    Freiburg (don't spell)   Friedrichstraße (spell Friedrich)
              Karl-Marx-Stadt (don't spell)

298 Mark, bitte.
Der Kurs heute ist 5,74 (read: 5 Komma 74)
Die Telefonnummer ist 33 06 11 (dreiunddreißig null-sechs elf)

Section I. Read ONCE

51. Kinder!	56. Wie heißt sie?
52. Die Amerikanerin	57. Die Äpfel? Wo?
53. Sind Sie Kanadier?	58. Sie muß nicht umsteigen.
54. Die Busse fahren um zehn Uhr.	59. Die Einzelzimmer sind zu teuer.
55. Warum schläft er so lange?	60. Unsere Gäste aus Amerika sind hier.

Section II. Read TWICE.

61. Wer ist Herr Schröder?
    Im Museum.

62. Die Kölner-Zeitung, bitte.
    Bitte schön, eine Mark zwanzig.

63. Wieviel kostet eine Fahrkarte nach Bonn?
    Zwei Stunden – drei Stunden mit dem Bus.

64. Wo waren Sie Donnerstag?
    Wir waren im Zoo mit unserem Sohn.

65. Wir haben keine Handtücher mehr.
    Rot ist heiß and blau ist kalt, aber das wissen Sie schon.

66. Muß ich umsteigen?
    Ja, sie muß umsteigen.

67. Fährt der nächste Bus direkt zum Krankenhaus?
    Nein, Sie müssen umsteigen.

68. Wo kann mein Mann warten?
    Im Hotel, oder auch im Stadtmuseum.

69. Wie lange müssen wir im Hauptbahnhof warten?
    2 Uhr.

70. Das Bad ist also im dritten Stock?
    Ja. Gehen Sie eine Treppe hoch.

Section III. Read ONCE.

71. Mein Vater ist 15 Jahre alt.

72. Moment. Das war für zwei Personen?
    Sie brauchen dann 500g Käse und 4 Brötchen.

73. Die Jugendherberge ist 10 Meter von hier. Sie müssen ein Taxi nehmen.

74. Ein Doppelzimmer mit Bad kostet 17 Schilling.

75. Wie weit ist es von Köln nach München? 500 Kilometer.

Section IV. Items 76–80. Read TWICE; read item number & ABCD in English.

76. Sie möchten schlafen? Gehen Sie zum . . .
    A) Jugendherberge   B) Konditorei   C) Hotel   D) Imbiß

77. Wo ist Kartoffelsalat billig? Im . . .
    A) Dom   B) Imbiß   C) Bank   D) Herrentoilette

78. Sie müssen Geld wechseln? Gehen Sie zum . . .
    A) Bank   B) Zug   C) Freiburg   D) Bahnhof

79. Der Zoo ist sehr weit von hier. Nehmen Sie Linie 4.
    Fahren Sie 20 Minuten. Sie sehen dann links ein . . .
    A) Haltestelle   B) Imbiß   C) Hotel   D) Zeitung

80. Oh, Sie haben ein Auto. Sie fahren *nicht* mit dem Zug.
    Dann brauchen Sie keine . . .
    A) Fahrkarte   B) Paß   C) Freund   D) Messer

READING TEST FOR CHAPTER 6

Use Part 1 of your SCAN-TRON form.   Time: 30 minutes.

Elementary spelling. By now you have seen enough German in print to know what the language looks like – its general pattern of spelling and also the basic rules of capitalization. For each of the items below,

mark "A" if spelling and capitalization ARE CORRECT
mark "B" if there is ONLY ONE ERROR
mark "C" if there are TWO OR MORE ERRORS.

1. Schwiez   2. ein Glas Wein   3. Halstelle recht um die Ecke
4. Bundesrepublik   5. Fraulein   6. Mitwoch   7. Shlussel
8. 200g Cäse   9. Munchen   10. Amerikanerinnen

Singular-Plural

Mark "A" if the words refer to ONE AND ONLY ONE person, thing, etc.

Mark "B" if the words refer to MORE THAN ONE person, thing, etc.

Mark "C" if the INFORMATION is INSUFFICIENT for one to make that distinction.

English examples: "she" – A; "them" – B; "you" – C; "fish" – C

11. Herren   12. Sind Sie Amerikaner?   13. die Doppelzimmer
14. meine Töchter   15. Sie schläft.   16. Gramm   17. die Ecke
18. die Kartoffeln   19. Sie muß umsteigen   20. die nächsten Züge

Days of the week. In both English and German, days of the week are often abbreviated when they appear in calendars, on signs, etc. For each item, select the answer – IF ANY! – which best describes the day named. If neither A, B, nor C fits, mark "D".

21. Di   A) Thursday   B) Tuesday   C) Sunday   D) none of the three

22. Mi   A) Wednesday   B) Tuesday   C) Saturday   D) none of the three

23. Sa   A) Sunday   B) Tuesday   C) Friday   D) none of the three

24. Mo   A) Wednesday   B) tomorrow   C) Monday   D) none of the three

25. What, then, does this sign mean? "Sa. u. So.: keine Züge"
    A) If you want to take the streetcar, don't plan to go on a weekend.
    B) If you want to take the freeway, don't plan to go on a weekend.
    C) If you plan to travel by train, you'd better go on a weekday.
    D) No trains on Friday or Saturday.

Here are some labels, signs, or other public notices that you might encounter. Use common sense when you answer the questions.

26. **ZIMMER FREI**
    What might you obtain at the place where you see the sign?
    A) a newspaper   B) a place to stay for the night
    C) cameras and tape recorders   D) a rent-free apartment

27. **Zu den Gleisen** →
    What sign might you see nearby?
    A) Fahrkarten – Inland u. DDR   B) Gleisen – ÖS 10,-/kg
    C) Gleisen fahren alle 20 Minuten.   D) 1 Glas Rotwein Sfr. 2,-

28. **Sommerferien – geschlossen**
    What does the sign likely mean?
    A) closed for summer vacation
    B) open during summer vacation
    C) ferry service only during summer
    D) town of Sommerferien closed

29. **CH**
    What country is meant?
    A) Mainland China   B) Taiwan   C) Czechoslovakia
    D) Switzerland

30. **DOM – 1 Stunde**
    After reading the notice, what might you say to those in your group who speak English?
    A) "According to the schedule, we've got just an hour to see the whole cathedral!"
    B) "This place is open just an hour during December, October and March."
    C) "We can get into the cathedral at 1 o'clock."
    D) "Good thing we're students. The admission price is lower."

Look at the ad for "Sam's" on page 197 of the Class Text. Answer items #31–33 on the SCAN-TRON in the blank space near your name. Write answers in ENGLISH.

31. Explain briefly the pun on the name of the bar.

32. How late is the bar open?

33. In which building is it located?

Look at menu on page 323 of the Class Text.

34. The document deals with food and beverage service.
    A) in train stations ONLY
    B) in dining cars and train compartments ONLY
    C) in German-speaking countries ONLY
    D) in train stations and dining cars ONLY

35. Which statement best describes the passenger's options in a train which has a dining car?
    A) Passengers must eat in the dining car. There is no other food/beverage service.
    B) The dining car provides food and beverages "to go." Passengers can fetch such items themselves.
    C) If passengers want something from the dining car, they must fetch it themselves.
    D) Food and beverages will not be served to passengers in sleeping cars.

What other items, symbols or words might you likely see near each of the following words?

36. Zeitungen
    A) *Time, Newsweek*
    B) clocks showing time in various cities of the world
    C) sign with opening/closing times
    D) *International Herald Tribune*

37. Kurs
    A) city map with a compass show-   B) öS, £, ¥
       ing north, etc.
    C) public notice prohibiting graffiti,   D) signs for doctors' offices
       obscenities, etc.
38. Stock
    A) WC, Frühstückssaal, Lift   B) farm, pet store, zoo
    C) BASF +2,5; Volkswagen −1,5   D) Äpfel, Orangen, Bananen
39. Quittung
    A) price tags for bargain items – a store is going out of business
    B) a locked gate, with a sign showing the hours the store is closed
    C) money
    D) D, DDR, CH, A
40. Umsteigefahrschein
    A) Jugendherberge   B) Dom   C) entwerten   D) wechseln

WRITING TEST FOR CHAPTER 3

time: 20 minutes; timing suggestion: skim entire test – 2 minutes; sections I & II – 3 minutes; section III: 5 min. – read task & think; 10 min. – write

I. Write the name, address and telephone number below in handwriting so that a hotel clerk in a small town in a German-speaking country could understand it.

Elisabeth Hartmann
7401 Tübingen
Zähringerstr. 11
Tel 0711 777 50 27

II. Write in German the names of:

2 meat dishes

2 vegetable dishes

any 2 other food dishes

3 beverages – one non-alcoholic, one containing neither alcohol nor caffeine

("dish" = prepared food, not just a grocery item; *English* examples: "beef" – *not* OK "beef teriyaki" – OK)

III. You and a companion are in the midst of a trip which includes travel in *three* German-speaking countries. You have two reasons to write a postcard to Aachen. The couple that ran the hotel you stayed in *last week* were friendly people, so you want to say something nice about your stay there and inform them about your subsequent travels. And you want to let them know you'll be passing through Aachen on your way home and would like to stay in their hotel. Here are some specific matters to address in your postcard – you need not cover them in the same order they are given here:

1. Report on your travels between Aachen and now – where you've been on which days, your opinion of noteworthy sights or cities, etc. Within the last day or so you've crossed an international border, and will do so again soon.

2. Compare the prices of similar accommodations you had in two different countries along the way, using appropriate currency units.

3. Sketch out your plans for tomorrow and the next couple of days/cities. Although you and your companion are on excellent terms still, you plan to split up for a few days later on. One of you wants a lengthier stay in city X, and will be traveling to Aachen a day or more later than the other.

4. Outline your desires for accommodations in Aachen; remember that one of you will get there before the other.

5. Maybe add some personal touches – like what the food and drink are doing to your weight.

   The task has been worded in such a way that you cannot translate it from English into German. Nevertheless, everything you need to do can be done with the German you have had in the course up to now. You will be graded not simply on the mistakes you make, but rather on your ability to communicate effectively. It is to your advantage to take risks and to try to demonstrate the range of what you have encountered in *Wie, bitte?* so far.

Write (PRINT!!) your note. Don't forget to sign it! Here are a few words to get you started –

Liebe Herr und Frau Thielen!

Gestern . . .

WRITING TEST FOR CHAPTER 11

DO NOT WRITE ON THIS PAGE.   TIME: 30 Minutes.

In this part of your final examination you are asked to write in German a message of the kind that adults often have to write. The task can be carried out with the German taught so far, but it is worded in such a way that you cannot simply translate its language. Instead, imagine yourself in the situation, and then express your meaning as best you can. You will be graded NOT simply on the number of mistakes you make, but rather on the good points too, above all your ability to communicate. It is therefore to your advantage to take some risks, and to try to demonstrate all that you have learned.

The situation: You took the plunge and went to Germany. You've been there long enough to know your way around and to have made friends whom you can address with *du*. A while back you and a German friend made plans to do something fun outdoors tomorrow, and this evening you have stopped by your friend's place to check on final arrangements. It is drizzling, and the high temperature today was 15° (Celsius/Centigrade, of course). You suspect that the weather will get better soon. Whatever the case, you don't let a few raindrops get in your way. You are concerned, though, about the health of your friend, who has had an off-and-on sniffle and slight fever.

Your friend is not home, so you have to leave a note – in German, of course. In your note do the following, in whatever order you think appropriate and in whatever detail you can handle:

1. Offer a greeting and explain why you are *writing* ("No one answered the door . . . ," etc.).

2. Remind your friend about the planned activity – is your friend still interested?

3. Comment about the weather and maybe show some concern about your friend's health.

4. Suggest what to do; pursue either (a) or (b), but NOT both:
   a) If you expect no change in plans, then discuss who brings what.
      (". . . And besides the corkscrew . . .")
   b) If you think you will have to change plans, discuss an alternate activity.

5. Suggest a time and place to meet, and outline what kind of transportation will be involved.

6. Arrange how you can be reached in the meantime to discuss things further if necessary.

7. Finish with a suitable farewell ("Got to go. Hang in there.")

Write your note on the paper provided. DON'T FORGET TO WRITE YOUR NAME.

Bibliography

American Council on the Teaching of Foreign Languages. *ACTFL Proficiency Guidelines.* Hastings-on-Hudson: ACTFL, 1986.

BARNETT, MARVA A. "How Receptive to New Ideas Are We? Reading and Listening Proficiency." *ADFL Bulletin* 19 (1988): 29–32.

BOYLE, JOSEPH P. "Intelligence, Reasoning, and Language Proficiency." *MLJ* 71 (1987): 277–88.

BRAGGER, JEANNETTE D. "Teaching for Proficiency: Are We Ready?" *Profession 87.* New York: The Modern Language Association, 1987.

BYRNES, HEIDI. "Grammar-Communicative Competence-Functions/Notions: Implications for and from a Proficiency Orientation." *UP* 17 (1984): 194–206.

———. "The Role of Listening Comprehension: A Theoretical Base." *FLA* 17 (1984): 317–34.

———, and Michael Canale. *Defining and Developing Proficiency: Guidelines, Implementations and Concepts.* ACTFL Foreign Language Education Series, vol. 18. Lincolnwood, Ill: National Textbook, 1987.

CARROLL, JOHN B. "Foreign Language Proficiency Levels Attained by Language Majors near Graduation from College." *FLA* 1 (1967): 131–51.

CARTER, ELAINE FULLER. "The Relationship of Field Dependent/Independent Cognitive Style to Spanish Language Achievement and Proficiency." *MLJ* 72 (1988): 21–30.

FISCHER, WILLIAM B. "Not Just Lip Service: Systematic Oral Testing in a First-Year College German Program" *UP* 17 (1984): 225–239.

Foreign Language Annals 17 (1984). Special issue on reading and listening.

FREED, BARBARA F. "Establishing Proficiency-Based Language Requirements" *ADFL Bulletin* 13.2 (1981): 6–12.

GAUDIANI, CLAIRE. *Teaching Composition in the Foreign Language Curriculum.* Language in Education: Theory and Practice Series, no. 43. Washington, D.C.: Center for Applied Linguistics, 1981.

HIGGS, THEODORE V. "The Input Hypothesis: An Inside Look." *FLA* 18 (1985): 197–203.

———. "Teaching Grammar for Proficiency." *FLA* 18 (1985): 289–96.

———, ed. *Teaching for Proficiency, the Organizing Principle.* ACTFL Foreign Language Education Series, vol. 15. Lincolnwood, Ill: National Textbook, 1984.

———, and RAY CLIFFORD. "The Push toward Communication." In Theodore V. Higgs, ed., *Curriculum, Competence, and the Foreign Language Teacher.* ACTFL Foreign Language Education Series, vol. 13. Lincolnwood, Ill: National Textbook, 1982.

HOFFMANN, ERNST FEDOR, and DOROTHY JAMES. "Toward the Integration of Foreign Language and Literature Teaching at All Levels of the College Curriculum." ADFL Bulletin 18 (1986): 29–33.

JAMES, CHARLES J. "Are You Listening? The Practical Components of Listening Comprehension." *FLA* 17 (1984): 129–33.

———, ed., *Foreign Language Proficiency in the Classroom and Beyond.* ACTFL Foreign Language Education Series, vol. 16. Lincolnwood, Ill: National Textbook, 1985.

JAMES, DOROTHY. "Toward Realistic Objectives in Foreign Language Teaching." *Profession 84.* New York: MLA, 1984. 33–36.

KAPLAN, ISABELLE. "Oral Proficiency Testing and the Language Curriculum: Two Experiments in Curricular Design for Conversation Courses: *FLA* 17 (1984): 491–97.

KRAMSCH, CLAIRE J. *Discourse Analysis and Second Language Teaching.* Language in Education: Theory and Practaice Series, no. 37. Washington, D.C.: Center for Applied Linguistics, 1981.

KRASHEN, STEPHEN. *Principles and Practice in Second Language Acquisition.* New York: Pergamon Press, 1982.

———, and TRACY D. TERRELL. *The Natural Approach.* Hayward, Calif.: The Alemany Press, 1983.

LANTOLF, JAMES P. and WILLIAM FRAWLEY. "Oral Proficiency Testing: A Critical Analysis." *MLJ* 69 (1985): 337–345.

LISKIN-GASPARRO, JUDITH. "The ACTFL Proficiency Guidelines: A Gateway to Testing and Curriculum.": *FLA* 17 (1984): 475–89.

MAGNAN, SALLY SIELOFF. "Assessing Speaking Proficiency in the Undergraduate Curriculum: Data from French." *FLA* (1986): 429–38.

Omaggio, Alice C. "Methodology in Transition: The New Focus on Proficiency." *MLJ* 67 (1983): 330–341.

———, ed., *Proficiency, Curriculum, Articulation: The Ties that Bind*. Reports of the Northeast Conference on the Teaching of Foreign Languages. Middlebury, Vt.: Northeast Conference, 1985.

———. *Teaching Language in Context. Proficiency-Oriented Instruction*. Boston: Heinle and Heinle, 1986.

Phillips, June K. "Practical Implications of Recent Research in Reading" *FLA* 17 (1984): 285–96.

Richardson, Peter N. "Proficiency-Based Curricula: The View from the Hill." *ADFL Bulletin* 18 (1986): 25–28.

Rickerson, Earl M. "Curriculum for Proficiency: Concepts to Build On." *UP* 17 (1984): 207–24.

Rogers, Carmen Villegas. "Improving the Performance of Teaching Assistants in the Multi-Section Classroom." *FLA* 20 (1987): 403–410.

Rosengrant, Sandra F. "A Hierarchy of Russian Writing Assignments.": *FLA* 18 (1985): 487–96.

Siskin, H. Jay, and Emily Spinelli. "Achieving Communicative Competence through Gambits and Routines." *FLA* 20 (1987): 393–401.

Swaffar, Janet K. "Reading Authentic Texts in a Foreign Language: A Cognitive Model." *MLJ* 69 (1985): 15–34.

Walz, Joel. "Is Oral Proficiency Possible with Today's French Textbooks?" *MLJ* 70 (1986): 13–20.

Instructor's Notes

Instructor's Notes

Instructor's Notes

Wie, bitte?

Ich zahle mit **POSTCHEQUE**

BITTE
nicht füttern

50 DDR
LEIPZIGER FRÜHJAHRSMESSE 1986

FREIWILLIG
80/100
DEM WALD ZULIEBE

Gleis 4 Karlsplatz

KÖLNER DOM
Turmbesteigung
Eintritt **1,-- DM**
Waren Sie schon in der
Domschatzkammer?

Wie, bitte?

INTRODUCTORY GERMAN
FOR PROFICIENCY

CLASS TEXT

William B. Fischer
Portland State University

Peter N. Richardson
Linfield College

WILEY

JOHN WILEY & SONS
New York   Chichester   Brisbane   Toronto   Singapore

Cover and Interior Text Designer: Dawn L. Stanley
Illustrator for Bildwörterbuch: Karin Erickson
Photo Researcher: Safra Nimrod
Photo Editor: Stella Kupferberg
Production Manager: Martin Bentz

Library of Congress Cataloging in Publication Data:

Fischer, William B.
  Wie, bitte?

  Includes index.
    1. German language—Grammar—1950–
2. German language—Textbooks for foreign speakers—
English. I. Richardson, Peter N. (Peter Nichols)
II. Title.
PF3112.F58   1989   438.2C421   89-17186
ISBN 0-471-84844-1

Printed in the United States of America

10   9   8   7   6   5   4   3   2   1

Preface

Wie, bitte? was created for people who want to be proficient in everyday German – that is, to understand, speak and write the language in ordinary situations, and to acquire a practical knowledge of the cultures of the German-speaking countries. The very first chapters teach "survival" German – how to identify oneself, get food, find shelter, and arrange transportation. By the end of the book students should be able to support their opinions, pursue academic and occupational discussion, and explore the special features of the German-speaking countries that open up to those who can use the language reasonably well: the artistic and historical heritage, the cuisine, the landscape.

Our intent has been to eliminate any obstacles to achieving that goal. The textbook is shorter than most, for it focuses on the demonstration of useful language rather than the discussion of grammar. It is also filled with samples of genuine printed German, so that if students do indeed travel to a German-speaking country they will almost feel as if they've been there before. The *Wie, bitte?* Class Text is accompanied by a Workbook, or Study Text, and other materials, including tapes and computer software, that offer detailed tutorials in listening, speaking, reading, and writing. Throughout *Wie, bitte?* we have striven not merely to present knowledge about German but rather to show *how* to gain such knowledge and practical facility.

Components of the Program

The **Class Text** is intended for intensive use in the proficiency-oriented classroom. After two preliminary chapters that present basic speech patterns and vocabulary, each chapter follows this organization: The first major theme of the chapter is presented in *Gespräche 1*, a set of model dialogs; then come *Struktur 1*, grammar patterns with brief comment; *Situationen 1*, an array of contextual communication tasks for pairs and groups of students; *Strategie – Kultur und Sprache*, cultural notes and useful advice on strategies for using language; *Gespräche 2*, presentation of the chapter's second major theme; *Struktur 2*; and *Situationen 2*. Each chapter is chock full of a wide array of realia, authentic texts, and photographs. After the 26 regular lessons, there is an afterword that assesses a student's progress and explores further possibilities for the study of German and travel in German-speaking countries, a special chapter on *Feste und Feiertage*, a visual dictionary (*Bildwörterbuch*), 40 pages of print realia, and a German-English glossary. The endpapers offer ready reference materials, including maps and charts, survival vocabulary, and basic grammatical patterns.

The **Instructor's Annotated Edition** includes a discussion of teaching methods, a course outline, a chapter classroom time budget, chapter-by-chapter teaching tips, testing advice and sample tests, and an estimate of attainable proficiency levels. Marginal annotations throughout the text offer classroom exercises, advice about teaching technique, and brief cultural enrichments.

The **Study Text** is a **Workbook** intended for individual use primarily outside the classroom, but also useful in it. The volume contains: 1) an orientation, with advice on study methods; 2) chapter-by-chapter study materials; 3) a reference grammar, to whose various sections the student is directed by marginal annotations in the brief grammar presentations in the Class Text; 4) a collection of recyclable realia which parallels that in the Class Text; 5) "props" (facsimile currency, tickets, etc.) suitable for situation exercises; 6) English renditions of the Class Text dialogs; and 7) chapter-by-chapter vocabulary lists. The Study Text is an integral part of the package. It contains many resources that are ordinarily found in the main textbooks of conventional packages.

The **tape set** is divided into two parts: 1) renditions and expansions of the textbook dialogs; and 2) aural realia and cultural offerings, organized by theme and linguistic structure. These items are the material for homework exercises, for listening tests, and for cultural enrichment. The development of listening comprehension with taped materials is an integral part of the package.

The **Test Bank** contains: 1) materials for proficiency-oriented speaking, listening, reading, and writing tests; 2) answer keys for selected tests and for Study Text exercises; 3) a set of realia suitable for use in the tests provided in the manual, or else in exercises and tests that the teacher devises. A script for the tape program is included in this manual.

The **computer courseware** is optional for both student and teacher. It includes: 1) contextualized grammar exercises and listening, reading, and writing tutorials; 2) computerized versions of selected tests in the testing manual; 3) administrative programs intended to aid the teacher in record-keeping, test administration, and development of auxiliary materials. Supported computers are the IBM PC and compatibles, Apple IIe/gs, and the Macintosh; for the last there is special courseware with natural speech recorded digitally on the disks.

Goals of the Program

For as long as anyone now alive can remember, Americans have been notoriously unfamiliar with languages other than English. In addition, we have been either unapologetic about our monolingual culture, or at least convinced that we as individuals do not have the right linguistic stuff to learn other languages. However, the economic, political, and social requirements of a global community of human beings underscore the necessity for reform in our attitude toward meeting other cultures on their own ground. As a nation we are finally beginning to reward those whose intercultural skills are based in a practical, functional knowledge of other languages. The impulse for fluency in other cultural settings springs in part from economic necessity, and also from the observations that we do not know our own culture well until we are familiar with another; that our horizons are limited only by the languages at our command; and that speaking only one language is like observing the world through one eye. For language is an expression of a cultural system, a means by which people organize the reality they observe. As such it is the key to understanding any culture, including one's own.

Fortunately, this is a very good time to be studying another language – and we must say that it is also a very exciting time to be teaching other languages. In recent years there has been a national call for language instruction that is first and foremost practical – stressing the need to survive and then thrive in a foreign culture – and that presents language as something living, genuine, and above all worth learning.

When ordinary people are asked why they want to learn a foreign language, the typical answer is something like, "I really want to be able to *use* the language. I want to speak to the people there, and I want to understand them." Language teachers, too, pride themselves on their own practical facility in communication, and dream of classes filled with fluent students who could successfully enter another society and thus be a credit to their own. All too often, though, students who have "taken" a foreign language bitterly tell how they were "took:" "I had two years of it, and even right afterwards I couldn't even order a meal." Almost everyone would like to be able to *speak* (or read, or write, or just understand) a foreign language, but many people regard *learning* a foreign language to be a mystery, and *studying* a foreign language to be a matter of boring memorization of vocabulary lists and grammar charts. The image of the monolingual speaker of English, whether the helpless tourist or the damaging "Ugly American," is well known. And yet there are – and always have been – classrooms in which foreign languages are well taught and learned.

Wie, bitte? was written with these classrooms in mind. It was also written with a careful eye to what we know today about second-language acquisition – what linguistic features and contexts are important as we move from the beginning level to the more advanced. It is our aim to teach students what they will need to know as mature adults functioning within a German-speaking culture. It is not our intention to teach everything there is to know about the German language, for that would be impossible in one year.

In writing *Wie, bitte?* we have heeded carefully the guidelines for proficiency in all skill areas established by the American Council on the Teaching of Foreign Languages (ACTFL) in conjunction with the Educational Testing Service (ETS). The ACTFL/ETS Guidelines, carefully adapted from performance criteria used for decades in the Foreign Service, show what we do with language within what cultural context and with what degree of accuracy. They also reflect our progress as we learn other languages. At the *Novice* level we learn the basics: numbers, colors, family members, the date and year, telling time – in other words, "survival" vocabulary. As we progress to the *Intermediate* level, the level at which we begin to create with language, we learn how to *describe* the things closest to our lives: our families, our home towns, and so on. We learn how to ask and give directions, arrange transportation, make social plans, and deal with the necessities of food and lodging. At the *Advanced* level we are acquiring the ability not just to describe, but to *narrate,* and with relation to past, present, and future time. Advanced speakers can talk in some depth about vacation plans, movie and book plots, their employment or daily routine, and similar topics that require the ability to speak in paragraphs, not just sentences. At the *Superior* level – a level students probably won't reach unless they have a good native gift for learning language and spend a substantial time abroad – we move with considerable ease in the language: The grammar and syntax are solid, the vocabulary is broad and varied, and we are able to hypothesize, to support our opinions, and to deal successfully with a broad range of topics from abortion to trade policy, tax amnesty, genetic research, and the ethics of political campaigns.

In spite of its decidedly practical orientation, *Wie bitte?* is not a phrase book for travelers – although we anticipate that students might want to take it along when they travel abroad. Contrary to typical quick-fix translation guides, *Wie, bitte?* stresses the importance of grammar, the skeleton that holds the linguistic body together and is absolutely central to effective communication. In doing so, the text program establishes a firm structural and lexical base for intermediate and advanced courses. The Class Text and Study Text are also full of exercises in listening, reading, speaking, and writing; of these the speaking exercises in particular are conceived for pairs of students, since the use of language implies involvement with others. Above all else, *Wie, bitte?* teaches strategy – the ability to be creative with language skills, to make linguistic facility at each level of proficiency serve the individual to the greatest extent possible in a wide range of contexts.

It should be clear by now that the learner is at the center of this book and at the center of the course in which it is used. Students cannot survive as passive observers of text and course, but must be ready to involve themselves in class activities as they may never have done before. The teacher's most valuable contribution to class will be not as a lecturer, but as a creative and productive helper as the students progress individually toward ever greater linguistic competence through group practice.

We have thoroughly enjoyed writing *Wie, bitte?*, and we trust that our pleasure in this project is evident. We are convinced that this new approach to language learning will be both challenging and fulfilling for both teachers and students, and we hope that both will continue for years to reap the harvest of the coming months' activities.

Acknowledgments

The authors would like to thank Gudrun Hommel-Ingram and David Fogg for their invaluable help in the preparation of many of the materials in this book. Without their expert counsel the task would have been much greater than it was. Our thanks go also to Tineka Bierma and the teaching assistants at Portland State University who helped field-test the book. We are proud that junior colleagues and students at both Portland State University and Linfield College could contribute to the development of *Wie, bitte?* Our personal thanks go as well to Angela Jung for her hospitality and pedagogical advice. In addition, both of our colleges gave us material administrative support. A stipend from the DAAD and assistance from the *Liga für Völkerfreundschaft der DDR* enabled us to gather up-to-date realia and information. Useful realia were also contributed by numerous *Verkehrsvereine*. We also want to compliment the editorial staff of John Wiley & Sons for their willingness to undertake a decidedly new sort of venture, and to commend them for the totally professional and sympathetic manner in which they dealt with a difficult project. We dedicate *Wie, bitte?* to our families, whose forbearance was always exemplary and who supported our undertaking wholeheartedly in spite of its heavy demands on our time and energy. As for the black bear that wandered out of the woods into Pete's back yard while we were working on Chapter 21, and that we – heady with the success of a well-turned phrase – pursued with shovels back into the firs: We hope that has been our greatest mistake in writing *Wie, bitte?*, and we swear to our families that we probably won't do that again.

For their reviews of the manuscript at various stages of development, the publisher and authors would like to thank the following professors: Mervin Barnes, University of Oklahoma; Richard Helt, University of Arizona; Ingeborg Henderson, University of California-Davis; Charles J. James, University of Wisconsin; Karen Kossuth, Pomona College; Thomas A. Lovik, Michigan State University; Janet K. Swaffar, University of Texas-Austin; Benjiman D. Webb, University of Miami.

W.B.F.
P.N.R.

Contents

Bildwörterbuch 284

Drucksachen 310

Glossary 350

Credits 378

Index 380

To the Student

Wie, bitte? is designed to make you proficient in basic German. You will be using the language for practical communication in real situations.

At first you will learn "survival" language — how to provide essential information about yourself and to arrange for food, shelter and transportation, as though you were merely passing through a German-speaking country or helping a visitor to your own society. Farther along you will deal with matters that occupy people when they live in a society for more than a few days, perhaps on a vacation trip or brief business assignment. Those matters include entertainment, greater efficiency in satisfying basic needs, and closer acquaintance with people and with the culture itself. At the end of the course you will rehearse the activities you might well pursue during an extended stay, such as a junior year abroad, a business transfer, or military service. Thus you will explore how to deal with complications that may arise in everyday situations: how to adapt to cultural differences; how to solicit, express, and defend opinions; and even how to make sure your laundry is taken care of and your pictures developed correctly.

Your most important resources, other than your teacher, will be your Class Text and your Study Text. The Class Text is not a book for study in a quiet intellectual atmosphere. It is for a classroom in which there should be a lot of lively talk and activity. The chief target of the Class Text is the spoken language. You can expect a good deal of conversation with a partner or in small groups. Sets of dialogs show how to perform particular communicative tasks, such as getting a hotel room, changing money, or discussing occupations. Each chapter has many situations, or "role-play" exercises, in which you will attempt to carry out variations of these basic tasks. The assignments in the Study Text consist largely of communicative tasks involving speaking, listening, reading, and writing. These exercises simulate genuine communication; they are not drills of vocabulary or grammar.

Learning a language for practical proficiency is not a matter of stumbling through complex discussions of grammar, memorizing vocabulary lists, reciting phrases, writing out artificial sentences, or translating long passages. You will attain proficiency by trying to use the language under realistic conditions. Though grammar and vocabulary are vital, the measure of your proficiency is not what you know or can say about the language, but rather *what you can do with it.* Thus in class and out you should *practice* the language, not just contemplate or discuss it. Speak it, listen to it, read it, write it, and learn enough about the culture to understand speakers of German as human beings.

We hope that for you *Wie, bitte?* will not be a dull textbook to be studied laboriously and then resold or exiled to a dusty shelf. It should be, rather, both a practical handbook to have in hand when you learn German in a German course and a convenient book to have at hand when you use the language, especially if you go abroad.

Preliminary Chapter

WIE, BITTE? WER? WAS?

Guten Tag!

If you wish to conduct your class in German, feel free to introduce here words like *Kapitel* and *Seite,* and also the necessary lower numbers.

You will probably want to take two days for each of the preliminary chapters. The material is for memorization – to be learned by rote for quick response. Try to avoid any discussion of grammar at this point. The overall goal of the two preliminary units is to bring the student up to the novice-mid-level in speaking and writing. We suggest you establish the one-on-one format (partners or small groups) as soon as possible, with the teacher as a roving monitor. You might intersperse occasional choral sessions or individual spot checks. Limit error correction to problems of pronunciation that would obstruct basic communication.

Exercise variations: one student covers column B, other student reads column A prompts; students with books closed respond to teacher's prompts.

Looking Ahead

In these preliminary units you will learn to talk simply about yourself and to describe your immediate world. You will also learn simple, polite expressions and a few basic strategies of communication.

You will be:

- asking for clarification of things you don't understand
- saying your name, age, nationality, and major
- saying simple courtesy formulas
- saying clock time
- identifying the days of the week
- counting money
- locating and naming major cities in Austria, East Germany, West Germany, and Switzerland
- asking questions about dates, times, and prices
- adjusting your handwriting slightly to fit German practices

DIALOGS — GESPRÄCHE

	A	B

Not Understanding

| You folks talk American? | Wie, bitte? |
| Meines Erachtens bedarf diese Aussage keinerlei Erklärung. | Wie, bitte? |

Greetings

Guten Morgen.	Guten Morgen.
Guten Tag.	Guten Tag.
Guten Abend.	Guten Abend.

Names

Wie ist der Name, bitte?	Schmidt. Anna Schmidt.
Guten Morgen, Herr _____ .	Guten Morgen, Frau _____ .
Auf Wiedersehen.	Auf Wiedersehen, Fräulein _____ .

| Wie ist der Familienname, bitte? | Mein Name ist _____ . |
| Danke. Und der Vorname? | _____ . |

| Wer ist das? | Das ist _____ . |

| Wie heißen Sie, bitte? | Schmidt. Ich heiße Benno Schmidt. |

Country and Nationality

Sind Sie Amerikaner?	Ja.
Sind Sie Amerikanerin?	Nein, Kanadierin.
Also, aus Kanada.	Ja, aus Toronto.

More Personal Information

| Und wie alt sind Sie? | Ich bin 22 (zweiundzwanzig). |
| Was studieren Sie? | Mathematik. |

It is important that students learn to respond when they do not understand, and that they learn that some German speakers cannot or prefer not to use English. You may or may not wish to let students indulge their humor with other versions of "You folks talk American?" Suggestion: With the print realia, such as a map or sign, have one student attempt to read a few words, with the other responding, "Wie, bitte?"

Guten Tag does not mean "Good day" in the sense of "Goodbye," nor in the sense of *"schönen Tag noch."* Save your discussion of various greetings in the German-speaking area (*Grüß Gott, Grüezi, Servus*) until later.

Perhaps use some of the realia that are rich in personal names (lists of doctors, hotel keepers, etc.). If so, this may be an opportune time to explain the relevant Study Text listening, reading, and writing exercises.
    You may wish to introduce – but without discussion of grammar – the third person singular pronouns and verb endings (*"Wer ist das?" "Er/Sie heißt* _____ *."*) We recommend that you *not* introduce the other possessive pronouns.

Resist the temptation to introduce many other nationalities, or to discuss noun formation and gender markers.

Introduce numbers 1 through at least 40. Emphasize listening comprehension and speaking. Ignore spelling mistakes unless they affect meaning (e.g., *neun/ nein*).

A list of academic subjects is provided in the Instructor's Guide. Additional annotations are presented chapter by chapter.

Dr. med. I. Druvins
Arzt f. Hals-Nasen-Ohrenheilkunde

Sprechst. Mo.- Fr. 9⁰⁰-12⁰⁰
    Mo.   9⁰⁰-12⁰⁰ u. 15⁰⁰-17⁰⁰
    Die. u. Do. 9⁰⁰-12⁰⁰ u. 15⁰⁰-18⁰⁰

Alle Kassen / Röntgen

O. Aguta
Arzt für Chirurgie
Durchgangsarzt

Sprechst. Mo - Fr 9 - 12 u. 15 - 18 Uhr
    Unfälle   8 - 18 Uhr
    außer Mittwochnachmittag

Erstkommunion

Weil die Geschichten schön sind.
Weil die Stunden lustig sind.
Weil ich viel von Gott lerne.
Weil ich gerne zeichne und spiele.
Weil die Geschichten von
Jesus spannend sind.
Weil ich gerne bete und singe.

```
ERSTKOMMUNIKANTEN         1984
=============================
AUFSCHNAITER Monika
BACHER Daniela
PERATHONER Daniela          EBNER Michaela
SINGER Gerhard              HAUSMEISTER Verena
TANZER Michael             KRISMER Verena
VILLGRATTNER Christoph     LAHARTINGER Richard
                          MAIR Karin
                          SARTORI Simone
                          TSCHIRNER Renaud
   MAURMAIR Roland
   PRASCH Thomas
   SEEBER Julia            GALLER Marion
   SCHMITT Mark            KLAUSNER Daniela
   SKINNER Andreas         LANER Gerald
                          PFISTERER Daniela
   GASSER Michaela         PLAWENN-SALVINI Sylvia
   GEISWINKLER Sabine      REDLICH Alexandra-Maria
   GREIL Marina
   ORTNER René
   ZOLLER Gerhard           AUGSCHÖLL Karin
                           BICHLER Ingrid
                           ELLER Petra
   PIRCHL Gerald           KRASNIK Alice-Helen
   PUTZ Reinhard           KURZTHALER Daniela
   SCHWAB Thomas           STUDIRACH Dominika
   STROBL Markus           WÖRGÖTTER Caroline
   WURZENRAINER Verena
```

HARTMANN AUGENOPTIK

BRILLEN KONTAKTLINSEN
FOTOARBEITEN

Schusterstraße 30–32 · 7800 Freiburg · Telefon 0761/30403

Augenkrankheiten

Austen, Dorothea, Dr. med.,
Auwaldstraße 90, Ruf 13 33 77
Birnbaum, Frank, Dr. med.,
Kaiser-Joseph-Straße 180, Ruf 3 38 85
Eidmann, U., Dr. med., und
Große-Ruyken, F. J., Dr. med.,
(Gemeinschaftspraxis)
Kaiser-Joseph-Straße 180, Ruf 2 38 93
Hallermann, Ch., Dr. med.,
Bertoldstraße 5, Ruf 3 02 25
Horn, Charlotte, Dr. med.,
Kaiser-Joseph-Straße 218, Ruf 3 39 27
Kotowski, Hartmut, Dr. med.,
Friedrichring 16/18, Ruf 3 37 85
Leu, Peter, Dr. med.,
Carl-Kistner-Straße 32, Ruf 44 22 11
Mackensen, Günter, Prof. Dr. med.,
Kilianstraße 5, Ruf 71 4 12
Mahler, Ulrich, Dr. med.,
Schwarzwaldcity, Ruf 2 64 44
Pausch, Adelheid, Dr. med.,
Sulzburger Straße 98, Ruf 49 13 31
Rilling, Franz, Dr. med.,
Goethestraße 50, Ruf 7 27 44
Roesen, Ulrich, Dr. med.,
Urbanstraße 4, Ruf 3 63 41
Schneider, Gustav, Dr. med.,
Schreiberstraße 20, Ruf 2 53 53
Schwiedeßen, Uwe, Dr. med.,
Sedanstraße 8, Ruf 2 48 28
Seydewitz, Frauke, Dr., und
Seydewitz, Robert, Dr. med.,
(Gemeinschaftspraxis)
Fritz-Geiges-Straße 22, Ruf 6 93 38
Sigmund, Erika, Dr. med.,
Goethestraße 18, Ruf 71 9 49
Treutler-Meyer, Ursula, Dr. med.,
Blumenstraße 2, Ruf 41 1 74
Unger, Hanns-Hellmuth, Prof. Dr. med.,
Günterstalstraße 9, Ruf 7 45 75
Velten, Herta, Dr. med.,
(Merzh.) Am Rohrgraben 5,
Ruf 40 72 22
Villinger, Helga, Dr. med.,
Schwarzwaldstraße 4, Ruf 71 5 51
Wagner, Johanna, Dr. med.,
Prinz-Eugen-Straße 4, Ruf 7 38 74
Wegner, Erika, Dr. med.,
Bertoldstraße 3, Im Bursengang,
Ruf 3 36 56
Wiesenack, Wolfgang, Dr. med.,
Leopoldring 5, Ruf 2 50 17

Dermatologie und Venerologie

Arnim, Ellen v., Dr. med.,
Kaiser-Joseph-Straße 244, Ruf 3 49 75
Bauch, Dagmar, Dr. med.,
Bertoldstraße 14, Ruf 2 44 88

Dubiel, Werner, Dr. med.,
Kaiser-Joseph-Straße 269, Ruf 3 33 63
Faber, Martin, Dr. med.,
Zähringerstraße 14, Ruf 3 56 01
Friedel, Gerd, Dr. med.,
Kaiser-Joseph-Straße 214, Ruf 3 69 51
Friedel, Stephan, Dr. med.,
Kaiser-Joseph-Straße 214, Ruf 3 75 18
Hartmann, Hans, Dr. med.,
Zähringer Straße 14, Ruf 5 66 99
Kaiser, Hans, Dr. med.,
Rathausgasse 38, Ruf 2 61 27
Kayma, Urte, Dr. med.,
Krozinger Straße 11, Ruf 48 45 00
Kühnl-Petzoldt, Christa, Dr. med.,
Rosastraße 9, Ruf 3 16 96
Meves, Christa, Dr. med.,
Kaiser-Joseph-Straße 248, Ruf 3 99 93
Schöpf, E., Prof. Dr. med.,
Direktor der Uni-Hautklinik,
Hauptstraße 7, Ruf 27 07 74 16
Stein, Botho, Dr. med.,
Kaiser-Joseph-Straße 205, Ruf 3 63 81
Waldermann, Franz, Dr. med.,
Zähringerstraße 14
Wintermantel, Volker, Dr. med.,
Kaiser-Joseph-Str. 180, Ruf 55 21 79

Frauenärzte

Barth, Christiane, Dr. med.,
Urbanstraße 4, Ruf 3 65 12
Baumgartner, Alfons, Dr. med.,
Schillerstraße 28, Ruf 7 45 22
Baymann, Ernst, Dr. med.,
Habsburgerstraße 59, Ruf 5 61 61
Deichsel, Wolfhard, Dr. med.,
Bertoldstraße 33, Ruf 3 74 22
Doerjer, Otto, Dr. med.,
Schwarzwaldstraße 146a, Ruf 7 03 03
Drägert, C., Dr. Dr. med.,
Christoph-Mang-Str. 18, Ruf 40 46 45
Drews, Christiane,
Mathildenstraße 16, Ruf 27 44 40
Eitel, Lutz, Dr. med.,
Kaiser-Joseph-Straße 269, Ruf 2 64 65
El-Ghussein, Helga, Dr. med.,
Krozinger Straße 11, Ruf 48 29 00
Frank, Peter, Dr. med.,
Dreisamstraße 13, Ruf 2 49 49
Freytag, Margarete, Dr. med.,
Beethovenstraße 8, Ruf 7 54 29
Friedrich, Heinz, Dr. med.,
Karlstraße 9, Ruf 2 58 48
Friedrich, Johanna, Dr.,
Schwarzwaldstraße 30, Ruf 7 38 58
Harsk, W., Dr. med.,
Oberlinden 1, Ruf 3 00 44
Hegar, Udo, Dr.,
Wilhelmstraße 10, Ruf 3 66 34
Hillemanns, Hans-G., Prof. Dr. med.,
Schlierbergstr. 3, Ruf 4 27 21
Huber, Richard, Prof. Dr. med. habil.,
Eggstraße 14, Ruf 7 50 91

Hugo, Jürgen, Dr. med.,
Schreiberstraße 20, Ruf 3 39 96
Keck, Heinrich, Dr. med.,
Schillerstraße 10, Ruf 7 39 55
Kloke, Wolf-Dietrich, Dr. med.,
Kaiser Joseph Straße 254, Ruf 2 35 55
Körner, Ursula, Dr. med.,
Marienstraße 13, Ruf 3 07 41
Körner-Liedke, Brigitte, Dr. med.,
Kaiser-Joseph-Straße 214, Ruf 2 50 01
Krako, Karoly, Dr. med.,
Sundgauallee 55, Ruf 8 15 77
Luckscheiter, Harald, Dr. med.,
Günterstalstraße 50, Ruf 7 35 21
Mayer, Gertrud, Dr. med.,
Bertoldstraße 3, Ruf 3 41 88
Medweth, Walter, Dr. med.,
Chefarzt der geb.-gyn. Abteilung des
Lorettokrankenhauses, Mercystraße,
Ruf 7 08 40
Michels, Gerd, Dr. med.,
Blochackerweg 5, Ruf 4 24 51/2
Müller, Rudolf, Dr. med.,
Greiffeneggring 1, Ruf 3 48 18
Prier, Gudrun, Dr. med.,
Münsterplatz 6, Ruf 3 41 46
Rosset, Wilhelm, Dr. med.,
Karlstraße 41, Ruf 3 22 62
Samman, R. M., Dr. med.,
Zähringer Straße 332, Ruf 55 10 61
Schmeling, Gerd, Dr. med.,
Zähringer Straße 14, Ruf 55 10 61
Schmitt, Rudolf, Dozent Dr. med.,
Karlstraße 41, Ruf 3 22 62
Schulte-Vallentin, M., Dr. med.,
Brunnenstraße 6, Ruf 3 91 99
Schwarz, H., Dr. med.,
Kornhaus, Ruf 2 40 03
Soliman, M., Dr. med.,
Schwarzwald-City, Ruf 3 13 51
Stix, Lothar, Dr. med.,
Andreas-Hofer-Str. 128, Ruf 47 17 70
Tettenborn, Klaus, Dr. med.,
Habsburgerstraße 131, Ruf 2 50 59
Wagner, Dieter, Prof. Dr. med.,
Diakoniekrankenhaus,
Ruf 13 01–245

Hals-, Nasen- und Ohrenkrankheiten

Beck, Chl., Prof. Dr. med.,
Direktor der Universitäts-HNO-Klinik,
Kilianstraße, Ruf 2 70-3206
Ebert, Bernd, Dr. med.,
Leopoldring 5, Ruf 3 23 00
Goller, Ferdo, Dr. med.,
Schreiberstraße 20, Ruf 2 55 22,
Killian, Wolfgang, Dr. med.,
Johanniterstraße 15, Ruf 2 40 47
Koch, Georgia, Dr. med.,
Kaiser-Joseph-Straße 255, Ruf 3 00 30
Martin, Günter, Dr. med.,
Bertoldstraße 5, Ruf 3 46 66
Mildt-Zimmerlin, Annelise, Dr. med.,
Tivolistraße 15, Ruf 2 47 25

Oertel, Werner, Dr. med.,
Dr. med. dent., Rotteckring 2,
Ruf 2 26 75
Paulus, Ernst, Dr. med.,
Friedrichstraße 44, Ruf 2 33 51
Schenck, Joachim, Dr. med.,
Greiffeneggring 1, Ruf 2 43 45
Schmidt, Hermann, Dr. med.,
Egonstraße 14, Ruf 27 24 95
Wulffen, Christoph, G. v., Dr. med.,
Albertstraße 1, Ruf 27 57 70
Zeiser, Robert, Dr. med.,
Krozinger Straße 7, Einkaufszentrum
Weingarten, Ruf 44 54 00
Zöllner, Fritz, Prof. Dr. med.,
Hugstetter Str 55, Ruf 2 70-1

Innere Medizin

Auwärter, Werner, Dr. med.,
Hagenmattenstraße 26, Ruf 6 74 95
Balig, Peter, Dr. med.,
Kaiser-Joseph-Str. 186-188, Ruf 3 33 03
Becher, Horst, Dr. med., Priv. Doz.,
Gerberau 6, Ruf 2 61 15
Becker, Heinrich, Dr. med.,
Münsterplatz 8, Ruf 3 08 00
Bilger, Rob., Prof. Dr. med.,
Chefarzt der Inneren Abteilung des
St.-Josefs-Krankenhauses,
Ruf 27 11-1
Brundies, Bernd, Dr. med.,
Habsburgerstraße 127, Ruf 2 20 99
Burmeister, Peter, Prof. Dr. med.,
Eisenbahnstraße 43, Ruf 3 66 14
Busse-Grawitz, E. G., Dr. med.,
(Merzh.) Im Ried 9, Ruf 40 31 66
Common, H., Dr. med.,
Gund., Feldbergstraße 17, Ruf 5 88 10
Daikeler-Meurer, Gabriele, Dr. med.,
Eisenbahnstraße 43, Ruf 3 66 14
Delker, Maria, Dr. med.,
Erasmusstraße 20, Ruf 3 66 27
Denz, Claus, Dr. med.,
Bertoldstraße 3, Ruf 3 33 00
Dietz, Helmut, Dr. med.,
Rheinstraße 25, Ruf 27 23 57
Dischler, Wolfram, Dr. med.,
Schwarzwald-City, Ruf 3 36 64
Fendrich, Klaus, Dr. med.,
Gund., Feldbergstraße 17, Ruf 5 88 10
Finck, Werner, Dr. med.,
Stadtstraße 55, Ruf 3 58 22
Frank, Dieter, Dr. med.,
Wölflinstraße 19, Ruf 3 48 80
Frank, Karl Th., Dr. med.,
Hermannstraße 2, Ruf 3 66 46
Fricke, Harald, Dr. med.,
Chr.-Mang-Str. 18–20, Ruf 40 20 34
Föhlich, Jürgen, Dr. med.,
Lorettokrankenhaus, Ruf 7 084-0
Gäng, Volker, Dr. med., habil.
Blochackerweg 5, Ruf 4 24 51
Gerok, W., Prof. Dr. med.,
Direktor der Med. Universitäts-Klinik,
Hugstetter Straße 55, Ruf 201-1

Preliminary Chapter 2

WO? WANN?
WIEVIEL?

Flughafen – Frankfurt am Main.

	A	B

Excuse me!

Demonstrate, explain, and energetically practice the two functions, including differences in intonation. This is a good opportunity to encourage natural gesture and emotion as integral parts of communication. Example: Have the students stand up and approach other students, either making an awkward motion or attempting to get their attention.

Oh, Entschuldigung.
Entschuldigung . . .

Bitte.
Bitte?

Where is . . . ?

If possible, show a wall map or overhead projection of the four German-speaking countries. The text realia also include many suitable maps or other realia. Underscore the importance of pronouncing names accurately to avoid offense or misunderstanding. (See Study Text for discussion and examples.) Teach approximate distances (in English or German), and perhaps establish the notion that by train 100 km = 1 hour, and vice versa; the aim should be to teach both language and culture (basic geography, initial treatment of metric system, and a little about transportation).

in the train:

Ist das Wiesbaden?

Nein, das ist nicht Wiesbaden.
Das ist Mainz.

reading a map:

Wo ist Aachen?
Wo?

Aachen? Da.
Da ist Köln, und hier ist Aachen.

Ist Freiburg in der Schweiz?
Wie, bitte?
Wo ist Frankfurt?

Nein, in der BRD.
In der Bundesrepublik.
Frankfurt an der Oder ist in der DDR.
Frankfurt am Main ist in der BRD.

Und Graz?

Das ist in Österreich.

Time and Day

Time and Day: Explain, practice, and encourage the facility to echo, vary, negate, and confirm as valuable rhetorical strategy. Use calendars in realia. Exercise variations: Student A: *"Gestern war Mittwoch."* Student B: *"Heute ist Donnerstag."* Practice time-telling on the hour only, leaving *halb* and *Viertel* for later. Introduce days of the week not given in the dialogs.

Wieviel Uhr ist es?
Entschuldigung. Wie spät ist es?
Was ist heute?
Morgen ist Mittwoch, ja?
Ist heute Freitag?

Ich weiß nicht. Tut mir leid.
Es ist zehn Uhr.
Montag.
Nein, nicht Mittwoch. Dienstag.
Nein, Donnerstag. Gestern war Mittwoch.

How much does that cost?

Optional for Cost: Fractional prices and other currency units – in moderation, and with appropriate realia (e.g., prices of common objects, especially if the generic term is cognate or the brand name familiar).

Wieviel, bitte?
Wieviel kostet das?

Fünf (5) Mark.
Das kostet sechzehn (16) Mark.

7

Blutenburger Frühling 1982

4.4.   So 16.00   Schloßkirche Blutenburg
Altbaierisches Passionssingen
mit den Fischbachauer Sängerinnen und
den Kreuther Musikanten
Verbindendes Wort: Georg Thurmair

10.4.   Sa 17.00   Schloßkirche Blutenburg
Das Blutenburger Osterspiel
Eine Bayerische Dichtung von und mit Matthias Pöschl
Susanne Steidle, Harfe; Mendlinger Dreigsang

15.4.   Do 20.00   Schloßkirche Blutenburg
Russische Osternacht
Münchner Madrigalchor
Werke v. Tschajkowski, Rimski-Korssakow,
Tschesnokow u. a. Osternachtgesänge im altslawischen
Ritus; Kanon d. hl. Joh. Damaszenus; Liturgie d. hl. Joh.
Chrysostomus (Komposition v. Nikolski); Tropar,
Kontakion, Kommunionpsalm
Ltg.: Franz Brandl – Einführende Worte:
Prof. Dr. Pietro Modesto (Mailand)

22.4.   Do 20.00   Schloßkirche Blutenburg
Musik alter Meister zur Osterzeit
für Orgel und Zinken
Werke v. Bach, Beneet, Sorge, Walther; Spielstücke a. d.
Renaissance-Zeit
Krummhorn-Quartett Ingolstadt; Friedrich Kneule a. d.
Blutenburg Orgel

28.4.   Mi 19.00   Bayer. Versicherungskammer, Sternstr. 3
Schülerkonzert

29.4.   Do und
30.4.   Fr, jeweils 20.00   Herkulessaal der Residenz
11. Symphoniekonzert
des Bayerischen Rundfunks
Mozart: Serenade B-dur f. 13 Bläser KV 361 – Strawinsky:
Les Noces; Scènes choreographiques Russes
Ltg.: Rafael Kubelik – Jane Marsh, Sopran; Glenys Linos,
Alt; Horst Laubenthal, Tenor; Andrew Foldi, Baß; Chor d.
Bayer. Rundfunks

29.4.   Do 20.00   Circus-Krone-Bau, Marsstr. 43
Maria Farantoure

29.4.   Do 18.00   Theater an der Leopoldstr. 17
Fünftes 6 Uhr-Konzert/XVI. Zyklus
d. Bayer. Vereinsbank i. V. mit dem Städt. Kulturreferat
Duo Ingrid Haus (Violine), Hans-Dieter Bauer
(Klavier)
Mozart: Violinsonate F-dur KV 376 – Ysaye: Sonate f.
Violine solo E-dur Nr. 6 – Stockhausen: Sonatine f.
Violine u. Klavier, 1951 – Beethoven: Violinsonate G-dur
op. 96

29.4.   Do 19.30   Theatersaal d. Wohnstiftes Augustinum
Mü.-Nord, Weitlstr. 66
Kammerkonzert
Werke v. Reger, Mozart, Rolla, Schubert
Kammerensemble d. Bayer. Staatsorch.: Klaus Holsten,
Flöte; Ulrich Grußendorf, Violine; Roland Krüger, Viola;
Gerhard Zank, Violoncello

29.4.   Do 20.00   St. Bonifaz, Karlstr. 34
Sonderkonzert des Philharmonischen Chores
Reger: Fantasie u. Fuge op. 52/3 – Dvořák: Messe D-dur
op. 86
Ltg.: Josef Schmidhuber – Solisten: Karl Maureen,
Rosemarie Stauder, Brune Femar, Heiner Hopfner, Rolf
Mertens

30.4.   Fr 20.00   Künstlerhaus am Lenbachplatz
Internationale Gitarrenkonzerte
Flöte-Gitarre Duo, Basel
Frank Nagel, Flöte; Walter Feybli, Gitarre

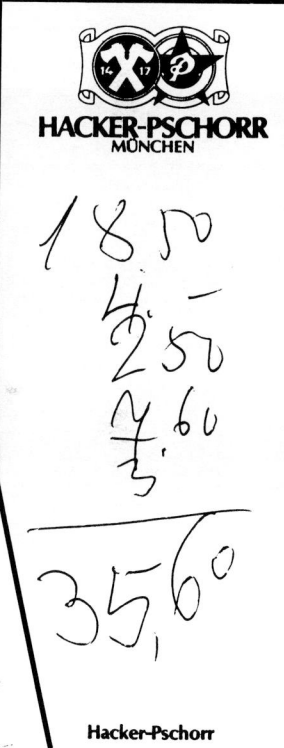

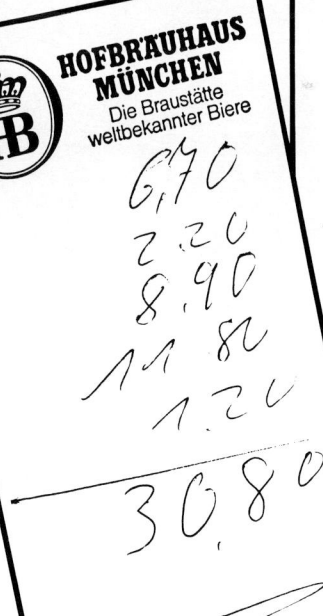

Chapter 1
FAHRKARTEN UND PÄSSE, BITTE/ IMBISS

Die Fahrkarten, bitte!

The dialogs in Chapters 1–26 are not necessarily meant for memorization. They provide realistic models of speech and are meant as patterns for carrying out certain functions in certain contexts. We suggest that you establish the basic vocabulary and patterns, and then proceed to situation work, either with your own setups or with the situations at the end of the chapter.

FUNKTIONEN – KONTEXTE – STRUKTUREN

Looking Ahead
You'll be performing simple transactions – asking questions, making polite requests, getting clarification, ordering simple meals, counting money, and identifying your possessions.

You will be using:
- question-words – many begin with "W"
- basic word-order principles
- subject-verb combinations
- forms of *sein* ("to be") and *haben* ("to have")
- the definite article ("the") for three types or "genders" of nouns

Fahrkarten und Pässe, bitte

Schaffner *conductor* **1**

Use the here/*hier* difference as a chance to do some contrastive pronunciation exercise. The insistence on accuracy of pronunciation should correspond to the target proficiency level.

Use tickets, etc., to practice handing things back and forth, with appropriate language. Demonstrate the difference in intonation of *bitte* and similar expressions. **2**

If necessary, inform students **3** that there is no capital ß.

Passbeamter *passport official*

Insist resolutely that students use the German **4** names, though perhaps not always when they speak English. Point out cities that have a common English name. Cologne (the perfume) is indeed named for the city, and has to do with the centuries-old scent industry: Eau de Cologne = Kölnisch Wasser. **5**

Briefly explain the difference between *um X Uhr* and *in X Stunden.* Exercise: show a simple timetable on the board (even hours only), with arrival times for several cities. Establish the time (*"Es ist X Uhr."*). Question: *"Wann sind wir in Y?"* Answer: *"Um A Uhr – in B Stunden."*

Expand the previous exercise to include times late in the day in order to practice the 24-hour clock.

SCHAFFNER	Die Fahrkarten, bitte.
JOHN	Huh?
WILL	Wie, bitte?
SCHAFFNER	Ihr Ticket, bitte.
JOHN	OK. Here. Uh, hier.
WILL	Bitte schön.
SCHAFFNER	Gut. Danke.
JOHN	Thanks.
WILL	Danke.
SCHAFFNER	Bitte schön.
JOHN	Well, I guess it's German from here on.
WILL	Wie, bitte?

SCHAFFNER	Guten Tag. Die Fahrkarten, bitte.
ANDREAS	Fahrkarten? Bitte sehr.
SCHAFFNER	In Ordnung. Danke schön. Wiedersehen.
ANDREAS	Danke. Auf Wiedersehen!

PASSBEAMTER	Guten Morgen. Paßkontrolle.
COLIN	Wie, bitte?
PASSBEAMTER	Paßkontrolle. Ihre Pässe, bitte.
COLIN	Oh. Yeah . . . Ja. Mein Paß. Bitte schön.
PASSBEAMTER	Ist gut. Danke schön.

PASSBEAMTIN	Tag. Die Pässe, bitte.
LOREN	Bitte schön. Uh, wann sind wir in Aachen?
PASSBEAMTIN	Ich weiß nicht. Ist das hier Ihr Gepäck?
LOREN	Das da? Nein, das ist nicht mein Gepäck.
PASSBEAMTIN	Ihr Gepäck ist das nicht. OK. Danke.
LOREN	Bitte sehr. Wiedersehen.

SCHAFFNER	Guten Abend. Ihre Fahrkarte, bitte.
TED	Meine Fahrkarte? Bitte schön.
SCHAFFNER	Danke sehr. In Ordnung.
TED	Danke schön. Wann sind wir in Köln?
SCHAFFNER	In zwei Stunden. Um zwanzig Uhr.
TED	Wie, bitte?
SCHAFFNER	Oh, Sie sind Amerikaner. Also heute abend um acht Uhr.
TED	Danke schön. Auf Wiedersehen.
SCHAFFNER	Wiedersehen. . . . So, Die Fahrkarten, bitte. . . .

STRUKTUR 1

Nouns §§1–3,5

Explain the relationship between the Class Text *Struktur* pages and the corresponding sections in the Study Text

This point is so important that nouns in the German-English dictionary in Wie, bitte? are listed separately by gender. When you look up a noun, you will have to consider its gender.

reference grammar. Please avoid lecture-style presentation of grammar. Demonstrate the structures and then make sure the students practice them with vocabulary variation, different tone of voice, etc. Many sections present only part of

Pronouns §§1,4,9,10

Use this occasion to review students' names and other material from the preliminary chapters: *"Ist das Hans?" "Nein, das ist George."*

3: Exercise: Teacher: *"Wo ist Nancy?"* Student: *"Da ist Nancy."* Teacher: *"Und wer ist das?"* Student: *"Das ist Lisa."* Use the same drill to review geography: Teacher: *"Wo ist Zürich?"* Student: *"Das ist in der Schweiz."*

4: Exercises: 1) Teacher: *"Sind Sie Amerikaner?"* Student: *"Ja,*

Verbs §14

ich bin Amerikaner/Nein, ich bin Kanadier." 2) Teacher: *"Sind Sie Amerikanerinnen?"* Student: *"Ich bin Amerikanerin; sie ist Kanadierin."*

1. Nouns

● spelling

Every German noun begins with a capital letter.

die <u>F</u>ahrkarte   das <u>G</u>epäck

● gender

Learn the definite article for each noun: **der/die/das.**

der Paß   **die** Flasche   **das** Gepäck
der Amerikaner   **die** Kanadierin   **das** Ticket

● singular and plural

ONE – SINGULAR		MORE THAN ONE – PLURAL
der Paß		Pässe
der Amerikaner		Amerikaner
die Fahrkarte	**die**	Fahrkarten
die Amerikanerin		Amerikanerinnen
das Ticket		Tickets

2. Pronouns

● *das*

Das is the all-purpose demonstrative pronoun. It points at something or someone. It is used for both singular and plural.

Ist **das** Ihr Gepäck?   Wieviel ist **das?**
Das ist Richard.   **Das** ist Elisabeth.
Das ist die Fahrkarte. **Das** sind die Fahrkarten.
    Eine Flasche Cola kostet zwei Mark zehn. Möchten Sie **das?**

● possessive pronouns

SINGULARS				PLURALS OF ALL NOUNS	
DER NOUNS	DIE NOUNS	DAS NOUNS			
Das ist mein Paß	mein<u>e</u> Fahrkarte	mein Gepäck	Das sind	Ihr<u>e</u> Pässe	
ihr Paß	ihr<u>e</u> Fahrkarte	ihr Gepäck		mein<u>e</u> Fahrkarten	
				Ihr<u>e</u> Tickets	

3. Question words (interrogatives)

<u>W</u>er?? <u>W</u>o?? <u>W</u>ann?? <u>W</u>ie?? <u>W</u>ieviel??

Wer ist das?   **Wo** sind wir?   **Wann** sind wir in Köln?
                   Wie alt sind Sie?   **Wieviel** kostet das?

4. The verb *sein* expresses "=".

ONE ONLY – SINGULAR	MORE THAN ONE – PLURAL
Ich **bin** Amerikaner.	Wann **sind** wir in Köln?
Sind Sie Amerikanerin?	**Sind** Sie Amerikanerinnen?
Mein Gepäck **ist** das nicht.	

what the advanced linguist considers to be a single larger grammatical topic. We urge you not to attempt to deal with the whole subject at once. The intent is to limit the material to what can be absorbed and produced with genuine proficiency. Error correction should be appropriate to the given proficiency level. The gender error in *"Das ist nicht meine Gepäck"* should not be singled out – here! – for stern correction, and the successful production of the sentence should be rewarded. Much can be accomplished with indirect correction and reinforcement modeling. Example: *"Oh – das ist nicht Ihr Gepäck. Das ist auch nicht mein Gepäck."*

SITUATIONEN 1 Fahrkarten und Pässe, bitte

Stage 1	Student **A**	Student **B**
1 *See the Introduction to the Instructor's Annotated Edition for advice about situation exercises.*	Asks for B's passport. Thanks B and starts to move on. Doesn't know; expresses regret.	Responds appropriately. Wants to know what time it is. Thanks A anyway; "Auf Wiedersehen."
2 *Solution to "born and raised in Manitoba": "Ja, [ich bin] aus Manitoba."*	Asks whether B is from Canada. Is flattered, but is from Graz. Tells B where Graz is.	Responds: born and raised in Manitoba. Asks same question of A. Doesn't know where Graz is. Concludes conversation politely.
3 *Use appropriate Zugbegleiter or map as prop. "Going through Köln" = Wann sind wir in Köln?, after which surprise that the train will arrive elsewhere at a certain time.*	Asks if train is going through Köln. Doesn't understand.	Sets A straight: it isn't; names a city south of Köln; B is from there. Tells when they'll be in Köln. Repeats the information.
4 *"Ist das die Paßkontrolle?"*	Sees uniformed official and anticipates passport check.	Is just checking tickets. Tells when and where passport check will be.

	A	**B**	**C**
1	(Enters train compartment to check tickets. It's evening.) Says it will be another hour.	(Is asleep.) Shows ticket, asks when they'll be in Bochum. Goes back to sleep.	Wakes friend, tells what's happening. Thanks and says goodbye.
2 *Solution to "Is suspicious, but leaves": "So? Hm. Danke schön. Auf Wiedersehen."*	Sees suitcase on luggage rack, asks if B is owner. Is not owner of suitcase.	Is not owner. Is not owner of suitcase.	Enters, asks for passports, tries to find out whose suitcase it is. Is suspicious, but leaves.

Stage 2

1

You are traveling to a major city. Your train is at the border. It is late at night. The passport official comes to check your papers. You need to know:

a) what time it is;
b) where you are;
c) when you will reach your destination.

2

You are traveling from Austria to Switzerland. You think you are near the border. You can see a town in the distance. Ask a passenger in your compartment

a) whether you are already across the border;
b) when passports will be checked;
c) which country the distant town is in;
d) whether she is from the town.

Versuchen Sie doch! (Now try this!)

You may think you do not have the vocabulary to carry out these tasks. Try to do the best you can with what you already know. You might also consult the Bildwörterbuch section "Transportation/Verkehr," pp. 292–3.

You have boarded a train and are searching for a seat. You enter a compartment. Four of the six seats are occupied by people. Two are occupied by someone's baggage. Can you obtain a seat without offending anyone?

You were in a hurry and boarded your train without buying a ticket. The conductor approaches. State your destination, inquire about the price, and complete the purchase. Can you say anything to maintain your dignity ("It was late and . . .")?

Greetings and farewells

These are an important part of German, just as bowing is essential for many functions in speaking Japanese. Always greet people (as a group) in shops, even if you feel self-conscious in front of others at first. Also, do not forget to say good-bye when you leave. After you return to North America, you will probably feel that something is missing from our commercial transactions.

Travel documents

We view **passports** as documents necessary for travel abroad. But Europeans carry an identification card (*der Personalausweis* or simply *der Ausweis*) as proof of permanent residence in a specific place. This card can suffice for travel to friendly neighboring countries (West Germany to Belgium, for example), but a passport (*der Paß*) is necessary for extended trips (a Swiss visiting Morocco, for example). Such trips may require a visa (*das Visum*) as well.

Currencies

Although the dollar is a well-known standard, each of the German-speaking countries has its own national currency:

Austria: 1 (ein) Schilling (öS) = 100 Groschen
East Germany: 1 (eine) Mark (M) = 100 Pfennige
West Germany: 1 (eine) (Deutsche) Mark (DM) = 100 Pfennige
Switzerland: 1 (ein) Franken (SFr) = 100 Rappen

Learn "ball-park" currency conversion rates (example: 1 öS = 10¢, 1 DM = 50¢, 1 M = 50¢, 1 SFr = 60¢). Coin and bill denominations vary from country to country; see Chapter 6.

Bitte

Note the frequency of *bitte* in the dialogs, and note the different English equivalents in the Study Text translations. Unusual for speakers of English is the virtual necessity of saying something (*"bitte," "bitte schön," "bitte sehr"*) when objects are passed:

"Meine Fahrkarte? . . . Bitte schön."   "Ein Bier . . . bitte sehr."

Some German-speaking learners of English say "please" when passing something in English-speaking countries. What mistake are they making?

Sausages

In a culture where around 1,000 different types of sausage (*Wurst*) are available, it is no surprise that one can expect a variety of sausages at fast-food stands. Sausage is generally ordered with potato salad (*der Kartoffelsalat*), French fries (*die Pommes frites*), or a hard roll (*das Brötchen*). In recent years *der Hamburger* has made its debut abroad, and some fast-food counters offer a new foreign sausage: *der Hot Dog. (Der Frankfurter,* by the way, is a man from Frankfurt.)

Using what you know

At every stage in your learning of German, you will want to get the most out of what you have. Remember:

1. We often use **sentence fragments,** and German speakers do also. They are a perfectly natural way of using language. If your delivery is fluent, your use of fragments in German can be quite effective:

Schmidt. Benno Schmidt.
Nichts, danke.
Zehn Mark.
Um sieben Uhr.
Aus Chicago.

2. You can **buy time** and give yourself a chance to think by asking for a repeat (*"Wie, bitte?"*) or by echoing and perhaps slightly changing what you have heard:

Ich komme aus Berlin.	So. Aus Berlin.
Nein, Tee haben wir nicht.	Hm. Tee haben Sie nicht. . . . Also Mineralwasser, bitte.

Listening for words you can echo from others can add to your effectiveness as a speaker of German.

Push this energetically, now and forevermore – it is a great rhetorical device, and can liven up a class.

3. You can **create questions** not only by using verb-first word order, but also simply by changing the intonation of a phrase or statement:

a) "Sind Sie Engländerin?"
   "Nein. Kanadierin."
   "Kanadierin?" ("Gee, are you really from Canada?")

b) "22."
   "22?" ("My, you don't look a day over 17.")

c) "Und drei Mark siebzig zurück."
   "Drei Mark siebzig?" ("I thought I'd get DM 4,70 back.")

d) Ich möchte Kaffee.
   Sie möchten *Kaffee?* ("I thought you hated it.")

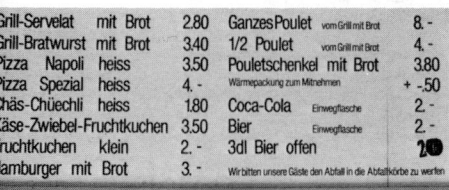

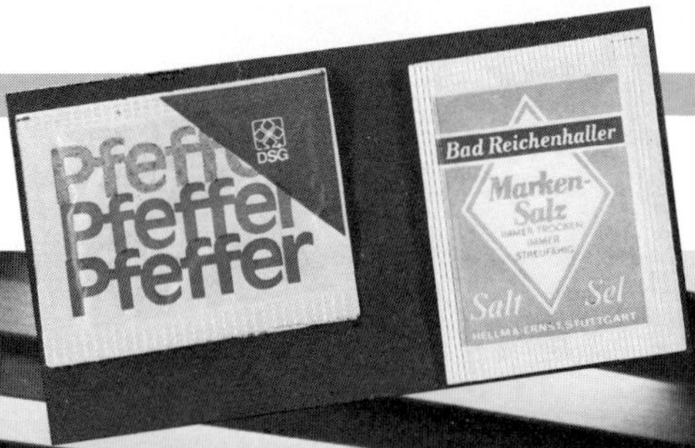

Jetzt kommt die Wurst zum Zug.

Im Juli und August Wurstspezialitäten-Wochen in allen Zugrestaurants.

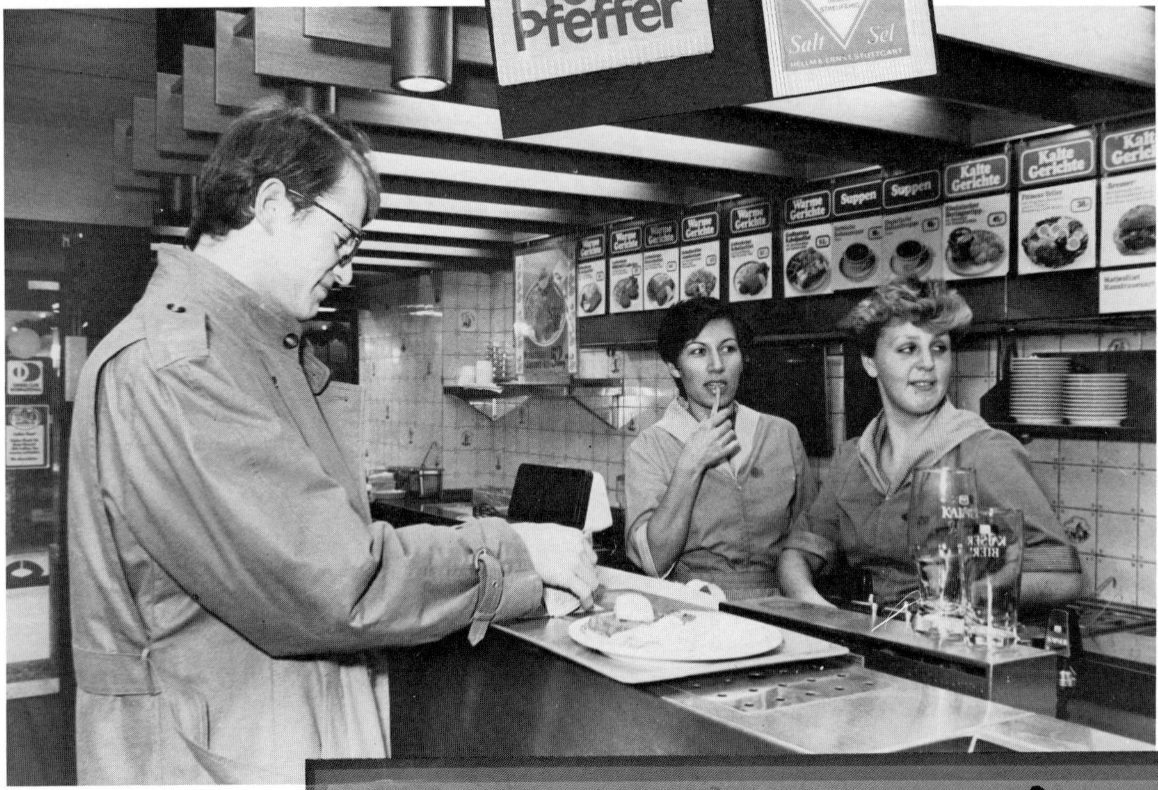

Bockwurst,
Senf, Art.-Nr.: 306
DM 2,60
Kartoffelsalat,
Art.-Nr.: 334 **DM 2,10**

Imbiß

<table>
<tr><td>*Inhaber* proprietor</td><td>**1**</td><td></td><td></td></tr>
</table>

Inhaber proprietor **1**

INHABER	Ja, bitte schön?
HERR FREI	Ein Glas Bier, bitte.
INHABER	Ein Bier. . . . Bitte sehr.
HERR FREI	Danke schön. Wieviel kostet das?
INHABER	2, –DM (Zwei Mark), bitte.

2

KELLNERIN	Also, Bratwurst, Kartoffelsalat und ein Bier. Sieben Mark zwanzig.
HERR GLATTHARD	Hier sind zehn Mark zwanzig.
KELLNERIN	Und drei Mark zurück. Danke schön.
HERR GLATTHARD	Danke schön. Auf Wiedersehen.
KELLNERIN	Wiedersehen.

3

FRAU SUTTER	Guten Abend.
INHABERIN	Guten Abend. Bitte schön?
FRAU SUTTER	Ich möchte bitte Currywurst mit Pommes frites.
INHABERIN	Und zu trinken?
FRAU SUTTER	Wieviel kostet eine Flasche Mineralwasser?
INHABERIN	Zwei Mark zehn. Möchten Sie das?
FRAU SUTTER	Ja, bitte.

4

FRL. HEBBEL	Haben Sie Tee?
INHABER	Nein, Tee haben wir nicht. Möchten Sie Kaffee?
FRL. HEBBEL	Ja, bitte, schwarz.
INHABER	Und zu essen?
FRL. HEBBEL	Nichts, danke.
INHABER	Also zwei Mark fünfzig.

5

INHABER	Also, drei Mark zehn.
FRAU SCHILLING	Bitte schön. Hier sind hundert Mark.
INHABER	Ach, hundert Mark? Ich weiß nicht, . . .
FRAU SCHILLING	Moment, ich habe zehn Pfennig.
INHABER	Danke sehr. Also drei Mark. . . . So, 20, 30, 40, 45, 50, 55, 70, . . . , nein, 60, 65, 70, 75, 80, 85, 90, 92, 94, 96, 97 Mark zurück. Bitte schön.

STRUKTUR 2

Nouns §6 **1. Nouns: pluralization patterns**

SINGULAR	PLURAL	SIGNAL	
der Paß	die Pässe	¨ + e	Umlaut over stem vowel, add -e.
der Engländer	die Engländer	none	The signal is the *der/die* difference.
die Fahrkarte	die Fahrkarten	-n	Many *die*-nouns form plural by
eine Flasche	zwei Flaschen	-n	adding -n.
das Ticket	die Tickets	-s	Many nouns borrowed from English or French form plural by adding -s.

Verbs §§1–4; W.O. §§1–4 **2. Word order**

Song: *"Mein Hut, er hat drei Ecken."*

● **position of verb in simple statements (declarative sentences)**

In simple statements the verb always appears in second position. This is the most important principle of German word order.

Verb second

1	**2**	**rest of statement**
Das	IST	nicht mein Gepäck.
Ihr Gepäck	IST	das nicht.
Tee	HABEN	wir nicht.
Ich	MÖCHTE	bitte Currywurst mit Pommes frites.
Hier	SIND	hundert Mark.
	VERB	

● **position of verb in questions**

Use menu or train travel realia to elicit contrastive structures and intonation with practice in echoing. Examples: 1) *"Haben Sie Tee?" "Oh, Sie haben Kaffee."* 2) *"Haben Sie Tee?" "Nein, Tee haben wir nicht. Wir haben X."* Continue this exercise with the next grammar item: 3) *"Wieviel kostet eine Flasche Bier?" "Eine Flasche Bier kostet X."* 4) *"Wieviel kostet eine Flasche Bier in Wiesbaden?" "In Wiesbaden kostet . . ."*

In **yes/no** questions

Haben Sie Tee?
Möchten Sie Kaffee?   **Verb first, then subject.**
Ist das hier Ihr Gepäck?

In **W**-Questions

Wann **sind** wir in Köln?   **W-word, then VERB, then SUBJECT**
　　1　　2　3　　　　　　　　　**1　　　　2　　　　3**

Wieviel **kostet** eine Flasche Bier?
　　1　　　　2　　　　　　3

Verbs §§5–7 **3. Verb endings (conjugation)**

Song: *"Wir sind zwei Musikanten."*

SINGULAR	PLURAL
Ich studiere Physik.	Tee haben **wir** nicht.
Herr Schmidt, haben **Sie** Ihre Fahrkarte?	So, meine Damen und Herren. Haben **Sie** Ihre Fahrkarten?
Mein Gepäck ist nicht hier. **Eine Flasche Mineralwasser** kostet . . .	

SITUATIONEN 2 Imbiß

Stage 1	A	B
1	Wants a wurst and a beer. Offers SFr 50 bank note. Finds and offers 20 Rappen. Apologizes.	Confirms order, gives price: SFr 5,20. Begins counting out change. Has to start counting again. Forgives.
2	Can't see menu, asks price of many alcoholic and nonalcoholic drinks. Orders the first thing she or he asked about. Has exact change, fortunately.	Tells prices, with growing impatience. Thanks for the change, says good-bye.
3	Asks what B would like. The *Imbiß* has no Currywurst. Suggests two substitutes, with prices. Serves items, gives price. Counts change, thanks.	Is uncertain, then asks for Currywurst. Confirms lack of Currywurst. Asks for French fries with soft drink. Confirms total, offers banknote. Concludes transaction.

Use a menu from the realia selection.

Encourage students to give examples of such drinks rather than to insist on specific vocabulary for "alcoholic" or "nonalcoholic." Illustrate the important skill of paraphrasing and enumerating in the absence of specific vocabulary.

	A	B	C
1	Orders Currywurst, potato salad, mineral water. Orders substitute.	Orders bratwurst, fries, coffee. Orders substitute.	(Works in *Imbiß*.) Don't have A's drink or B's fries. Confirms orders.
2	Orders sandwich. Asks for apple juice. Orders coffee (no cream).	(Isn't listening.) (Still not listening.) Asks for hotdog and apple juice.	Asks what A wants to drink. Out of apple juice; offers orange juice. Confirms order; turns to B. Patiently repeats: no apple juice.

Tagesplatte
Art-Nr. 640
Ungarisches Gulasch
Spaghetti, Salatteller
DM 14,–

in Ⓑ	in Ⓕ	in ⓃⓁ
FB 304,–	FF 37,90	Hfl 16,–
in Ⓘ	in Ⓐ	in ⒸⒽ
Lit 7900,–	öS 100,–	Sfrs 11,80

Als Menü zuzüglich:
Hühnerbrühe mit Einlage,
1 Brötchen oder 1 Scheibe Brot
und Eiskrem.

DM 19,10

in Ⓑ	in Ⓕ	in ⓃⓁ
FB 415,–	FF 51,70	Hfl 21,80
in Ⓘ	in Ⓐ	in ⒸⒽ
Lit 10800,–	öS 137,–	Sfrs 16,10

TEE/IC/D-Züge
ab 6.82

The phrase "so you won't miss your train," like many others in the *Situationen*, merely helps to set the stage. It is not necessary for the student to say anything about a train here, but appropriate emotion should be encouraged.

Stage 2

1

Enter an *Imbiß* and greet the person working there.

a) Order food and drink for lunch. The drink should be nonalcoholic.
b) After you get your change, find out what time it is so you won't miss your train.

3

You're at the snack bar.

a) You're thirsty, but not hungry.
b) Find out anything you can about when you will reach your destination or how far it is.
c) Remember to order the items you offered to fetch for others.

2

You're setting off to find the *Imbiß* buffet in the train. Offer to fetch something for the elderly couple who are sharing your compartment. Repeat what they ask you to get, just to be sure you have understood.

4

Return to your train compartment and distribute the various items you have fetched for others.

a) Settle money matters.
b) Continue the conversation with polite small talk about destinations, nationalities, and so on.

Versuchen Sie doch

Right after leaving the *Imbiß*, where you consumed food and drink for which you were charged DM 8,50, you realize that you have paid for a second bottle of a beverage that you neither ordered nor consumed. The total should be DM 6,50. Can you go back and make your point? If you think you need a past tense, do you have one? If you don't have one, can you work around the gap?

19

Chapter 2

IM HOTEL/
RESTAURANT
IM HOTEL

FUNKTIONEN – KONTEXTE – STRUKTUREN

Looking ahead

You will be asking more detailed questions, especially about shelter and meals, and you will learn how to express judgments and make comparisons. Be sure to remember your greetings and courtesy phrases from earlier chapters, as well as ways to request clarification and identify your possessions.

You will be using:

- more subject-verb combinations (I need, you need, she need<u>s</u>)
- conjunctions (and, or) to join sentence elements
- expressions that give commands (the imperative)
- terms that express quality, equality, and inequality
- compound nouns (words constructed from simpler words)
- *kein* to express negation (no, not any)

Im Hotel

1

HERR AMRHEIN	Guten Abend. Bitte schön?
HERR JÖRY	Ein Doppelzimmer, bitte.
HERR AMRHEIN	Gern. Und wie lange bleiben Sie?
HERR JÖRY	Nur eine Nacht.

2

HERR BECK	Guten Abend. Wir brauchen zwei Einzelzimmer zusammen, bitte.
FRAU RANCKE	Ist recht. Mit Bad?
HERR BECK	Mit Dusche – haben Sie eins mit Dusche und eins ohne Dusche?
FRAU RANCKE	Natürlich. Das macht zusammen 145 Mark pro Nacht.

Use hotel realia to review names and lower numbers. Try to enable the student to handle transactions involving even-unit amounts of currency, including simple change-making and multiplication (*DM 75 pro Nacht. Also DM 150 für zwei Nächte*). Do not assume that facile recitation of numbers in sequence indicates true proficiency in either comprehension or production. Note also that exercises or tests whose items involve numbers can be used to check for many other linguistic features (e.g., negation, prepositions, tense distinctions).

3

HERR GELLERT	'n Abend.
FRL. ZIPPERT	Guten Abend. Haben Sie ein Zimmer für eine Nacht?
HERR GELLERT	Ja. Möchten Sie ein Einzelzimmer oder ein Doppelzimmer?
FRL. ZIPPERT	Um . . . Wieviel kostet ein Doppelzimmer mit Bad?
HERR GELLERT	Also, ein Doppelzimmer mit Bad kostet hundert Mark.
FRL. ZIPPERT	Ich glaube, das ist ein bißchen zu teuer. Und ohne Bad?
HERR GELLERT	Achtzig Mark.
FRL. ZIPPERT	Also, das Doppelzimmer ohne Bad, bitte.

4

FRAU LANDOLF	Und Sie möchten es für zwei Nächte, ja?
FRAU QUIESE	Ja, für heute und morgen. Wieviel kostet das, bitte?
FRAU LANDOLF	Für zwei Nächte? Das macht zusammen neunzig Mark – mit Frühstück, natürlich.
FRAU QUIESE	Schön.
FRAU LANDOLF	Also, Zimmer Nummer sieben. Hier ist der Schlüssel. . . . Und ist das Ihr Gepäck da?
FRAU QUIESE	Nein, mein Gepäck ist noch im Taxi.

Hotel Kistenpass Brigels
Für ruhige Ferien im idyllischen Bergdorf

Das Drei-Stern-Hotel mit prämierter Küche und Familientradition.

Alle Zimmer mit Bad oder Dusche, WC und Telefon. Bankett- und Konferenzräume, Kegelbahn, TV-Raum, Garage und Parkplätze. Das ganze Jahr offen.

Zirka drei Minuten von der Talstation Péz d'Artgas entfernt.

Besitzer: F. Caduff, Telefon 086 4 11 43 oder 4 16 26

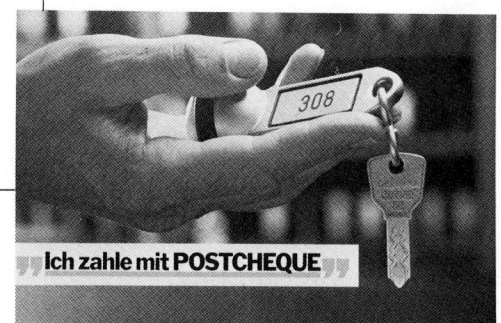

Ich zahle mit POSTCHEQUE

STRUKTUR 1

1. Being polite

bitte

Bitte can be used in several places: before a sentence, after a sentence, or between phrases in the middle of a sentence. But *never split the subject and verb.*

Return to Gespräche 1 to demonstrate and discuss where else *bitte* might appear in various utterances. Maybe point out that the bond between subject and verb is much tighter in German than in English.

(**bitte**) Ich möchte (**bitte**) ein Einzelzimmer (**bitte**).

Wieviel kostet das, **bitte**? **Bitte,** wieviel kostet das?
Bitte, haben Sie ein Doppelzimmer mit Bad?
Haben Sie **bitte** ein Doppelzimmer mit Bad?
Haben Sie ein Doppelzimmer mit Bad, **bitte**?

Verbs §7

2. Present tense

Verbs have endings. They must fit the subject.

Recommend and perhaps discuss a dictionary and maybe even a verb-conjugation reference source.

dictionary form (*infinitive*): **brauchen** *stem*: **brauch-**

SINGULAR	PLURAL
ich **brauch** + **-e** ich **brauche**	wir **brauch** + **-en** wir **brauchen**
Sie **brauch** + **-en**	Sie **brauch** + **-en**
Brauchen Sie ein Doppelzimmer, Frau Braun?	Herr Schwarz, Herr Weiß – Sie **brauchen** zwei Einzelzimmer, ja?

der Herr / die Frau } **brauch** + **t** { der Herr / die Frau **braucht**

die Herren / die Frauen } **brauch** + **-en** { die Herren / die Frauen **brauchen**

W.O. §7

3. Conjunctions

Conjunctions are words that join sentence elements.

Use realia (menus, etc.) to set up exercises: 1) student wants many items ("*und*"); 2) student is not sure what is available ("*Haben Sie X oder Y?*"). Point out how simple enumeration can substitute for higher-level vocabulary or structures not yet learned (e.g., *Samstag und Sonntag = das Wochenende; Montag, Dienstag, . . . Freitag = jeden Tag*). Note too, for future reference, that *und* can often fulfill the function of *wenn* ("You do that and I'll do this."), just as *oder* can express *wenn + nicht* ("You do that or I'll do this" = "If you don't do that, I'll do this."). We strongly recommend that students be taught early and explicitly that function has priority over form, and that facile use of lower-level structures and vocabulary is often more effective than halting attempts at higher-level language.

und für heute **und** morgen
oder ein Einzelzimmer **oder** ein Doppelzimmer

113	GERÄUCHERTES FORELLENFILET mit Sahnemeerrettich, Butter und Toast *Smoked fillet of trout with creamed horseradish and butter, toast*	11.50
155	SEELACHSFILET in Senfsauce mit Kartoffeln und Kopfsalat *Fish-fillet in mustard-sauce with potatoes and lettuce*	13.50
164	ROTBARSCHFILET gebacken mit Remouladensauce und Salaten *Fried fillet of perch with sauce remoulade and mixed salad*	14.20
150	FRISCHE FORELLE 'blau' mit zerlassener Butter, Kartoffeln und Kopfsalat *Steamed trout with melted butter, potatoes and lettuce*	16.00
151	FRISCHE FORELLE 'Müllerin Art' mit Kartoffeln und Kopfsalat *Fried trout with poatoes and lettuce*	16.50
020	RAHMHACKBRATEN mit Salzkartoffeln und Salat *Meat loaf in cream-sauce with potatoes and salad*	10.20
030	SCHWEINSBRATEN mit Semmelknödel und Salat *Roast pork in gravy with Bavarian dumpling and salad*	11.50
032	KASSELER RIPPCHEN mit Sauerkraut und Kartoffeln *Smoked pork-chop with sauerkraut and potatoes*	12.00
236	JÄGERSCHNITZEL mit hausgemachten Spätzle und Salat *Steak of pork in mushroom-sauce with Swabian noodles and salad*	14.50
240	WIENER SCHNITZEL mit pommes frites und Salat *Fried steak of veal with french fried potatoes and salad*	16.80

SITUATIONEN 1 Im Hotel

Stage 1

	A	B
1	(Enters hotel.) Gives greeting. Inquires about single room with bath. Needs the room for four nights. Makes sure breakfast is included.	(Works in hotel.) Responds to greeting. Tells price, asks about length of stay. Tells total price. "Of course." Does A want the room?
2	Wants a room with a shower. Has only SFr 48. Doesn't want to change any more traveler's checks – is leaving early tomorrow for Austria.	Room with shower is SFr 65. Suggests a solution.
	A and B conclude the transaction – one way or another.	
3	(Has taken room at hotel.) Needs to know when breakfast is served, and also where. Looks in wrong direction. Thanks, gets set to go.	(Is hotel clerk.) Tells when. Points toward the hotel restaurant, with appropriate comments. Gently corrects A. Reminds A not to forget passport and room key.

Family Hotel Thielen
Tourist-Hotel
garni

Brandenburger Straße 1-5 · 5000 Köln 1 · Tel. 0221/123333 + 121492

Use realia that includes *bis*, or just accept *"um X Uhr"* as the starting hour.

Don't teach *vergessen*, or at least not immediately; let students find some other way *("Oh, Herr _____ . Ihr Schlüssel.").*

Challenging the student to converse about two topics at once has several advantages: 1) it probes for genuine proficiency; 2) it permits realistic review of lower-level skills; 3) it is indeed realistic – such conversations occur often; 4) it can be great fun and can enliven the classroom.

	A	B	C
4	Negotiates for room: double without bath, cheap.	(Hotel clerk.) Explains price and so on.	(Hotel manager.) Interrupts: don't have any more rooms of that kind/price.
	Checks alternatives.	Just don't have much left.	Explains why (example: "It's Friday").
	Asks for directions to another hotel listed in tourist information.	Doesn't know the place.	Gives directions to other hotel.

Stage 2

Make sure students have realia handy. If the exercise proves difficult, give standard utterances a hotel clerk would use. Many are in the *Gespräche*.

3 b): Solutions: use *glaube, oder.*

4: Don't teach hotel jargon *"anschließend."* The notion of "adjoining" can be approached quite fluently in several ways, for example: 1) *"Wo sind die Zimmer?"*; 2) *"Nr. 2? Wie weit ist das von Nr. 7"* or *"Nr. 321? Ich möchte auch Nr. 322.";* 3) *"zwei Zimmer zusammen."*

1
Arrange accommodations for yourself.

a) Double-check the price.
b) Confirm the breakfast time – you intend to leave early next morning.

If you have to leave before breakfast, can you negotiate a price reduction?

2
It's your last day in the country before you fly home, and you're strapped for cash. You inquire about accommodations. It turns out the price is too high. Make a graceful exit.

3
Negotiate for accommodations for your group of five. You've had a long, hot day of travel.

a) Is it worth getting one room with a shower, which everyone could then use? Showers for those who do not have them in their rooms cost DM 2,00 extra. Is it worth it?
b) You mention that you might like to stay in the city a few days, but you don't want to commit yourself.

4
You (= two couples traveling together) would like two adjoining rooms, but price is more important. The clerk offers two double rooms; both have baths.

Versuchen Sie doch

You are in a remote region of Austria, and the waiter does not speak English. The American couple at the next table has found out that you speak some German and they want you to help them. It seems that the waiter has totally confused their order and therefore has brought each of them a meal that contains some of the right items but also some items that belong to the other person.

Learn how to say something when you don't know how

When you are using your German, you will probably think that you don't have all the words to do the job. Many language learners share this apprehension. But there are some things you can do to help yourself.

Instead of plowing full-tilt into an absent word (*"ich brauche ein . . . ein . . . ich brauche ein . . ."*), back up a bit, rephrase, and try to get around the obstacle. If you use similar words and establish a context for what you mean to say, a sympathetic listener will help you out. If you listen carefully for situations like this in English, you will see that this speaker-listener interaction is very common in your own language as well. Body language is important, too. The preceding dialog involving the fellow who drops his knife shows that many people speak eloquently with their hands. But beware: nonverbal language, although it is a necessary complement to verbal language, can never substitute entirely for the real thing.

Remember the strategy advice from Chapter 1: See whether you can make the other person carry some of the burden of the conversation, and then echo part of what you have heard. You can become a skillful learner of both vocabulary and structure this way.

In hotels

• Your passport

When you register in West Germany, Switzerland, and Austria, you will be asked to provide your passport number on the registration form. In East Germany you will likely be asked to leave your passport at the desk during your entire stay.

• Your room key

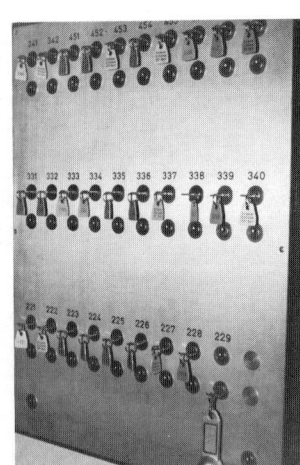

When you leave your room, do not plan to tote your heavy room key with you. Instead leave it at the registration desk on your way out. Many hotels have a theftproof key board for this purpose.

In restaurants

• *ich möchte*

When you order, use the expression you have learned here: "**Ich möchte** . . ." Do not say "*Ich habe* . . ." for English "I'll have . . ." (If you already have that, why are you ordering it?)

• the check

When you want the check, simply summon the waitress or waiter: *"Fräulein!/ Herr Ober? – Zahlen, bitte!"* Pay that person when the bill is presented; do not expect to take it to a cashier. Quite likely you will see on the menu that a 15% tip (*Bedienung*) is regularly included in the price of the meal. You should, however, round up to the next currency unit. Do not flinch when you pay a nominal extra charge for bread and rolls; see "Restaurant im Hotel," p. 27, dialog 8.

GESPRÄCHE 2

Restaurant im Hotel

Reinforce the gestures and patterns of intonation that accompany the conventional expressions. Encourage students to act out the interchanges. This is a good time to break such comfortable habits as always remaining seated and quiet, speaking always with the same partner, saying everything in the same tone, depending slavishly on the book dialogs, etc.

Point out the advantages of being able to describe a specific item by referring to a larger category, the tactic complementary to that of circumlocution by enumeration introduced earlier. Use appropriate menus to illustrate how to identify key words in long compounds, and to show classification of food dishes by larger categories (*Vorspeisen*, etc.).

The dialog is intentionally "hokey" so that its vital point will be both evident and palatable. The student must learn to communicate at any cost, and to do so without constant, time-wasting recourse to dictionaries and grammars. Follow-up exercises: How to get another spoon, how to express a nationality or an academic subject not yet learned.

1

OBER	Zum Wohl, die Herrschaften.
HERR UND FRAU BÜHLER	Danke sehr.

2

OBER	Also, bitte schön. Zweimal Kotelett, zwei Glas Rotwein. Guten Appetit.
HERR UND FRAU MÄHDER	Danke.

3

HERR BLATTER	Ich möchte bitte Nummer 1.
OBER	Und für die Dame?
HERR BLATTER	Uh . . .
FRAU BLATTER	Nummer 4, bitte.

4

TIM GRADY	Herr Ober!
OBER	Ja, bitte schön.
TIM GRADY	"Seelachsfilet." Was ist das, bitte?
OBER	Oh, das ist Fisch. Und sehr gut heute.

5

FRL. MEISTER	Wir möchten beide das Kotelett mit Salzkartoffeln und Bohnensalat, bitte.
KELLNERIN	Also die Tagesspezialität. Und zum Trinken?
FRL. MEISTER	Bringen Sie uns bitte zwei Glas Rotwein.

6

FRAU WITTKOWSKI	Das Restaurant ist doch wunderbar, nicht?
FRAU ENGEL	Ja, und das Kotelett schmeckt fantastisch.
FRAU WITTKOWSKI	Der Wein auch. Trinken wir noch ein Glas?
FRAU ENGEL	Warum nicht? Herr Ober!? Noch zwei Glas, ja?
OBER	Wie, bitte?
FRAU ENGEL	Bringen Sie uns bitte noch zwei Glas Weißwein.
OBER	Ja, gerne.

7

BILL	Drat! I dropped my knife and I don't know the word to use to get another one.
JACK	Let me try something. Herr Ober!
OBER	Ja, bitte. Brauchen Sie etwas?
JACK	Ja. Für das Kotelett. Der Herr braucht . . .
OBER	Salz?
JACK	Nein, das haben wir schon. . . .
BILL	Ich brauche ein . . . für mein Kotelett brauche ich ein . . .
OBER	Oh, ein Messer! Sie haben kein Messer!
BILL	Ja, ein Messer. Ich brauche ein Messer.
OBER	Das bringe ich sofort.

8

FRAU CAMENISCH	Fräulein! Zahlen, bitte.
KELLNERIN	Also, zweimal Wurstsalat und zwei Bier, ja?
FRAU CAMENISCH	Und auch die zwei Brötchen.
KELLNERIN	Zwei Brötchen, ja. Das macht zusammen dreizehn Mark, bitte.

9

HERR FRISCH	Herr Ober, wir möchten zahlen, bitte.
OBER	Ist das alles zusammen? . . .

27

Rather than translating, illustrate the meanings of the new expressions by citing examples from the dialogs. See note in Instructor's Guide.

1. More interrogatives

Wo? Wer? Wie? Was? Was ist das? Wie lange? Warum? Warum nicht?

Verbs §§47–49

See note in Instructor's Guide.

2. Imperatives: direct (but often polite) commands

infinitive + *Sie*

Bitte, **bringen Sie** uns noch zwei Glas Rotwein.
Moment! **Essen Sie** das nicht!

Maybe point out that in German the negation of a command does not involve rewording, as it does in English (Eat/Don't eat).

3. Judgments and comparisons: expressing quality, equality, and inequality

QUALITY	EQUALITY	INEQUALITY
Das ist teuer.	Das ist auch teuer.	Das ist zu teuer.
Das ist nicht teuer.	Das ist auch nicht teuer.	Das ist nicht zu teuer.

Reading/listening/speaking exercise: Have students gain a "benchmark" impression of typical prices by perusing appropriate realia (menus, product labels, hotel listings). Then student or teacher

GREATER PRECISION
Das ist nicht so teuer.
Das ist ein bißchen zu teuer.
Das ist viel zu teuer.
Das ist sehr teuer.

proposes a price for something to elicit *"nicht so teuer,"* etc. The same format could be used, with different realia, to exercise complex phrases involving other adjectives (*viel, weit, groß*, etc.).

Nouns §11

Use appropriate realia (menus, etc.) to demonstrate the importance of compounding in German. The best examples are close cognates, either because they are drawn from the everyday realm (*Kochbuch*, *Gulaschsuppe*), or because they involve the international vocabulary of science and technology (*Computerprogrammierer*).

4. Compound nouns

- ### adjective + noun

  der Wein   der Rotwein   der Weißwein
  das Zimmer   das Einzelzimmer   das Doppelzimmer

- ### noun + noun

  das Hotel + <u>das</u> Zimmer > <u>das</u> Hotelzimmer
  die Wurst + <u>der</u> Salat > <u>der</u> Wurstsalat
  das Salz + <u>die</u> Kartoffeln > <u>die</u> Salzkartoffeln
  die See + <u>der</u> Lachs + <u>das</u> Filet > <u>das</u> Seelachsfilet

- ### verb + noun

  fahren + <u>die</u> Karte > <u>die</u> Fahrkarte

A.A. §8

5. *Kein*: negating things (nouns) — "no," "not any"

Haben Sie ein Messer? Nein, ich habe **kein** Messer.
Möchten Sie ein Zimmer mit Bad? Nein, wir brauchen **kein** Bad.
Tut mir leid, wir haben **keine** Bratwurst. Möchten Sie eine Bockwurst?

Exercises: 1) Inquiry about and listing of all those things (from previous vocabulary) that one does not have. 2) Similar conversations about items in realia or in *Bildwörterbuch* pages. The important linguistic features are "kein- + NOUN" and verb-subject combinations reflecting incipient sentence creation. Of lesser importance, so not yet introduced, is the accusative case. Apply reinforcement and error correction accordingly. Above all, do not attempt to teach the accusative system here!

SITUATIONEN 2 Restaurant im Hotel

Stage 1

	A	B
1	(Seats self at restaurant table.) Briefly orders light meal and drink.	(Works at restaurant.) Greets and waits. Confirms order.
2	Is in a hurry. Asks what time it is. Checks to see if restaurant has Imbiß-type menu items. Orders quick bite.	Gives time. Yes. Gives prices. Reassures A: right away.
3	Searches for table. Passes by B's table, looking somewhat desperate. Sits down and ponders menu. Requests advice about menu items.	Lets A know that the seats at the other end of the table are unoccupied. Is curious about A but asks questions politely. Gives advice. ("Yesterday the fish . . .")

	A	B	C
4	(Works in restaurant.) Greets A and B. (It's dinnertime.) Takes orders for drinks. Confirms order and departs. Returns with beverages, takes dinner order. Confirms order.	(Doesn't speak German.) Mumbles something. Gets by by saying "beer." Asks C a few questions in English about menu. (To C:) Tell him I want. . . . Requests C to ask A about substituting vegetable items.	(Does speak German.) Returns the greeting. Requests beverage. Explains: X is fish, etc. Begins to relay the order. Relays the request.

Sidebar (left column, Stage 1):

In Stage 2 situations, encourage use of any of the several menus in the Class Text or Study Text, especially the comprehensive menus. If a new menu is used, it might be a good idea to conduct a quick "skimming" session to orient the students to the menu's format and to refresh basic vocabulary. Maybe also review standard lines used by restaurant personnel, though many are illustrated in the *Gespräche*.

Solutions: 1) *Nicht X, Y. Ist das OK?* 2) *Aber nicht mit X, mit Y, bitte.* Resist the temptation to teach *sondern*. Ignore slight problems with third person (**möchtet, für den *Herr*).

Stage 2

1

(Use your menus for the following situations.)

Summon the waiter or waitress.
Order dinner for yourself.
Get advice about the main course.

2

You think you might like to take advantage of the special of the day, but you're still suffering from jet lag and don't know what day it is.

a) Find out what day it is; maybe save face by explaining why you don't know.
b) The special of the day turns out to be pork liver. Turn it down diplomatically.

3

The food was good, but you have eaten as much as you care to.

a) Request your bill.
b) Explain why you didn't eat everything.

4

You *think* your dinner bill is too high. No doubt the mistake – if there was one – was honest; there were eight of you at dinner, and you have been there several hours. Perhaps there was a mistake about which dish you had, or how much you drank.

a) Summon the waitress.
b) Explain the problem to her.
c) If it turns out you're wrong, be ready to apologize.

Sidebar (left column, Stage 2):

3 b): Solutions: *Das war wunderbar, (aber) (das ist) zuviel,* etc.

2 a): One solution: *Gestern war ich in New York, und heute bin ich hier.*

2 b): One solution for "diplomatically:" *"Ich glaube, ich möchte . . ."* But this is also a good occasion to reinforce the importance of the tone of voice.

Versuchen Sie doch

Tell someone else about what you ate and drank yesterday – where you ate, how much it cost, and so on.

29

Chapter 3

FAHRKARTENSCHALTER/ REISEPROVIANT

Guten Appetit & Gute Reise

FUNKTIONEN – KONTEXTE – STRUKTUREN

Looking ahead

You'll be telling time (official and casual), making travel arrangements, asking for clarification, buying food, listening carefully for travel directions, and looking for key words in written materials.

You will be using:

- a variety of basic verbs
- imperative forms (commands)
- vocabulary essential to train travel and purchase of food
- the metric system
- expressions of quantity

Fahrkartenschalter

Pop listening quiz (nongraded), perhaps 5 items: clock time, some items within longer **1**

der Beamte, die Beamtin *official*

utterances, some utterances containing more than one time indication (*"Der nächste ist um 11.55, weitere Züge dann um 12.35, 13.15."*) Students can also check comprehension with each other, using timetables in realia as sources of items. **2**

Expansion: repeat dialog 3 using Austrian, Swiss, or East German cities and currency. **3**

Blackboard or overhead projection: sketch of large train station, with various trains on various tracks. Students repeat the situation, with a different destination, etc., each time. Encourage them to change conversational partners. **4**

Vary with inquiries about other station facilities. (Use blackboard, overhead sketch, appropriate *"Bildwörterbuch"* display, or München station floor plan from realia). Encourage estimation of distances in metric units. **5** **6**

| FRAU HOFFMANN | Wann ist der nächste Zug nach Köln, bitte? |
| BEAMTER | Dreizehn Uhr siebzehn. |

HERR SAXEN	Wieviel kostet eine Karte nach Köln, bitte?
BEAMTIN	Neun Mark siebzig. Neunzehn Mark vierzig hin und zurück.
HERR SAXEN	Wie, bitte?
BEAMTIN	Aachen nach Köln, neun Mark siebzig. Aachen – Köln – und zurück nach Aachen, neunzehn Mark vierzig.

DR. VAZER	Guten Morgen. Eine Karte nach Köln, bitte.
BEAMTIN	Einmal nach Köln. Einfach oder hin und zurück?
DR. VAZER	Einfach, bitte.
BEAMTIN	Ist recht. Acht Mark zehn, bitte. Gleis sieben um elf Uhr fünfundzwanzig.
DR. VAZER	Gleis sieben. Wo ist das?
BEAMTIN	Gehen Sie hier links und dann fünfzig Meter weiter.

HERR STEIGER	Zweimal nach Düsseldorf, bitte, hin und zurück.
BEAMTER	Hier ist geschlossen. Schalter 4, bitte.
HERR STEIGER	Oh, Entschuldigung. Danke.

| FRL. FELDER | Entschuldigung. Wo ist die Damentoilette? |
| FRAU UHLIG | Ich weiß nicht. Fragen Sie die Frau da. |

FRL. FELDER	Entschuldigung. Wo gibt es hier eine Damentoilette?
FRAU SZADROWSKY	Toiletten finden Sie da rechts, um die Ecke.
FRL. FELDER	Wie, bitte?
FRAU SZADROWSKY	Rechts um die Ecke da. Verstehen Sie das?
FRL. FELDER	Ach, ja, rechts. Ist gut. Vielen Dank.

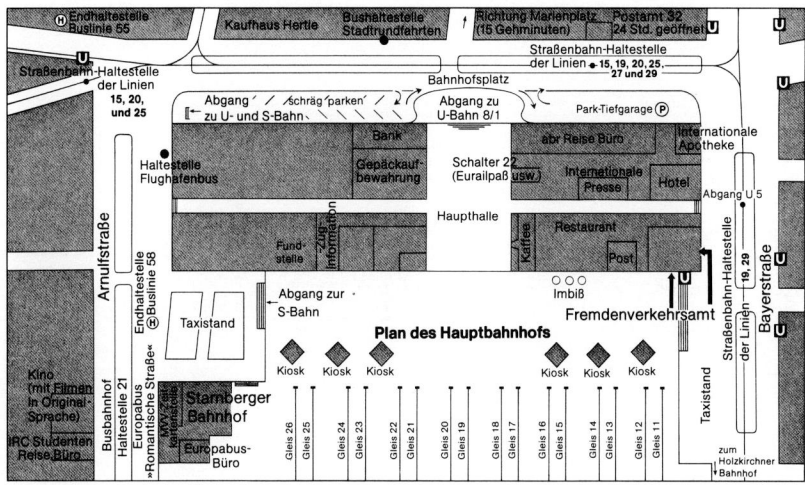

31

STRUKTUR 1

Preps. §§5,8

1. Prepositions: *in, aus, nach* with cities and countries

Sind Sie aus Stuttgart?
Entschuldigung. Sind wir in Köln?
Heute sind wir in Aachen.

Nein, ich bin aus Heidelberg.
Nein, hier ist Aachen.
Morgen fahren wir nach Köln.

2. Interrogatives: *wohin* and *wo*

Wo sind wir heute? – In Köln.

Wohin fahren wir morgen? – Nach Bonn.

wo = location

wohin = direction

3. Telling time: standard pattern — *"X Uhr Y"*

	SPOKEN		WRITTEN
CASUAL	OFFICIAL		
Es ist 3 Uhr.	Es ist 15 Uhr.		3.00/15.00
Es ist **3 Uhr 40**.	Es ist **15 Uhr 40**.		3.40/15.40

4. Pronouns

● **pronouns you already know: *ich, wir, Sie, es, das***

● **new (singular): *er* = he or it   *sie* = she or it**

Er, sie, and es reflect the gender of the nouns they represent:

SINGULAR			
Masculine	der Zug	**er**	Kommt der Zug spät? Ja, er kommt spät.
Feminine	die Wurst	**sie**	Schmeckt die Wurst gut? Ja, sie schmeckt gut.
Neuter	das Zimmer	**es**	Ist das Zimmer teuer? Ja, es ist teuer.

PLURAL			
All genders	{ die Züge / die Würste / die Zimmer }	**sie** = they	Ja, sie sind teuer

Hinfahrt Reisetag:		
Abfahrt in		Uhr
	ab	
umsteigen in	an	
	ab	
Ziel	an	

Rückfahrt Reisetag:		
Abfahrt in		Uhr
	ab	
umsteigen in	an	
	ab	
Ziel	an	

Name:
Straße:
Wohnort:

Vary by introducing realia (maps, etc.), by having students change partners, and by asking for reportage (perhaps even with encapsulation [but no *daß*]: *"Sie sagt, sie ist aus Mannheim."*) If you use country names, avoid digression into explanation of complications like *"aus den Vereinigten Staaten"* or *"Wir fahren in die Schweiz."*

Section 2 can be introduced by extension from 1, with useful practice in strategies of echoing and eliciting repetition (*"Morgen fahren wir nach Köln." "Wohin?" "Nach Köln." "Oh, nach Köln."*) While such exercises may seem

Pronouns §5

childish, they reinforce important production skills and resemble genuine speech. They also help convince students that real language is replete with redundant information, and that therefore one need not panic if one fails to understand every word.

The pattern can be exercised with the customary clock face (blackboard, etc.). More realistic and dynamic might be an exercise with attendant realia: Student A is taking X train, which is to leave at Z time. When someone asks what time it is, it is always M minutes before or after that time.

Avoid discussion of the overlap between casual use of *das, es* for all sorts of things, and the precise use of *er, sie, es* to correspond with the gender of the named antecedent.
    If you find yourself lapsing into colloquial use of the demonstrative (*"Ja, der kommt spät"*), don't worry. The demonstratives are indeed used often in real speech, and for that reason they are introduced early in this text. Here cultivation of listening comprehension is more important, since only rarely do beginning students produce demonstrative pronouns independently.

Stage 1

The Stage 1 exercises in earlier chapters often included directions for "small talk" – greetings, thank yous, farewells, and so on. Now that the situations are getting more complicated, we will often not mention those details. But don't forget to say such things where they would be useful or even necessary in a real conversation.

"Persists" = "Nein . . ." or *"Ja, die Damentoilette ist links. Aber wo ist die Herrentoilette?"*

	A	B
1	Asks when next train to Bonn is. Points out that it's now 11:40. Confirms information by repeating it. Thanks B.	Thinks it is at 11:37. Trains depart for Bonn every 15 minutes. Gives times for next three. "Don't mention it."
2	Wants a ticket to Leipzig. Where is the right counter? Uses the opportunity to find out where to get something to eat.	Explains that this is wrong counter for tickets to East Germany. "Number 5, to the left." It's late, so the restaurant is closed. Recommends another place for a quick bite. Tells where it is and why it's good.
3	Needs to find bathroom – not for self, but for companion of opposite sex. Persists. Is very grateful.	Somewhat surprised at the question. Provides information; bathrooms are beyond the *Imbiß*, and on opposite sides.

	A	B	C
4	(B's child: speaks no German.) Grumbles about the trip.	(Speaks some German.) Greets C. Negotiates transportation from Köln to Hamburg.	(Works at ticket counter.) Greets. Waits expectantly. Provides information about trains and prices. Offers directions.
	Hears word "Hamburg," gets hungry. Needs bathroom.	Asks where to get fast food. Asks about bathroom.	Tells where bathroom is. Asks how old A is.
	Doesn't understand.	Tells how old A is.	Sympathizes.

Stage 2

Set up by having each student construct own timetable, track listing, and, with help, rate schedule. Encourage double-checking, money-counting, etc. Similar setups are useful for other situations.

2a): Checking for discounts: *"Ich bin Student/19 Jahre alt. Wieviel kostet . . ."*

VSd. Some solutions: *"Sie finden ___, und dann . . ."; "Da ist ein ___, und dann ein ___."*

1

You have just purchased your train ticket, and have just a few minutes to catch your train – and to haul a lot of baggage. You notice that your train is posted for *"Gleis 10a,"* not just *"Gleis 10."*

a) Zip back to the ticket counter and clarify matters. (Apologize to those in line ahead of you.)
b) If you have to deal with left/right distinctions, make sure you know whether "left" means *your* left or that of the person talking to you.

2

Your group of four wants to make a side trip from Aachen to Amsterdam/Luxemburg/Utrecht before going on to Köln, and is buying a package tour. Go to the station and make all the arrangements, as follows:

a) Purchase tickets for the group. Check about student/youth discounts.
b) Check whether passports are needed. How about visas (*das Visum, die Visen*)?

Versuchen Sie doch

Use the floor plan of the München train station and the *"Bildwörterbuch"* displays *"Transportation/Verkehr"* and *"Money and Store/Geld und Geschäft."*

You have found that the public restroom is at the other end of the train station, past various shops, the snack bar, etc. On your way back you bump into someone who is carrying a cane, wearing a yellow armband with three black dots, and is – as you can well see – blind. The person inquires about restrooms. Give directions.

Problem: Even if you could name all the shops along the way, and did somehow know that the word for "see" is *"sehen,"* would it do any good to give directions that way? (*Hint:* There are other verbs that do not rely on vision.)

Quantities – ordering and estimating

● You can use rough estimates for metric measures.

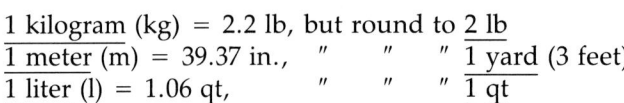

1 kilogram (kg) = 2.2 lb, but round to 2 lb
1 meter (m) = 39.37 in.,   "   "   " 1 yard (3 feet)
1 liter (l) = 1.06 qt,   "   "   " 1 qt

To order or estimate quantities:

● another of the same = *noch ein(e)*

noch ein Bier, bitte = *another beer, please*
noch eine Flasche Wein = *another bottle (of the same) wine*

● X quantities of Y = *Xmal Y*

dreimal Kaffee, bitte = *3 coffees, please*

● Masculine and neuter nouns of quantity never change form.

ein **Becher** Vanille-Eis – zwei **Becher** Vanille-Eis
ein **Glas** Cola – zwei **Glas** Cola
(also: **Päckchen, Stück, Pfund**)

● But feminine nouns of quantity show their plurals.

eine **Tasse** Tee – zwei **Tassen** Tee
eine **Flasche** Wein – zwei **Flaschen** Wein

Note that, particularly in colloquial or regional speech, some English quantity-nouns do not show a plural ("Gimme 50 foot of that rope there." "Three dollah."). Cf. also the adjectival patterns like "a ten-foot pole."

Der Bahnhof

Because European railroad stations are usually vital transportation hubs, they provide a wide variety of services in addition to train tickets and information (*die Auskunft/die Information*). In larger stations you will see signs for:

Blumen – a flower shop to buy gifts for friends
Imbiß – the ever-present fast-food stand
Kiosk – a newsstand with an international selection of newspapers and magazines; also beverages, some packaged food items, and sundries
Post – a post office, including phone booths for local and long-distance (and international) calls
Reisebüro – a travel agency
Restaurant – ranging from the essentials, cafeteria-style (typical: *Bahnhofbuffet*), to an elegant meal
Schließfächer – coin-operated baggage lockers
Verkehrsverein – chamber of commerce office with information about local sights and events, maps, and so on
Zimmervermittlung – a central room reservation office, with information about accommodations ranging from private rooms to hotels

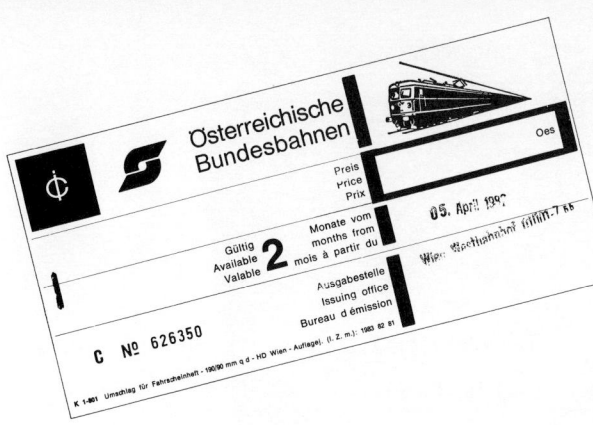

Aachener-Familien-Sommer

Ein Großstadtaufenthalt für die ganze Familie! Aachen, die alte Kaiserstadt im Dreiländereck lädt ein zu Kunst, Geschichte und Atmosphäre zum Sonderpreis.
Vom 14. 7. - 31. 8. 1986, jeweils von Freitag Abend bis Montag Mittag gilt das neue Arrangement des Verkehrsvereins Bad Aachen e.V.

Bei diesem Angebot haben wir besonders an Familien mit Kindern gedacht: Bis zu 2 Kinder unter 16 Jahre übernachten im Zimmer der Eltern kostenlos und auch das Frühstück vom Buffet ist im Preis einbegriffen.
Außerdem enthält das Arrangement ein Paket an Leistungen, die einen Aufenthalt in Aachen zu einem Erlebnis werden lassen:
Begrüßungscocktail im Hotel
Stadtführung mit Anekdoten und Sagen aus der Aachener Geschichte
Besuch der Aachener Museen
Besuch des Internationalen Spielcasinos (erst ab 18 Jahre)
Aachen Souvenir
Aachen - Informationsmappe
Sie wohnen in einem Hotel der gehobenen Mittelklasse. Die Unterbringung erfolgt in komfortablen Doppelzimmern mit französischem Bett und einem Einzelbett. Zusatzbett auf Anfrage. Alle Zimmer verfügen über Bad/WC, TV-Gerät, Weckuhr, Minibar und Selbstwähltelefon. Das reichhaltige Frühstücksbuffet ist ebenso im Preis inbegriffen, wie der Parkplatz vor der Tür.

Der Preis für dieses Arrangement einschließlich aller genannten Leistungen beträgt pro Zimmer und Nacht **DM 99,–**

Buchen können Sie dieses Arrangement beim
Verkehrsverein
Bad Aachen e.V.
Bahnhofplatz 4
5100 Bad Aachen

Bei Rückfragen steht Ihnen Frau Jaquet, Tel. 0241/30600 gerne zur Verfügung.

Fahrplanauszug
Winter 1985/86

München → Köln DB

29. September 1985 bis 31. Mai 1986

634 Km

Verkehrszeiten	ab	Zug	an	Service	Umsteigen in	an	ab	Zug
nicht 25., 26.XII., 1.I.	1.24	D 14164	9.53		Stuttg	5.12	6.06	IC 518
nicht 25.XII., 1.I.	4.03	D 718	10.53	🍷				
nicht 25.XII., 1.I.	4.03	D 718	11.37	🍷	Mannh	8.28	8.32	IC 500
Mo bis Sa, auch 13.IV., nicht 25.XII. bis 1.I., 29. bis 31.III., 19.V.	5.43	D 786	11.59	🍷				
Mo bis Fr, nicht 21.XII. bis 1.I., 28. bis 31.III., 19.V.	5.51	IC 616	11.53					
	6.51	IC 516	12.53					
	7.00	D 814	15.33	🍷				
Mo bis Sa, nicht 25.XII. bis 1.I., 29. bis 31.III., 19.V.	7.52	IC 696	13.53					
	7.57	IC 628	1?.59		Mannh	11.28	11.32	IC 108
	8.52	IC 614	14.53					
	8.57	IC 524	14.59					
	9.52	IC 514	15.53					
	10.27	D 716	17.29	🍷				
	10.52	IC 694	16.53					
	10.57	IC 522	16.59		Mannh	14.28	14.32	IC 102
	11.08	FD 722	18.23	🍴				
	11.41	TEE 16	17.47	🚌				
	11.52	IC 512	17.53					
	11.57	IC 124	17.59					
	12.37	IC 624	18.59					
	12.37	FD 210	19.23	🍴				
	12.52	IC 692	18.53					
	13.52	IC 612	19.53					
	13.57	IC 520	19.59		Mannh	16.28	16.32	IC 106
	14.52	IC 110	20.53					
täglich außer Sa, nicht 24. bis 31.XII., 28. bis 30.III., 18.V.	15.52	IC 690	21.53					
	15.57	IC 620	21.59		Mannh	19.28	19.32	IC 104

1. Klasse → 174,00 DM ↔ 348,00 DM Vorzugskarte ↔ 280,00 DM IC Zuschlag 5,00 DM
2. Klasse → 116,00 DM ↔ 232,00 DM Vorzugskarte ↔ 186,00 DM IC Zuschlag 5,00 DM

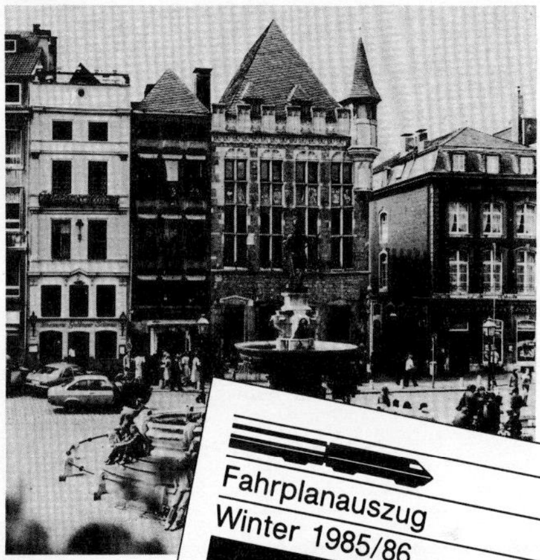

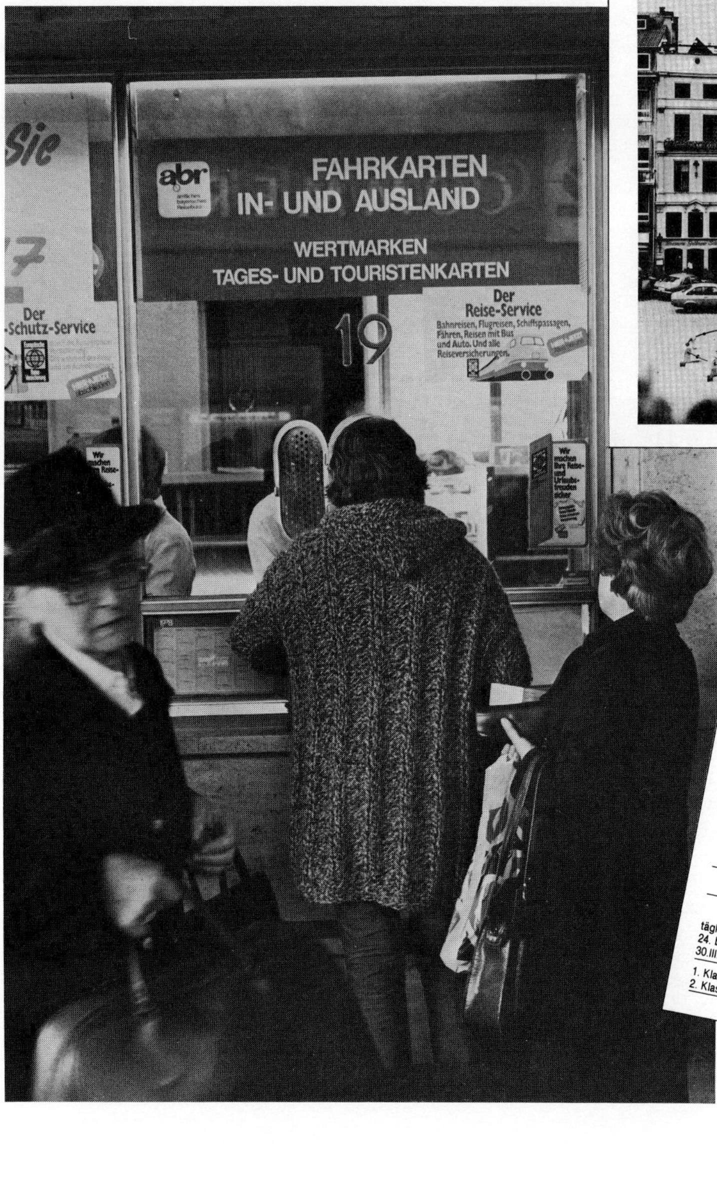

Intercity
Abteilservice

  DSG–Tochter der Bahn

Art.-Nr			DM

Herzhaftes
| 426 | Gulaschsuppe, Brot oder Brötchen | | 5,20 |
| 568 | 3/2 Brötchen oder 3/2 Scheiben Brot mit Butter, gek. Schinken, Edamer Käse und Mettwurst | | 4,80 |

Süßes
828	Packung Leibniz-Keks (100 g)		1,80
829	Packung Ritter-Sport-Täfelchen (150 g)		2,70
440	Marmorkuchen (2 Scheiben)		2,65
441	Stück Käsekuchen		2,65
443	1 Schoko-Kokos-Makrone		1,60
445	1 Mandelhörnchen		1,60
431	Portion Eiskrem		2,80

Heißes
470	Kännchen Kaffee		4,70
472	Kännchen entcoffeinierter Kaffee (HAG) mit löslichem Kaffee		4,70
473	Kännchen Tee		4,70
475	Kännchen Trinkschokolade		4,70

Erfrischendes
871/875	Flasche Pilsbier	0,33 l	3,40
872/873	Flasche Exportbier	0,33 l	3,40
880	Flasche Apollinaris Mineralwasser	0,33 l	2,60
882	Flasche Staatl. Fachingen Mineralwasser	0,33 l	3,50
891	Flasche Coca-Cola	0,20 l	2,60
893	Flasche Fanta	0,20 l	2,60
900	Flasche Vaihinger Apfelsaft	0,20 l	2,60
902	Flasche Vaihinger Orangensaft	0,20 l	2,90

Scharfes
800	Fläschchen Weinbrand „Dujardin Imperial"	2 cl	3,00
802	Fläschchen Doornkaat	2 cl	2,90
801	Fläschchen Jägermeister	2 cl	3,10

Belebendes
921	1984er Kenzinger Hummelberg oder Müller-Thurgau Qualitätswein 1985er -trocken-	Baden 0,25 l	6,20
944	Le Patron Französischer Tafelrotwein	Frankreich 0,25 l	5,20
822	Kupferberg Gold	0,20 l	7,20

Ihr IC-Betreuer vermittelt Ihnen gern einen Platz im Zugrestaurant.
Wählen Sie dort aus unserem umfangreichen Speisen- und Getränke-
angebot. Wir empfehlen in diesem Monat besonders:

Hähnchenbrust „à la King" in heller Rahmsoße,
Butterreis, Salatteller_____ **DM 14,80**

Alle Preise sind Inklusivpreise.
DSG Deutsche Schlafwagen- und Speisewagen-Gesellschaft m.b.H.
Guiollettstraße 18-22 · 6000 Frankfurt am Main 1

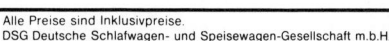

Reiseproviant

Vary using consumer-goods realia and different currency (especially Austrian, to exercise higher numbers).

Vary using other possessions. **1**
Don't try to teach the accusative case here. If you wish, inculcate it by mild indirect correction, or else limit the list to F/N nouns or any plurals. Note that the function of *"Vergessen Sie Ihr-X [accusative] nicht!"* can be carried out by the simple reminder, *"Ihr-X [nominative],"* or by *"Ist das Ihr-X [nominative]?"*

2

"Emmenthaler" is a variety of Swiss cheese. In or near Switzerland, where many varieties of cheese are produced, it's insufficient to identify a cheese as just "Swiss cheese."

3

Suggest intensive exercise, with variation in items, number of people for whom they are being bought, and currency units. Encourage "guestimates" or "ball-park" management of metric units.

4

HERR WIESER	Guten Tag. Zwei Orangen und eine Tafel Schokolade, bitte.
FRAU REINIG	Bitte schön. Sonst noch etwas?
HERR WIESER	Nein, danke, das ist alles.
FRAU REINIG	Vier Mark dreißig, bitte.
HERR WIESER	Vier Mark . . . und . . . zehn, zwanzig, dreißig Pfennig.
FRAU REINIG	Danke. Auf Wiedersehen. Moment – vergessen Sie Ihre Fahrkarte nicht!
HERR WIESER	Danke vielmals. Auf Wiedersehen.
HERR CASPAR	. . . und zwei Brötchen und ein bißchen Schweizerkäse.
FRAU STOPS	Das Stück Emmenthaler hier ist 180 Gramm. Ist das genug?
HERR CASPAR	Nein, nicht für zwei Personen. Ein bißchen mehr, bitte. Sagen wir 250 oder 300 Gramm.
FRAU STOPS	Also das Stück hier. 280 Gramm. Und sonst noch etwas?
FRL. HEUSS	So. Das macht drei Mark neunzig.
HERR BITZBERGER	Hier sind hundert Mark.
FRL. HEUSS	Oh, hundert Mark! Haben Sie es nicht kleiner?
HERR BITZBERGER	Moment mal. . . . Ja, ich glaube. Eine Mark, zwei Mark, zwei Mark fünfzig, drei Mark, drei Mark fünfzig, sechzig, siebzig, achtzig, neunzig.
FRL. HEUSS	Vielen Dank.
FRAU KITZHABER	Und wir nehmen auch ein Päckchen Nüsse.
FRL. BERNHARD	Die Nüsse auch? Ist das nicht zuviel?
FRAU KITZHABER	Nein, ich liebe Nüsse. Ich glaube, ich esse sie schon hier.
FRL. BERNHARD	Aber die Schokolade essen wir später im Abteil, ja?

STRUKTUR 2

Verbs §§47–49

1. More about imperatives (command forms)

Don't forget **Sie!**

The reference grammar addresses the exception of *Seien Sie* (vs. **Sein*). The difference is far greater in spelling than in actual speech (cf. standard regional forms like Bavarian *"Sei'n S'"*). Be cautious in error

The basic form for the imperative is the *infinitive* + **Sie.**

Vergessen Sie Ihre Fahrkarte nicht, Herr Meier!
Geben Sie mir eine Tafel Schokolade, bitte.
Die Herrentoilette? Gehen Sie hier rechts 50 m.
Herr Ober! Bitte, bringen Sie uns noch zwei Glas Wein.
Meine Herrschaften, Frühstück ist um 7 Uhr. Bitte, seien Sie da!

Pronouns §6

2. More about pronouns: "person," perspective, verbs

correction – certainly in the students' speech and perhaps even in their writing. The aim is to establish the imperative *pattern.*

Suggest *heavy* contextual work with the *sie/sie/Sie* distinction, especially in listening. Point out and encourage students to reproduce the difference in body language (eye orientation, etc.) between second and third person discourse.

A few students will find it difficult to switch from second person (within a conversation) to third person (reporting the conversation). More, perhaps, will have trouble with the first-to-third transformation, especially in speaking. Thus when asked a question about themselves they may fail to make the transformation at all (**Ja, studieren Sie Mathematik*), or they will in effect use the *"-enSie"* as a verb ending (**Ja, ich studierenSie Mathematik*).

- **Pronouns reflect the person and number of the nouns they refer to.**

	SINGULAR	PLURAL
First person	**ich**	**wir**
Second person	**Sie**	**Sie**
Third person	**er/sie/es**	**sie**

- **Pronouns change when viewpoint changes.**

Sind *Sie* Amerikanerin?   Ja, *ich* bin Amerikanerin.

- **Pronouns and verbs together: watch the endings!**

PERSON	SINGULAR		PLURAL
First	**ich** brauch<u>e</u>		**wir** brauch<u>en</u>
Second	**Sie** brauch<u>en</u>		**Sie** brauch<u>en</u>
Third	**er** (der Ober) **sie** (die Kanadierin) **es** (das Zimmer)	brauch<u>t</u>	**sie** brauch<u>en</u>

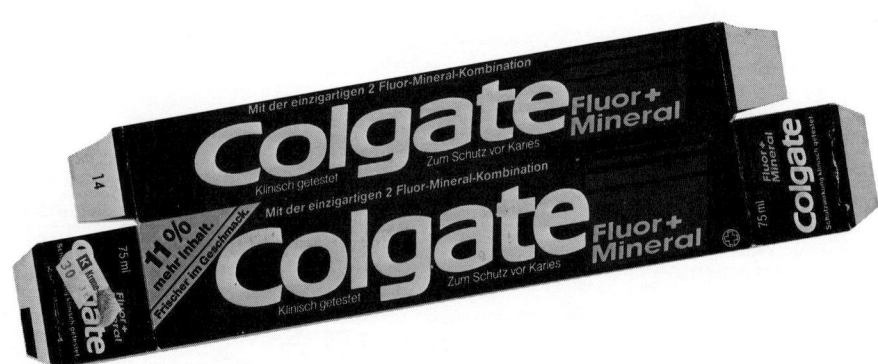

SITUATIONEN 2 Reiseproviant

	A	B
Remind students to make use of menus and product labels.		
1 (Traveler) Greets. Requests two bottles of beverage. Adds on a bar of chocolate.		(Works at train station kiosk.) Greets. Waits for A to ask for something. Fetches them; totals price so far – 3,- DM. Fetches it and revises the total. "Anything else?"
"No." Offers next higher banknote.		Counts change, thanks, says farewell.
2 (Traveler) Requests bread and cheese (250 g) for two lunches. Requests bottled beverages – non-alcoholic. Wonders if they have oranges. Asks price.		(Store employee) Fills the request; doesn't mention price. "No. Not today. Sorry." "7,50 DM; oops, forgot the bread; 8,50 DM."
	(They complete the transaction.)	

A	B	C
3 (Traveler) Begins to order lunch materials (to go) for self and two others.	(Store employee) Obliges. Is curious about A's foreign accent. Is A from England?	(Traveler – enters later.)
"No." Tries to tell about self but is in somewhat of a hurry.	Is helpful.	Enters, greets, and wonders if they have any nuts.
Somewhat annoyed but polite.	Tries to help A and C.	Realizes error and apologizes.
4 (Traveler – speaks no German.)	(Traveling with A – speaks a little German.) Greets.	(Store employee) Greets. Waits to serve.
Steadily plies B with questions about what X is; ideas for things to get; changes in what to get; other things for B to ask C, including restroom location.	Attempts to get picnic food and drink for self and A. (B and C eventually complete the transaction; B is even able to tell C a little about himself/herself, about A, and about their trip.)	Has most of what B asks for.

Stage 2

2: Partners can help by asking questions like *"Ist das auch für Sie?"* *"Ist das nicht ein bißchen viel?"*

1
Obtain food and drink for four people going on a picnic in the city park. You don't know the other people very well, so you should provide for a range of tastes in food and drink.

2
A fellow passenger in your train compartment is preparing to make the long trip through the train to the snack bar, and has indicated a willingness to pick up something for you. Make your request politely.

Versuchen Sie doch

The fellow passenger in situation #2 above has returned, juggling the items and the change from the transaction. You realize that one of the items is not the one you requested – wrong beverage, chocolate bar with nuts instead of without, etc. What do you say, if anything? What do you say when that nice person realizes the error?

Chapter 4

IM ZUG/
WO IST DIE STRASSE?

Wie, bitte? Das ist der Zug nach Rom?!

FUNKTIONEN – KONTEXTE – STRUKTUREN

Looking ahead

You'll be getting a seat on the train, talking about your trip, describing family and friends, asking and giving directions in a city, and comparing qualities and quantities.

You will be using:

- verb forms in the third person (he, she, it, they)
- time phrases that refer to the future (Until July I'll . . .)
- forms that compare things (pretty, prettier – good, better)
- word order for emphasis (In ten minutes you'll be there)
- conjunctions to speak and write more efficiently (and, or, but)

Im Zug

1

FRAU PRINZ Guten Tag. Ist hier noch frei, bitte?

FRAU WAGNER Nein, es tut mir leid. Der Platz ist besetzt.

FRAU PRINZ Oh, danke schön. Auf Wiedersehen.

2

HERR FILZER Bitte, wie spät ist es?

HERR WETTSTEIN Umm, ich glaube, Viertel vor zehn. Moment mal . . . Ja, es ist neun Uhr sechsundvierzig.

3

HERR HAMBURGER Reisen Sie auch nach Basel?

DOKTOR SCHLUMPF Nein, nur nach Köln.

HERR HAMBURGER Köln? Wunderbar, die Stadt. So viel zu sehen. Der Dom ist natürlich fantastisch, aber das wissen Sie schon, oder? Und der Zoo für die Kinder! Und . . .

4

With dialog 4 or soon after introduce kinship terms; see *"Bildwörterbuch"* display *"People/Leute."* Vary the dialog to fit students' families, and perhaps allow them to say a few words about family members. Point out – but don't harp on – the distinction between *o* and *ö*, and between the *ch-* sounds in *Tochter* and *Töchter*. Standard for correction: allow wide range of allophones, but correct errors that would convey wrong information or irritate the native speaker used to dealing with foreigners.

usw. (und so weiter) *etc., and so on*

Quickly introduce seasons and months; for weather, see *"Bildwörterbuch"* section on *"Nature/Natur."*

HERR BLOCH Tag. Sind diese Plätze schon besetzt?

HERR TRÄGER Nein, hier ist noch frei. Bitte, nehmen Sie Platz.

HERR BLOCH Danke schön. Ich hole meine Familie und komme gleich wieder.

. . .

HERR BLOCH So. Hier bin ich wieder. Das ist meine Familie – meine Frau, mein Sohn und meine zwei Töchter.

5

FRAU BRÜCKNER Und sind Sie Amerikaner?

MARK FRY Ich ja, aber mein Freund ist Kanadier. Ich arbeite für eine Bank in Köln, und er studiert bis Juli in München.

FRAU BRÜCKNER Ach, Köln ist sehr interessant. Der Dom, das Museum, der Zoo usw. . . . Mmm . . . Sagen Sie mal, schläft er immer so lang?

MARK FRY Nein, aber wissen Sie, er arbeitet jetzt so viel. Er studiert Physik.

FRAU BRÜCKNER So – das ist schade. Er sieht jetzt nichts, und die Reise nach Köln ist doch so schön – aber noch schöner im Sommer.

STRUKTUR 1

Verbs §12

1. Stem-changing verbs

er/sie/es forms

Point out that the *e* in *does* is the equivalent of an umlaut (often represented earlier by *e* instead of diaeresis), and that *says* involves an umlaut (to "sez") that is not evident in spelling.

Some German verbs change their stem in the third person singular, as does English (do – d<u>oe</u>s).

● e > i	**essen**	ich esse	wir essen
		Sie essen	Sie essen
	BUT	er/sie/es **ißt**	sie essen
	vergessen	ich vergesse	wir vergessen
		Sie vergessen	Sie vergessen
	BUT	er/sie/es **vergißt**	sie vergessen
	nehmen	ich nehme	wir nehmen
		Sie nehmen	Sie nehmen
	BUT	er/sie/es **nimmt**	sie nehmen
● e > ie	**sehen**	ich sehe	wir sehen
		Sie sehen	Sie sehen
	BUT	er/sie/es **sieht**	sie sehen
● a > ä	**schlafen**	ich schlafe	wir schlafen
		Sie schlafen	Sie schlafen
	BUT	er/sie/es **schläft**	sie schlafen

Set up small-group exercise with a map or picture of people: A (to B): "*Sehen Sie* [city/person name]?" B (to A): "*Ja, ich sehe . . .*" A (to C): "*Er/sie sieht . . .*" Vary with questions; similarly with *essen*. Perhaps combine with kinship terms.

W.O. §7

2. Coordinating conjunctions

aber/und/oder

There are advantages and disadvantages to using (or not using) such connectors. Structural sophistication, if actual performance is slow, should not be ranked above fluent production of less sophisticated language – and conversely. Various methods of connections are presented later. Here you might point out that conjunctions are useful, but that facile creation of two simpler sentences is also effective. See the section in "*Strategie*."

Coordinating conjunctions can join entire sentences as well as sentence elements. They have no effect on word order.

Der Dom ist fantastisch. Das wissen Sie schon, ja?
Der Dom ist fantastisch, **aber** das wissen Sie schon, ja?

Ich hole meine Familie. Ich komme gleich wieder.
Ich hole meine Familie **und** komme gleich wieder.

SITUATIONEN 1 Im Zug

Stage 1	A	B
1	Enters train compartment, greets. Asks if there is room. Is polite, asks if there is room for his (her) family. Is thankful, responds positively.	Responds with greeting. Says there's still room left, invites A to sit down. Responds positively.
2	Doesn't want to disturb fellow passenger, but has to know the time; mumbles question. Restates question, guesses time. Asks for clarification. Is very grateful.	Asks for clarification. Gives correct time. Gives time another way. Is glad to have helped.
3	Is showing pictures of family to fellow passenger. Identifies parents and siblings. Gives ages of family members. Tells what parents do. Responds animatedly.	Is mildly interested. Asks name of each. Responds politely; asks occupations of parents. Is interested; asks what siblings study in school.
4	Thinks Köln is pretty. Thinks Marburg is too small. Disagrees. Is from Köln; asks if B is going to be staying in Köln until the weekend. Expresses regret – the city is more interesting on the weekend.	Agrees, but finds Marburg prettier. Thinks Marburg is small, but more interesting. Asks if A is from Köln. B's ticket is round-trip; is returning to Hamburg on Friday.

Push for something more than just "Ja."

Exercise 2 could easily be expanded to three people by having a partner C who echoes A's and B's utterances. See note in Instructor's Guide.
"Time another way:" "X Uhr Y" becomes "Y nach X," "21 Uhr" becomes "9 Uhr," etc.

See "Bildwörterbuch," "People/**Leute**"

Avoid introducing "Beruf," etc.; a low-level way to elicit the information is to ask a yes/no question like, "Ist Ihr Bruder Arzt?"

Encourage comparisons (either with the comparative or with "[nicht so] . . . wie" or "auch," and correct only indirectly (by repetition or modeling) failure to umlaut adjective stems.

Stage 2

Introduce appropriate realia (train menus and pictures, "Bildwörterbuch" displays).

See note in Instructor's Guide.

1
You think you see an empty seat in a train compartment. Open the door and

a) greet the occupants;
b) inquire about the seat.
If the seat is free, explain that you will go back and get your baggage.

2
You and three friends who don't speak German are sharing a compartment with an elderly couple. Introduce your friends and say a little about them.

3
Find out where food and drink can be obtained on your train. Check the prices.

4
You are seated in the train. There are several empty seats in your compartment, though some of your belongings are on them. A couple pauses near your door, obviously looking for a place to sit.

a) Attract their attention and inform them that the seats are vacant, despite the baggage on them.
b) After they are seated, offer some small talk – names, nationalities, destinations.

Versuchen Sie doch

See note in Instructor's Guide.

You learn that someone in your train compartment is planning to visit the city you have just left. Offer some advice drawn from your own experiences – accommodations, meals, activities, attractions, people. Can you fit your advice to the seasons?

Where to go for information

The downtown areas of European cities are vital centers of activity. Extremely important are the train station and – usually right near it – the *Verkehrsbüro* (or *das Verkehrsamt*). In the *Verkehrsbüro* you can obtain advice about getting the most out of your stay. There you will find out important information about the city, including directions to places of special interest, and you can ask for a map (*der Stadtplan*) to take along with you. You can learn about schedules and tickets to performances as well. The *Verkehrsbüro* may also include the *Zimmervermittlung*, a central office where you can reserve a room in a hotel, boarding house (*die Pension*), or private home throughout the city. (You will learn more about *die Zimmervermittlung* in Chapter 15.)

Writing exercise: prepare a skeleton letter for a request for information from the *Verkehrsamt*. See relevant forms (inquiry cards, etc.) in the realia.

How to ask for information – ways to elicit details, description, and comparison

You already know *"Wie, bitte?"* as a means of getting clarification. (*"Was?"* is very impolite, incidentally.) Other phrases that will bring help are

"Entschuldigung . . ."   "(Tut mir leid,) ich verstehe nicht"
"Moment, bitte, was ist das?"   "Ist das . . . (ein[e] . . .)?"

"Ist das wie . . . ?" asks for comparison.

"Bohnensalat. Ist das wie Kartoffelsalat?"

It's a good idea to repeat information you have been given, both so that you will remember it better and so that any misunderstandings will show up.

"Also, das Hotel Krone ist um die Ecke und dann links 200 Meter."

When you are sure you have understood, you should make that obvious; remember also to be courteous.

"Ist gut/ist recht."   "Das verstehe ich."
"Schön."   "Vielen Dank/Danke vielmals/Danke sehr."

Metrics: some handy time and distance conversions

Stundenkilometer (km/h) = km per hour

100 meters = about 100 yards = about 1 minute at walking pace (*zu Fuß*)
1000 m = 1 km = 10 minutes on foot (without suitcases!)
express train – average speed (including stops!): 100 km per hour = 1 mile per minute

Straße = block

The word *Straße* will do quite nicely as an equivalent for "city block." But as your maps will show, European cities often have irregular layouts; few were designed according to a grid. Therefore the phrase *zwei Straßen weiter* is more an indication of landmarks than a close estimate of distances.

If you can get a copy, play the Karl Valentin comic song, "*Die vier Jahreszeiten*," both for the content and for the exaggerated "stage" accent and the chance it gives to check pronunciation in a nonthreatening way.

The point is to provide a communicative *function* before teaching the customary grammatical-lexical equivalents, which involve notorious word-order problems. You might also point out that the functions of *wenn* and *obwohl* can be conveyed with some good basic rhetoric: "*Sind die Plätze frei? Ich hole (dann) meine Familie.*" = "*Wenn die Plätze frei sind, hole ich meine Familie.*" This does not mean that first-year students should never be taught *wenn* and verb-last word order; the subject is covered later in the text. Rather, they should be encouraged to communicate. Like native speakers, they can do without *wenn* for quite a long time. Perhaps remark that *dann* and *also* can be effective aids, since they help establish the notions of temporal or logical connection that are not explicit in *und*.

die Jahreszeit, die Jahreszeiten / der Monat, die Monate

der Winter	der Januar, der Februar, der März
der Frühling	der April, der Mai, der Juni
der Sommer	der Juli, der August, der September
der Herbst	der Oktober, der November, der Dezember

Creative use of *und* and *aber*

You don't yet know words for "if" and "although," but *und* and *aber* can serve the purpose well enough in many instances, just as "and" and "but" can be used in English to express those meanings. So don't let the lack of some vocabulary tie your tongue.

Sie finden die Plätze, und ich hole das Bier.	If you'll find the seats, I'll get the beer.
Im Sommer ist es schön, aber im Winter schöner.	Although it's nice in the summer, it's nicer in the winter.

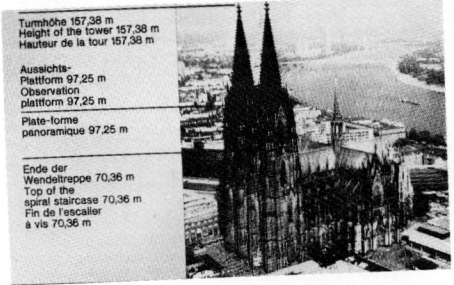

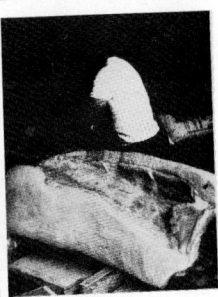

Turmhöhe 157,38 m
Height of the tower 157,38 m
Hauteur de la tour 157,38 m

Aussichts-
Plattform 97,25 m
Observation
plattform 97,25 m

Plate-forme
panoramique 97,25 m

Ende der
Wendeltreppe 70,36 m
Top of the
spiral staircase 70,36 m
Fin de l'escalier
à vis 70,36 m

Zahlen zum Dom
Der Dom ist 144 m lang, im Querhaus 86 m breit und im Mittelschiff 43,35 m hoch.

Der Dachfirst ist 61 m, der Dachreiter 109 m hoch. Die Fassade ist 61 m breit und 157,38 m hoch. Zur Aussichtsplattform, die man durch das um 1375 entstandene Petersportal erreicht, steigt man 509 Stufen empor. Dabei kommt man an den großen Glocken vorbei, von denen 9 läutbar sind. Die größten sind: St. Peter (1923) 24 t, Pretiosa (1448) 11,2 t, Speciosa (1449) 6 t.

Der Dom bedeckt eine Fläche von fast 8.000 m² und hat eine innere Nutzfläche von 6.166 m². Alle Fensterflächen machen über 10.000 m², alle Dachflächen 12.500 m² aus. Der umbaute Raum beträgt ohne das aufwendige Strebwerk 407.000 m³.

La cathédrale en chiffres
La cathédrale a 144 mètres de longueur, son transept lui donne une largeur de 86 mètres et la hauteur de sa nef principale est de 43,35 mètres. La hauteur du faîtage est de 61 mètres et le lanterneau de 109 mètres. La façade est large de 61 mètres et haute de 157,38 mètres.

La galerie que l'on atteint par le portail Saint Pierre datant de 1375, en gravissant 509 marches, permet de passer devant les grandes cloches dont neuf sont battantes. Les plus grandes sont celles de St. Peter (1923) pesant 24 tonnes, Pretiosa (1448) 11,2 tonnes, Speciosa (1449) 6 tonnes. La cathédrale recouvre une surface de près de 8.000 m² et a une surface utile intérieure de 6.166 m².

Tous les vitraux ont une superficie totale de plus de 10.000 m², toutes les surfaces de toit de 12.500 m². Le volume intérieur est de 407.000 m³, si l'on excepte les contreforts.

Die Dombauhütte
Die traditionsreiche Dombauhütte beschäftigt heute über siebzig Mitarbeiter. Davon sind 36 Steinmetzen und Bildhauer, 10 Glasrestauratoren, weitere Handwerker verschiedener Bauberufe und 6 Angestellte einer kleinen Verwaltung. Aufgabe der Hütte ist es, die schweren Kriegs- und Verwitterungsschäden zu beseitigen und den Bau innen und außen pfleglich zu unterhalten. Die Mittel werden durch kirchliche, staatliche und städtische Zuschüsse, zu einem erheblichen Teil aber durch freiwillige Spenden aufgebracht. Diese kommen hauptsächlich vom 1841 gegründeten Zentral-Dombauverein, der überhaupt erst den Ausbau des Domes 1842 bis 1880 ermöglichte, indem er zwei Drittel der gesamten Kosten trug.

La Dombauhütte
Cet organisme de longue tradition emploie de nos jours plus de soixante-dix personnes, et notamment 36 sculpteurs et marbriers, 10 restaurateurs de vitraux, d'autres artisans de différentes disciplines et six employés d'administration. La tâche de la »Dombauhütte« est de veiller à la réparation des graves dommages dus à la guerre et aux intempéries, ainsi qu'à l'entretien intérieur et extérieur de l'édifice. Les fonds proviennent de subventions de l'Eglise, de l'Etat et de la municipalité, mais une grande part provient aussi de dons de particuliers. A cet égard, l'association »Zentral-Dombauverein« fondée en 1841 joue un rôle important. C'est grâce à elle que les travaux de la cathédrale ont pu être exécutés de 1842 à 1880, travaux dont elle prit en charge les deux tiers des frais.

Fußgängerzone

Cologne
Keulen
Köln
Oslo 1000 km
Kopenhagen 630 km
Stockholm 1200 km
London 470 km
Berlin 500 km
Dublin 900 km
Amsterdam 230 km
Brüssel 180 km
Paris 400 km
Wien 720 km
Barcelona 970 km
Zürich 400 km
Rom 1000 km
Entfernungsangaben = Luftlinie
N
KÖLN
Rhein
Chorweiler
Merkenich
Flittard
Pesch
Longerich
Stammheim
Niehl
Höhenhaus
Ossendorf
Nippes
Riehl
Holweide
Mülheim
Buchforst
Braunsfeld
Merheim
Junkersdorf
Lindenthal
Kalk
Deutz
Ostheim
Sülz
Klettenberg
Bayenthal
Poll
Zollstock
Marienburg
Westhoven
Rodenkirchen
Hürth
Meschenich
Sürth
Porz
Langel

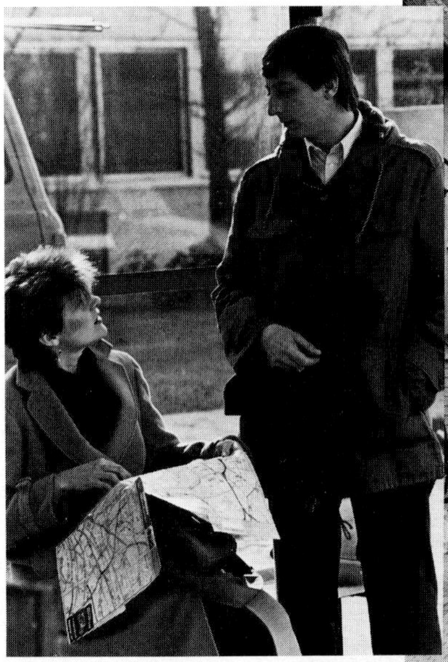

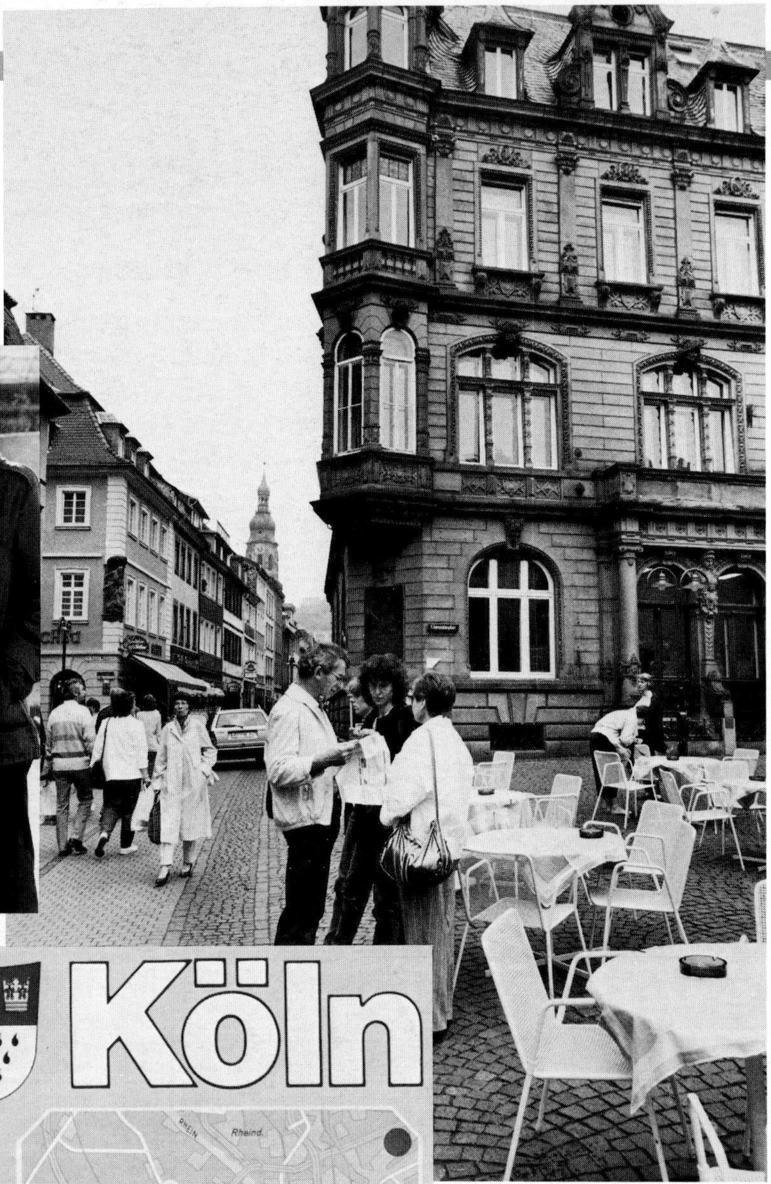

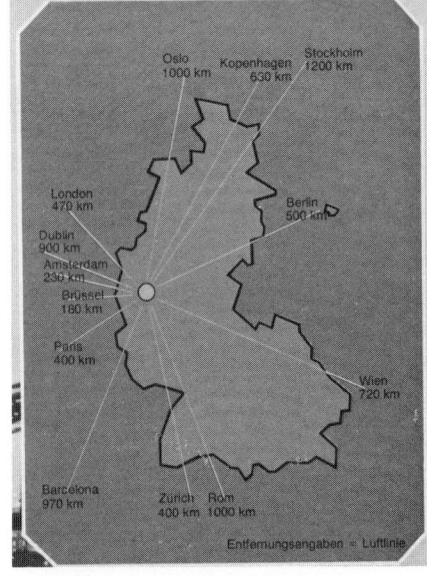

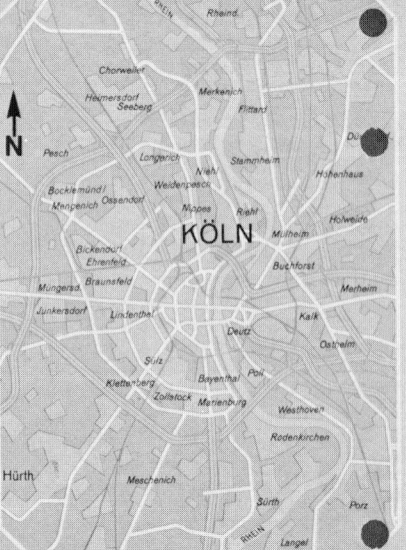

Wo ist die Straße?

The dialogs can be varied
endlessly with maps, hotel lists,
and the *"Bildwörterbuch"*
displays. Good chance to
remind students of the
importance of polite expressions like *"Entschuldigung"* or
"bitte schön." By Chapter 4 they
may have come to think they
needn't worry about material
from the earliest chapters. Here,
as always, recall the concept
of the *"spiral syllabus."*

Aim for lexical reproduction
of the masculine accusative.
Explain the grammar only if
pressed. Most students will not
raise the point, unless they have
had German before.

1

| FRAU BENJAMIN | Bitte, wo ist das Hotel Krone? |
| HERR WEISHAUPT | Hotel Krone. Tut mir leid, das weiß ich nicht. Das Verkehrsbüro ist um die Ecke. Fragen Sie dort. |

2

| HERR REICH | Entschuldigung. Wissen Sie, wo das Hotel Thielen ist? |
| HERR BEERLI | Nehmen Sie die Linie 10 bis zum Bahnhof. In zehn Minuten sind Sie da. |

3

| FRÄULEIN SCHALLER | Die Jugendherberge? Das ist nicht weit von hier. Gehen Sie hier ein paar Straßen weiter. Dann sehen Sie eine Konditorei. Gehen Sie dann links 200 Meter. |
| JACK ALIN | Moment mal. Also zwei Straßen weiter. . . . |

4

FRAU FISCHER	. . . So finden Sie es leicht.
FRAU MOHR	Danke. Und wo finde ich hier ein Taxi?
FRAU FISCHER	Das kostet zu viel. Sie gehen besser zu Fuß.
FRAU MOHR	Aber ich habe zu viel Gepäck. Ich glaube, ich nehme ein Taxi.

5

FRAU STOLZBODEN	Fahren Sie also weiter durch die Stadt. Immer geradeaus. Sie sehen links das Hotel Hessen, . . . eine Bank, . . . die Post . . . und dann den Hauptbahnhof.
FRÄULEIN METZGER	Also gut. Links ein Hotel, die Post, dann eine Bank . . .
FRAU STOLZBODEN	Nein. Das Hotel, dann die Bank – die Deutsche Bank ist das – und jetzt die Post.
FRÄULEIN METZGER	Und dann finde ich den Hauptbahnhof.
FRAU STOLZBODEN	Richtig. Dann finden Sie den Hauptbahnhof. Fahren Sie aber immer geradeaus.

6

| GIANNI STRUMOLO | Entschuldigung. Wir suchen das Stadtmuseum. Hier ist die Adresse. |
| HERR CHRISTOPH | Das ist nicht weit von hier. Aber heute ist Montag. Ich glaube, es ist heute geschlossen. |

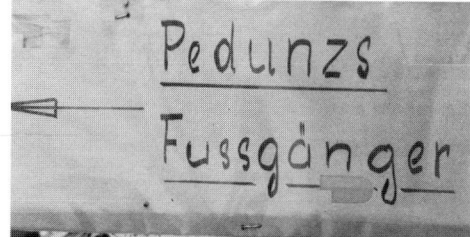

STRUKTUR 2

See note in
Instructor's Guide.

Verbs §10

1. Future time

To express future time you can just use the present tense + a time phrase.

Ich <u>komme</u> gleich wieder.
I'm coming back right away.

In zehn Minuten <u>sind</u> Sie da.
You'll be there in 10 minutes.
} will, going to

A.A. §§23,24

2. Comparing things: use *-er.*

Die Reise nach Köln ist doch so **schön** – aber noch **schöner** im Sommer.

Map exercise: A: *Wie weit ist*
[city, etc.]? B: [estimate]. C:
[comment:] *Nein, weiter/nicht so
weit.*

Das ist nicht **weit** von hier. Gehen Sie ein paar Straßen **weiter**.

A.A. §36

3. Adverbs: often the first word in a sentence

Multistage map exercise: point
out landmarks on way to X.
Narration exercise: make up an
itinerary with time phrases –
outline an itinerary on the
board, with time phrases (days,
times) in left-hand column; for
present tense: also list of verbs

Verbs §27

Pattern occurs often in giving directions.

In zehn Minuten sind Sie da.
Links sehen Sie eine Konditorei.
Dann finde ich den Hauptbahnhof.

for emphasis

(*sehen, essen*); first stage: wir;
second stage: individuals
comment (*Aber ich . . .*); third
stage: third person discussion.
Targets: "*Montag sind wir in
Hamburg*," "*In 2 Minuten sind
wir da*," etc.

4. *Wissen:* two very important irregular forms

ich **weiß** wir wissen
Sie wissen Sie wissen
er/sie **weiß** sie wissen

4: Student A: states a fact
(especially a self-evident fact,
e.g., "*Es ist 10 Uhr*" or "*Heute
ist Dienstag*"), perhaps with
intonation appropriate to
reminding someone of the
obvious. Student B: echo the
fact, beginning "*Ich weiß, . . .*"
(without *daß*!!). Variations
include ensuring that the initial
fact involves first or second
person, so that B has to
transform the perspective;
having student C talk about
student B ("*Ja, sie weiß, . . .*).
An adept speaker can convey
the sense of *ob* without actually
knowing the conjunction or
anything about verb-last word
order: "*Ist das Mainz oder
Wiesbaden? Wissen Sie?*" Caution:
Don't put the student in the
position of saying "*Ich weiß
nicht, . . .*," since the
introduction forces *ob*, with
attendant word-order
complexity; thus the setup with
obvious facts.

Inselstadt Lindau

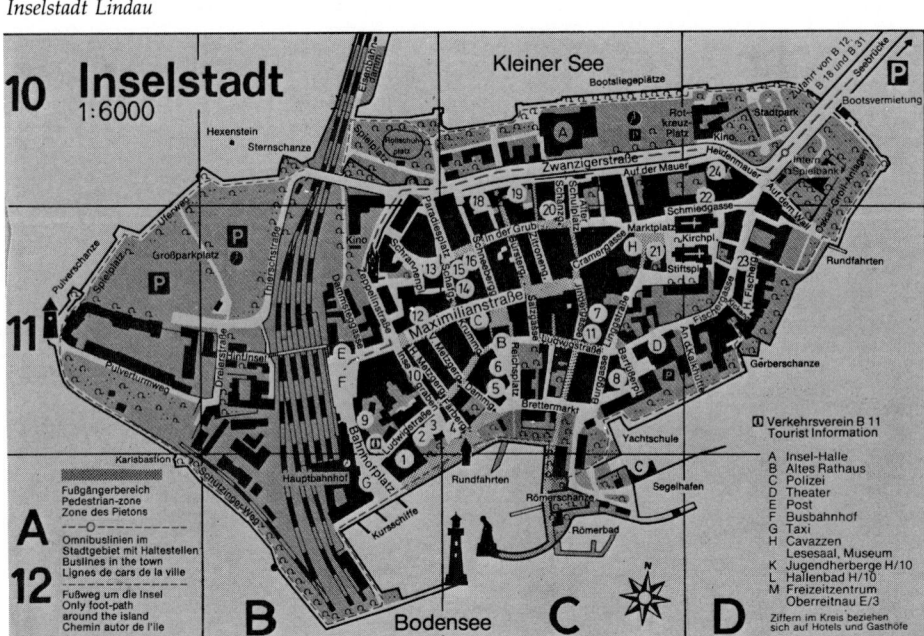

SITUATIONEN 2 Wo ist die Straße?

Stage 1	A	B
1	Is looking for the Albula Hotel. Asks where the tourist office is. Is very grateful for the help. Says good-bye.	Doesn't know where it is. Says it's right around the corner. Is glad to help. Says good-bye.
2	Asks where there is a taxi. Asks how long a walk that is. Is satisfied; starts to go left. Sees a bakery, resolves to ask there.	Knows there's a taxi stand a couple of streets farther on. Remarks that A has lots of luggage; says it's a five-minute walk. Interrupts; the taxi is in the opposite direction.
3	Is looking for the youth hostel. Asks for the address. Asks for landmarks. A repeats, confuses the order. Asks which bus line goes there. Is grateful; asks when the bus comes, and where to catch it.	Says it's far from there, on bus line 4. Doesn't know the address. Says A will see a bank, the post office, two hotels, and a bakery. Repeats slowly. "Number 4 gets there in ten minutes." "Around the corner to the left."

Whether partner A says anything here is a matter for debate. You might ask the class how they would diplomatically say they were going off to find a second opinion.

Use the realia and maps provided. Two reasons: 1) overt – point out how gestures and introduction of real-world materials can be used to buy time; 2) covert – by now the verve of the first few units, where progress seemed to be stunning, may have diminished, and the class may have sunk back into well-behaved apathy, sitting quietly at desks with noses in books and hands neatly folded. Get them up and moving, draw them away from their textbooks, and break up cozy partnerships.

A	B	C
4	(Husband of C.)	(Wife of B.)
Asks where the museum is.	Says it's to the left and six blocks.	Says it's to the right and four blocks.
Repeats, confusing the two.	Corrects self – it's only five blocks.	Says her husband doesn't know.
Asks for clarification.	Says it's five blocks to the right. Says his wife doesn't know.	Disagrees – it's straight ahead.
Confirms that it's straight ahead.	Disagrees – it's to the right.	Remembers it's closed today.
Thanks them both, says good-bye.		

Stage 2

See the various realia items having to do with zoos and similar attractions. This is a good time to prepare for Chapter 11 – and to reinforce the notion of compounds and cognates – by introducing a few animal names. The *Duden Grammatik* has a nice list of animal sounds.

1

You are new in town. Someone approaches you and asks for directions to some street.

a) You didn't catch the name of the street.
b) Even when you understand the name of the street, you don't know where it is, but you try to help anyway.

2

You have been to the zoo and are now back at your hotel in the center of town. Another hotel guest asks you for advice, including:

a) how to get to the zoo, and under what weather conditions;
b) things to see along the way if on foot;
c) your opinion of the zoo.

Versuchen Sie doch
See the map of the Vienna region in Chapter 13.

You are visiting Klosterneuburg, a suburb to the northwest of Vienna. An Italian gentleman and his wife ask you how to get to Wiener Neustadt, south of the city. Do the best you can. They'll have to walk to the bus stop and take a bus into the city, then change. . . .

49

Chapter 5
HALTESTELLE/
HOTEL – BAD ODER DUSCHE?

FUNKTIONEN – KONTEXTE – STRUKTUREN

Appropriate songs: "Himmel und Erde," "Muß i denn," "Heut' kommt der Hans zu mir."

Looking ahead

You'll be dealing with public transportation, discussing hotel facilities, and finding out how things work.

You will be using:

- modal verbs (can, should, have to)
- prepositions used to talk about destinations (toward, to)
- words that indicate sequence and direction (then . . . to the)
- pronouns and nouns as subjects or "doers" (I, he, she, we)

50

Haltestelle

Brühl Castle 13 km SE of Köln.

1

Some students may need help with the fundamentals of using maps, timetables, and public transportation, regardless of which language is used. Maybe take a few minutes to locate Köln landmarks.

2

Named for Jacques Offenbach (1819–1880), composer born in Köln. Works include *Tales of Hoffmann* (inspired by E.T.A. Hoffmann's stories). Some students would recognize his famous "can-can" melody.

3

Point out how German vocabulary is often based on variations of a root, where English may have quite different words (*einsteigen* – "get on" or "board"; *aussteigen* – "get out" or "get off"; *umsteigen* – "transfer" or "change").

4

5

HERR KÜNDIG	Wann kommt der nächste Bus nach Brühl?
HERR MUHMENTHALER	Um 10 Uhr 23 und dann um 10 Uhr 43. Also alle 20 Minuten.
FRAU ZIPPERT	Entschuldigung. Fährt dieser Bus zum Bahnhof?
FRAU MÜTTERL	Nein, aber die S-Bahn Linie 12 fährt direkt dahin.
FRÄULEIN WEIDELI	. . . Nein, die Nummer 13 fährt nicht direkt zum Offenbachplatz. Sie müssen umsteigen.
HERR AMBACH	Umsteigen? Wo?
FRÄULEIN WEIDELI	Also, Nummer 13 bis Bachstraße. Dort müssen Sie aussteigen. Und dann nehmen Sie Nummer 9.
HERR ROHR	Muß ich umsteigen?
FRAU RANKE	Ja, am Marktplatz. Die Haltestelle sehen Sie links, wenn Sie aussteigen.
HERR ROHR	Und wie lange muß ich da warten?
FRAU RANKE	Nicht sehr lange. Die Busse fahren alle 30 Minuten.
HERR ROHR	Alle 30 Minuten? Aber es ist doch so kalt.
FRÄULEIN BÜRGER	Entschuldigung. Ich suche das Krankenhaus. Ist das weit von hier?
FRÄULEIN LEUTHOLD	Nein, das ist nicht sehr weit. Aber es regnet so stark. Nehmen Sie ein Taxi. Das ist besser.

STRUKTUR 1

Verbs §§18–21,23

1. "Modal" verbs

müssen

Müssen expresses *have to, need to, got to, must*. An infinitive (for example, **gehen**) completes the idea.

* **forms:**

	SINGULAR	PLURAL
1	ich **muß**	wir müssen
2	Sie müssen	Sie müssen
3	er/sie/es **muß**	sie müssen

* **word order:** same principle as before

a) simple statement: Sie **müssen** umsteigen.

b) question: **Muß** ich umsteigen?

c) after question words: Wie lange **muß** ich da warten?

2. Giving directions

Use a word like **dann, da, dort, hier.** Then use a verb followed by its subject.

Steigen Sie dort aus. **Dann** nehmen Sie Nummer 9.

3. Destinations

* **nach** with names of cities:

Eine Karte **nach** Köln, bitte.

* **zum** or **zur** with specific locations:

masculine	der Bahnhof –	**zum** Bahnhof, bitte.
neuter	das Krankenhaus –	**zum** Krankenhaus
feminine	die Haltestelle –	**zur** Haltestelle

Exercise: list schedule and obligations (*Um zwei muß ich arbeiten;* simpler still: A: *Um X Uhr?* B: *ich muß* _____); error control: demonstrate but don't dwell on *u/ü* distinction, take it fairly easy on **er/sie mußt* (indirect correction), do come down *hard* on **myussen* and **Ich müsse.*

Don't worry about management of the inner field. Correct infinitive placement only indirectly. Chief concerns here are conjugating and placing the modal.

Exercise: direction giving (temporal order; spatial order; have students point carefully on map to produce *"da/hier"*).

Itinerary exercises: 1) with map and timetable: *Wir fahren nach X, und dann nach Y.* (Interruptions: *"Wann sind wir in X?"*); 2) with map and list of landmarks on board or overhead (two groups of nouns: a. masculine and neuter; b. feminine). *"Fahren Sie nach [suburb, other city]?"* *"Nein, zum Campingplatz."* Expansion: continue with prompt, *"Und dann?"* Maybe review verb-second word order by encouraging a time phrase as first element. Ignore plurals. Avoid: 1) explanation of dative case – the aim here is to establish *zum* and *zur* as lexical (rote) elements in preparation for later expansion with grammatical discussion; 2) use and explanation of other directional prepositions, especially the accusative/dative ones; 3) country names that are not used with *nach.*

SITUATIONEN 1 Haltestelle

Stage 1	A	B
1 Deutz is directly across the Rhine from Köln. The situations can be done with realia in hand, or else you can set up a blackboard or overhead or handout chart of your own – either for everyone to see, or else for just the partner who is playing the native speaker.	Wants to know when the bus to Deutz will come. Asks what time it is now. Is grateful for the information.	Isn't sure, but thinks it's every 15 minutes. It's 3:22 P.M. The bus comes at 3:29. Responds politely.
2	Wants to take a tram to the museum. Asks how often – and where to find one. Asks how long he'll have to wait. Asks if he'll have to change buses.	Says that only buses make the trip. Says museum buses leave from the train station on the half hour. Responds – it's 3:15 P.M. No transfer will be necessary.
3	Asks whether the hospital is far. Says it's nicer in the summer, then asks where the bus stop is. Asks where she'll have to get off. Expresses regret; thanks B.	Says it's too far to walk; A should take a bus or a taxi, since it's raining. Says it's just around the corner to the left. Get off at the Rathausplatz and take another bus. Is polite; says good-bye.

	A	B	C
4 Solution: *"Sie müssen umsteigen."*	Wants to go to the train station. Doesn't understand the idea of transfer. Mentions the winter weather. Asks whether it's really necessary to get off here. Gets off, thanks B and C.	Says: will have a long trip. Says: will have to get off the bus, Agrees weather is nasty. Says this is the stop. Acknowledges thanks.	Agrees – transfer is necessary. . . . and get on another for the station. Says A should get out at this stop. Says A should take the Number 13 bus. Says good-bye.

Stage 2

2: Use the maps provided, or draw a schematic map on the board.

Versuchen Sie doch notes: Check to see whether the student can express a range of "wanting," from insistent (but polite) demand through forthright wanting to modest preference.

Versuchen Sie doch

Solution: *"Sie brauchen keine Dusche,"* or just *"ohne Dusche."*

For second paragraph: maybe set up a comical confusion by covertly encouraging the "clerk" to distract the "guest" with a reminder that what Americans would call the fifth floor would be the fourth <u>Stock</u> for German speakers.

1

You're in the *Verkehrsbüro* in the train station, asking for directions to two restaurants you've heard about.

a) Which of the two does the clerk think is the better?
b) Find out whether they have a special restaurant map of the city.

2

You have rented a car in Köln and have driven to the zoo, which is north of the city. Now you want to go to the university, which is southwest of the city.

Ask about routes. The main question: Should you attempt to drive straight through the city? Also: how much time will you need?

Ten of your old friends from Sackville, N.B., are planning to visit you soon in Bonn, where you are doing your best to arrange rooms for them. Unfortunately, the youth hostel is booked solid for that week. Three friends want to be sure to stay in the same room; they are not fastidious about personal hygiene. Another four would like to room together, probably in adjoining doubles with a shower in one room and a bath in the other. The last three require singles; a simple washbasin will do for each, but it would be nice to have a shower available nearby. Because Bonn is louder than Sackville, they will want to be on the 5th or 6th floor, away from the street noise.

Jot down some notes to help you negotiate the rooms with the sympathetic hotel clerk, and practice the exchange until you are confident that you will say just the right thing.

Transit

European cities usually have an extensive network of buses and streetcars to service all parts of the downtown and outlying areas. Schedules are available at many stops. The *Bahnhof* (*Hauptbahnhof*) is normally the hub of the system, allowing you to reach your destination within the city soon after your arrival at the train station. You buy your ticket from a machine (*der Fahrkartenautomat*) before boarding a bus, and then you validate it (*entwerten*) either at the machine (*der Entwerter*) or on the vehicle itself. City transit officers check tickets regularly, and there's a fine for riding without a valid ticket (*schwarzfahren*).

Showers

Most larger European hotels have modern facilities, and the accommodations are priced accordingly. But not all rooms in smaller hotels or *Pensionen* have showers, especially in older buildings. If you arrange for a room without a shower or bath, you may well have to pay extra – the equivalent of a dollar or so – to use a shower down the hall from your room or on another floor. You may arrange for this at the desk, or there may be a coin- or token-operated meter on the shower that gives you a limited bathing time. Too much money in the meter is better than too little! Even if a bath or shower is not available, you will still find a washbasin in your room.

Beds

Do not expect a queen-size or king-size bed in your room. European beds are twin-sized. A *Doppelzimmer* will simply have two of them, though of course they can be put side by side. Covers include a thick feather comforter (*die Federdecke, das Federbett*).

Other amenities

Television sets and telephones are not found in all hotel rooms, especially in older ones. Be forewarned that calls from hotel rooms are very expensive. Especially if you are calling long-distance, a trip to the phone at the post office (*die Post*) will be worthwhile. You will learn about telephoning in Chapter 12.

Finding out how things work

Do not be afraid to ask when you do not understand how something works. *"Wie mache ich das?"/"Was muß ich machen?"/"Und was dann?"* will evoke helpful information about doing things. Note that *machen* is a good all-purpose verb for "do."

If you are reading directions about how to do or operate something, pay attention to nouns and verbs. Fortunately, such words are often easy to find. Nouns will be capitalized, and verbs are often given in their infinitive form at the ends of sentences. Be sure to pay attention to the word *"nicht"*!

LINKS GEHEN, RECHTS STEHEN

Bitte vorne an der Kasse zahlen.

Nicht aussteigen, bevor der Zug hält.

Colors

weiß	white	blau	blue	grün	green
schwarz	black	**rot**	red	**gelb**	yellow
grau	gray	**rosa**	pink	**braun**	brown

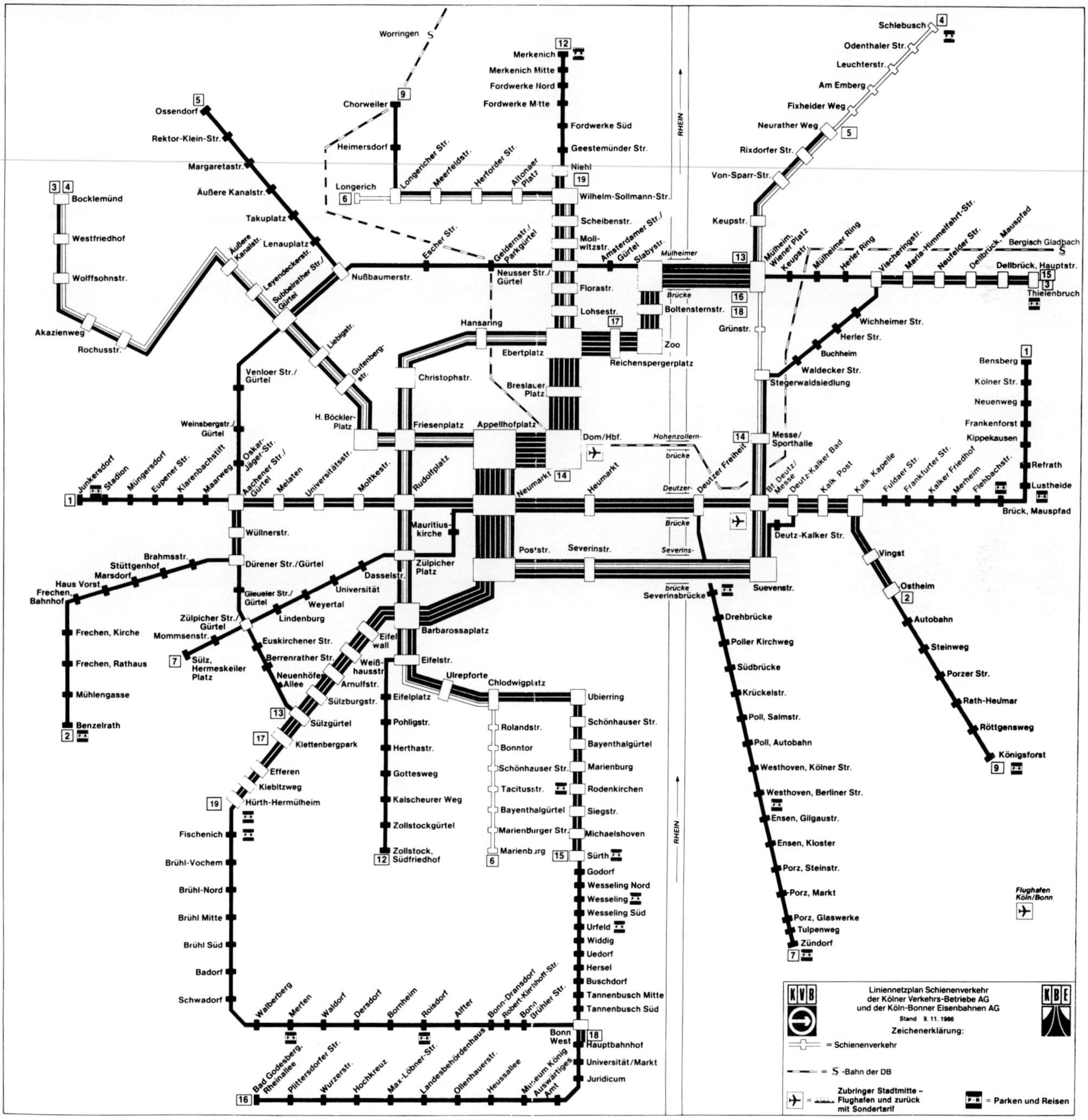

Worringen S

Merkenich

12

Merkenich Mitte

Fordwerke Nord

Fordwerke Mitte

Schlebusch 4

Odenthaler Str.

Leuchterstr.

Am Emberg

Fixheider Weg

Ossendorf 5

Chorweiler 9

Fordwerke Süd

Neurather Weg

Rektor-Klein-Str.

Heimersdorf

Geestemünder Str.

Rixdorfer Str.

5

Margaretastr.

Longericher Str.

Meerfeldstr.

Herforder Str.

Altonaer Platz

Niehl

19

Von-Sparr-Str.

Bocklemünd 3 4

Äußere Kanalstr.

Longerich 6

Wilhelm-Sollmann-Str.

Keupstr.

Mülheim, Wiener Platz

Mülheimer Ring

Herler Ring

Vischeringstr.

Maria-Himmelfahrt-Str.

Neufelder Str.

Dellbrück, Mauspfad

Bergisch Gladbach S

Westfriedhof

Takuplatz

Scheibenstr.

Amsterdamer Str.

Moll-

Slabystr.

Keupstr.

Wolffsohnstr.

Äußere Kanalstr.

Lenauplatz

Leyendeckerstr.

Escher Str.

Geldern-str./Parkgürtel

witzstr.

Gürtel

Mülheimer

Brücke

13

Dellbrück, Hauptstr.

15

3

Thielenbruch

Nußbaumstr.

Neusser Str./ Gürtel

Florastr.

16

Wichheimer Str.

Akazienweg

Subbelrather Str./Gürtel

Lohsestr.

Boltensternstr.

18

Herler Str.

Rochusstr.

Liebigstr.

Hansaring

17

Buchheim

Venloer Str./ Gürtel

Gutenberg-str.

Ebertplatz

Zoo

Grünstr.

Waldecker Str.

Stegerwaldsiedlung

Bensberg 1

Kölner Str.

Weinsbergstr./Gürtel

Christophstr.

Reichensperperplatz

Neuenweg

H. Böckler-Platz

Breslauer Platz

Frankenforst

Kippekausen

Friesenplatz

Appellhofplatz

Dom/Hbf.

Hohenzollern-brücke

14

Messe/ Sporthalle

Junkersdorf 1

Stadion

Müngersdorf

Eupener Str.

Klarenbachstift

Ottokar-Jäger Str./ Gürtel

Aachener Str./Gürtel

Melaten

Universitätsstr.

Moltkestr.

Rudolfplatz

Neumarkt

14

Heumarkt

Deutzer Freiheit

Deutz/ Messe

Bf. Deutz/ Messe

Deutz-Kalker Bad

Kalk Post

Kalk, Kapelle

Fuldaer Str.

Frankfurter Str.

Kalker Friedhof

Merheim

Fliehbachstr.

Refrath

Lustheide

Brück, Mauspfad

Deutzer Freiheit

Maarweg

Wüllnerstr.

Mauritius-kirche

Post-str.

Severinstr.

Severins-brücke

Brück, Mauspfad

Brahmsstr.

Stüttgenhof

Dürener Str./Gürtel

Zülpicher Platz

Deutz-Kalker Str.

Vingst

Marsdorf

Dasselstr.

brücke

Severinsbrücke

Suevenstr.

Haus Vorst

Frechen Bahnhof

Gleueler Str./ Gürtel

Universität

Weyertal

Ostheim

2

Zülpicher Str./ Gürtel

Lindenburg

Barbarossaplatz

Drehbrücke

Autobahn

Frechen, Kirche

Mommsenstr.

Euskirchener Str.

Eifel wall

Poller Kirchweg

Steinweg

Frechen, Rathaus

7

Sülz, Hermeskeiler Platz

Berrenrather Str.

Weiß-hausstr.

Eifelstr.

Südbrücke

Porzer Str.

Mühlengasse

Neuenhöfer Allee

Ulrepforte

Krückelstr.

Rath-Heumar

Arnulfstr.

Eifelplatz

Chlodwigplatz

Ubierring

Poll, Salmstr.

Röttgensweg

Benzelrath 2

Sülzburgstr.

Schönhauser Str.

Poll, Autobahn

Königsforst 9

Sülzgürtel

13

Pohligstr.

Rolandstr.

Bayenthalgürtel

Westhoven, Kölner Str.

Klettenbergpark

17

Herthastr.

Bonntor

Marienburg

Westhoven, Berliner Str.

Efferen

Gottesweg

Schönhauser Str.

Rodenkirchen

Ensen, Gilgaustr.

Kiebitzweg

Kalscheurer Weg

Tacitusstr.

Siegstr.

Ensen, Kloster

Hürth-Hermülheim

19

Zollstockgürtel

Bayenthalgürtel

Michaelshoven

Porz, Steinstr.

Fischenich

Zollstock, Südfriedhof

12

Marienburger Str.

Marienburg

6

Sürth

15

Porz, Markt

Brühl-Vochem

Godorf

Porz, Glaswerke

Brühl-Nord

Wesseling Nord

Tulpenweg

Flughafen Köln/Bonn

Brühl Mitte

Wesseling

Zündorf

Brühl Süd

Wesseling Süd

7

Badorf

Urfeld

Schwadorf

Widdig

Uedorf

Hersel

Buschdorf

Tannenbusch Mitte

Tannenbusch Süd

Walberberg

Merten

Waldorf

Oersdorf

Bornheim

Roisdorf

Alfter

Bonn-Dransdorf

Bonn, Robert-Kirchhof-Str.

Bonn, Brüher Str.

Bonn West

18

Hauptbahnhof

Universität/Markt

Juridicum

Bad Godesberg, Rheinallee

Plittersdorfer Str.

Wurzerstr.

Hochkreuz

Max-Löbner-Str.

Landesbehördenhaus

Ollenhauerstr.

Heussallee

Museum König

Auswärtiges Amt

16

Liniennetzplan Schienenverkehr der Kölner Verkehrs-Betriebe AG und der Köln-Bonner Eisenbahnen AG

Stand 9.11.1986

Zeichenerklärung:

= Schienenverkehr

S = S-Bahn der DB

Zubringer Stadtmitte – Flughafen und zurück mit Sondertarif

P·R = Parken und Reisen

Novotel und Freiburger Mineral-Thermalbad

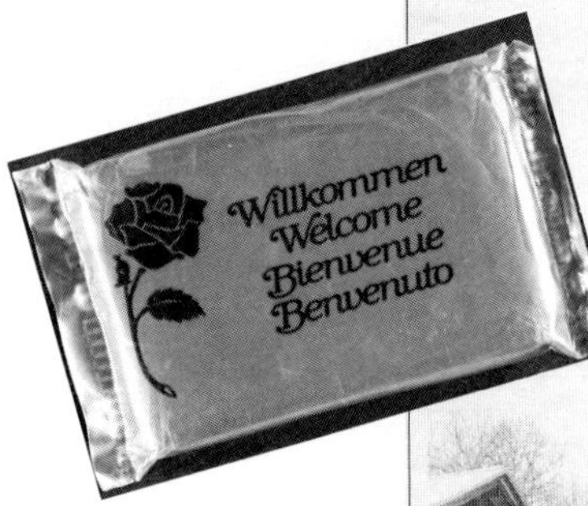

Den Streß wegbaden

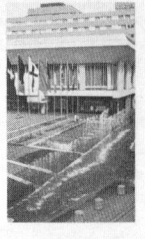

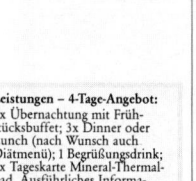

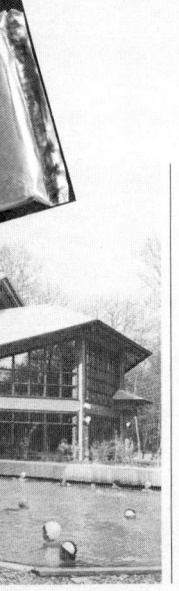

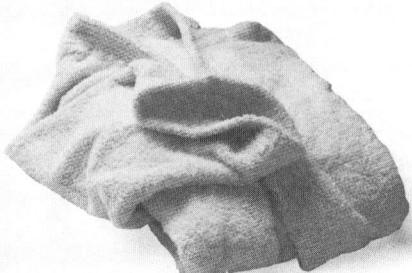

Ihr Freiburger Novotel liegt direkt in der Altstadt neben dem Stadtpark und der Fußgängerzone. Gemeinsam mit dem Freiburger Eugen-Keidel-Mineral-Thermalbad bieten wir ein vier- oder siebentägiges „Programm gegen den Streß" an. Warme Quellen gegen den kalten Alltag. Lassen Sie das Auto daheim oder in der Hotelgarage. Wenige Schritte vom Hotel wartet der Bus, der Sie direkt zum Thermalbad und natürlich zurück bringt. Streßfrei. Lassen Sie einfach alles an sich abperlen wie warmes Wasser.

Leistungen – 4-Tage-Angebot:
3x Übernachtung mit Frühstücksbuffet; 3x Dinner oder Lunch (nach Wunsch auch Diätmenü); 1 Begrüßungsdrink; 2x Tageskarte Mineral-Thermalbad. Ausführliches Informationsmaterial zu Ihrem Kurangebot. Prospektmappe Freiburg.

Preise pro Person:
Einzelzimmer
349,– DM **Code 1039**
Doppelzimmer
295,– DM **Code 1040**

Leistungen – 7-Tage-Angebot:
6x Übernachtung mit Frühstücksbuffet; 6x Dinner oder Lunch (nach Wunsch auch Diätmenü); 1 Begrüßungsdrink; 3x Tageskarte Mineral-Thermalbad. Ausführliches Informationsmaterial zu Ihrem Kurangebot. Prospektmappe Freiburg.

Preise pro Person:
Einzelzimmer
655,– DM **Code 1041**
Doppelzimmer
547,– DM **Code 1042**

Möglichkeiten der Tageskarte Mineral-Thermalbad Freiburg:
1. *Bewegungsbad*
2. *Solarium (30 Min.)*
3. *Med. Fußpflege*
4. *Römisch-Irisches Dampfbad*
5. *Sportmassage*
6. *Wannenbad mit CO_2-Quellwasser*
7. *Wannenbad mit Ruhe*
8. *Sprudelwanne (Hydroxeur)*
9. *Wannenbad mit Zusätzen (Fichtennadel, Heublume, Baldrianextrakt, Moorbad)*

Termine:
Ganzjährig, täglich.

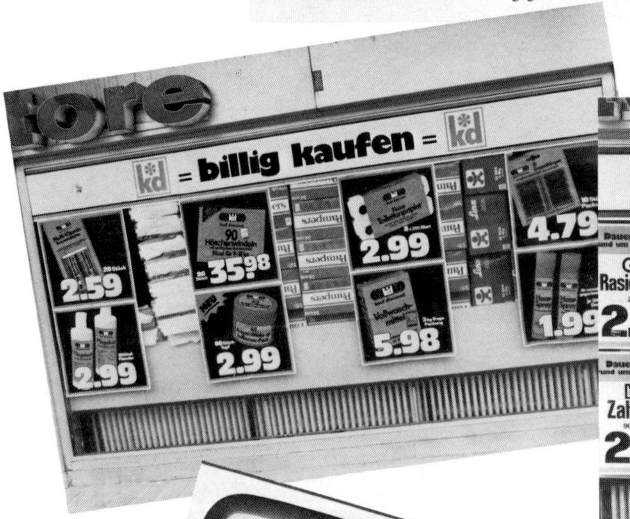

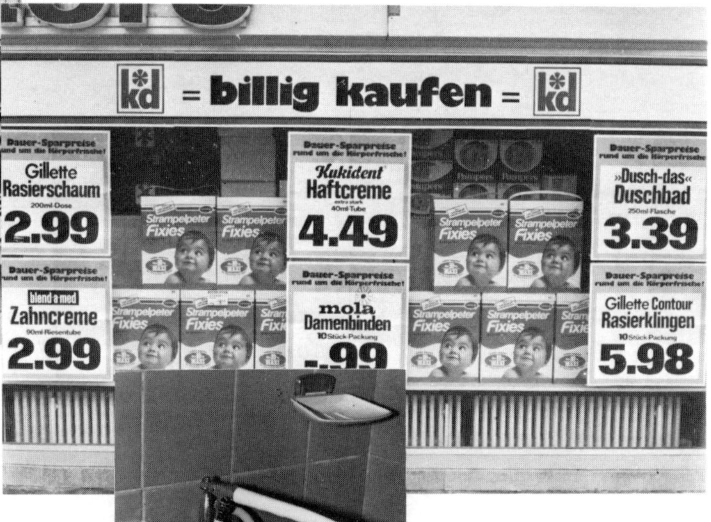

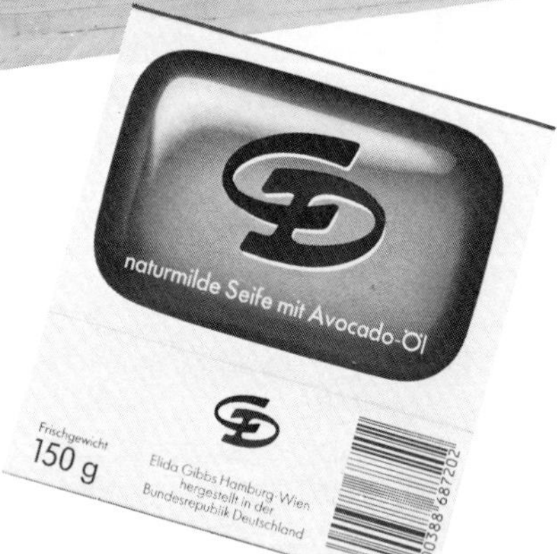

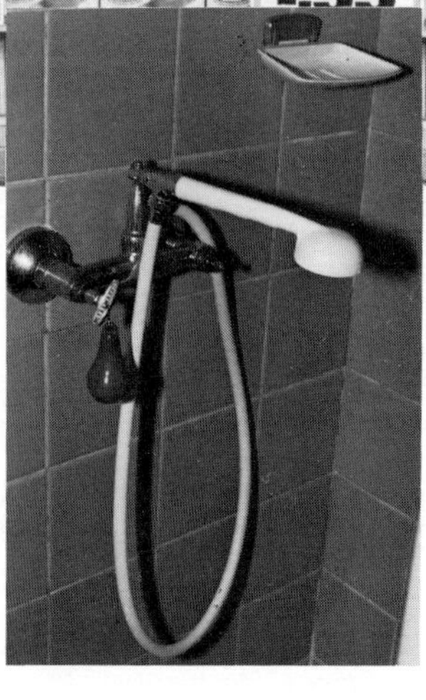

Hotel – Bad oder Dusche?

Nächstes WC
Ebertplatz-Innenhof
Öffnungszeiten: ganzjährig
täglich
von 7.00 - 22.00 Uhr

1

Usual variations, with realia and with drawing of imaginary hotel, showing stories in cutaway and floor plan from bird's-eye view. Teach colors at will; see "Strategie" section.

FRAU MIXNITZ	Guten Tag. Bitte schön?
HERR STREBEL	Ein Einzelzimmer mit Dusche, bitte.
FRAU MIXNITZ	Ja, gern. Und für wie lange?
HERR STREBEL	Für zwei Nächte, bitte . . .

2

FRAU PENNE	Abend, die Herrschaften.
FRAU ALBRECHT	Guten Abend. Wir brauchen ein Doppelzimmer, bitte.
FRAU PENNE	Gern. Und soll das mit Bad oder Dusche sein?
FRAU ALBRECHT	Mit Dusche, bitte.
	. . .
FRAU PENNE	So. Bitte schön. Das macht DM 64,-. . . . Und hier ist Ihr Schlüssel.

3

Avoid discussing the dative and accusative cases. Teach "im-X-ten Stock" as a lexical pattern. Correct der/den error only indirectly; the structure will be presented formally very soon.

FRAU GRATWOHL	Also, das Bad finden Sie im zweiten Stock rechts. Das kostet 5 Franken extra.
HERR DAETWYLER	OK. Und wo ist unser Zimmer, bitte?
FRAU GRATWOHL	Im ersten Stock links. . . . Moment mal, Sie haben noch keinen Schlüssel für das Zimmer.
HERR DAETWYLER	Und für das Bad? Brauchen wir einen Schlüssel?
FRAU GRATWOHL	Ja. Den Schlüssel gebe ich Ihnen gleich. Seife und Handtücher bekommen Sie hier unten.

4

ANGELA SPROUL	Und wo kann ich duschen?
FRÄULEIN REISER	Die Dusche ist im gleichen Stock, links um die Ecke. Wissen Sie, wie das funktioniert?
ANGELA SPROUL	Was meinen Sie genau? Heiß und kalt und so weiter? "Heiß" ist "H" und "kalt" ist "K," ja?
FRÄULEIN REISER	Nein. Nicht alle Gäste im Hotel verstehen Deutsch so gut wie Sie. Es ist ganz einfach. Heiß ist links und rot, und kalt ist rechts und blau. Vergessen Sie nicht: rot ist heiß, blau ist kalt.
ANGELA SPROUL	Also: rot – heiß, blau – kalt. Vielen Dank!

5

FRAU GIRSBERGER	. . . Gehen Sie also eine Treppe hoch, und dann links.
FRAU TIEMENS	Das ist Nummer 28?
FRAU GIRSBERGER	Ja, 28. Und Handtücher finden Sie im Zimmer oben.
FRAU TIEMENS	Und Seife auch?
FRAU GIRSBERGER	Ja, das auch.
	. . .
FRAU TIEMENS (am Telefon)	Ja, hier ist Zimmer 28. Bitte, ich habe keine Handtücher. Ich möchte doch baden.
FRAU GIRSBERGER	Ach, das tut mir aber leid. Ich bringe sie sofort hoch. Brauchen Sie auch Seife?
FRAU TIEMENS	Das kann sein. . . . Nein, Seife haben wir schon. . . . Moment. Mein Mann sagt, wir brauchen auch Toilettenpapier.

57

STRUKTUR 2

Point out major contrasts to English: German statements are based on the verb-second principle, English statements on subject-verb-object sequence. The subject in a German statement often comes after the verb; seldom does that happen

A.A. §§1–3

in English. Consequently, some students will assume that a noun or pronoun appearing after a verb in a German statement must be an object; when they learn the accusative case in the next chapter, they may conscientiously put such

A.A. §8

subjects in the accusative, while poorer students, who may have no command of case, will use the nominative.

Contextual exercises:
1) introduce and ask about members of real or imaginary families – students bring photos; 2) identify possessions (use the "Bildwörterbuch" resources). Encourage some plural possessives by having the speaker address more than one person at a time. This is a good time to review noun plurals.

Verbs §§22,24

Songs: *Muß i denn; Ich bin ein Musikant . . . Ich kann spielen;* exercises: discuss a transit map with several possible routes (*Sie können umsteigen,* etc.); "*Und wo kann ich [essen,* etc.]?" "*Gehen Sie zum . . .*"; describe a child's current development ("*Kann Ihre Schwester schon sprechen?*") or prescribe behavior ("*Kinder/Wir/Sie sollen . . .*"). This is a good chance to reinforce *nicht.*

Reinforce location of infinitive by modeling and indirect correction; avoid above all a discussion of inner field, verb complement, etc. Watch for and correct tendency to double-conjugate (**"Ich muß gehe.")

1. Subjects: actors in the sentence – "doers"

subject   subject
Ich suche das Krankenhaus.   **Das** ist nicht sehr weit.

            subject   subject
Wann kommt **der Bus**?   **Die Busse** fahren alle 20 Minuten.

            subject
Dann finden **Sie** den Hauptbahnhof.

2. Endings of <u>d-</u> "the" for <u>subjects</u>: they sound like the pronouns.

		ENDING	PRONOUN
masculine:	Wann kommt d<u>er</u> Bus?	**-er**	**er**
feminine:	Wo ist d<u>ie</u> Damentoilette?	**-ie**	**sie**
neuter:	D<u>as</u> Kotelett schmeckt fantastisch.	**-as**	**es**
plural:	D<u>ie</u> Brötchen kosten zwei Mark.	**-ie**	**sie**

3. Subject endings: *ein, kein, mein, unser, Ihr.*

		ENDING
masculine:	Das ist mein __ Sohn.	-
(*der* nouns)	Hier ist Ihr __ Schlüssel.	-
feminine:	Wieviel kostet ein<u>e</u> Karte?	**-e**
(*die* nouns)	Das ist mein<u>e</u> Frau.	**-e**
neuter:	Ist das Ihr __ Gepäck?	-
(*das* nouns)	Nein, das ist nicht mein __ Gepäck.	-
	Wieviel kostet ein __ Doppelzimmer?	-
plural:	Das sind mein<u>e</u> zwei Töchter.	**-e**
(all nouns)		

4. Two more modal verbs: *können, sollen*

Können expresses ability. **Sollen** expresses obligation.

- **forms:** like those of **müssen**

		SINGULAR	PLURAL
können	1	ich **kann**	wir können
	2	Sie können	Sie können
	3	er/sie/es **kann**	sie können
sollen	1	ich **soll**	wir sollen
	2	Sie sollen	Sie sollen
	3	er/sie/es **soll**	sie sollen

- **word order:** the <u>infinitive</u> completes the idea

                 infinitive
Wo **kann** ich <u>duschen</u>?

                        infinitive
Soll das mit Bad oder Dusche <u>sein</u> ?

SITUATIONEN 2 Hotel – Bad oder Dusche

Stage 1

	A	B
1	Says the shower is on the second floor. Price is S10,-.	Asks how much the shower is. Agrees on price; asks where the room key is.
	Hands over the key for the room.	Wants to shower right away. Asks about key.
	Key is not necessary. Hands them over gladly; reminds B that breakfast room is on the same floor. Breakfast starts at 6:00.	Thanks; asks for soap and towels. Asks when breakfast is.
2	Would like a double for her parents and a single for self.	Gives information about room rates, bath and shower, breakfast.
	Parents have to have a bath; wants a shower for self.	There's a double with a bath, but no single with a shower – only a single without a shower.
	Expresses disappointment, but will take the single anyway.	Is delighted, gives room prices – Fr 90,- for the double, 50 for the single.
	Says they want the rooms for two nights.	Is even more delighted, tallies the bill.

Be thankful if the student produces "Das brauchen Sie nicht," or even *Sie brauchen kein Schlüssel; reward that, rather than directly correcting the error in the accusative.

"Wants a shower for self" – "Ich brauche/möchte . . ."

	A	B	C
3	(Looking for hotel room.)	(Hotel guest; already has room.)	(Works at hotel desk.)
	Special desire: wants to inspect room.	Wants to shower.	Offers A key for room 23; offers B key to shower.
	Asks how much breakfast costs for children.	Asks how much shower costs.	Breakfast for kids: no charge; shower: Fr 2,00 for 10 min.
	Thanks C.	Thanks C with different phrase.	Turns to another person waiting for help.

Stage 2

1

You know that, when you stay in a small hotel, it will be appreciated if you eat in the hotel's own restaurant, if it has one. But you're not very hungry now, though you may be later.

a) Find out if the restaurant has *Imbiß*-type items.
b) Find out how late it's open.

2

The shower didn't work. Report that fact to the management.

a) Greet politely, though with dampened enthusiasm.
b) Report the malfunction.
c) Describe how to operate the shower when it's working, so that the clerk can't accuse you of ignorance.
d) You'd still like to shower/bathe. Does the clerk think all the showers aren't working?

Encourage the use of days of the week, phrases like "heute abend," and fractional time, especially in the front field.

Versuchen Sie doch

(You don't have much past tense yet (just *war* = was). But still, you may need to talk about things that have happened (or failed to happen!). So go right ahead and use the present tense – right now it's better than nothing, and in the heat of vivid recollection people indeed do that in both English and German.)

Tell how you got lost on your way from the train station to the hotel – what you or others were doing, looking for, saying, etc. ("So then I ask . . . , and she says . . .").

59

Chapter 6

GELDWECHSEL/ KIOSK

USA					
Devisenkurse					42-013/19 186
1,– US$ = DM 2,40			DM 1,– = 0,42 US$		
US$	DM	US$	DM	DM	US$
0,05	0,12	30,–	72,–	0,10	0,04
0,10	0,24	40,–	96,–	0,20	0,08
0,15	0,36	45,–	108,–	0,50	0,21
0,25	0,60	80,–	192,–	1,–	0,42
0,50	1,20	95,–	228,–	2,–	0,83
1,–	2,40	120,–	288,–	5,–	2,08
1,50	3,60	150,–	360,–	10,–	4,17
2,–	4,80	180,–	432,–	20,–	8,33
2,50	6,–	200,–	480,–	50,–	20,84
3,–	7,20	230,–	552,–	100,–	41,67
4,–	9,60	400,–	960,–	150,–	62,51
5,–	12,–	450,–	1.080,–	200,–	83,34
7,50	18,–	800,–	1.920,–	250,–	104,18
10,–	24,–	1.000,–	2.400,–	300,–	125,01
20,–	48,–	5.000,–	12.000,–	400,–	166,68

Bitte berücksichtigen Sie, daß sich die Kurse kurzfristig ändern können.

Deutsche Bank ☑

Please remember that exchange rates can change quite suddenly. (For the German, look at the rate card above.)

Song: *"Herbstlied"* (*"Zeit der Reife"*) by Karl (not *the* Karl) Marx. Poem: *"Herbstlied"* by Rilke.

If your local newspaper reports exchange rates, or if foreign currency is exchanged at the airport or a main bank, some students may have noticed the rates. You might explain that rates will be given in reverse (reciprocal) fashion. That is, something like ".50" ($.50 buys DM 1,-), rather than "2.00" ($1 buys DM 2,-). Given time and interest, discuss *Ankauf/Verkauf* difference, *Spesen,* and other things the traveler should know to handle money wisely. See *"Strategie"* section for details.

FUNKTIONEN – KONTEXTE – STRUKTUREN

Looking ahead

You'll be exchanging money, making small purchases, counting change, dealing with minor problems, and improving your small talk.

You will be using:

- demonstrative pronouns to point out things and people (Do you mean that one over there? Yes — *her,* not *him.*)
- direct objects — what the subject directly acts on (Do I need my *passport?* Don't forget the *date.*)
- the modal verb *wollen* — to want to
- negations (no, not, not any, none, no more)

Geldwechsel

Since exchange rates can fluctuate greatly, the rate given here may not be current. You **1** might mention that to the class, and point out the overall downward trend over the dollar, from about 4:1 (DM: US$) in the sixties to even fewer than 2:1 in the eighties. Not **2** inappropriate would be a brief comment that America's weakness in foreign languages contributed to the decline. **3**

Do fast-paced counting exercises to reinforce numbers. 1) Set a fictional exchange rate that is relatively simple (e.g., 3.00 or 2.50); student A declares a rather large but relatively even sum of currency to exchange (e.g., 150); student **4** B announces the conversion; elaboration: have the "clerk" set the rate. 2) Student A names a rather large odd sum (e.g., DM 123,45); student B either counts out the sum in appropriate currency units (50, 100, 120, 122, 123, 123 + 45), or else tenders the next largest bill that could be used to pay such a sum, after which A returns and counts the change. Maybe covertly instruct one partner to make a counting error. If **5** necessary, remind students that a busy cashier's line is no place to have to fumble for numbers.

Das Datum: Explain American vs. European date conventions. Encourage the ability to write the full date in numerals and to say the month. Don't get bogged down in discussions of the accusative and dative cases in time phrases. But by all means feel free to model such phrases, especially *"Heute ist der ___ e Oktober,"* etc.

HERR SCHORER	Geldwechsel? Ja, Schalter eins, bitte.
TOM GREEN	Danke schön. Brauche ich meinen Paß?
HERR SCHORER	Na, vielleicht. Den haben Sie mit, ja?
TOM GREEN	Leider nicht. Der ist im Hotel.

| ALLEN KRILL | 1,78. Ist das der Kurs für Reiseschecks? |
| FRÄULEIN HOSTETLER | Nein, für bar. . . . |

VINCE JACOBS	Ich möchte 350 Dollar wechseln, bitte.
HERR JACOBI	350 Dollar in D-Mark. Moment mal. . . . Also 722,85. Möchten Sie einen 500 Mark Schein, oder wollen Sie es klein haben?
VINCE JACOBS	Geben Sie mir bitte fünf Hundert-Mark-Scheine und dann vier Fünfziger.
HERR JACOBI	Also, 1, 2, 3, 4, 500 Mark, 550, 600, 650, 700 Mark . . . zehn, zwanzig . . . zwei fünfundachtzig. Und da die Quittung. Bitte schön.

FRAU BRAUNER	Also, 5 Reiseschecks, 100 kanadische Dollar, macht DM 182,-. Unten links müssen Sie noch unterschreiben, und bitte schreiben Sie das Datum oben rechts.
BILL BRADLEY	Brauchen Sie auch meinen Paß? Der ist im Hotel.
FRAU BRAUNER	Nein, den brauche ich nicht. Die Unterschrift ist genug. Aber Sie sollen bitte das Datum nicht vergessen.
BILL BRADLEY	Ist gut. Unten links unterschreiben, Datum oben rechts.

FRÄULEIN DRECHSLER	Bitte 20 Mark klein.
HERR KAISER	Ja, gern. Möchten Sie einen 10-Mark Schein und zwei 5-Mark Stücke?
FRÄULEIN DRECHSLER	Nein. Geben Sie mir bitte vier 5-Mark-Stücke. Die sind für den Fahrkartenautomat.
HERR KAISER	Also, bitte schön. 5, 10, 15, 20.

bfrs	hfl	£	US-$	FF		Kurs	Kurswert % Ab-wicklungsgeb.	DM-Betrag
			TC 200			218	436 - 5	431 -

ANKAUF

Datum -6. März 1986   E 634566 ✳

REISEGELD FÜR ALLE WELT

DEUTSCHE VERKEHRS-KREDIT-BANK
AKTIENGESELLSCHAFT
Wechselstube Aachen Hbf

STRUKTUR 1

Pronouns §4

1. Demonstrative pronouns

After a noun has been used in conversation, you can refer to it

1) Students point to people in class. One student says, or two students converse: *Das ist* (name). *Der ist _____, Die studiert _____.* At the end, recall the conversation and summarize it. 2) Student A points to a person or common object and says, *"Das ist mein(e) X."* Student B offers a comment, like *"Oh, die ist schön."*

To illustrate how the connotation can easily include contempt or dismissal: Student A (pointing to something, with surprise): *Das ist Ihr X?* Student B: *Der? Nein. Der ist zu klein,* etc.

- **simply by repeating it**

If you do this too much, you'll sound childish. ("See the dog? The dog is big. The dog is nice.")

- **by using *er* (for *der*-nouns), *sie* (for *sie*-nouns), or *es* (for *das*-nouns)**
- **by using demonstrative pronouns: *der, die, das***

Use them to refer with <u>emphasis</u> to someone or something or to lend an <u>informal</u> tone to your German.

    <u>emphatic:</u> Hansjörg? **Der** ist hier. (But his friend Theodor isn't.)
            Schweizer Brot? **Das** schmeckt gut! (But *this* bread is lousy.)

    <u>informal:</u> Ihr Ticket? Oh, **das** habe ich hier. Tut mir leid.
           Das ist meine Schwester. **Die** ist 18.

A. A. §§4,8

2. Direct objects: what the subject acts on

verb	subject		dir. obj.		subject	verb	dir. obj.

Braucht Ihr Mann auch **Seife?**   Ich bringe **sie** sofort.

A. A. §4

3. Direct object endings   `d- the`

See note in Instructor's Guide.

	SUBJECT	OBJECT	ENDING
der-nouns (masculine)	Sie sehen	de<u>n</u> Hauptbahnhof.	**-en**
die-nouns (feminine)	Wir möchten	di<u>e</u> Tagesspezialität.	**-ie**
das-nouns (neuter)	Ich suche	da<u>s</u> Krankenhaus.	**-s**
all plurals	Ich möchte	di<u>e</u> Salzkartoffeln.	**-ie**

Pronouns §§9,10

4. Direct object endings   `ein, kein, mein, Ihr`

Similar to previous exercise: Hotel (blackboard: list of nouns in context) – *"Ich habe kein X." "Ich bringe ein X." "Bringen Sie Ihr X." "Ich bringe mein X."*

		ENDING
masculine	Brauchen Sie Ihre<u>n</u> Schlüssel?	**-en**
feminine	Ich hole mein<u>e</u> Familie.	**-e**
neuter	Wir brauchen ein Doppelzimmer.	[none]
plural	Ich habe kein<u>e</u> Handtücher.	**-e**

Verbs §25

5. The modal *wollen* expresses "want (to)."

Exercise: *"Wollen Sie X [noun]?" "Nein, ich brauche kein X."* Expansion: have a third student echo: *"Y braucht/will kein X."*

- **forms**

		SINGULAR	PLURAL
	1	ich **will**	wir wollen
	2	Sie wollen	Sie wollen
	3	er/sie/es **will**	sie wollen

- **word order:** An infinitive completes the action.

    50 Mark? Wollen Sie es klein **haben?**

SITUATIONEN 1 Geldwechsel

Stage 1

Maybe introduce complications that check solidity of Chapter 6 knowledge and also review earlier material (e.g., covertly tell "clerk" to make a counting error, or instruct a third student to join the conversation – needs quick information, in a hurry to conduct own exchange, just wants to ask friendly questions; third student could play role of American who speaks no German and wants the German-speaking compatriot to translate).

A	B
1 Wants to change dollars to öS.	Asks for identification.
Shows passport.	Asks A to sign form.
Asks if B needs the date.	No date is needed – just the signature.
Asks exchange rate for DM.	Says rate is 5.22.
Says: will be right back with DM, which are in hotel room.	Thanks; says good-bye.
2 It's evening; wants to cash traveler's checks for trip.	Says they're closed.
Says: just has to cash checks.	Is sorry, but it's past six.
Says: has only $50; train is leaving soon.	Relents, gives DM 95. Counts out bills (4 × 20, 1 × 10) and a 5-DM coin.
Asks for five 1-DM coins for change.	Counts them out – briskly.
Thanks effusively, then asks for receipt.	Gives receipt; says farewell.
Says farewell.	

A	B	C
3 Is going to Innsbruck for the weekend; asks to change DM 165 to öS.	Wants to add DM 45.	Wants to know whether DM 165 or 210.
Says 165 is enough to pay for the room.	Says they'll need more for room and meals; asks C's advice.	Asks where they're staying.
Hotel Goldener Adler.	Says Restaurant "Goethe-Stube."	Advises DM 210 – and more.
Agrees, adds DM 90.	Asks for öS 100 in change.	Rate is 5,25; counts out öS for DM 300, including eight 10-öS coins and four 5-öS coins.
Thanks; says good-bye.	Thanks; says good-bye.	Thanks; says good-bye.

(A, B, and C say thanks and good-bye, each in a different way – to avoid sounding like parrots or machines.)

Stage 2

1

You are planning a concert weekend in Salzburg. Go to the *Geldwechsel* counter at the Dresdener Bank.

a) Ask for DM 200 in öS.
b) Get the largest bills you can.
c) Remember that you will need some change for public transportation when you arrive.

2

You enter the *Kreissparkasse*, or savings & loan.

a) Ask what today's exchange rate is for US$ into DM.
b) Ask to change enough US$ to yield DM 125.
c) Ask whether you will have to sign anything, and if so, where.

Versuchen Sie doch

Your family is about to visit you from Albany. You want to show your brothers what Austrian currency looks like. a) Ask for a variety of bills for the $50 traveler's check you are exchanging. b) Tell the bank official you want a variety of small coins for each of your younger brothers. c) Tell the official you don't need the receipt just handed you. Be polite.

Currency

Don't bother to deal with the rare currency denominations, like the West German 1/4 and 1/2 Pfennig coins. Explain only if requested the two plurals of *Stück.*

Encourage use of facsimile currency; do some transaction exercises (money-changing, purchases, cost estimates, change-counting).

You should be familiar with the appearance and value of the most commonly used denominations of coins (*das Stück, -e, die Münze, -n*) and bills (*der Schein, -e*) for the currency of the four German-speaking countries. Of course, currency units and conversion values vary from country to country, but all the currencies are decimal. And unlike U.S. paper money, the banknotes as well as the coins of each country are of different sizes.

You will remember from Chapter 1 that Austria's unit of currency is the *Schilling* (öS), which consists of 100 *Groschen.* In common use are coins for 5, 10, and 50 *Groschen,* and bills for 20, 50, 100, 500 and 1000 *Schilling.* Currently the value of the Schilling varies between 7¢ and 9¢.

The East German unit of currency is the *Mark* (M), consisting of 100 *Pfennig.* You will find coins for 1, 5, 10, 20, and 50 *Pfennig,* as well as for 1, 2, 5, 10, and 20 *Mark,* and bills for 5, 10, 20, 50, and 100 *Mark.* Currently the official value of the East German *Mark* is about 50¢. The black market rate in East Germany is about 5 East German marks to 1 West German mark, and West German banks exchange at a rate of about 4 East to 1 West. Currency smuggling is treated severely by the authorities.

In each Swiss *Franken* (SFr) there are 100 *Rappen.* There are 1, 2, 5-, 10-, 20-, and 50-*Rappen* coins, coins for 1, 2, and 5 *Franken,* and colorful bank notes in denominations of 10, 20, 50, 100, 500 and 1000 *Franken.* Each Swiss *Franken* is worth about 60¢.

The West German *Deutsche Mark,* or *Mark* (DM), consists of 100 *Pfennig.* There are coins for 1, 2, 5, 10, and 50 *Pfennig* as well as for 1, 2, and 5 *Mark.* Common bills are issued in denominations of 10, 20, 50, 100, 500 and 1000 *Mark.* Each *Mark* you buy will cost about 50¢.

You can change money at a number of places, paying various rates of exchange. Transportation hubs like train stations and airports offer exchange services (*die Wechselstube, -n*) with generous hours of operation. If you travel by car, there are numerous opportunities to exchange currency near border crossings. In cities and towns all banks offer exchange services. In general, banks offer the best exchange rates; smaller (but perhaps more convenient) places charge more.

Wherever you change money you will find a *Kurstafel,* a signboard that lists the day's exchange rates. If you are staying in one place for a long time, you will soon find out which place offers you the best rate – although for smaller amounts the differences are minimal. The charts list two columns of figures. If you want to buy local currency, consult the *Ankauf* ("buy") column opposite the currency you have; if your stay is ending and you want to change your local money into another currency, you will find the appropriate rate under *Verkauf* ("sell"). But try to avoid double-changing of this sort. Not only does the bank charge a fee (*Spesen*) for each transaction; as a commercial enterprise it buys money at a lower rate than it sells it. Because East Germany wants "hard" Western currency to improve its balance of payments, you will be required to change 25 marks (*der Pflichtumtausch*) for each day of your stay in that country. The 25 marks may well be covered by your hotel reservations or other pre-arranged travel costs.

Here are some more useful terms when money is changed:

der **Reisescheck (-s)**	traveler's check
die **Note**/die **Banknote (-n)**	bill
das **Bargeld**	cash
in bar	in cash
wechseln	to change money

Der *Kiosk:* the European newsstand – and more

At a *Kiosk* you find not only magazines and newspapers, but also street maps, postcards, chocolate bars, cough drops, aspirin – and a few unexpected items for the traveler such as stamps, transit tickets, toilet paper, fruit, and miniature bottles of liquor. Just ask for what you need; if it is unavailable at the *Kiosk*, the person behind the counter will surely know where you can find it.

More about "I'd like . . . "

In Chapter 2 you learned that when you are ordering food or negotiating a purchase, you should be sure to say *"Ich möchte . . . "* rather than *"Ich will . . . "* or *"Ich habe . . . "*.

Ich möchte is polite and says "I'd like . . . ". Don't use *wollen* – it doesn't mean "will"!

Ich will . . . haben is too demanding. It does not mean "I'll have . . . " It would mean "I want X and I don't mean maybe!"

IM WAGEN DIESES ZUGES **BUFFET-BAR**   NELLA VETTURA DI QUESTO TRENO **BUFFET-BAR**

MENU ZUM FESTPREIS

FRÜHSTÜCK	DM	Ö Sch.
Kaffee mit Milch o. Tee Butter · Marmelade · Keks	4,10	31,–
MITTAGESSEN oder ABENDESSEN		
Pasta asciutta Fleisch oder Geflügel Beilage · Käse · Obst (ohne Getränke)	17,50	130,–

GERICHTE A LA CARTE SIND NICHT ZU BEKOMMEN —

CAFETERIA UND GETRÄNKE

Kaffee	1,00	6,50
Kaffee mit Milch oder Tee oder Schokolade	1,50	10,–
Sandwich »einfach«	1,70	12.50
Sandwich »feinsmecker«	2.30	15.–
Banane	1.70	12.50
Engl. Kuchen	1.50	13.–
Keks	1.80	13.–
Schokolade	1.50	10.–
Drops · Kaugummi	0.70	5.–
Wein 1/4	2.20	18.–
Wein 36 cl.	5.20	45.–
Italienische Bier 1/3 »flasche«	2.20	18.–
Mineralwasser 1/2	1.20	9,–
Italienische Bier 1/3 »dose«	2.50	22.–
Erfrischungstrunk »flasche«	1.80	14.–
Erfrischungstrunk »dose«	2.20	17,–
Fruchtsäfte	1.80	14.–
Aperitive	1.80	14.–
Züsatzbecher	0.20	1.–
Einsatz	0.20	1.–

BEDIENUNG UND STEUERN INBEGRIFFEN

PASTI A PREZZO FISSO

PRIMA COLAZIONE	
Caffellatte o Tè Burro · Marmellata · Biscotti	L. 2.050
COLAZIONE o PRANZO	
Pasta asciutta · Carne o pollo Contorno · Formaggio · Frutta (bevande escluse)	L. 8.800

NON E' PREVISTO IL PASTO ALLA CARTA —

BEVANDE E CAFFETTERIA

	Lire
Caffè	450
Caffellatte · Tè	700
Cioccolato	700
Panino imbottito	850
Panino gastronomico	1.050
Banana	850
Pasticceria	800
Cioccolata	650
Biscotti	800
Caramelle · Chewing gum	350
Vino 1/4 con bicch.	1.100
Vino pregiato 36 cl.	2.300
Birra naz. 1/3 »bottiglia«	1.050
Acqua min. 1/2	600
Birra naz. 1/3 »lattina«	1.250
Bibite »bottiglia«	900
Bibite »lattina«	1.050
Succhi di frutta	900
Apertivi	900
Liquori nazionali	1.100
Cognac	1.700
Whisky	2.000
Bicchiere supplementare	50
Deposito vuoti	50

SERVIZIO E TASSE COMPRESI

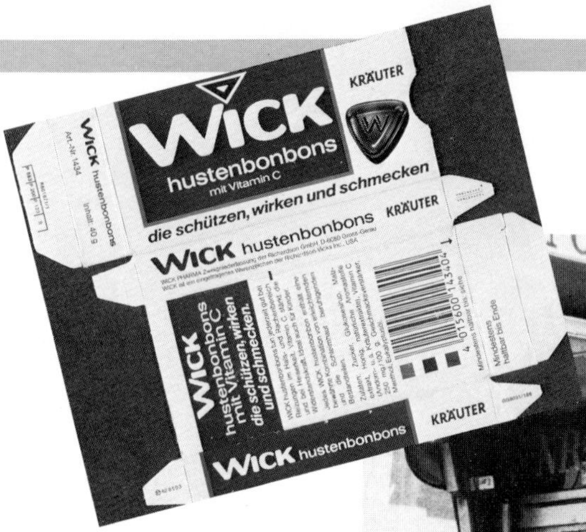
WICK
hustenbonbons
mit Vitamin C
KRÄUTER
die schützen, wirken und schmecken
WICK hustenbonbons
KRÄUTER
WICK
hustenbonbons
mit Vitamin C
die schützen, wirken
und schmecken.
KRÄUTER
WICK hustenbonbons

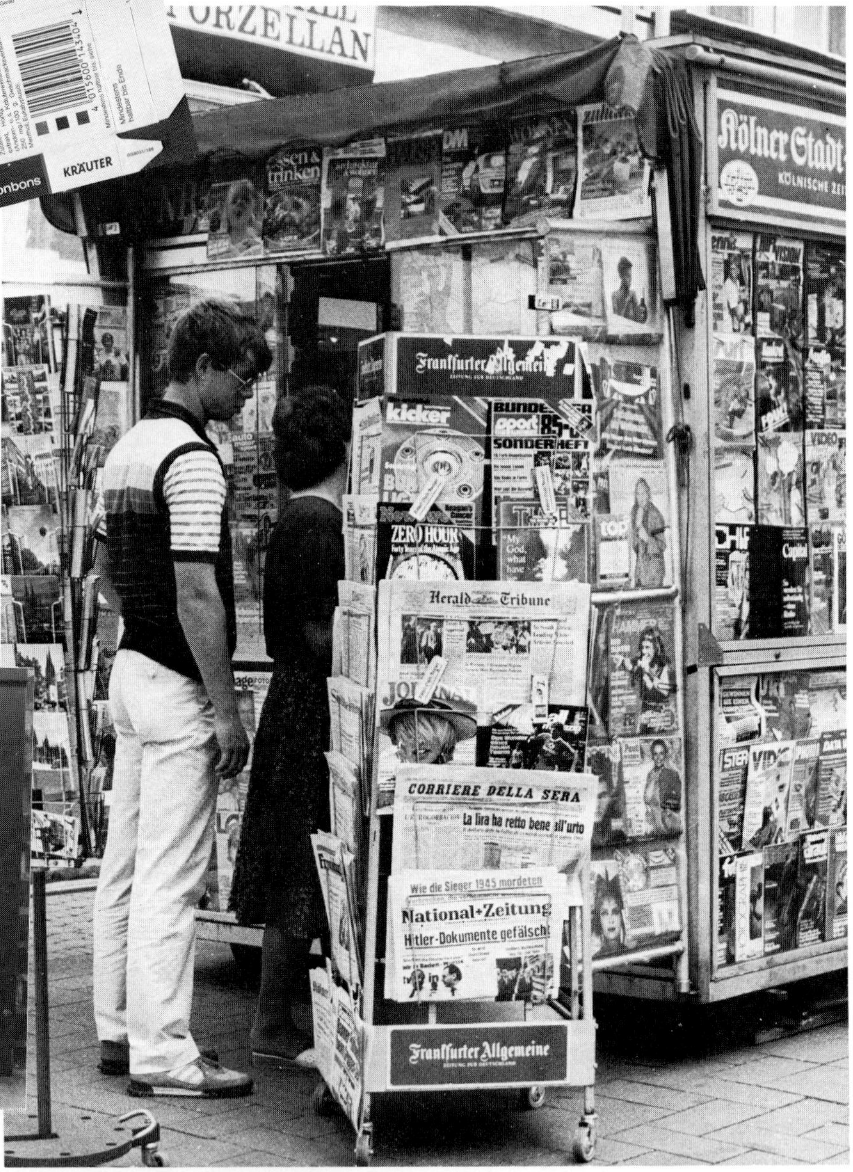
PORZELLAN
Kölner Stadt-
KÖLNISCHE ZEI
essen & trinken
Frankfurter Allgemeine
kicker
SONDERHEFT
ZERO HOUR
Herald Tribune
CORRIERE DELLA SERA
La lira ha retto bene all'urto
Wie die Sieger 1945 mordeten
National-Zeitung
Hitler-Dokumente gefälscht
Frankfurter Allgemeine

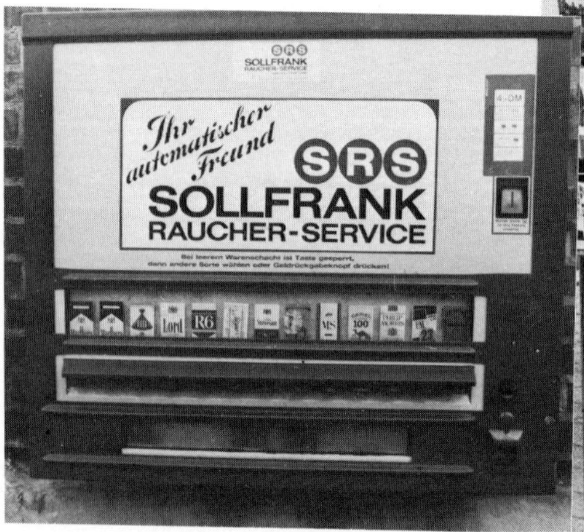
SRS
SOLLFRANK
RAUCHER-SERVICE
Ihr automatischer Freund
SRS
SOLLFRANK
RAUCHER-SERVICE

NEU: SOFT-TUBE
Colgate
Klinisch getestet
Zum Schutz vor Karies
Fluor+
Mineral
67,5 ml
NEU: SOFT-TUBE
Colgate
Klinisch getestet
Zum Schutz vor Karies
Fluor+
Mineral

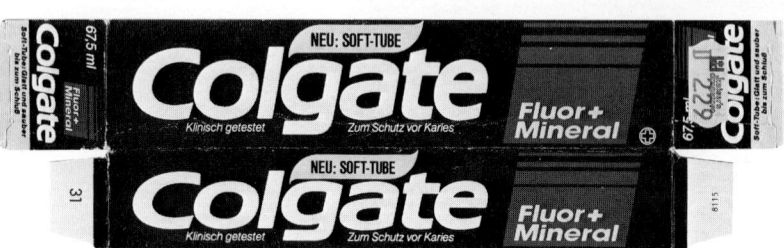

Kiosk

1

Rosinen = raisins.

Introduce productive levity by illustrating how German speakers might well pronounce American brand names. See realia for more (e.g., Colgaht-uh toothpaste); explain the transformation of Vick's to Wiks coughdrops at your own risk. Point out that German brand names have their own connotative system (Rama dairy products, Vizier cleaner [Middle Eastern potentate: *"nimmt den Schmutz ins Visier"*]). Try to promote some knowledge of brand names (*"Jakobs Kaffee," "Dr. Oetker"*) and "visual fluency" in recognition of packaging (Knorr soups, mustard and mayonnaise in tubes). Obviously, use of realia is vital. Ancillary points: reinforcement of metric system, familiarization with international vocabulary (e.g., names of chemicals in lists of ingredients). See ACTFL/ ETS *Provisional Proficiency Guidelines* for German (reading: intermediate-mid, culture: intermediate and advanced). Tests should be constructed accordingly.

In dialog 4: Have students translate the broken English back into German and identify the recurrent error patterns of Germans attempting English.

2

3

4

HERR EISLER	Bitte eine Tafel Schokolade, ein Päckchen Rosinen und . . .
FRAU GOTTWALD	Moment mal. Hier sind die Rosinen. Und dann die Schokolade – war das mit Nüssen?
HERR EISLER	Ja, bitte. Und haben Sie auch die *International Herald Tribune*?
FRAU GOTTWALD	Nein, die von heute haben wir nicht mehr. Oder wollen Sie die von gestern?

MARIANNE WOLZ	Ja, ich brauche eine Fahrkarte für die Straßenbahn. Der Automat nebenan funktioniert nicht.
HERR SARTORIUS	Ja, der ist immer kaputt – oder so scheint es. Also eine Karte – wollen Sie eine 24-Stundenkarte?
MARIANNE WOLZ	Ist das viel teurer?
HERR SARTORIUS	Eine Fahrkarte kostet 1,50, die 24-Stundenkarte 12 Mark. Die ist billiger, wenn Sie viel fahren.

HERR SCHÜRER	Sonst noch etwas für die Reise?
PROFESSOR LOCHER	Mm, Obst vielleicht. Ja, Äpfel.
HERR SCHÜRER	Ja, gern. Wie viele denn?
PROFESSOR LOCHER	Zwei, bitte, und eine Orange. Und ich sehe, Sie haben keine Bananen, oder?
HERR SCHÜRER	Ja, wir haben keine Bananen. Das heißt, wir haben heute keine Bananen. Gestern ja. Aber heute nicht. Tut mir leid.

TED ADORNO	Entschuldigung. Haben Sie die Zeitschrift *Time*?
FRAU KNÜSEL	Newspapers and journals from the States are left over there. Do you not see them?
TED ADORNO	Ja, wir können Deutsch sprechen. Ich verstehe Sie schon. Aber die *Time* ist nicht da.
FRAU KNÜSEL	Entschuldigung. Sie sprechen ja gut Deutsch. Die *Time* ist also nicht mehr da. *Newsweek* haben wir noch.
TED ADORNO	Naja, die nehme ich. Und auch eine Kölner-Zeitung.

Synopsis exercises: 1) (to contrast nominative and accusative): one- or two-person items: *"So. Da ist der X. Oh, Sie haben (Ich habe) schon einen X."* (Student C: interfere or confirm – *"Sie hat schon einen X."* 2) (to strengthen front-field

W.O. §3

management) student A: *Wir brauchen einen X.* Student B: *Den X bringe ich sofort. Brauchen Sie auch eine Y?* Encourage better students to help with indirect correction by serving as commentators: *Sie sagt, sie braucht einen X. Ja, aber haben Sie eine Y*, etc.

W.O. §20

Negation exercises: Shopping (*Reiseproviant, Kiosk*, etc.): *"Haben Sie (ein-) X?" "Nein, wir haben kein- X"* (don't forget plurals). Orientation: *"Gibt es hier eine X-Straße?" "Nein, hier gibt es keine X-straße."* Hotel: *"Haben Sie ein Einzelzimmer?" "Nein, wir haben kein Einzelzimmer; möchten Sie ein Doppelzimmer?/möchten Sie es mit Bad/Dusche?" "Nein, ich brauche kein Bad/keine Dusche."* (List on blackboard things in a hotel room.)

Exercises: *Was funktioniert nicht?; Soll ich zum X gehen? Nein, gehen Sie nicht zum X, gehen Sie zum Y.* Emphasize pattern emulation with attention to natural intonation; avoid analytical discussion of placement of *nicht*; don't introduce *"nicht ein"* as an emphatic form; if you wish, model but do not discuss the pattern *"Ein X haben Sie nicht"* as an alternate to *"Sie haben kein X."* In short, try to get *nicht* going toward where it belongs, and be pleased if the students on their own produce *kein* at all.

STRUKTUR 2

1. Direct objects: word order

subj. 2   direct object
Sie haben noch <u>keinen Schlüssel</u>.
Wir brauchen <u>ein Doppelzimmer</u>.

or for greater emphasis

direct object 2 subj.
<u>Das Bad</u> finden Sie im zweiten Stock.
<u>Den Schlüssel</u> bringe ich sofort.

2. *Kein* and *nicht*

GLAS-SAMMELSTELLE
Bitte an Sonn- und Feiertagen
sowie nachts 20.00 – 07.00 Uhr
<u>Kein</u> Glas in die Mulde werfen.

- ● **Kein** negates **nouns.** It comes **before** them.

  Sie haben **kein Messer**!
  Sie haben noch **keinen Schlüssel** für das Zimmer.
  Ich habe **keine Fahrkarte**.
  Wir haben heute **keine Bananen**.

- ● **Nicht** negates elements other than nouns, or the entire idea. It usually comes **late** in the sentence.

Der Automat funktioniert. Der Automat funktioniert **nicht**.
Ich weiß.   Ich weiß **nicht**.
Vergessen Sie das Datum. Vergessen Sie das Datum **nicht**.
Sie können hier aussteigen. Hier können Sie **nicht** aussteigen.
Die haben wir.   Die haben wir **nicht** mehr.
Den brauche ich.   Den brauche ich **nicht**.

English word order is not so flexible, because case signals are very weak. Infrequent, but not considered abnormal, is the placement of the direct object in a front field for contrastive emphasis: "The sofa we (indeed) bought – the table we didn't."

SITUATIONEN 2 Kiosk

Stage 1

By now some may be finding these exercises tedious; others may still find them difficult. Vary the fare and perhaps raise morale by reviewing similar tasks in earlier units, such as Chapter 1 (*Imbiß*) and Chapter 3 (*Reiseproviant*). There you might insert complications derived from Chapter 6 situations, or push for grammar presented in Chapter 6.

1

A	B
Would like two apples and a chocolate bar.	Asks what kind of chocolate – with raisins?
Wants milk chocolate.	Asks if A wants anything else.
Says B shouldn't forget the apples.	Asks what color – red or green.
Wants red apples.	Says price – DM 5,20.

2

A	B
Will be taking the streetcar twice, wants the appropriate ticket.	Says ticket machine is around the corner.
Says ticket machine is broken.	Is surprised. Asks if A would like anything else.
Wants a *Süddeutsche Zeitung* also.	Today's is sold out.
The ticket will be enough.	Thanks A. Ticket costs ÖS 8.
Thanks B; says good-bye.	Thanks A; says good-bye.

3

"Lots" – sample solution: *"Wir haben"* + list of combinations.

Suggest having students prepare "shopping lists," both to improve fluency in speaking and to review writing skills.

A	B	C
(traveler)	(traveler)	(Works in Kiosk.)
Wants an apple.	Wants one also.	There are no apples.
Is about to start a long trip from Frankfurt.	Trip will be to Locarno.	Suggests another fruit – has lots of oranges.
Doesn't like oranges.	Asks about nuts.	
Says nuts are more expensive.		Says raisins don't cost more. Lots of packages are available.
Asks price.	Wants two packages.	Price is DM 6 each.
Asks for one package.	Still wants two packages; says: would just as soon stay in Frankfurt.	Suggests two packages of raisins and an orange for DM 12.
Agrees; hands over DM 20.		Makes change; good-bye.
Says good-bye.	Thanks C; says good-bye.	

Stage 2

VSd: This task is intended to anticipate themes of later chapters and thus to suggest to students that they often have enough German to carry out more advanced functions, just as they are frequently encouraged to redo tasks from earlier chapters – presumably much more effectively. You

Versuchen Sie doch

might examine a few such items in detail, showing how the structures and vocabulary learned in the interim can be used most effectively.

1

You are in the airport *Kiosk*, about to return home to Cleveland. Buy appropriate souvenirs for

a) Mom, who loves Swiss chocolate;
b) Dad, who thinks he can read German and likes the *National Enquirer*;
c) Uncle Ned, who likes a snort or two before supper;
d) your brother, who has the biggest stamp collection in Cuyahoga County.

2

The *Kiosk* clerk would like to sell you

a) a newspaper (you don't know whether it's today's);
b) a street map, which the clerk compares favorably with the one put out by the chamber of commerce (you don't know if it's cheaper or not);
c) a *Time* magazine (you wonder whether they still have *Newsweek*).

You and some friends are planning a two-week tour of two other German-speaking countries. Enter a travel agency and ask about room, meal, and transportation prices in the various places you would like to visit. Remember that the agent will indicate expenses not in US$ or CAN$, but instead in the currencies of the country you are presently visiting, and that of the country you are considering visiting.

Chapter *7*
STADTRUNDFAHRT/ KONDITOREI

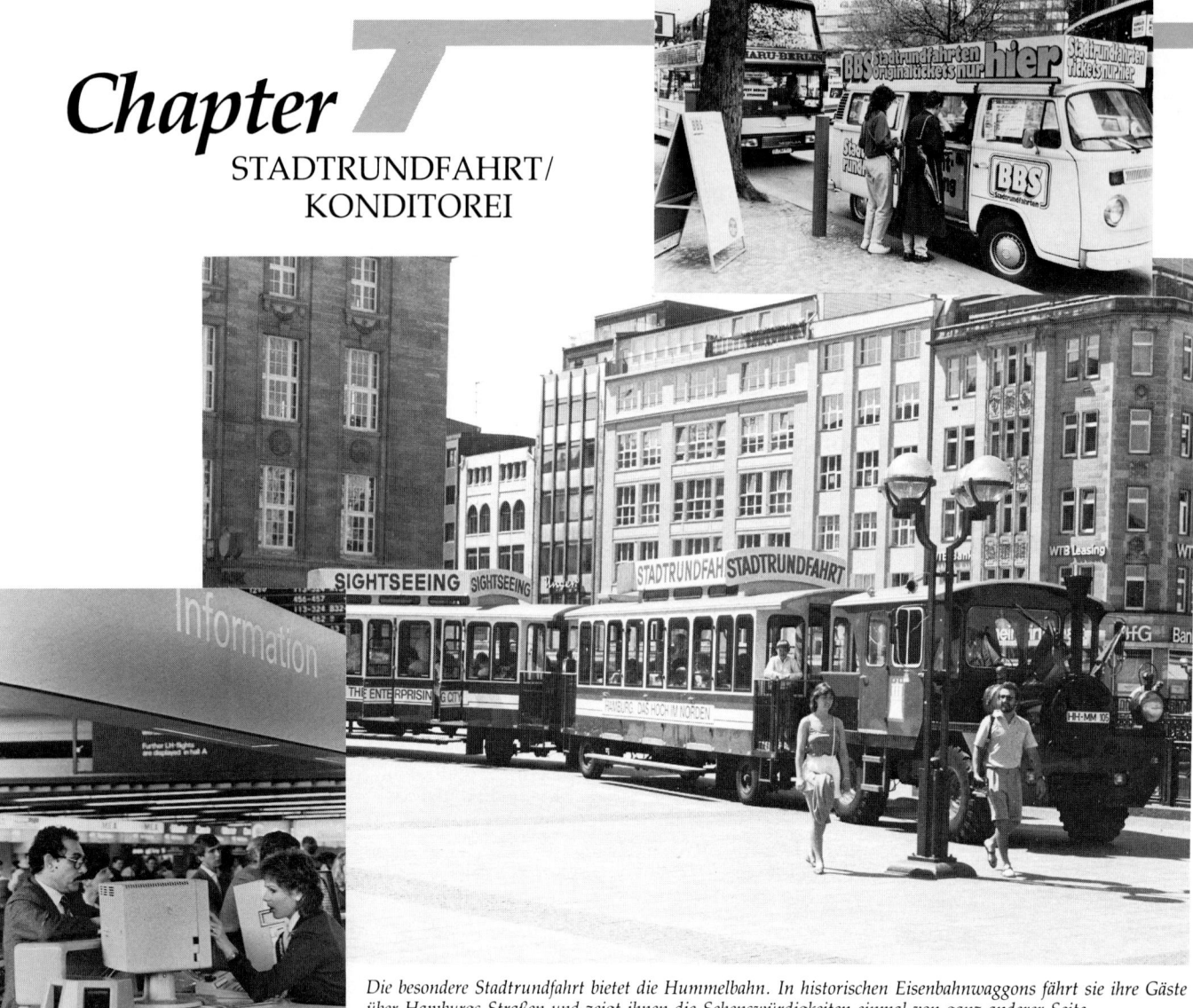

Die besondere Stadtrundfahrt bietet die Hummelbahn. In historischen Eisenbahnwaggons fährt sie ihre Gäste über Hamburgs Straßen und zeigt ihnen die Sehenswürdigkeiten einmal von ganz anderer Seite.

FUNKTIONEN – KONTEXTE – STRUKTUREN

Appropriate song for *Konditorei* section: "C-A-F-F-E-E trink nicht so viel Kaffee." The antiquated spelling C̢AFFEE corresponds to musical notes.

Looking ahead

You'll be arranging city tours, inquiring about tickets, making plans, ordering bakery goods, and asking for more advice about what to see and do.

You will be using:

- prepositions to tell about where and when (at, in, after)
- the modal verb *dürfen* to express permission (may, can, allowed to)
- separable verb prefixes (call *up*, come *back*)
- time phrases on the half and quarter hour
- modal verbs in longer sentences

70

Stadtrundfahrt

1

This is a good time to go back to similar situations in earlier chapters; redo them, this time introducing overt questions with polite phrases like *Können/ Würden Sie mir sagen, Wissen Sie, wann/wo* . . .

Review *wissen* and ways of asking names.

Feel free to introduce other ordinals. At most explain how they are formed with -(s)t; teach the adjective-ending pattern as lexical knowledge.

Maybe take a minute to vary the "*Dann . . . an*" pattern, with its long inner field, by changing the time phrases. But don't offer to explain the structure.

Students will readily sense the similarity between "*rufe . . . an*" and "call . . . up." Apparent lack of similarity elsewhere may trouble them. Here there is a parallelism, "start up," though most often *anfangen* is glossed as "begin." Use schedule-type realia (church, concert, etc.) as foundation for exercises with *anfangen* and *der/die/das nächste.*

Review time-telling in the *X Uhr Y* pattern; push students to express the same time as many ways as possible.

Dialog is particularly suitable to variation, because many versions can be generated by low-level changes (the attraction, entrance location, where and when to meet, what to do afterwards). Use a combination of realia: map, tourist brochure, tour schedule.

1

HERR DIMITZ	Ja, guten Tag. Die Stadtrundfahrt – können Sie mir sagen, wann sie ist?
FRÄULEIN NEFF	Die nächste beginnt um 14 Uhr 30 – also, in einer Stunde. Für wie viele Personen soll das sein? Wir haben nicht mehr viele Plätze.
HERR DIMITZ	Haben Sie noch vier frei? Wir wollen die Stadtrundfahrt heute machen. Morgen müssen wir schon wegfahren.
FRÄULEIN NEFF	Moment mal, ich sehe nach. Unser Computer weiß alles. . . . Ja. Vier Plätze haben wir noch. Darf ich die Namen wissen?

2

FRAU STROBEL	. . . Nein. Für die erste Stadtrundfahrt morgen sind alle Plätze schon reserviert. Eine zweite Rundfahrt gibt es aber um 15 Uhr. Möchten Sie die machen?
PROFESSOR RAU	Na, vielleicht. Ich muß zuerst meinen Mann fragen. Er ist noch im Hotel, und ich möchte ihn nicht anrufen. Die Kinder schlafen noch.
FRAU STROBEL	Machen wir das so: Fragen Sie Ihren Mann, und dann rufen Sie uns morgen früh um 9 Uhr an.
PROFESSOR RAU	Vielleicht kann ich heute nachmittag zurückkommen.

3

DOKTOR PFANNER	. . . Natürlich. Wir bleiben eine Stunde im Dom. Dort gibt es viel zu sehen.
HERR RIEMER	Darf man dort fotografieren?
DOKTOR PFANNER	Ja, aber nur nicht mit Blitz. Das stört den Gottesdienst. Der nächste fängt schon um 11 Uhr an.
HERR RIEMER	Dann muß ich mein Stativ holen. Habe ich genug Zeit?
DOKTOR PFANNER	Ja, unser Bus fährt erst um Viertel nach 9 ab.
HERR RIEMER	Gut. Ich treffe Sie unten in 5 Minuten.

4

FRAU ISSLER	Also, die Herrschaften. Eine Stunde im Museum. Den Eingang sehen Sie hier links.
FRÄULEIN KAUL	Und wo treffen wir uns dann?
DOKTOR ZÄHNER	Und wann ist das Mittagessen?
FRAU ISSLER	Treffen Sie mich vor dem Restaurant am Domplatz-so um Viertel nach 12. Ich reserviere uns einen Tisch.
FRÄULEIN KAUL	Und was machen wir nach dem Essen?
DOKTOR ZÄHNER	Können wir einkaufen gehen? Ich möchte ein paar Ansichtskarten vom Fluß.
FRAU ISSLER	Unser Bus holt uns um Viertel vor zwei ab. Wenn Sie schnell essen, . . .

STRUKTUR 1

A.A. §§5,8; Preps. §§4,5,7,8, 10,11

Rapid-fire exercise: Student A says a location-noun (e.g., Bahnhof); student B says, "*Ich gehe zum Bahnhof.*" Student A says, "OK. Sie gehen zum Bahnhof." Student A: "*Oper* [or switch tasks]." Can be expanded to set up *von . . . zu* phrases. Try to keep the pace fast enough that the student has little time to go gender-hunting and must instead commit to a pattern; that is, a gender error, if a dative form is used, is less

1. Prepositions *aus, mit, nach, von, zu*: followed by the dative case

- articles for masculine and neuter nouns = *dem/einem*

der Bahnhof	zu **dem** Bahnhof
das Essen	nach **dem** Mittagessen
das Museum	von **einem** Museum

serious than producing the correct gender but failing to transfer to the dative case.

Point out that the contractions, unlike many English contractions, are not considered inappropriate in serious spoken or even written language.

- articles for feminine nouns = *der/einer*

| die Oper | aus **der** Oper |
| die Stunde | nach **einer** Stunde |

- contractions: **zum = zu dem, zur = zu der, vom = von dem**

zum Bahnhof   **vom** Bahnhof   **zur** Marienkirche

Preps. §§20,21,22,24,28
See note in Instructor's Guide.

Bitte dem Chauffeur die Sicht nach rechts freilassen
———
Prière de laisser au chauffeur la vue libre sur la droite
———
Favorite lasciare libera la visuale a destra al conducente

Preps. §8

The intermediate-mid student will still have difficulty with past time, and will still confuse *vor* and *für* with "for." Model and drill accordingly. Here you can feel relatively free to use plurals, since most time-unit

Verbs §26

nouns are feminine nouns whose plurals end in *-n* anyway.

2. Using prepositions *in, an, vor* and *auf* to talk about location:

Wo?

- preposition is followed by dative case

- contractions: **im = in dem, am = an dem**

der Dom	Wir bleiben eine Stunde **im** Dom.
die Kirche	Ich treffe Sie **vor der** Kirche, ja?
das Hotel	Er ist noch **im** Hotel.
der Bahnhof	. . . um 3 Uhr **am** Bahnhof.

3. Using *nach, in, vor, an* to talk about location in time

Wann?

- preposition is followed by dative case

Was machen wir **nach dem** Essen?   **In einer** Stunde kommen wir zurück.

Am Dienstag reisen wir nach Basel.   **Vor einer** Woche war sie in Aachen.

4. The modal verb *dürfen* suggests having permission.

Don't get hung up on – and waste class time on – the intricacies of *dürfen, können,* "may", "can", "be allowed to", etc. Most students will not produce this modal anyway without very overt prompting. Should it actually appear, though, look out for the relatively serious error "*Ich darf sie (nicht)*," which might appear in a situation where the speaker

- forms:

		SINGULAR	PLURAL
1		ich **darf**	wir dürfen
2		Sie dürfen	Sie dürfen
3		er/sie/es **darf**	sie dürfen

- word order: like that of other modals

verb at end
Darf ich die Namen <u>wissen</u>?

Darf man dort <u>fotografieren</u>?

was asked to comment about child-raising. The speaker might well mistake the dictionary equivalent (passive voice) "be permitted to" for (active voice) "permit" or "let," and thus try to express the idea, "I won't let them," as *"Ich darf sie nicht."* Far easier, of course, is a construction with *verboten.* And far more important is exercise with the more common modals.

	Stage 1	**A**	**B**

Stage 1

A — **B**

1

Sold out = *keine Karten/Plätze mehr.*

A	B
Asks for tickets for four on the next day's tour.	Says morning tour is sold out, but tickets are available for 3:15.
Would like to go in the morning; train is leaving town at 6:10 P.M.	Says that's plenty of time – tour lasts only two hours.
Agrees, but will have to ask friends.	Suggests A call later to confirm.
Gives B name to hold places until the call.	Copies down A's name, repeats understanding that A will call.
Wants to leave öS 100 to hold places.	Says that's not necessary.
Thanks; says good-bye.	Responds in kind.

2

"Encourages A to hurry": could be done simply by saying that they have only a few minutes.

A	B
It's 2:00; wants to take the tour at 2:30, but has to get children in the hotel.	Encourages A to hurry, but says there's enough time.
. . .	
Returns without children, who are still asleep.	Suggests A return with family for evening tour at 7:00.
Asks if there is still room for eight.	Is surprised at number, but will check the computer list.
Asks B to reserve eight places for them.	There is room; asks A for name.
Begins to name children.	Needs only last name.

A simple exchange of sincere *Danke* and *Bitte schön* would do.

3

A	B
Asks when the first tour leaves.	Says it's at 9:20; asks whether A wants a ticket.
Doesn't know; asks whether tour goes to the cathedral.	Tour begins at the cathedral; asks what else A would like to see.
Wants to see the waterfront, the city museum, and the university.	That tour leaves in an hour; asks whether A wants a ticket.
Doesn't know; asks where that tour begins.	That tour begins down by the river, then goes to the museum and to the university.
Would like to buy two tickets; asks if any are available.	Doesn't know; checks computer; is sorry, but they are out of tickets; asks if A would like to try tomorrow.
Will be in Hamburg tomorrow. Thanks B for the trouble.	Has been glad to help.

Stage 2

1	**2**
You are at the tour office in Karlsruhe. Find out	You have had to cancel your reservations on the Frankfurt city tour.
a) whether there is much to do there;	a) Express your regrets to the official.
b) whether your ticket for a drive around the city is still reserved;	b) Ask whether there is another tour in an hour or so.
c) whether you can return a bit later for the second tour at 2:00.	c) You find out there is none. Say you'll be back tomorrow at this same time.

Versuchen Sie doch

You've taken the bus tour of the city. Now tell someone else the highpoints – what and why.

You've taken the bus tour, but you didn't really have time to explore everything that interested you. Pick out a major locale covered by the tour. Then get out your map and plan a walking tour of the interesting area. Discuss: what transportation you will use to get there; where and what you will eat; things you might want to buy.

Städte, Straßen und Stadtpläne

Cities like München, Wien, Zürich, and Dresden do resemble North American cities in their larger features. That is, there is a central city surrounded by various districts and suburbs. But a glance at a city map will show major differences between a typical city in the German-speaking countries and one in the United States or Canada, particularly in the central and western regions of North America. The chief reason for the cultural difference in city layout is, of course, historical. Cities in the German-speaking countries have been inhabited much longer than those in North America. Seldom were they laid out according to a single overall plan that has remained unchanged. Köln, for example, exhibits at least three stages: a small, squarish Roman settlement; a larger circular medieval walled city; and a modern urban-suburban sprawl.

The focus of the traditional city layout is usually the main church, though in some cities other buildings may equal or exceed it in importance. Thus the city hall (*das Rathaus*) is important in cities with a strong tradition of municipal government, while a prominent palace (*die Pfalz, die Residenz*) or court (*der Hof*) is found in cities long controlled by the nobility. Still other cities are dominated by natural features, as Hamburg is by its harbor.

Orderly street grids with square blocks are extremely rare. Often several streets intersect, sometimes forming a large open space or "*Platz*." Ancient city walls or other fortifications, even where all direct trace of them has vanished, may have left their mark on street patterns and landmark names. Thus the word for a city gate (*das Tor*) is found in names like "Eigelsteintor" in Köln. Similarly, the commercial structure of earlier times is evident in spaces whose names end in *-markt* (market). Downtown Köln has an "Alter Markt," a "Heumarkt," a "Holzmarkt," a "Buttermarkt," and a "Fischmarkt"; near the center of München is the "Viktualienmarkt," in which groceries ("victuals") are indeed still sold outdoors.

Suburbs or other city *regions* are often designated by compass terms (*Nord, Süd, Ost, West, Nordost,* etc.) or by district names (Köln–Ehrenfeld, München–Nymphenburg). In Wien, the districts (*Bezirke*) are numbered rather than named, with District I being the *Stadtmitte* and the others surrounding it in inner (II–IX) and outer (X–XXII) zones. It is customary to use the district number when giving directions: "*In welchem Bezirk ist die Kurrentgasse, bitte? Im Ersten.*" Postal ZIP codes (*die Postleitzahl, -en*) also denote districts; thus *8 München 1* (or *8000 München 1*) is an address in the city's central district.

Many larger cities are circled by one or more main perimeter roads. The inner may well follow a much earlier medieval wall; names of the segments will likely end in the word *-ring* (*der Ring*). An outer parkway is often termed a "beltway" (*der Gürtel*).

As one might expect, many streets and other features are named for prominent cultural figures. The poets Goethe and Schiller, the philosopher Kant, and composers like Mozart are commemorated in street names in many a city. Changes in political systems have their effect as well. Thus the name "Hitler" was imposed on many locations during the Third Reich, and quickly removed after 1945. Names of socialist heroes like Marx, Lenin, and Ernst Thälmann appear everywhere in East Germany. Still other features are named for other cities or regions; note the invariable ending *-er* in such names (Bonner Platz, Potsdamer Straße). Of considerable cultural and human interest are two widespread names. *Judengasse* attests clearly to both the presence and the segregation of Jews in earlier times. A *Rosengasse* or *Rosenstraße* was often a district of houses of prostitution.

Urban geography – some useful vocabulary

See *Bildwörterbuch* display "Stadt – Straße – Haus."

die Stadtmitte, das Zentrum, die Innenstadt	*downtown or central city*
das Viertel	*section ("quarter") of a city*
Wohnungsviertel	*residential district*
der Bezirk (-e)	*administrative section of a city, district*
der Vorort (-e)	*suburb*
die Umgebung (-en)	*surroundings*
die Kreuzung (-en)	*intersection*
die Querstraße (-en)	*cross street*
die (Verkehrs)ampel	*traffic light*

The use of letters or numbers as street names is unheard of in the German-speaking countries. Should you need to express such information in German, perhaps to a visitor to North America, any of these patterns will work:

1. Cite the name in English – *"Ja. Das ist die Fifth Avenue."*
2. Give the cardinal number (or letter) after the word *"Straße"* – *"Ich wohne in der Straße Acht/Straße K* (or *in der K-Straße)*.
3. Treat the number-name as an ordinal ("-th") number – *"Ich wohne in der Achten Straße."*

Verkehr: Transit and Traffic

Despite the love of automobiles encountered in all German-speaking countries, familiarity with the operation of public transit systems is virtually a survival skill for both long-time residents and those spending only a few days in urban areas. Larger cities may have several types of transit conveyance: bus, streetcar, subway (*U-Bahn = Untergrundbahn*), and urban-suburban high-speed line (*Schnellbahn*). The last is often abbreviated *S-Bahn*, as it is in München. The same abbreviation, however, may be used elsewhere for streetcar (*Straßenbahn*); another common term, *Stadtbahn*, also begins with *S* and might therefore lead to confusion. Generally, though, tickets are valid on all conveyances within a transit system.

Die Konditorei

Die Konditorei – insufficiently expressed in English as "pastry shop" – is an important cultural institution in German-speaking countries. It differs from a normal bakery (*die Bäckerei*) in that it offers not only baked goods like bread, cakes (*Kuchen, Torten*), and cookies (*Plätzchen, Kekse*), but also pastries (*Feingebäck*), ice cream, and beverages from soft drinks to coffee, tea, and light alcoholic refreshments. It also provides a place to sit for a rest or to meet someone. The *Konditorei* thus offers a public equivalent to the household coffee break (*die Kaffeepause*) in midafternoon, usually around four o'clock, for a light snack. Inviting someone in (or out) for coffee is for many people the equivalent of the North American supper invitation; the European custom, though, is less costly and often less formal – and it preserves the family's privacy in the evening.

Thoughtful students will not appreciate the common insinuation that America's underdeveloped or poorly maintained mass transit systems are an indication of general cultural inferiority. You might encourage them to use their new-found knowledge and resources (realia – maps, etc.) to explore the issue. Sample argument: the well-developed modern public transportation systems found in the German-speaking countries owe their existence to several factors that point up differences between North America and Europe: far greater population density, more centralized government, the opportunity for radical redesign brought by World War II devastation, and even the narrow streets and old buildings, which greatly impede auto traffic. You might challenge better students to formulate such arguments in simple but effective German. Certainly those who spend any time at all in German-speaking countries will encounter the need to discuss the more controversial aspects of such comparative topics. Moreover, distance lends enhancement; visitors to other cultures may discover in themselves a heightened resolve to argue the merits of their own.

Nr.	Tour	Abfahrt	Dauer ca.	Preis in öS	Kinder
1	Große Stadtrundfahrt / Grand City Tour	9.30, 10.30, 14.30 Uhr / 9.30, 10.30 a. m., 2.30 p. m.	3 Std. hours	280,–	100,–
12	Wien informativ Abfahrtsstelle: 10.30 11.45 Uhr / Vienna – getting acquainted ❶ 15.00 · 16.30 Uhr		1 1/4 Std. hours	150,–	50,–
30	日本語大パノラマコース ❷		4時間 13時30分	380,–	200,–
31	Wiener Potpourri / Vienna Potpourri Departure point: 13.30 Uhr	10.00 Uhr	3 Std. hours	190,–	50,–
41	Wienerwald-Impressionen / Vienna Woods Impressions ❶	13.00 Uhr	3 1/2 Std. hours	230,–	50,–
2	Spanische Reitschule / Spanish Riding School	9.30 Uhr / 9.30 a. m.	3 Std. hours	350,–	100,–
3	Panoramatour mit Donau / Panoramatour with Danube	9.30, 14.30 Uhr / 9.30 a. m., 2.30 p. m.	3 Std. hours	280,–	100,–
33	Panoramatour – Operette / Panoramatour – Operetta	14.30 Uhr / 2.30 p. m.	8 Std. hours	800,–	400,–
4	Wienerwald – Mayerling / Vienna Woods – Mayerling	9.30, 14.30 Uhr / 9.30 a. m., 2.30 p. m.	4 Std. hours	350,–	100,–
44	Wienerwald – Operette / Vienna Woods – Operetta	14.30 Uhr / 2.30 p. m.	9 Std. hours	800,–	400,–
5	Beleuchtetes Wien / Illuminated Vienna	20 Uhr / 8 p. m.	3 1/2 Std. hours	350,–	100,–
6	Wiener Serenade – Grinzing / Viennese Serenade – Grinzing	20 Uhr / 8 p. m.	4 Std. hours	600,–	300,–
7	Wiener Serenade – Nachtklub / Viennese Serenade – Night Club	20 Uhr / 8 p. m.	5 Std. hours	800,–	–
8	Romantisches Donautal – Wachau / Romantic Danube Valley – Wachau	9.30 Uhr / 9.30 a. m.	8 Std. hours	800,–	400,–
10	Pusztatour / Pusztatour	9.30 Uhr / 9.30 a. m.	8 Std. hours	800,–	400,–
11	Ausflug in die Alpen / Alps and Nature Tour	9.30 Uhr / 9.30 a. m.	8 Std. hours	800,–	400,–
13	Salzburg – Festspielstadt / Salzburg – Festival Town	7 Uhr / 7 a. m.	ca. 12 Std. hours	1500,–	900,–
14	Bratislava – mit Schiff / Bratislava – by boat		10 Std. hours	800,–	500,–
17	Budapest informativ / Budapest – getting acquainted	7 Uhr / 7 a. m.	Tage	1490,–	900,–
50	Alpenflug – Tirol, Olympiastadt Innsbruck / Flight over the Alps – Tyrol – Olympic City Innsbruck			3000,–	–
21 22	Spanische Reitschule, Sängerknaben / Spanish Riding School, Boys' Choir	8.30 Uhr / 8.30 a. m.		500,–	300,–
25 32	Spanische Reitschule / Spanish Riding School	14.30, 18.30 Uhr / 2.30 p. m., 6.30 p. m.		600,–	300,–

5 Tage Österreich   4360,–   Prag   ab 1.160,–

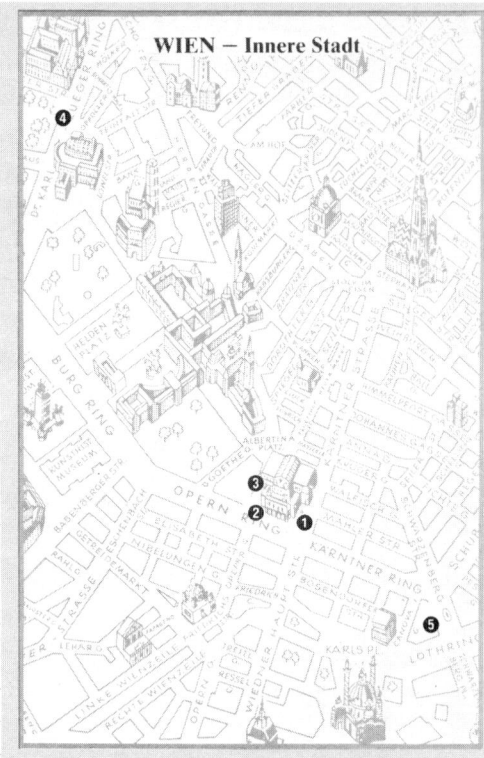

WIEN – Innere Stadt

HAUPTABFAHRTSZEITEN · MAIN DEPARTURE TIMES
Zentrale Abfahrtsstelle · Central Starting Point:
Autobusbahnhof Wien-Mitte
9.30   10.30   14.30   20.00
Zubringerstellen · Starting Points:

❶ ganzjährig	❷ ganzjährig	❸ ganzjährig	❹ vom 2.5.–31.10.	❺ vom 2.5.–31.10.
Oper, RB Austrobus	Oper, Österr. Verkehrsbüro	Operngasse, Elite Tours	Universität, RB Austrobus	Schwarzenbergplatz bei McDonalds
9.20	9.20	9.20	9.15	9.15
10.20	10.20	–	10.15	–
14.20	14.20	14.20	14.15	14.15
19.50	–	–	–	–

Telefon 72 46 83-0, 75 11 42-0 Serie   Telex: 135417 VISIT

Konditorei

1

Review *oben* and *unten*, and ask for contextual descriptions that are likely to produce compound location phrases like *"vorne am Fenster."*

2

Point out the changing position of women and the persistence of traditional roles; note that in dialogs elsewhere in *Wie, bitte?* other behavior is exhibited. Perhaps bring in expressions like *gnädige Frau* and *Küss' die Hand.*

Himbeeren *raspberries* **3**

Mention a few other kinds of berries, and offer equivalents of common North American berries (blackberries = *Brombeeren*).

4

5

FRAU MAHLER	Gibt es einen Tisch da vorne am Fenster? Dann können wir sehen, wann unser Bus kommt.
FRAU HAUPTMANN	Dort gibt es zu viele Leute. Suchen wir hinten etwas. Oder wollen Sie nicht neben den Toiletten sitzen?

HERR SCHERER Ich möchte ein Stück Nußtorte, bitte, und Mineralwasser.

Generate pastry names by setting up combinations of ingredients and flavors with -torte or -kuchen.

FRÄULEIN GALLER Sehr gut. Und für die Dame?
HERR SCHERER Auch Nußtorte, bitte.
FRAU SCHERER Aber mit Kaffee.
FRÄULEIN GALLER Also, zweimal Nußtorte, Mineralwasser, Kaffee. . . . Soll ich eine Tasse oder ein Kännchen bringen?

MS. CONNORS Ich möchte Himbeereis, bitte.
HERR LUTZ Und der Herr?
MR. CONNORS (. . .)
MS. CONNORS Pardon. Er spricht kein Deutsch. Für ihn bitte Schokoladeneis.
HERR LUTZ Wollen Sie einen Becher oder eine Tüte?

HERR SCHULZ Sie fahren schon übermorgen weg?
HERR GRAUNING Ja. Was sollen wir noch machen?
HERR SCHULZ Also, Sie waren schon im Dom, natürlich, und auch im Rheinpark.
HERR GRAUNING Und auch im Museum neben dem Dom, und in der Synagoge am Rathenau-Platz.
HERR SCHULZ Ja. . . . Was gibt es dann noch zu sehen?
HERR GRAUNING Vielleicht etwas für unsere Kinder? Der Zirkus oder . . .
HERR SCHULZ Ach, der Zoo! Den Zoo müssen Sie bestimmt noch sehen. Und heute abend können Sie eine Fahrt auf dem Rhein machen.
HERR SCHULZ Schön, wenn wir einen Babysitter finden.

HERR FREUDENBERG Naja. Zwei Konzerte, drei Museen und fünf Kirchen in zwei Tagen – das ist viel.
FRÄULEIN DANZER Für mich ist das zu viel. Und dann sitzen wir am Nachmittag in einer Konditorei und essen zu viel.
HERR FREUDENBERG Vielleicht sollen wir tanzen oder wandern gehen.
FRÄULEIN DANZER Oder auch schwimmen gehen – wenn nicht im Fluß, dann in einem Schwimmbad.

77

STRUKTUR 2

Verbs §§30,31

Explain if necessary, but only briefly, that another thought may come later in the sentence. See exercise in note in Instructor's Guide.

1. Separable prefixes

- **modify the meaning of the verb**
- **appear at the end of the thought (as often in English)**

    weg "away" + **fahren** = **wegfahren** "go/drive *away*"
    Er fährt **weg.**
    Wann fahren Sie **weg?**
    Morgen müssen wir schon **wegfahren.**

    aus "out of" + **steigen** "climb" = **aussteigen** "get *off*"
    Sie steigt in Bonn **aus.**
    Wo steigen wir **aus?**
    Sie müssen also in Köln **aussteigen.**

    an "at, on, to" + **rufen** "call" = **anrufen** "phone, call *up*"
    Sie ruft mich morgen **an.**
    Rufen Sie uns . . . **an.**
    Möchten Sie Susanne später **anrufen?**

See note in Instructor's Guide.

2. More about telling time: *Viertel* and *um*

- **_Viertel_ = "quarter," "15 minutes"**

    Est ist **Viertel** vor drei.   Es ist **Viertel** nach drei.

- **When things take place: *um* _____ (*Uhr*)**

    Die Dombesichtigung fängt erst **um Viertel nach 10** an.

Verbs §21

Two kinds of exercise: 1) addition of modal to simple sentence; 2) expansion of inner field. Try to do both within a communicative context (e.g., student A is directed to present the plans for the day in short sentences ["*Wir essen im Hotel*"], student B is directed to probe

Preps. §25

for detail and modification ("*Müssen wir im Hotel essen?*" "*Wann wollen wir essen?*").

3. Modal verbs in longer sentences

- **The verb that completes the thought comes last.**

    Wir <u>wollen</u> das unbedingt heute **machen.**
    Morgen <u>müssen</u> wir schon **wegfahren.**
    <u>Darf</u> ich die Namen **wissen?**
    Vielleicht <u>kann</u> ich heute nachmittag **zurückkommen.**
    <u>Soll</u> ich eine Tasse oder ein Kännchen **bringen?**

4. *Neben* shows location ("next to").

- **Used with the dative (just as *in, an,* and *vor*)**

    Oder wollen Sie nicht **neben** <u>den Toiletten</u> sitzen?
    Die Konditorei steht **neben** <u>der Marienkirche.</u>

Usual speaking task: describe the hotel floor plan, location of items on *Kiosk* shelves, etc., with blackboard sketch, overhead projection, realia, or *Bildwörterbuch* display. Listening check: Can the student sketch a floor plan from a rapid

description (maybe including distractions like, "*Letztes Jahr war der Tisch neben dem Bett, den haben wir aber nicht mehr.*"). Writing task: a note to friend, telling where you left the keys and books you yourself can't go back to fetch.

SITUATIONEN 2 Konditorei

Stage 1

	A	B
1	Is very thirsty, asks for suggestions. Orders tea with lemon. Prefers a pot of hot tea.	Suggests tea, beer, Fanta, and Radler (beer and 7-Up). Asks whether hot or iced tea. Responds politely.
2	Would like a fruit torte for self and a cup of ice cream for the child. Strawberry, if they have it. Chocolate.	Asks what kind of fruit torte. They do; asks what kind of ice cream. Confirms both orders.
3	Suggests a seat next to the magazine rack, asks B to sit down. Orders two beers; suggests they go to a park and take some pictures. Raises beer glass, says something fitting.	Answers politely; wonders what else they should go see. Suggests they read a magazine while they have their beer; A shouldn't forget supper at 6:15. Responds appropriately.

"Next to the magazines" will do.

	A	B	C
4	Is very hungry; orders wurst, potato salad, beer, then pastry and hot chocolate.	Is diet-conscious; orders tea, salad, and a roll. Reprimands A – who really shouldn't eat so much.	Repeats order, thanks; leaves.
	Is defensive; says B should eat more. Asks C not to forget rest of order. Is enthusiastic; mentions possible menu.	Changes subject, suggests a Rhine cruise that night. Changes mind, suggests dancing instead.	Brings most of order; is polite. Brings rest of order.

Stage 2

If student can't produce mitnehmen, then Muß ich den Kaffee hier trinken? will certainly do. It is assumed that students will be using realia, which often includes useful clues, and that they will have been told to steal vocabulary where they can.

1

You're in the *Konditorei* Bachmann with a friend who doesn't speak German.

a) Address the proprietor.
b) Ask whether the nut cake is fresh.
c) Order some fruit ice cream for yourself and another kind for your friend.
d) Ask whether you could buy some coffee to go.

2

You and your friend are discussing the calorie-laden pastries on the table in front of you and wondering whether all that caffeine is really good for your health. Suggest some ways to change your sinful habits and still enjoy life.

Versuchen Sie doch

The waiter has just brought the wrong kind of ice cream. Set him straight in a polite way, using your stock of courtesy formulas.

You are ordering midafternoon snacks for your four Italian friends, who don't speak much German. You want to impress them with the variety of goodies available in northern Europe. Do the best you can.

79

Chapter 8
OPERNKASSE/ALTSTADT

Frankfurt am Main: Alte Oper.

Some students may not find "highbrow" culture appealing. Explain briefly the importance of classical music in German-speaking countries, a topic dealt with at length in Chapter 20. Remark also that the Chapter 8 material provides the foundation for attending many types of events, including rock concerts and soccer games. Reinforce the point with appropriate realia, such as *Veranstaltungskalender*, playbills, and sports news.

Song for Ch. 8: "Der Leiermann" from Schubert's *Winterreise*.

FUNKTIONEN – KONTEXTE – STRUKTUREN

Looking ahead
You'll be buying entertainment tickets, expressing emotion, making alternate arrangements, planning a walk through a city, and talking a little about history.

You will be using:
- ordinal numbers – numbers that tell sequence (first, second, . . .)
- more negations
- the word *noch* to express *still, yet,* and *more*
- more complicated time phrases (tomorrow morning)
- adverbs that tell where things go (down there, up there)
- more prepositions (equivalents of through, for, without)
- direct-object pronouns (me, us, you, him, her, them)

Opernkasse

Realia include several calendars of events and items with seating information. See also the "*Bildwörterbuch*" display on "*Kultur.*" Once again, review transaction procedures, this time with occasional complications (e.g., don't have this or that item, or have unexpected choices).

1

FRAU ALTORF	Haben Sie noch Karten für den *Freischütz?*
FRÄULEIN DORPEN	Für heute abend? Mal sehen. . . . Ja, ich habe noch vier vorne.
FRAU ALTORF	Sind die alle in einer Reihe zusammen?
FRÄULEIN DORPEN	Nein, zwei sind in der dritten Reihe, zwei direkt hinter ihnen in der vierten Reihe.

2

HERR DIENER	Gibt es noch etwas für heute abend?
FRAU WEISS	Nein, leider nicht. Für heute abend habe ich nichts mehr.
HERR DIENER	Ach, schade. Aber für morgen abend?
FRAU WEISS	Ja, das geht noch. Wieviele Karten möchten Sie denn?

3

DOKTOR HUMBERT	Guten Tag. Ich möchte zwei Karten für heute abend, wenn Sie noch etwas haben.
HERR DEUTSCH	Oh, das tut mir leid, aber für heute sind wir schon ausverkauft.
DOKTOR HUMBERT	Aber nein! Den *Freischütz* wollen wir aber bestimmt sehen!
HERR DEUTSCH	Für den zwölften haben wir noch Karten.
DOKTOR HUMBERT	Erst für den zwölften? Aber wir müssen schon am elften wegfahren.

4

FRAU DR. KOPP	Guten Tag. Haben Sie noch Karten für *Aïda* am 5ten Oktober?
FRÄULEIN GRÄDEL	Nein, für den 5ten haben wir leider keine Karten mehr. Auch keine für den 7ten.
FRAU DR. KOPP	Ach, schade. Für wann haben Sie denn noch etwas?
FRÄULEIN GRÄDEL	Für den 6ten, aber das ist dann nicht *Aïda*. Und am 8ten gibt es keine Vorstellung. Für den 9ten haben wir nur noch Stehplätze.
FRAU DR. KOPP	Und für nächste Woche? Vielleicht können wir noch ein paar Tage bleiben. . . .
FRÄULEIN GRÄDEL	Für nächsten Montag und Mittwoch haben wir noch viele gute Plätze. Was ist besser für Sie? Montag ist der 10te, Mittwoch der 12te.
FRAU DR. KOPP	Ich glaube, wir möchten sie früher haben, also am 10ten.

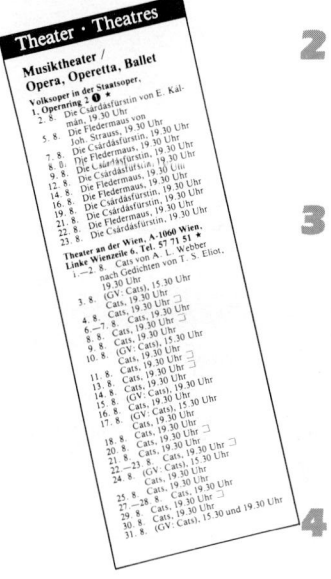

We have chosen the superscript $^{-ten}$ to help the student in the transition from *fünften* to *5.* Remark that the dialogs are not reading selections, but introductions to new linguistic and cultural structures. Also remark that German does not use the superscript convention.

STRUKTUR 1

A.A. §§16,17

1. Ordinal numbers: the ____ th of the month

Ignore irregularities (*achte*, not *acht + te*, etc.); exercise: sketch calendar on board: *Was ist heute? Der . . . . Und gestern?* etc. (Maybe suggest that one partner make erroneous suppositions.) Expansion: intense contrast of *der -(s)te* with *am -(s)ten* (e.g., with alternating *Wann/Was* questions ["*Wann ist Fidelio? Am dritten. Ist das Montag? Nein, Montag ist der vierte. Und was spielt am vierten?*"]).

1–19: der ____ te

der **erste**	der elfte
der zweite	der zwölfte
der **dritte**	der dreizehnte
der vierte	der vierzehnte
der fünfte	der fünfzehnte
der sechste	der sechzehnte
der **siebte**	der siebzehnte
der achte	der achtzehnte
der neunte	der neunzehnte
der zehnte	

20–100: der ____ ste

der zwanzigste
der einundzwanzigste
der zweiundzwanzigste
. . .

SIMILAR
der nächste
der letzte

Expand previous exercise with setups like "*Haben Sie etwas für den ____ (s)ten?*" Also: "*OK, Montag ist der dritte. Was ist der nächste Montag?*" and similar calculation exercises. The system for giving dates will exasperate some students, but the skill is vital; so grasp the nettle firmly, and push rapid-fire drill – practice rather than discussion.

- **Express "What day is it?" with NOMINATIVE case: " ____ ist der ____ -te (-ste)"**   **-e**

Montag ist **der zehnte**, Mittwoch **der zwölfte**.

- **Express "On what day is it happening?" with DATIVE case: "am ____ -ten (-sten)"**   **-en**

. . . am 5. Oktober   (am fünften)   schon am 11.   (am elften)
und am 8.   (am achten)   Am 22. erst?   (am zweiundzwanzigsten)

- **Express "For which day?": with *für* and the ACCUSATIVE case – "Ist das für den ____ -ten (-sten)?"**   **-en**

für den 5.   (für den fünften)
für den 7.   (für den siebten)
für den 9.   (für den neunten)
für den 21.   (für den einundzwanzigsten)

Pronouns §19

2. Expressing nothing, something, everything   **nichts/etwas/alles**

Haben Sie **etwas** für den ersten?
Für den ersten habe ich **nichts** mehr.
Für heute abend ist auch **alles** ausverkauft.

Verbs §52

3. Making suggestions to someone ("Let's . . .")

Use map or pictures to stimulate discussion of plans. Expand with echoing and reformulation. Examples: Student A: *Gehen wir zum Dom.* Student B: *Sie wollen also zum Dom gehen?* Student C: *Ja, sie will zum Dom gehen. Ich auch.* Student B: *Also, gehen wir zum Dom.*

Just use the **wir**-form of a verb according to this pattern:

Gehen wir zum Dom.
Nehmen wir die Straßenbahn.
Kaufen wir Karten für die Oper.

Martin Luthers Sterbehaus
in der Lutherstadt Eisleben

Stage 1	A	B
1	Wants four tickets for *Der Rosenkavalier* for the next evening.	Is sorry, but tickets are sold out.
	Is obviously disappointed; asks about next performance.	Next performance is on the 5th.
	Has been planning to leave on the 3rd; asks for advice.	Suggests a concert on the 2nd – Mozart, Sibelius, Bruch.
	Loves Sibelius; asks for two tickets, asks time of concert.	Concert is at 8 P.M.; tickets cost SFr 44.
	Would like seats for 2 couples if possible.	There are 2 seats together in row 17, and 2 together in row 22.
	Pays with a SFr 500-note; thanks.	Makes change; thanks.
2	Asks for six student tickets to *Die Hochzeit des Figaro*.	Asks whether for the 16th, 18th, or 20th?
	For the 18th.	The only tickets left are for standing room way up high.
	Thinks that will be fine; asks price.	Price is öS 10 each.
	Pays with an öS 100-note, asks for some coins in the change (for the streetcar ticket machine).	Counts out change.
3	Says last night's performance of *Parsifal* was terrific, wants to buy tickets for two friends.	No tickets are available until Friday evening.
	Friends are leaving on Friday morning.	Suggests they come on Wednesday evening; perhaps some tickets will be turned in at the box office.

Use *wollen* for "planning."

Some students may sniff at all the items with classical music, or will just be perplexed. Let your music students shine! Play a few appropriate excerpts.

3: Special vocabulary for "turn in tickets" is not needed. The clerk can say simply that they don't have any now for Wednesday, but that they might in a while, leaving the customer to figure out the obvious reason. Or the clerk can explain the notion in simpler language: people buy tickets and then don't want to see the opera.

Stage 2

One of the authors, who indeed likes *Die Meistersinger*, recalls a performance in Nürnberg. It began at 6 P.M., ended at 11.15, and included two intermissions, one of 30 minutes and one of 40, during which substantial snacks were sold.

1

You realize that many feel *Die Meistersinger* to be insufferably long.

a) Suggest to your business associate that you could talk better in a *Konditorei* than in the opera house.
b) Suggest that you talk either before or after the opera.
c) You find out to your delight that she loves Wagner; suggest that she prolong her stay in Hamburg to take in the production of *Parsifal* as well. It's on the 8th, the 11th, and the 14th.

2

You have just been to the box office at the *Staatsoper* in Vienna.

a) Tell your unhappy friend that *Die Zauberflöte* is sold out.
b) Suggest an alternative. Gershwin's *Porgy and Bess* is playing at the *Theater an der Wien*; there's an outdoor concert of Brahms and Mozart at the *Rathaus*; you could hear an all-Schubert program of chamber music at the *Universität*; and Brecht's *Mutter Courage* can be seen at the *Burgtheater*.
c) You agree on the Schubert. Tell your friend how you will get to the university.

Versuchen Sie doch

Unforeseen events of a fairly serious though not necessarily unpleasant nature make it impossible for you to attend the event for which you bought tickets some time ago. The tickets were expensive, at least for your budget. Take them back to the box office and negotiate a refund.

STRATEGIE – KULTUR UND SPRACHE

Music

Because opera and classical music play a more important cultural role in German-speaking countries than in ours, tickets to performances may be difficult to find. This is especially true during the summer festival season, when tickets to popular programs may be sold out months in advance. Be ready to name alternative dates or to buy standing-room tickets (*der Stehplatz, Stehplätze*), which, although they may be uncomfortable for long operas, are very inexpensive. Be ready to tell the person at the box office whether you want to sit *oben* or *unten*, *vorne* or *hinten*.

It is regarded as impolite to take coats and packages to your seat. These should be left at the *Garderobe,* for which you pay a modest charge. And when – inevitably – you have to disturb others to get to your seat, it is good manners to face *them*, not the *stage*, as you squeeze by.

Larger cities have a number of concert halls, each with its own program of events. Some halls specialize in certain kinds of music. In Vienna, for example, you can hear operettas (such as Lehár's *Die lustige Witwe*) and musicals (such as *Cats*) in the *Theater an der Wien* and operas (such as Strauß's *Der Rosenkavalier* or Berg's *Wozzeck*) in the *Staatsoper*. The entire range of musical entertainment will be listed in the current *Stadtkalender*. Be sure to read the date correctly! Remember that 2.7. = July 2, not February 7.

In a theater (*das Theater*) you will find live stage productions. Movies are found in a movie theater (*das Kino*).

Asking directions

Keep in mind a strategic check list:

- get the person's attention (*"Entschuldigung . . . ?"*)
- show the person your map and make your inquiry (*"Wie finde ich . . . ?" "Wie komme ich zum/zur . . . ?"*)
- have the person repeat anything you don't understand (*"Wie, bitte?"*)
- echo the directions (*"Gut. Also zwei Straßen. . . . ?"*)
- ask about landmarks underway (*"Und was sehe ich?"*)
- anticipate errors you might make (*"Vielleicht gehe ich zu weit. Was sehe ich dann?"*)
- make a final run-through to make sure you have everything

Identifying streets

Most street names have the word *Straße* in them. Smaller streets sometimes are named -*gasse* (*Marktgasse, Blumengasse*) or -*weg* (*Steinweg, Martinsweg*). A larger street, more like a boulevard, frequently carries the name -*allee* (*Kennedyallee, Berliner Allee*). A square, usually located in front of a public building, and often named for a prominent citizen, is *der Platz: Rathausplatz, Marx-Engels-Platz*. Street signs frequently mistaken for true street names by foreigners indicate one-way streets (*Einbahnstraße*) and dead-end streets (*Sackgasse*). Many cities have managed to reclaim and beautify their historic districts by building outdoor pedestrian malls (*Fußgängerzonen*).

Use a concert listing (not necessarily classical), poster, etc., for a comprehensive check of skills, structures, and vocabulary. Examples: pronunciation of performers' names, clock time, addresses, transportation. Such material is suitable for a variety of exercises focusing singly on speaking, listening, reading, or writing, or else requiring facility in combinations of them (e.g., read the printed schedule and then compare it with spoken information, or write a note to a friend about the evening's plans).

This is a good opportunity to teach vocabulary of clothing and personal possessions; see "*Bildwörterbuch.*" Can the students describe such possessions well enough that the attendant would find them more readily; more difficult, of course, but worth a try, would be to attempt description of a lost item.

Since students frequently fail to import their discourse strategies into a new language, you might well take time for a solid exposition of the skills here, and even a detailed "walk through" of a conversation so organized.

Perhaps mention the Austrian use of *Gasse* as variant of *Straße*, especially if your students commonly participate in study programs there.

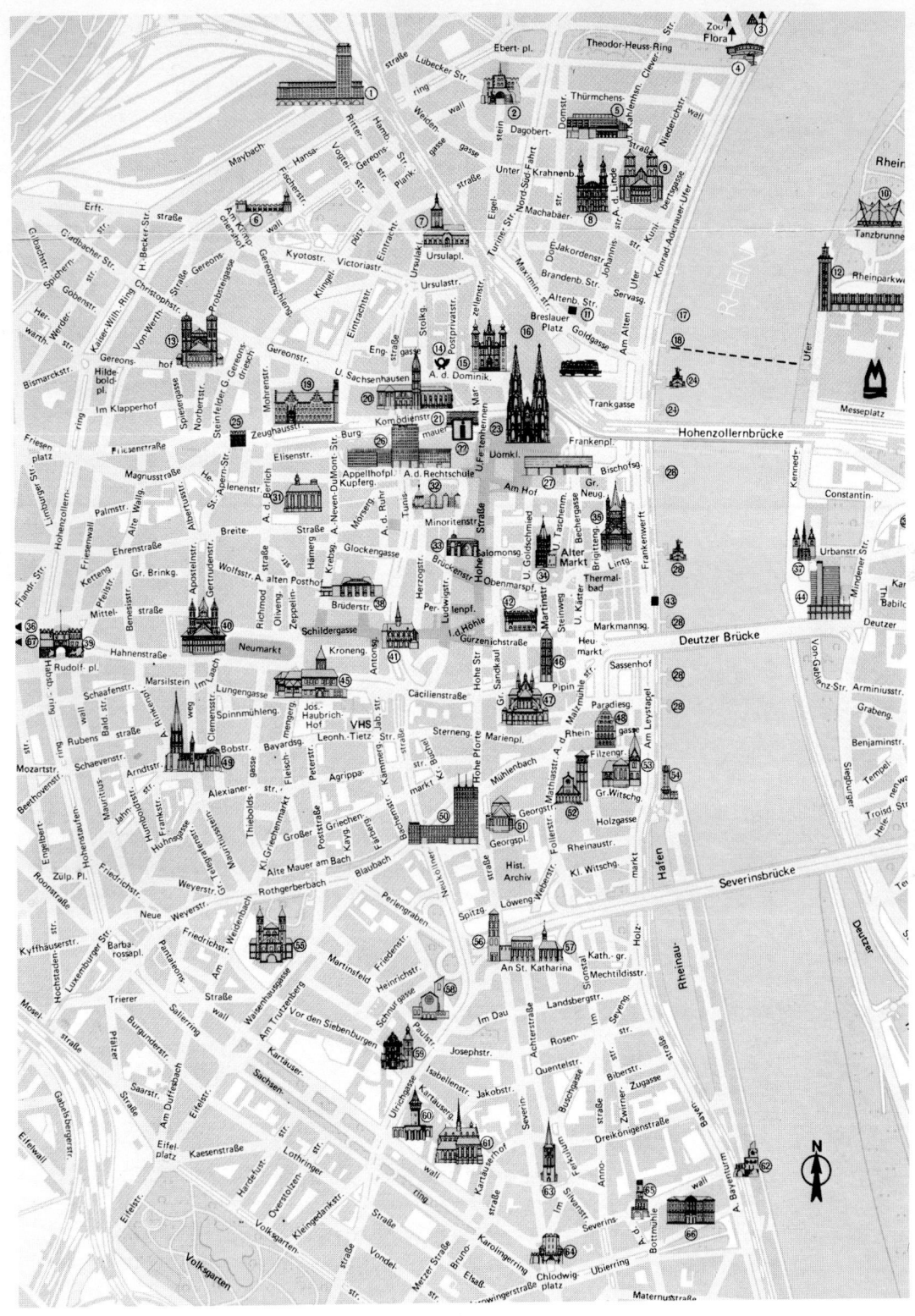

86

GESPRÄCHE 2

Altstadt

1

HERR BIRKEL	Ach, das war wirklich fantastisch – der Dom, die Parks, das Museum, . . .
FRAU BIRKEL	Und hier in Köln gibt es immer Altes und Neues zusammen, eine moderne Stadt und eine Stadt aus dem Mittelalter.
HERR BIRKEL	Ja, und eine Altstadt ohne so viele Autos. Hier ist es leicht, ein Fußgänger zu sein.
FRAU BIRKEL	Das stimmt. Die Fußgängerzone in der Hohen Straße ist sehr schön. Und die Promenade am Rhein muß kilometerlang sein.
HERR BIRKEL	Nun? Wie sieht es für heute abend aus? Wollen wir Karten für die Abendfahrt auf dem Rhein kaufen? Die Stadt war so schön gestern abend, ich möchte sie vom Fluß sehen.

2

FRAU KURSTEINER	Gehen wir da hinauf zum Rathaus.
KARL KURSTEINER	Nein, ich bin zu müde. Ich will nichts mehr sehen. Wie weit ist das Hotel von hier?
FRAU KURSTEINER	Nur 15 Minuten zu Fuß. Und wir sehen das Rathaus sowieso, wenn wir direkt zum Hotel gehen wollen.
KARL KURSTEINER	Na, heute nachmittag bleibe ich im Hotelzimmer.

3

FRÄULEIN KLEE	Schon Viertel nach zwölf. Wollen wir noch durch die Altstadt bummeln und dann später essen?
HERR KANDINSKY	Schön. Ich bin noch nicht hungrig, aber um eins oder so möchte ich etwas essen.
FRÄULEIN KLEE	Prima – aber das Essen gestern abend war furchtbar. Heute wollen wir nicht wieder im Hotel essen, oder? Vielleicht am Domplatz. . .
HERR KANDINSKY	Ja, gute Idee. Aber wohin wollen wir jetzt zuerst?
FRÄULEIN KLEE	Also, ich möchte die Sankt-Aposteln-Kirche besichtigen. Ich glaube, die ist am Neumarkt, nicht weit von der Oper. Und nach einer Stunde finden wir etwas zu essen. Geht das?
HERR KANDINSKY	Natürlich geht das. Ich glaube, die Treppe hier führt zur Mittelstraße hinunter. Von dort ist die Kirche wahrscheinlich leicht zu sehen.

4

FRÄULEIN HAMELN	So. Dies ist also die Sankt-Aposteln-Kirche. Wie alt ist sie denn? Ich sehe kein Schild.
HERR MEINRAD	Lesen wir den Stadtführer . . . "Neumarkt – 11. Jahrhundert; Kirche – romanisch."
FRÄULEIN HAMELN	Also nicht gotisch wie der Dom, und nicht römisch wie die Mauer in der Nähe vom Stadtmuseum.
HERR MEINRAD	Nein. Diese Kirche ist aus dem 12ten Jahrhundert. "Im zweiten Weltkrieg stark zerstört."
FRÄULEIN HAMELN	Wahrscheinlich schon vor 1945.
HERR MEINRAD	"Altar 1975."
FRÄULEIN HAMELN	So alt ist das nicht. Ich bin ja 1970 geboren.

Dialog 4: Reinforce simple ordinal patterns by eliciting short responses to a chart of real or contrived architectural history: (chart) "St. Martin – 1363"; spoken response – "Also, vierzehntes Jahrhundert."

Feel free to present the facts and discuss the issues of wartime destruction, the *Wirtschaftswunder*, etc. Although some students will regard such matters as ancient history, any adult who has a more than momentary contact with the culture must have some familiarity with the topic to avoid appearing inexcusably ignorant. Here, though, just basic facts and issues will suffice, since the topic is treated again in later chapters.

STRUKTUR 2

A.A. §38

1. *Noch:* "still, yet, left over"

Review exercise: *"Herr Ober, bringen Sie mir noch ein* _____ [container] [beverage]." Similarly, *"Gibt es noch* [food item]?"

Gibt es **noch etwas** für heute abend?
. . . , wenn Sie **noch etwas** haben.
Haben Sie **noch Karten** für *Aïda* am 5.?
Für den 12ten haben wir **noch Karten**.
Für Mittwoch haben wir **noch viele gute Plätze**.

Here, as elsewhere in similar exercises, you can use a third student to prompt the other two (e.g., *"Ja, gestern, sagen Sie, aber wann?"*). The student can also double check that the intended information was conveyed: *"Oh, gestern abend? Um wieviel Uhr?"*

2. Defining time more precisely

gestern	heute	morgen
gestern morgen	heute morgen	
or gestern früh	*or* heute früh	morgen früh
gestern nachmittag	heute nachmittag	morgen nachmittag
gestern abend	heute abend	morgen abend

Für **heute abend**? Mal sehen . . .
Aber **morgen abend** . . .
Na, **heute nachmittag** bleibe ich im Hotelzimmer.

A.A. §41

First-year students will not readily produce *hinauf*, etc. Make the point, but then maybe concentrate on their ability to listen for such directions in longer contexts.

3. More about directions

hinauf, hinunter, an . . . vorbei

Ich glaube, wir müssen hier **hinunter** gehen.   *down*
Gehen wir da **hinauf** zum Rathaus.   *up*
Wir müssen sowieso **am** Rathaus **vorbei** laufen.   *past, on by*
    an dem

Preps. §§13,15,16,18

At the Intermediate level, *für, durch,* and *ohne* are vital prepositions. *Gegen* is not.

Push fast-paced production of short items. For *durch:* with map, city drawing, etc. – *"Wie kommen wir zum/zur X?" "Gehen Sie durch . . ." "Und dann um . . . ?"* For *für:* ticket-purchasing and calendar, or discussion of objects and recipients (*"Der Schlüssel da – ist der für Sie oder*

Pronouns §7

für Ihren Mann?" You could use familiar vocabulary, or perhaps introduce new nouns, such as those for professions or more distant relatives (*"Bildwörterbuch"*). Expand then to include the new accusative personal pronouns below.

Redo earlier discussion about arrival plans, this time with focus on third person, who is either the person arriving (*"Er kommt um 9 Uhr an. Er soll mich sofort anrufen."*) or else the contact person (*"Soll ich sie sofort anrufen?"*).

4. The ACCUSATIVE prepositions

durch, für, ohne

Wir machen einen Spaziergang **durch den** Park.   masculine: **-en**
Haben Sie Karten **für den** *Freischütz*?

Wollen wir noch **durch die** Altstadt bummeln?
Und **für die** Dame?   feminine: **-e**
Und **für nächste** Woche?

Wir haben nur eine Stunde **für das** Museum   neuter: **-s**

Ja, und eine Altstadt **ohne so viele** Autos.   plural: **-e**
Für wie viele Personen ist das?

5. Accusative personal pronouns

	SINGULAR	PLURAL
1	mich	uns
2	Sie	Sie
3	ihn/sie/es	sie

- **with accusative prepositions**
  Für mich Himbeereis, bitte.
  Und **für ihn** bitte Schokoladeneis.

- **as direct objects**
  Mein Mann? Ich möchte **ihn** nicht anrufen.
  Meine Frau? Ich möchte **sie** nicht anrufen.
  Treffen Sie **mich** vor dem Restaurant um 12.
  Unser Bus holt **uns** um Viertel vor zwei ab.

Treffen wir uns im Schwimmbad!

SITUATIONEN 2 Altstadt

Stage 1	A	B
1	Suggests they go to the *Stadtpark*. Thinks they might be able to go by the *Marienkirche* on the way. Suggests they take a walk along the river the next day.	Agrees – it was fantastic last night. Good idea, since Köln is so easy to get around in. Will probably be too tired, and will probably want to stay in hotel room.
2	Asks how far the *Römisch-Germanisches Museum* is. Suggests they go; maybe there'll be a *Konditorei* on the way, and they can get something to eat. Likes the variety in the old part of town, suggests they explore it tomorrow.	Doesn't know, but thinks it's probably a half-hour walk. Sounds fine; isn't hungry quite yet anyway; wants to see more. Agrees; likes the pedestrian malls.
3	Would like to take a good look at the *Neumarkt*. Thinks it's not far from the *Sankt-Aposteln-Kirche*. Suggests they find tickets for a cruise on the Rhine that evening.	Thinks that sounds interesting, asks where it is. Remembers that church from last night, thinks she knows how to find it again. Is terribly tired, but agrees that a cruise sounds like fun.
4	Says the city hall is probably very easy to find. Suggests they saunter through the city and ask. Notes that it's already 11:30, suggests they find lunch in about an hour.	Can't find it on the city map. Finds that a good idea – not everyone here is a foreigner. Agrees; suddenly finds the *Rathaus* on the map, looks at the picture in the guide book – but still thinks the cathedral prettier and more interesting.

"Get something to eat" = finden etwas zu essen; können etwas essen.
"Likes variety" = "Wir sehen so viel hier," "Hier gibt es so viel," said with gusto.

"Easy to find" can be done with "können . . . finden."

Stage 2

2 c): Correct errors in adjective endings very conservatively, and mostly by echoing with correct forms in a realistic conversational manner.

1

You have been exploring Köln all day.

a) Suggest that you and your friends find a restful activity for the evening.
b) Ask them if it's all right if you don't accompany them to the symphony.
c) Say you would like to meet them for a snack after the concert, though.

2

You are planning a walk through Köln. Suggest you go

a) down to the Rhine, then
b) to the cathedral and through the old part of town, then
c) up to the old city wall, then
d) back to your hotel.

Versuchen Sie doch

How well can you describe a historic building of the type one might see in an *Altstadt*: appearance? age? location? How can one get to it from a major city landmark like the station or cathedral?

You're not interested in buying for your family junky souvenirs that often turn out to have been made on the other side of the world. Ask someone – perhaps the hotel clerk – to help you. Discuss the members of your family and the sorts of things they might like.

Chapter 9

FRÜHSTÜCK/
WAS EMPFEHLEN SIE?

FUNKTIONEN – KONTEXTE – STRUKTUREN

Appropriate song: Schiller's *An die Freude* in the last movement of the Ninth (Choral) Symphony of Beethoven. Also *"Der Lindenbaum"* from Schubert's *Winterreise.*

Looking ahead

You'll be expressing food and drink preferences in greater detail, commenting on present and past activities, asking for advice, dealing with more complex city directions, and asserting your ability to use German.

You will be using:

- common verbs in a past tense form (was, had, wanted to)
- indirect object ("dative") pronouns (Bring *me* something)
- more prepositions (with, from)
- more adjectives for greater precision in description (a *softboiled* egg, *better* weather)
- more units of measurement (*half* past two, hours *long*)

90

Frühstück

1
Remind students of this point of frequent interference between English and German: *bekommen* ≠ become. Mention also *stehen* ≠ stay and encourage careful monitoring of "false friends."

2
1: Treat *ruhig* lexically, as a flavoring particle with the meaning "go ahead and. . . ." Other contexts: at a *Kiosk* (*Sie können mir ruhig den* Stern *geben*), a bank or post office (*Sie können mir ruhig zwei Zwanziger geben*). It would be confusing to bring up the meaning of "quiet" here.

Direct students to *Strategie* section for discussion of polite requests.

Treat the adjective ending lexically (i.e., do not present the declension of adjective endings after *der*-words, since it would be confused with the *ein*-word declension given in this chapter).

3

Drill the use of *es gibt* with accusative: "*Gibt es ein X bei Ihnen zu Hause?*" "*Nein, bei uns gibt es kein X. Es gibt einen Y.*"

Encourage the student to pursue the "*Na, . . .*" line with a comparison.

4
The use of preterite modal forms enables students to talk extensively about the past without having to learn the preterite forms of other verbs. Drill suggestion: Two columns on the board: "*Ich wollte gestern . . .*" and "*Ich mußte . . .*", later supplemented by column "*Warum?*" The "*Warum?*" column gives reasons for either of the other two, using either modal preterites or *war* and *hatte. Ich wollte gestern ins Kino gehen, aber ich mußte zu Hause bleiben. Es war schon zu spät und ich hatte kein Geld.*

HERR BOSSART	Zo, good morning. You sleep very late, yes. I was think we have to knock up your room. Do you become coffee or tea?
MR. SPALDING	Sie können ruhig Deutsch sprechen, wenn Sie wollen.
FRAU LEUTENEGGER	So, die Herrschaften. Zweimal Frühstück. Und haben Sie sonst noch einen Wunsch?
HERR HOLLINGER	Ich hätte gern Tee statt Kaffee.
FRAU LEUTENEGGER	Schwarztee. Kommt sofort.
FRAU HOLLINGER	Und ich möchte ein Vierminutenei, bitte.
FRAU LEUTENEGGER	Also, einmal Tee und ein weichgekochtes Ei. Bitte schön.
HERR HOLLINGER	Hm. . . . Ich habe kein Messer. Würden Sie mir bitte ein Messer bringen?
FRAU LEUTENEGGER	Bitte schön. Ich gebe Ihnen auch einen Löffel für das weichgekochte Ei. Gabeln haben Sie ja schon. Brauchen Sie sonst noch etwas?
FRAU HOLLINGER	Unsere Tochter möchte eine kleine Tasse Schokolade.
MR. ROTH	Guten Morgen. Ist hier noch frei?
HERR RICHIGER	Na, guten Morgen, Herr Roth. Nehmen Sie doch Platz.
MR. ROTH	Danke. . . . Guten Appetit.
HERR RICHIGER	Danke, gleichfalls.
MR. ROTH	. . . Ein schöner Tag, wenn es so bleibt.
HERR RICHIGER	Das war doch herrlich gestern abend, nicht?
MR. ROTH	Ein wunderbarer Abend war das. Ich finde Köln wirklich sehr interessant.
FRAU RICHIGER	Gibt es so etwas bei Ihnen zu Hause?
MR. ROTH	Bei uns in Amerika? Na, . . .
FRÄULEIN KUPPER	Würden Sie mir bitte die Brötchen reichen?
FRAU LEHMANN	Gerne. Möchten Sie auch Marmelade?
FRÄULEIN KUPPER	Nein, danke. Ich habe schon genug. . . . Übrigens, waren Sie auch gestern abend in der Oper, beim *Freischütz?*
FRAU LEHMANN	Nein, leider nicht. Wir wollten Karten kaufen, aber sie hatten keine mehr für gestern abend.
FRÄULEIN KUPPER	Ach, schade. Konnten Sie für heute abend etwas bekommen?
FRAU LEHMANN	Ja, aber die Plätze waren sehr teuer. Wir mußten pro Karte 60 Mark ausgeben.

1. Talking about yesterday: the past tense of *sein, haben,* and the MODALS

• *sein*

> **war** = was

War adds an **-en** where you would expect it:

	SINGULAR	PLURAL
1	Ich **war** in Bonn.	Wir **waren** in Bonn.
2	**Waren** Sie in Köln?	Sie **waren** in Köln, nicht?
3	Er/sie/es **war** nicht hier.	**Waren** sie zu Hause?

• *haben*

The verb **haben,** like **sein,** is irregular. The important past signal is the ending **-te.** Again, note the **-en** endings where you would expect them:

	SINGULAR	PLURAL
1	**Ich hatte** kein Geld.	Wir **hatten** nur 20 Mark.
2	Sie **hatten** ein Auto.	**Hatten** Sie keine Zeit?
3	Er/sie **hatte** genug.	Zehn Pfennig **hatten** sie nicht.

• modals

The modals also use **-te** to indicate past tense. These past forms look very much like those for **haben:**

MODAL	PAST STEM	
wollen	woll**te**-	
können	konn**te**-	no umlaut
müssen	muß**te**-	no umlaut

Wir **wollten** Karten kaufen, aber sie hatten keine.
Konnten Sie für heute abend etwas bekommen?
Wieviel **mußten** Sie denn bezahlen?

2. Dative pronouns

	singular		plural	
	NOMINATIVE	DATIVE	NOMINATIVE	DATIVE
1	**ich**	**mir**	**wir**	**uns**
2	**Sie**	**Ihnen**	**Sie**	**Ihnen**
3	**er**	**ihm**	**sie**	**ihnen**
	sie	**ihr**		
	es	**ihm**		

Exercise: Teacher says sentence with name in dative, student replaces name with pronoun. T.: "Ich kaufe Lisa eine Karte" S.: "Ich kaufe ihr eine Karte." T.: "Ich kaufe Lisa und Frank zwei Karten." S.: "Ich kaufe ihnen zwei Karten." Variation: T.: "Bitte, bringen Sie mir ein Messer." S.: "Gut. Ich bringe Ihnen ein Messer." T.: "Bitte, bringen Sie meinem Mann eine Gabel." S.: "Gut. Ich bringe ihm eine Gabel."

• as indirect objects: something is done for someone

Geben Sie **mir** bitte auch zwei 5-Mark-Stücke.
Würden Sie **ihm** bitte ein Messer bringen?
Den Schlüssel gebe ich **Ihnen** gleich.
Ich gebe **ihr** auch einen Löffel.

• as objects of prepositions that require the dative

Gibt es so etwas **bei Ihnen** zu Hause?
Bitte, kommen Sie **mit mir.**

SITUATIONEN 1 Frühstück

	A	**B**
Stage 1		

Refer to breakfast menus for variations of these situations.

1

A	**B**
Asks if there's room at B's table.	Says there is; asks A to sit down.
Thanks; comments that yesterday was a fine day.	Agrees, but says children were tired, so they couldn't go for an evening stroll.
Says that's too bad, because they really wanted to do that.	Predicts that today will be even better—fine weather.
A's family plans to spend the day at the *Rheinpark*.	B's children want to go swimming today—yesterday they didn't have time to swim.
Suggests they do some things together.	

2

A	**B**
Calls to waiter.	Responds.
Says the egg was to have been soft-boiled, not hard-boiled.	Apologizes, will correct order right away.
Would like a spoon for the egg, as well as salt and pepper.	Repeats what will bring; asks if there is anything else.
Asks if there's any ham in the kitchen.	Doesn't know; will check.
Says always has ham at home.	Brings order, names items while putting them down.

3

A	**B**	**C**
Is in a good mood in the morning — comments about the weather.	Agrees, remarks positively about last night's activities.	Doesn't care about last night.
Is eager to change the subject, predicts a fine day ahead.	Asks what C would like to eat.	Wants just a pot of tea; didn't want to eat last night, either.
Agrees, suggests a large breakfast (states items).	Says C has to eat something.	Tells them not to do anything with him (her); plans to stay there for a few hours and will join them later.
	Asks C what they're going to do with him (her).	
Says C can go ahead and stay there if C really wants to.	Says they'll meet C in front of the cathedral at 11:15.	Repeats plan, agrees.

Stage 2

1

Your business associate and you sit down to breakfast.

a) Tell her you hope she enjoys her meal.
b) Mention that you wanted to eat something before the tour today.
c) Ask her her opinion of the city. Is it like her hometown?

2

There is no one in the breakfast room; you are afraid it might not be open yet.

a) Ask the person at the counter if breakfast is being served yet.
b) Ask if you should sit in any special place.
c) You need a jolt: ask the waiter to make sure the coffee is black, and ask for a standard breakfast.

Versuchen Sie doch

You drove 20 km since leaving the city after breakfast, and suddenly realized that you had left your traveler's checks on the chair next to you in the breakfast room. Having driven back to the hotel, find the person who served breakfast, identify yourself (you had an unusual breakfast), explain the problem, and ask if he (she) can help you.

More about *would like*

You have been using **möchte** as a way to ask politely for something. Another common phrase is **ich hätte gern:**

> Ich **hätte gern** Tee statt Kaffee.
> Wir **hätten gern** zwei Karten zum *Freischütz*.

Still another way of asking politely is to use the verb form **würden** with an infinitive completing the idea:

> **Würden Sie** mir bitte ein Messer **bringen?**

Meals

The breakfast conversations in this chapter illustrate a fundamental difference between European and American breakfasts. In German-speaking countries a standard breakfast consists of rolls (*das Brötchen, die Brötchen*), butter (*die Butter*), preserves (*die Marmelade* or *die Konfitüre*), and coffee, tea, or cocoa (*heiße Schokolade*). There may be an extra charge for anything else, such as eggs or perhaps a plate of cold cuts and cheese. North German breakfasts tend to be more generous than those in the south.

On menus in more rustic places you may see listed *Bauernfrühstück*, or "farmer's breakfast." It will likely include eggs, bacon, cheese, and even potatoes.

Eggs are cooked in several ways:

weichgekochtes Ei = soft-boiled
hartgekochtes Ei = hard-boiled
Spiegeleier ("mirror eggs") = sunny-side up
Rühreier ("stir-eggs") = scrambled

The noon meal (*das Mittagessen*) is typically the largest meal of the day. It is so important that many families still manage to have lunch together at home in spite of busy work and school schedules. Lunch is a hot meal, the equivalent of an American supper in its completeness; and a glass of beer with lunch is not considered degenerate. In many towns offices and businesses close for two hours at noon; this facilitates relaxation in the middle of the day, as preparation for a long afternoon. Businesses are frequently open until 6 P.M.

Supper (*das Abendessen*) is generally a lighter meal, reflecting the older term *das Abendbrot:* usually just cold cuts (*der Aufschnitt*) and cheese with bread, but sometimes with a warm sausage as well. Wine or beer frequently accompanies the evening meal. Evening meals in restaurants may well be more elaborate, as they often are in America.

Don't explain Subjunctive II here. *Möchte, hätte,* and *würde* are introduced as formulaic expressions that need no additional explanation. Exercise: Make multiple requests (*"Ich hätte gern Tee, bitte, und ich möchte auch ein weichgekochtes Ei."*) or echo question in response (A: *"Was möchten Sie, bitte?"* B: *"Ich hätte gern Kaffee, bitte."*)

cutlery use

It is customary to keep the fork in the left hand, even for bringing food to the mouth. At that point the fork is, in the common American view, upside down: the tines point down somewhat, and the fingers of the left hand are above instead of below the thumb. Both hands are kept above or on the table, not in the lap. For some odd reason, potatoes are cut with a fork, never with a knife.

Therefore the equivalent of American parents' ''Keep your hand in your lap!'' is *''Die Hände gehören auf den Tisch!''* The teacher can illustrate this easily in class. See drawing in *''Bildwörterbuch.''*

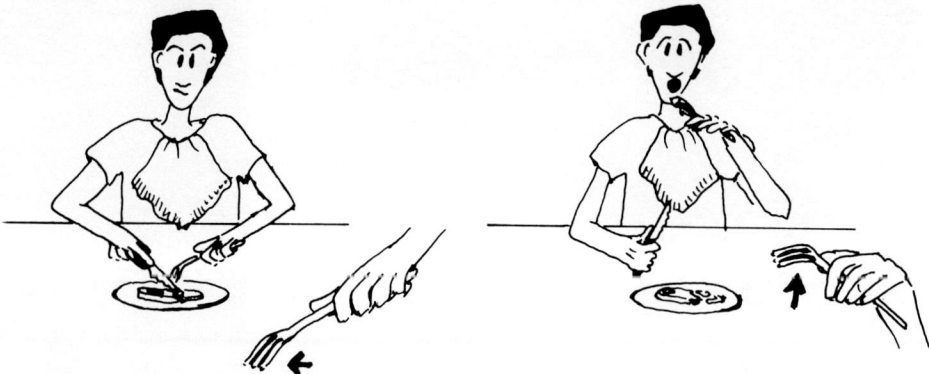

how to decline another helping . . .

Das ist zu viel.   *That's too much*

Danke, ich habe schon genug.   *Thanks, but I'm full.*

Das ist sehr nett von Ihnen, aber ich habe schon genug.   *That's really nice of you, but I'm full.*

. . . or explain why you didn't finish a meal

Das war alles sehr gut, aber zu viel für mich.   *Everything was wonderful, but there was just too much for me.*

		M
Unser Angebot vom Frühstücksbüfett:		
1 Portion Rahmbutter	20 g	0.50
1 Portion Butter	20 g	0.59
1 Portion Konfitüre	50 g	0.45
1 Portion Bienenhonig	30 g	0.90
1 Brötchen		0.05
1 Fettbrötchen		0.07
1 Kuchenbrötchen		0,09

Außerdem stehen für Sie verschiedene Brotsorten zur Auswahl bereit.

		M
1 weichgekochtes Ei		0.95
2 Eier im Glas		1.90
1 Scheibe Schweinebraten	30 g	1.01
1 Scheibe Kalbsbraten	30 g	1.53
1 Scheibe geräuchertes Roastbeef . . .	30 g	1.28
1 Scheibe Roastbeef „rosa"	30 g	1.34
1 Scheibe Kaßlerbraten	30 g	1.13
1 Scheibe Pökelzunge	30 g	1.22
1 Scheibe Schinkenspeck	30 g	0.69
1 Scheibe gekochten Schinken	30 g	0.93
1 Scheibe Lachsschinken	20 g	0.56
1 Scheibe Nackenschinken	30 g	0.95
1 Scheibe Nußschinken	30 g	0.78

		M
1 Scheibe Hausmacher-Leberwurst . .	30 g	0.61
1 Scheibe Jagdwurst	30 g	0.62
1 Scheibe Hausmacher-Blutwurst . . .	30 g	0.59
1 Scheibe Teewurst	30 g	0,62
1 Scheibe Knackwurst	30 g	0.81
3 Scheiben ungarische Salami	20 g	0.68 / 0
3 Scheiben Bauernsalami	30 g	0.83
1 Paar Halberstädter Würstchen . . .		3.75
1 Ecke Camembert		0.54
1 Ecke Schmelzkäse		1.11
1 Scheibe Schnittkäse	30 g	0.72
1 Portion Frischkostsalat		1.45

Frisches Obst und Südfrüchte bieten wir Ihnen nach Saison und Angebot.

	M
Wir bereiten gern auf Wunsch:	
1 Teller Haferflockensuppe	2.25
1 Teller süße Grießsuppe mit Butter	2.80
2 Spiegel- oder Rühreier, natur	2,40
2 Spiegel- oder Rühreier mit Saftschinken .	4,00

	M
Unsere Empfehlung ab 9.00 Uhr:	
Sektfrühstück:	
1 kleine Flasche Sekt — Rotkäppchen halbtrocken	17,70
Sechs belegte Weißbrotecken, nett garniert .	18,95
Katerfrühstück:	
1 Glas Wernesgrüner Pilsner, 0.25 l	1,02
Frühstücksteller	8,35

Kräuterheringsfilet auf einer Apfelscheibe, zwei heiße Partywürstchen, Schinkenwürfel auf Bauernbrot und Setzei, Gewürzgurke, Sahnemeerrettich, Butter und Bauernbrot

Sollten Sie Appetit auf ein kräftiges Frühstück haben, bieten wir Ihnen:

	M
Ukrainische Soljanka mit Sahne und Zitrone	2,60
Deutsches Beefsteak auf Landbrot, Zwiebel und Gewürzgurke	4,05
Kongreß-Toast	4,65
(Putenbruststreifen mit Pfirsich und Käse überbacken)	
Paniertes Kalbsschnitzel mit Spiegelei . . .	7,55
Filetsteak mit Grillwürstchen auf Bauernbrot und Salatvariation	10,00

Benötigen Sie Reiseverpflegung, lassen Sie es uns bitte wissen. Wir bereiten sie gern nach Ihren Wünschen.

Geistliches Konzert

Lesar: Domine, ne in furore tuo
        arguas me
Purcell: Der Herr, ist groß
        Aus der Tiefen, rufe ich, Herr,
        zu dir. Kantate BWV 131
Bach: Ave Maria

Liszt: Warum toben die
Mendelssohn: Heiden
        Pater noster
        Ich hebe meine
        Augen auf
Verdi:
Burkhard:

Ausführende: Chor und Orchester der Pädagogischen Hochschule Reutlingen
Leitung: Michael Goldbach

Spende erbeten

Der Jäger aus Kurpfalz
lädt ein:

**Auf, auf,
in den
Mannheimer
Luisenpark!**

So kommen Sie hin:
Mit Auto und Bus: Kostenloser Großparkplatz direkt rechts an der Autobahnausfahrt
Mannheim-Mitte, unmittelbar am Haupteingang Friedensplatz. Mit Bahn und Stra-
ßenbahn: Hauptbahnhof Mannheim, Straßenbahnlinie 47 direkt bis Luisenpark.
(Mo.-Fr. 6-18 Uhr, Sa. 7-14.30 Uhr, So. u. Feiertag 13-18.30 Uhr) oder Linien 30
und 46 bis Tattersall, Weiterfahrt mit Linie 36 bis Luisenpark.

Öffnungszeiten:
Täglich von 9.00 Uhr bis kurz vor Eintritt der Dunkelheit, Mai-August bis 21.00 Uhr,
bei sehr ungünstiger Witterung früher. Verlassen des Parks danach über Drehkreuze.

Eintrittspreise:
Erwachsene 2,50 DM · Begünstigte 2,– DM · Kinder 10-15 Jahre 1,– DM · Schüler
im Klassenverband –,50 DM (freier Eintritt für begleitende Lehrkräfte). Jahresdauer-
karten, Abend- und Winterkarten noch preiswerter.
Freier Eintritt für Kinder unter 10 Jahren und für 100%-Behinderte.

Nicht gestattet: Hunde, Rundfunkgeräte u. ä., Rollschuhe u. ä., Schlitten.

Das alles erwartet Sie:
41 Hektar herrliche Parklandschaft. Faszinierende Tulpenblüte, weiträumiger Som-
merflor, farbenprächtiger Herbst. Seebühne (1000 Sitzplätze), Veranstaltungsmit-
telpunkt von April bis September (Monatsprogramm anfordern). Festhalle Baumhain (800-1000 Personen) für Betriebs- und Vereinsausflüge. Bunte Nachmittage
und Konzerte. Fernmeldeturm (205 m) mit Aussichtskanzel (121 m). Gondoletta-
Anlage mit 45 Booten (1,7 km Rundfahrt, 45 Minuten). Freizeit- und Kinderparadies,
z.B. Freizeithaus, Grillplätze, Minigolf, Kleinkinder-, Burg- und Wasserspielplatz.
Gehege für Tiere des Bauerhofes, Pflanzenschauhaus mit subtropischen und tropi-
schen Pflanzen, Seerosenteiche, Aquarium und Terrarium. Affen, Krokodile, Fla-
mingos, Pinguine. Großflugvolieren, Stelzvogelgehege. Sommernachtsfest und
Herbstfest.

Gastronomie:
Seerestaurant mit Terrassen und Gartenhof, Café Pflanzenschauhaus mit Terras-
se, Weinstube mit Weinlauben, Festhalle Baumhain mit Gartenhof, Drehrestaurant
im Fernmeldeturm (125 m), Kioske.

Planetarium nur 400 m vom Haupteingang Friedensplatz.

Stadtpark Mannheim GmbH
Gartenschauweg 12, 6800 Mannheim 1, Tel. (0621) 411087

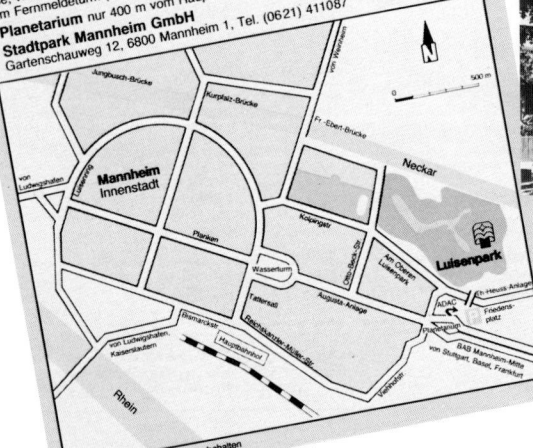

Stand März 1985, Änderungen vorbehalten

Römisch-Germanisches Museum

Was empfehlen Sie?

1

MR. SLOANE	Wir kennen die Stadt noch nicht sehr gut. Was empfehlen Sie, Herr Pfenninger?
HERR PFENNINGER	Ja, zum Zoo müssen Sie unbedingt.
MR. SLOANE	Gut, aber sagen Sie uns bitte, wie wir dahinkommen.
HERR PFENNINGER	Also, Sie gehen zum Dom. Von dort nehmen Sie Straßenbahn Linie 11 oder 16. Es ist egal: Beide Linien fahren direkt dahin.
MR. SLOANE	Und die 11 oder die 16 wieder zurück?
HERR PFENNINGER	Selbstverständlich. . . . Schönen Tag noch!

Select list of events from realia (e.g., Mannheim *Tagesveranstaltungen*) to refer to other possibilities. The class can compare events and discuss which is better (comparative drill).

das Orgelkonzert (-e)
organ concert

2

FRÄULEIN BACH	Nun, schönes Wetter heute, die Herrschaften. Also zurück zum Dom?
DOKTOR GROB	Nein, das machen wir vielleicht Sonntag, wenn es regnet.
FRÄULEIN BACH	Sonntag? Dann können Sie dort um halb 3 am Nachmittag ein Orgelkonzert hören.
DOKTOR GROB	Schön. Aber heute wollen wir mit der Fähre zum Rheinpark. Und wir wollten auch Karten für die Abendfahrt auf dem Rhein kaufen.
FRÄULEIN BACH	Sie wissen schon, wo die Kasse ist?
DOKTOR GROB	Direkt am Rhein, ja, nicht weit vom Dom?
FRÄULEIN BACH	Ja, oder man kann die Karten auch im Verkehrsamt kaufen. Das ist gar nicht weit von hier.

Amerikahaus
American cultural center

3

HERR WIESEL	Das Amerikahaus? Geben Sie mir mal Ihren Stadtplan. Na, sehen Sie. Sie wissen schon, wo die Oper ist, ja?
SUSAN PETERS	Ja. Wir waren schon zweimal dort. Also zur Oper. Und dann?
HERR WIESEL	Dann müssen Sie weiter zur Sankt-Aposteln-Kirche – das sind vier-fünf Straßen – etwa 250 Meter.
SUSAN PETERS	Und wie kommen wir dahin?
HERR WIESEL	Sie gehen besser durch den Neumarkt. Dann sehen Sie also rechts die Kirche-
SUSAN PETERS	Die Kirche ist also rechts.
HERR WIESEL	Dann ein bißchen weiter links das Amerikahaus in der Hahnenstraße.
SUSAN PETERS	Und so kommen wir zum Amerikahaus?
HERR WIESEL	Ja. Passen Sie nur auf, und da sehen Sie es schon.

Neumarkt "New Market"

Refer to city map of Köln. Use this dialog to pose tasks of finding different buildings and points of interest.

4

HERR GRETHEN	Guten Morgen, die Damen. Also, wie war's gestern?
FRAU OERTIG	Sehr schön, die Stadtrundfahrt.
HERR GRETHEN	Die Turmbesteigung auch?
FRAU OERTIG	Leider nicht. Wir konnten den Turm nicht besteigen. Das Wetter war zu schlecht. Zuviel Nebel.
HERR GRETHEN	Ach, schade. Das wollten Sie doch so gerne machen. Aber heute ist bestimmt besseres Wetter.
FRAU OERTIG	Sagen Sie mir mal – regnet es hier immer so viel?

See "*Bildwörterbuch*" section "Nature/*Natur*" for weather vocabulary.

STRUKTUR 2

A.A. §§10–12

Please do not succumb to the temptation to present the entire declension of preceded adjectives at this time. We introduce unpreceded adjectives and adjectives after *ein*-words here because the similarity between endings and pronouns makes sense to the student. When this pattern is fully understood we introduce adjectives after *der*-words in Chapter 16.

Classroom activity includes simple transformations: Teacher: *"Das ist ein Student. Er ist klug."* Students: *"Das ist ein kluger Student."* Continue for possessions, articles of clothing, other objects in the room. After every five objects/people, repeat the entire chain: *"Das ist ein kluger Student, eine weiße Bluse, ein toller Ring,* etc.

1. Adjectives in front of nouns

• nominative: after a form of *ein* (or *mein*, etc.)

	DEFINITE ARTICLE	NOMINATIVE ENDING	(LIKE PRONOUN)
masc. ein schöner Tag	**der** Tag	**-er**	er
fem. eine interessante Stadt	**die** Stadt	**-e**	sie
neut. ein weichgekochtes Ei	**das** Ei	**-es**	es

• without *ein* or *der/die/das*

	DEFINITE ARTICLE	NOMINATIVE ENDING	(LIKE PRONOUN)
masc. Das ist guter Kaffee.	**der** Kaffee	**-er**	er
fem. Nächste Stadtrundfahrt	**die** Stadtrundfahrt	**-e**	sie
neut. Heute ist besseres Wetter.	**das** Wetter	**-es**	es
pl. zwei weichgekochte Eier	**die** Eier	**-e**	sie

• accusative: after a form of *ein* (or *mein*, etc.)

	DEFINITE ARTICLE	ACCUSATIVE ENDING	(LIKE PRONOUN)
masc. Einen schönen Tag	**den** Tag	**-en**	ihn
fem. Eine interessante Stadt	**die** Stadt	**-e**	sie
neut. Ein weichgekochtes Ei	**das** Ei	**-es**	es

• without *ein* or *der/die/des*

	DEFINITE ARTICLE	ACCUSATIVE ENDING	(LIKE PRONOUN)
masc. Ich liebe schwarzen Kaffee	**den** Kaffee	**-en**	ihn
fem. Wir trinken frische Milch	**die** Milch	**-e**	sie
neut. Wir haben besseres Wetter	**das** Wetter	**-es**	es
pl. Sie haben nette Kinder	**die** Kinder	**-e**	sie

Prepositions §§7,10–12

2. Dative prepositions — contractions　　　`zu, mit, von`

You have already seen *nach, aus, von,* and *zu* in Chapter 7.

- • *zu + dem* contracts to *zum, zu + der* contracts to *zur*
- • *von + dem* contracts to *vom*
- • no contraction: *von + der, mit + anything*

Exercise: rapid-fire conversion. Student A: *"um halb drei?"* Student B: *"Ja, um 2 Uhr 30,"*

3. Telling time　　　`halb`

Halb leads ahead to the next hour. It does not mean half *past* but half *before.*

　　12:30 = halb eins　　　2:30 = halb drei

　　Sie können **um halb drei** ein Orgelkonzert hören.

4. Showing possession with *von* and the dative case

　　Der Großvater **von** mein<u>em</u> Vater war mein Urgroßvater.
　　　　　My father's grandfather was my great-grandfather.

　　Ein Freund **von** <u>mir</u> war im Juli in Österreich.
　　　　　A friend of mine was in Austria in July.

SITUATIONEN 2 Was empfehlen Sie?

Stage 1

	A	B
1 Consult weather vocabulary in *"Bildwörterbuch"* for dialog variations.	Asks advice on how to get to the zoo. Asks if there's a bus. Asks how often the buses run.	Suggests a taxi because of the weather. Bus No. 16 goes there. Isn't sure, but says there won't be much of a wait.
	Asks how much a ticket costs.	Guesses 60 Pfennig; says ticket machine is right around the corner.
	Corrects self; meant to ask how much a ticket to the zoo costs.	Doesn't know — but says it's not too much.
2 Refer to realia listing cruise schedules and prices.	Asks about the cruise on the Rhine.	Recommends it enthusiastically. Says how beautiful the city is from the river.
	Asks whether B recommends a day trip or one at night.	Says both are wonderful. The river shines at night and there is dancing on board. In the daytime everything can be seen.
	Asks where to buy tickets, wonders how much they cost.	Pulls out a brochure, shows prices; says ticket office is down by the river.
	Thanks B.	Hopes A has a nice day.

	A	B	C
3	Would like to see the Sankt-Aposteln-Kirche.	Says that's a beautiful church, starts to explain how to get there from the opera house.	Interrupts — B's directions are not right. It's through the *Neumarkt*.
	Repeats what B and C have said.	Interrupts — the church is on the left about 100 meters from the opera. Says it doesn't matter. You can't miss it.	Says B is wrong: it's farther than 100m — more like 250m.
	Suggests asking a taxi driver for help.	Says it's better just to take a taxi.	Says the taxi is expensive. Asks for A's city map to find it for A.
	Says it's too bad they don't know the city very well yet.	Says knows the city well, but just not from this place.	Says B doesn't know the city well, and probably doesn't know where the Roman wall is.

Stage 2

1

You were not at all impressed with your city tour. It was too hurried, and since this is the off-season, some things were either uninteresting or else simply closed. Advise other hotel guests what to do.

2

You were greatly impressed with your walking tour of the city. There were few participants, and you got to do a lot of extras. Tell about those extras, and give some advice to others who are considering taking the same tour.

Versuchen Sie doch

See *"Bildwörterbuch"* sections on "People/*Leute*" and "Activities – general/*Was tut man?*" for vocabulary of emotions and actions.

Tell your hotel clerk about the differences between hotels (and hotel clerks) in North America and Europe.

Describe the various folks at home for whom you want to buy gifts.

Chapter 10

DOM/ GESCHENKE

DIN = Deutsche Industrie Norm; cf. discussion in Chapter 25. DIN 21 is the equivalent of ASA 100.

Appropriate song: *"Ein' feste Burg ist unser Gott"*

Looking ahead

You'll be discussing historical landmarks, specifying locations, discussing concrete objects in considerable detail, learning parts of buildings, and obtaining things for other people.

You will be using:

- prepositions to specify locations (at, from)
- modal verbs in longer sentences
- emphasized items to begin sentences (And postcards you will find . . .)
- two-part locational phrases (around the corner to the left)
- the principles by which longer German words are constructed
- expressions for "like to" and "would like to"
- basic adjectives to point out one item among many (which? this)
- *sagen, glauben,* and *wissen* to introduce other statements

Dom

See realia *"Zahlen zum Dom,"* **1**
Chapter 4, page 45.

HERR ENGELS	So ein Wetter! Tut mir leid, die Herrschaften, aber den Turm dürfen wir nicht besteigen. Bei diesem Wetter ist es zu gefährlich, besonders für Kinder.
FRAU VON SCHOLZ	Ach – und ich wollte so gerne von dort oben die Stadt fotografieren.
HERR ENGELS	Natürlich wollten Sie das. Aber das geht viel besser an einem sonnigen Tag. Dann sind die Straßen nicht so naß.
FRAU VON SCHOLZ	Na gut. Vielleicht könnte ich morgen zurückkommen, oder auch übermorgen.

The Hohenzollern family, **2**
whose ancestral castle (Burg Hohenzollern) lies about 25km south of Tübingen, ruled Brandenburg, Prussia, and Germany from the fifteenth century to the end of World War I, when Wilhelm II abdicated. The most distinguished members of the royal family were Friedrich Wilhelm I (reigned 1713–40) and Friedrich II (reigned 1740–86). **3**

HERR BRIEST	Und links sehen Sie also, meine Herrschaften, die Sankt-Ursula-Kirche, und weiter rechts . . .
FRAU GÜRLÜK	Entschuldigung. Wie alt ist diese Kirche? Tausend Jahre?
HERR BRIEST	Fast tausend Jahre alt. Sie stammt aus dem 12. Jahrhundert. Und von der Ostseite haben wir eine schöne Aussicht auf die Hohenzollernbrücke. . . .
LEVENT GÜRLÜK	Mensch! Ist die aber lang!
HERR BRIEST	Ahem! . . . Diese Brücke stammt aus dem Jahre 1907 und ist mehr als 500m lang.

FRAU WERDENBERG	Also das war wirklich einmalig. Und nun möchte ich gern ein paar Ansichtskarten kaufen.
FRÄULEIN SACHSEN	Gut. Die finden Sie hier vorne am Eingang.
Farb/Dias HERR WERDENBERG	Und auch Farbdias vom Dom?
FRÄULEIN SACHSEN	Wahrscheinlich. Aber wenn Sie keine finden, können Sie überall in den Geschäften Touristenartikel bekommen.
Touristen/Artikel FRAU WERDENBERG	Und Briefmarken? Auch hier am Eingang?
FRÄULEIN SACHSEN	Ja, ich glaube schon. Aber neben dem Café ist ein Kiosk. Da finden Sie ganz sicher Ihre Briefmarken.
HERR WERDENBERG	Und da bekomme ich auch Polaroid-Film?
Foto/Geschäft FRÄULEIN SACHSEN	Mm. Leider nicht. Da müssen Sie zum Fotogeschäft. Das ist aber auch hier in der Nähe, am Bahnhof.

KÖLNER DOM
Turmbesteigung
Eintritt 2,-- DM
87745
Waren Sie schon in der
Domschatzkammer?

4

FRAU VON HAAG	Ja, ich brauche bitte zwei Diafilme, DIN 21.
FRÄULEIN BETTNER	Bitte schön. Welche Marke denn, und mit wievielen Aufnahmen?
FRAU VON HAAG	Agfa, bitte. Mit 24 Aufnahmen, wenn Sie die haben.
FRÄULEIN BETTNER	Haben wir ganz bestimmt. . . . Ja, doch, hier sind sie. Und wollten Sie sonst noch etwas?
FRAU VON HAAG	Ja, ich hätte auch gern Ansichtskarten von der Stadt, aber ich sehe sie hier nicht.
FRÄULEIN BETTNER	Doch, wir haben eine große Auswahl. Schauen Sie doch da vorne am Eingang, an der großen Tafel.
FRAU VON HAAG	Ach, Entschuldigung. Und Briefmarken haben Sie auch, ja?
FRÄULEIN BETTNER	Die haben wir natürlich auch. Soll das für das Ausland sein?

STRUKTUR 1

Prepositions §§5,6

1. More about prepositions: their basic meanings and English equivalents

- **bei:** close proximity in space or time – by, at, in, during

  Bei diesem Wetter ist es zu gefährlich.   *in this weather*

- **aus:** not just "out"; also "from"

  Die Kirche stammt **aus dem 12. Jahrhundert.**⎫
  Das Museum stammt **aus dem Jahre 1907.**⎬ *is or dates from*

Word Order §6

2. Word order: modal verbs and their infinitives

phrase **modal** [other words and phrases] *infinitive*.
(*second*)   (*last*)

Den Turm	**dürfen**	wir	nicht	*besteigen.*
Ich	**wollte** so gern von dort oben die Stadt			*fotografieren.*
Vielleicht	**könnte**	ich	morgen	*zurückkommen.*
Nun	**möchte** ich gern ein paar Postkarten			*kaufen.*

Word Order §3

3. Word order: emphasizing something by placing it first.

emphasized element	verb	subject	rest of sentence
Den Turm	können	wir	nicht besteigen.
Natürlich	wollten	Sie	das.
Neben dem Café	ist	ein Kiosk.	
	2		

It's a good idea to confine exercises to the prepositions' meanings given in the text and not to try to be exhaustive in your treatment of the semantic field of each preposition.

Ignore the less frequent pattern: adverb – verb – pronoun object – noun subject (*Heute hat mir mein Bruder zehn Mark gegeben.*).

Remember: In simple statements the main verb is in second position no matter what the first element is. If the subject does not precede the verb, it must follow the verb immediately.

4. Using two elements to describe location more exactly

Drill this thoroughly by using the classroom as a point of departure. Student A: "*Wo ist . . . ?*" Student B: "*Das ist . . . .*" Use short phrases at first (*vorne links*, etc.). Then use one of the city maps (Trier, perhaps) to describe the location of points of interest.

vorne ⎫ ⎧ am Eingang
überall ⎪ ⎪ in den Geschäften
hier ⎬ ⎨ in der Nähe
links ⎭ ⎩ um die Ecke

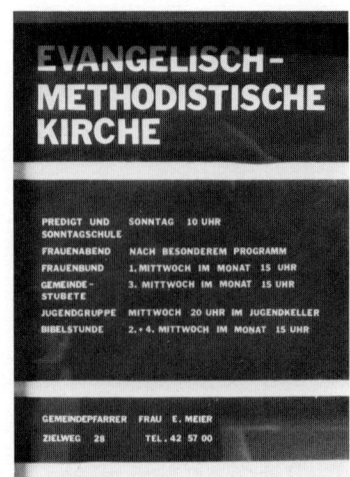

Geschenke

1

Treat *dachte* lexically, noting the similarity to English *thought*.

Rhein/Schiff

FRAU KNECHT	So, bitte schön. Der Nächste?
BOB KAUFMANN	Ich möchte ein T-Shirt mit einem Bild von Köln.
FRAU KNECHT	Ja, wir haben viele mit Bildern. Wollten Sie eins mit dem Dom?
BOB KAUFMANN	Vielleicht, aber ich dachte an etwas anderes. Etwas mit dem Rhein oder . . .
FRAU KNECHT	Hier ist eins mit einem Rheinschiff. Hübsch, nicht?
BOB KAUFMANN	Oh, das ist schön. Haben Sie es in meiner Größe?
FRAU KNECHT	Ich glaube schon. Welche Größe haben Sie denn?

2

Video/Spiele

FRÄULEIN MEYER	Guten Tag. Sind Sie die Nächste?
FRAU KÜTTEL	Ja. Ich suche ein Geschenk für meinen Sohn. Er ist 10.
FRÄULEIN MEYER	Schön. Liest er gern? Wir haben gute Kinderbücher.
FRAU KÜTTEL	Nein, nicht so gern.
FRÄULEIN MEYER	Welche Hobbys hat er? Sport, vielleicht? Wir haben auch alles für junge Sportler.
FRAU KÜTTEL	Das ist wirklich egal. Nur keine Videospiele. Er soll nur nicht so viel fernsehen.

3

Spiel/Waren/Abteilung

rollen/Treppe

HERR ZELLJADT	Entschuldigen Sie. Wie komme ich zur Spielwarenabteilung?
FRAU BEHLER	Spielwaren sind oben, im vierten Stock. Gehen Sie eine Treppe höher.
HERR ZELLJADT	Danke schön. Und die Herrenabteilung?
FRAU BEHLER	Die finden Sie unten, im ersten Stock.
HERR ZELLJADT	Wie, bitte? In welchem Stock?
FRAU BEHLER	Im ersten Stock. Von der Rolltreppe aus gehen Sie links um die Ecke.

4

Plastik/Tasche

FRAU BÜHLMANN	. . . So, 11,20 Mark zurück. Da haben Sie Ihre Quittung und hier die vier Weingläser.
TOM TANKERSLEY	Danke schön. Das sind Geschenke für meine Eltern in Amerika. Können Sie sie bitte gut einpacken?
FRAU BÜHLMANN	Gerne. Brauchen Sie auch eine Plastiktasche?
TOM TANKERSLEY	Ja, danke. Und noch eine Frage: Wo finde ich Kassetten mit Kölner Volksmusik?
FRAU BÜHLMANN	Kassetten und Platten finden Sie im Untergeschoß. Dort gibt es auch Bilderbücher, Plakate und Ansichtskarten, wenn Sie andere Geschenke für Ihre Familie suchen.

STRUKTUR 2

Nouns §11

With realia: signs *"Kein Zugang,"* etc.

1. Word formation

Many of the compound nouns you have seen so far have parallel English equivalents: *Postkarte, Videospiele, Bilderbücher.*

In addition, German has many compound nouns that are not so obvious in meaning. These may seem difficult at first, but very often they are simply combinations of easily understood root words.

Mention *Schreibwaren.*

Mention *Jahrzehnt, Jahrtausend.*

ROOT/MEANING	+ ROOT/MEANING	> COMPOUND/MEANING
aus out of ⎫ **ein** into ⎬ **-gang** going **zu** to ⎭		⎧ der **Ausgang** exit (way out) ⎨ der **Eingang** entrance (way in) ⎩ der **Zugang** access (way to)
spielen play	die **Waren** goods	die **Spielwaren** toys
aus out of	die **Wahl** choice	die **Auswahl** selection
aus out of	das **Land** country	das **Ausland** foreign country, -ies
das **Jahr** year	**hundert** 100	das **Jahrhundert** century
fern distant	**sehen** see	**fernsehen** watch TV

A.A. §40

2. verb + *gern(e)*

You might want to postpone *gern haben.* See note in Instructor's Guide.

- expresses liking to do something

    Liest er **gern?**   Does he like to read?

Remember that **möchte** means *would like.*

    Ich **möchte** Himbeereis, bitte.
    Wir **möchten** um drei im Dom sein.

A.A. §16; Nouns §13

3. *der Nächste/die Nächste* — an important pattern

Teach *Nächste* as a fossil form without going into an exegesis of adjective endings after *der*-words. Adjectives following the definite article are treated in Chapter 12.

The article (**der/die**) reflects the gender of the person:

Frau Knecht:	So. Bitte schön. **Der Nächste?**	
Bob Kaufmann:	Ich möchte . . .	(masculine = **der**)
Fräulein Meyer:	Guten Tag. Sind Sie **die Nächste?**	
Frau Küttel:	Ja, guten Tag. . . .	(feminine = **die**)

4. Identifying things among other similar things   welch-?/dies-

A.A. §18

Again, avoid teaching adjectives between *welch-/dies-* and the noun until Chapter 12. Exercises using *welch-* can include long comprehension questions involving class members, because the students will know each other well by this time. *"Welcher Student sieht gern fern, hat sieben Geschwister und studiert englische Literatur?" (class points) "Dieser Student."* Or 20 questions: Teacher: *"Diese Studentin hat zwei Brüder."* Student: *"Hat diese Studentin auch Schwestern?"* etc. Remind students of the function of *dies* alone to point to things nearby, both singular and plural: *Dies ist meine Mutter, dies sind meine Eltern.*

The endings of **welch-** and **dies-** echo the forms of the corresponding definite articles **der/die/das.**

	ARTICLE	
Diese Brücke stammt aus dem Jahre 1907.	**die**	(nominative)
Bei **diesem** Wetter ist es zu gefährlich.	**dem**	(dative)
Welche Größe haben Sie denn?	**die**	(accusative)

5. Introducing one statement with another:

says ⎫		
believes ⎬ that	Herr Briest sagt, diese Brücke ist mehr als 500m lang.	
knows ⎭	Ich glaube, wir können sie überall finden.	
	Ich weiß, wir haben viele T-Shirts mit Bildern.	

SITUATIONEN 2 Geschenke

Stage 1

	A	B
1	Is looking for something for husband. Likes to read, play golf, watch TV.	Asks about husband's interests. Books are on the third floor, sports on the . . . , and video games on the . . .
	Repeats, confuses the three locations. Apologizes, says thanks.	Repeats correctly.
2	Shows B something, indicating A thinks it quite pretty. Shows something else in another size. Indicates that it's quite reasonably priced.	Is not inspired; asks to see something else. Thinks that looks better. Agrees; asks if A has it in the next larger size as well – a present for B's mother.
3	Asks advice about a present for parents. They are wine connoisseurs. Agrees that sounds like a good idea. Likes the first set; asks B to pack for shipment to Canada. Would like something to carry them in.	Asks what parents like to do. Suggests some wine glasses. Shows three different sets of four. Is happy to accommodate. Suggests something appropriate.

"Ich glaube nicht," "Das ist zu X," etc.

"Gar nicht so teuer," "nicht zu teuer," etc.

"Meine Eltern trinken gern Wein – viel Wein."

Sorten, Gruppen, Möglichkeiten; or simply *drei Gläser.*

	A	B	C
4	(Is cashier.) Asks what B would like.	(Is male customer.) Says the woman standing there is next.	(Is female customer.) Thanks B; begins to ask for something.
	Says C was not there before B; insists that B was next.	Says he was not really there first.	Thanks B again, begins again to order.
	Interrupts C; asks what B wanted.	Says he doesn't know – something for his son.	Now is able to complete order – a T-shirt, size 10, for her daughter.
	Says they have size 10. Size 8 is not in stock.	Gets advice.	Says she'd also like a size 8.

"Größe 8 haben wir nicht (mehr)."

Stage 2

1

You have been waiting in line for some time, and others keep cutting in front of you. Finally you decide to become assertive.

a) Tell the person in front of you that you were already here.

b) Tell the clerk that you are next, and describe the relative positions of the three other people waiting in line.

" . . . und dann . . . und dann . . ." "und der Nächste . . ."

2

You wanted to find a nice table setting for yourself and your beloved – a knife, fork, and spoon for each of you, and perhaps a soup spoon and small butter knife as well. Tell the clerk what you were looking for (you don't see anything that strikes your fancy), make the purchase, and ask to have it gift-wrapped as a surprise. Be sure to ask for a receipt.

Versuchen Sie doch

You have arranged to make a purchase, which is now gift-wrapped on the counter in front of you. Suddenly you realize to your horror that you didn't exchange enough money at the bank, which is now closed. You plan to leave town within the hour, but somehow you have to pay for your items before you go. Discuss the possibilities.

"Er soll nicht so viel trinken," "Er trinkt gern, aber zu viel."

The clerk suggests a set of beer glasses as a present for your uncle. You have said he likes to drink, but would prefer that he cut down on his drinking. Tell the clerk some other things he likes to do – hike, swim, travel – and solicit other suggestions.

Chapter 11

ZOO/ ABENDFAHRT AUF DEM RHEIN

KD Köln-Düsseldorfer

Kontrollkarte
für Einfache Fahrt № 010804

Nur gültig mit dem Gruppenfahrausweis

Vollständig oder teilweise nicht benutzte Kontrollkarten werden nur erstattet, wenn eine entsprechende Bestätigung des Schiffsinspektors auf dem Gruppenfahrausweis eingeholt wurde.

Bitte offen und persönlich vorzeigen und bei Beendigung der Fahrt abgeben.

Im übrigen gelten die Allgemeinen Beförderungsbedingungen

Achtung Löwen kreuzen
die Fahrbahn

BITTE
nicht füttern

FUNKTIONEN – KONTEXTE – STRUKTUREN

Songs, poems, children's rhymes appropriate to chapter: "Jonny, wenn du Geburtstag hast" (Dietrich); "In dem Walde da steht ein Haus"; "Die Forelle" (Schubert); "Die Lorelei"; "Ich bin dein"; "Eene deene Tintenfaß"; "1, 2, 3, du bist frei"; "Ich und du, Müllers Kuh"; "Maikäfer flieg"; "Schwesterchen, komm tanz mit mir"; "Der Panther" and "Herbsttag" (Rilke).

Looking ahead

You'll be learning animal and clothing names, making detailed comparisons, handling more formal introductions, and, above all, learning a new form of address – the familiar *du*.

You will be using:

- familiar address (*Du gehst, Du siehst* rather than *Sie gehen, Sie sehen*) to talk to people you know well
- comparative forms (good, better) and words that explicitly relate the items in a comparison (X is better *than* Y)
- more separable-prefix verbs (get *up*, come *along*) in more complex patterns (You *have to* get up)

1

Regenschirm umbrella

Affen/Haus

FRÄULEIN HUBER	. . . So, 2 Erwachsene, 2 Kinder - 17 Mark, 3 Mark zurück.
	Und möchten Sie einen Regenschirm mieten? Es ist sehr naß.
FRAU VON SALIS	Auch ziemlich kalt. Sind alle Tiere draußen?
FRÄULEIN HUBER	Nein, nicht alle. . . . Darf ich etwas empfehlen?
	Wir haben ein berühmtes Affenhaus, und drinnen ist es auch wärmer als draußen.
FRAU VON SALIS	Ach, das klingt gut.

2

Eis/Bären

Nashorn rhinoceros

HERR FRANZEN	Nun, wollen wir zuerst die Bären sehen? Die Eisbären sind gleich da drüben.
FRÄULEIN GLATT	Nein, ich möchte lieber die Fische und dann die Vögel besuchen. Die sind interessanter.
HERR FRANZEN	Oh nein. Ich finde große Tiere besser. Vielleicht gehe ich zu den Elefanten und dann zum Nashorn. Und du gehst die Enten sehen.
FRÄULEIN GLATT	Also gut. . . . Siehst du den Imbiß da? Ich treffe dich dort in einer Stunde.

Seehund seal **3**

See/Löwe

Illustrate the use of the definite article before personal names in

Fütterung feeding

Viertel/Stunde

colloquial German. You might stress, however, that to many speakers of German this sounds sloppy. Students should practice using names *without* the definite article, but should be aware **4** of the pattern.

Remind students of the difference between *fressen* and *essen*, but don't be overly strict in enforcing it in class interchanges. Gentle correction strategy: Student: *"Der Seelöwe ißt Fisch."* Teacher: *"Ja, richtig, der Seelöwe frißt Fisch. Und was frißt ein Löwe?"*

Mention implicit *"gehen"* here. Other examples: *"Ich will/möchte nach Hause"*; English: "I want down, I want out of here."

KÖBI FÄSSLER	Guck mal! Ein Seehund. Oder ist das ein Seelöwe?
FRAU FÄSSLER	Das muß ein Seehund sein. Seelöwen sind größer und haben längere Zähne.
KÖBI FÄSSLER	Der sieht wie der Onkel Max aus. Gib ihm etwas zu fressen. Was frißt er gern?
FRAU FÄSSLER	Siehst du das Schild nicht? "Nächste Fütterung 15.00 Uhr." Warten wir eine Viertelstunde. Ich kaufe ein paar Fische und du wirfst sie zum Seehund.
KÖBI FÄSSLER	Und der fängt sie immer, nicht wahr? Und der hat keine Hände!

ANGELIKA STOCK	Schau mal, Mutti. Ein Krokodil. Es sieht tot aus.
FRAU STOCK	Das Krokodil schläft gerade. Zuerst frißt es viel, und dann schläft es lange.
ANGELIKA	Du Krokodil! Sei nicht so faul! Steh doch auf!
FRAU STOCK	Sprich nicht so laut! Lies mal das Schild: "Krokodile springen und beißen. . . ." Weißt du, Krokodile fressen jeden Tag Menschen in Afrika. Besser, du nimmst jetzt meine Hand.
ANGELIKA	Mutti, ich will auch mal zu den Schlangen.

Verbs §8

See note in Instructor's Guide.

1. *Du* – "you"

Du is used to address family members, close friends, children, animals, and even God.

> Siehst du den Imbiß da?
> Du Krokodil!
> Inge! Du!

- **add *-st* to the verb stem**

$$du + \text{-}st$$

> Und **du gehst** die Enten sehen.
> Ich kaufe ein paar Fische und **du wirfst** sie zum Seehund.
> Was **möchtest du** jetzt machen?

Verbs §13

2. *Du* and stem-changing verbs

In Chapter 4 you learned about stem-changing verbs:

See note in Instructor's Guide.

INFINITIVE	THIRD PERSON SINGULAR STEM CHANGE
essen	er/sie ißt
vergessen	er/sie vergißt
nehmen	er/sie nimmt
sehen	er/sie sieht

These verbs change their stems for *du* also:

> du **ißt**
> du **vergißt**
> du **nimmst**   Besser, **du nimmst** jetzt meine Hand.
> du **siehst**   **Siehst du** den Imbiß da?

3. *Draußen/drinnen:* where things are located

Use this opportunity for a vocabulary check. Name a zoo animal, asking the class to say whether it lives outside or inside at the zoo. "*Das Krokodil.*" "*Das wohnt draußen.*" "*Die Fische.*" "*Die wohnen drinnen.*" Follow-up: "*Warum wohnt der Eisbär draußen?*" etc. (tests adjectives, comparatives).

draußen	think **aus**		out/in ⎰ there / -side / -doors
drinnen	think **in**		

> Sind alle Tiere **draußen**?
> **Drinnen** ist es auch wärmer als **draußen**.

Wilhelma
in Stuttgart

Deutschlands einziger Zoologisch-botanischer Garten

Das Erlebnis mit 8000 Tieren und herrlichen Pflanzen aus aller Welt

● ganzjährig täglich geöffnet ●
große Schauhäuser ● kein Wetterrisiko

Stuttgart-Bad Cannstatt, Neckartalstraße, Postfach 501227
Telefon (0711) 540 20
Anfahrt über B10 bzw. B14
S-Bahn: Bahnhof Bad Cannstatt oder Nordbahnhof
Straßenbahn: Linie 14 und 13
Bus: Linie 52, 55 und 56

Öffnungszeiten:	Hauptkasse:	Tierhäuser:
Mai bis August	8.00–18.00	8.00–19.00
April und September:	8.00–17.30	8.00–18.30
März und Oktober	8.00–17.00	8.00–18.00
November bis Februar:	8.00–16.00	8.00–17.00

Das Aquarium öffnet um 9.00 Uhr. Dienstags wird es 1 Stunde vor den Tierhäusern geschlossen. Der Park bleibt bis Einbruch der Dunkelheit – spätestens 20.00 Uhr – geöffnet.

Eintrittspreise:

Tageskarten:		Jahreskarten:	
Erwachsene	7,— DM	Erwachsene	40,— DM
Rentner	6,— DM	Rentner	20,— DM
Kinder, Schüler und Studenten,		Beikarte für Ehefrau	20,— DM
Schwerbeschädigte mit Ausweis	3,— DM	Kinder	10,— DM
Gesellschaften ab 20 Personen:		Studienkarten für Schüler und Studenten	20,— DM
Erwachsene	6,— DM		
Kinder	2,50 DM		
Schulen, je Schüler	2,50 DM		

SITUATIONEN 1 Zoo

Stage 1	A	B
1	(little brother of B) Wants to be inside, where it's warmer. Wants to see snakes and bears. Yes – they don't sleep as much. Would like something to drink, too. Says that sounds great.	Agrees; asks what A would like to see. Good idea – how about the polar bears? Right – brown bears sleep more. Suggests some hot chocolate.
2	(Is 12 years old) Asks B to recommend something to see. Likes animals with teeth. Asks what they like to eat. Says would rather see birds. Thanks B for advice.	(Is zoo visitor, unknown to A) Asks what A likes. Suggests crocodiles. Says "children." Says birds are outside and inside.
3	(daughter of B) Asks B what bears like to eat. Asks when bears will eat breakfast. Wants to give fish to bears. Asks who feeds them. Asks if fish eat bears, too.	(mother of A) Says bears eat lots of fish. Says soon – at 9:00. Says visitors aren't allowed to. A man comes and throws the fish to them. Suggests it's time to go see the seals.
4	(14-year-old friend of B) Says the strawberry ice cream is great. Wants to see the skunks. Says his (her) sister looks like a skunk. Asks if raccoons really wash their food.	(14-year-old friend of A) Agrees, says always likes to eat ice cream at the zoo; asks what A would like to see now. Good idea – refers to skunks' little eyes (like those of their biology teacher). No – she looks more like a raccoon. Of course they do – and they like to take showers and sleep in hotels, too.

Be sure to enforce *du/Sie* distinction here.

"Was findest du interessant?"
"Was siehst du gern?"

Infinitive phrase is not necessary. *"Es ist X Uhr. Gehen wir zu den Seehunden." "Was machen die Seehunde? Was meinst du?"*

Stage 2

1
You are at the zoo with your brother, who wants to walk as little as possible. Tell him

a) he shouldn't be so lazy;
b) he ought to get up;
c) he ought to feed the seals with you;
d) he can sit here if he wants; you'll see him back here in two hours.

2
You and your beloved are at the zoo, where you're deciding on the day's activities. It's a blustery day with intermittent showers.

a) Discuss how to keep dry outside.

b) Most of your favorite animals are outside, but there are some interesting ones indoors as well. Make a plan for seeing as much as you can without getting soaked or frozen.

3
You are standing in front of the bears' cage with your friends' little boy. He's taunting the sleeping animals. Tell him:

a) bears are not really very lazy;
b) they like to bite children;
c) bears can run faster than children;
d) every day bears in Canada eat people;
e) people don't like to eat bears because they are so dangerous.

Versuchen Sie doch

You are entertaining the young son of friends in Basel. It is his first visit to the zoo. Tell him what the animals in the zoo do all day, what the people do, and what the people are not allowed to do if they value their lives. Tell him how what the animals do in the zoo differs from what they do in their natural habitats.

113

Animal names

Many German animal names are nearly identical to English ones:

der		*die*	*das*
Hund Elefant	Wolf Fuchs	Katze	Insekt
Affe Büffel	Schimpanse	Giraffe	Schwein
Bulle Ochse	Wurm Fisch	Kuh	Kalb
Bär Tiger		Henne	Känguruh

Some names are deceptive. They sound like English words, but refer to different animals. For example, *der Elch* means "moose," not "elk."

There are also some common German animal names that are quite unlike their English counterparts:

der Vogel "bird"   der Dachs "badger"   das Pferd "horse"
   der Igel "hedgehog"   der Hirsch "stag" or "elk"

Another group of names describes animals by their appearance or habits:

der Seehund "seal" ("sea-dog")
das Stachelschwein "porcupine" ("barb-pig")
das Nashorn "rhinoceros" ("nose-horn")
der Vielfraß "wolverine" ("much-gobble")
das Stinktier "skunk" ("stink-animal")
der Waschbär "raccoon" ("wash-bear")
der Eisbär "polar bear" ("ice-bear")
das Eichhörnchen "squirrel" ("little-oak-horn")
das Faultier "sloth" ("lazy animal")
das Nilpferd "hippopotamus" ("Nile horse")
die Schlange "snake" ("ropelike one")

"mountain cat." Here the habits of this omnivore caused the popular association of *fjeld-* with *viel-* and *-fross* with *-fraß* (*<*fressen*).

Note the Bavarian dial. *Ohrkatzenschwoaf* "squirrel" (*Ohr + Katzen + Schweif*, "Ear-cat-tail-"); use this in class at your own risk.

Du and *Sie* – when to use what

Du is reserved for intimates. When in doubt, use *Sie*. Overuse of *Sie* may make you sound too formal, but improper use of *du* can be taken as an insult. Like overreadiness to use first names, it might be considered too "palsy-walsy."

A very young child will address everyone as *du*, including strangers. Gradually the child learns to say *Sie* to all but very familiar adults. Whether a child addresses you with *du* or *Sie*, say *du* to the child.

Teenagers and young adults who are even slightly acquainted readily use *du* among themselves. University students customarily address each other that way, and if you are in a university setting you may well be called *du* by strangers of your own age.

• the German concept of "friend"

Speakers of standard German distinguish between *Freunde* and *Bekannte*. *Freunde* (*der Freund, die Freundin*) are close friends. *Bekannte* (*der Bekannte, die Bekannte*) are more casual acquaintances. While American English tends to use "friend" for both kinds, in German the difference is important, and is reflected in the reservation of *du* for *Freunde* and the use of *Sie* with *Bekannte*. Adult German

---

Margin notes (left column):

List some idioms using animals if you wish: for example, *Schwein haben, Schlange stehen;* use of *sau* as intensifying prefix: *saukalt, -blöd*, etc. Also include verbs: *muhen, miauen, bellen, brüllen, schreien, piepsen, heulen,* etc.

Maybe point out the underlying cognate and word family (*Vogel/fowl; Vogel – fliegen – Flügel*).

Seehund is a folk etymology from Old High German *sëlah* (> *sele* > *seel* > *seel-hund* > *Seehund*); the first element was incorrectly believed to have something to do with the sea; and the *h* was associated with *Hund* – logically enough, since to many people the heads of dogs and seals are similar. Note English dial. *selkie*, "seal."

Vielfraß is another folk etymology, this time from Scandinavia: Norw. *fjeldfross,*

When you write a note or letter to a du, *be sure to capitalize the* D *in all forms:* Du, Dein, Dir, Dich.

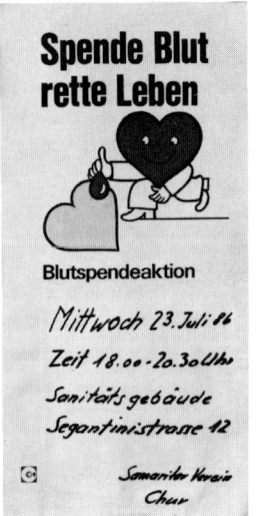

Spende Blut rette Leben

Blutspendeaktion

Mittwoch 23. Juli 86
Zeit 18.00-20.30 Uhr
Sanitätsgebäude
Segantinistrasse 12

Samariter Verein
Chur

speakers do not lightly change from *Sie* to *du* in addressing the same person. The change, which reflects a distinct deepening of the relationship, is often accompanied by an informal ceremony, perhaps a toast. The difference between *Sie*- address and *du*-address is even trickier when romance is a possibility.

More formal introductions – some standard phrases

Students practice introducing: 1) themselves (*darf ich mich vorstellen?*), 2) a friend (*darf ich Bill vorstellen?*). Enforce handshaking custom.

The key word in making introductions is *vorstellen*, "introduce" or "present."

Darf ich vorstellen?	May I make the (or some) introductions?
Darf ich meinen Mann vorstellen?	May I introduce my husband?
Darf ich mich vorstellen?	May I introduce myself?

Here are two proper replies to an introduction:

Guten Morgen, Herr Fuchs. *or* Freut mich sehr, Frau Wolf.

Gestures are important in introductions. A handshake is virtually obligatory between adults, be they men or women, and there is usually a slight bow of the head. Children being introduced to adults are often expected to look them directly in the eye and make a more distinct bow (boys) or a curtsy (girls).

Der Rhein

Time for a geography review. Trace other major rivers in all four countries from source to mouth. Locate major cities on each.

die Quelle: Der Tomasee (2345m) in den ostschweizerischen Alpen
die Länge: 1300km (Potomac 460km, Hudson 500km, St. Lawrence 1225km, Colorado 1350km, Columbia 2000km, Mississippi 4000km, Amazon 6300km)
die Länder: die Schweiz, die Bundesrepublik Deutschland, Frankreich, Holland

Wines and wine names

Bring wine labels to class. Practice reading names and finding towns on the map.

Both West Germany and Austria are major wine producers, though only West German wine is exported in quantity to North America. White wine is encountered far more frequently than red wine, and in general German wines are quite light in taste and body. Chief wine-producing regions are denoted by river names – der Rhein, die Mosel (accent on first syllable). *Rheinwein* comes in brown bottles, *Moselwein* in green.

Although many North Americans have heard of "Liebfraumilch," German wines ordinarily have names consisting of two or even more words. The first is likely to be a geographical name, very often that of the town where the vineyard is located. The second is the actual name of the wine. Thus the name of the most famous (and expensive) German wine: Bernkasteler Doktor. Wine names can be very fanciful, sometimes even playfully coarse (Kröver Nacktarsch – Bare Bottom) or fondly sacrilegious (Liebfraumilch – Milk of the Blessed Virgin).

Chapter 20 includes a more detailed discussion of wine.

City names as adjectives: the invariable ending -er

Very often a wine's vintage year is indicated along with the wine name. If so, the invariable ending -er is added to the year: 1985er (often printed 85er and usually pronounced "*fünfundachtziger*"). Note that the same ending -er is used to make adjectives of city names.

Other examples: Nürnberger Lebkuchen, Wiener Schnitzel, Berner Troubadours, and many newspaper names such as Stuttgarter Zeitung.

der Kölner Dom   die Baseler Nachrichten   Frankfurter Würste

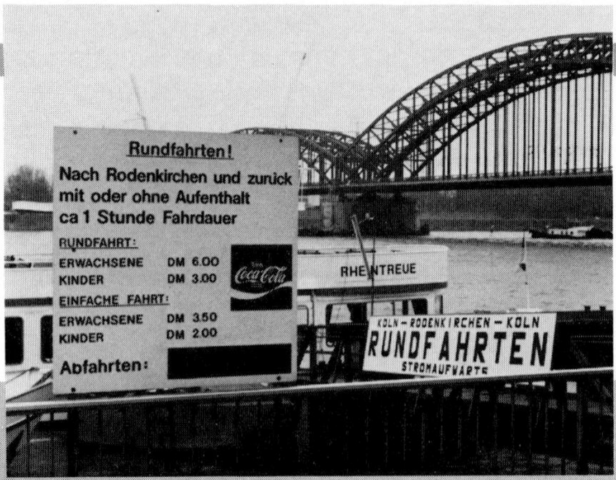

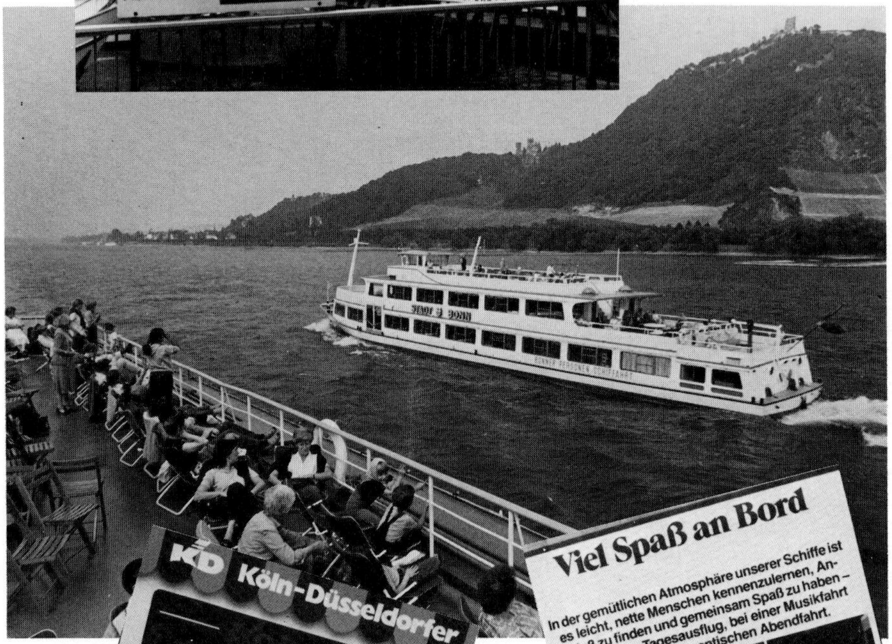

Saisoneröffnung
Ostern 1986

Bei Vorbestellung sind Sonderfahrten jederzeit möglich.

Ermäßigungen

auf Sammelfahrschein Gruppenrabatte für fahrplanmäßige Fahrten:

ab 15 Personen 5%
ab 35 Personen 10%
ab 100 Personen 15%
ab 250 Personen 20%

Ermäßigungen für Schulklassen mit mehr als 15 Schülern:

Schüler unter 12 Jahren:
Kinderfahrpreis abzüglich 15%

Schüler über 12 Jahren:
Erwachsenenfahrpreis abzüglich 20%

Berufsschüler und Schüler über 18 Jahren:
Erwachsenenfahrpreis abzüglich 10%

Auf die unter Sonderfahrten stehenden Schiffsausflüge kann kein Rabatt gewährt werden.

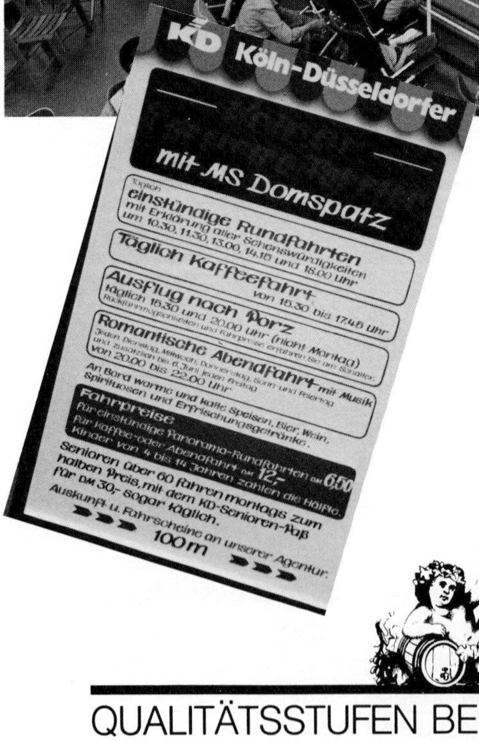

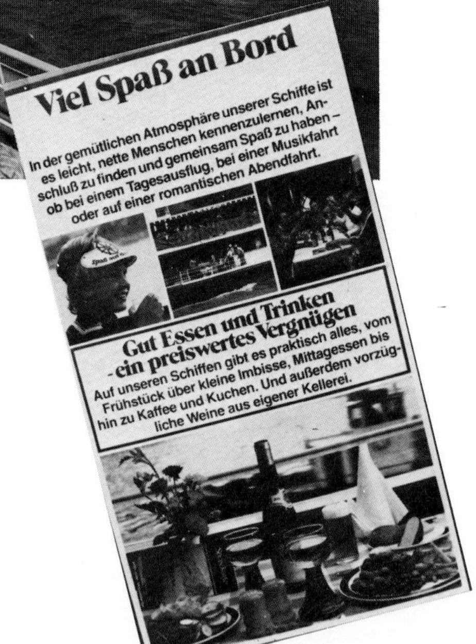

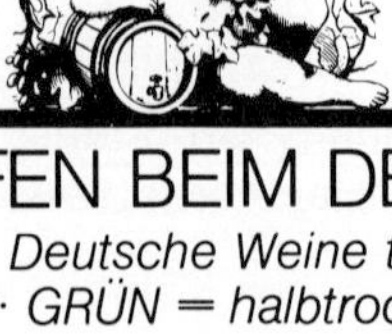

QUALITÄTSSTUFEN BEIM DEUTSCHEN WEIN

Viele Deutsche Weine tragen das Weinsiegel
GELB = trocken · GRÜN = halbtrocken · ROT = lieblich

DEUTSCHES WEINSIEGEL trocken Rheinhessen

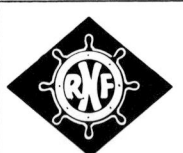

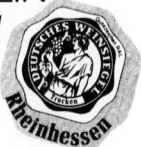

<table>
<tr><td>Student A tells temperature and weather conditions, Student B tells appropriate clothing. Refer to Bildwörterbuch.</td></tr>
</table>

1

Fahr-/Plan
Sonderfahrt special trip

Pulli Pullover

FRAU DACHSEN	Mach doch schnell. Unser Schiff fährt in 20 Minuten ab.
HERR DACHSEN	Ich dachte, erst um 19.30.
FRAU DACHSEN	Nein, lies mal den Fahrplan. "Sonderfahrt Rhein in Flammen. Abfahrt von der Rheinbrücke 19 Uhr."
HERR DACHSEN	Ich komme schon. Gib mir den Zimmerschlüssel. Und vergiß diesmal deine Jacke nicht!
FRAU DACHSEN	Die habe ich schon, den Hut auch. Nimmst du deinen Pulli auch mit?
HERR DACHSEN	Ja. Es ist schon ziemlich kühl – nicht mehr als 15 Grad.

2

HERR MARTENS	Guten Abend. Ist hier noch frei, bitte?
HERR SIEBERT	Ja, bitte schön. Hier ist noch Platz.
HERR MARTENS	Ach, danke. Übrigens – ich heiße Martens.
HERR SIEBERT	Siebert, freut mich sehr. Meine Frau . . .
HERR MARTENS	Abend, Frau Siebert. Und darf ich Fräulein Behrens vorstellen?

3

Reise/Führer

Drachen dragon
Fels rock

FRAU MAREK	Schönes Wetter für eine Abendfahrt, nicht?
FRAU BAUER	Herrlich – und am Abend viel kühler und frischer als am Tag. . . . Machen Sie die Fahrt auch zum ersten Mal?
FRAU MAREK	Das ist unsere erste Rheinfahrt überhaupt. Übrigens, wissen Sie, wie das Schloß da drüben heißt?
FRAU BAUER	Moment. Ich schaue mal in unserem Reiseführer nach. . . . Köln, Königswinter, Rolandseck. . . . Das muß ja der Drachenfels sein.

4

Schiff/Kapelle

KARL BRUGGMANN	Gabi, wir kennen uns schon eine Woche. Wir müssen feiern! Wollen wir noch eine Flasche Wein oder Sekt bestellen?
GABRIELE FLICK	Ja, und die Loreley kommt bald. Das ist alles so romantisch, besonders wenn die Schiffskapelle spielt. Und ich tanze so gern mit dir.
KARL BRUGGMANN	Herr Ober, was würden Sie uns empfehlen, die Steinberger Auslese oder den Fuchsmantel Wackenheimer Riesling Kabinett?
HERR STALDER	Das kommt darauf an. Die sind beide ausgezeichnet. Die Steinberger Auslese ist etwas süßer, der Fuchsmantel trockener. Ich selber trinke lieber den Fuchsmantel – der 81er ist besonders gut.

Großveranstaltung: Rhein in Flammen (Koblenz)

Samstag, 9. 8. 1986

mit Musik

Abfahrtsstelle Heidelberg 10.30 Uhr	Abfahrtsstelle Mannheim 12.30 Uhr

Unsere Gäste erleben die Veranstaltung »Rhein in Flammen« von unseren Schiffen aus (bis ca. 23.00 Uhr). Danach Ausschiffung und Rückfahrt mit Bussen. Ankunft Mannheim ca. 2.30 Uhr, Heidelberg ca. 3.00 Uhr

---

STRUKTUR 2

A.A. §§24–29

No matter how long the adjective, just add -er.

See note in Instructor's Guide.

Point out the origin of *die Eltern* from *die Älteren.*

Other useful irregular comparative forms: *viel – mehr, nahe – näher, hoch – höher.*

1. More about comparing things

● As you learned in Chapter 4, most comparative forms end in **-er:**

Die Vögel sind interessanter.
Am Abend ist es viel kühler und frischer als am Tag.

● Some comparatives **umlaut the vowel** in the stem:

groß: Seelöwen sind **größer.**
lang: Sie haben **längere** Zähne.

> like English:
> old → elder

● A few forms are **irregular** and must be memorized:

gut: Ich finde große Tiere **besser.**
gern: Die Stinktiere möchte ich gern sehen. Ich möchte **lieber** die Affen besuchen.

● Use of *so . . . wie* and *-er als*

You can extend the "nicht so ____" you learned in Chapter 2 by adding <u>wie</u> and then naming the second item:

Die Wurst ist <u>nicht so teurer</u> **wie** das Kotelett.

> denying equality
> **nicht so** ____ **wie** ____

TPR exercises work well with imperatives, especially those with separable prefixes. "Judy, *stehen* Sie *auf* und gehen Sie

You can say much the same thing by using the comparative and *als:*

Das Kotelett ist <u>teurer</u> **als** die Wurst.

> asserting inequality
> ____-er als

Verbs §§30,31

zum Fenster. Bill, *stehen* Sie *auf* und gehen Sie zur Tür – und *nehmen* Sie Karen *mit*. Bleiben Sie dort bitte *stehen*. Judy, *kommen* Sie *zurück* – und Bill auch, aber *bringen* Sie Karen nicht *mit*. Karen, *bleiben* Sie bitte dort *stehen*. Mike, . . .

2. More about separable-prefix verbs

● With a modal, the prefix joins the main verb:

(**vorstellen**)   Darf ich Fräulein Behrens **vorstellen?**

● Remember from Chapter 7, though: when the separable prefix verb is the *only* verb, the **prefix** comes **at the end of the sentence:**

(**aussehen**)   Der Seehund **sieht** wie der Onkel Max **aus.**
(**nachschauen**) Ich **schaue** mal in unserem Baedeker **nach.**

Pronouns §11; Verbs §50

See note in Instructor's Guide.

3. Even more about *du*

● **case forms**

nominative	**du**
accusative	**dich**
dative	**dir**
possessive	**dein**

Tell students to give *du*-commands to other students. Teacher: *"Jane, sagen Sie Ralph, er soll aufstehen."* Jane: *"Ralph, steh auf."* Combine and vary with TPR exercises.

● **imperative (command) with *du***

WITH SIE: VERB + SIE	WITH DU: VERB STEM ONLY
Stehen Sie doch auf!	Steh doch auf!
Kommen Sie zu mir!	Komm zu mir!
Machen Sie schnell!	Mach schnell!
Seien Sie nett!	Sei nicht so faul!

Note vowel changes in some verb stems:

Sprechen Sie lauter!	**Sprich** nicht so laut!
Lesen Sie weiter!	**Lies** mal das Schild!

Stage 1	A	B
1	Is on the way to the boat; tells B not to forget her hat.	Has her hat; tells A not to forget his windbreaker.
	Asks B whether she has the room key.	Says she thought A had it.
	Thinks it's in her pocket.	No – says they have only 15 minutes before the boat leaves.
	Finds the key on the table; says they should hurry.	Says she knows that – it's already 6:45.

Here, as elsewhere, "etc." is a cue to inspire student's imagination.

	A	B
2	Greets, then tries to make conversation with a woman he has admired from afar – talks about weather, the boat, etc.	Gives noncommittal responses to A's statements.
	Introduces himself (name is Marti).	Acknowledges Mr. Marti, doesn't give her name.
	Says he's never taken this boat trip before.	Says she and her husband were here last year, indicates that he's approaching now with her coat.

Double infinitive is not necessary here: "*Ich kann die Schiffskapelle nicht hören.*"

Während is unnecessary: "*am Tag*" or "*heute nachmittag*" will suffice.

See if students catch the humor if you suggest using *Sie* here.

	A	B
3	Says they must be sitting too far toward the front of the boat – can't hear the ship's orchestra playing.	Suggests they sit inside, where it's warmer.
	Agrees – it's not as warm now as during the day.	Asks if A would like him to fetch her coat.
	No – they'll just snuggle a bit.	Orders a bottle of Piesporter Michelsberg for the occasion – they've been in Köln for exactly two days.
	Wonderful idea – he's so romantic.	Is also hungry, suggests fruit and cheese.

Stage 2

1

You don't know what time the cruise begins.

a) Ask your companion to read the schedule and find out how much the cruise costs.
b) Say you're not sure whether you have that much cash on you.
c) Suggest you go down to the dock; perhaps they'll take a traveler's check.
d) Remind your companion to take along a sweater and jacket because of the temperature on the river.

2

You suggest an evening cruise on the Rhine to your companion. Cite all the advantages you can.

3

The boat is beginning its trip back down the Rhein to the dock at Köln. You have had a wonderful evening with the other couple at your table, and are grateful to them and happy to have gotten to know them. Express your feelings and arrange to meet them the next day for coffee at that pastry shop you found yesterday near the university.

Versuchen Sie doch

You've now been in Köln for a week. Think back over the past several days and recall

a) the things you wanted to do both indoors and outdoors when you arrived at the train station;
b) the things you were able to do because of favorable weather, friendly people, and the good transportation system;
c) the things you couldn't do because of bad weather, surly people, and the traffic.

119

Chapter 12

POST/ IM ABTEIL

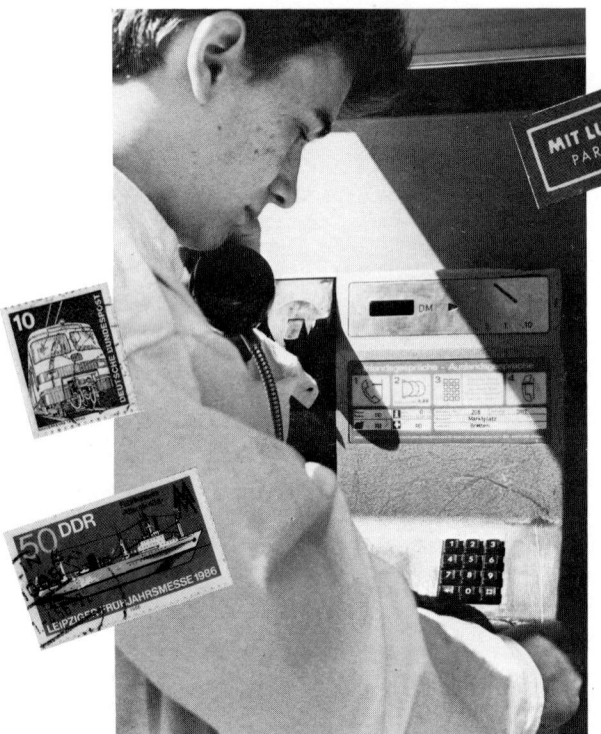

FUNKTIONEN — KONTEXTE — STRUKTUREN

Appropriate songs:
"Die Post" (from Schuberts
"Winterreise" #13);
*"Wir eilen mit schwachen, doch
emsigen Schritten zu Dir"* (Bach
cantata, BWV78);
*"Mein Freund ist mein, und ich
bin Dein"* (BWV140);
"Du bist die Ruh" (Schubert);
*"Horch, was kommt von draußen
rein?"*

Looking ahead

You'll be conducting postal transactions, learning how to use the telephone, finding out more about trains and other public facilities, expressing plans, and discussing the past.

You will be using:

- *wenn* in longer constructions
- pronouns and nouns together (I'll give *you* some *airmail stickers.*)
- *gehen* + a verb to express plans for the immediate future
- more *du* forms
- the present perfect — the fundamental German past tense
- the connector (conjunction) *daß* (I heard *that* the train is late.)

Post

Treat *per* only in combination with *Luftpost*. Mention *mit Luftpost* and illustrate with an airmail envelope.

1

CATHY KERNER	Ich möchte diese zwei Briefe und die Ansichtskarten per Luftpost nach Amerika schicken, bitte.
FRAU WENNE	Bitte schön. Dieser kostet 1,10, der andere Brief ist schwerer, der kostet 1,70. Und zehn Ansichtskarten, 7 Mark. Das macht zusammen 9,80, bitte.
CATHY KERNER	Wie, bitte? Ich habe Sie nicht verstanden.
FRAU WENNE	9 Mark und 80 Pfennig.
CATHY KERNER	Danke. Und wieviel kostet eine Ansichtskarte nach Kanada?
FRAU WENNE	Auch 70 Pf. Das wäre also zusammen 10 Mark 50.

2

PROFESSOR NEU	Ich möchte bitte zehn Siebziger.
HERR STALDER	Im Moment habe ich keine Siebziger mehr. Darf ich Ihnen Fünfziger und Zwanziger geben?
PROFESSOR NEU	Die sind für Ansichtskarten, aber ich glaube, es geht schon.
HERR STALDER	Und brauchen Sie sonst noch etwas?
PROFESSOR NEU	Ja, bitte – einige Luftpostaufkleber.

Post/Paket **3**

RICHARD LYMAN	Ich möchte ein Postpaket Größe 3, bitte.
FRAU STEINER	Bitte schön. Und Sie müssen diese Formulare ausfüllen, wenn Sie das nach Übersee schicken.
RICHARD LYMAN	Gibt es eine Ermäßigung für Bücher?
FRAU STEINER	Ja, wenn das Paket nicht mehr als 5 Kilo wiegt.
RICHARD LYMAN	Noch eine Frage. Ich habe Geschenke für meine Familie gekauft – Weingläser und so weiter. . . .
FRAU STEINER	Dann ist es besser, wenn Sie ein Paket mit Plastikschaum kaufen.

Plastik/Schaum

4

HOWARD LEICHTER	Ich möchte bitte meine Familie in den USA anrufen. Könnten Sie mir erklären, wie man das macht?
HERR THIELE	Gehen Sie in Kabine 2. Die Vorwahl für Amerika ist 0 01. Sie wählen also die ganze Nummer. Dann kommen Sie zurück, wenn Sie fertig sind.
HOWARD LEICHTER	Vielen Dank. Und wieviel kostet das, bitte?
HERR THIELE	Ein Ferngespräch nach Amerika kostet 4,80 Fr pro Einheit. Eine Einheit ist eine Minute.
HOWARD LEICHTER	Kann sein, daß ich nicht genug Geld bei mir habe.
HERR THIELE	Das geht schon. Ihre Familie kann den Anruf bezahlen.

Vorwahl international telephone access code

fern/Gespräch

Show students the connection between *anrufen* and *der Anruf*.

5

BARRY GOODMAN	Wieviel ist denn das kleine Paket?
HERR BOENINGER	Das weiß ich noch nicht. Moment mal.
BARRY GOODMAN	Ach, geben Sie mir bitte den ersten Brief und das große Paket wieder. Ich muß die Postleitzahlen schreiben.
HERR BOENINGER	So, ist gut. Also die beiden Briefe sind DM 4,60. Und für die beiden Pakete macht das DM 26,90. Zusammen DM 31,50, bitte.

STRUKTUR 1

W.O. §9

1. Word order: *wenn*

after **wenn:** verb at end

Wenn-clauses are treated here only in sentence final position. Front-field subordinate clauses are introduced in Chapter 14.

Sie müssen diese Formulare ausfüllen, **wenn** Sie das nach Übersee **schicken**.

Ja, **wenn** das Paket nicht mehr als 5 Kilo **wiegt**.

Dann ist es besser, **wenn** Sie ein Paket mit Plastikschaum **kaufen**.

W.O. §19

2. Pronouns and nouns together

pronouns come first

Practice this structure with menus as well: *"Bringen Sie mir bitte ein Pils." "Bringen Sie uns bitte zweimal Kasseler Rippchen."*

pronoun   noun   noun

Darf ich **Ihnen Fünfziger** und **Zwanziger** geben?

pronoun   noun

Könnten Sie **mir** bitte auch einige **Luftpostaufkleber** geben?

Verbs §§34,36

3. *gehen* + infinitive: "to go do (something)"

Contexts for exercise: city/zoo/ household. *"Ich gehe X sehen/ besuchen/finden/und du gehst Y*

Und **du gehst** den Storch **sehen**.   Ich **gehe** mein Gepäck **holen**.

A.A. §16

4. Adjectives after definite articles

kaufen/füttern/kochen," etc. For contexts see Stuttgart Wilhelma zoo (p. 112) and *Bildwörterbuch* *"City/Stadt"* (p. 286–287) and *"Rooms/Zimmer"* (p. 288–289).

• nominative

masculine	**-e**	Der ander**e** Brief ist schwerer.
feminine	**-e**	Wieviel kostet die groß**e** Ansichtskarte?
neuter	**-e**	Wieviel war denn das groß**e** Paket?
PLURAL	**-en**	Also – die beid**en** Briefe sind DM 4,60.

Assign students, each with different adjectives and professions: Tom = *Lehrer, alt;* Betty = *Ärztin, müde;* Diane = *Pilotin, jung;* Dave = *Fußballspieler, schnell.* Teacher points to each; class identifies: *"Tom ist der alte Lehrer,"* etc. For accusative use the same exercise, but with Teacher: *"Wen sehe ich?"* Class: *"Sie sehen den alten Lehrer,"* etc.

• accusative

masculine	**-en**	Geben Sie mir bitte den erst**en** Brief.
feminine	**-e**	Sie wählen also die ganz**e** Nummer.
neuter	**-e**	Geben Sie mir bitte das groß**e** Paket wieder.
PLURAL	**-en**	Für die beid**en** Pakete macht das DM 26,90.

Briefe
(Beförderung auf dem Luftweg inbegriffen)

	Taxe Europa und Mittelmeer-länder Fr.	übrige Länder Fr.	Höchst-gewicht
bis 10 g	1.10*	1.40	2 kg
über 10 g bis 20 g	1.10*	1.70	
über 20 g bis 50 g	1.80	3.––	
über 50 g bis 100 g	2.50	4.––	
über 100 g bis 250 g	5.––	8.60	
über 250 g bis 500 g	10.––	16.60	
über 500 g bis 1000 g	17.––	29.––	
über 1000 g bis 1500 g	23.––	41.––	
über 1500 g bis 2000 g	28.––	52.––	
* nach Ländern, die zur **CEPT**[1] gehören: bis 20 g	0.90		

Aerogramme	Taxe eines Briefes bis 20 g	1.20	––

Postkarten/Ansichtskarten
(Beförderung auf dem Luftweg inbegriffen) 0.80 1.10 ––

Ansichtskarten, Besuchs- sowie Glückwunsch- und Beileidskarten mit Grüssen oder Höflichkeits-formeln in höchstens 5 Wörtern: Taxe der Drucksachen

Drucksachen zur ermässigten Taxe
Bücher, Broschüren, Musikalien und geographische Karten

bis 20 g	0.60	0.70	500 g
über 20 g bis 50 g	0.80	1.––	
über 50 g bis 100 g	0.90	1.25	
je weitere 50 g	0.20	0.35	

Sondersack[1]
für Drucksachen zur ermässigten Taxe

je kg (Sackgewicht inbegriffen)	2.80	5.30	30 kg

POST PAC

Bei Ihrer Poststelle und in Papeterien gibt's für jedes Paket die richtige Verpackung: Faltschachteln in vier verschiedenen Grössen und eine spezielle Flaschenverpackung. Klebeband und Schnur sind selbstverständlich auch dabei.

Grösse	Innenmasse	Verkaufspreis
Grösse 1	19,5 x 13,5 x 9,5 cm	Fr. 1.50
Grösse 2	30,5 x 21,5 x 11 cm	Fr. 2.––
Grösse 3	38,5 x 21,5 x 13,5 cm	Fr. 2.50
Grösse 4	48,5 x 26 x 18,5 cm	Fr. 3.––
Grösse 5	Flaschenverpackung (7 dl, 1 l)	Fr. 2.50

	A	**B**
Stage 1		

1

"Dieser Brief" or "der Brief."

A	**B**
Would like to send two letters airmail to North America. Would also like stamps for six postcards. Gives B a DM 20-note. Responds appropriately.	Says how much they'll cost; one is heavier than the other. Add the totals: DM 1,30 for one letter, 1,50 for the other; 70 Pf for each card. Counts appropriate change.

2

A	**B**
Has to have stamps in denominations of 70 Pf and DM 1,10; wants as many as possible for DM 25. Decides on 10 of 70 Pf and 15 of DM 1,10. Says that would be all right; thinks the stamps will probably fit onto postcards. Gives two DM 20-notes.	Says the order has to be more precise; asks how many of each A would like. Has only eight 70s left; asks if A would accept two 40s and two 30s instead. Counts total: DM 7 + DM 16,50 makes DM 23,50. Counts change.

3

For example, *"Meinen Vater – und nur meinen Vater"*

Don't expect *Wen*; *"Wie heißt [Ihr Vater], bitte?"*

A	**B**
(People keep cutting in line) Says is next in line. Wants to place a person-to-person call to Harrisburg, Pa.; asks what must do. Thinks B has misunderstood; stresses that the call has to be person-to-person.	Confirms that A is the next customer; asks what A would like. Tells A to enter booth No. 4, dial the number, and come back to pay for the call. Understands now; offers to place the call; asks A for name of person called.

Stage 2

1

The post office is crowded, and the lines are all quite long. You don't want to spend too much time waiting in the wrong line. Approach the head of the line and

a) politely excuse yourself for butting in;
b) check to see whether you are at the right counter for long-distance phone calls to Canada;
c) thank those whom you have inconvenienced.

2

It's summer, and you have completed your junior year abroad. You want to ship home some books, some heavy clothes, and some souvenir beer glasses. Go to the post office and

a) find out whether there's a special rate for books, and whether there are any weight limitations.
b) ask whether the clerk thinks you can pack the glasses with the clothes, or whether you should have special packaging.

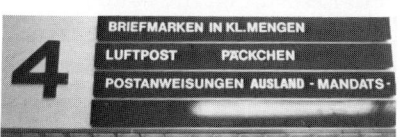

Can you find a misspelled word?

Versuchen Sie doch

You want to send four packages to Halifax, Nova Scotia. You want to insure them, but don't know the word for "to insure." Try to get your point across to the clerk. (Remember, if you don't know a word, your strategy is to "talk around it.")

Two people are ahead of you in line at the post office, and your train is leaving in just a few minutes. You want to ship some things home, and you simply must mail your package before you depart. It is quite bulky, and you will be crossing a border and want to use up the rest of your local currency. Persuade the people ahead of you to let you do your business first.

STRATEGIE – KULTUR UND SPRACHE

*The pictures in this chapter show typical post office signs. Key words to look or listen for, or to use in inquiries, are: **Scheck, Schalter, Paket, Ferngespräche, Briefmarken** (or **Postwertzeichen**), **Inland/ Ausland**.*

Die Post: not just the post office

As might be expected, the postal services of the German-speaking countries are operated by their national governments. But some other services and facilities, unlike their counterparts in the United States, are also government-operated, even in the quite definitely capitalistic countries of West Germany, Austria, and Switzerland, and certainly in the officially socialistic German Democratic Republic. Among those entities are the railroads and airlines and, in the area of telecommunications, the radio, TV, and telephone systems. In Austria, Switzerland, and West Germany the postal service also operates a widely used checking account service. Thus in the post office one not only mails letters and packages but might also place a long-distance telephone call or make direct payments by depositing money in someone else's postal checking account. Many firms and even some individuals list their *Postscheckkontonummer* on their stationery.

Since post offices are often busy places, you will want to be sure you are in the right line. One word for "stand in line" is *anstehen*. Since the word for the "line" itself is *die Schlange* (= "snake"!), another expression is *Schlange stehen*.

More about trains

Do a Socratic tutorial about distances and population densities.

Compared with the United States and Canada, the German-speaking countries are very densely populated and internal distances are short. Thus the government maintains a modern and efficient rail network, of which passenger service is a major part. Train travel is a mainstay of ordinary life, and not just for tourists. Correspondingly, the automobile is not quite as vital as it is in the United States and Canada, and domestic air travel is not nearly as prominent as it is in larger and less densely populated countries. The language of train travel is therefore of relatively greater importance in German than in American English.

Interurban IC trains (*Inter-City-Züge*) and Trans-European-Express (*TEE*) trains have their own special schedules and charge extra (ticket surcharge = *der Zuschlag*). Information about the composition of trains (*die Zugordnung*) and the facilities they offer is readily available at tourist offices, in station ticket lobbies, at the train platform (*der Bahnsteig*), in the customized pamphlet (*der Zugbegleiter*) placed in the compartments of major trains, and in the book-length master timetable (*das Kursbuch*). Often the *Zugordnung* is displayed visually on a large panel at the boarding platform. Facilities noted include first- and second-class (*erste, zweite Klasse*), smoking or nonsmoking sections (*Raucher, Nichtraucher*), dining and snack cars (*Speisewagen, Büffet*), and sleeping cars (*Liegewagen*).

*See **Bildwörterbuch:** "Transportation/**Verkehr**" p. 292.*

Double-checking, guarding against miscomprehension, asking for details

When you fail to understand something, *"Wie, bitte?"* is a good all-purpose expression – which is why it is the title of this book. But unvaried repetition makes one sound like a machine. Here are other ways to do the job:

1. In a questioning tone repeat what you think you heard, and either ask for confirmation or indicate that you didn't catch the rest.

(Sie sagen,) es gibt keine Ermäßigung für Bücher?

2. Directly admit your lack of comprehension, perhaps with an introductory phrase that will slow the other person down.

(Moment). Ich verstehe Sie nicht. / Ich habe Sie nicht verstanden.

3. To request repetition or amplification, use either *erklären* or *beschreiben*:
Bitte, könnten Sie das erklären?   Können Sie das bitte beschreiben?

Don't forget *aussehen* as another way to ask for description:
Wie sieht das aus?

If all else fails, simply pose yes/no or either/or questions.
Ist es braun? Ist es blau oder grün?

Of course, this is quite inefficient and could lead to a long guessing game. This is why *erklären, beschreiben,* and *aussehen* are such important verbs.

How to talk around missing vocabulary

Examples: junk, watch, bank.

Thumbing through a dictionary is often time-consuming, and it can be dangerous, since a given word may have several wildly different equivalents in a foreign language. It is useful to develop skill in *circumlocution,* the knack of talking around a gap in your vocabulary. Here are some pointers:

1. Very often you can get the other speaker to do most of the work by implying what you need. List similar items in the same context, or give examples of a similar kind, and then lead the other person into making intelligent guesses. Perhaps you need an envelope; one possibility:
Ich habe Papier und Briefmarken, aber ich brauche ein . . .

2. Don't get hung up on specialized terminology, brand names, and other such details. If you have learned that "envelope" = *der Umschlag,* then here's how to get a Manila envelope:
Ich brauche einen großen (braunen) Umschlag.
or: Der Umschlag muß größer sein. Der ist nicht für einen Brief. . . .

3. Sometimes you can work around the lack of a specific term by finding some larger or more general category to which it belongs, and then adding its special characteristics. Suppose you know that the postal service sells padded cartons for fragile objects, but you don't know the words for "padded," or "fragile," or much less for "antique enamel snuffbox." Try this:
Ich brauche ein Paket für . . . oh, für Weingläser und so weiter.

4. A very useful skill is the ability to describe at fair length a situation or set of conditions that leads up to the item for which you lack an expression. Very valuable is the connector *wenn* ("if"). But even without using *wenn,* you can still group your utterances in a way that suggests the idea "if . . . then." Similar strategies can substitute for a lack of other generic words, such as *"wie."*

An example: You want to make a collect call to North America but don't know the word for "collect" in this sense; the word *sammeln,* which is no doubt in your paperback dictionary, means "gather items of interest" (stamps, coins, etc.). Here are but a few of the many ways to do it:
(without *wenn* or *wie*) Ich möchte meine Familie in Amerika anrufen.
  Aber ich habe kein Geld. Kann ich meine Familie anrufen?
(with *wie,* without *wenn*) Wie kann ich meine Familie in Amerika
  anrufen? Ich habe kein Geld. *or:* Ich möchte meine Familie anrufen.
  Aber wie? Ich habe kein Geld.
(with *wie* and *wenn*) Wie kann ich meine Familie in Amerika anrufen,
  wenn ich kein Geld habe?

Zahlen und Fakten zum Schweizer Gletscher-Express

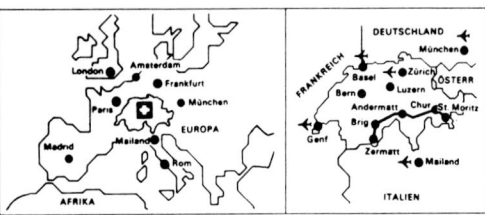

Information

- Schweizerische Verkehrsbüros
- Verkehrsbüro, CH-7500 **St. Moritz**, Tel. 082 3 31 47, Tx 74 429
- Verkehrsbüro, CH-3920 **Zermatt**, Tel. 028 67 16 25, Tx 38 130
- Furka-Oberalp-Bahn, CH-3900 Brig
- Rhätische Bahn, CH-7000 Chur
- BVZ-Bahn, CH-3900 Brig

3 Private Bahnen: die Rhätische Bahn, die Furka-Oberalp-Bahn und die Brig-Visp-Zermatt-Bahn bilden zusammen das grösste Meterspurnetz Europas mit einer Länge von

500 km. Der Gletscher-Express, der «langsamste Schnellzug der Welt», ist ein

8 stündiges, nostalgisches und spektakuläres Abenteuer. Die

270 Bahn-Kilometer von St. Moritz nach Zermatt führen über

291 Brücken, durch

91 Tunnels und Galerien, inklusive den am 25. Juni 1982 eröffneten Furka-Basistunnel, mit einer Länge von

15 km, der längste Meterspur-Bahn-Tunnel der Welt; mehrere über

50 Jahre alte, restaurierte Speisewagen sind auf dieser Strecke eingesetzt. Einzeln reisende Fahrgäste bezahlen für die Strecke St. Moritz–Zermatt (oder umgekehrt)

103 Franken für eine Fahrkarte erster Klasse. Den Fahrgästen wird in St. Moritz, bzw. Zermatt,

1 vom Bahnhofvorstand unterzeichnete, fortlaufend numerierte Erinnerungsurkunde überreicht. Das offizielle Pauschalangebot des Gletscher-Express beinhaltet neben den vorreservierten Hotelzimmern auch

1 originelles schrägstehendes Weinglas, das auf dem Speisewagentisch in steilen Kurven so gedreht werden kann, dass trotz Schräglage des Wagens kein kostbarer Tropfen verlorengeht . . .

1

HERR WIDNER	Guten Tag. Sind hier noch zwei Plätze frei, bitte?
DOKTOR VON SPOHR	Ich glaube schon, wenn sie nicht reserviert sind. Schauen Sie mal das Schild draußen an.
HERR WIDNER	Hier steht nichts. Ich gehe mein Gepäck holen und komme gleich wieder.
DOKTOR VON SPOHR	Na gut, aber passen Sie auf. Der Zug fährt bald ab.

2

BEATE	Also, Köln war wirklich toll! Und wir haben so viel gesehen.
KONRAD	. . . und gegessen und getrunken und gesungen.
BEATE	Aber nicht viel geschlafen.

3

SVEN	Bitte, mein Herr, dieses Abteil ist für Nichtraucher.
HERR BLATTER	Das ist ein Nichtraucherabteil? Verzeihung, ich habe das Schild nicht gesehen.

4

FRAU BECK	Warum fahren wir nicht ab?
HERR BECK	Ich habe gehört, daß der Zug aus Bremen Verspätung hat.

5

Speise/Wagen

KÄTHE	Ach, du bist schon wieder da. Hast du den Speisewagen gefunden?
SUSANNE	Nein. Der Schaffner hat mir gesagt, es gibt keinen.
KÄTHE	Aber sicher gibt es ein Büffet.

6

HERR BURCKHARDT	Haben Sie gesagt, Sie kommen aus Kanada? Das habe ich nicht gewußt. Ich habe gedacht, daß Sie Amerikanerin sind.
MS. THOMPSON	Wie, bitte? Ich habe Sie nicht verstanden. Es gibt so viel Lärm.

Checkliste vor der Abreise

☐ Pass – wenn nötig verlängern
Ausweis-Nummer notieren (Verlust)
☐ Visa einholen
☐ Internationalen Impfausweis – wenn nötig – besorgen
☐ Billette besorgen, Versicherungen abschliessen
☐ Fällig werdende Zahlungen erledigen
(die Schweizerische Volksbank erledigt das für Sie)
☐ Reisezahlungsmittel besorgen
☐ Wertsachen in einem Tresorfach der Schweizerischen Volksbank deponieren

☐ Autofahrer: wenn nötig internationalen Führerausweis und grüne Versicherungskarte besorgen
☐ Regelmässige Hauslieferungen abbestellen (z. B. Milch)
☐ Leerung des Briefkastens organisieren oder Post nachsenden lassen
☐ Reiseplan, Kontaktadresse und Reserveschlüssel hinterlegen (Hauswart)
☐ Persönliche Medikamente nicht vergessen
☐ Gas, Wasser und Strom abstellen
☐ Kühlschrank (je nach Modell) zurück- oder ganz abstellen (Achtung: Tiefkühltruhe braucht Strom)
☐ Sorge für Pflanzen und Haustiere

Damit Sie mehr von Ihren Ferien haben

SCHWEIZERISCHE VOLKSBANK

STRUKTUR 2

Verbs §§15,17

Teacher to Student A: *"Fragen Sie Bill, ob er eine Schwester hat/ob er schläfrig ist."* Student B: *"Bill,*

Verbs §§68–70

hast du eine Schwester?/bist du schläfrig?" No explanation of word order after *ob* is necessary; when students know that every command means "Ask him/her if . . . " they will concentrate on their task.

Don't get bogged down in a discussion of *haben* vs. *sein*. The matter is addressed in Chapter 14. The important thing here is establishing the pattern "auxiliary + participle," and emphasizing the equivalence of German present perfect to English preterite. Have students practice using present perfect by having in mind when they come to class three things they did the previous day or evening; gradually expand to four, etc. A short discussion of the previous day's happenings can easily become a regular feature of the first few minutes of class. Variation: have students guess what others did the evening before. This will provide constant reinforcement of the most common verbs: *arbeiten, sprechen, spielen, schreiben, lesen, schlafen,* etc.

Additional exercise: The teacher asks one half of the class *"Was machen wir, wenn wir in Köln sind?"* The second half of the class takes notes in response and answers the teacher's next question, *"Was haben wir in Köln gemacht?"* Add similar exercises that recount past events.

Part of the class tells a chain of events; the other part pretends impatience, answering *"Ich weiß schon, daß . . . "*

1. *Du* forms of the common irregular verbs *haben* and *sein*

du **hast**   du **bist**

2. The present perfect tense – the common German past tense

● **use:** talking about things that happened in the past – from a few seconds ago to a long time ago

● **basic form:** *haben* with appropriate endings + past participle

● **participles of regular verbs – standard pattern:**

ge- + verb stem + **-t**

INFINITIVE	PAST PARTICIPLE	
kaufen	gekauft	Ich **habe** Geschenke für meine Familie **gekauft.**
hören	gehört	Ich **habe gehört,** daß der Zug Verspätung hat.
sagen	gesagt	**Haben** Sie **gesagt,** Sie kommen aus Kanada?

● **participles of irregular verbs – another standard pattern**

ge- + verb stem + **-en**
　　　　　　　　\ **stem vowel often changes**

INFINITIVE	PAST PARTICIPLE	
sehen	gesehen	Und wir **haben** so viel **gesehen**
trinken	getrunken	– und **getrunken** und **gesungen.**
singen	gesungen	
schlafen	geschlafen	Aber wir **haben** nicht viel **geschlafen.**
finden	gefunden	**Hast** du den Speisewagen **gefunden?**

● Some irregular past participles end in **-t.**

INFINITIVE	PAST PARTICIPLE	
wissen	gewußt	Das **habe** ich nicht **gewußt.**
denken	gedacht	Ich **habe gedacht,** Sie sind Amerikaner.
bringen	gebracht	Moment – er **hat** uns Vanilleeis **gebracht.**

There are about 50 extremely common irregular verbs. Their forms are unpredictable and must therefore be memorized.

3. *Daß*

The conjunction *daß* ("that") links two clauses.

> like **wenn,** verb at end

Kann sein, **daß** ich nicht genug Geld bei mir habe. → verb

Ich habe gehört, **daß** der Zug aus Bremen Verspätung hat. → verb

SITUATIONEN 2 Im Abteil

Stage 1	A	B
1	(elderly gentleman with cigarette) Enters train compartment, greets passenger already there.	Responds politely, then sees cigarette; says this is a no-smoking car.
	Doesn't understand; asks B to repeat.	Repeats slowly.
	Says he's not smoking.	Says A is holding a cigarette.
	Says he doesn't intend to smoke it.	Responds appropriately.
2	(Is close friend of B) Says things will be better if B sleeps a little bit.	Has a headache. Says he can't sleep – it hurts too much.
	Says B celebrated too much the night before.	Says A drank a lot, too.
	Says slept very well.	Is happy that one of them slept well.
3	(Is about to board the train) Asks conductor if there is a sleeping car on the train – companion is tired.	(Conductor) Says this isn't an IC train, and there's no sleeping car.
	Says didn't know that.	Says A can read that on the sign next to the train.
	Says thought this was the IC 125 to München.	No, this train is going to Lübeck. The München train is on the adjacent track.
	Is upset, says it's leaving in three minutes; calls to companion, tells her the news.	

Stage 2

1

You are traveling to Freiburg. Tell the person in your compartment what your plans are.

a) If it's raining when you get there, you're going to go to the youth hostel and try to catch up on the sleep you lost in Köln. It was worth losing the sleep.

"unless" = wenn . . . nicht

b) If it's not raining, you're going to take a walk around the city, unless it's cold. You have some errands to do.

c) In any case, you're certainly going to go find a good meal right away; the snack car on the train doesn't really fill the bill.

2

You are on the train from Zürich to Bern. You are curious about a youngster in your compartment, and he is curious about you.

a) Ask him why he's reading a book in English.

b) Ask whether he's traveled much.

c) Tell him you didn't know that Swiss children like to read so much.

d) Tell him where you're from, what you're doing in his country, and why you're getting up to leave the compartment (you're hungry).

e) Ask him whether he would like you to bring him something from the snack car.

Versuchen Sie doch

While you were in Köln a funny thing happened: You were just leaving your hotel for the train station, and you picked up the wrong luggage by mistake. The rightful owner told the police, who approached you and began asking questions. You misunderstood at first, but then saw the problem and traded for your luggage, which was still back at the hotel desk. You just made your train in time. You meet your Dutch friend at the station; tell him what happened.

129

Chapter 13

JUGENDHERBERGE/ KRANKHEIT

Songs appropriate to Chapter 13: Schubert: *"Du bist die Ruh"*; Dietrich: *"Ich bin von Kopf bis Fuß auf Liebe eingestellt."*

FUNKTIONEN – KONTEXTE – STRUKTUREN

Looking ahead

You'll be learning about youth hostels, talking about an excursion, and dealing with minor medical problems.

You will be using:

- the pronoun *ihr* (= *du* + *du* . . .) to talk to friends
- ways of modifying adjectives to give more detail (*really* nice)
- *beim* to express simultaneous action
- *seit* + verb in *present* tense to express *continuing* action
- longer clauses after subordinating conjunctions
- verb complements in longer sentences
- *bleiben* and *weiter* to express continuing action or condition

Jugendherberge

<table>
<tr><td>*Bettwäsche* bed linens **1**</td><td>FRAU HENTSCHEL</td><td>Habt ihr Schlafsäcke oder eure eigene Bettwäsche mit, oder wollt ihr sie mieten?</td></tr>
<tr><td></td><td>HANS KRÖGER</td><td>Wir möchten gerne Decken haben, wenn's geht, und Kissen auch. Bettwäsche haben wir schon.</td></tr>
<tr><td>*Schlaf/Raum*</td><td>FRAU HENTSCHEL</td><td>In Ordnung. Also nur noch zwei Sachen: Ab 10 Uhr muß es in den Schlafräumen ruhig sein, und morgen geht es nicht vor 7 Uhr los.</td></tr>
<tr><td>*Ruhe/Stunde*</td><td>HANS KRÖGER</td><td>OK, gut. Also die gewöhnlichen Ruhestunden. Ich bin sowieso totmüde. Wir waren heute lange unterwegs.</td></tr>
</table>

<table>
<tr><td>**2**</td><td>HERR HENTSCHEL</td><td>Und hast du denn deinen Ausweis dabei?</td></tr>
<tr><td></td><td>ERNA GÄBLER</td><td>Ja, ich glaube schon. Doch, da ist er. Bitte schön.</td></tr>
<tr><td>*Hausordnung* house rules</td><td>HERR HENTSCHEL</td><td>Und die Hausordnung findest du hier an der Tafel links.</td></tr>
<tr><td></td><td>ERNA GÄBLER</td><td>Mm – ich habe noch eine Frage: mein Freund und ich wollten heute abend zum Konzert im Stadtpark, und —</td></tr>
<tr><td></td><td>HERR HENTSCHEL</td><td>– und ihr wollt bis spät ausbleiben, ja? Aber bitte nicht später als 22 Uhr. Wir schließen pünktlich um 10 ab. Und bitte keine Sachen wie Geld oder Kameras im Zimmer lassen, wenn ihr ausgeht.</td></tr>
</table>

<table>
<tr><td>**3**</td><td>BRIGITTE LOOS</td><td>Und was hast du dort alles gesehen?</td></tr>
<tr><td></td><td>ERIKA WOLFEN</td><td>Oh, Mensch, das war toll. Da waren ein paar Jungen vom Münchner Touring-Club. Mit denen haben wir eine wunderschöne Radtour durch Oberbayern gemacht.</td></tr>
<tr><td>*Oberbayern* upper Bavaria
Voralpenland Alpine foothills</td><td>BRIGITTE LOOS</td><td>Herrlich, du. Ich liebe das Voralpenland. Mit meiner Schulklasse habe ich letztes Jahr eine Wanderung von Oberammergau nach Innsbruck gemacht.</td></tr>
<tr><td></td><td>ERIKA WOLFEN</td><td>Oh, prima. Aber ich fahre eigentlich lieber rad – und immer von Jugendherberge zu Jugendherberge, weil's so billig ist. Und ich lerne auch so viele Leute kennen.</td></tr>
<tr><td></td><td>BRIGITTE LOOS</td><td>Und es ist auch sauber in den Jugendherbergen. Nur helfe ich nicht so gern in der Küche.</td></tr>
<tr><td></td><td>ERIKA WOLFEN</td><td>Aber wenn alle zusammen kochen oder nach dem Essen Geschirr spülen, macht es wirklich Spaß.</td></tr>
</table>

<table>
<tr><td>Introduce *Das macht mir/uns* [etc.] *Spaß* as an idiom often</td><td></td><td></td></tr>
<tr><td>*Aufenthaltsraum* lounge **4**
requiring dative personal objects. Block attempts to equate *Spaß* with *fun*; otherwise students will be saying, *"Das ist Spaß."*</td><td>ANGELA PASSAU</td><td>Nein, im Aufenthaltsraum darf ich nicht rauchen. Die Herbergseltern haben das schon gestern abend gesagt.</td></tr>
<tr><td></td><td>CHRISTIANE JUNG</td><td>Ja, ich finde, die haben ganz recht: du kannst rauchen, wenn du irgendwo in der Stadt ein Hotelzimmer findest. Hier geht's nicht.</td></tr>
<tr><td>*Drogen* drugs</td><td>ANGELA PASSAU</td><td>Und Trinken geht natürlich auch nicht – und selbstverständlich keine Drogen.</td></tr>
<tr><td>Introduce *recht haben* and *unrecht haben* if you want. Students with French or Spanish will learn the first easily.</td><td>CHRISTIANE JUNG</td><td>Ja, und das finde ich eigentlich recht gut an den Jugendherbergen. Die Herbergseltern sind da und sind auch fast wie Eltern – nur nicht *unsere* Eltern.</td></tr>
<tr><td></td><td>ANGELA PASSAU</td><td>Genau. Mit denen kann ich gut reden, wenn ich etwas auf dem Herzen habe. Ich hatte heute morgen ein Problem, und wir haben es beim Geschirrspülen diskutiert.</td></tr>
</table>

STRUKTUR 1

Students prepare questions to be directed to two or more

Pronouns §12

classmates. Pairs of students take turns asking questions: *"Wohin geht ihr heute abend?" "Wir gehen ins Kino. Was macht ihr?"*, etc.

1. *Du* + *du* = *ihr*: verb ending *-t.*

SINGULAR		PLURAL
1	Ich gehe nach Köln.	Wir gehen alle nach München.
2	Gehen Sie auch?	Sie gehen auch mit, ja?
	Gehst du mit uns?	**Geht ihr** zusammen?
3	Er/Sie geht nicht mit.	Gehen sie jetzt oder später?

2. Participles of verbs ending in *-ieren*

Verbs §69

NO **ge**; just verb stem + **t**

Wir diskutieren → Wir haben es *diskutiert.*

3. Modification of adjectives and adverbs for greater precision

A.A. §§1,37

sehr müde   *totmüde*   *wunderschön*   *wirklich* gut

4. Using *beim* (= *bei dem*) to express two simultaneous actions

Nouns §16

beim Essen   beim Geschirrspülen

Common English equivalents: *while, at, during, as, when.*

Question students about what they think of during various activities: *"Was denken Sie beim Musikhören/beim Schlangestehen in der Mensa/abends beim Spazieren (Einschlafen)/morgens beim Aufwachen?"*

MARBURG

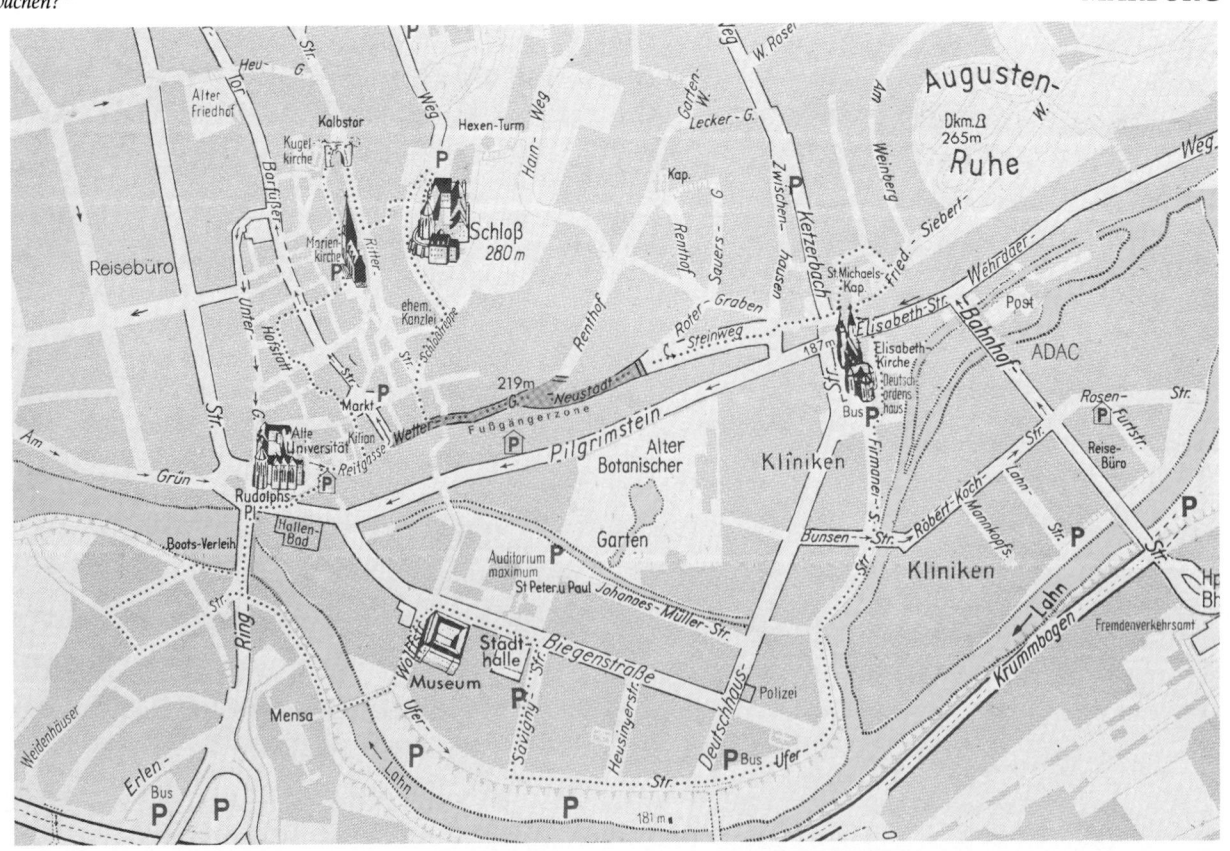

SITUATIONEN 1 Jugendherberge

Stage 1	A	B
1	*(Herbergsvater)* Asks B to sign in guest register. Bottom; asks if B has a youth hostel card. Didn't know B was American – speaks very good German. Is flattered; asks if B needs any sheets or a pillow for the night.	Asks where – top or bottom? Shows card to A. Is flattered; compliments A on nice-looking youth hostel. Has a sleeping bag and doesn't sleep with a pillow.
2	Asks about house rules. Agrees it's a good idea. Is very grateful – has had a long bike ride today. Says likes to work in the kitchen.	Says guests must be quiet after 10 P.M. Guests should also be quiet if they leave before 7 A.M. Says *Herbergseltern* expect that the young people will help out in the kitchen. Says washrooms must be left clean.
3	Says didn't know there was a youth hostel in this town. Says youth hostels are great places to meet people from all over the world. Thinks that when you're abroad you should meet new people. Bought it in München. Responds affirmatively.	Saw a youth hostel sign in town and found the way on foot. Agrees; met someone from own hometown at the youth hostel in Karlsruhe. Agrees; asks where A found T-shirt. Would like to have one with the Alps on it; asks if A likes to hike.

"Shows card to A": By now, the student readily says something appropriate in such situations; good time for a close check and, if necessary, reminder. "Is flattered": "*Ach, danke, das ist sehr nett von Ihnen*" would be wonderful, but an embarrassed smile could work just as well – provided the student does not always resort immediately to body language rather than speech.

Stage 2

1

You have been chosen to wash the dishes, since you didn't help with supper.

a) Try to make the others believe that your hands are allergic to water.
b) When that doesn't work, tell them that you never learned how to wash dishes in your country.
c) Tell them that you weren't serious.
d) To smooth things over, say you're looking forward to the sing-along in the common room after the dishes are done.

2

It's the middle of the night, and you've just awakened. Two of the other girls in bunks near you have been giggling and are about to start a pillow fight.

a) Ask them politely to be quieter.
b) If that doesn't work, tell them why you have to get some sleep tonight.
c) Tell them you'll go fetch the *Herbergsmutter* if they aren't quiet very soon.

Versuchen Sie doch

You are on a bicycle tour of Schleswig-Holstein with four friends, and are poring over a map. You decide to see some ocean while you're in the north, and think it might be nice to take the boat from Hamburg to Cuxhaven on the coast, stay in the youth hostel in Cuxhaven, then take the ferry to the island of Helgoland, a 2 1/2-hour trip. On Helgoland you could stay in the "Haus der Jugend." The next day it would be fun to continue by boat to the North Frisian island of Sylt, do some sunbathing, and spend the next night in the little town of Hörnum. The next day you would push on to Flensburg, load your bikes on a train, and complete the circle to Hamburg. Ask the *Herbergsvater* in Hamburg for some advice about your plans: How long will all this take? How much food should you take along? What is the weather on the islands at this time of year? Are there special youth rates on the ferryboats? Do you have to make reservations for the hostels?

Kneippkur- und Erholungshelme der Marienschwestern
vom Karmel

4101 **Bad Mühllacken**
Telefon (0 72 33) 215

5252 **Aspach - Innkreis**
Telefon (0 77 55) 315

4362 **Bad Kreuzen**
Telefon (0 72 66) 281, 282

bieten alle Kneipp-Anwendungen, Bäder, Unterwasser- und
Heilmassagen nach ärztl. Verordnung. Hallenbad in
Bad Kreuzen vorhanden. Die Häuser sind modern eingerichtet,
individuell geführt und bieten in guter Atmosphäre beste
Gewähr für erfolgreiche Behandlung und gute Erholung.

The language of tourist accommodations

Tourism is an intensely cultivated activity and industry throughout Europe. During the summer months, of course, visitors from abroad can be found at the major tourist attractions. Then, and at other times during the year, many Europeans themselves take vacations. In West Germany, Switzerland, and Austria *Urlaub* or *Ferien* (vacation) is a three- or four-week respite from employment or study. Most jobs guarantee such a paid leave. Typically the *Urlaubsreise* is a carefully planned and orchestrated event, not the casual jaunt familiar to many in North America.

Correspondingly, those going *auf Urlaub* expect excellent facilities and service, and they want to know ahead of time what they will get. Travel brochures and advertisements offer detailed descriptions of accommodations, and also of nearby recreational facilities and the landscape itself. Typically the language is rich in the specialized vocabulary of tourism, particularly adjectives and nouns, and many abbreviations are used. We offer here, with a glossary and explanation of abbreviations, a typical vacation hotel description and an entry from a youth hostel listing.

Medical insurance and services

Virtually everyone in German-speaking countries is a member of a generous health and hospitalization insurance program. This implies higher taxes, of course, but there are many benefits. Health care is efficient and readily available, and someone who is sick needn't have any qualms about incurring the expense of a visit to the doctor.

Under this system, health professionals in West Germany, Switzerland, and Austria are paid directly by the insurance company (*die Krankenkasse*). Generally the company requires patients to obtain a *Krankenschein* to take along to the doctor's office, and the office personnel process this "certificate of illness" and send it on to the *Krankenkasse*. Foreign students become members of a *Krankenkasse* as part of their matriculation at a university. Tourists are given an *Einzahlungsschein* to pay into the doctor's account at the post office.

Medical services are generous and varied. Visitors from North America are surprised that European *Krankenkassen* routinely pay for their members' trips to a *Kurort*, a town usually located in the mountains with mineral springs and a range of healthful activities for guests (*Kurgäste*). A *Kur* can last from several days to several weeks, and often includes physical therapy. The few equivalents in North America include White Sulphur Springs, West Virginia, Hot Springs, Arkansas, and Sun Valley, Idaho.

2

Jugendherberge Wien 7
<u>Neubau</u>

A-1070 Wien, Myrthengasse 7,
Tel. 93 63 16, 93 94 29

123 Betten, **ganzjährig geöffnet;**
behindertengerecht, Aufenthalts-
räume, Tischtennisraum, Musik-
raum.
Nächtigung mit Frühstück 130 öS;
Menü oder Lunchpaket 48 öS.

123 beds, **open throughout the year;**
handicapped welcome, recreation
rooms, table tennis, music room.
Bed and breakfast 130 AS; menu
or lunch-box 48 AS.

123 lits, **ouvert toute l'année**, aussi
pour handicapers, salles de séjour,
tennis de table, salle de musique.
Lit avec petit déjeuner prix 130 SA;
menu ou repas piquenique 48 SA.

Medical vocabulary you may find useful includes

das Krankenhaus/die Klinik/das Spital	hospital
die Ambulanz	outpatient clinic
der Krankenwagen	ambulance
der Facharzt/die Fachärztin	specialist
die Krankenschwester	nurse
der Krankenpfleger	male nurse
die Versicherung	insurance
das Rezept	prescription
verschreiben	prescribe
untersuchen	examine
die Untersuchung	examination
das Medikament	medicine (medication)
Medizin	medicine (subject of study)

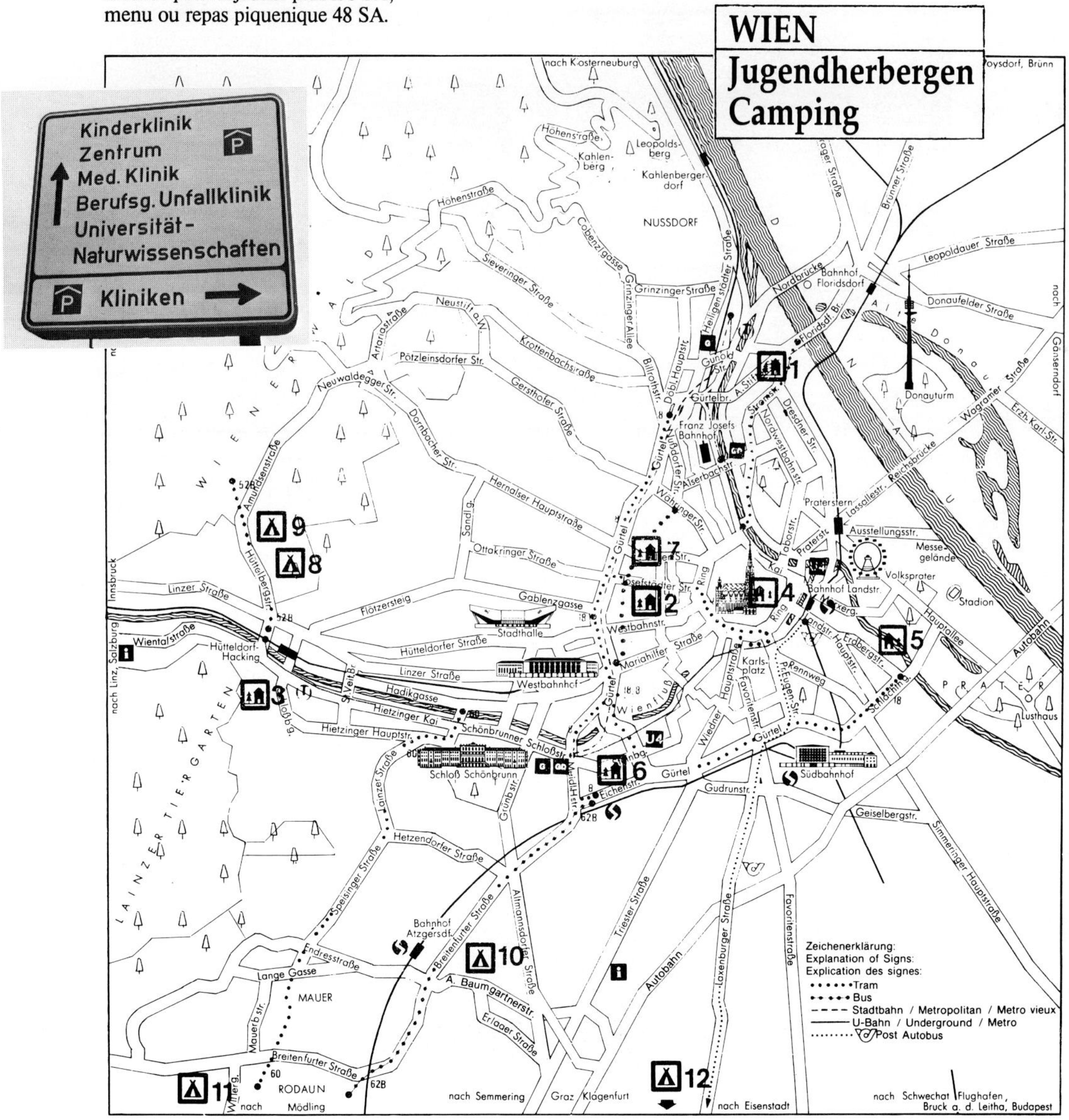

**WIEN
Jugendherbergen
Camping**

**Kinderklinik
Zentrum
Med. Klinik
Berufsg. Unfallklinik
Universität-
Naturwissenschaften**

Kliniken →

 7

Hostel Zöhrer

A-1080 Wien, Skodagasse 26,
Tel. 43 07 30

29 Betten, **ganzjährig geöffnet;**
getrennte Unterkünfte für Frauen
und Männer; Küchenbenützung.
Nächtigung ohne Frühstück 110 öS.

29 beds, **open throughout the year.**
Separate quarters for women and
men, kitchen available, bed without breakfast 110 AS.

29 lits, **ouvert toute l'année,**
chambres pour femmes et hommes
séparées. Usage de la cuisine
possible. Nuit sans petit déjeuner
110 SA.

11

Schwimmbad
Camping Rodaun

A-1238 Wien-Rodaun,
An der Au 2, Tel. 88 41 54
15.000 m²

geöffnet / open / ouvert:
20. 3.–16. 11. 1987
10 km vom Stadtzentrum,
Steckdosen, Gastwirtschaft.
10 kilometers from city center,
electric plugs, inn, pool.
Situé 10 km du centre de la ville,
prise de courant, restaurant,
piscine.
Preis / Price / Prix:
1 Person 40 öS; 1 Kind / child /
enfant 22 öS;
1 Auto / car 12 öS.
Zeltplatz 47 öS.
Site for tent 47 AS.
Place pour la tente 47 SA.

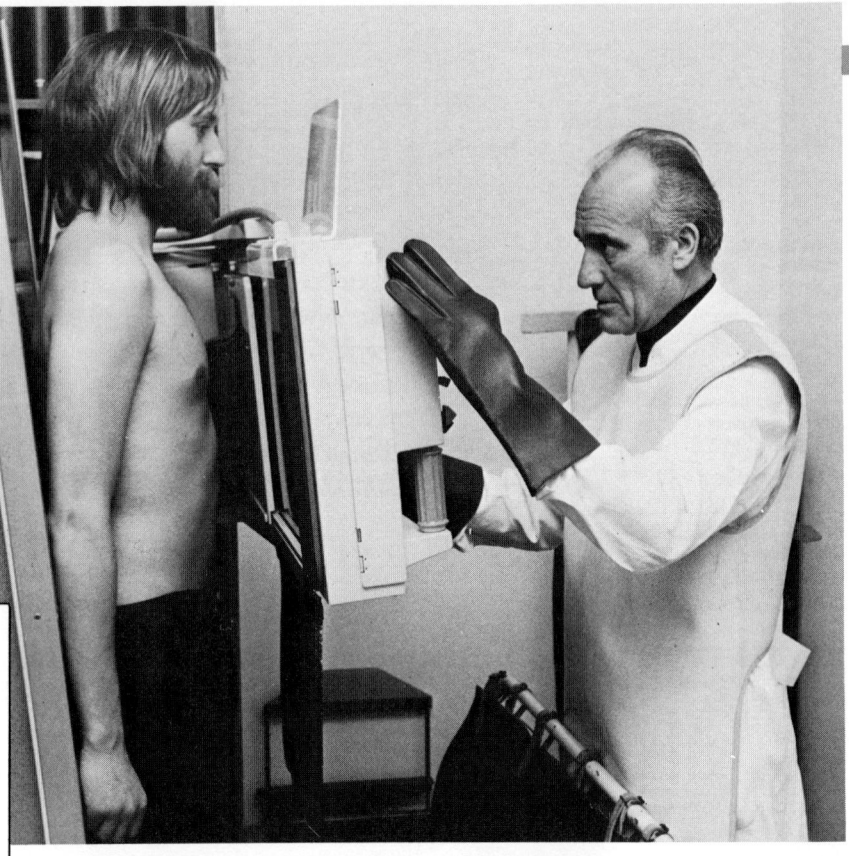

Notrufe

110	Notruf
112	Feuerwehr
88 21	Polizei
3 33 33	Rettungsleitstelle Deutsches Rotes Kreuz
2 66 00	Malteser Hilfsdienst Rettungsdienst/Krankentransporte
27 01	Uni-Klinik (Sammelruf)
270-43 61	Vergiftungs- Informationszentrale
8 50 85	Ärzte-Notfalldienst
1 11 01	Telefonseelsorge
31323	ADAC

Krankheit

1

HARALD	Ich glaube, ich bin erkältet.
UTE	Was, schon wieder?
HARALD	Ja, seit Dienstag. Die Jugendherberge war furchtbar kalt.
UTE	So – seit drei Tagen. Es ist vielleicht besser, wenn wir heute zu Hause bleiben.

2

LISELOTTE	Also wie geht es dir?
CHRISTIANE	Ich habe Kopfschmerzen, auch wenn ich im Bett liege.
LISELOTTE	Vielleicht weil du gestern abend zu viel getrunken hast.
CHRISTIANE	Naja. Aber die Magenschmerzen . . . und ein wenig Fieber habe ich seit gestern früh.
LISELOTTE	Schade, daß du so tief ins Glas geschaut hast.
CHRISTIANE	Ach, laß mich doch in Ruhe! Haben wir denn kein Aspirin oder so?
LISELOTTE	Ja, ich habe Tabletten da, aber vielleicht sollst du zum Arzt, wenn es wirklich ernst ist.
CHRISTIANE	Nein, ich glaube, für mich sind ein paar Stunden Ruhe der beste Arzt.
LISELOTTE	Na, das meine ich auch. Morgen geht's dir schon wieder besser.

so tief ins Glas geschaut = so viel getrunken

Call attention to the connection between *schmerzen* and *Schmerz.*

3

Hüfte hip

HERR HIRT	Bitte, sagen Sie mir, wo es ihnen weh tut. . . . Hier?
HERR RUDOLF	Nein, etwas höher, so am Knie. Und meine Hüfte schmerzt jetzt auch furchtbar. Mensch, das tut aber weh!
HERR HIRT	Und das wird noch schlimmer, wenn Sie weiter laufen. Bleiben Sie also bitte hier sitzen. Ich rufe einen Arzt.
HERR RUDOLF	Ja, ich glaube, ich will mal inzwischen ein bißchen liegen. Aua!
HERR HIRT	Sie müssen sofort zum Arzt. Ich rufe das Krankenhaus an. Sie fahren besser mit einem Krankenwagen als bei mir im Auto.

Student A tells which kind of doctor he or she is visiting (see Freiburg doctors' list in realia); Student B asks *"Tut Ihnen/dir das Auge (der Hals, etc.) weh?"*

Refer to *Reference Grammar,* Nouns §12 if there are questions about "weak nouns."

4

FRAU BETHKE	Ja, ich sage ihnen, das ist schlimm, Frau Vogt. Sie sollten wirklich zu einem Spezialisten gehen, zum Augenarzt.
FRAU VOGT	Aber wissen Sie, Frau Bethke, ich war sonst noch nie in meinem ganzen Leben krank, und jetzt so auf einmal . . .
FRAU BETHKE	Da müssen Sie aber gut aufpassen. Wenn Sie nicht sofort zum Augenarzt gehen, kann das noch viel schlimmer werden.
FRAU VOGT	Ja, ja, ich weiß, das sagt mein Mann auch. Aber wissen Sie, ich habe etwas Angst, wenn ich das Wort "Klinik" höre.
FRAU BETHKE	Ach, was – warum denn? Sie düfen doch nicht ängstlich sein. Sie sind ja in einer Klinik geboren!

Call attention to the relationship between *Angst* and *ängstlich.*

ängstlich fearful

STRUKTUR 2

Verbs §11

1. *Seit*

present tense with **seit**

Use *seit* for talking about what has been happening and is still happening.

Begin sentences with a *seit*-phrase, varying time from recent past (*Seit zwei Minuten . . .*) to distant past (*Seit 1972 . . .*); divide the class; see which half can complete more sentences.

> Ich <u>bin</u> **seit Dienstag** erkältet. (I *have been and am still* sick.)
> Ein wenig Fieber <u>habe</u> ich **seit gestern früh.** (I *still have it.*)

This is one of the chief sources of interference between English and German. Error can lead to serious misunderstanding.

Meine Großeltern **wohnen seit** 40 Jahren in Ohio.	My grandparents **have lived** (have been *living*) in Ohio for 40 years. (the grandparents are definitely alive and still live there.)
Meine Großeltern **haben** 40 Jahre in Kalifornien *gelebt*.	My grandparents **lived** for 40 years in California. (The grandparents don't live in California and may not even be alive.)

2. Word order: present perfect tense after subordinating conjunctions (*weil, daß, wenn, etc.*).

W.O. §13

The verb that agrees with the subject goes last.

> Vielleicht **weil** du gestern abend zuviel getrunken **hast.**

> Schade, **daß** du so tief ins Glas geschaut **hast.**

One student guesses what another has done recently by beginning statements: "*Ich glaube, daß . . .*" The student in question affirms or denies with an entire sentence. Student A: "*Ich glaube, daß Ed gestern abend*

3. Verb complements

Verb complements complete what the verb starts.

- In a simple sentence or question, they appear **at the end.**

  > Ich bin seit Donnerstag <u>erkältet</u>.
  > Seit wann sind Sie <u>erkältet</u>?

Verbs §§34–36

einen Film gesehen hat." Ed: "*Wie, bitte? Du denkst, daß ich einen Film gesehen habe? Das ist falsch/ Unsinn/Quatsch,*" or "*Ja, es stimmt, daß ich einen Film gesehen habe.*" Perhaps introduce with a lower-level exercise: Student A makes virtually any statement about the past; Student B feigns lack of comprehension – "*Wie, bitte? Was sagen Sie?*" Student A repeats with encapsulation – "*Ich sage* (or *habe gesagt*), *daß. . . .*" This can be expanded to include more people: Student A asks B, "*Was sagt er/sie?*"
The "*Schade, daß . . .*" construction deserves more than casual attention, since the phrase can often be used to emulate the function of the subjunctive, and yet requires no subjunctive.

- After subordinating conjunctions, they appear **near the end.**

  > Es ist vielleicht besser, wenn wir heute <u>hier</u> bleiben.
  > Ich habe Kopfschmerzen, auch wenn ich <u>im Bett</u> liege.
  > Und das wird noch schlimmer, wenn Sie <u>weiter</u>laufen.

4. Expressing continuing action or condition

> Und das wird noch schlimmer, wenn Sie <u>weiter</u>laufen.
> <u>Bleiben</u> Sie hier sitzen.

Common English equivalents are *keep on [verb-]ing, remain, stay [verb-]ed.*

5. Verbs used with the dative case

leid tun/weh tun

You have already seen

(Es) tut *mir* leid.	*I'm sorry.* (Literally: It does **to me** sorrow.)

New:

Es tut **mir** weh.	*It hurts me.* (Literally: It does **to me** pain.)

Similar:

> Es tut **ihr/ihm/uns/ihnen/ihnen** weh.

SITUATIONEN 2 Krankheit

Stage 1	A	B

1

"Ich bin sehr krank." Sich fühlen is unnecessary at this stage.

"Wieso? Was meinst du? Was ist denn los?"

A	B
Says he feels really sick.	Asks what the symptoms are.
Has headache and stomachache.	Suggests A go to the doctor.
Doesn't want to go; wants to stay in bed.	Suggests no concert that evening.

2

"Ist das alles – nur Fieber?" Use your own judgment in exercising skills of circumlocution by exploring ways to describe such common symptoms as nausea; similarly with body parts. Some students may be discomfited by the topic, while others – particularly those who have traveled or will be traveling – will want to pursue the matter and will regard failure to do so as an indication that the teacher is not completely serious about promoting genuine proficiency in the "real-world" use of the language.

Quickly review the difference between (verb) + *gern* and *möchte*.

Begin with *"Dann . . ."*

A	B
Feels feverish.	Asks how long that's been going on.
For three days.	Any other symptoms?
Pains in arms, back, and legs.	Asks if A has taken pain reliever.
Just aspirin.	Says A should drink lots of liquids.
Admits having had a good deal of beer at the party three nights ago.	Didn't mean that kind of liquids.

3

A	B
Asks B where the pains are.	In the shoulder, and a little lower on the back.
Asks if it's very painful.	Yes, pain is acute.
Says B should continue lying down.	Agrees willingly.
Will call a doctor.	Says that would be fine, is grateful.
B should be sure not to get up.	A shouldn't worry about that!

4

A	B
Is worried about pains in ears.	Says that can be serious.
Has had pains for two weeks now.	Says A should see an ear specialist.
Doesn't want to – has never seen one before.	Says A shouldn't be afraid – B went to a knee specialist last week.
Asks why B went.	Likes to walk and was afraid there were problems with one knee.
Loves listening to music and doesn't want to have ear problems.	Says that's why A should go see a doctor.

Stage 2

1

You have been planning an evening in town, but suddenly feel terrible.

a) Tell your friends how you feel.
b) Tell them to go ahead and have fun – you'll recover soon.
c) Ask them to bring you a nice dessert from the pastry shop nearby.

2

Your nose has hurt for five days now.

2b: "Einen Arzt/eine Ärztin." Don't hold out for *"Spezialist(en),"* but if it does come without the weak ending, leave it unremarked.

a) Explain your problem to the *Herbergsmutter* and ask her advice.
b) Ask her whether she can recommend a specialist.
c) Get her to reassure you about seeing a doctor in a foreign country.

3

You have checked into the *Hals-Nasen-Ohrenklinik* at the university and have inquired about your appointment with the staff and about arrangements for paying for treatment. Now tell the person who has brought you to the hospital that

a) soon you'll be able to see a doctor.
b) after your appointment you'll take an *Einzahlungsschein* to the post office and pay into the clinic account there;
c) then you'll write to your insurance company at home for reimbursement;
d) then you'll probably have to pick up a prescription at a pharmacy;
e) then you'll want to get some food.

Versuchen Sie doch

You were biking on a back road in the Austrian Alps when you came upon an accident scene. A car had driven off the road and hit a tree; the driver was unconscious, but the other person in the front seat, although hurt, was able to speak to you. One passenger in the rear seat had cut his chin and was bleeding slightly; another had hurt her leg and was unable to walk. After seeing that you could do little to help, you rode like the wind to the next town to find a doctor. Now you are in the doctor's office and must describe the scene as accurately as possible so appropriate help can be sent. Do the best you can.

Chapter 14

MUSEUM/ WANDERUNG

DEUTSCHES JAGDMUSEUM MÜNCHEN
NEUHAUSER STRASSE 53

EINTRITTSKARTE

DM 3.—

Von Mitte Juni bis Mitte Oktober täglich 9.30 – 17 Uhr geöffnet.
Von Mitte Oktober bis Mitte Juni täglich 9.30 – 16 Uhr geöffnet,
außer Montag.

85772

DIE ERSTEN AUTOMOBIL

18087   BMW Museum
Zeltmotor

Tageskarte

nicht übertragbar

Appropriate music and poetry:
"Der frohe Wandersmann"; "Durch die Wälder, durch die Auen" (aria from *Der Freischütz*); *"Das Wandern ist des Müllers Lust"; "In dem Walde steht ein Haus"* (children's song).

FUNKTIONEN – KONTEXTE – STRUKTUREN

Looking ahead

You'll be finding out what you can see and do (or not do) in museums, going on a hike, and talking about your experiences in both activities.

You will be using:

- more subordinating conjunctions (as, before, so that)
- equivalents of *when* (*als* = one time in past; *wenn* = if, whenever)
- the pronoun *man* (= indefinite you, they, people, one)
- the present perfect of verbs of motion
- the pronoun *ihr* in commands
- subordinate clauses to begin sentences (When I was young, . . .)
- verbs that require the dative case

140

Museum

Remind students that *was für* is a fossil and does not automatically govern the accusative case. Its object is determined by sentence syntax.

Review the use of *es gibt* with accusative.

Museen: Note the unusual plural. Many *-um* nouns of Latin origin have *-en* plurals.

1

HERR ZELIKOWITSCH Bitte, was für Museen gibt es hier in Freiburg?

FRAU WALTHER Ach, eigentlich alles – wir haben hier acht Museen. Ich gebe Ihnen einen Stadtführer und ein paar Prospekte. Wissen Sie schon, was Sie sehen möchten?

HERR ZELIKOWITSCH Ja, also, wir sind gerade von Köln gekommen. Wir haben das Kunstmuseum und das Römisch-Germanische Museum gesehen, als wir dort waren.

FRAU WALTHER Dann schlage ich vor, daß Sie unser Museum für Stadtgeschichte besuchen. Und wenn Sie noch länger hier bleiben, müssen Sie auch das Museum für Neue Kunst sehen.

2

BOB ROSENKRANTZ Zwei Erwachsene, bitte, und zwei Kinder. Gibt es eine Ermäßigung für ausländische Studenten?

FRÄULEIN STOFFEL Selbstverständlich. Alle Studenten bezahlen die Hälfte. Und für Kinder ist der Eintritt frei.

BOB ROSENKRANTZ Schön. Möchten Sie unsere Studentenausweise sehen?

FRÄULEIN STOFFEL Nein, das ist unwichtig. Also, zweimal 2,50 Mark, bitte. Und geben Sie bitte Ihre Taschen und Mäntel an der Garderobe ab, bevor Sie hineingehen. Den Kinderwagen können Sie auch dort lassen, wenn Sie wollen.

BOB ROSENKRANTZ Danke. Darf ich meinen Photoapparat mitnehmen?

3

Matthias Grünewald, late Gothic painter (early sixteenth century).

FRAU ZANGERL Entschuldigung. Die Kamera da. Gehört die Ihnen?

FRAU KIESEMANN Ach ja. Die gehört mir. Ich habe sie fast vergessen.

FRAU ZANGERL Hier darf man leider nicht mit Blitz fotografieren, weil das die anderen Museumsbesucher stört.

FRAU KIESEMANN Oh, Verzeihung. Das wußte ich nicht. Und ich wollte so gern eine Aufnahme vom Grünewald-Altar machen.

FRAU ZANGERL Schade, daß Sie kein Stativ mitgebracht haben. Aber Postkarten und Plakate kann man vorne am Eingang kaufen.

4

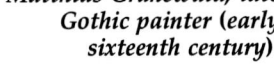

HERR LAUTENBACH Ja, man hat uns gesagt, daß Sie hier Bilder vom Grünewald-Altar verkaufen. Wir durften ihn nicht fotografieren, weil ich nur einen Blitz und kein Stativ hatte.

FRÄULEIN FEHR Schade. Aber von dem Altar haben wir eine Menge Bilder, weil er so berühmt ist. Wollten Sie Postkarten, Plakate oder Farbdias?

HERR LAUTENBACH Wahrscheinlich Postkarten, aber das große Plakat da gefällt mir sehr. Haben Sie es etwas kleiner? Wir sind auf der Reise.

FRÄULEIN FEHR Kleiner haben wir es leider nicht. Aber man kann es auch in einer Postverpackung kaufen. Das Plakat ist schon für die Post verpackt, damit man es nach Übersee schicken kann.

1. More subordinating conjunctions

als   bevor   damit

All these conjunctions place the verb at the *end* of the clause.

Wir haben das Kunstmuseum gesehen, **als** wir dort **waren.**
Geben Sie bitte Ihre Taschen ab, **bevor** Sie **hineingehen.**
Das Plakat ist verpackt, **damit** man es nach Übersee schicken **kann.**

2. *als* and *wenn*: an important difference

● **als** = "when" only in past time – for things that happened once

. . . , **als** wir dort **waren**   **Als** ich 18 Jahre alt **war**, . . .

● **wenn** = "when" in any time; also "if" or "whenever"

Wir gehen immer ins Konzert, **wenn** wir in Köln **sind.**
Wir haben immer den Dom besucht, **wenn** wir in Köln **waren.**

3. *Man*: the universal "you," "they," "people," "one"

● **Man** is a third person <u>singular</u> pronoun.

● **Man** is no one in particular.

Hier darf **man** nicht mit Blitz fotografieren.	"You can't take pictures . . ."/ "There's no picture-taking . . ."
Postkarten kann **man** vorne am Eingang kaufen.	"You can buy . . ."/ "Postcards can be bought . . ."
Man hat uns gesagt, . . .	"We were told . . ."/ "Someone told us . . ."
Man kann es in Postverpackung kaufen.	"You can buy it . . ."/"It's available . . ."/"It's for sale . . ."
. . . damit **man** es nach Übersee schicken kann.	" . . . for shipping overseas."/ " . . . so you can ship it . . ."

Individual students become the subject of sentences formed with *als* clauses: " . . . , *als Betty gestern abend in der Stadt war.* The class suggests ways to complete the sentence; finally Betty gets her chance to complete the sentence to her liking. Similar exercise: the class   *W.O. §11*

suggests ways to begin the sentence to end " . . . *damit man besser schlafen/essen/arbeiten kann,*" or " . . . *bevor man schlafen geht.*" Begin the sentence with "*Man muß* . . ." Style note: once you have begun a sentence with *man*, you must carry the *man* through; don't change pronoun horses in midstream.   *Pronouns §17*

The presence of *immer* is often a clue to the use of *wenn.*

Zürcher Spielzeugmuseum

(Sammlung Franz Carl Weber)
Fortunagasse 15/Ecke Rennweg 26
(5. Stock, Lift), 8001 Zürich,
T 01/211 93 05, Tram 6, 7, 11, 13 bis
Rennweg/Augustinergasse

Öffnungszeiten
Mo–Fr 14–17

Eintritt frei

Dienstleistungen
Führungen von Gruppen nach
Vereinbarung, auch ausserhalb der
Öffnungszeiten.

	Stage 1	**A**	**B**

1

You can vary the museum situations easily by introducing the many relevant realia – change not just entrance prices and opening/closing times, but also what kind of things to photograph and buy, reasons for seeing X, etc.

A

(Enters museum)
Wants to buy tickets for four adults.
Reconsiders – two adults and two students; apologizes for changing.
Asks if B needs proof of student status.
Has been shopping; asks B about leaving packages.
Asks where the restroom is.
Thanks; gives B DM 20,- and asks for single DM coins in change.

B

Repeats request: DM 16,-.
Repeats request: DM 12,-.

Says none is needed.
Says in the check room.

One flight down and to the left.
Counts change.

2

Don't expect *"nicht mehr lange." "Ja, aber morgen früh müssen wir schon wegfahren."*

A

Wants to rest a spell; they've been walking since early this morning.
Suggests they stay until late tomorrow.

Repeats suggestion; would like to see the Museum of Natural History and knows B would like to go to the anthropological exhibits.
Suggests staying until late Tuesday then.

B

Understands, but they won't be in Freiburg very much longer.
Isn't sure – they're due in Basel tomorrow evening.
Suddenly remembers that museums in Freiburg aren't open Mondays.

Thinks that's possible, but they'll have to call friends in Basel.

Stage 2

Deutsches Jagdmuseum, München

Versuchen Sie doch

See also sets of materials in Class Text and Study Text *Drucksachen.*

1

You are standing in front of the Art Institute in Chicago with friends from Austria. As part of their introduction to life in America, you explain to them

a) what it costs to visit the museum;
b) what the special prices are for students, seniors, and children;
c) whether visitors are permitted

   1. to smoke
   2. to take pictures
   3. to take snacks or chewing gum with them inside.

Quite likely you are not familiar with the Art Institute. Can you say something using common sense and any museum experience you might have?

2

You made a purchase for a friend at the museum store. When you gave it to her you saw that she had the identical picture on her wall. Now you have taken it back to exchange it for another.

a) Explain your predicament.
b) Ask whether they will exchange it.
c) Ask whether other pictures by the same artist are available.
d) A picture in another size strikes your fancy, and you decide to buy that for your friend. Ask whether another like it is available packed for shipping to Grandma in Calgary.

You are just walking out of a museum when you encounter two couples who are considering spending an hour or so inside. They ask you whether you liked the museum, and what especially pleased you. Using the various museum materials you have seen from the Augustinermuseum, tell them how they might best spend their hour inside.

You were just in the *Museum für deutsche Geschichte* in East Berlin. You didn't know that you were supposed to leave your attaché case at the entrance to the museum, or that you weren't allowed to take pictures of some of the things inside. Now the officials have stopped you on your way out and are asking questions. Bearing in mind that you have agreed to meet the other members of your group at the Weltzeituhr on Alexanderplatz at 5:00, do the best you can. It's now 5:10.

143

Do appropriate oral exercises with maps (Student A: *Wo ist X?"* B: *150km südlich von Y,* etc.). Remind students that they may well have to locate their own North American regions, unless they live in states or provinces well known to the average speaker of German; exercise accordingly, but *without* a map of North America. In real life the student in Europe may well not have such a map handy, and this is also a chance to remind some students of what they should have been taught before going to college.

Recall Oberammergau song: *"Heut' kommt der Hans zu mir . . ."*

Some geographical terms

When you are traveling you will have good reason to talk about where you are and where you are going. You will find the general geographical vocabulary presented here essential for describing not only your stay in Europe, but also your home in North America (*Nordamerika*). Four of the most basic words are

der Norden   der Osten   der Süden   der Westen

Most often you will use these in combination with *im* to tell location: *im Norden, im Osten, im Süden, im Westen.* In abbreviated form they most frequently appear in combination with each other or with other geographical terms:

der Nordwesten   Südbayern   Westeuropa   Südostasien

When you are speaking of geographical location, you usually use the verb *liegen*:

Schleswig-Holstein **liegt** im Norden.   Georgia **liegt** im Südosten.

The compass points have adjectival forms as well; note the umlauted stems:

Hessen liegt **nördlich** von Baden-Württemberg.
Die Schweiz liegt **südlich** von der BRD und **westlich** von Österreich.
München liegt **östlich** von Freiburg.

Other important terms are *Ober-, Unter-, Nieder-,* and *Mittel-*:

Der Chiemsee liegt in *Oberbayern.*
Untertürkheim liegt in der Nähe von Stuttgart.
Linz ist eine Stadt in *Niederösterreich.*
Dieses Jahr war sie im Urlaub am *Mittelmeer* ("on the Mediterranean").

These prefixes correspond to English Upper, Lower, Nether- (as in the Netherlands, *die Niederlande* – the low lands), and Middle (Illinois liegt im amerikanischen *Mittelwesten*).

Many German speakers refer to their written and spoken standard language, the language you are learning now, as *Hochdeutsch* ("High German"). This term is misunderstood by many to have social implications (higher on the social ladder than the colloquial language). However, *Hoch-* is a purely geographical term, referring to the historical standard language that has been used for centuries in various forms in the southern (higher) three quarters of what now constitutes the two Germanies. There is a *Niederdeutsch* as well, called "Low German" in English. It used to be a language of great importance, but it is no longer spoken by many people and is confined to largely rural areas of northern West and East Germany, where elevations are lower approaching the North Sea (*die Nordsee*) and the Baltic (*die Ostsee*).

German borders

Freiburg and several other cities such as Stuttgart, Heidelberg, and Ulm are located in the West German state (*das Land*) of Baden-Württemberg. As the name suggests, this state is a union of two former provinces. Because the alliance is so recent (1952), many people still refer to the older regions of *Baden*, to the west, bordering on France, and *Württemberg*, to the east, between Baden and the state of *Bayern* (Bavaria). Older political realities are often still present in

SPIELZEUGMUSEUM
im Alten Rathausturm, Sammlung IVAN STEIGER
Marienplatz,MÜNCHEN

names. The full name of Freiburg is *Freiburg im Breisgau,* identifying the city within a region already important in medieval times. The city's name is often written *Freiburg i. Br.* or *Freiburg/Br.*

Hikers looking west from the Schauinsland lookout above Freiburg see across the Rhine valley into the French region of Alsace (German *Elsaß*). The unstable, even bloody history of this entire area illustrates the precarious existence of small districts located between two or more powerful political entities. Alsace belonged to France before 1871, when it and part of Lorraine (German *Lothringen*) to the north were ceded to Prussia after the French defeat in the Franco-Prussian War. Nearly 50 years later, in 1919, Alsace and Lorraine were restored to France after Germany's defeat in World War I. In 1940 German troops occupied Alsace, which was finally liberated in 1945. Today all Alsacians speak French, but many still speak German as well. Place names of German origin in Alsace are clear reminders of its checkered past: Strasbourg (German *Straßburg*), Munster, Illkirch.

A particularly striking example of a political seesaw is the present West German state of the *Saarland* (Saar). In 1797 it was united under French rule, then was divided between Bavaria and Prussia (*Preußen*) in 1815. After World War I the Saar became independent, only to be restored to Germany in 1935. In 1940 it was united with the French province of Lorraine as the *Westmark* ("western border"). In 1947 the *Saarländer* voted for economic union with France, and the Saar became autonomous in 1954. Finally, the Saar became fully integrated into West Germany in 1957 as one of its ten *Länder.*

In view of political upheavals of this sort, it is small wonder that West Germans often appeal to the relative stability of older names to identify themselves and their regions. Citizens of Baden-Württemberg do not call themselves Baden-Württemberger, but *Schwaben* (Swabians), using the name of the Suebi, one of the Germanic tribes that settled the region in the early centuries A.D. The dialect spoken in the southwest of the BRD is called *Schwäbisch.* Similarly, the large lake on the Rhine between West Germany and Switzerland, *der Bodensee,* is known to many as *das Schwabenmeer,* "the Swabian ocean."

The political patchwork that was united under Bismarck before World War I no longer exists as a single entity. From its nominal heir, Hitler's Third Reich, the agreements that marked an end to World War II separated the territories extending from East Prussia (*Ostpreußen*) west to a line formed by the Oder and Neiße rivers. This area, including the old German cities of Danzig (Polish Gdańsk) and Stettin (Polish Szczecin), is now part of Poland. Königsberg, once the northeasternmost German city on the Baltic, is now Kaliningrad, part of the Soviet Union. The area to the west of the Oder-Neiße line and to the east of a jagged line extending south from near Lübeck was under Soviet occupation after World War II and became the modern state of East Germany (*die Deutsche Demokratische Republik,* [DDR]) in 1949. West Germany (*die Bundesrepublik Deutschland* [BRD]) had been formed earlier that year from the British, French, and American occupation zones. The former German capital of Berlin was also divided after the war, with the three Western zones making up West Berlin and the former Soviet zone being East Berlin, the capital of the DDR.

The end of World War II brought an influx of nearly ten million ethnic Germans into the present-day BRD from the eastern part of the former German Reich. For this reason you will encounter many West Germans whose families were part of this mass migration some forty years ago, and many more who trace their ancestry to areas far removed from West Germany's present borders.

By now some students may feel bogged down in unnecessary history. You might remind them that the issue of borders is still a volatile one – if not always with the governments involved, then often still with individuals.

Do a quick calculation of ratios – which can easily be conducted in German – to show what the proportional number of refugees would be for America. That hypothetical figure far exceeds the number of refugees our society – in peacetime! – has had to manage.

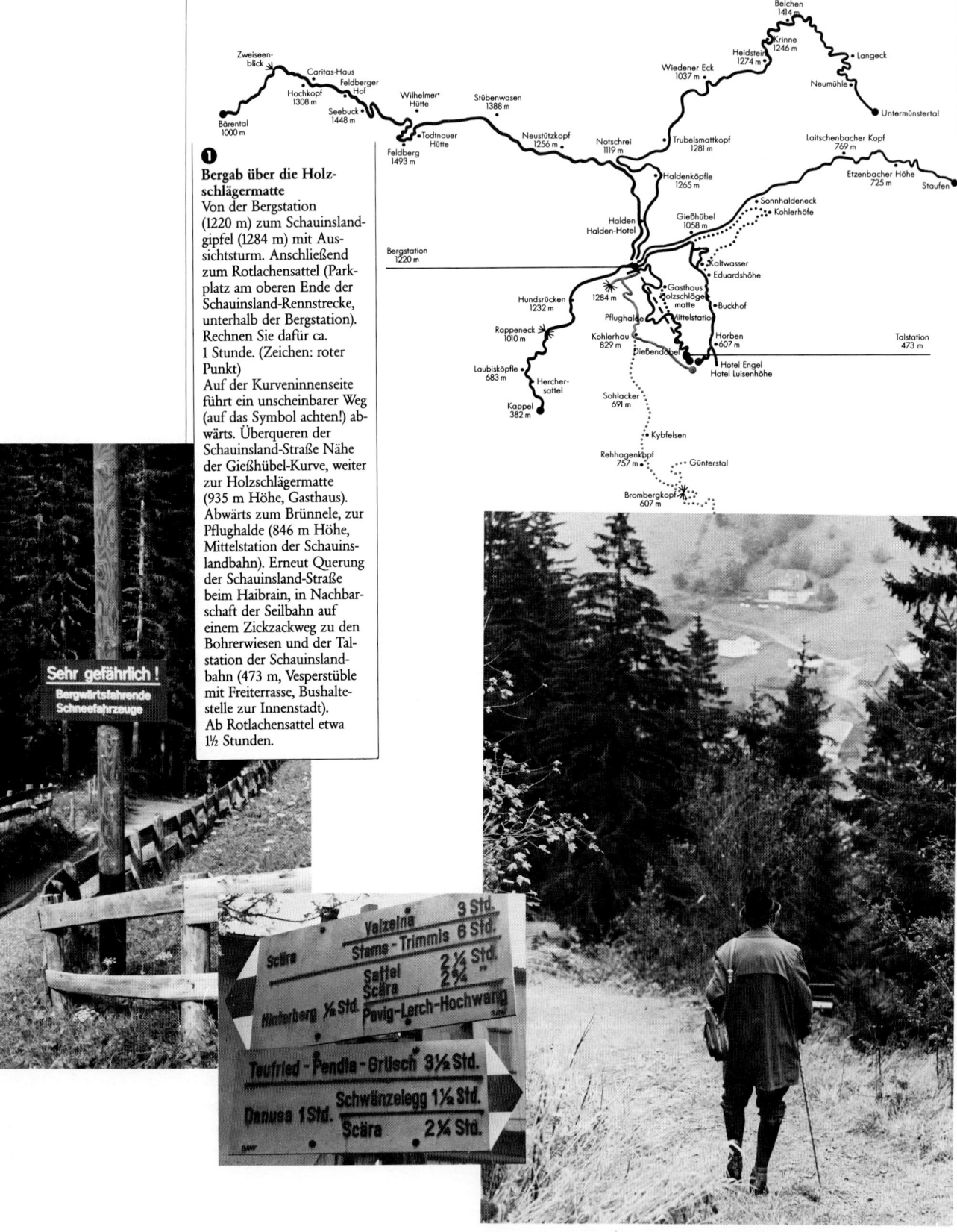

❶

Bergab über die Holz-schlägermatte
Von der Bergstation (1220 m) zum Schauinsland-gipfel (1284 m) mit Aus-sichtssturm. Anschließend zum Rotlachensattel (Park-platz am oberen Ende der Schauinsland-Rennstrecke, unterhalb der Bergstation). Rechnen Sie dafür ca. 1 Stunde. (Zeichen: roter Punkt)
Auf der Kurveninnenseite führt ein unscheinbarer Weg (auf das Symbol achten!) ab-wärts. Überqueren der Schauinsland-Straße Nähe der Gießhübel-Kurve, weiter zur Holzschlägermatte (935 m Höhe, Gasthaus). Abwärts zum Brünnele, zur Pflughalde (846 m Höhe, Mittelstation der Schauins-landbahn). Erneut Querung der Schauinsland-Straße beim Haibrain, in Nachbar-schaft der Seilbahn auf einem Zickzackweg zu den Bohrerwiesen und der Tal-station der Schauinsland-bahn (473 m, Vesperstüble mit Freiterrasse, Bushalte-stelle zur Innenstadt).
Ab Rotlachensattel etwa 1½ Stunden.

Sehr gefährlich !
Bergwärtsfahrende
Schneefahrzeuge

Wanderung

1

Bergstation *top of the lift*

2

"Der Ton macht die Musik."
Students may want to sound
petulant in practicing this
sentence, recalling their early
youth. How many ways can the
sentence be read?

Note the implied *"-fahren"*
or *"-kommen."*

3

Tragetasche *shopping
bag with handles*
Küche/Tisch

Point out an example of
declarative word order but
question intonation. The
intonation wins.

4

Tannen *fir trees*
"Robinson spielen," playing
Robinson Crusoe marooned on
an island. *"Indianer"* = cowboys
and Indians. Both the
"Robinsonade" and Western
fiction have enjoyed widespread
popularity in the German-
speaking countries.

5

See notes in Instructor's Guide.

JENS	Du, Hans-Dietrich! Warst du schon mal auf dem Berg da?
HANS-DIETRICH	Doch ja – der heißt Schauinsland. Von da oben kannst du kilometerweit sehen. Daher der Name: Schau-ins-Land.
JENS	Und wie hoch liegt die Bergstation?
HANS-DIETRICH	1220m – und der Gipfel ist noch höher: 1284m. Aber mit der Seilbahn ist man in wenigen Minuten da oben.
JENS	Aber – kann man nicht hinunterfallen?
HANS-DIETRICH	Nein, Jenschen, die Bahn ist gar nicht gefährlich.
FRAU DÄNIKEN	Christa, wenn du mit willst, mußt du den Pullover anziehen. Die Bluse ist einfach nicht warm genug.
CHRISTA	Aber ich möchte lieber hier bleiben und mit Katrin spielen.
FRAU DÄNIKEN	Aber wir wollen ein Picknick machen. Wir nehmen unsere Rucksäcke und wandern, bis wir müde sind, dann essen wir irgendwo in der Sonne –
CHRISTA	Und können wir dann mit der Seilbahn zurück?
FRAU DÄNIKEN	Ja, bestimmt, Christa. Aber wir wandern erst noch weiter, bevor wir zurückfahren.
ERIKA	Setz dich doch hin, Emil. . . . Hast du etwas vergessen?
EMIL	Du, Erika, du glaubst es nicht. Aber die Tragetasche mit dem Essen steht noch zu Hause auf dem Küchentisch.
ERIKA	Aber nein! Und ich habe soviel Hunger! Naja, fahren wir mal wieder hinunter. Da können wir das Essen holen und schnell zurückkommen. Ich habe dir aber immer gesagt –
EMIL	Du bist doch nicht böse mit mir?
ERIKA	Wieso böse, Emil? Nein, ich muß sowieso eine Jacke holen – hier oben ist es ziemlich kühl bei dem Wind.
EMIL	Ja, das stimmt. Ich habe heute früh die Wolken nicht gesehen. Ich hoffe, es regnet nicht.
HERR SCHILLER	Schaut mal. Seht ihr die Bäume links vom Wanderweg?
ANNAGRET	Meinen Sie die Tannen da unten, Herr Schiller?
HERR SCHILLER	Ja, als ich jung war, haben wir Kinder dort Indianer oder Robinson gespielt. Wir haben auch eine Hütte gebaut.
ANNAGRET	Ist Ihre Hütte noch da?
HERR SCHILLER	Nein, ich glaube nicht. Aber lauft mal hinunter, da könnt ihr nachsehen.
FRAU DR. ZAHND	Sind Sie hinaufgestiegen, Herr Professor, oder sind Sie mit der Seilbahn gefahren?
PROF. LENZEN	Wir haben die Seilbahn genommen – mein Fuß tut mir immer noch weh.
FRAU DR. ZAHND	Ihr Fuß? Was ist denn passiert?
PROF. LENZEN	Ja, das war auf einer kurzen Wanderung vom Schauinsland hinunter, wissen Sie, so durch den Wald. Und da habe ich den Fuß gegen einen Stein geschlagen. Und seit drei Wochen tut er mir weh.

STRUKTUR 2

Verbs §71

Trace one student's way around
the campus or into town and
back, making heavy use of both
gehen and *kommen*. Be careful
with *steigen*, which students will
want to use transitively. Resist
the temptation to mention
besteigen; the present perfect of
inseparable prefix verbs is
treated in Chapter 22.

1. More about the present perfect tense: verbs with *sein*

- **The subject is usually moving.**

    steigen   gehen   kommen

- **The auxiliary is *sein*, not *haben*.**

    steigen (participle = **gestiegen**)
    Sind Sie hinauf**gestiegen**?

    fahren (participle = **gefahren**)
    Oder **sind** Sie mit der Bahn **gefahren**?

    passieren (participle = **passiert**)
    Was **ist** denn **passiert**?
        (motion is implied: change over a period of time)

Verbs §51

This is another opportunity for
TPR exercises. Students give
orders to two other students at
once: *"Geht zur Tür,"* *"Bringt
mir Jacks Buch,"* etc.

2. The *ihr*-imperative

- **gives commands to two or more people who are *du***

- **formed with verb stem + −*t***

    (Schau mal, Annagret!)
    Schaut mal, Annagret und Hans-Rudolf!

    (Lauf mal hinunter, Hans-Rudolf!)
    (**Lauft** mal hinunter, Annagret und Hans-Rudolf!)

W.O. §17

Set up hypotheses for class
activities at the end of the day:
*"Wenn es regnet,/Wenn die Sonne
scheint,/Wenn es nicht zu weit ist,/
Wenn wir genug Geld haben,/
Wenn Audrey ihr Auto fährt,/
Wenn Joe nicht schläft, . . . "* The
class gives as many result
clauses as possible. It is
important to establish the

3. Subordinate clauses in first position

The main verb is still the second element in the sentence.

WENN-CLAUSE FIRST	VERB SECOND
1	2
Wenn du mit willst,	mußt du den Pullover anziehen.
Als ich jung war,	haben wir Kinder dort gespielt.

Verbs §37

pattern of *wenn* usage without
the subjunctive – "if" clauses in
real situations. Other exercises:
pick a student and begin a
sentence with *"Als X gestern
abend in seinem Zimmer/in der
Stadt/bei Y war, . . . "* Continue
in the present perfect.

Stress that *"Wie geht es dir?"* is
not the exact cultural equivalent
of "How are you?" and is not
said when meeting someone for
the first time. The question
often implies that the other
person has not been well
recently.

4. Verbs used with the dative case

These verbs take dative, not accusative objects.

Nun, wie geht es **dir**, Annagret?
    (Wie geht es **Ihnen**, Herr Kunz?)

Mein Fuß tut **mir** immer noch weh.
    (Sein Fuß tut **ihm** immer noch weh.)

Aua! Das gefällt **mir** nun gar nicht.
    (Das gefällt **der** Frau gar nicht.)

Es tut **mir** leid, aber wir haben keine Karten mehr.
    (Er sagt, daß es **ihm** leid tut.)

Die Kamera da. Gehört sie **Ihnen**?
    (Gehört sie **dir**?)

Begin using *gefallen* to find out
students' likes and dislikes.
Write a list of verbs on the
board and ask opinions of them:
*"Schwimmen? Das gefällt mir sehr
gut."* *"Tony spielt seine Trompete
immer. Und das gefällt mir gar
nicht."* The next question is
"Warum?"

Gehören: Use this pattern to
identify owners of articles of
clothing in the classroom. Feel
free to use *Wem* in your
questions, but don't require it of
students yet. *Wem* and *Wen* are
treated in Chapter 22.

SITUATIONEN 2 Wanderung

Stage 1

	A	B
1	Wants to leave soon; asks B to get ready.	Isn't sure about going; might like to stay home and sleep.
	Says B has to come along; asks B to get sleeping bag and pack and not to forget jacket.	Asks what they'll do if it rains.
	Says they'll have their picnic anyway.	Will go along if absolutely necessary.
2	Would like to visit Schauinsland.	OK, but doesn't want to hike to the top.
	Says B must be too old.	Reminds A that he (she) is only 23; suggests they meet at the top.
	Asks B and others to meet at the restaurant at the *Bergstation*.	Applauds A's idea; says they'll see A at the top in two hours.
	Says they should wait if he (she) is not there in exactly two hours.	Says they'll find something to do. . . .

"Naja, dann . . ." will do; so will a nonchalant reiteration of the plan to have a picnic.

	A	B	C
3	(All are in the Gondola high above the ground between the *Talstation* and the *Bergstation*)		
	Asks how B is feeling.	Not at all well.	Asks B why not.
	Remembers B was fine when they were on the ground at the *Talstation*.	Agrees, but that was on the ground. Now they're in the air.	Says they can't get out now; B will just have to wait.
	Agrees with C.	Is afraid; if they fall –	Says they won't fall.
			Jokes: if they do, there's a doctor in Freiburg.
	Says they didn't fall in Switzerland.	Agrees; but that was in Switzerland.	Says B shouldn't be afraid; they'll be on top very soon.
		Doesn't like "on top."	Tells B not to be a child.

Stage 2

If the students cannot recall the word for "skunk," or even if they can, this is an opportune time to exercise the skills of circumlocution: Can they describe the animal (perhaps chosen from a list of other animals) well enough that a partner can name it? Suggestions for other animals: buffalo, opossum, Gila monster, crayfish, Siamese cat, sasquatch; note the opportunity for use of

1

You are talking with a friend about the hiking possibilities in the hills above Freiburg. You want to know more about Schauinsland.

a) Ask about the altitude of both the city and the *Bergstation*.
b) Ask how often the gondola leaves from the *Talstation*.
c) Ask in what directions things can be seen from the top.
d) Suggest that the two of you hike up to the top, eat lunch, and ride down.

2

You are now halfway up the mountain and would like to stop for a rest. A couple of Swiss hikers come along, and you decide to

a) ask them how much longer it will take you to reach the top;
b) ask them whether it looks like rain up on top;
c) tell them they should consider turning around and going back: you think you saw a skunk about 100m back.

Versuchen Sie doch

compass-direction and other geographical terms.

You're now back at the youth hostel in Freiburg. While you're helping out with supper preparations, tell the others what you did today. Don't forget to mention what you thought was a skunk.

Chapter 15

ZIMMERVERMITTLUNG / WOHNUNG

Direkt an Vermieter

Wir möchten unseren Urlaub in Ihrem Haus verbringen. Machen Sie uns bitte ein Angebot für die Zeit vom _____ bis _____
    Anreisetag   Abreisetag

Wir sind _____ Erwachsene und _____ Kinder im Alter von _____ Jahren und wünschen Übernachtung mit ☐ Frühstück ☐ Halbpension ☐ Vollpension

_____ Einbettzimmer _____ Zweibettzimmer _____ Dreibettzimmer _____ bzw. Unterbringung in einer

☐ fl. W. w. u. k. ☐ fl. W. w. u. k. ☐ fl. W. w. u. k. ☐ Ferienwohnung
☐ Dusche/Bad ☐ Dusche/Bad ☐ Dusche/Bad ☐ in einem
☐ Du./Bad/WC ☐ Du./Bad/WC ☐ Du./Bad/WC Ferienappartement

Besondere Wünsche _____

Ort _____ Datum _____ Unterschrift _____
Zutreffendes bitte ankreuzen

LANDGANG FÜR INFORMATIKER

Fremdenverkehrszentrale e.V. Bieberhaus, Hachmannplatz.
Mo.-Fr. 7.30–18.00 Uhr.
Sa. 8.00–15.00 Uhr,
Tel. 040/24 87 00
Touristische Auskünfte, Informationsmaterial, Betreuung von Hamburg-Besuchern, Vermittlung von Unterkünften, Reservierung von Theaterkarten etc. sowie allgemeine Rundfahrten.

Hamburg-Information am Flughafen
Ankunftshalle D, täglich 8.00 bis 23.00 Uhr, Tel. 040/5 08 24 57
Vermittlung von Unterkünften, Informationsmaterial über Sehenswürdigkeiten, Unterhaltungsprogramme, Gastronomie usw. Auskünfte über den Hamburger Verkehrsverbund, Verkauf der Touristenkarten (HVV).

Hotel-Reservation im Hauptbahnhof
Wandelhalle, täglich 7.00–23.00 Uhr, Tel. 040/24 87 00
Vermittlung von Unterkünften nach Ankunft, Informationsmaterial über Sehenswürdigkeiten. Auskünfte über den Hamburger Verkehrsverbund, Verkauf der Touristenkarten (HVV).

Hamburg-Information am Hafen
St.-Pauli Landungsbrücken, täglich 9.00–18.00 Uhr, Tel. 040/31 39 77
Info-Pavillon für Touristen und Hamburger im Hafenbereich, tägl. Hafenbericht und Tidenkalender, Verkauf der Touristenkarten (HVV), Informationsmaterial.

Hamburg-Information in der City
Gerhart-Hauptmann-Platz.
Mo.-Fr. 9.00–18.00 Uhr,
Sa. 9.00–14.00 Uhr bzw.
18.00 Uhr, Tel. 040/32 47 58
Informationspavillon für Touristen und Hamburger, Verkauf der Touristenkarten (HVV), Informationsmaterial über Sehenswürdigkeiten, Ausstellungen.

Hamburg-Information Autobahn-Raststätte Stillhorn
ADAC-Vertretung,
Februar–Oktober täglich
10.00–18.00 Uhr,
Tel. 040/7 54 46 03
Vermittlung von Unterkünften, Informationsmaterial über Sehenswürdigkeiten, Gastronomie usw.

Explain the common use of room-finding service: location in or near transportation facilities; options available (*Preislage, privat*); deposit.

FUNKTIONEN – KONTEXTE – STRUKTUREN

Looking ahead

You'll be arranging for accommodations through a room-finding office, talking with a landlord, planning for a longer stay in one place, and setting up an apartment.

You will be using:

- subjunctive verb forms to express hesitation or politeness (Could you . . . ?, Would you . . . ?, Would it be . . . ?)

- comparative forms of adjectives and adverbs to say the same thing in a different way or to express distinctions more precisely (far better, much better, not so good)

- common prepositions to show motion toward an object (into the city, onto the table)

- separable verbs in the present perfect tense (have called up)

Zimmervermittlung

1

With dialog work or elsewhere: use realia (maps and hotel listings) as raw material for comparisons. Example: Student A suggests hotel(s), B comments on the appealing features (price, distance, quiet, appearance), C comments on the disadvantages. Encourage summary statements that include more than one

2

privat arrange a room in a private home – a common practice

adjective, and also formulations that intensify single comparatives ("*weit* billiger"). Can also be used to review structures likely in expressing opinion: first/second/third person transformation ("She says it's much farther than that."), encapsulation (with or without *daß*), and *wenn* and *weil.*

(am Telefon) **3**

Check and exercise ability to correlate map distance with travel time; review strategies for giving/getting directions, especially with complications (weather, alternate modes of transportation). Reinforce *wenn*-constructions by remarking that it is helpful to tell people what they will see if they go too far or in the wrong direction. Check management of third person forms by having students redo dialogs from the perspective of one who is negotiating on behalf of others who do not speak German.

Immanuel Kant (1724–1804), philosopher; major influence on political theory and psychology.

HERR LAUCH	Für zwei Nächte? Und wieviel wollten Sie ausgeben?
HERR GROSS	Nicht mehr als 60 Mark, wenn das ohne Bad ist.
HERR LAUCH	Moment mal. Ich hätte zwei Möglichkeiten. Die Krone – die ist ganz in der Nähe – und das Lamm – das liegt aber etwas weiter von der Stadtmitte.
FRAU GROSS	Nun, näher wäre besser. Aber ist die Krone ruhig? Wir konnten gestern im Bahnhofshotel nicht gut schlafen.
HERR LAUCH	Nun, sie liegt in der Königstraße, und da ist viel Verkehr. Das Hotel Lamm ist weit ruhiger und kostet weniger.
FRAU GROSS	Na, Schatz, wollen wir das Lamm probieren?
HERR GROSS	Ich glaube schon. Würden Sie da für uns bitte anrufen?
FRÄULEIN AMBRUGG	Schade, daß die Hotels alle voll sind. Privat wäre eine Möglichkeit. Möchten Sie es privat versuchen?
HERR MARTIN	Ja, also, wenn alle Hotels in der Bahnhofsnähe schon belegt sind. Hätten Sie etwas für 50 oder 60 Franken?
FRÄULEIN AMBRUGG	In der Heidengasse, im südlichen Stadtteil, sind ein paar Möglichkeiten in dieser Preislage – und vielleicht etwas noch billiger. Da fahren Sie mit der Nr. 5 hin.
HERR MARTIN	Und wie teuer etwa?
FRÄULEIN AMBRUGG	Die sind beide sehr preiswert: pro Person pro Nacht 25 Franken, inklusive Frühstück.
HERR MARTIN	Also, für eine Nacht, 2 Personen: 50 Franken mit Frühstück. Schön.
FRÄULEIN AMBRUGG	Soll ich also die Leute anrufen? Sie fahren sofort hin, ja?
FRAU LATTIG	Aber wenn Sie das Zimmer haben wollen, dann müssen Sie sofort kommen. Ich muß in die Stadt.
HERR HANSEN	Wir kommen gleich, wenn Sie noch 20 Minuten warten können.
FRAU LATTIG	Ist recht, Herr Hansen. Also, nehmen Sie die S-Bahn Linie 10 zur dritten Haltestelle, Mozartstraße. Das Haus steht direkt gegenüber. Die S-Bahn fährt alle 5 Minuten.
HERR HANSEN	So. Nummer 10 bis zur dritten Haltestelle. Danke schön, Frau Lattig. Auf Wiederhören.
FRAU LATTIG	Wiederhören. Bis bald.
FRÄULEIN PFAFF	Also, ein Doppelzimmer im Hotel Europa.
DOKTOR FORSTER	Wo ist das genau?
FRÄULEIN PFAFF	Ich zeige es Ihnen auf der Karte. Wir sind hier in der Ringstraße. Das Hotel ist keine 200 Meter von hier, in der Kantstraße, auf der rechten Seite.
DOKTOR FORSTER	Bis wann hält man das Zimmer frei? Unser Gepäck ist immer noch am Bahnhof im Schließfach.
FRÄULEIN PFAFF	Sie müssen in einer Stunde dort sein. Ich gebe Ihnen also diesen Zettel. Sie bezahlen hier 5 Mark, und Sie bekommen es später in der Hotelrechnung zurück.

4

Verbs §§53,54

Set up sequences or hierarchies of sentences that contrast blunt with polite language. Example: 1) terse phrase (*"Currywurst, bitte"*) or crass command (*"Bringen Sie . . ."*); 2) more polite version. Encourage variation of polite formulas, as occurs in reality, by posing tasks that require several sentences (e.g., order food for several people); prohibit immediate repetition of same formula. Beyond the level of polite requests, encourage expansion of single clauses to complex utterances by requiring encapsulation of *W*-questions. Thus *"Wo ist das Hotel Europa?"* becomes *"Könn(t)en Sie mir sagen, wo . . . ?"*; or in an exchange of opinion an overt inquiry like *"Ist das Zimmer zu teuer?"* becomes *"Würden Sie sagen, daß das Zimmer zu teuer*

A.A. §29

ist?" Such exercises present a good opportunity to review earlier chapters: earlier tasks can be done now in their original formulation, but much more fluently, or they can be attempted using new structures and vocabulary, with the greater effectiveness readily apparent.

See note in Instructor's Guide.

To locate some of these accommodations, use the map on page 48.

1. Expressing politeness or hesitation with subjunctive forms

● for greater persuasiveness or to be cautious

"would you, could you please," instead of "will you, can you"

● verb forms: Similar to past tense; many stem vowels have umlaut

You have already seen *würde* and *könnte* used this way with a following infinitive:

Würden Sie da für uns bitte anrufen?
Könnten Sie mir auch einen Fahrplan geben?

New in this chapter:

Näher **wäre** besser. *"It **would be** better closer [to town]."*
Hätten Sie etwas für zwei Personen? *"**Would** you **have** something for two?"*

Note the difference in tone:

CONFIDENT TO PUSHY		POLITE TO INSECURE
"Haben Sie . . . ?"	vs.	"**Hätten** Sie . . . ?"
"Do you have . . . ?"	vs.	"**Would** you **have** . . . ?"
"Ist das für . . . ?"	vs.	"**Wäre** das für . . . ?"
"Is that for . . . ?"	vs.	"**Would** that **be** for . . . ?"

2. More about the comparative

● saying the same thing a different way

Näher wäre besser. – Weiter ist nicht so gut.
Das Hotel Lamm ist ruhiger. – Das Hotel ist nicht so laut.
Das Zimmer ist preiswerter. – Das Zimmer ist nicht so teuer.
Das Zimmer kostet weniger. – Das Zimmer kostet nicht so viel.
Das Zimmer ist teuer. – Das Zimmer ist nicht so preiswert.

● using a supplemental adverb for greater precision

viel ruhiger	**noch** billiger	**weit** ruhiger
much quieter	*even cheaper*	*far quieter*

● PRIVATZIMMER (Telefon-Vorwahl Lindau: 0 83 82)

Name und Anschrift des Vermieters 8990 Lindau (B)	Planquadrat	Telefon-Nummer Vorwahl (0 83 82)	Geöffnet in den Monaten (von/bis)	Mindestaufenthalt (Tage)	Einzelzimmer	Doppelzimmer	Dreibettzimmer	Inklusivpreis pro Bett mit Frühstück DM min.	max.	mit Bad/WC oder Dusche/WC	mit Bad oder Dusche	mit Bad/WC oder Dusche/WC außerhalb des Zimmers	mit Warmwasser	mit Warmwasser im Bad	Dusch- oder Bademöglichkeit	Parkmöglichkeit	Liegewiese	Balkon	Aufenthaltsraum	Fernsehmöglichkeit	Heizung	Aufnahme von Tieren nach Rücksprache	Ferien auf dem Bauernhof
Alt Paula Eichbühlweg 25	F/8	43 26	4-10	3		1		17.--	19.--				•			•	•	•			•		
							1	17.--	19.--				•			•	•	•			•		
Baumeister Hedwig Kapellenweg 24	E/9	2 67 38	1-12		1			21.--	22.50		•		•			•	•	•	•	•	•	•	
						1		21.--	22.50		•		•			•	•	•	•	•	•	•	
Dr. Behrendt Winfriede Am Alpenblick 9	E/3	48 44	1-12		2			18.--				•				•	•			•	•	•	
		58 63				1		18.--					•			•	•			•	•	•	
Bichler Berta, Ludwigstraße 62	B/11	55 56	2-11		1			23.--				•					•			•	•		
Böcher Waltraud, Gruberweg 2c	E/9	2 10 08	3-10	5		1		26.--	28.--	•						•	•	•		•	•		

SITUATIONEN 1 Zimmervermittlung

Stage 1	A	B
1	Would like a room for three nights, but not in a youth hostel.	Asks where in the city – near the station?
	Says no, it has to be quiet – is very tired and has to sleep in.	Suggests the Hotel Drei Könige.
	Asks where that is.	On Bischofstraße, north of the St.-Ursula-Kirche.
	Thinks that sounds fine. Asks the price.	Says DM 65, –, including breakfast.
2	Wants a room for two for two nights, but not in a hotel.	Is surprised that A doesn't want to stay in a hotel; asks why not.
	Says a hotel is too expensive.	Is sympathetic; suggests a private room.
	Agrees, but it must be near the station.	Asks if A really means that – it's fairly noisy in the center of town.
	Says that doesn't matter; has to catch a train at 6:15 tomorrow.	Suggests the Pension Eiger a single with breakfast for SFr 32, –.
	Asks location.	Pension is two blocks from the station.
3	Asks if there are any rooms in the eastern part of town, near the stadium.	Says there are lots. For how many, how long, and in what price range?
	For two, for four nights, and with breakfast if possible.	Repeats question about price – apparently A didn't hear or understand *"Preislage."*
	Says not more than SFr 85, –.	Suggests a room on Schafgasse, SFr 68, – with breakfast.
	Says that sounds fine; asks how far it is from the stadium.	Only about a five-minute walk.
	Is very interested; asks B to call and ask if the room is still available.	Is happy to do so.

Stage 2

1

You and two friends are staying in Nürnberg for a few days, and are at the room reservation office. The youth hostel was a bit noisy last night, and you didn't sleep very well.

a) Ask whether you can transfer your things to a *Pension* or private room for the next three nights. Tell why.
b) Tell the clerk you'd like to be near the city wall. You just love to walk around in the old sections of cities.
c) A shower isn't necessary, but it would be nice.

2

You are in Hamburg, where you want to spend a week seeing the sights and conducting some business for your company. In three days you will be joined by your spouse, who will stay the rest of the week with you.

a) Arrange for a private room in a quiet part of town.
b) Make sure public transportation is available.
c) A room with a bath will be hard to find, but you don't often get to Hamburg and want to relax in style. Make sure the clerk in the room-finding office knows this.

Versuchen Sie doch You have now gained considerable experience with accommodations in German-speaking countries. At the *Hauptbahnhof* in München you are approached by an elderly Japanese couple who think you are a native and who need some advice about room possibilities. They speak no English but learned surprisingly good German at the Goethe-Institut in Tokyo. Do your best to outline their options.

153

Living accommodations

A German speaker inviting a friend "home" for a visit may well say "*Komm zu mir.*" But the home in Europe, even for a well-settled family, is likely to be an apartment. Although most families in German-speaking countries want to own a one-family house, most live in apartments because of the high price and scarcity of land for building. By North American standards, most of the German-speaking area of Europe has been overpopulated for 1000 years or more. Europeans visiting even our most densely populated areas are surprised by the amount of land available here.

Those living in apartments may have a *Mietwohnung*, which is rented, or an *Eigentumswohnung*, which they own. Rent in an urban apartment is usually about DM 10 per square meter (*pro Quadratmeter*), or about one DM per square foot. Rents are lower in the country, more like DM 6,50/m². Government involvement in housing is less apparent in North America than in Europe, where a small percentage of apartments are owned outright by the state. In East Germany, where there is still an acute shortage of apartments, the state is involved to a much greater degree in housing construction and financing. Rents range from M 0,80 to 1,25/m², and virtually all apartments are state property. The average East German family pays about 5 percent of its M 2000 monthly income for rent and utilities. In both east and west, many apartments are in tall buildings (*Hochhäuser*, sometimes sarcastically termed *Wohnsilos*), where the elevator (*der Lift, der Aufzug*) is a daily fact of life.

Land is sold not by the acre, but by the square meter. Building lots are very small, with houses occupying almost the entire area, save for a token strip of lawn or small garden. In view of these circumstances, it is hardly surprising that many people have a small garden plot (*das Wochenendgrundstück, der Schrebergarten*) some distance from their homes, a weekend retreat that may measure only 20 m² but that includes a miniature cottage (*das Gartenhäuschen*, or, in East Germany, *die Datsche*). These colonies of *Schrebergärten* form something like a discontinuous green belt surrounding urban areas.

The human consequences of these circumstances are varied. One result of a dense population, and of public concern about overpopulation, is the negative birth rate in West Germany – the only major industrialized country in which the population is actually decreasing. Yet the BRD actively encourages family growth: a monthly subsidy for each child, called *Kindergeld*, is paid to all families on a graduated scale according to income. East German couples are encouraged to begin families early. An interest-free state marriage subsidy of M 5000 is forgiven over time as each couple produces children.

Another consequence of high population density is the tradition of quiet hours in urban areas between 1 and 4 P.M. and between 10 P.M. and 7 A.M. Sundays are unofficial days of relaxation, when it is possible in some areas to receive a police citation for overindulging in work, such as washing a car or mowing a lawn.

If students find the statistics and unit conversions tedious, point out that such "nuts and bolts" comparisons of possessions and living conditions are common topics when one enters another culture, especially when one has attained the intermediate-level proficiency that is not unlikely in students now in Chapter 15. Set up such comparisons, in English at first if necessary, particularly where the metric system and complex calculations are involved. Encourage use of the grammatical comparative, but remember that the function of comparing can be undertaken without it.

Apartment rental – useful vocabulary

die Miete	rent
der Mieter/der Mietnehmer	tenant
mieten	to rent (as a tenant)
vermieten	to rent (as a landlord)
in Untermiete wohnen bei X	to sublet from X
der Mietgeber/die Mietgeberin	landlord/landlady
der Mietvertrag	lease, rental agreement
die Nebenkosten	utilities
der Strom, das Wasser, die Heizung	power, water, heat

The East German government now subsidizes housing loans—especially for families with many children.

How much do people spend on rent? Do improvements in housing conditions result in rent increases?

Since the GDR's foundation on 7 October 1949 rents have not changed. They are low and remain low. Costs for construction, modernization, maintenance and repairs are financed from annually increasing appropriations from the state budget.

On average, some three to five per cent of family income are spent on the monthly rent including heating, depending on the size of a dwelling and its fittings. The rent is between 0.80 and 1.25 marks per square metre in a new building, the low heating costs not included.

The modernization of old buildings does not result in rent increases. When hot water supply and central heating is added, the tenant pays only for the use of these conveniences but does not contribute to the building costs.

Also other improvements in housing and living conditions, e.g. better public transport, the erection of shopping centres, child-care facilities, swimming pools, sportsgrounds or other public facilities, do not affect rents in the respective housing area.

Wie hoch sind die Mieten? Ist die Verbesserung der Wohnbedingungen mit Mieterhöhungen verbunden?

Die Mieten haben sich seit Bestehen der DDR (gegründet am 7. Oktober 1949) nicht verändert. Sie sind und bleiben für den Bürger niedrig. Die Kosten für Neubau, Rekonstruktion, Werterhaltung und Reparaturen an Wohnungen werden durch jährlich wachsende Ausgaben aus dem Staatshaushalt gedeckt.

Im Durchschnitt werden – je nach Größe und Komfort – für die Wohnungsmiete einschließlich Heizung drei bis fünf Prozent des Familieneinkommens aufgewendet. Für einen Quadratmeter Wohnraum müssen in Neubauwohnungen zwischen 0,80 und 1,25 Mark gezahlt werden. Hinzu kommen die ebenfalls sehr niedrigen Kosten für Heizung.

Mit der Modernisierung von Altbauten ist keine Mieterhöhung verbunden. Erhält die Wohnung Warmwasserversorgung oder Zentralheizung, so trägt der Mieter lediglich die Kosten für die Nutzung, jedoch in keiner Form die Baukosten.

Auch die Verbesserung der Wohn- und Lebensbedingungen durch neue Verkehrseinrichtungen, den Bau von Kaufhallen, Kindereinrichtungen, Schwimmbädern, Sportplätzen oder anderen dem Gemeinwohl dienenden Einrichtungen hat keine Auswirkungen auf die Mieten in dem jeweiligen Wohngebiet.

From a brochure issued by the East German government.

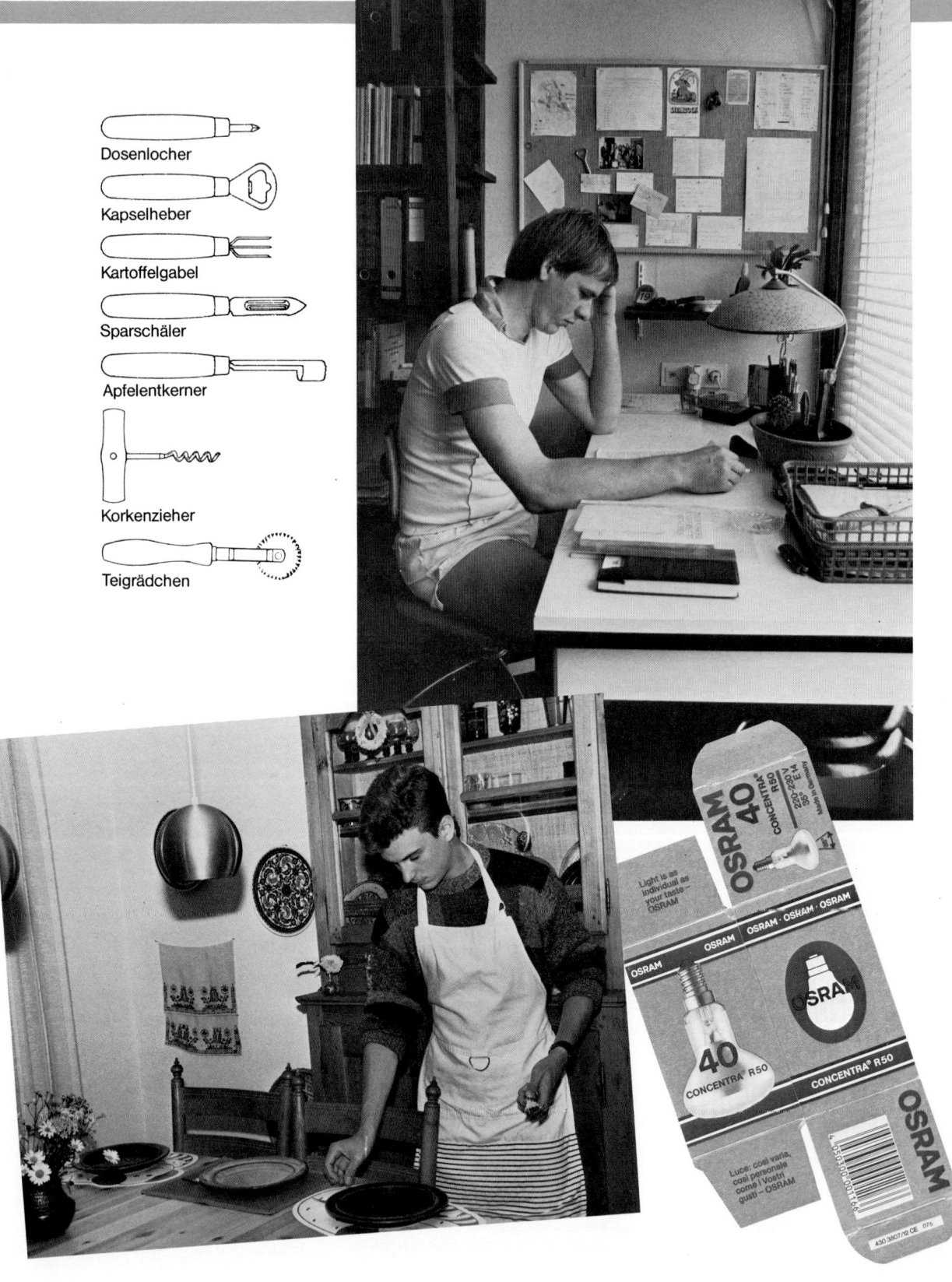

Dosenlocher

Kapselheber

Kartoffelgabel

Sparschäler

Apfelentkerner

Korkenzieher

Teigrädchen

Wohnung

1

Try similar exercises with the arrangement of other spaces, for example, a refrigerator as the groceries are unpacked. See *Bildwörterbuch* displays for vocabulary.

der Flur corridor or hallway

HERR BÜRGEN	So. In dem Schrank gibt es genug Platz für Ihre Sachen, würde ich meinen. Den Koffer können Sie dann da oben auf den Schrank legen, wenn Sie alles ausgepackt haben.
HERR SOHLICH	Und der Rucksack? Der ist ziemlich groß.
HERR BÜRGEN	Den können Sie unten in den Schrank legen.
HERR SOHLICH	Und die Toilette ist draußen auf dem Flur?
HERR BÜRGEN	Ja auf dem Flur. Die Dusche finden Sie unten im Keller. Aber Sie sagten, Sie wollten sofort in die Stadt?
HERR SOHLICH	Ja. Der andere Koffer ist immer noch im Schließfach. Und wir wollten im Supermarkt einige Sachen kaufen.

2

Kochnische very small kitchenette

Use *Bildwörterbuch* displays (house, common objects, activities) for enrichment exercises involving inquiries about household items, their location, and what one does with them.

X ist an der Reihe. It's X's turn.

FRAU JANKUHN	Die Kochnische finden Sie dann dort neben der Stube. Einen Schrank haben Sie zwischen dem Herd und dem Sofa. Dann sieht man nicht so direkt in die Kochnische.
FRÄULEIN KÖHLER	Und der Kühlschrank. Wo . . .
FRAU JANKUHN	In der Ecke, sehen Sie, da links vom Becken.
FRÄULEIN KÖHLER	Prima, sehr praktisch. . . . Und zum Saubermachen – haben Sie einen Staubsauger im Haus?
FRAU JANKUHN	Ja, den Staubsauger finden Sie unten neben der Hintertür.
FRÄULEIN KÖHLER	Also beim Ausgang zur Garage. Gut.
FRAU JANKUHN	Jeder räumt selber das eigene Zimmer auf und trägt seinen Müll hinaus. Und alle vier Wochen müssen Sie die Treppe putzen, damit sie sauber bleibt.
FRÄULEIN KÖHLER	Und wann bin ich an der Reihe?
FRAU JANKUHN	In zwei Wochen, also am fünfzehnten. Und die Miete ist immer am ersten fällig.

3

HERR KRAUS	So. Sie sind schon wieder da. Alles in Ordnung?
MS. SEITZ	Wunderbar. Ich habe meinen Koffer ausgepackt, und dann haben wir unsere Freunde angerufen.
HERR KRAUS	Sie können jetzt duschen, wenn Sie wollen. Ich habe im Badezimmer ein bißchen aufgeräumt.
MS. SEITZ	Das ist sehr nett von Ihnen.
HERR KRAUS	Aber darf ich Sie bitten, nicht allzu lange in der Dusche zu bleiben? Der Strom ist hier teurer als in den USA.
MS. SEITZ	Bestimmt. Übrigens – es scheint, daß die Lampe neben meinem Bett nicht funktioniert.
HERR KRAUS	Aha – es scheint, daß die Lampe nicht scheint.

Birne 1) light bulb, 2) pear

MS. SEITZ	Komisch, nicht? Hätten Sie vielleicht eine neue Birne?

4

FRAU BURGER	Wenn Sie ausgehen, geben Sie den Schlüssel bitte im Hotelrestaurant oder an der Theke ab. Das ist hier etwas anders als in Amerika.
MR. DRABKIN	Selbstverständlich. Das haben wir schon in Aachen gelernt, oder besser gesagt, im Zug nach Köln. Ich habe den Hotelschlüssel in meiner Tasche gefunden.

STRUKTUR 2

Preps. §§20–30

Remind students that the dative-only prepositions still take the dative case, even if they involve motion.

Only the best students are likely to grasp the motion-rest distinction, and fewer still will produce it *without overt prompting* in task-oriented writing or, much less, speaking. The present treatment is intended to lay the groundwork for later – in the course, or else in subsequent years. This might

Verbs §69

be a good time to review other, more tractable prepositional problems, like *nach/zu,* and to illustrate the distinction between *zu* (distant destination) and *in* (nearby destination). We suggest you avoid entirely the topic of abstract or idiomatic use of prepositions.

2: Establish the case distinction – at least for short-term memory – by setting up "moving exercises," mostly for the high-frequency prepositions *in* and *auf.* Student A: "*Wir bringen die Bücher in die Küche*" (much huffing and puffing). B: "*OK. Die Bücher sind jetzt in der Küche.*" Assign other students to echo and comment: "*Wohin? In das Wohnzimmer?*" or "*Wo? Auf dem Flur.*"

Ausgepackt: Treat this pattern as the "normal" one. Don't try to contrast it with that of inseparable prefix verbs. Most students – that is, most of those who have any functional command of participle formation – will not try to separate inseparable prefixes and add a *ge-* to their participial stems. Here modeling and contextual exercise, with appropriate reinforcement, will accomplish far more than will analytic presentation. Exercise: Proudly (or ruefully) tell what you've already done, unbeknownst to your nagging partner.

1. Prepositions with the accusative case   `Wohin?`

- **motion toward ⟶ the object**

in   English: *into*

Sie sagten, Sie wollten sofort **in die Stadt** fahren?
Sie sollten den Schlüssel nicht einfach **in die Tasche** stecken.
Der Rucksack kommt auch **in den Schrank.**

auf   English: *on (top of), onto*

Den Koffer können Sie oben **auf den Schrank** legen.

Other prepositions that require accusative case when *motion* is involved are:

| an | hinter | neben | über | unter | vor | zwischen |

2. The present perfect with separable-prefix verbs

- **past participle and prefix appear *together***

                                                  prefix past participle
auspacken: ausgepackt

Ich habe schon alles **ausgepackt.**
Müssen wir noch **auspacken?**

PRESENT TENSE	PRESENT PERFECT TENSE
Wieviel **geben** Sie **aus?**	Wieviel **haben** Sie **ausgegeben?**
Ich **rufe** die Leute **an.**	Ich **habe** die Leute **angerufen.**
Ich **mache** selber **sauber.**	Ich **habe** selber **saubergemacht.**
Wir **räumen** dann **auf.**	Wir **haben** dann **aufgeräumt.**
Ich **gebe** den Schlüssel **ab.**	Ich **habe** ihn **abgegeben.**

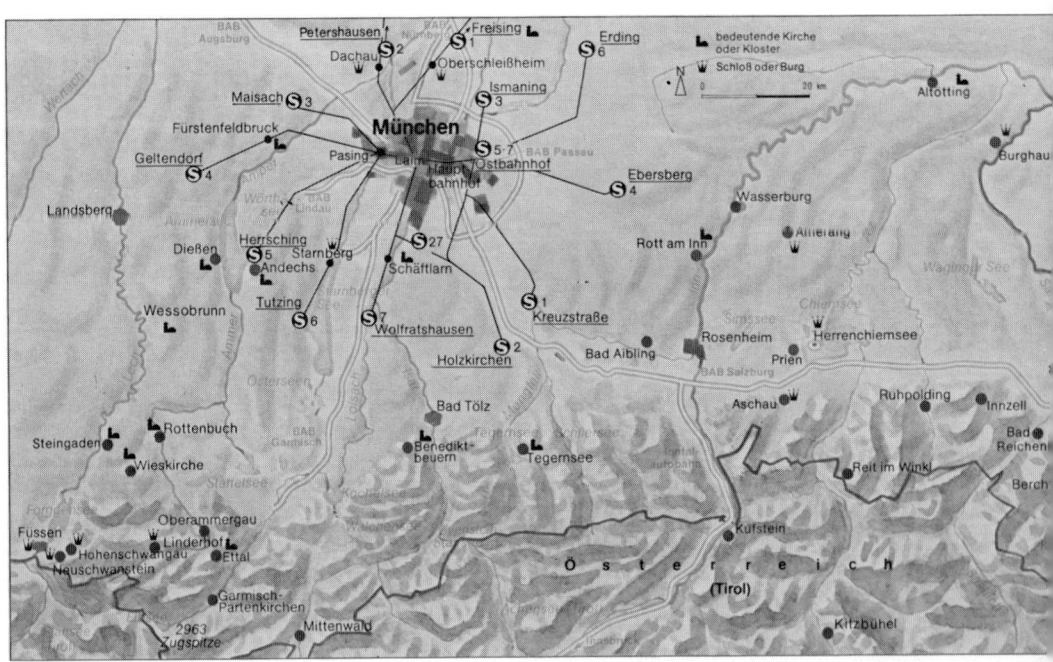

SITUATIONEN 2 Wohnung

Stage 1	A	B
1 Note that here and elsewhere in the *Situationen* the student may – but need not absolutely – use a preposition with the accusative case for motion. "Suggests the closet" could also be expressed by "*Sehen Sie den Schrank da?*" or even "*Da im Schrank – da gibt es genug Platz für Ihren Koffer,*" or "*Der Koffer bleibt besser im Schrank.*"	Says she has unpacked her suitcase. Asks where to put it. A's clothes are already in the closet.	Is delighted. Suggests the closet. Then A should put it on the sofa – they can take it to the basement later. Thought A wanted to drive downtown.
	Asks B to put B's things on the floor because would like to sleep on the bed. Yes, but after an hour or so.	Understands – is tired too.
2	Says the bedroom doesn't have a door.	Says that's no problem – no one can see into the bedroom from the living room.
	Notes that there's only a table between the kitchen and the living room. Says the apartment's very small – maybe too small.	Says that's typical – but you don't have to carry the food very far. Adds that they didn't pay too much for the rent.
	Agrees, says it's also much quieter than the apartment on Wolfgasse.	Adds that it's not as expensive, either.
3	Says apartments are different from the ones in the U.S. Says they're smaller. Says the rent is higher.	Asks what A means.

Thinks they're larger. Says that's because they're in a city; in the U.S. they lived in a town. |
| | Says electricity is more expensive – they'll have to be more careful. Notes that the bathroom and kitchen are more modern than in the U.S. | Agrees, says they won't be able to take long showers. Agrees – the kitchen is very modern, but you still have to take out the garbage . . . |
| | – and pick up the apartment and clean | . . . but it's still better than in a hotel. |

Stage 2

1

You are considering renting a furnished apartment with a fellow student at the university in Göttingen. You have a clear choice of places: a two-room apartment in the center of the city, in an old building that was newly renovated, or a new three-room apartment located on the edge of the city on a bus line. The apartments cost about the same. Considering your plans, outline the advantages and disadvantages of each.

2

You want very much to rent a room for six weeks in Konstanz, but you don't have much money. Tell a prospective landlady that you're very good at keeping things clean, and will gladly do much more than your share of chores around the house in exchange for a reduction in the room rent. Make sure she knows you understand exactly what one must do to keep a house clean.

Versuchen Sie doch

You have now moved into your apartment, only to find that the bed is very uncomfortable, the light in the living room doesn't work, and the refrigerator doesn't keep your food very cold – especially the ice cream that dripped out of the freezer compartment onto the flowers you were keeping fresh to take to your friends' house this evening. Unfortunately, the landlady is not at home, but has left a note that any problems should be taken to the neighbor. Explain to the neighbor what has happened to you and what you would like the landlady to do about it. Remember to be polite – it's not the neighbor's fault.

159

Chapter 16

STADTPLAN – FAHRPLAN/ U-BAHN – S-BAHN

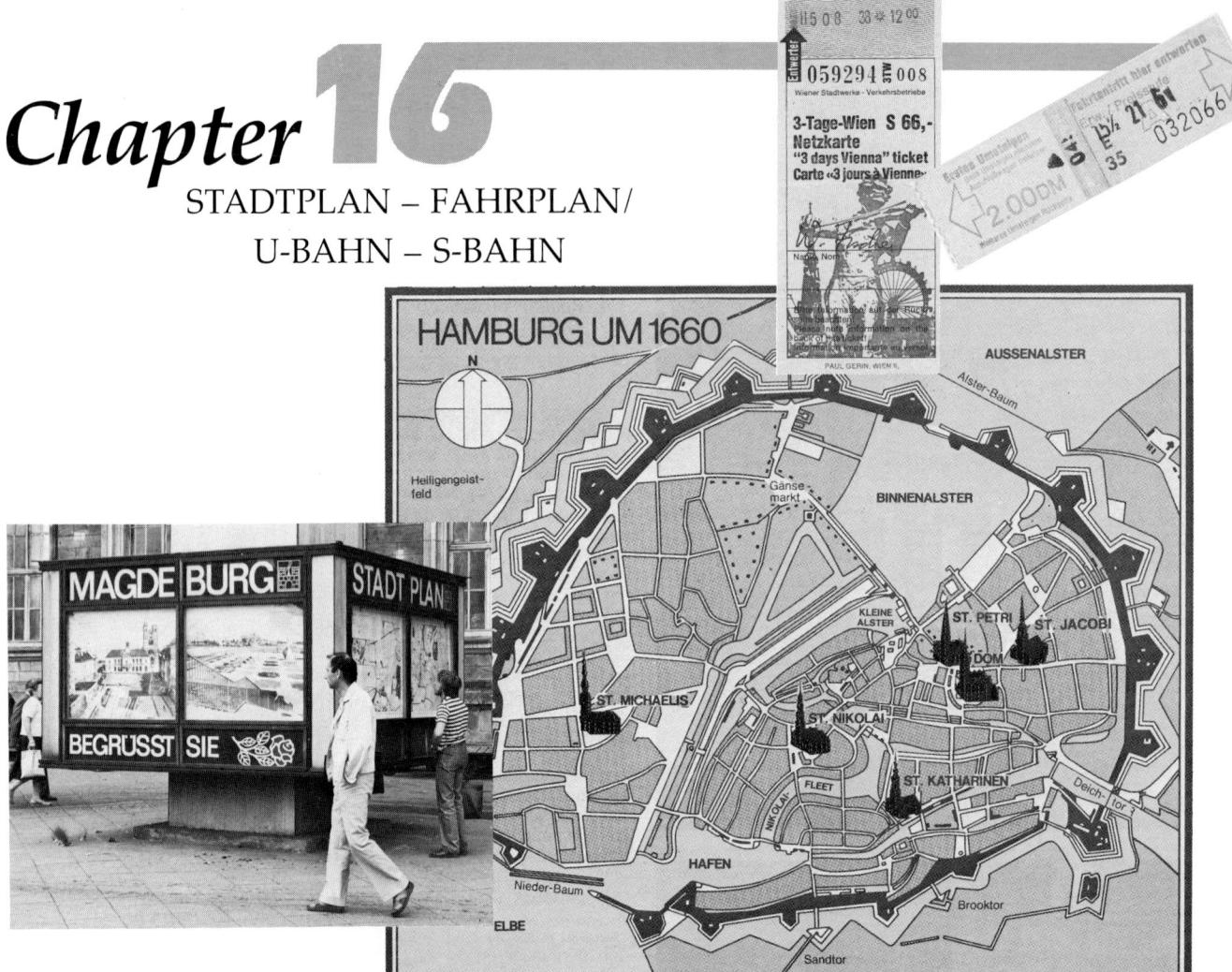

Appropriate songs: *"Am Brunnen vor dem Tore"*; *"Der Wegweiser"* (from Schubert's *"Winterreise"*); *"Auf der schwäbischen Eisenbahn"*; *"Der Mond ist aufgegangen"*; *"Lili Marlen."*

FUNKTIONEN – KONTEXTE – STRUKTUREN

Looking ahead

You'll be obtaining maps and timetables, locating landmarks, discussing parking facilities, and learning how to use mass transit.

You will be using:

- the subjunctive to express doubtful or hypothetical possibilities (*"We could"* rather than *"We can"*)
- the present perfect tense of separable-prefix motion verbs (*Wir sind eingestiegen* – We got on)
- the several meanings of *vor* (in front of, before, ago)
- the dative case with an article and a following adjective (*Mit dem nächsten Bus* – on the next bus)
- the conjunction *ob* ("if" in the sense of "whether")
- prefixes and suffixes to expand your vocabulary (<u>in</u>valid, normal<u>ly</u>)

Stadtplan – Fahrplan

1

Monats/programm

The Michelin tire company produces an extensive series of travel guides. The shorter green guides focus on history and tourist attractions, the longer red ones on hotels and restaurants.

HERR BLOCH	Möchten Sie den großen Straßenplan, oder wollten Sie das Monatsprogramm mit dem kleinen Stadtplan?
GRETE ERNST	Du, Thomas, wir haben ja schon den Michelin-Führer. Der hat Straßenpläne für jede große Stadt.
THOMAS BENEDIKT	Ja, ich weiß. Aber das Monatsprogramm steht nicht drin. Und wir wollen doch etwas unternehmen, oder?
GRETE ERNST	Ja, stimmt. Aber heute ist schon der 29. Wir sollten fragen, ob er das neue Programm hat.

2

Review basic compass directions, and then expand by setting up conversations in which two landmarks are described in relation to each other. Student A: *Das ist also X. Aber wo ist Y?* B: *Y ist* (e.g., *nordöstlich*) *von X, vielleicht* (distance/travel time).

FRAU LAMPRECHT	Bayerisches Nationalmuseum. Schauen wir mal – M29. Also im nordöstlichen Stadtteil. Das wäre ziemlich weit vom Bahnhof.
HERR LAMPRECHT	Nun, wir könnten ja mit der 55 direkt hinfahren.
FRAU LAMPRECHT	Ich fahre nicht so gern mit dem Bus. Wieviel würde ein Taxi kosten?
HERR LAMPRECHT	Machen wir es so. Wir fahren zuerst mit der S-Bahn zum Marienplatz. Das ist in der Stadtmitte.
FRAU LAMPRECHT	Gut. Vor dem Mittagessen können wir das Rathaus und das Spielzeugmuseum besuchen.
HERR LAMPRECHT	Und nach dem Essen könnten wir einen Spaziergang durch den Hofgarten machen.
FRAU LAMPRECHT	Aber wir müssen um vier Uhr bei meiner Kusine sein.

Spiel/zeug toy(s)

Hof (royal) court

Point out other *-zeug* nouns (*Flugzeug, Werkzeug, Schlagzeug*), and the general meaning of *Zeug* as ''stuff,'' ''things,'' or even ''junk.''

3

FRÄULEIN OTT	Das Parkhaus ist doch viel zu teuer, findest du nicht?
HERR THALMANN	Ja, besonders wenn wir nicht nur ein paar Stunden bleiben wollen.
FRÄULEIN OTT	Du, ich habe einen Vorschlag. Michael, Georg und Konrad waren vor einem Jahr in München. Das Auto haben sie bei der Endstation von einer Buslinie geparkt.
HERR THALMANN	Und dann sind sie mit dem Bus in die Stadt zurückgefahren. Sehr schlau. Machen wir das.

4

HARALD WEINRICH	So. Da seid ihr endlich! Ist denn was passiert?
MONIKA LERNER	Wir haben in der Stadt gegessen und dann sind wir zum Nationalmuseum gegangen.
MARTIN LERNER	Dann wollten wir mit der Straßenbahn zu dir fahren – Linie 55 hast du uns gesagt.
MONIKA LERNER	Wir haben das Schild falsch gelesen. . . .
MARTIN LERNER	*Du* hast das Schild falsch gelesen. Dann sind wir in die 53 eingestiegen. Wir sind bis zum Josephsplatz gefahren.
HARALD WEINRICH	Also. Dort seid ihr ausgestiegen, und . . .
MONIKA LERNER	Wir mußten auf die nächste U-Bahn warten. Und die ist erst um 17.33 angekommen. . . .
HARALD WEINRICH	Ist nicht so schlimm. Aber warum habt ihr mich nicht angerufen?

Verbs §§53–54

The speaker modestly implies that what is desired is not possible, and thus lets the other person have the pleasure of turning a wish into reality. The suggestion is something like, "I know it's impolite of me to ask, and in any case you probably can't do it, but it sure would be nice if . . ."

See note in Instructor's Guide.

Review of the basic principle of *sein* + motion verbs will almost certainly be necessary, since weakness here is characteristic of even the intermediate-high level in speaking, which few if any students will have reached by Chapter 16. Useful, too, would be contrastive exercise of the separable-prefix verbs that take *haben*. Nucleus for situation

Preps. §28

work: "Tell how you got wildly lost on the transit system, despite the attempts you made to get an early start and to contact someone at your destination." If necessary provide the verbs *aufstehen, abfahren, ankommen, gehen, fahren, einsteigen, aussteigen, umsteigen, anrufen.* While emphasizing the management of *sein*, be tolerant of errors in participle formation, and of minor flaws in word order. If the exercise goes well, encourage formulations with time phrases in the front field.

1. Main function of the subjunctive

The subjunctive is used to express something tentative, distinctly unlikely, or contrary to fact.

Wir **könnten** ja mit dem Bus Nummer 55 direkt hinfahren.
Wieviel **würde** ein Taxi kosten?

- **verb endings**

1	ich könn<u>te</u>		wir könn<u>ten</u>
2	{ du könn<u>test</u>		ihr könn<u>tet</u>
	{ Sie könn<u>ten</u>		Sie könn<u>ten</u>
3	er/sie/es könn<u>te</u> (no *t!!*)		sie könn<u>ten</u>

- **already familiar: subjunctive for extra politeness**

Könn<u>ten</u> Sie [*not* **können** Sie] mir noch ein Bier bringen?
Could you [not *Can you*] *bring me another beer?*

- **voice tone and body language**

The intonation and gestures that accompany the subjunctive are distinctly different from those associated with the indicative.

SUBJUNCTIVE	INDICATIVE
cautious tone	evident emotion
tentative gestures	expansive gestures

2. Separable-prefix verbs with sein   sein + motion verbs

- **form:**   sein + [other elements] + prefix + participle
                                        └─ one word ─┘

Wo **seid** ihr denn **ausgestiegen?**

Dann sind sie mit dem Bus in die Stadt zurückgefahren.
. . . Und dann sind wir in die 53 eingestiegen.
Die U-Bahn ist erst um 17.33 angekommen.

3. *Vor* before, in front of, ago   3: See note in Instructor's Guide.   dative case

- **to indicate location**

vor dem Hotel   *in front of* (or *before*) the hotel

- **to indicate time**

vor dem Essen   *before* the meal (*before* eating)
vor drei Tag*en*   three days *ago*

das/ein Jahr	**vor** ein*em* Jahr	**vor** 2 Jahren
der/ein Monat	**vor** ein<u>em</u> Monat	**vor** 2 Monaten
die/eine Woche	**vor** ein<u>er</u> Woche	**vor** 2 Wochen

Even when it means "ago", **vor** is still a preposition and therefore comes *before* its object. Compare the other German temporal prepositions:

nach einem Jahr   *after a year*
in einem Jahr   *in a year*
vor einem Jahr   _____ *a year AGO*

The English construction with "ago" *after* the time unit is an oddity.

SITUATIONEN 1 Stadtplan – Fahrplan

Stage 1

Obviously, exercise will benefit from use of appropriate realia. Vary by replacing "walk" with some other activity; student will then have to discuss other destinations (e.g., *Museum*).

Perhaps have the students read the entire "script" before beginning to speak, if such is not your regular practice. Ask them to check their realia (map, etc.), and to consider what they might say in the more thought-provoking parts ("explains why," "explains need to get going"). Maybe provide B with some generic utterances ("sympathetic remarks" = "*Oh, ja, also nicht zum Marktplatz*," "*Das ist nicht schlimm*," "*Ja, ich weiß*"); group exercise before partner conversations: develop and list on board models for B's more complex utterances (reasons for being in a hurry [*müssen*]; vocabulary for summarizing A's error [*aussteigen*, etc.]; list of likely attractions and review of prepositions/cases [*zum Zoo*, etc.]).

3: See notes in Instructor's Guide.

	A	B
1	Wants to take a nice long walk. Are both within walking distance? Prefers to do something else after all.	Suggest two places – one near, one far. Gives directions, transportation cost.
2	Politely accosts a stranger. May be lost. Tells what was looking for. Yes. Explains why. Tells what route was taken.	In a hurry but polite. Confirms the problem. Is A on foot? Asks where A started out. Makes sympathetic remarks, then explains A's errors.
	Decides to make the best of it; asks what there is to do nearby. Apologizes for detaining B; thanks.	Suggests something, or explains lack of attractions. Explains need to get going.

	A	B	C
3	(Has broken glasses but managed to locate center of town on map)	(Is with A; has worse map skills, better German skills)	(Knows city well)
	Needs to find an optician. Suggests that B ask the person over there.	Gently corrects A, who is pointing to a mannequin in a clothing store.	Approaches and offers help.
	Begins to say something about glasses.	Explains the problem.	Not sure, believes there's an optician near station.
	Gestures with map and says a few words. Worried about distances.	Asks C to orient them on the map. How far from here to there.	Does so, briefly. Explains map scale and converts distances to time needed (walking, public transit, taxi).
	Many thanks.	Yes, says C has been lots of help. Many thanks.	Reassures them; offers a backup plan if they have trouble.

Stage 2

1b): Alternate subjects: museums, churches, outdoor recreation, beer halls.

2: If you have not already done so, conduct a close orientation with a map of München. Let the students locate Platzl on their own. This is a good chance to play some folk (or pseudofolk) music.

1

Enter the *Verkehrsbüro* and ask about city maps they have. Your preferences:

a) You don't need the comprehensive city guide.
b) You would like one that shows walking or cycling tours. Could the clerk suggest a specific attraction or activity?
c) Do they have one in French for your new acquaintance at the youth hostel?

2

You're in München and would like to go to "Platzl" – the Bavarian equivalent of the Grand Old Opry in Nashville.

a) Ask for the address and landmarks.
b) Figure out how far it is from where you are now, wherever that is.
c) Ask for information about tickets and reservations.

Versuchen Sie doch

Use München Map: Show route from station to Lenbachplatz. Vary combinations of origins and destinations. Add complications: one-way streets, construction zones.

As you are walking on the street, a car pulls up and the driver asks you for directions. You know the place – you've walked from here to there often. But you aren't sure about the one-way streets and pedestrian zones. Do the best you can with your map or your memory. Maybe the people in the car should just park it and walk with you.

163

PARKHAUS
A

Ihr Fahrzeug
befindet sich im

Geschoss
04

Vielen Dank
und gute Fahrt!

Flughafen Zürich
Amt für Luftverkehr
park and fly

sicher durch den
Lauf der Zeit.

NATIONAL
VERSICHERUNG

Situation: invite a friend to a
party to be held at X's place.
Discuss location, time, what to
bring, etc. Maybe mention *"bei
uns in Amerika,"* used tacitly in
Chapter 9; cultural enrichment:
Dietrich song, *"Jonny, wenn du
Geburtstag hast."*

STRATEGIE – KULTUR UND SPRACHE

Words for "place"

- der **Ort** (-**e**)

Ort refers to a specific location or locale, identifiable as a spot on a map.

> Wo liegt der Ort? Am Rhein, nicht weit von Koblenz.

Where you can, though, use a more specific word: *die Stadt, das Städtchen* (small city or town), *das Dorf* (¨er) (village).

- der **Platz** (¨e)

Platz refers to a place or seat in a restaurant, train, etc., or location in a city: *am Stefansplatz.*

- place of residence

The official term is der *Wohnort* – place of residence or domicile. More casually, the rooms and building are named by their type – Haus, Wohnung, Zimmer.

> Really nice *place* you have here. Sie haben ein sehr schönes *Haus.*

The residence viewed as a personal space that might be visited by others is commonly expressed with a preposition and a personal pronoun:

> *bei* + pronoun (dative) = *at* X's place, house, etc.
> Wo ist die Party? Bei mir.

> *zu* + pronoun (dative) = *to* X's place, house, etc.
> Kommen Sie zu uns am Sonntag.

The indefinite *someplace* or *somewhere* is expressed as *irgendwo.*

> Das Hotel ist irgendwo im Schwarzwald.

Transit systems – advanced vocabulary

The word for "ticket" varies, but generally contains the word *Fahr-* (*Fahrschein, Fahrkarte, Fahrausweis*). Tickets are widely available, and vending machines are even more common.

Key terms are

Fahrziel wählen	*select destination*
Knopf drücken	*press button*
Münze	*coin*
Münzeinwurf	*coin slot*
einwerfen	*insert*
Innenzone, Innenraum	*inner region*
Außenzone, Außenraum	*outer region*
Netz	*network, system*
Gesamt (as in **Gesamttarifgebiet**)	*comprehensive, systemwide*

There are tickets to suit virtually every transportation need. Some common types are:

24-Stundenkarte (Tageskarte)	**Wochenendkarte**
Wochenkarte	**Monatskarte**
Seniorenkarte	**Stadt-Familienkarte**

*Mehrfahrt*karten (multiple ride), *Streifen*karten, and *Sammel*karten are blocks or strips of tickets used in systems that have multiple zones and charge according to distance. Thus an adult may pay two units for a short trip and five for a much longer one. Commonly one folds over the required number of zone tickets and then a conductor or machine validates the ticket.

Tickets are not valid (*gültig*) until they are validated. The action is *entwerten* (*Sie müssen die Karte entwerten*); the machine that does it is *der Entwerter*.

More than a few strangers find themselves heading the *wrong* way on the *right* transit line. Typically, station displays and signs on vehicles carry not only the line *number* (*Liniennummer*) but also the name of the stop at the end of the line (*Endstation*). The key word is *Richtung* – direction (*in beide Richtungen* = in both directions).

Signs of importance inside conveyances include the following key words:

Notbremse   *emergency brake*
Behindertensitz   *seat reserved for the handicapped*
(alternate terms: **[Schwer]beschädigte**)

The common symbol for "handicapped" is three black dots in a yellow triangle.

Young people are still expected to yield their seats to the elderly; in Vienna the rule has been known to be enforced vigorously by the elderly themselves, perhaps with an umbrella swat.

Schwarzfahren

Many transit networks are governed by the honor system, which is backed up by roving inspectors. Riding without a valid ticket is termed *schwarzfahren*. The penalty is fairly large – often more than $20. The inspector's brief lecture may well be made more unpleasant by the common tendency of other passengers to get involved and to discuss the shortcomings of the offender and perhaps the offender's country, either among themselves or directly with the offender. Once, in a hurry to catch the *U-bahn* after gathering some material for this book, one of the authors was sorely tempted to board with a 24-hour ticket that had expired just a few minutes before. That trip was the only time in a month that he encountered a ticket inspector. Fortunately, he had decided at the last minute to buy a new 24-hour ticket and to validate it as he boarded.

Use realia that present the various choices; particularly useful are the several "Touristen-ABC" and transit-system overview items.

More thoughtful students may be intrigued by the notion that, while their own culture *validates* tickets at the beginning of a trip on the transit system, the other culture *de-validates* them. A similar contrast can be found in the terms "screw*driver*" and *Schraubenzieher* ("screw*puller*"); some might suggest that the former term suggests construction, the latter proclivities toward de-construction or even destruction. Here, though, one should proceed cautiously, despite the arguments advanced by Ralf Dahrendorff in *Gesellschaft und Demokratie in Deutschland*. But *Spaß und höheren Blödsinn beiseite:* superior students interested in such issues of comparative sociology should be encouraged to read the Dahrendorff book, which is available in English translation.

Mention related terms *schwarzer Markt, schwarzarbeiten* ("moonlight" – but something beyond that, since *schwarzarbeiten* directly suggests that taxes are not paid, where moonlighting can be an aboveboard job).

American and German Driving Habits
Donald D. Hook

Germans give a better performance on the road than Americans do. Their skill in handling their vehicles is in abundant evidence, and a pervasive regard for the law makes Germans safer drivers than Americans. Even though an entire generation much more intimately associated with the automobile has matured since the war ended, there is evidence that other factors have come into play as well.

The oft-heard argument that Germans, by their very nature, view various social structures with unquestioned respect is not without some validity. (That this presumed inborn rigidity has at times contributed to misfortune for many cannot be denied.) And there is little doubt that their ethnic homogeneity has facilitated the acquisition and promotion of certain national characteristics. With as much—or as little—certainty it can probably be conversely argued that the mixed nature of American society has produced, over many years, a measure of tolerance for our different backgrounds which is demonstrated by our refusal to establish for all a single set of mores—or even one set of traffic laws.

What is not entirely clear is why, in such a country as West Germany, where the density of population is roughly that of southern New England, incidents of rudeness and crudeness have virtually disappeared. Perhaps as suggested earlier, people are calmer, more satisfied, when there is considerable national stability. It is also a matter of having lived with crowded conditions longer than we in America and having learned, of necessity, to cooperate and to be careful not to offend. For the Germans police themselves. In contrast to the United States, it is rare to see a policeman, but it is virtually impossible to get away with anything—even a minor traffic violation. *Somebody* will witness the event and step up to instruct the violator, if not to report him or her to the authorities. Under crowded conditions criminals and scofflaws simply cannot be tolerated.

Journal of Popular Culture Vol. 19 #1 Summer 1985

Schnellbahnen im Münchner Verkehrs- und Tarifverbund

Entwurf : MVV / HA 1 Stand : September 1985

In die Freizeit, zum Wandern, zu Sport und Spiel, für Einkauf, Stadtbummel, Besorgungen, Besuche:

Der MVV bringt Sie sicher, schnell und bequem hin und heim. Ihre problemlose Fahrkarte: Das 24-Stunden-Ticket. 24 Stunden (ab Entwertung) fahren so oft und wohin Sie wollen.

24-Stunden-Tickets gibt's aus den Automaten, beim abr, beim Fremdenverkehrsamt und an der Rezeption der Münchner Hotels, die in diesem Verzeichnis mit dem Servicezeichen **K** versehen sind.

Nur im Stadtnetz Zürich gültig, gelber und blauer Bereich des Automatenplans

●

Billett für eine Fahrt mit Umsteigen.
Retour- und Umwegfahrten verboten.
Gültigkeitsdauer ab Stempelzeit:

Kurzstreckenbillett
Kennzeichen: 3 Randkerben   30 Min.
Billett für Tarifstufe 1
Kennzeichen: 2 Randkerben   60 Min.
Billett für Tarifstufe 2
Kennzeichen: 1 Randkerbe   90 Min.
Tageskarte, keine Randkerbe   24 Std.
Nur im Stadtnetz Zürich gültig,
gelber und blauer Bereich des
Automatenplans
●

Billett für eine Fahrt mit Umsteigen.
Retour- und Umwegfahrten verboten.
Gültigkeitsdauer ab Stempelzeit:
Kurzstreckenbillett
Kennzeichen: 3 Randkerben   30 Min.

U-Bahn – S-Bahn

1

2

Exercise: Today is the (x)th; single trip costs A, *Wochenkarte* B, and *Monatskarte* (for this month) C. Which is the best buy? *Monats/ende*

3

Botanischer Garten collection of plants, just as a zoo is a *Zoologischer Garten* or collection of animals.

4

Explain various terms for transportation ticket: *Fahrkarte* for longer trips (train, etc.); *Flugkarte* for air travel; *Fahrschein, Fahrausweis* for local transit.

die Güte goodness
Geld/strafe fine (penalty)

WILLIAM LEWIS	Entschuldigung, wissen Sie, ob man hier eine S-Bahnkarte kaufen kann?
FRAU ACKERMANN	Die bekommen Sie am Automat dort. Wissen Sie Bescheid?
WILLIAM LEWIS	Nein, ich weiß nicht, wie man das macht. Könnten Sie das bitte erklären?
FRAU ACKERMANN	Sicher. Sehen Sie, in der gelben Zone – das ist dieser Stadtteil hier – kostet es DM1,20. In der blauen ist es teurer – DM2,00.
WILLIAM LEWIS	Ich muß zum Leopoldplatz fahren.
FRAU ACKERMANN	Das liegt in der blauen Zone. Drücken Sie also den blauen Knopf und werfen Sie Ihre Münze hier ein. Da bekommen Sie die Karte.
FRL. FELLMANN	Grüß Gott. Kann ich hier eine S-Bahnkarte kaufen?
FRAU EISENHAUER	Natürlich. Was für eine Karte wollen Sie – eine Wochenkarte, eine Monatskarte, . . . ?
FRL. FELLMANN	Ich bleibe ein paar Wochen hier und fahre täglich drei- oder viermal.
FRAU EISENHAUER	Dann wäre eine Monatskarte am besten. DM65 bitte.
FRL. FELLMANN	Wie lange ist sie noch gültig? 30 Tage oder nur bis zum Monatsende?
HERR JAEGER	Bitte, der junge Herr. Wollen Sie bitte aufstehen? Die Dame möchte sich setzen.
HERR POST	Wie, bitte? Ach ja, bitte schön. Setzen Sie sich. Kann ich mit den Paketen helfen?
FRAU KNIEBEL	Danke, das ist sehr nett von Ihnen.
HERR POST	Bitte schön. Übrigens, ich will zur Heidestraße. Wissen Sie, ob ich umsteigen muß?
FRAU KNIEBEL	Heidestraße? Ach, das liegt nicht weit vom Kunsthaus, hinter dem Botanischen Garten. Ich glaube nicht, daß Sie umsteigen müssen.
HERR HOFER	Darf ich bitte Ihren Fahrschein sehen?
FRÄULEIN KELLER	Meinen Fahrschein? O ja, sicher, bitte schön.
HERR HOFER	Umhh. Der ist aber ungültig für diese Strecke.
FRÄULEIN KELLER	Aber ich habe ihn gerade vor zehn Minuten gekauft.
HERR HOFER	Aber Sie sind am Bärenplatz eingestiegen. Auf dieser Seite vom Fluß ist er nicht gültig. Da brauchen Sie eine andere Karte für die blaue Zone.
FRÄULEIN KELLER	Ach, du meine Güte, was mache ich jetzt?
HERR HOFER	Naja, da müßten Sie normalerweise eine Geldstrafe zahlen – und die richtige Karte kaufen.
FRÄULEIN KELLER	Ich wußte nicht, daß das eine andere Zone ist. Ich bin hier fremd.
HERR HOFER	Ist nicht schlimm. Jetzt wissen Sie Bescheid. So . . . Ich wünsche Ihnen einen schönen Aufenthalt in unserer Stadt.

167

STRUKTUR 2

A.A. §§13,17

1. Adjectives after articles: dative case　　　　-en

pattern for all genders and plural: article + adjective + **-en**

Main point: through exercise even more than explanation, establish -en as the characteristic "throwaway" ending for the oblique or less important dative (and genitive) case, just as -e is the characteristic signal for the vital nominative and accusative cases after an article with a "strong" ending, at least in the singular, which itself is so much more important than the plural. See note in Instructor's Guide.

MASCULINE
{ am sieb<u>ten</u> Dezember
das Monatsprogramm mit dem klein<u>en</u> Stadtplan
ein Monatsprogramm mit einem klein<u>en</u> Stadtplan?

FEMININE　in der zehn<u>ten</u> Reihe
in der gelb<u>en</u> Zone

NEUTER　in dem klein<u>en</u> Hotel
in einem klein<u>en</u> Hotel

PLURAL　in den groß<u>en</u> Hotels

W.O. §12

2. Conjunction *ob*　　　*if* only in the sense of *whether*

Übrigens, wissen Sie, **ob** ich für die Heidestraße umsteigen muß?

Return to earlier chapters for material to set up exercises in which questions are encapsulated with introductions employing ob. Examples: A) Student A poses a yes/no question; B feigns lack of comprehension; A restates, introducing with, "Ich wollte wissen/fragen, ob . . ."; B) Student A remarks, "Wir sollten fragen, ob [er das neue Programm hat, etc.]"; B poses the question directly to C ("Haben Sie das neue Programm?"; C answers the question, or feigns lack of comprehension, as in A above.

- **requires verb-last word order**

Hat er das neue Programm?
Wir sollten fragen, *ob* er das neue Programm *hat*.

- **provides a politer and therefore more effective way of asking Yes/No questions**

- **frequently used with words that describe getting and giving travel or "tourist" information**

Wissen Sie, **ob** . . .　　Könnten Sie mir sagen, **ob** . . .

- **not interchangeable with *wenn***

For enrichment point out the immense irregularity (and variety!) of English as compared with German. Ordinarily we use only the forms "weekly" and "monthly"; seldom do we employ "diurnal(ly)" in favor of "daily"; but often we alternate "yearly" with "annual(ly)," and most students will recognize "nocturnal(ly)" as a partial equivalent of "night(ly)." See note in Instructor's Guide.

3. Word formation with common prefixes and suffixes　　often corresponds to English *-ly*.

- **-*lich***

täglich *daily*　　freundlich *friendly*
endlich *finally*　　natürlich　*naturally*

- ***un-***

Student A: X ist nicht (adjective); B: Nein, X (or pronoun) ist un- (adjective). In some instances the exercise can be expanded with a modal paraphrase, whether near or distant. Thus "X ist unglaublich" = "Man kann das nicht glauben," and "Y ist unmöglich" = "Man kann das nicht tun." If you teach the suffix -bar (-able, -ible, etc.) you can also work with untrinkbar = Man kann das nicht trinken, etc.

The prefix *un-* can be added readily to many adjectives or adverbs to create opposites. English uses several negating prefixes (*un-, in-, im-, non-*); German has only one.

gültig – <u>un</u>gültig (= "<u>in</u>valid" or perhaps just "<u>not</u> valid")
natürlich – <u>un</u>natürlich (= "<u>un</u>natural")

NOTE: Often a single German word may function as either an adjective or an adverb. Thus *natürlich* may mean either "natural" (adjective) or "naturally" (adverb), just as *gut* can mean either "good" (adjective) or "well" (adverb).

Das Essen ist wirklich sehr *gut*.　　　　adjective
Die Pianistin hat wirklich sehr *gut* gespielt.　　adverb

Stage 1	A	B
1	Needs tickets for self and two others. Provides the information.	Children? Students? Adults? Seniors? If children, how old? If students, need ID.
Most students should have sufficient imagination to make up such information, and by now the class should have been trained not to have any inhibitions about speaking, even extemporaneously. If you encounter difficulty, list some possibilities – autobiographical sketches – on the board.	Has left passports in hotel; begins to explain why. Concludes transaction.	Willing to trust them. Counts out change, offers helpful map.
2	Needs some kind of transit pass. Confused by all the possibilities. Three weeks, with some two-night side trips out of the city. Intends to use the transit system heavily some days, others not at all.	Lists the options and their prices. Asks how long A plans to be in the city. Suspects the monthly pass would still be a good idea, but asks for more details. Calculates a trial case ("Say, for example, you take X trips a day for Y days . . . ").
1: "Has left . . ." does not require past tense, though that would be nice; "Unsere Pässe sind im Hotel" will do.		
3	(Has dropped transit pass, unaware)	(Sees transit pass, thinks it might be A's, but isn't sure. Picks it up.) Politely gets A's attention.
"Somewhat standoffish" could be expressed in many ways: a cool "Ja?"; "Ja, was wollen Sie?"; "Wollten Sie mit mir sprechen?." Once someone has gotten your attention, silence is virtually impossible.	Somewhat standoffish. Checks and realizes pass is missing. Maintains dignity by explaining why the pass is still unsigned. Thanks profusely to make up for earlier coolness.	Quickly explains. Wonders whether it is indeed A's. Ready to hand over pass, but notices it is unsigned. Offers a gentle reminder. Sympathizes – has seen conductor approaching to check tickets (always happens that way). Concludes conversation.

Stage 2

1: For a challenge, redo as "You are with a group of children . . ."

2: Try it as a phone call (students sit back to back).

1

You are with a child and have just viewed the extensive collection of Christmas manger scenes at the Bayerisches Nationalmuseum. You now want to go to the Toy Museum near Marienplatz.

a) Tell the child where you will be going, and how you plan to get there.
b) Find out whether the child would like to walk part of the way or is tired.
c) You could both use a snack; discuss whether you want one now or later.

2

With a transit map and a schedule of cultural events, plan an evening out for yourself and someone else.

a) Select the event and find out time, place, cost, etc.
b) Find the location on the map and determine the route to take.
c) Agree when and where to meet.
d) What about dinner before or a snack after?

Versuchen Sie doch

Supplemental situation and model for similar review: Redo *Stadtplan/Fahrplan Stage 2 Situation 2*, this time by exploring at least two public transportation routes. If you contemplate going on foot, could you make it in an hour?

The Austrian military officer you thought you were addressing politely as "Herr Schaffner" is not at all amused at being mistaken for a subway conductor and asked the price of a ticket to the amusement park (*der Prater*). (Would you be able to tell the story later?)

You've lost your new monthly pass for the transit system. You think you may have left it at a kiosk when you were buying the monthly events program. You hope you remembered to sign it. Go back and prove that you are you.

You're at the S-7 station in Wolfratshausen south of München. Someone you know has found a new, unsigned transit pass. You look it over and offer advice about what can and should be done with it.

Chapter 17

MENSA / UNIVERSITÄT

Mensa der Universität

Stiftung Berner Studentenheim

Ist das die Mensa der Universität München? (Or is it the student union at the University of Oregon?)

Wie kann man wissen, daß das Foto wahrscheinlich nicht amerikanische, sondern deutsche Studenten zeigt? (Tip: die Hände.)

Top photo: It's Munich. Lower photo: Refer to discussion of cutlery handling in Chapter 9.

FUNKTIONEN – KONTEXTE – STRUKTUREN

Looking Ahead

You'll be eating in a student cafeteria, talking about living accommodations, and discussing university studies.

Songs and poems appropriate to chapter: "*Alt Heidelberg du Feine*"; "*O alte Burschenherrlichkeit*"; "*Doktor Eisenbart*"; "*Die heiße Schlacht am kalten Büffet*" (Reinhard May); *Faust I*, ll. 355ff.: "*Habe nun, ach! . . .*"

You will be using:

- nouns made from adjectives to denote nationality (Austrian, the Austrians)
- words that indicate indefinite agents (someone, no one)
- reflexives – words that refer back to the subject of a sentence (I'm going to buy *myself* some books)
- adverbs of definite time (every day, last week)
- the conjunction *sondern* to substitute one thing for another (not math, *but rather* physics)

Mensa

1

Friesland: on the North Sea
coast, near the Dutch border.

ERICH KOPP	Mahlzeit. . . . Ist hier noch frei?
GEORG FRANZEN	Ja, sicher, setz dich doch.
ERICH KOPP	Erich Kopp, aus Friesland.
GEORG FRANZEN	Georg Franzen, freut mich, Erich.
GISELA MAUTNER	Dann muß ich mich auch vorstellen: Gisela Mautner.
ERICH KOPP	Grüß Gott, Gisela. Bist du von hier?
GISELA MAUTNER	Nein, aus Baden-Baden.

2

Spätzle
type of noodle
saftig juicy
Bohnen beans

Encourage description of
American dishes (taco, etc.) by
listing of ingredients, either in
straight series or in the pattern
"X mit Y."

THOMAS RICHTER	Also, das würde ich nicht empfehlen. Es sieht so . . . wie soll ich das sagen . . . unnatürlich aus. Das kann niemand essen.
GISELA BRUSECKI	Vielleicht hast du recht: ein bißchen mehr Farbe im Gemüse wäre schön.
THOMAS RICHTER	"Brathuhn mit Spätzle" – das klingt viel besser. Und einen grünen Salat nehme ich auch.
GISELA BRUSECKI	Sind die Würste gekocht oder gebraten? Ich möchte mir ganz gern eine saftige Bratwurst mit Bohnensalat kaufen.
THOMAS RICHTER	Schau mal: "Tageskarte: zwei Wiener mit Brötchen und Kartoffelsalat DM 4,70." Nicht schlecht. Das ist billiger als Bratwurst und schmeckt auch viel besser.
GISELA BRUSECKI	Na, vielleicht. . . . Nimmst du auch einen Traubensaft?

3

indisch Indian (Eastern);
Indianer American Indian
Reis/Fleisch
Lust haben feel like; have a
yen or hankering for
Mittel/Klassen/Mahlzeit
Amerikanistin
American Studies major
griechische Austern
Greek oysters

HANNI KLINGER	"Indisches Reisfleisch" – was ist denn das?
UTE NELZ	Also, Hackfleisch mit Reis, Rosinen, Paprika, Curry –
HANNI KLINGER	Na, mal sehen. Etwas aus Mexiko wäre auch gut.
UTE NELZ	Nicht für mich – das wäre viel zu scharf. Außerdem habe ich Lust auf einen guten amerikanischen Hamburger.
HANNI KLINGER	So – Mittelklassenmahlzeit für die Amerikanistin, aber mich interessiert etwas Exotisches.
UTE NELZ	Oh, fein. Etwas Exotisches in der Mensa – und bei McDonalds kaufen wir uns griechische Austern, wie?

4

Studentendorf student housing
development

Wohngemeinschaft
communal apartment group

FRANZ MOSER	Na, was meint ihr: "Gesucht: Untermieter für den Monat August. Nette, möblierte Zwei-Zimmerwohnung im 7. Stock." – das ginge, oder?
BENEDIKT GERBER	Mal sehen. Das ist doch im Studentendorf, und in dem Hochhaus hätten wir wahrscheinlich Ehepaare mit Kindern –
HEINZ KONRAD	Wenn ihr da sonst nichts seht, sollten wir uns die Wohnung mal anschauen. Wir wären sowieso nicht viel zu Hause.
FRANZ MOSER	Stimmt. Und wenn die Wohnung gut eingerichtet ist –
HEINZ KONRAD	Oder wollen wir es lieber bei einer Wohngemeinschaft versuchen? Ein älteres Haus, jemand von der Uni . . .

171

1. Using adjectives to show national origin

A.A. §§20,21

Set up two-column exercise: column A – national adjectives; column B – food items. Target: *"französische Zwiebelsuppe,"* *"amerikanische Austern,"* etc. Don't worry about culinary verisimilitude; just practice the pattern "national adjective + noun."

Rätoromanisch: *Switzerland's fourth national language, an archaic Romance idiom closely related to Italian.*

Point out common error:* *"Ich bin amerikanisch."*

See note in Instructor's Guide.

Point out that, while it is considered "low class" to talk about talking American instead of English (see the very first

Pronouns §18

dialog of Preliminary Chapter 1), German translations of American literature may well carry the description, *"aus dem Amerikanischen."*

COUNTRY	LANGUAGE	ADJECTIVE	CITIZEN (MALE, FEMALE)
USA	Englisch	amerikanisch	Amerikaner, -in
Kanada	Englisch	kanadisch	Kanadier, -in
	Französisch		
Österreich	Deutsch	österreichisch	Österreicher, -in
BRD	Deutsch	westdeutsch	Deutscher, Deutsche
DDR	Deutsch	ostdeutsch	Deutscher, Deutsche
die Schweiz	Deutsch / Französisch / Italienisch / Rätoromanisch	schweizerisch or Schweizer + Noun	Schweizer, -in

Most adjectives of nationality describe the national language as well.

- adjective **X-isch** often = **aus, in,** or **von X**   don't capitalize the adjective

  japanisch = aus Japan

- Many countries have the **-er/-erin** form for citizens.

2. Indefinite pronouns ending in -mand

"no one," "someone"

Pronouns ending in *-mand* are third person singular pronouns, like *man.*

- ***niemand:*** "no one (at all)"

  Das <u>kann</u> **niemand** essen.

- ***jemand:*** "someone (or other)"

  Ich gehe nur mit, wenn **jemand** mit dem Proviant <u>hilft</u>.

  NOTE: The word for every*one* is **alle**. The word for every*thing* is **alles**.

Stage 1

	A	B
1	Thinks the pork chop with curry sounds a bit spicy.	Disagrees; thinks it's very tasty (had it yesterday).
	Would rather have something from South America or maybe Korea.	Finds Korean food too sharp – no one can eat it.
	Thinks Korean food is very exotic.	Korean food isn't B's cup of tea. Has a craving for cheap but good local food.
	Says that's not very international.	So what? – just wants to buy some food.
	Invites B over for a French meal.	Would like to come; asks what to bring.
	Asks B to bring something to drink.	Sure . . . Almost forgot – what day and when?

How many ways can your class rephrase this high-level idiom in the German presented up to now?

	A	B	C
2	Is all ready to go hiking.	Asks if A can't wait for a couple of hours.	Agrees, would like to buy a big meal before going.
		Needs to clean up in the house so the landlord won't be angry.	
	Has a better idea. Suggests a plan: C goes to eat, A and B go to B's house for supplies.	Interrupts, says it's A's turn to bring supplies.	Will try to bring something from the Mensa.
	Thinks C is right, suggests C bring some international gourmet food.	Says A shouldn't be that way.	Is terribly hungry, starts listing Mensa food to buy.
		Still needs to clean up the house.	Keeps listing Mensa food.
	Says the house looks so unnatural when it's clean.	Says A should just wait a bit. B will find someone for the housecleaning, and then they can go.	Keeps listing Mensa food. Starts repeating self.

Stage 2

1

You've just sat down at a table in the Mensa, and begin a conversation with the other student there.

a) Tell her essentials about yourself and ask her for similar information.
b) Discuss the food – you think it's good (she thinks it's too bland).
c) Suggest another food item to suit her taste.
d) Tell her what five different countries have foods you like, even though she prefers five other ones.

2

You need an apartment. Tell the person in the *Auslandsamt* (foreign student office) that you're considering renting either

a) a furnished two-room apartment with a friend in the high-rise dormitory; or
b) an unfurnished one-room apartment alone near the center of town.

3

You're at the market, buying supplies for an exotic meal for a few friends. Tell the person with you how much of each food item to buy. (Remember that quantities must be in metric units.)

1 b): *Nicht scharf/heiß genug.*

3: Recommend *Bildwörterbuch* displays about food and transactions.

Versuchen Sie doch

You've just ordered a heavy meal in the Mensa and are confronted by a slim vegetarian friend who questions your sanity. Give a good reason for ordering each of the things on your tray. Then see if you can give the vegetarian's reply to each.

STRATEGIE – KULTUR UND SPRACHE

Die Mensa: not just a student cafeteria

The Mensa (Latin: "table") serves many purposes as a focus of student life in German-speaking countries. Its function varies from university to university, but it can range from a cafeteria to a student union with a variety of services.

Because the Mensa is subsidized by the state, food is inexpensive. For the equivalent of $2 or so it is possible to eat reasonably well – in a culture that spends a large percentage of its income on food. Survival meat-and-potatoes fare (*Stammessen*) is also available, and for a correspondingly low price: about DM 2,40. Students from North America are surprised that beer, because it is considered a food, is available in the Mensa.

The Mensa is also frequently the only university building that provides a common meeting place for students. There may also be offices for insurance, travel, cultural groups, political organizations, and in some cases the all-important *Auslandsamt,* the foreign student office. Because the Mensa is such a central part of the university, it is a magnet for messages of all kinds – from the *Schwarzes Brett* ("Black Board") with handwritten notices (housing, bicycles for sale, etc.) to tables with pamphlets about academic, political, and social affairs.

Die Universität = Die Hochschule

The North American system of colleges and universities was patterned after European – and very often German – institutions of higher education, but today there are striking differences between the two systems.

Older American institutions were often patterned on the British model, "newer" ones (e.g., land-grant colleges, many state universities) on the German model.

Because students enter German-speaking *Universitäten* and *Hochschulen* at a later age (generally 20 or 21), the tenor of instruction and the learning environment are more like those at the advanced undergraduate and graduate level in America. Students enter a university with a major and minor firmly in mind, and rarely take courses outside those fields. University study is intended to be specific and career-oriented rather than general and broadening, because much of what is accomplished here during the first two years of general college study is done in the high school or, as it might better be called, the preparatory school (*das Gymnasium*). A far smaller proportion of university-age people become *Studenten* in Europe than on this side of the Atlantic.

Perhaps remark – especially if the point is relevant to your own type of institution – that the German university system lacks equivalents of either the small liberal arts college or the junior college, and that older, "returning" students recommencing (or just commencing) study after years engaged in other pursuits are extremely rare, as are those with full-time commitments to jobs or family.

Just as there are individual graduate institutions in North America specializing in law, medicine, theology, and business, there are a variety of *Hochschulen* that allow entering students to pursue specific career interests; examples are *die Wiener Hochschule für Musik, die Theologische Hochschule* in Frankfurt, *die Eidgenössische Technische Hochschule* (*ETH*) in Zürich, similar respectively to the Peabody Conservatory, the Yale Divinity School, and Cal Tech. There is also a *Sporthochschule* in Köln.

Rarely does a university in Europe have something like a campus, and rarely is there a feeling of close community. Individual academic departments or divisions (*Institute, Fakultäten*) may be scattered widely throughout a city; most students do not live in dormitories (*Studentenheime*); and fraternities (*Verbindungen*) or sororities (*Frauenverbindungen*) are unimportant. Big-time sports programs do not exist.

Maybe mention the importance in earlier times of *Burschenschaften* (social and political fraternities) and the dueling and drinking societies.

There is now one private institution in the BRD.

There are no private colleges in the North American sense, and the prospect of paying large sums of money yearly for a university education is difficult for European students to comprehend. All advanced study in the four German-speaking countries is virtually free. But classes tend to be large and impersonal, especially on the lower level.

Education – some tricky vocabulary

Beginning students (*Studenten im ersten, zweiten, dritten Semester*) take introductory classes in their specific disciplines: *Übungen* ("practice sessions"), *Proseminare* (low-level seminars), and *Vorlesungen* (lectures), the latter sometimes with hundreds of students enrolled. "Classes," unless specifically noted, are called *Vorlesungen* ("*Ich habe eine Vorlesung um 10*"), never *Klassen*.

"*Was studierst du?*" is a familiar question: "What's your major?" – for *studieren* means "to follow a course of study at a university." It does not describe what one does each night; that is *arbeiten*:

Ich kann nicht zum Konzert gehen. Ich muß *arbeiten*.

The verb *machen* is used in enumerating the courses one is taking:

"Dieses Semester *mache* ich Psychologie, Biologie und einen Kurs über Psychiatrie in Wien um 1900."

NOTE: High School is not *Hochschule;* use the word *Oberschule*. "Grade," in the sense of group of students, is expressed by "*die Klasse,*" or also by "*Schuljahr.*" "Grade," in the sense of marks on a report card or transcript, can be expressed by *die Note* (*-n*).

Words for "people"

To express "the people in (country)," use the nationality word – *not "Leute," "Menschen," or "Volk."*

The people in Austria are friendly. *Die Österreicher sind freundlich.*

● *die Person, -en* – neutral or "official" term, both male and female

Die Stadtrundfahrt? Für wie viele **Personen**?
Sie/Er ist wirklich eine nette **Person**.

● *die Leute* – specific people, such as a group; often casual; can mean "folks" (though not in the sense of "parents")

"Die **Leute** da drüben sind Freunde von meinen Großeltern."

● *der Mensch, -en* – human being, as opposed to members of other species

Die **Menschen** sind interessanter als die Affen.

● *man* – indefinite: people, you, they, one

Das macht **man** nicht.

● *das Volk, ⁻er* – a national group

Das Schweizer **Volk** liebt seine Berge.

Maybe mention the *numerus clausus,* which sets grade qualifications for admission to the majors and for assignment to a university.

See Bildwörterbuch: Universität, p. 291.

6

Universität Bern

Philosophisch-historische Fakultät

Seminargebäude I

Note the common student errors in attempted renditions of "the people in Germany": **Die (deutschen) Leute/Die Männer/ Menschen/Die Völker (in Deutschland).*

Good time for a chorus of Beethoven's Ninth: "*Alle Menschen werden Brüder. . . .*" Emphasize that *Männer* pertains only to males, and thus would not be used to express such sentiments as "All men are created equal." Remark that German has nonsexist terms for generic "man" or "(hu)mankind" (*die Menschheit*). Maybe point out the difference between *Menschheit* (humanity – species) and *Menschlichkeit* (humanity – humaneness), and even *Männlichkeit* (manliness, masculinity – whatever that means these days). See note in Instructor's Guide.

SCHWEIZERISCHE VOLKSBANK

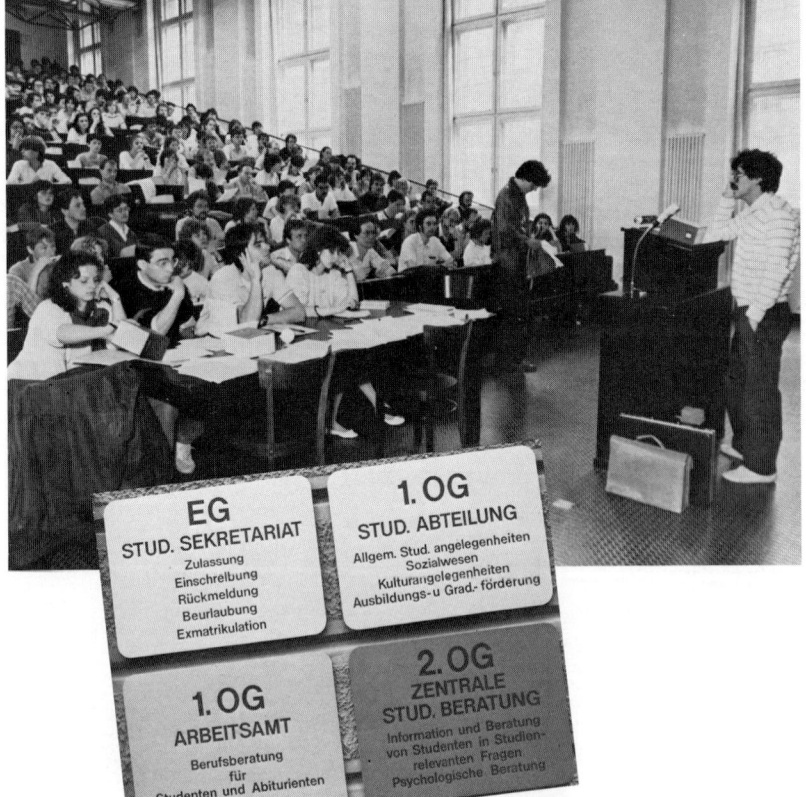

JOHANN WOLFGANG GOETHE
UNIVERSITÄT

Hochschul-
sport

Ethnologie

Erziehungs-
Bibliothek

Sprach

Psychologie
Erziehungs-u.
Unterrichts-
wissenschaft

German
Romanistik
Geschichte

Capitol Kino

Soziale
Medizin

Rechts-
medizin

U

EG
STUD. SEKRETARIAT
Zulassung
Einschreibung
Rückmeldung
Beurlaubung
Exmatrikulation

1. OG
STUD. ABTEILUNG
Allgem. Stud. angelegenheiten
Sozialwesen
Kulturangelegenheiten
Ausbildungs-u Grad.-förderung

1. OG
ARBEITSAMT
Berufsberatung
für
Studenten und Abiturienten

2. OG
ZENTRALE
STUD. BERATUNG
Information und Beratung
von Studenten in Studien-
relevanten Fragen
Psychologische Beratung

Universität

1

Austausch
exchange

DAVID HENSLEY — Nein, das ist kein Austauschprogramm. Unser College schickt jedes Jahr 15 Studenten nach München.

ANNI REICHARDT — Und die dürfen hier alles studieren?

DAVID HENSLEY — Ja, aber im ersten Semester haben wir Sonderkurse.

ANNI REICHARDT — Aber im zweiten Semester macht ihr dann an gewöhnlichen Kursen mit, oder?

*Kurs "course" as well as
"currency rate"
Kurs < Latin cursus, from
currere, "to run"*

DAVID HENSLEY — Ja, die meisten von uns schon. Aber das sind meistens Vorlesungen und Seminare über Geschichte, Kunst, Literatur, – also die Geisteswissenschaften.

ANNI REICHARDT — Und auch Kurse in den Naturwissenschaften?

DAVID HENSLEY — Die können wir zu Hause machen. Hier haben wir die beste Möglichkeit, europäische Kultur kennenzulernen.

2

PETER PEISER — Sprachwissenschaft? Wirklich? Warum denn?

RALPH BIERMANN — Nun, Sprachen interessieren mich einfach. Ich bin ja im Ausland geboren. Jeden Tag hatten wir andere Sprachen im Haus: Italienisch, Französisch, auch Schwedisch.

PETER PEISER — Du willst also Dolmetscher werden oder so?

RALPH BIERMANN — Nein, nicht unbedingt. Die wissenschaftliche Seite der Linguistik interessiert mich: Sprachgeschichte, Struktur, wie man eine Sprache lernt usw.

PETER PEISER — Also nicht unbedingt *was* man sagt, sondern *wie* man es sagt. Ich selber finde das Was interessanter als das Wie. Aber jedem Tierchen sein Plaisirchen. . . .

*Aber . . . to each his own,
different strokes for different
folks*

3

SANDY PALMER — Also kommt ihr auch mit 5 Jahren in die Schule?

ALEX SCHIWOW — Nein, meistens erst, wenn wir sechs sind. Und dann dauert unsere Schulzeit ja auch ein Jahr länger.

SANDY PALMER — Ihr seid also erst mit 19 fertig? Und dann beginnt das Studium an der Universität?

Zivildienst
alternative service

ALEX SCHIWOW — Nicht unbedingt. Nach dem Abitur müssen wir Jungen in die Armee gehen oder Zivildienst machen.

4

KAREN STEEN — Und wann müßt ihr ein Hauptfach wählen? Auch vor dem dritten Jahr?

BERT BRANDT — Nein, sofort. Aber wenn man das Abitur gemacht hat, weiß man meistens, was man studieren will.

KAREN STEEN — Ist es also unmöglich, das Hauptfach zu ändern? Bei uns macht man das oft.

BERT BRANDT — Ja, das finde ich gut bei euch. Es ist aber auch hier möglich. Nur darf man nicht das ganze Leben lang studieren!

KAREN STEEN — Das sagen meine Eltern auch immer.

BERT BRANDT — Und hier sagt der Staat, daß man nicht immer Student bleiben darf. Der Staat finanziert nämlich das Studium.

KAREN STEEN — Für alle?

BERT BRANDT — Ja, aber hier studieren nicht so viele Leute wie bei euch.

177

STRUKTUR 2

Verbs §41
See note in Instructor's Guide.

1. Doing something for oneself rather than for others

reflexive actions

● actions that reflect on the actor (subject) **are reflexive.**

Ich möchte *mir* ganz gern eine Bratwurst kaufen. "(for) myself"
same person

Bei McDonalds kaufen *wir uns* auch Austern. "(for) ourselves"
same persons

● Doing something for someone else is **not reflexive.**

Ich habe *dir* Kartoffelsalat gebracht. "(for) you"
different people

● **sich**

To transfer the action clearly requires a special pronoun in the third person and *Sie*-forms.

Ute möchte *ihr* griechische Austern kaufen.
Ute   some other (female) person

(She wants to buy her some Greek oysters.)

Er/Sie möchte *sich* griechische Austern kaufen.
"(for) himself/herself"

Ich glaube, sie möchten *sich* eine Flasche Wein holen.
"(for) themselves"

Möchten Sie *sich* noch eine Wurst holen?
(for) yourself/yourselves

Nouns §15

Just plant the seed with regard to case, since the feature is evident only with the masculine. More important are vocabulary (*jed-*) and the notion that such time phrases almost never use *für* where English uses *for*. Don't get involved in explanations of the legitimate use of *"für/auf zwei Monate,"* etc.

2. Telling when things happen or how long they last: definite time

accusative

Jeden Tag hatten wir andere Sprachen im Haus.
Unser College schickt **nächste Woche** 15 Studenten nach München.
Unsere Schulzeit dauert **ein Jahr** länger.

Similarly:

Wir bleiben ein<u>e</u> Minute / zwei Minuten bei Ihnen. (die Minute)

        ein<u>e</u> Stunde / ein paar Stunden   (die Stunde)

        ein<u>e</u> Woche / viele Wochen   (die Woche)

        ein<u>en</u> Monat / einige Monate   (der Monat)

W.O. §8

3. The conjunction *sondern*

"but (rather)," "instead"

The *aber/sondern* distinction is difficult to target for production, in practice or in testing, unless one chooses to do translation exercises, which runs counter to the concept of proficiency. See note in Instructor's Guide.

● *aber* – expresses objection, modification, reservation (Yes, but . . .)

Aber hier studieren nicht so viele Leute wie bei euch.

● *sondern* – rejects A, substitutes B

Sondern often appears with a negation.
    nicht Schweinefleisch, sondern Hackfleisch
    Also nicht unbedingt was man sagt, sondern wie man es sagt.

178 CHAPTER 17

SITUATIONEN 2 Universität

Stage 1	A	B

1

See if your students can list such countries. There is no need to teach the terms Entwicklungsland, unterentwickelt, and dritte/vierte Welt.

A	B
Says his group of students isn't taking regular university courses.	Asks why not.
Says regular courses are too hard for foreigners in the first term – no one understands German well.	Asks why A's group of students is here if they're not studying at the university.
Says the purpose of the stay in Europe is to study European history and art.	Says has seen foreign students all over the university in both terms.
Says has also seen them, asks what countries they all come from.	From all over the world, especially underdeveloped countries.

2

A	B
Asks why B is interested in biology.	Wants to work in a laboratory.
Thought B wanted to be either a doctor or a dentist.	Finds the scientific side of medicine more interesting.
Asks whether B's interest in biology came from someone in the family.	Had good science instruction in high school.
Own science teachers were good, but finds the humanities more interesting.	Asks what A would do with that in a career.
Says humanities students can do anything.	Agrees, but still finds physical sciences more interesting.

3

At most the student is prepared by the dialogs to outline the basic military obligation. The exercise can end here, or you yourself may take over the B role and provide more information.

A	B
Tells B when American students begin school and how long they go.	Mentions differences in West Germany.
Asks if all students go right on to the university.	Says all beginning students have to have passed the entrance examination.
Tells what most American students do after high school.	Finds that interesting; asks about military service.
Tells situation; asks about military service in West Germany.	Mentions basic military obligation.

Stage 2

1

You are in the Mensa in Tübingen, talking with a student you just met during lunch. Tell him how long you've been there already, why you are majoring in what you have chosen, and what you hope to accomplish through your studies.

2

Sie sprechen gerade mit einigen österreichischen Studenten in Graz. Sagen Sie ihnen

a) warum Sport an amerikanischen Universitäten so wichtig ist;
b) warum viele amerikanische Studenten in Studentenheimen wohnen;
c) was Sie in Österreich besonders interessiert.

Versuchen Sie doch

Don't attempt this unless you have earlier discussed numerus clausus.

You have been studying for a term at the Universität Konstanz and find yourself at a table in the Mensa with a student from Madrid who has just matriculated. Explain to the student something you've just encountered yourself: the term *numerus clausus*, the policy that limits the number of students in – generally – technical fields because of shortages in teaching facilities; and the ZVS, the office in Dortmund that attempts to distribute students in various fields throughout the BRD according to the facilities available at each university.

Berater adviser

Sie sind Austauschstudent an der Universität Kiel. Sagen Sie dem Berater im Auslandsamt etwas über Ihre Stadt in Nordamerika und über Ihre Familie. Fragen Sie ihn dann, was er Ihnen in den ersten Semesterwochen empfiehlt.

179

Chapter 18

KAUFHAUS/ FUNDBÜRO

Use *Bildwörterbuch* "City-Street-Building/*Stadt-Straße-Haus*" (pp. 286–287) and "Money and Store/*Geld und Geschäft*" (p. 290).

⚓KaDeWe Etagenplan

6.OG. Feinschmeckeretage · Bestellannahme
Party-Service · Übergang Parkhaus II

5.OG. Lampen · Gardinen · Betten · Teppiche · Künstliche
Blumen · Gourmetrestaurant »Silberterrasse«
Übergang Parkhaus II

4.OG. Haushaltwaren · Küchen · Elektrogeräte · Porzellan
Glas · Geschenkartikel · Kunstgewerbe · Bilder · Hobby
Autozubehör · Alles für das Bad · Übergang Parkhaus II

3.OG. Radio/Fernsehen · Schallplatten · Musikinstrumente
Computer · Foto · Uhren · Spielwaren · Kinderwagen
Bücher · Schreibwaren · Verpackungsservice
Restaurant · Übergang Parkhaus I und II

2.OG. Damenkonfektion · Herrenkonfektion · Junge Mode
Pelze · Damenhüte · Modeschmuck · Boutique International · Sammelkasse · Übergang Parkhaus I und II

1.OG. Sport · Stoffe · Alles für das Kind · Damenwäsche
Miederwaren · Weißwaren · Handarbeiten · Kurzwaren
Kundendienstcenter · Reisebüro · Bank · Theaterkasse
Friseur · Lotto-Toto · Fernsprecher
Übergang Parkhaus II

Erdgeschoß
Parfümerie · Süßwaren · Modewaren · Herrenartikel
Lederwaren · Schuhe · Echtschmuck · Modeschmuck
Hundesalon · Absatzbar · »Wiener Café« · Charles
Jourdan · Fogal · Escada · Davidoff/Intern. Presse
Fendi · HCL Taschen · Samsonite · Bree

KaDeWe – Kaufhaus des Westens – in Berlin.

FUNKTIONEN – KONTEXTE – STRUKTUREN

Looking ahead

In this chapter you'll be making inquiries in department stores, negotiating purchases, trying to find lost items, talking about the recent past, and making spur-of-the-moment decisions or changes in plans.

You will be using:

- the dative case with special verbs and adjectives (It's pleasing *to me,* Don't be angry *with him*)
- subjunctive verb forms to express politeness and to hypothesize (It *would be* better, then, if . . .)
- more reflexive constructions (Can you identify *yourself?*)
- question words to introduce indirect questions (I don't know *where* she went last night)

Kaufhaus

Review Chapter 6 (*Kiosk*) and Chapter 10 (*Geschenke*) using the new skills presented in this chapter (i.e., don't just purchase something, tell about the purchase: compare it, tell why, where else it's available, etc.).

1

Use dialogs 3 and 4 as models for classroom variations. Students in pairs: Student A (customer) refers to something Student B (clerk) is wearing; carry out try-on and purchase. Then have clerk hint that the

2

3

lila light purple

Lieblings + (*noun*) = *favorite* (*noun*)

customer is oversize for garments; customer reacts; clerk explains comment: not meant as customer understood – poor ordering/stocking strategy, perhaps.

Gern geschehen glad to (*have helped/have done it*)

4

5

So ein Pech what bad luck

HERR RUNKEL	Guten Tag. Womit kann ich Ihnen helfen?
HERR ZDANEK	Guten Tag. . . . Ich schaue mich nur um, danke.
HERR HOHLER	Grüß Gott. Vielleicht können Sie mir helfen. Ich suche ein paar Hemden für meinen Sohn – der ist acht – aber ich sehe hier noch nichts.
FRAU NIEHOFF	Ach, nein, hier nicht. Die Größen für sein Alter sind dort drüben an der Wand.
HERR HOHLER	Oh, schön. Ich habe sie nicht gesehen.
FRAU ZSCHAMMER	Nun, das gefällt mir wirklich sehr gut, muß ich sagen.
FRÄULEIN KOHL	Nicht wahr? Ich finde es auch recht hübsch.
FRAU ZSCHAMMER	Hätten Sie es auch in lila? Das ist meine Lieblingsfarbe.
FRÄULEIN KOHL	Tja, dieses Jahr hatten wir ganz wenig in lila. Leider ist in lila nichts mehr da.
FRAU ZSCHAMMER	Ach, schade, daß ich nicht früher gekommen bin. Aber wir waren im Urlaub. Wüßten Sie vielleicht, wo ich in der Stadt sonst noch suchen könnte?
FRÄULEIN KOHL	Ja, also probieren Sie es bei Aschinger oder im neuen Mode-Hof in der Severinstraße.
FRAU ZSCHAMMER	Ach, Aschinger, natürlich. Ich bin Ihnen sehr dankbar für die Hilfe.
FRÄULEIN KOHL	Bitte. Gern geschehen.
FRÄULEIN ROHR	Was würden Sie sagen? Meinen Sie, es geht so, oder ist es mir zu klein?
FRAU WINKLER	Ja, also ich glaube, Sie könnten ruhig eine Nummer größer tragen.
FRÄULEIN ROHR	Meine ich auch – das wäre auch viel bequemer, nicht?
FRÄULEIN WIRTZ	Nein, leider sind die neuen Sommeranzüge schon ausverkauft. Es tut mir leid.
HERR HOELSCHER	Ach, so ein Pech –
FRÄULEIN WIRTZ	Aber wir haben immer noch eine gute Auswahl an schönen Anzügen. Sehen Sie hier links, die kann man auch im Herbst und im Frühling tragen.
HERR HOELSCHER	Naja, das müßte ich mir mal überlegen. Ich habe nämlich schon zwei Anzüge für den Herbst – und diese Farben gefallen mir auch nicht so gut.
FRÄULEIN WIRTZ	Ja, also ich verstehe schon, was Sie meinen – heller wäre natürlich besser, aber es wäre auch schön, wenn man den Anzug nicht nur im Sommer tragen könnte.
HERR HOELSCHER	Ja, das schon. Naja, ich glaube, ich warte lieber. Aber vielen Dank für die Hilfe.

STRUKTUR 1

1. Special uses of the dative

Verbs §37

Be sure students don't say just *"Das ist zu klein,"* which is perfectly good German but not the mature expression targeted here. Establish a context that forces them to talk about someone *for whom* clothing is being selected, someone *to whom* they are thankful, etc.

- **with adjectives:** indicates **who** is affected – **by, for, to, at**

Das ist <u>mir</u> zu **klein.**
Ich bin <u>Ihnen</u> sehr **dankbar** für die Hilfe.
Ist <u>dir</u> das **recht?**

- **after certain verbs:** *gefallen, helfen, dienen*

Das **gefällt** <u>mir</u> wirklich sehr gut.
Vielleicht können Sie <u>mir</u> **helfen.**
Womit kann ich <u>Ihnen</u> **dienen?**

Now is the time to talk in more detail about what students like and dislike. Drill this function thoroughly in subsequent days and chapters. See additional note in Instructor's Guide.

2. Subjunctive reminder

Verbs §§53–56

Illustrate the difference between *"Sind Sie schon bedient"* and *"Wären Sie schon bedient."* Tone: "perhaps," "do you suppose," etc. Review easy situations in early chapters, pointing out where the subjunctive might be more effective. Emphasize the

- **politeness**

Hätten Sie es auch in lila?
Die **hätten** bestimmt noch etwas.
Was **würden** Sie sagen?
Wüßten Sie vielleicht, wo ich in der Stadt sonst noch suchen könnte?

notion that being polite is not the equivalent of being wishy-washy, but rather contributes to one's power with language.

Functions of hypothesis and politeness intersect in some cases, such as *". . . wo ich sonst noch suchen könnte."* There is no implication here of *". . . wenn ich Zeit hätte"* or another sort of hypothesis.

- **hypothesis**

Wissen Sie, wo ich in der Stadt sonst noch suchen **könnte?**
Sie **könnten** ruhig eine Nummer größer tragen.
Das **wäre** auch viel bequemer.
Es **wäre** auch schön, wenn man den Anzug nicht nur im Sommer tragen **könnte.**

3. Using *nicht* to invite confirmation

W.O. §20

Parallel in colloquial American English *". . . , no?"* Exercise: teacher says true or false sentences with *". . . nicht?"* and students respond. *"Graz liegt in der Schweiz, nicht?" Nein, das stimmt nicht." "Heute ist Dienstag, nicht?" "Ja, das stimmt/ Ja, richtig."*

Das wäre auch viel bequemer, **nicht?**

- added as an **afterthought,** with a pause

- **many English equivalents,** most of them unique to the associated sentence

That would also be a lot more comfortable, **right?**
That would also be a lot more comfortable, **wouldn't it?**

- **variations**

Nicht wahr?
Nit? Ni? Na? Gell? – casual, even sloppy:
　　　　　　(Huh? Ain't it? Don't it, though?)

Gell is typical of southern speech, and is sometimes shortened to *ge?* It comes from *gelten,* probably *"Gilt das/nicht?"*

SITUATIONEN 1 Kaufhaus

Stage 1	A	B

1

"Welche Interessen hat er denn?"
"Was findet er interessant?" (*Sich interessieren für* is not necessary.)

Optional complication: include questions about gift-wrap, practice counting change.

	A	B
1	Asks whether B has been helped.	Is just looking. Then remembers brother's birthday, needs present.
	Asks about brother's interests.	Describes interests.
	Suggests the perfect thing.	Agrees, asks price.
	Completes sale.	

In the absence of *Umkleidekabinen* use *"Wo kann/darf ich es anprobieren?"*

2	Wonders whether B has the same article in a larger size.	Brings article, suggests A try it on.
	Doesn't have time right now.	Will hold for A to come back later.
	Decides not to wait, asks where dressing rooms are.	Tells location.
	. . .	
	Returns; larger size is a perfect fit.	Asks whether A wants anything else, completes sale.

3	Wants to buy a fall suit.	Those aren't in the store yet.
	Thanks B; starts to leave.	Suggests A try one of the summer suits, which are on sale.
	Isn't sure; asks about colors.	Suggests colors appropriate to fall.
	Decides to try one on.	Asks A's size.
	Gives size.	Regrets that only another color in that size is left.
	Decides to wait a few weeks for the new fall suits.	Thinks A ought to think about it a bit – those summer prices can't be beaten.
	Rephrases decision more forcefully.	

Stage 2

1

You are looking for presents for your family at home.

a) Ask the salesperson for help.
b) Say that the things suggested are not just what you're looking for.
c) Say you'll look around for a while and ask again for help later.

2

It's just hours before your flight leaves for Minneapolis–St. Paul, and you haven't bought presents for your friends back home. You are at Globus, a popular department store in Zürich. Ask to find appropriate departments for gifts for

a) your beloved, who fancies hand-made items;

b) your best friend, who loves jigsaw puzzles with mountain motifs;

c) Enrique, the exchange student from Colombia who just arrived to spend a year living with your family, and who has already been wearing your clothes in your absence.

3

You are in Innsbruck, where you plan to spend a few days hiking in the Alps. Unfortunately, you've forgotten to bring much of your hiking apparel and accessories with you from Erlangen, where you are studying. Tell your hiking partner how nice it would be if you had the various items, and then suggest how to remedy the situation.

3: See *Bildwörterbuch* displays about clothing and leisure activities and realia having to do with sports and outdoor activities.

Versuchen Sie doch

Through a set of bizarre misunderstandings, you have been locked in for the night at the Kaufhof department store. When you try to get out the front door the alarm sounds, and the police soon discover you cowering behind the jewelry counter near the door. Tell them a believable set of excuses – what you wanted to do that afternoon, what happened then to thwart those plans, and so on. (Some people in this fix would not be above citing their foreign citizenship in an appeal for mercy.)

Words for "thing"

English uses the word "thing" very frequently and with many meanings. Although there are precise German equivalents of "thing" in its more restricted and formal meanings, those words are not used where English uses "thing" in a more casual sense. Here are some useful words and expressions.

Don't get bogged down in a discussion of capitalization irregularities in these patterns. The contrast in ending between the adjective after *nichts/etwas* and after *das* need not be explained at length – demonstration and brisk exercise are far better – and complexities of other cases should not be mentioned at all. The pattern *"alles [adjective]-e"* should be taught only lexically (see special chapter *Feste und Feiertage*).

Der/die Dingsda: what's his/her name, whoozits.

Return to student situations in clothing store, with students buying each other's clothes. Augment with these expressions. For patterns (striped, checked, etc.), see *Bildwörterbuch* section on Categories/*Kategorien*, pp. 308–309.

- ***das Ding* (-e)** – a very concrete object

  So. "Socket wrench." Wie heißt das Ding auf deutsch?

- ***die Sache* (-n)** – a general or indefinite thing, an abstract entity, subject, matter, or issue

  Wir gehen jetzt. Bring deine Sachen!
  Geld, Arbeit, Zeit mit der Familie – das sind ja wichtige Sachen.

- **"-thing" in expressions of quantity**

  nichts = nothing
  etwas = something   *irgendetwas* = anything
  alles = everything

Nichts and *etwas* are often combined with a following adjective.

  nichts anderes = nothing else   etwas anderes = something else
  etwas Billigeres = something cheaper

- **"things" as specific personal possessions – name the item precisely**

  I'll get my things [= baggage, rather than clothes].   **Ich hole mein Gepäck.**

- **indefinite "stuff" or "junk"**

  das Zeug (no plural) = *stuff, junk, things*
  der/die/das Dingsda = *gadget, doodad, thingamajig*

Clothing sizes and fitting terms

Größen

Herren – Anzüge	**USA**	36	38	40	42	44	46	48	
	D	46	48	50	52	54	56	58	
Herren – Hemden	**USA**	14	14 1/2	15	15 1/2	16	16 1/2	17	
	D	36	37	38	39	41	42	43	
Herren – Schuhe	**USA**	8	8 1/2	9–9 1/2	10–10 1/2	11–11 1/2	12–12 1/2		
	D	41	42	43	44	45	46		
Damen – Kleider	**USA**	8	10	12	14	16	18		
	D	36	38	40	42	44	46		
Damen – Schuhe	**USA**	6	6 1/2	7	7 1/2	8	8 1/2	9	
	D	36	37	38	38	39	40	41	

- ***anprobieren*** – to *try on* or fit before making alterations

  Darf ich das anprobieren?   *May I try it on?*

- ***passen*** – to fit or *suit* when tried on

  Das paßt mir sehr gut.   *That feels pretty nice to me.*

- ***hell*** – light in color   ***dunkel*** – dark   ***bunt*** – colorful

Description in detail – a vital skill

Bare survival requires only that we be able to name necessary things and actions; details are unimportant. But the ability to describe with some precision is essential for even everyday life.

In our native language we develop this ability early:

> Santa, please bring me a big shiny sled, some of those little plastic things for my hair, and one of those dolls that talks like the one I saw in the store yesterday when Mommy and Daddy were looking at clothes for me.

Learners of a foreign language may or may not transfer their native strategic skills to the new language. Here, therefore, is some advice about how to describe.

A. You may well know how to name the thing you wish to describe, for example, a lost possession. Your task here is to give basic physical information (dimensions, etc.) and then perhaps mention a feature that sets the item apart.

Ich suche einen Koffer – braun, etwa 80 cm lang und ganz neu.

B. Describing more complex physical objects, concepts, and other intangible entities is more difficult. The skill is often necessary when we begin comparing another culture with our own. In such cases a close German equivalent may not be readily available. The essential skill is the ability to find a way around the missing vocabulary. Here are some suggestions:

1. Create a series of known words that then lead logically to the idea or thing you wish to introduce. Your listener may well supply the word.

target: the word for "great-grandmother"
series: **Tochter, Mutter, Großmutter, . . .**

2. Use a larger category, accompanied by a significant feature, to suggest a specific member. The distinguishing feature might be expressed by an adjective, prepositional phrase, or additional clause with its own subject and verb.

target: word for "street-sweeper"
description: **Das ist eine Maschine. Sie macht die Straßen sauber.**

3. Enumerate specific examples to suggest a category. Here the expression "*zum Beispiel*" is useful.

target: the word for "profession"
set of examples: **Arzt, zum Beispiel, oder Professor, Ingenieur, . . .**

4. Compare and contrast the target item with another item for which you do know the word.

target: "gift-wrap"
description: **Das ist Papier, aber für Geschenke.**

5. Describe a situation in which the item or idea plays a significant role. The conjunction *wenn* and the indefinite pronoun *man* are extremely useful, but you can manage without them if their use makes things too complicated.

target: "gift-wrapping ribbon"
situation: **Meine Tochter hat Geburtstag. Ich habe das Geschenk und das Geschenkpapier schon, aber ich brauche noch . . ."**

The equivalent of this technique, when you are actually describing a lost object, is a narration in which you retrace the events associated with the loss. Of course the narration is intended not to describe the object, but to refresh the memory so the object can be traced and found.

---

lang · long
die Länge · length
breit · wide
die Breite · width
tief · deep
die Tiefe · depth
hoch · high
die Höhe · height
groß · large
die Größe · size

See *Bildwörterbuch* "Categories/*Kategorien*" pp. 308–309.

Use these words again and again in describing things.

🛒 KaDeWe Service

6. OG. Feinschmeckerservice · Bestellannahme
Party-Service · Internationale Journale

5. OG. Gourmet-Restaurant Silberterrasse
Möbel-Einrichtungsberatung
Gardinen- und Auslegewarenservice
Kundengarderobe · Telefon · Toiletten

4. OG. KaDeWe Küchenstudio · Berlin-Souvenirs
Auto-Reifenmontage · Toiletten

3. OG. Café-Restaurant · Zillestube (Self-Service-Restaurant)
Fotokopierer · Passbildautomaten
Gepäckschließfächer · Verpackungsservice · Toiletten

2. OG. Sammelkasse · Kundengarderobe · Baby-Wickeltisch
Pelzkonservierung und Aufbewahrung
Erste Hilfe · Toiletten

1. OG. Kundendienst-Center · Fundbüro · Telefon
Kredit – Versicherungsvermittlung · BHI Bankschalter
Reisebüro · Lotto – Toto · Theaterkasse
Herrenmaßkonfektion · Premier Coiffeur · Toiletten

Erdgeschoß
Wiener Café · Christ Juweliere und Uhrmacher
Mister Minit Absatzbar und Schlüsseldienst
Ansbacher Straße: KaDeWe Blumen- und Pflanzenmarkt
Mal-Atelier Liebenau · Kosmetikstudio
Passauer Straße: Nähzentrum · Fahrradspezialist
Hundesalon

Wichtige Rufnummern
IMPORTANT TELEPHONE NUMBERS
NUMÉROS IMPORTANTS DE TÉLÉPHONE

Funkstreife · Police Squad Cars · Police-secours   Tel. 1 10
Feuerwehr · Fire Dept · Sapeurs-pompiers   Tel. 1 12
Rettungsdienst · Ambulance Service · Secours d'urgence   Tel. 22 26 66
Kassenärztlicher Notfalldienst · Medical emergency service ·
Service médical d'urgence   Tel. 55 86 61
Apotheken-Notdienst · Pharmacy emergency service ·
Service pharmaceutique d'urgence   Tel. 59 44 75
ADAC-Information   Tel. 28 01 01
ADAC-Pannendienst · Emergency Service · Service routier   Tel. 76 76 76
ACE-Pannendienst   Tel. 53 65 02
Telefonseelsorge
   evangelisch   Tel. 1 11 01
   katholisch   Tel. 1 11 02
Kirchl. Informationen der evang. u. kath. Kirche
   (Fernspr.-Ansage)   Tel. 11 57
Drogenberatung · consultation on drugs ·
service de consultation sur les stupéfiants   Tel. 2 33/32 36
Drogenprävention   Tel. 2 33/81 63
Alkoholikerberatung   Tel. 52 07/3 42, 3 44 u. 3 93
   consultation on alcoholism · consultation sur l'alcoolisme

Fundbüros · Lost-property-offices · Bureaux des objet trouvés
Fundbüro der Stadtverwaltung, Ruppertstr. 19   Tel. 2 33-1
(Funde auf Straßen und in städt. Verkehrsmitteln). Mo mit Fr 8.30 – 12, Di
auch 14 – 17.30 Uhr, Fei geschlossen.

Bundesbahn, Hauptbahnhof, Bahnhofpl. 2,   Tel. 1 28/58 59
gegenüber Gleis 26 (Funde im Bereich der Bundesbahn)
Mo mit Fr 8 – 16 Uhr, Fei geschlossen.

Fundstelle im Ostbahnhof   Tel. 1 28 84/4 09
(Funde im Bereich der S-Bahn)
Mo mit Fr 8 – 17.45, Sa 8 – 11.45 Uhr, Fei geschlossen.

Bundespost, Arnulfstr. 195, Zimmer 105   Tel. 1 39/5 52
(Paketpostamt) Funde im Bereich der Post einschl. Telefonzellen
Mo mit Fr 8 – 11.30 u. 12.30 – 15 Uhr, Fei geschl.

Deutschland
Deutschland

Erforderliche Reisedokumente
Personen: Pass (nicht länger als 5 Jahre abgelaufen) oder Identitätskarte. West-Berlin: **nur** gültiger Pass. (Bei Einreise mit dem Flugzeug: wie bei Reisen in die BRD.)
Fahrzeuge: Grüne Versicherungskarte (nicht obligatorisch).

Zollfreie Einfuhr (ab 17 J.)
Waren im Wert von DM 115.–, inkl.: 200 Zigaretten oder 50 Zigarren oder 250 g Tabak, 2 l Spirituosen bis 22°, über 22° nur 1 l oder 2 l Schaumwein und 2 l sonstiger Wein. 500 g Kaffee, 100 g Tee, 50 g Parfum. Üblicher Reiseproviant.

Trinkgeld / Service
Hotel / Restaurant: inbegriffen.
Taxi / Träger / Coiffeur: 10%

Taxispesen
Basistarif: DM 3.70 bis 4.– und DM 1.60 bis DM 1.90 pro km.

Posttaxen nach der Schweiz
Karte: DM –.60.
Brief bis 20 g: DM –.80.

Automiete (Richtpreis)
7 Tage (inkl. Versicherung): Grundpreis: ab ca. DM 300.– bis DM 1300.– plus ca. DM –.43 bis DM 1.48 pro km.

Geschwindigkeitsbeschränkungen
Innerorts generell 50 km/h (Beginn und Ende bei gelber Ortstafel). Ausserorts beschränkt auf 100 km/h. Auf Autobahnen und auf Strassen mit mindestens 2 Fahrstreifen in jeder Richtung frei, Richtgeschwindigkeit 130 km/h. Parkieren nur in der Fahrtrichtung gestattet.
Das Anschnallen ist obligatorisch.

Stromspannung: 220 V.

Reiseandenken
Holz- und Elfenbeinschnitzereien (Oberammergau), Schwarzwälder Kuckucksuhren, Porzellan, Kameras, Lederwaren, Spielzeuge, Halbedelstein-Verarbeitung (Idar Oberstein), Musikinstrumente, Bayerische Dirndl, Antiquitäten.

Währung

1 Deutsche Mark (DM) = 100 Pfennige		
sFr. 100.– = DM 119.–		
DM 100.– = sFr. 84.95	(Stand 1. 86)	

Ein- und Ausfuhr von Zahlungsmitteln

	Einreise	Ausreise
Deutsche Mark	frei	frei
Fremde Währungen	frei	frei

Bargeldlos reisen mit:

Reisechecks:	Swiss Bankers Travellers Cheques und andere
Checks:	eurocheque
Kreditkarten:	Eurocard und andere

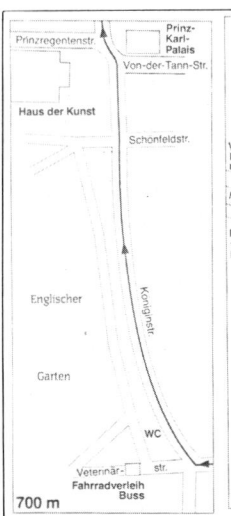

700 m

1050 m

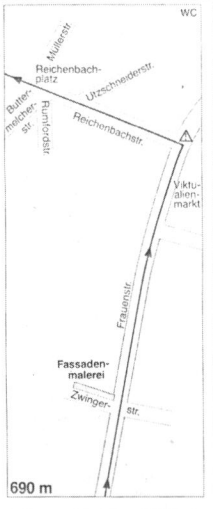

690 m

790 m

An der Königinstraße rechts. Diese Straße führt am Englischen Garten, der seinen Namen nach der im englischen Gartenbaustil gehaltenen Anlage erhielt und zu den größten europäischen Parks zählt, entlang. Er umfaßt eine Fläche von 373 ha und erstreckt sich auf über 5 km Länge nach Norden. An der Von-der-Tann-Straße rechts das Generalkonsulat der Vereinigten Staaten von Amerika. Wir sehen das Prinz-Karl-Palais rechts und das Haus der Kunst links (siehe S. 5). Wir überqueren die Von-der-Tann-Straße und fahren auf dem Altstadtring weiter.

Rechts die Kuppel des ehem. Armeemuseums. Wir kreuzen die Maximilianstraße, eine elegante Einkaufsstraße, die König Max II. nach den Plänen von Friedrich Bürklein anlegen ließ. Rechts führt sie zur Residenz und zur Oper, links über die Isar zum Maximilianeum. Unmittelbar an der Kreuzung sehen wir links den Sitz der Regierung von Oberbayern und gegenüber das Museum für Völkerkunde. Wir treffen nun auf den Isartorplatz mit seinem alten Stadttor (1337, Teil der zweiten Stadtummauerung). Das Außenfresko auf dem Tor stellt den Einzug Ludwig

des Bayern nach der Schlacht bei Mühldorf im Jahre 1322 dar. Im Südturm das höchst originelle Valentin-Musäum (mit zahlreichen Erinnerungen an den Münchner Humoristen Karl Valentin und andere Volkssänger, im obersten Stockwerk ein „Kuriositäten-Café"). Ein Stück weiter (Ecke Frauen-/Zwingerstraße) an einer Brandmauer interessante Fassadenmalerei. Am Viktualmarkt bietet sich nun rechts ein herrlicher Blick über die bunten Verkaufsstände auf die Türme der Altstadt. Bei Ampel (Reichenbachstraße) links abbiegen.

Wir kommen zum städtebaulich neugestalteten Gärtnerplatz (einheitlich Farbgestaltung der Häuser) mit schöner Grünanlage. Den Platz beherrscht das Staatstheater am Gärtnerplatz (1865), wo leichte Opern, Operetten, Musicals und Ballett aufgeführt werden. Der Baumeister Friedrich von Gärtner gab dem Platz seinen Namen. An ihn erinnert eine Büste in der Anlage gegenüber dem Theatereingang. Wir fahren nun durch die Klenze- und Ickstattstraße zurück zum Ausgangspunkt in der Hans-Sachs-Straße.

Fundbüro

1   HERR LECHNER   Und Sie erinnern sich wirklich nicht mehr?

DR. STIERLE   Nein, und das ist mir einfach unverständlich. Wie ist es möglich, zwei so große Koffer im Bahnhof zu verlieren?

HERR LECHNER   Denken Sie noch einmal nach, vielleicht erinnern Sie sich doch. Am Fahrkartenschalter hatten Sie die Koffer noch.

DR. STIERLE   Und da hatte ich sie noch. Und dann sind wir zum Imbiß marschiert, und ich habe sie dort in eine Ecke gestellt.

HERR LECHNER   Ja, genau. Sind sie nicht dort in der Ecke?

DR. STIERLE   Nein, ich habe schon nachgeschaut.

HERR LECHNER   Dann wäre es besser, wir melden uns beim Fundbüro. Vielleicht wissen die dort, was wir machen können.

2   DR. STIERLE   Also setzen wir uns mal hin. Hier hat man die Hände voll.

HERR LECHNER   Na, gut. Aber wir müssen uns eigentlich beeilen. Der Zug fährt ja in 25 Minuten ab.

DR. STIERLE   Ja, aber wenn ich meine Koffer nicht finde, kann ich nicht mitfahren. . . . Ach, nun sind wir an der Reihe!

FRAU MEINERT   Bitte schön?

DR. STIERLE   Guten Tag. Ich habe zwei große Koffer verloren, so dunkelgrüne. Haben Sie sie gesehen?

FRAU MEINERT   Meinen Sie die da? Die waren auf einem Gepäckkarren beim Imbiß, und der Träger hat sie hierher gebracht.

3   FRAU DR. BECK   Können Sie mir helfen? Ich habe meine Tasche verloren.

HERR STEINER   Wir wollen mal sehen. Wie sieht Ihre Tasche aus?

Wildleder suede

FRAU DR. BECK   Sie ist eine hellbraune Tasche aus Wildleder.

Review usage of *Herr Dr.* and *Frau Dr.* as explained in the first preliminary chapter. *Frau Dr. Beck* could be a *Doktor* in her own right or simply married to *Dr. Beck.*

HERR STEINER   Und der Inhalt?

FRAU DR. BECK   Mein Geldbeutel, Sonnenbrille, Schlüssel, Kosmetik und so – und mein Personalausweis.

HERR STEINER   Hm. Ohne Ausweis können Sie sich nicht ausweisen. Wir haben eine solche Tasche, aber ich kann sie Ihnen nicht geben, wenn ich nicht genau wissen kann, wer Sie sind.

FRAU DR. BECK   Nun, warum schauen Sie sich nicht einfach das Bild auf dem Ausweis an?

HERR STEINER   Hm. Ja – warum nicht? Machen wir es so.

4   FRAU GLATTHARD   Ja, guten Tag, ich kann meinen Sohn nicht finden. Können Sie mir bitte helfen?

HERR KOCH   Hm, Sie sollten sich bei der Polizei melden – hier im Fundbüro gibt man nur Gepäck ab und so, keine Personen.

FRAU GLATTHARD   Gut. Und wo finde ich die Polizei?

HERR KOCH   Das Büro finden Sie zwischen dem Fahrkartenschalter und dem Reisebüro Kühne, also im ersten Stock oben.

FRAU GLATTHARD   Vielen, vielen Dank.

HERR KOCH   Bitte schön – nur keine Angst. Sie finden ihn schon.

FRAU GLATTHARD   Ja, und wenn ich ihn finde, . . .

Verbs §§42,43

Exercise: list several reflexive constructions on the board. Students in pairs have the task of devising different kinds of situations using all the constructions: shopping, restaurant, youth hostel, hospital, museum, etc. Each pair is responsible for one context.

You could mention some more distant equivalents – *sich beeilen* (get oneself moving), *sich anziehen* (dress oneself).

Despite your best efforts, it is unlikely that any but the best students will consistently produce reflexives in contextual use of the language or a proficiency-oriented test, though they could be made to parrot

W.O. §15

reflexive patterns and walk through transformation/ translation exercises. Teaching, therefore, should emphasize lexical command of high-frequency reflexive formulations (*"Setzen Sie sich," "Darf ich mich vorstellen?"*) and the situations in which they may well appear. Remember that you are laying the groundwork for later courses, in which the reflexive can be explored more deeply, particularly if the students have a ready stock of lexical patterns.

2: See exercise suggestions in Instructor's Guide.

1. More about reflexive constructions

● Some have exact or close equivalents in English.

Dann muß ich **mich** auch **vorstellen.**	*Then I'll have to **introduce myself,** too.*
Ohne Ausweis können Sie **sich** nicht **ausweisen.**	*You can't **identify yourself** without an I.D.*
Wir **kennen uns** schon seit drei Jahren.	*We've **known each other** for three years.*

● Most do *not* have exact equivalents in English.

Also **setzen** wir **uns** mal **hin.**	*So let's **sit down** a while.*
Aber wir müssen **uns** eigentlich **beeilen.**	*But we really do have to **hurry.***
Ich kann **mich** wirklich nicht mehr **erinnern.**	*I just can't **remember** any more.*
Ich **schaue mich** nur **um,** danke.	*I'm just **looking,** thanks.*
Sie sollten **sich** bei der Polizei **melden.**	*You ought **to report** to the police.*

2. Question words that introduce dependent clauses:

wo, was, wie, wer, wann, warum, welche, wieviel

● Inclusion of a question in another utterance involves a **change in word order,** as in English.

Where *could I* look elsewhere in the city?
Do you know where *I could* look elsewhere in the city?

Wo *könnte ich* in der Stadt sonst noch suchen?
Wissen Sie, wo *ich* in der Stadt sonst noch suchen *könnte*?

● The verb goes at the end of the clause.

(Independent clause: Wo könnte ich . . . suchen?)
Wissen Sie, **wo** ich in der Stadt sonst noch suchen **könnte**?

(Independent clause: Was können wir machen?)
Vielleicht hat man dort eine Ahnung, **was** wir machen **können**.

(Independent clause: Wer sind Sie?)
. . . wenn ich nicht genau wissen kann, **wer** Sie **sind**.

SITUATIONEN 2 Fundbüro

Stage 1

A	B
1 Is very sad.	Asks why A is so sad.
Has lost suitcase belonging to father.	Asks where A lost it.
Doesn't know.	Asks where A looked.
Has looked all over the station, doesn't know what to do now.	Suggests going to the lost-and-found office.

"Das Paket – ich kann es nicht finden."

A	B	C
2 Tells B they have to hurry; train is leaving soon.	Says can't hurry more; has to look for lost package.	Greets A and B; asks whether they've seen her (his) suitcase.
	Says they have to find his (her) package.	Says saw a package.
Says train is leaving in ten minutes.	Asks what package looked like.	Tells what suitcase looks like.
	Doesn't care about suitcase.	
Saw a suitcase like that at the lost and found.	Wants to know about package.	Asks where lost and found is.
	Implores C to tell about package that C saw.	
Tells C where lost and found is.	Says will inquire at the police station; asks if C has the package.	Asks whether B has the suitcase.
Says the train just left.		

Stage 2

2: Use *wahrscheinlich, vielleicht,* or other adverbs, which also talk around the new feature of subordination after interrogatives.

1

You are on the train from Stuttgart to München. Suddenly you notice that one of your bags is missing, but you don't have any idea where you could have left it. Go over the possibilities with your traveling companion, and then discuss what steps you will take.

2

You are in the Hamburg *Hauptbahnhof.* One of the people you're traveling with has lost a hat, and another is missing a briefcase. You suspect a group of people who have been sitting near you, but you can't prove anything. Discuss the situation with either the police or the lost-and-found official. It's frustrating to have to begin to answer most of their questions with "I don't know . . ."

Versuchen Sie doch

Assume that you are Monika or Martin Lerner in the Gespräche 1, #4, dialog in Chapter 16. You took the wrong S-Bahn in München and were late to your cousin's house. You made some purchases before lunch, and now – at your cousin's – you notice that you no longer have them with you. Using the map of München, discuss where you might have left your things and what you will have to do to recover them. (Expressions of anguish would not be inappropriate.)

Sie haben vor einer halben Stunde das Haus von Ihren Freunden in Hamburg verlassen und sind jetzt am Bahnhof. Auf einmal sehen Sie, daß Sie irgendwo unterwegs Ihren Regenschirm und einen Sack voll Geschenke für Ihre Verwandten in Bonn verloren haben. Sind die Sachen noch bei den Freunden? In der S-Bahn? Hat sie jemand im Bahnhof gestohlen? Gehen Sie zum Fundbüro am Bahnhof und besprechen Sie die Sache mit dem Beamten.

Chapter 19

FREIZEIT: NATUR UND SPORT/ FREIZEIT: HOBBYS UND MUSIK

Use *Bildwörterbuch* "Hobbies-Sports-Special Interests/*Hobbys-Sport-Sonderinteressen*" (pp. 304–305) and "Culture/*Kultur*" (pp. 298–299).

FUNKTIONEN – KONTEXTE – STRUKTUREN

Looking ahead

You'll be talking about leisure time activities, both indoor and outdoor – making plans, describing how things are done, and recalling your experiences.

You will be using:

- infinitive phrases ("That's easy *to do.*")
- the form *euch* as accusative and dative of *ihr* ("you")
- the time adverbs *schon, noch,* and *nicht mehr/kein- mehr* ("already," "still," and "not any longer")
- reflexive verbs used with prepositions ("I'll have to *inform myself about* it.")
- nouns in the dative plural (most add *-n*)
- adverbs for more precise meaning ("absolutely," "at least," "very probably")

Freizeit – Natur und Sport

1

Freibad outdoor pool

HERR ROFFLER	Badeanzüge finden Sie im Sportgeschäft Roffler in der Bahnhofstraße. Oder billiger im Kaufhaus nebenan. Aber im Fachgeschäft hat man die beste Auswahl.
FRÄULEIN HARDT	Also bei Roffler. Und könnten Sie mir auch sagen, wie ich zum Freibad komme?
HERR ROFFLER	Ach, zum Freibad wollen Sie? Von Roffler gehen Sie die Bahnhofstraße hinauf, zirka 200m.
FRÄULEIN HARDT	Und wüßten Sie, wie lange die noch geöffnet sind?
HERR ROFFLER	Die machen schon in knapp einer Stunde zu.
FRÄULEIN HARDT	Also, besten Dank für die Information, Herr . . . uh . . .
HERR ROFFLER	Roffler. Schöne Grüße an meinen Bruder.

2

Lift ski lift (elsewhere also "elevator")
in Betrieb in operation, working
Langlaufschier cross-country skis

FRAU SCHWERIN	Ich wollte noch heute schilaufen. Sind die Lifte alle in Betrieb?
FRÄULEIN BUCHHOLZ	Ja, nur die Rothornbahn noch nicht. Erst ab Dienstag.
FRAU SCHWERIN	Schön. Und dann hätte ich noch eine Frage. Ich habe nämlich auch Langlaufschier . . .
FRÄULEIN BUCHHOLZ	Das geht natürlich auch. Sie machen die schöne Tour zum Schwarzsee hin, dann östlich, Richtung Reute –
FRAU SCHWERIN	Moment, bitte. Das klingt ein bißchen kompliziert. Hätten Sie vielleicht eine Karte von der Gegend?

3

Klasse great!

See note on *Aufstieg* in Instructor's Guide.

STEFAN MARX	Treffen wir uns also nächste Woche wieder hier?
TRINA SEILER	Klasse, du. Und ich bringe etwas zu essen mit.
STEFAN MARX	Schön – aber das sollst du vielleicht mit den anderen Mitgliedern besprechen. Nächstes Wochenende ist ja der große Schwarzhorn-Aufstieg.
TRINA SEILER	O, toll. Meine Eltern haben mir geschrieben, daß ich am Schwarzhorn-Aufstieg teilnehmen soll.
STEFAN MARX	Schade, daß sie ausgewandert sind. Sonst könnten sie mitmachen.
TRINA SEILER	Ja, das mit dem Wander-Klub ist besonders schön. Ich habe wirklich Lust, den Tag mit euch zu verbringen.
STEFAN MARX	Du, mehr als nur den Tag. Wir fangen den Aufstieg nachts um 10 an. Dann sehen wir den Sonnenaufgang vor dem Abstieg.
TRINA SEILER	Fantastisch! Ich freue mich schon darauf.

Sonnenaufgang sunrise

4

ASS. ROXANNE AG
Schlankheits-Institut
Bräunungs-Zentrum
Sportgeräte-Vertrieb
Fitness-Center
Kindergarten
Body-Shop
Sauna

HERR SPENGLER	. . . und das wäre also für das ganze Wochenende, ja?
ARTUR ZSCHOKKE	Ja, bis Sonntag abend, so um 5 oder 6.
HERR SPENGLER	Also wir schließen den Laden pünktlich um 18 Uhr. Sie müssen spätestens um 17.45 hier sein.
EMMA ZSCHOKKE	Das können wir sicher schaffen.
HERR SPENGLER	Ist gut. Das wäre also 20 Mark täglich, und 50 Mark Pfand. Haben Sie sonst noch Fragen?
ARTUR ZSCHOKKE	Ja, der Reifen hier scheint etwas Luft zu brauchen.

Verbs §39

See note in Instructor's Guide.

1. Infinitive phrases end in *zu* + infinitive.

Ich habe wirklich Lust, *den Tag mit euch zu verbringen.*
Der Reifen hier scheint *etwas Luft zu brauchen.*
Wie ist es möglich, *zwei so große Koffer im Bahnhof zu verlieren?*

Pronouns §12

Students work in groups of two pairs each. Each couple suggests that the other two do something

2. *Euch:* the accusative and dative of *ihr* ("you")

Im Zoo habe ich **euch** leider nicht gesehen.
accusative

Ich habe wirklich Lust, den Tag mit **euch** zu verbringen.
dative

A.A. §§38,39

with them or for them. The other two give a reason why they can or cannot do that with the first couple. See earlier chapters (especially chapter 11)

History lesson: students ask each other whether certain events are still taking place. (*"Lebt Kaiser Wilhelm noch?"*) Answers may be positive or negative. Review *kein- X mehr* as a means of negating nouns: *"Haben Sie noch Karten?" "Nein, wir haben keine Karten mehr."* Similarly with *nicht* + verb. *Schon* can be pushed by asking for responses to querulous comments like *"Ich glaube, du hast die Karten noch nicht gekauft."*

3. Time phrases with *schon* and *noch*

- comment about the continuation of an action

- *Schon* shrinks time.

  Sie machen schon um 18 Uhr zu.
    (They close at [*as early as*] 6.)
  Fantastisch! Ich freue mich schon darauf.
    (I'm *already* looking forward to it.)

- *Noch* stretches time.

  Wissen Sie, wie lange die heute noch geöffnet sind?
    (They have been open today; are they <u>still</u> open?)

  Und dann habe ich noch eine Frage.
    (I had one *before,* and now I have *yet* another one.)

for situations that can be redone, with specification to change singular informal to plural informal.

Hunde sind in der Ladestraße an der Leine zu führen
Der Grundeigentümer . A .ÖBB.

Willkommen auf Vorarlberger Bauernhöfen!

In diesem Prospekt, der zum ersten Mal erscheint, finden Sie die Adressen von fast 450 Vorarlberger Landwirten verzeichnet.
Sicherlich werden Sie darin einen Bauernhof finden, auf dem Sie einen erholsamen Urlaub oder angenehme Ferien mit Ihrer Familie und Ihren Kindern verbringen können.
Auf den klein- bis mittelbäuerlichen Familienbetrieben, die sich überwiegend im Bergbauerngebiet befinden, wird Grünlandwirtschaft mit einer intensiven Viehzucht und Milchviehhaltung betrieben.
Das leistungsfähige Braunvieh und die vorzüglichen Emmentaler- und Bergkäse sind in zahlreichen Staaten bekannt und begehrt. In den Talgebieten gibt es bekannte Textilindustrie- und Gewerbebetriebe, die sich umweltfreundlich in die Landschaft einfügen. Der abwechslungsreiche und schöne Erholungsraum mit seinen grünen Wiesen, Weiden und Wäldern erstreckt sich vom Bodensee und dem jungen Rhein über das Voralpengebiet bis zu den teils vergletscherten Hochgebirgszonen.
Durch vorzüglich geführte und bestens ausgestattete Gasthöfe, Hotels und Pensionen sowie durch gepflegte Sommer- und Wintersportorte ist Vorarlberg aber auch zu einem international bekannten und beliebten Fremden- verkehrsland geworden, das die Partnerschaft mit der Landwirtschaft und deren Leistungen zu schätzen weiß.

𝔘rlaub am 𝔅auernhof
in Vorarlberg Österreich

Gemeinde, Name, Adresse	ZIMMER			FERIENWOHNUNGEN		
	Ein-bett	Zweibett	nähere Angaben	An-zahl	Personen	nähere Angaben
Wittwer Josef, Argenzipfel Nr. 54	1	2 + kb 1 - Bett	Wfl, Kfl, Wr, WC, Hz, K, gj			
A-6780 BARTHOLOMÄBERG 1 087 m Tel.-Vorwahl : 05556						
Battlogg Quido, Haus Nr. 116		5 + kb	Wfl, Kfl, D, WC, Hz, K, Ss	1	6	Fl, Ss
Loretz Benedikt (Bühel ob Würfel) Haus Nr. 75		2 + kb	Wfl, Kfl, K, B, WC, Hz	1	3 - 5	Fl, Hz

	A	B
Stage 1		
1	Asks about a good place to buy a pair of hiking boots.	Suggests either the sporting goods store or the shoe store on the corner.
	Asks which one is the better.	Neither quality nor price varies much.
	Asks about interesting hiking trails.	Isn't sure what A is interested in – mountains?
	Is more interested in bird watching.	Shares A's interest.
	Asks what B would recommend.	Suggests the hike around the Schwarzee – there are lots of birds.
2	Wants to go skiing, asks B for directions.	Asks what kind of skiing.
	Likes to go cross-country skiing.	Says there are wonderful trails on the east side of the Rothorn.
	Asks how to get there.	Says the cable car starts about 20 m to the south of the train station.
	Asks if the lift is still running.	Everything is running – until 5 P.M.
	Asks where to buy a map of the ski area.	Says maps are available at the lift.
3	Is very excited about spending the next day with B and other friends.	Says it will be a fine day, describes perfect weather for a hike.
	Asks B about the Calandaberg climb next weekend.	Describes the night climb and the view of the sunrise from the peak.
	Is really looking forward to it.	Says it will be a hard climb.
	Says it's easy for B and friends, because they do it every year.	Says that doesn't make any difference – after 20 years it's still hard.
	Asks if B would still like to come to A's apartment for supper – they need to take a look at some maps.	Says that would be great; asks if A still has some of that tasty Mexican food.

Im Sportgeschäft kostet es nicht viel mehr/weniger; Sie zahlen vielleicht DM 60 im Sportgeschäft und DM 62 im Schuhgeschäft.

Sie finden die Seilbahn . . .

Und kann ich mit der Seilbahn fahren? (In Betrieb is unnecessary.)

Ich freue mich; das ist prima, wunderbar.

Das ist egal/nicht wichtig; feel free to teach "das spielt keine Rolle."

Stage 2

1
Your friends in the *Wohngemeinschaft* are curious about what sorts of outdoor activities you enjoy. Tell them about your interests, assuming you are from a) Tallahassee, Florida; b) Detroit; c) Vancouver, B.C.

2
After supper you decide that it would be fun to get to know these students better. Make appropriate suggestions for some outdoor activities for the six of you, assuming you are studying in a) Köln; b) Freiburg; c) Zürich.

3
Your friends are just about to leave for a long weekend of sunning and windsurfing on the *Ostsee*. You have been planning to go along with them, but are quite surprised – and a bit upset – that they are leaving already. You still have some chores to do and a few errands to run. Let them know your situation and do your best to leave on time with them all. Perhaps you can convince them to help you with what you have to do.

4
Let your roommate know what a poor idea the ski trip was and whose idea it was ("*Schade, daß du . . .*").

A good check of whether your students are really making progress would be whether you have to remind them what attractions are to be found in the three areas. If you have to, get out the realia once again.

Versuchen Sie doch By a happy coincidence, that nice Japanese couple you met and helped in the München train station (Chapter 15) has reappeared in Köln, where you have been studying. You recognize each other and decide to have a cup of tea together. Tell them what sorts of outdoor activities you think they would enjoy, bearing in mind that they are not as young and flexible as you are. Tell them an anecdote about your own participation in one of these activities earlier in the semester.

STRATEGIE – KULTUR UND SPRACHE

Source of statistics: *Kursbuch Deutschland 85/86* (Goldmann Verlag, München 1985), pp. 490–531.

Spiegel-Verlag (ed.): Freizeitverhalten, Hamburg 1983. (Spiegel-Verlagsreihe "Märkte im Wandel," vol. 11), Beilage.

Leisure activities

Europeans tend to relax in much the same way Americans do: by watching television and listening to music. A recent survey showed that over 46 percent of adults in West Germany spent their leisure time in one of these two passive pursuits. The ten most popular activities were

AKTIVITÄT	ANTEIL (%)
1. Fernsehen	28,4
2. Musik hören	17,8
3. Freizeitsport	8,7
4. Bücher lesen	8,3
5. Zeitungen lesen	5,7
6. Besuche bei/von Verwandten und Freunden	4,9
7. Gartenpflege	4,8
8. Gaststättenbesuche (Kneipen)	4,4
9. Gaststättenbesuche (Restaurants)	3,4
10. Zeitschriften lesen	2,8

Urlaub – quite a business

Hundreds of clubs and associations promote leisure activities – from stamp collecting (*Bund deutscher Philatelisten*) to cat breeding (*Deutscher Edelkatzenzüchter-Verband*) and falconry (*Deutscher Falkenorden*). But the free-time activity most obvious to the foreign observer is travel. In spite of bottlenecks on the *Autobahnen*, long lines at borders, and overflowing tourist accommodations at the most popular vacation centers, each year about 16 million West Germans, one-fourth of the country's population, travel abroad. Their reasons vary:

GRUND FÜR DEN AUSLANDAUFENTHALT	ANTEIL (%)
Sportliche Aktivität	52
Im Meer baden, am Strand liegen	39
Mit anderen Menschen zusammensein	35
Die nationale Küche kennenlernen	35

The countries visited vary as well. The most popular are

RANG	LAND	ANTEIL (%)
1	Italien	12
2	Spanien	11
3	*Österreich*	10
4	Frankreich	5
5	Jugoslawien	4
10	*die Schweiz*	1,5
12	*DDR*	0,9

West Germans who vacation in the BRD prefer the extreme north and south, with *Bayern* being the favorite region, followed by *Baden-Württemberg* in the southwest and *Schleswig-Holstein* on the North and Baltic Seas.

Poor families with children in the BRD are eligible for a vacation subsidy. The amount of money granted to help with vacation expenses varies according to family income, number of children, and *Land* of residence.

Use the biographies to review ordinal numbers and expressions for years and centuries. Use names of composers and their works to fine-tune pronunciation.

Maybe mention how classical music actually pervades popular culture. It provides, for example, background music for Disney cartoons and melodies for advertising jingles.

See note in Instructor's Guide.

Schiller's *"An die Freude"* ("Ode to Joy"), from the last movement of Beethoven's 9th Symphony, is also used as an American church hymn, though with different words ("Joyful, Joyful, We adore Thee"). Depending on the composition of your class, you might explore the contributions of German poets and composers to American sacred music.

Nephew of Moses Mendelssohn (1729–1786), major German philosopher and one of the first German Jews to enter the mainstream of German culture.

Plus ça change: When *Tristan* was first performed, some suggested that the music was so sensuous that women should not be allowed to attend, not because they would be offended, but because they – supposedly creatures of passion rather than reason – might become too aroused.

Giants of German music – vital cultural knowledge

The list offered below focuses on the centuries when German music rose to international prominence, and when many considered music to be a particular glory of German culture. You will note that almost every composer wrote something that has become widely known in America *outside* the realm of classical music, though quite often people are not aware of the source.

- **Beethoven, Ludwig van (1770–1827).** Nine famous symphonies, including above all the Fifth and the Ninth, the latter with its triumphal chorus. Thirty-two piano sonatas, among them the "Moonlight" (*Mondschein*) and the Pathétique. Sixteen string quartets. Born in Bonn, resided for many years in Wien.
- **Bach, Johann Sebastian (1685–1750).** Huge body of sacred music, including cantatas, the *B-minor Mass,* oratorios, and passions (gospels set to music). *Brandenburg Concertos* and a setting of the famous hymn *"Ein' feste Burg ist unser Gott"* ("A Mighty Fortress Is Our God"). Twenty children, several of whom became prominent musicians. Long residence in Leipzig.
- **Mozart, Wolfgang Amadeus (1756–1791).** Child prodigy in composition and performance. Incredibly prolific composer of diverse works, both sacred and secular. Wrote 41 symphonies and operas such as *Don Giovanni, The Marriage of Figaro,* and *The Magic Flute.* Born in Salzburg, performed internationally, settled in Wien. Died in poverty; gravesite unknown.
- **Brahms, Johannes (1833–1897).** Wide range of works, including four symphonies, two piano concertos, a violin concerto, and a large body of chamber music. Popularly known works include the Hungarian Dance No. 5 and, even more, his "Lullaby" (*Wiegenlied*). Born in Hamburg, lived in Wien.
- **Mendelssohn, Felix (1809–1847).** Symphonies, overtures, concertos, songs, and incidental music for dramas. The wedding march for Shakespeare's *A Midsummer Night's Dream* is played often in America. Born in Hamburg, performed internationally (especially London), resided in Leipzig.
- **Wagner, Richard (1813–1883).** "Bad boy" of German music. In his youth a political revolutionary, and posthumously a favorite composer of Adolf Hitler. Gigantic operas, among them *Tristan und Isolde, Die Meistersinger von Nürnberg, Der Ring des Nibelungen* (four parts), and *Lohengrin,* which is the source of one of the most popular wedding marches in America ("Here Comes the Bride"). Born in Leipzig, political exile from 1848 to 1861, settled in Bayreuth. His dramatic style has led to the use of his melodies in computer games and science-fiction films.
- **Schubert, Franz (1797–1828).** Master of the art song (*das Kunstlied*) for piano and voice (about 600 works). Also wrote The *Unfinished Symphony* and a setting for the sacred text *Ave Maria.* Spent entire life in Wien.
- **Strauß, Johann (1825–1899).** "The Waltz King" of Wien. Famous for "The Blue Danube Waltz" and "Tales of the Vienna Woods."
- **Haydn, Franz Joseph (1732–1809).** Wide range of works, including the oratorios "The Creation" and "The Seasons" and 104 symphonies, among them the "Surprise Symphony." Spent several years in England, much of the rest of his life in Wien.
- **Händel, Georg Friedrich, name anglicized to George Frederick Handel (1685–1759).** Born in Halle, settled in England (1712). Oratorios, operas, songs, church and chamber music. Excerpts from *The Messiah* (1742), especially the "Hallelujah Chorus," are played widely in America at Christmas and Easter.

Samstag, 5. Juli

Meßplatz, Durlacher Allee
7.00 Flohmarkt

Wildparkstadion und Sportstätten
der Universität Karlsruhe
8.30 Sportfest der Strafvollzugsbedien-
steten des Landes Baden-Württemberg

Festplatz Knielingen
10.00 Start und Ziel
*Große Veteranen-Rallye (1200 Jahr-
feier Knielingen)*

Karlsruher Marionettentheater
15.00 „Die Orchideenhexe"
Märchenspiel von Trude Rehse

Festplatz Knielingen
18.30 Großer Europäischer Folkloretreff
(1200 Jahrfeier Knielingen)

Oberrheinisches Dichtermuseum,
Röntgenstraße 6
19.00 Vortrag „Was uns Tugend wert sein
kann"
*Veranstaltung des Parvati-Vereins,
Karlsruhe*

Sonntag, 6. Juli

Badisches Staatstheater, Großes Haus
11.00 Vorkonzert zum 8. Sinfoniekonzert
*Werke von Christobal Halffter, Ben-
jamin Britten und Hector Berlioz*

Rennwiesen Knielingen
14.00 Pferderennen des Zucht und Renn-
vereins Knielingen
(1200 Jahrfeier Knielingen)

Karlsruher Marionettentheater
15.00 „Die Orchideenhexe"
Märchenspiel von Trude Rehse

Festzelt, Festplatz Knielingen
17.30 Blasmusik mit der Kapelle „La Union Filarmonica"
*aus Amposta/Tarragona (1200 Jahr-
feier Knielingen)*

Kinder- und Jugendtheater
18.00 „Der kleine Prinz"
von Sait Exupéry

Badisches Staatstheater, Kleines Haus
19.30 „Oedipus der Tyrann"
*Tragödie von Sophokles, Übertra-
gung: F. Hölderlin*

Sandkorn-Studiotheater
20.00 „Der Kontrabaß"
von Patrick Süskind

Universität Karlsruhe, Gerthsen-Hörsaal
20.00 Konzert des Sinfonieorchesters an
der Universität Karlsruhe
*Werke von Borodin, Tschaikowsky
und Mozart*

Kammertheater Karlsruhe
20.15 „Komm raus aus dem Schrank"
Lustspiel von Philip King

Montag, 7. Juli

Festzelt, Festplatz Knielingen
19.00 Festausklang mit Hitparade
(1200 Jahrfeier Knielingen)

Badisches Staatstheater, Großes Haus
20.00 8. Sinfoniekonzert
*Werke von Christobal Halffter, Ben-
jamin Britten und Hector Berlioz*

Festzelt, Festplatz, Knielingen
21.30 „Die Globetrotter" — Eine Kiste voll
Musik, Parodien, Imitationen, Ge-
sang und Stimmung
(1200 Jahrfeier Knielingen)

Dienstag, 8. Juli

Kinder- und Jugendtheater
15.00 „Der kleine Prinz"
von Sait Exupéry

Badisches Staatstheater, Großes Haus
20.00 „Julius Caesar"
Oper von Georg Friedrich Händel

Badisches Staatstheater, Kleines Haus
20.00 „Oedipus der Tyrann"
*Tragödie von Sophokles, Übertra-
gung: F. Hölderlin*

Freizeit – Hobbys und Musik

Only a few interests could be dealt with here; the main intent was to provide language with which basic leisure activities **1**

Münzen/Sammler
großartig terrific

might be described, and to highlight music for its importance in German culture.

Sammlerwert collector's value
selten rare

Try to give attention to the hobby of each student, and **2**

in discussion to push for something beyond the mere naming of the hobby – why the student likes it, what other activities are associated with it, the people one encounters.

3

Liebhaber enthusiasts

4

Kopfhörer headphones

PROFESSOR ZEHNDER	Ach, sind Sie auch ein Münzensammler?
HERR PETERS	Ja, ich sammle schon seit elf Jahren.
PROFESSOR ZEHNDER	So? Sie müssen eine großartige Sammlung haben.
HERR PETERS	Na, sie ist ziemlich groß, aber ich interessiere mich nicht so sehr für Quantität. Qualität ist viel wichtiger.
PROFESSOR ZEHNDER	Ja – die besten Münzen sind schön und auch selten.
HERR PETERS	Ja, aber leider hat der Sammlerwert mehr mit Seltenheit als mit Schönheit zu tun.
FRAU MAURER	Und was für Hobbys hat denn eigentlich Ihr Sohn?
HERR FRINGS	Na, er bastelt gern – Flugzeuge und so.
FRAU MAURER	Und wissen Sie, wieviel Sie ausgeben wollen?
HERR FRINGS	Oh, mehr als 50 Mark sollte es nicht sein.
FRAU MAURER	Ich zeige Ihnen ein paar Sachen. Dann können Sie sich überlegen, was Sie genau wollen. Und Sie sagen mir dann Bescheid, ja, wenn Sie etwas gefunden haben.
GABI VON WEBERN	Hast du dein Instrument mitgebracht?
WALTRAUT SABIN	Ja, ich bleibe sechs Monate hier, und ich wollte es nicht zu Hause lassen. Ich übe jeden Tag – seit Jahren.
GABI VON WEBERN	Nun, was hast du Donnerstag abend vor? Ich spiele in einer kleinen Gruppe. Wir treffen uns bei mir um 8 Uhr. Du könntest mitmachen, wenn du willst.
WALTRAUT SABIN	Gerne. Was für Musik spielt ihr? Ich interessiere mich hauptsächlich für klassische Musik, aber ich habe auch in Kneipen Jazz gespielt.
GABI VON WEBERN	Wir spielen eigentlich alles: klassische Sachen, Jazz, auch Musicals. Es ist vor allem eine Gruppe für Liebhaber. Du bist also herzlich willkommen.
FRAU ASCHINGER	So, nun paßt Ihnen der Kopfhörer aber perfekt. Wollten Sie den so mitnehmen, oder soll ich ihn wieder einpacken?
FRÄULEIN TRÜB	Den können Sie so an dem Kassettenrekorder lassen. Ich möchte mir im Zug Musik anhören.
FRAU ASCHINGER	Haben Sie nicht gesagt, daß Sie nach Ost-Berlin reisen?
FRÄULEIN TRÜB	Ja. Wir wollen mal selber sehen, wie man dort lebt.
FRAU ASCHINGER	Na, Sie sollten dort auch die Deutsche Oper besuchen. Nach der Renovierung soll sie ganz schön sein. Und dort kann man sich sehr billig gute Schallplatten kaufen.
FRÄULEIN TRÜB	Mm – eine weitere Frage: Gibt es Schwierigkeiten an der Grenze, wenn man so einen Apparat mitbringt?
FRAU ASCHINGER	Keine Angst. Die Kontrolle ist nicht mehr so streng.

STRUKTUR 2

Verbs §§44,45

1. Even more about reflexive constructions

Many reflexive verbs are used with prepositions. Often the preposition must be learned individually along with the verb.

"I'm interested in"
Ich *interessiere mich* nicht so sehr **für** Quantität.
Ich *interessiere mich* hauptsächlich **für** klassische Musik.

"I'm looking forward to"
Ich habe *mich* so **auf** einen neuen Anzug *gefreut*.

Sometimes the pronoun is in the dative case – you do something *for yourself*.

Ich möchte **mir** im Zug Musik **anhören.**
Direct object is Musik

Dann kannst du **dir überlegen,** was du genau willst.
Direct object is was du genau willst

Nouns §14

2. Noun dative plurals

Basic form: Nouns in the dative plural add an *-n*.

Ich sammle schon **seit** elf Jahren.
(das Jahr, die Jahre)

Das sollst du vielleicht **mit** den anderen Mitgliedern besprechen.
(das Mitglied, die Mitglieder)

3. Sentence adverbs convey the speaker's attitude.

Das sollst du **vielleicht** mit den anderen organisieren.
(polite suggestion; maybe you don't want to)

Ich wollte **unbedingt** mitmachen.
(I just *had* to!)

Was für Hobbys hat denn **eigentlich** Ihr Sohn?
(I'm really curious about him)

Ich interessiere mich **hauptsächlich** für klassische Musik.
(But I have other interests as well)

A.A. §38

4. *Noch* and its negatives *nicht mehr/kein- mehr*

Ist die Kontrolle **noch** sehr streng? – Nein, heute **nicht mehr.**
(Die Kontrolle ist **nicht mehr** so streng.)

Haben Sie **noch** Bananen?
Heute haben wir **keine** Bananen **mehr.**

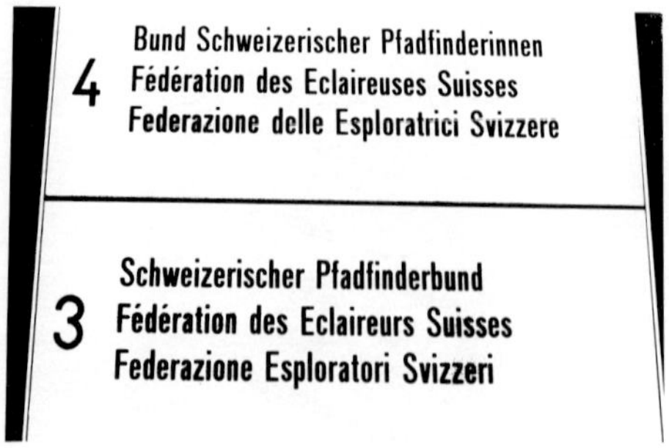

4 Bund Schweizerischer Pfadfinderinnen
Fédération des Eclaireuses Suisses
Federazione delle Esploratrici Svizzere

3 Schweizerischer Pfadfinderbund
Fédération des Eclaireurs Suisses
Federazione Esploratori Svizzeri

Marginal notes (left column):

Students see how many ways they can complete the sentence *"Ich freue mich auf. . . ."* Combine with *sich interessieren für* in logical sentence pairs. *"Ich interessiere mich für Musik, und ich freue mich aufs Konzert am 23."* Resist the temptation to contrast *sich freuen auf* with *sich freuen über*; the meaning "to be happy about something" will be provided with several easier expressions, among them *X freut mich.*

Don't complicate class presentation by bringing up nouns like *Auto* that form their plural with *-s*. The matter is dealt with in the reference grammar. Consider yourself fortunate if the student, at this stage, shows any inclination to add the *-n* to a fairly accurate plural in uncued production.

Stage 1	A	B
1 *normale*	Asks whether B would like to show B's stamp collection to A. Has been interested in stamps for about 15 years; also collects coins. Agrees they're very interesting; thinks it's better to have a few superb stamps than lots of common ones. Professes modesty about own collection.	Didn't know that A was interested in stamps. Likes rare stamps from the Scandinavian countries. Says A is quite right; A must have a terrific collection. Is now eager to show A the collection.
2 *ganz oben*	Is shopping for her husband, who likes to make model airplanes. Would like to take a look at a large model on the top shelf. Says her husband still likes to play with model planes after he has made them. Suggests the two "boys" get together.	Says her little boy also loves model planes. Says her little boy made that. Says her little boy does, too. Says that sounds like a good idea, asks where they could meet.
3 *Gruppe*	Asks what instrument B plays. Asks what kind of music B prefers. Says there's a combo that plays every Friday evening at her (his) house. Invites B to join the group if B would like to. Asks how long B has been playing. Thinks that sounds terrific.	Plays piano and violin. Plays everything, but prefers jazz. Is enthusiastic, would love to hear them. Has played jazz violin in bars; would love to jam with a new group. Piano – 12 years; violin – 8 years.

Stage 2

Complication/continuation: explore what questions the clerk might ask about the child.

Use the Bildwörterbuch, pp. 304–305.

1

You are in a department store in Basel, shopping for a present for your little brother or sister. After you greet the clerk, tell her what sort of present might be appropriate. Be sure to stay within your tight budget.

2

You have found someone in Dortmund who has a collection of old VWs. You have an old VW at home in Grand Rapids, too, but this person's cars are in much better condition. Find out as much as you can about the collection and the collector, and ask for advice about improving the condition of your car.

3

You are planning a get-together with four friends from the university. The evening will be spent playing several different styles of music. The five of you represent strings, brass, woodwinds, and percussion, and each of you is able to play more than one instrument. Suggest to Urs, Reto, Silvia, and Heidi.

a) what the order of the evening should be – jazz first? rock first?;
b) what each of you should play for each part of the evening;
c) when and where you should meet;
d) why you have chosen that time and place.

Versuchen Sie doch

Give as many reasons as you can for your belief that reading is the best indoor hobby.

Now argue that it isn't. Suggest something else.

Describe the musical organizations at your college or university. How do they compare with those you saw and heard in high school?

Discuss with a companion the relative merits of hobbies that involve a) collecting things; b) making things; c) playing music.

Chapter 20

KONZERT/WEINPROBE

Top Left: *"Radio-Symphonie Orchester Berlin unter der Leitung von Lorin Maazel."* Top Right: *"Deutsche Staatsoper."* Bottom: *"Die Tschechische Philharmonie gastiert in Berlin (Ost)."*

Songs and poems appropriate to this chapter: *"Himmel und Erde müssen vergehen," "Trink, Brüderlein, trink."* Drinking songs from Ch. 17, *Universität:* Early Beatles songs, Elvis Presley's *"Muß i denn," "Daumen neig dich, Finger streck dich"* (kiddie rhyme), Hofmannsthal's *"Die Beiden,"* Rilke's *"Herbsttag."*

FUNKTIONEN – KONTEXTE – STRUKTUREN

Looking Ahead

You'll be making arrangements to hear a concert, talking about things to do inside the concert hall, and discussing the quality of the productions. You'll also do some wine tasting and explore the process of wine making.

You will be using:

- *da-* compounds to abbreviate prepositional combinations (*für das* → *dafür*)
- verb + preposition combinations (*warten auf* – wait for)
- more reflexive verbs
- the superlative form of adjectives: their great<u>est</u> degree
- infinitive phrases in some new ways: with separable verbs, with *um*, and with *brauchen*

200

Konzert

See the *Bildwörterbuch* display on "Culture/Kultur" for illustrations and lists of musical terms. **1**

die Messe *mass*
(church and music)

If not right now, then sometime during the chapter introduce the *Bildwörterbuch* display of musical terminology. This is obviously the chapter in which to emphasize musical enrichment, particularly items that contain language that can be understood readily. Since **2** cultural knowledge is regarded as a component of proficiency, such materials – and not just the "highbrow" items – are actually more than enrichment; they contribute significantly to one's ability to communicate within the culture. You might choose to go beyond merely preaching the point, and instead make cultural (and specifically musical) knowledge part of your tests. See note in Instructor's Guide. **3**

wechseln *(ex)change money*
tauschen *exchange or trade items*

Porgy and Bess: **Oper von George Gershwin (1898–1937) aus dem Jahre 1935.** *Songs: "Summertime," "I Got Plenty of Nothin'," "Bess, You is My Woman Now."*

im Taxi **4**

Wegen dem Verkehr: See note in Instructor's Guide.

Frei/Licht/Theater outdoor theater

Opern/Kenner opera lovers, connoisseurs

HERR WEGMANN	In der Zeitung steht, daß es immer noch einige Karten für die Bach Messe in h-moll gibt. Wärst du dafür?
FRAU WEGMANN	Das kommt darauf an. Müssen wir in die Stadt, nur um die Karten abzuholen? Dann bin ich dagegen.
HERR WEGMANN	Ich glaube, wir können sie telefonisch bestellen. Hier steht aber nichts darüber. Soll ich anrufen?
FRAU WEGMANN	Meinetwegen. Wenn es aber nur Stehplätze gibt, dann müssen wir uns überlegen, ob es sich lohnt.
FRAU STRAUSS	So, bitte schön. Zwei Plätze nebeneinander im Parkett, in der dritten Reihe links. Die Garderobe ist unten.
LISA VOGEL	Ja, danke. Habe ich Zeit, eine Zigarette zu rauchen?
FRAU STRAUSS	Hm – die Aufführung fängt in wenigen Minuten an.
LISA VOGEL	Na, man kann eine Stunde auf eine Zigarette warten.
FRAU STRAUSS	Eigentlich dauert es 90 Minuten bis zur ersten Pause. Sie wissen, daß die *Meistersinger* eine sehr lange Oper ist. Die Aufführung dauert viereinhalb Stunden.
LISA VOGEL	Kann ich mir während der Pause etwas zu essen kaufen? Sonst wäre das zuviel Wagner auf einen leeren Magen.
MR. KARSTEN	Ich hätte eine Bitte. Könnte ich den Platz mit Ihnen tauschen? Dann kann ich neben meiner Frau sitzen.
HERR BOENISCH	Aber selbstverständlich. Schon vor der Pause habe ich selber daran gedacht. Sie sind größer als ich, und ich konnte nicht die ganze Bühne sehen.
MR. KARSTEN	Besten Dank. Das ist sehr nett von Ihnen.
HERR BOENISCH	Ich nehme an, Sie sind Amerikaner. Wie gefällt Ihnen unsere Aufführung von *Porgy and Bess*?
MR. KARSTEN	Ausgezeichnet. Ich habe nicht gewußt, daß man sich hier so für amerikanische Komponisten interessiert.
HERR NILITSCHKA	In die Baslerstraße? Das dauert ein bißchen, wegen dem Verkehr nach der Oper. Hat's Ihnen gefallen?
PROF. FLEISCHMANN	Ja, *Aïda* ist immer etwas Herrliches, auch wenn ich nicht viel verstanden habe.
HERR NILITSCHKA	Ja, italienische Opern singt man sehr oft bei uns in der deutschen Übersetzung. Die Musik ist weit wichtiger als der Text. Manchmal verstehe ich auch selber die deutschen Worte nicht.
PROF. FLEISCHMANN	In Rom haben wir *Aïda* auch gesehen, mit den Elefanten auf der Bühne im Freilichttheater.
HERR NILITSCHKA	Naja. Man kann die beiden Aufführungen nicht direkt miteinander vergleichen. Elefanten auf die Bühne bringen. Das gibt es nur in Rom. Das sind Aufführungen für Touristen, nicht für Opernkenner.

STRUKTUR 1

Pronouns §14

See note in Instructor's Guide.

Expand the exercise in the note above to a systematic drill of the replacement of prepositional phrases with *da-* compounds. Emphasis on a summary echo isolates and strengthens the transformation. A: *X ist auf dem Y.* B: *Oh, darauf.* Expansion: A: *Nein, X ist nicht auf dem Y, sondern . . .* B: *Oh, nicht darauf* [+ corrects A].

You might occasionally use the so-called "anticipatory *da-*compound" structure (*Ich bin dagegen, daß . . .*), but you should not attempt to teach it overtly.

Verbs §35

See note in Instructor's Guide.

See note in Instructor's Guide.

Verbs §§41–46

See note in Instructor's Guide.

Resist resolutely an urge to contrast *sich* (acc.) *jemandem vorstellen* (to introduce) with *sich* (dat.) *etwas* (acc.) *vorstellen* (to imagine something).

If your class seems reasonably adept, you might contrast reflexive and nonreflexive instances of these verbs by asking students to describe (and some to act out) what people do who are responsible for dressing not only themselves but also someone else (e.g., child or invalid). See note in Instructor's Guide.

1. *da-* compounds: used to talk about things without naming them again

"with, for, after (etc.) that/it"

● **Da- + preposition often replaces prepositional phrases.**

Wärest du [*für das* →] **dafür**? "for that/it"

A *da-* compound can replace – very efficiently! – an entire prepositional phrase, or even a whole subject-verb clause.

Sollen wir heute abend ins Konzert gehen? Ich bin **dafür**.
(dafür = für die Idee, daß wir heute abend ins Konzert gehen)

NOTE: An -r- is added if the preposition begins with a vowel:

Hier steht nichts [*über das* →] **darüber**.

NOTE: *Da-* compounds never refer to people.

neben meiner Frau → *neben ihr* (not *daneben*)

2. Verb-preposition combinations

● **The preposition changes or completes the meaning of the verb.**

NOTE how prepositions change the meaning of the English verb *take:*

Take after a relative, *take out* a pizza, *take down* a number, *take in* money, *take over* a company.

● **The preposition must be learned along with the verb. You can't count on parallels to English.**

Ich *interessiere* mich *für* (not *in*) klassische Musik.

Man kann ja eine Stunde *auf* (not *für*) eine Zigarette *warten*.

3. Reflexives: review and expansion

● **Doing something for oneself** dative case

Kann ich *mir* während der Pause etwas zu essen kaufen?

● **Actions clearly performed upon the actor** accusative case

Darf ich *mich* vorstellen? May I introduce *myself?*

● **Actions not obviously reflexive to a speaker of English**

Ich *schaue mich* nur *um*, danke. "looking around"
Dann müssen wir *uns überlegen*. "consider"

Dann können Sie *sich entscheiden*. "decide"
. . . , ob es *sich lohnt*. "if it's worthwhile"

● *sich an/aus/umziehen — an important reflexive verb family*

Er **zieht** sich immer sehr elegant **an**. "gets dressed"
Er **zieht** sich immer abends **aus**. "gets undressed"
Er **zieht** sich immer vor dem Essen **um**. "changes clothes"

Stage 1

A	B
1 Asks if B would like to go to a concert. Says there are still tickets.	Isn't very interested, says it all depends. Isn't in favor if tickets are available only at the box office.
Says B can think it over until later.	Says A should call to order tickets.
2 Tells B where seats are located. Tells B where cloakroom is.	Asks where to leave things (coat, etc.). Asks whether concert is very long – is very hungry.
B can get something to eat at the intermission.	Asks what sorts of things are available.

A	B	C
3 Loves Orff's *Carmina Burana*.	Agrees, but doesn't understand it. Doesn't understand the words.	Asks what B doesn't understand.
Read the text last week, but doesn't understand the music. Offers to trade seats.	Would like a better view. Says it's not worthwhile – not much time left.	Says this is an especially good production. Offers to trade seats.
Asks what B and C want to do after the concert.	Suggests what to do.	Is hungry, wants a substantial snack.

Carmina Burana: *scenic oratorio (1937) by Curl Orff (1895–1982) based on medieval Latin songs.*

"... would like a better view" = "*Wenn ich (man) besser sehen könnte.*"

Stage 2

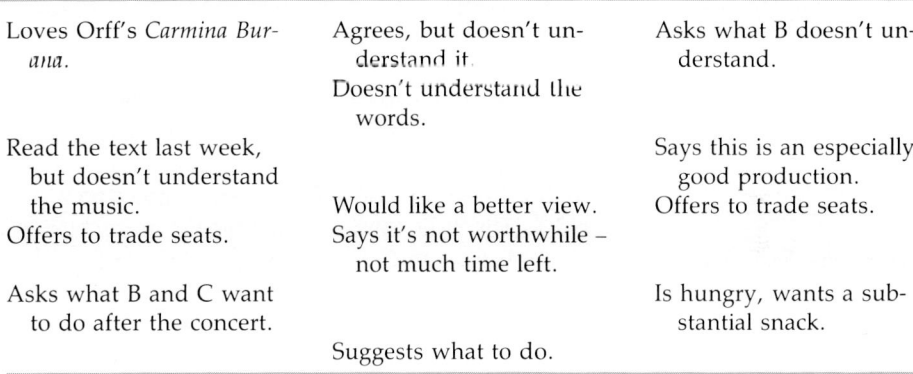

Versuchen Sie doch

One intent of the first item is to suggest that there are times when speaking German might be advantageous even in America. No doubt you can devise similar situations.

Direct students to appropriate realia for second item.

1

You're in Wien, where you are finally going to get to hear the Vienna Choir Boys (Wiener Sängerknaben). (You heard them in the big city once when you were in a choir yourself at the State Line Good News Full Gospel Tabernacle.) Ask your hotel clerk to call for tickets for you. Say when you want to go, where you want to sit, and how much you're willing to pay for tickets. Remind the clerk how special the Choir Boys are to you.

2

You're afraid it's too late to get good seats to hear the Tokyo String Quartet. Another possibility would be the Stuttgarter Kammerorchester, playing at the same time elsewhere in the city. Discuss the alternatives with your friends, suggesting possibilities for buying tickets on short notice. You prefer the quartet, but the chamber orchestra is a close second.

3

You want to go to a concert of something other than classical music. Discuss the possibilities.

You've always wanted to talk with one of the Vienna Choir Boys, and now the chance is at hand – they're performing near your hometown. You just have to convince the chaperone at the dressing room door to let you by. Say what you must.

You're in the Deutsche Oper in East Berlin, waiting for a performance of Weber's *Oberon* to begin. The person sitting next to you is making noise eating a snack and dropping crumbs on the velvet seats. Try to correct the situation in as positive a manner as you can. (For models of what to say, look ahead to the dialogs for *Höflichkeit/Unhöflichkeit* in Chapter 26.)

Maybe teach "Music alone shall live" ("Himmel und Erde müssen vergehen"); other appropriate enrichment: children's songs, "An die Freu(n)de" from Beethoven's Ninth Symphony.

Mention *Volkslied* and *Kunstlied*.

You could mention the fondness for Western fiction (Karl May) and the clubs that stage reenactments of cowboy, Indian, and cavalry days.

Note the extension of such patterns to America when immigration from central Europe was heavy. Immigrants formed choirs and bands, and for a time German was the dominant language of opera production in New York, even of Italian operas.

"Music Alone Shall Live" – Music in German culture

It is virtually impossible to overestimate the importance of music – both classical and popular – in German culture and society. A lack of basic familiarity with the subject, particularly the classical heritage, may well be regarded with surprise or even irritation, as though one were somehow deficient in education and ordinary human appreciation for beauty and excellence.

Of course, not every German, Austrian, or Swiss plays the violin, sings operatic arias, or loves to attend concerts, but respect for "serious" music is emphasized more than it is in our own culture. Classical music is subsidized heavily by government. There are dozens of opera companies and even more professional orchestras. Several of the latter, such as the renowned Bavarian Radio Symphony, are maintained by the broadcasting industry, as was once the case in the United States. Still of supreme prestige in music are Wien and Berlin (both East and West), though those cities have lost much of the political importance they once enjoyed when Germany and Austria were world powers.

Other types of music are pursued enthusiastically in the German-speaking countries, though none openly rivals classical music in prestige. Most familiar to North Americans, of course, is the "oom-pah" band of festivals and beer halls. The folk tradition, including many distinct regional forms, has always been strong, and has at times contributed to the classical current. Jazz is taken quite seriously as an artistic form, though its popularity is due in some part to the general interest in things American. "Swing" and big-band sounds, like Glenn Miller's "In the Mood," have been widely known since World War II. Rock has been a part of the popular music scene ever since Elvis served a hitch with the U.S. Army in Germany and the Beatles got their start in Hamburg ("Komm gib mir Deine Hand"). In the seventies and eighties the music of the *Neue Deutsche Welle* ("New German Wave") began attracting attention outside the German-speaking realm. Even country-western music is appreciated and imitated. There are German versions of American hits, such as *"Der Feigling des Jahrhunderts"* ("The Coward of the County") or *"Wer Liebe sucht"* ("Stand by Your Man"), and original songs as well, like *"Texas-Town, die Western Stadt, liegt mitten in Berlin"* or *"Ich möcht so gern nach Nashville, Tennessee."* Curiously enough, several features of country-western music – certain instrumentations, the waltz form, and of course the yodel – are of German origin, so the export of country music to Europe is in part just the return of a favor. Last, *"Tingeltangel"* ("honky-tonk" or "easy-listening") music is immensely popular. Sentimental titles like *"Mein Liebeslied muß ein Walzer sein," "Weißt Du, sie spielen unser Lied,"* or *"Der liebste Platz, die Rasenbank am Elterngrab"* suggest that such music, like its American equivalent, is often so bad that it's good.

A striking feature from the larger perspective is the coexistence of the many types of music in the taste of an individual or the activities of a group. The breadth of interest can be seen – whether as a cause or an effect – in social dancing. Casual dancing is common, but so is ballroom dancing. Accordingly, a dance band will offer many types of music.

Cultivation of classical music, its integration into everyday life, and the encouragement of tolerance in musical tastes are reflected in widespread music and speech training in the schools, by amateur musical groups, particularly the very common choral societies or *"Sängervereine,"* and even by the structure of the broadcast media. Television offerings commonly include orchestral perform-

das Evergreen golden oldie

Program (broadcast event) = *die Sendung, -en.*

"Öffentlich-rechtlich"; to encourage the independence of the medium, the tax-generated funds for it are channeled through a supposedly "blind" trust.
Feel free to designate some or all these pieces as *Kitsch*, as cultural offerings that in themselves lack lasting value. One should be aware, though, of the social significance of *Kitsch*.

From Bayern 1, 25 March 1986, 7 P.M.

ances. More intriguing is the pattern in radio, which is relatively more important in the German-speaking countries than it is in North America. There is no real equivalent to the American "special interest" pattern of programming, where a given station concentrates almost exclusively on one type of music such as country, soul, top forties, easy listening, or old favorites. In the large West German province of Bavaria, for example, there are four main radio stations, or actually just four channels (*das Programm, -e*) of what is in effect a single station. All four, and the local television channels as well, are operated by Bavarian Broadcasting (Bayerischer Rundfunk), which is a governmental institution rather than a private corporation. One channel, Bayern 4 Klassik, offers only classical music. The other channels are more or less "middle-brow." Characteristic of their musical offering are two features. Although there are some specialty programs, the ordinary musical fare covers practically the entire spectrum in a single session. Thus one recent edition of the *"Deutsche Schlagerparade"* included the following hits (*der Schlager, -*): the group "Münchner Freiheit" with *"Tausendmal Du"* (easy listening/soft rock); Andrea Jürgens singing *"Shy, Shy Sugarman"* (sixties-style soft rock, German lyrics); the ever-popular Peter Alexander and the West German national soccer team singing *"Mexiko, mi amor"* in commemoration of the team's departure for Mexico to play for the World Cup; the Austrian group "Erste Allgemeine Verunsicherung" with *"In der Provinz bin ich der M-M-M-M-Märchenprinz"* (comic talk song); the Austrian Adolf Meyer (stage name Andy Bogg) singing *"Ich will Deine Tränen weinen"* (Elvis imitation); Nikki with *"Wenn ich mit dir tanz"* (bebop); and "Die Flippers" performing *"Ein kleines Lied vom Sonnenschein"* (sugar-coated folk). The classics, too, find their way into everyday programming. Entire concerts or lengthy pieces may be broadcast, especially on Sunday. Light classics are mixed in with other types of music on some programs. Thus a *"Glückwunschkonzert"* broadcast of birthday and wedding anniversary announcements accompanied by musical requests might include Brahms's *"Ungarischer Tanz Nr. 5."*

STADTPLAN WIEN

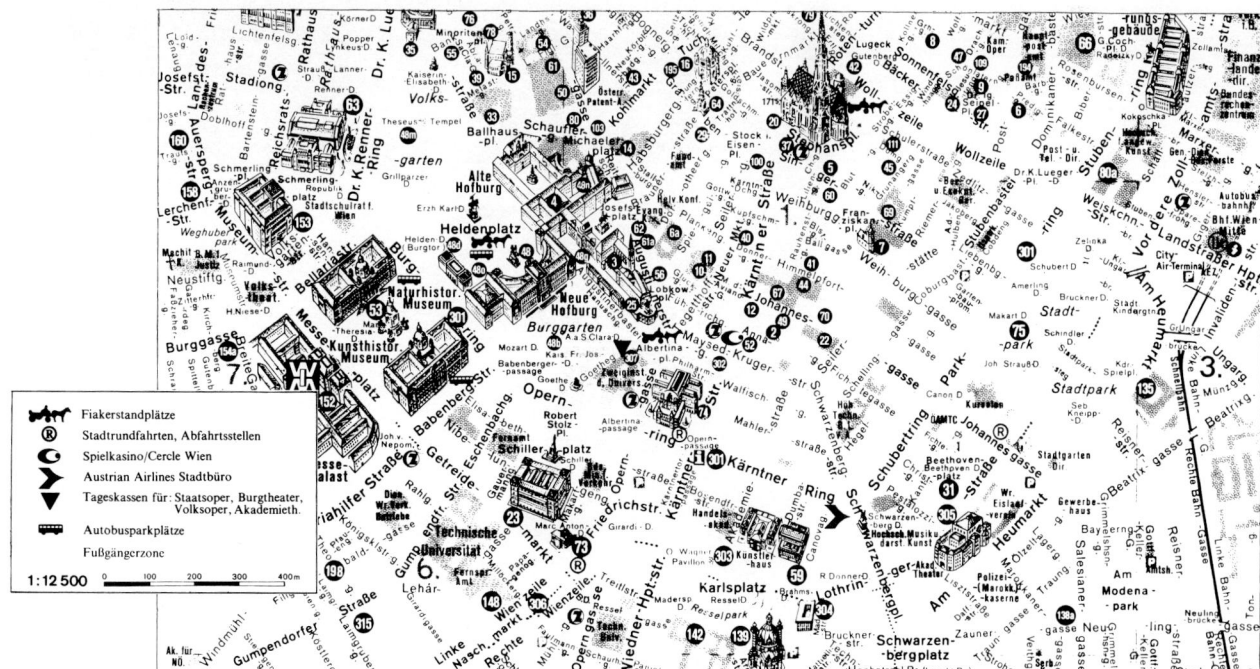

Prädikat »Kabinett«

Das Mindest-Mostgewicht für einen Kabinett-Wein muß 73 bzw. 76 Grad Oechsle betragen.

Prädikat »Spätlese«

Die Trauben müssen nach Beendigung der Hauptlese im vollreifen Zustand geerntet werden. Das Mindest-Mostgewicht beträgt 85 Grad Oechsle.

Prädikat »Auslese«

Dies ist ein Wein ausschließlich aus vollreifen Trauben, bei denen alle kranken, unreifen oder fehlerhaften Trauben von Hand „ausgelesen" werden. Der Mindest-Mostgehalt beträgt 95 Grad Oechsle.

Prädikat »Trockenbeeren-Auslese«

Edelste und teuerste Wein-Raritäten: Denn nur eingeschrumpfte, rosinenartige, edelfaule Beeren können verwendet werden. Das ergibt naturgemäß sehr geringe Mengen, aber absolute Spitzen!

Eiswein

In gefrorenem Zustand – bei mindestens minus 8 Grad – gelesene und sofort gekelterte Trauben. Das in den Beeren enthaltene Wasser bleibt zu Eis gefroren in den Kelterrückständen. Dadurch wird der Most – im Gegensatz zu Beerenauslesen – nicht nur im Zuckergehalt, sondern auch in der so wichtigen Säure konzentriert.

		Abhol-preis	Versand-preis
Anbaugebiet	Rheinpfalz		ab 60 Fl. frei Haus
Trockene und Halbtrockene Weine		DM/Fl. 0,75 l	DM/Fl. 0,75 l
110	1986er Ungsteiner Osterberg Müller-Thurgau QbA TROCKEN frisch, mit feiner Art	4,80	5,70
120	1986er Kallstadter Kronenberg Silvaner Qualitätswein TROCKEN durchgegoren, bekömmlich	5,00	5,90
140	1986er Ungsteiner Weilberg Riesling Qualitätswein HALBTROCKEN elegant, herzhaft	5,90	6,80
180	1986er Kallstadter Steinacker Riesling Qualitätswein TROCKEN spritzig, rassig	6,10	7,00
190	1986er Kallstadter Steinacker Muskateller Qualitätswein HALBTROCKEN sortentypisch, ausdrucksvoll	6,50	7,40
210	1986er Kallstadter Kobnert Muskateller Qualitätswein TROCKEN mit ausgeprägtem Duft	6,60	7,50

Weinprobe

You, your students, or the institution for which you teach may not condone the consumption of alcohol. In earlier chapters abundant attention was paid to nonalcoholic beverages. Here the focus is on a prominent feature of the culture. Should you have moderate reservations about the material, you might, for example, treat the dialogs as samples of speech that might be heard – rather than necessarily produced – by persons sojourning in German-speaking countries. Thus the teetotaling tourist might accompany others to a winery without partaking, and might still be interested in what is going on. Should you wish or need to alter the focus radically, without sacrificing the linguistic targets of the material provided, you might offer material that is similar in structure, vocabulary, and function, such as exposition of cheese production.

Rosen im Frühling: Encourage similar colorful (if trite) comparisons, not just because they are expected when one tastes wines, but because beginning students often have a very meager store of adjectives; their tendency under production pressure is to reduce the world to *gut* and *schlecht*.

Should someone ask why *-lese* in wine terminology so much resembles *lesen,* explain that the root meaning of both is "to gather." The Germanic seer who sought to divine the unknown would cast down wooden staves (*Buch-staben*) engraved with letters ("write" is related to *ritzen*), and would then *gather* them up for interpretation.

FRÄULEIN LASSWITZ	Darf ich Ihnen jetzt den 83er anbieten? Das war ein ausgezeichneter Jahrgang – vielleicht der beste in den letzten 10 Jahren, und auch der teuerste.
FRAU WIESINGER	Kann man den 83er mit dem 81er vergleichen?
FRÄULEIN LASSWITZ	Der 81er ist mir zu süß. Ich trinke lieber einen trockenen Wein.
FRAU WIESINGER	Mir schmeckt der Wein besser, wenn er etwas süßer ist. Und mit ein bißchen Käse und Obst.
FRÄULEIN LASSWITZ	Ja, Sie scheinen sich für unsere Weine zu interessieren. Darf ich Sie zur nächsten Weinprobe einladen?
FRAU WIESINGER	Aber gern. Wann wäre das denn?
FRÄULEIN LASSWITZ	Sie findet am vierten Oktober statt, um 14 Uhr.
HERR NIKOLAUS	Haben wir noch Zeit, die Spätlese zu probieren? Unser Bus fährt in wenigen Minuten ab.
FRÄULEIN MÖHN	Das sollten Sie unbedingt tun, bevor Sie wegfahren. Dann können Sie sich noch entscheiden, ob Ihnen die Spätlese oder die Auslese besser schmeckt. Darf ich einschenken?
HERR NIKOLAUS	Ja, gerne. Soll man diesen Wein kühl servieren?
FRÄULEIN MÖHN	Gewöhnlich trinkt man Moselweine zwischen 15 und 17 Grad. Sie dürfen nicht allzu kalt sein.
HERR NIKOLAUS	Dieser Wein schmeckt mir sehr. Wie Rosen im Frühling.
FRÄULEIN MÖHN	Nicht wahr? Wollen Sie ein paar Flaschen mitnehmen?
FRAU DÖRFLER	Wann erntet man eigentlich die Trauben im Herbst?
FRÄULEIN MEISTER	Es kommt darauf an. Die Trauben für einen "Kabinett"-Wein erntet man früher als für die "Spätlese," und die "Auslese"-Ernte findet noch später statt, wenn die Trauben wirklich vollreif sind.
FRAU DÖRFLER	Und wie lange bleibt der Wein im Faß, bevor er in die Flasche kommt?
FRÄULEIN MEISTER	Das ist ganz verschieden. Manchmal schon nur einige Monate, aber die Rheinweine fast nie mehr als 3 Jahre.
CHARLES PORTER	Wir waren letzte Woche hier und haben den Johannisberger Kabinett sehr gut gefunden.
HERR SCHMÜCKING	Sie haben also am Weinfest teilgenommen?
CHARLES PORTER	Ja, und wir hatten eine Frage: Wie schwer ist es denn, Wein nach Amerika zu schicken?
HERR SCHMÜCKING	Es lohnt sich eigentlich nicht für ein paar Flaschen. Die können Sie selber durch den Zoll bringen.
CHARLES PORTER	Aber wir wollten eine ganze Kiste. Das ist zu schwer.
HERR SCHMÜCKING	Das können wir alles für Sie erledigen. Sie brauchen nur ein paar Formulare auszufüllen.

207

Targeted exercise is necessary but should not consist predominantly of transformational chanting

A.A. §§31,32

(Teacher: "*schnell*"; Students: "*Das schnellste Auto.*"). Establish contexts and use props – consumer product labels are helpful, as are ads. Student A points out a quality in one item, thus introducing the noun (*Dieser Wein ist süß*); B quickly describes the item that is superlative in that category (*Aber dieser Wein ist der süßeste*). Enrich the exercise by adding questions (*Ist dieser Wein süß?, Aber warum trinken Sie ihn nicht oft?*).

1. Superlative forms of adjectives: their greatest degree

adjective forms:

POSITIVE	COMPARATIVE	SUPERLATIVE
soft	soft<u>er</u>	soft<u>est</u>

● **standard pattern:** adjective comparative stem + **-st**

Remember: sometimes there will be an umlaut on the stem vowel.

adjective	*comparative*	*comparative stem*	*superlative*
klein	kleiner	klein	**kleinst-**
lang	länger	läng-	**längst-**
jung	jünger	jüng-	**jüngst-**

die *kleinsten* Kinder   die *längsten* Tage

● **alternate pattern: -est** after adjectives ending in **-d, -t,** or an **s**-sound

die *ältesten* Weine
die *spätesten* Weine
die *heißesten* Tage
exception: die **größten** Städte

● **irregulars:** new stem + **-st**

gute Weine   bessere Weine   die *besten* Weine

Verbs §40

2. More about infinitive phrases

See note in Instructor's Guide.

If students are quite capable, exercise the contrast between *X scheint + zu + infinitive* and *Es scheint, daß X . . .* conjugated verb.

● Remember that **zu** + infinitive comes at or near the *end* of the phrase (which may be quite long). In English the *to* + verb comes at the *beginning* of the infinitive phrase.

Habe ich Zeit, *eine Zigarette zu rauchen?*
Wie schwer ist es denn, *Wein nach Amerika zu schicken?*

● **zu** appears as a part of a separable-prefix verb.

Müssen wir in die Stadt, nur um die Karten *abzuholen?*

● An infinitive phrase introduced by **um** expresses *purpose* ("in order to").

. . . nur um die Karten *abzuholen.*

● **brauchen nicht . . . zu ___ = müssen nicht**

Sie müssen nicht hier bleiben, wenn Sie keine Zeit haben.
Sie *brauchen nicht hier zu bleiben,* wenn Sie keine Zeit haben.

Note that *nicht müssen* = "don't have to," NOT "must not."

● **zu** + infinitive often follows *scheinen.*

Sie *scheinen* sich für unsere Weine *zu interessieren.*

THE BEST GRAPES

1. Riesling	5. Ruhlander	9. Kerner
2. Muller-Thurgau	6. Morio Muskat	10. Faber
3. Silvaner	7. Weißburgunder	11. Bacchus
4. Scheurebe	8. Gewürztraminer	12. Huxel
		13. Optima

MOST IMPORTANT WINE REGIONS

1. Rheinpfalz	4. Nahe
2. Rheinhessen	5. Rheingau
3. Mosel Saar Ruwer	6. sonstige

SITUATIONEN 2 Weinprobe

Stage 1	A	B
	1	
Encourage attention to at least the major geographical distinctions (Rhein vs. Mosel). Employ any available bottle labels or wine lists – many medium-price American restaurants have wine lists, and most contain at least one German wine (often misspelled by the waiter, and even more often grossly mispronounced by the personnel). Use the occasion to fine-tune pronunciation; it won't hurt to suggest associations of *savoir faire*.	Offers B a wine to taste. Suggests a Johannisberger. Says it's drier, tells vintage.	Likes dry wines better – this wine is too sweet. Asks about it – vintage, sweetness. Asks for a glass.
	2	
	Would like something to go with the meal. Asks B to compare the '85 with the '87. Asks to try the '85.	Suggests something appropriate: an '85 and an '87. Suggests the '87 is too young – needs more time in the bottle. Says the '85 is bound to be good, too, wants to sell A a case.
	3	
	Wants to order some wine. A has come to appreciate the wine. Gives details.	Asks particulars. Is interested; asks for more details. Asks why A chose this wine over one other that is especially good.
3: See note in Instructor's Guide.	Gives reasons.	
	4	
	Would like to send a case of wine back to Louisville. Money is no object; loves the wine. Has tried all over to get it, but it isn't available at home.	Says that's rather expensive. Asks why A wants to take so much. Isn't the wine marketed in the U.S? It's not impossible to send the wine; will be happy to accommodate A.

Stage 2

1

You don't really care for the wine you have been given but are too polite to say anything about it. You'd like to try another, perhaps another vintage. Tell the vintner – perhaps a comparison of the two would be useful. What would you say if the second wine were not as good as the first?

2

You are a nondrinker, on a tour of the Mosel region with friends, and have stopped in at a winery for an advertised tasting. The owners of the winery are gracious hosts and immediately give you a glass of their favorite wine. But your church forbids drinking wine.

a) Do your best to be complimentary about the wine without tasting it.
b) Explain your church doctrine to the winemaker and her husband, who have never heard of such a thing.

You might remind students that they are perfectly free to promote goodwill by praising the smell of the wine and the color and shape of the glass, by asking about the wine production process or the pretty woodcarvings on the shelf, etc.

Versuchen Sie doch

See note in Instructor's Guide.

You're sure the wine you ordered for your meal has gone bad. You don't want to drink it and you don't want to pay for it. Tell the serving person your position firmly but politely, and offer an informed explanation.

What can you say about the production of wine or beer in your own locality? Explain how drinking and driving are dealt with where you live.

You have found an excellent wine, and are sure that your parents would love some of it for their anniversary in two months. You would also like to have some along on the rest of your trip, which will last for another six weeks. Make suggestions about purchase, packaging, and shipping to accommodate a) your plans for your parents; b) your greedy self-indulgence.

209

Chapter 21

AUSFLÜGE/REISEBÜRO

Songs and poems appropriate to
this chapter: West German
national anthem (text by
Hoffmann von Fallersleben),
*"Als wir jüngst in Regensburg
waren,"* Goethe: *"Heidenröslein,"*
Kästner: *"Sachliche Romanze."*
Also short passages from Martin
Luther's Bible that illustrate past
tenses. Mention Luther's role in
the evolution of the modern
German standard.

FUNKTIONEN – KONTEXTE – STRUKTUREN

Looking Ahead

You'll be planning and discussing excursions, talking about activities in various cities, and arranging for travel to East bloc countries.

You will be using:

- different ways of expressing causation (Because . . . , due to)
- different ways of expressing simultaneity (While . . . , during)
- *noch nicht* and *noch kein-,* the negatives of *schon*
- stretch of time phrases, in which *seit* and *noch* express continuing action
- past tense forms of common verbs (was, knew, asked, etc.)

210

Ausflüge

der Hochzeitstag
wedding anniversary

The Karl Valentin sketch, "Der neue Buchhalter," is built upon an outrageous variation of spellings for the common name "Meyer," "Meier," etc. It can be used both for comic relief and for an intensive check of spelling skills.

Point out how German combines a native root, *steigen*, with prefixes to form complex words that are nevertheless easily understood by even children. English *ascent* and *descent* are not readily comprehensible, and of course few adults know what the root syllable *scandere* means.

1

HERR FREUDENBERG	Grüß Gott. Schöne Aussicht, nicht? Dürfen wir uns zu Ihnen setzen?
FRAU FREUDENBERG	Wir wollen uns auch ein bißchen ausruhen. Der Berg wird jedes Jahr höher.
TOM DOOLEY	Ja, bitte, nehmen Sie doch Platz.
HERR FREUDENBERG	Danke. Ich muß erst mal den Rucksack ablegen.
KWANG KIM	Darf ich Ihnen dabei helfen? Der sieht schwer aus.

. . .

FRAU FREUDENBERG	Ja, die Wanderung machen wir seit vierzig Jahren, jedes Jahr an unserem Hochzeitstag.
HERR FREUDENBERG	Mit den Jahren hat sich alles geändert. Vor vierzig Jahren gab es keine Autobahn durch das Tal.
FRAU FREUDENBERG	Na, Schatz. Es wird spät. Höchste Zeit, daß wir gehen.
HERR FREUDENBERG	Hat uns sehr gefreut. Wir wünschen Ihnen also noch einen schönen Tag. Auf Wiedersehen.

2

MR. SAWYER	Darf ich mich zu Ihnen setzen?
HERR BEHRENS	Sicher. In diesem Gasthaus ist es immer schwer, einen freien Tisch zu finden.
MR. SAWYER	Ich bin erst heute angekommen. Vielleicht könnten Sie mir eine Wildspezialität empfehlen.
HERR BEHRENS	Das Hirschfilet ist ausgezeichnet. Hier serviert man das mit einer wunderbaren Beerensoße.
MR. SAWYER	*Bärensoße?* Bären haben wir im Zoo gesehen, aber . . .
HERR BEHRENS	Nein, nein. Sie haben mich mißverstanden. Das sind Beeren – also Pflanzen, nicht Tiere.
MR. SAWYER	Also, Hirschfilet mit Beerensoße. Danke, Herr . . .
HERR BEHRENS	Behrens. Ich heiße Behrens. Tatsächlich. Komisch, nicht?

3

FRÄULEIN MARTI	Entschuldigung. Ich glaube, wir haben uns verlaufen. Wir wollten die Burg Hohenfels besichtigen.
FRAU SCHREIBER	Ach, Sie haben den falschen Weg genommen.
FRÄULEIN MARTI	Aber nein! Wie ist das möglich?
FRAU SCHREIBER	Nun, Sie haben wegen dem steilen Aufstieg nicht bemerkt, daß Sie immer weiter nach Süden gewandert sind.
FRÄULEIN MARTI	Na ja, wissen Sie, ob man die Burg auch auf diesem Weg erreichen kann?
FRAU SCHREIBER	Also dieser Weg hier führt weiter durch den Wald und dann zur Paßhöhe hinauf. Den Weg zur Burg hinunter können Sie dann nicht verfehlen.

4

| HERR ZAUCHER | Aber wenn Sie hinaufsteigen, brauchen Sie mindestens zweieinhalb Stunden. Beim Aufsteigen werden Sie müde, und Sie genießen den Abstieg nicht mehr. |
| FRAU KARLEN | Du, das stimmt schon. Wir würden nur an die nächste kleine Strecke denken. Wenn wir am Paß anfangen, haben wir mehr Spaß an der ganzen Sache. |

211

Review the use of *weil* and associated grammar. Chief aim of error correction: *weil* with verb last in second clause. Similarly with *wenn* in next suggestion. Set up exercises in which Student A begins with two simple statements; B then pushes for clarification of temporal relationships; other students vary the structure using the alternatives provided.

1. Flexibility in answering "Why?" — four ways to express <u>causation</u>

X happened. Y happened.   inference: Y because of X
Der Aufstieg war steil. (   ) Wir haben nicht bemerkt, daß . . .

X happened, therefore Y happened.   "and so, therefore . . ."
Der Aufstieg war steil – **also** haben wir nicht bemerkt, daß . . .

Because X happened, Y happened.   "because . . ."
Weil der Aufstieg steil war, haben wir nicht bemerkt, daß . . .

Because of X, Y happened.   "because of . . ."
Wegen dem steilen Aufstieg haben wir nicht bemerkt, daß . . .

If you use any one of these all the time, you will sound monotonous, even childish. Natural adult speech exhibits a variety of constructions:

Well, it rained, and so we left.
We left because it rained.
It was raining, so we just decided to leave.
Because of the rain, we had to leave.

Nouns §16; W.O. §§9,13

2. Flexibility in answering "When?" — five ways to express <u>simultaneity</u>

**Beim Schlafen reisen –
beim Reisen erholen**
Verlängern Sie Ihren Urlaub. Reisen Sie nachts im bequemen Schlaf- oder Liegewagen. Ein Platz im Liegewagenabteil mit 6 Personen kostet 23 DM, im Abteil mit 4 Personen (in den meisten Verbindungen) 29 DM (incl. Bettzeug). Die Preise für ein Schlafwagenbett richten sich nach der gewünschten Klasse und der Länge des Schlafwagenlaufs. Der Schlafwagen- und Liegewagen-Fahrplan informiert Sie über Verbindungen und Preise. Fragen Sie bitte nach der "Ortfahrer-Karte 9 + 1" für Schlafwagen-Reisende.

X happens. Y happens.   Simultaneity is only *implied.*
Sie steigen auf. Sie werden müde.

X happens. Meanwhile, Y happens.   Add **dabei.**
Sie steigen auf. **Dabei** werden Sie müde.

In the process of X-ing   **beim** (= **bei dem**) + infinitive
Beim Aufsteigen werden Sie müde.
_{capitalize the infinitive}

When(ever) you X   **wenn** + subject and . . . verb
Wenn Sie aufsteigen, werden Sie müde.

During the time that you X   **während** + subject and . . . verb
Während Sie aufsteigen, werden Sie müde.

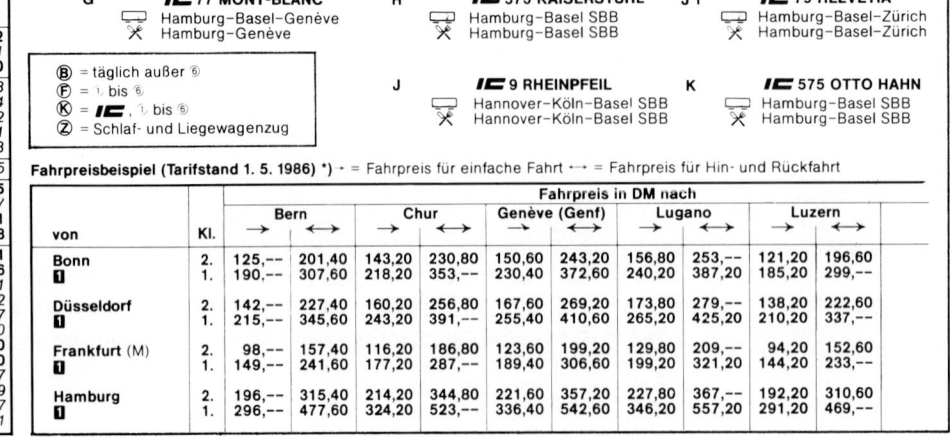

über Basel	G **IC** ←
Hamburg Hbf	10.02
Bremen Hbf	▲10.11
Hannover Hbf	11.20
Dortmund Hbf	▲11.48
Essen Hbf	▲12.04
Düsseldorf Hbf	▲12.32
Köln Hbf	▲13.01
Bonn Hbf	▲13.23
Berlin Zoo	7.15
Frankfurt (M) Hbf	14.45
Saarbrücken Hbf	◪13.47
Karlsruhe Hbf	16.01
Basel Bad Bf ⊞ ○	17.38
Basel Bad Bf	17.41
Basel SBB ○	17.46
Bern ○	▯19.31
Spiez ○	20.52
Interlaken Ost ○	21.27
Brig ○	22.00
Lausanne ○	20.10
Genève ○	20.50
Zürich HB ○	18.57
Chur ○	20.39
Luzern ○	19.07
Lugano ○	21.51

G   **IC** 77 MONT-BLANC   H   **IC** 573 KAISERSTUHL   J 1   **IC** 79 HELVETIA
Hamburg–Basel–Genève   Hamburg–Basel SBB   Hamburg–Basel–Zürich
Hamburg–Genève   Hamburg–Basel SBB   Hamburg–Basel–Zürich

Ⓑ = täglich außer ⑥
Ⓕ = ①, bis ⑥
Ⓚ = **IC** , ① bis ⑥   J   **IC** 9 RHEINPFEIL   K   **IC** 575 OTTO HAHN
Ⓩ = Schlaf- und Liegewagenzug   Hannover–Köln–Basel SBB   Hamburg–Basel SBB
Hannover–Köln–Basel SBB   Hamburg–Basel SBB

Fahrpreisbeispiel (Tarifstand 1. 5. 1986) *) ← = Fahrpreis für einfache Fahrt ←→ = Fahrpreis für Hin- und Rückfahrt

von	Kl.	Bern →	←→	Chur →	←→	Genève (Genf) →	←→	Lugano →	←→	Luzern →	←→
Bonn ▯	2.	125,--	201,40	143,20	230,80	150,60	243,20	156,80	253,--	121,20	196,60
	1.	190,--	307,60	218,20	353,--	230,40	372,60	240,20	387,20	185,20	299,--
Düsseldorf ▯	2.	142,--	227,40	160,20	256,80	167,60	269,20	173,80	279,--	138,20	222,60
	1.	215,--	345,60	243,20	391,--	255,40	410,60	265,20	425,20	210,20	337,--
Frankfurt (M) ▯	2.	98,--	157,40	116,20	186,80	123,60	199,20	129,80	209,--	94,20	152,60
	1.	149,--	241,60	177,20	287,--	189,40	306,60	199,20	321,20	144,20	233,--
Hamburg ▯	2.	196,--	315,40	214,20	344,80	221,60	357,20	227,80	367,--	192,20	310,60
	1.	296,--	477,60	324,20	523,--	336,40	542,60	346,20	557,20	291,20	469,--

SITUATIONEN 1 Ausflüge

Stage 1	A	B
1	Has been hiking long and hard, would like to rest.	Is happy to offer A a seat.
	Asks where B is from.	Tells A.
	Asks whether B comes here often.	Is here for the first time; asks A same question.
	Has been coming here for many years; things are different now.	Asks what A means by that.
	Tells B; says it's time to be going.	Wishes A a pleasant day.
2	Asks B for permission to sit down.	Offers A a seat; makes small talk about crowd.
	Asks whether B comes here often.	Was one of the first customers here.
	Asks about specialties.	Says poultry dishes are superb, with a good choice of domestic wines.
	Asks B what attractions B thinks are especially interesting here.	Names some outdoor activities; prefers indoor activities – especially eating.
	Says B doesn't show it.	Does a lot of swimming; doesn't like to hike – always gets lost.
	Asks for directions to nearby castle.	Gives directions.
	Thanks; hopes to see B tomorrow.	Likewise, B's sure.
3	Says it's really time to be off – they have a long way to walk today.	Feels a bit slow this morning – didn't sleep very well and is tired.
	Can hardly wait to hit the trail.	Doesn't want to think about the hike.
	Portrays the view from on top.	Thinks a postcard would do just as well.
	Suggests a compromise – take the bus to the pass, have a bite to eat, and walk back down.	Says A always was very smart; thinks that's an excellent idea; talks about advantages of the plan.

Stage 2

Students will need some props here. Direct them to use any of the landscape pictures in this or other chapters (e.g. 13, *Wanderung*).

1

You are on a hike in the Alps with a blind Austrian friend, and you have stopped for a snack. Your view encompasses a broad valley that has been thickly settled, but you are mercifully far above the hubbub down below. Describe for your friend what you see, being as careful as possible to include details.

2

You have had a nice hike in the woods and have found an inviting – although crowded – inn for some refreshments. An inquisitive person at your table is eager to hear your impressions of leisure activities in German-speaking countries. Do the best you can.

3

A couple of Dutch hikers have been within sight all morning as you struggled up the trail from Kandersteg to the Gemmipaß. Now they have finally caught up with you. They are excited about the mountains, and so you decide to tell them about what happened to you yesterday on the steep trail that leads up to the Gemmipaß from Leukerbad to the south. They'll want to hear all about the animals, your clothing and hiking gear, and the other hikers who came to your rescue. (Don't forget that what happens when is very important in an exciting story.)

Versuchen Sie doch

By now you will have begun to suspect that the sheer difference in size between North America and Europe determines what sorts of trips one takes here and abroad. Suppose you are a student at the Universität Leipzig. Discuss with your East German roommate the restrictions or possibilities implied by linguistic, geographical, and political environments in Europe that are different from the ones you grew up with.

STRATEGIE – KULTUR UND SPRACHE

Expressions for "right" and "wrong"

It might be a good time to introduce the serious students to Farrell's *German Synonyms*.

Things and information are *richtig* ("correct") or *falsch* ("incorrect").

> Heute ist Dienstag, ja?   Ja, richtig.
> Sie haben den falschen Weg genommen.

To describe people who express opinions, use *haben + recht* or *unrecht*

> Ja, du hast recht. Wir haben den falschen Weg genommen.

Remind students of the confirmatory use of *nicht* (*wahr*), among whose many equivalents is the colloquial " . . . , right?" Use your own judgment about *Sie haben Mist gebaut* – You did that all *wrong*.

Words for "pleasure" and "fun(ny)"

Das macht (mir) Spaß.	*That's fun [for me]. (note the dative case)*
Viel Spaß!	*Have fun!*
Das tun wir zum Spaß.	*We're doing that for fun.*
Ich finde es lustig.	*I think it's funny [humorous].*
Das ist sehr komisch.	*That's funny [odd].*

It is probably time to review *gern* again.

Genießen is used particularly for pleasures of the senses or of items that can be consumed.

> Wir genießen es sehr.   *We really enjoy [relish, savor] it.*

In response to information, accomplishments, etc., use *sich freuen*.

> Das freut mich sehr.   *I'm really happy [greatly pleased] about that.*

You could introduce *Freut mich sehr* in response to an introduction; see special chapter "Feste und Feiertage."

Words for "country" and "government"

Das Land (¨er) is the geographical country, as found on a map.

> auf<u>s</u> (= auf *das*) Land gehen, fahren, etc.
> = to go or drive into the country (away from the city)
> auf *dem* Land = location in the countryside

Der Staat (-en) refers to a country or nation as a political entity.

> Die zwei deutschen Staaten heißen die BRD und die DDR.

Der Staat also means government, as a long-term system:

> Ich habe ein Stipendium vom Staat.   *I have a government scholarship.*

Maybe point out the meaning of *Regierung* as "political administration," since many dictionary-thumbing students imply that they are in the pay of the current power-wielders by using that word to describe their scholarships or the government as an employer.

   Explain *Staat* (or *Bundesstaat*) as U.S. "state," and *Land* ("-er) as West German "state" or "province."

Die "Deutsche Frage," oder: Was ist "deutsch?"

Refer to previous chapters on history (10, 14).

See note in Instructor's Guide.

A thoughtful traveler might be puzzled at signs over the ticket windows in the München train station. The categories are *Inland* (domestic), *Ausland* (foreign), and between the two, *Berlin und DDR.* At least in West Germany, East Germany is considered to be something other than a foreign country.

Maybe mention that the sign also conveys the notion that Berlin (whether East or West) is not part of East Germany.

See note in Instructor's Guide.

   The ambivalent relationship between East and West Germany surfaces elsewhere in the language and the culture of those for whom German, in one form or another, is a native tongue. East and West Germany share a single system of postal "ZIP" codes (*die Postleitzahl, -en*), though automobile license plate codes are quite different. In West Germany relations with East Germany are officially termed "*deutsch-deutsche Beziehungen*," as though the two parties were indeed but halves of a larger whole. "*Deutsch*," too, is the word commonly used to describe the language spoken by Austrians and Swiss. But Austrians and Swiss may also use the word *deutsch* in an uncomplimentary way. Thus a

West German tourist trying to get business to move along more rapidly in a Swiss post office might finally be told, *"Ach, seien Sie nicht so furchtbar deutsch!"* – "Don't be so doggone German," so pushy and efficient.

The often agonized, even bloody dispute about *"deutsch"* and *"Deutschland"* has deep historical roots. The word *deutsch* itself is derived from the ancient Germanic word for "people," and thus means simply "of the people." Our English words "German" and "Germany" are derived from the Latin word *germania*, whose origin is uncertain. The Romans applied the term "Germani" to the "barbarians" they encountered in certain regions north of Italy – but they also used many other terms to identify particular groups or tribes. French and Spanish use words for "German(y)" that are derived from *"alemanni,"* originally the name for the people living in what is now southwestern West Germany and western Switzerland, near the present French border.

Over recorded history European borders have changed radically, and some countries disappear and reappear on the map – notions difficult for many North Americans to comprehend intellectually, much less grasp emotionally. The word *Deutschland* itself is relatively new, and the absence of a unified Germany – regardless of boundaries and geographical or political terms – is not the exception but the rule in European history, as it is today. Only for brief periods has there been a relatively unified political entity encompassing even a large minority of German speakers, even within the area that modern non-Germans commonly think of as "Germany." The first such "Germany" carried a confusing name. Ordinarily mentioned by its shorter name, the "Holy Roman Empire," its full name was *"Das Heilige Römische Reich Deutscher Nation"* – the Holy Roman Empire of the German Nation. Its rulers – first among them Charlemagne (*Karl der Große*) – claimed the prestige of being the successors to the emperors of the dead Roman Empire. But the important phrase in this name is *"Deutscher* Nation." It expresses the vague but powerful notion that speakers of German, regardless of where they live, somehow belong to a larger whole or "Nation," with the word understood in a sense far different from our concept of "nation."

It is also difficult for us to understand that the idea of "nation" could also have implications for a culture's concept of its art (*die Kunst*). Much of the greatest German art was created when there was no united Germany of any kind. Consequently, there is in German culture a common conception that political unity and artistic greatness are contradictory, and indeed that art should be prized above politics. A phrase often encountered in discussions of *"die Deutsche Frage,"* and known to almost every adult German, is *"Das Land der Dichter und Denker"* – Germany defined as "the land of poets and thinkers." The ultimate expression of the same notion in music occurs at the end of Wagner's opera *Die Meistersinger*, whose hero addresses his people:

zerging' in Dunst	*Should the Holy Roman Empire*
das heil'ge röm'sche Reich,	*vanish in smoke and haze,*
uns bliebe gleich	*we would still have*
die heil'ge deutsche Kunst!	*Holy German Art.*

An ovation greeted the lines at what was perhaps the most spectacular recent staging of the opera, in 1963 at the rededication of the restored Nationaltheater in München. The opera house had been reduced to ruins by Allied bombers on October 2, 1943. *Die Meistersinger* was to have been performed that very evening. The year 1943 was one of the few in which there was indeed a large, unified Germany. By 1963 many Germans had come to prefer the art to the empire.

Maybe remark that often enough a culture's name for itself expresses – implicitly or explicitly – the notion that its members are the true "people."

Point out that the word *France* is by origin a German word. Maybe mention the use of *allemand* in the square-dance step "allemand left."

Note that the Latin origin of "nation" emphasizes an ethnic rather than a geographical or political definition: *natio* is derived from the past participle of *nasci*, "to be born."

Mit der Bahn sollten Sie Ihren Landgang beginnen, wenn Sie dieses
Zeichen finden. Abfahrt ab Altona
oder Hauptbahnhof.

Allgemeine Auskünfte,
Tel. 33 99 11

Ausflüge und Sonderfahrten
der DB, Tel. 1 15 38

Reisevorschläge und Sonder-
angebote der DB,
Tel. 1 15 39

Autovermietung

(Auswahl)

Autorent
City – Gertrudenstraße 3,
Tel. 33 59 98

Auto Sixt
Ellmenreichstraße 26,
Tel. 24 14 66
Flughafen,
Tel. 50 82–3 05/3 40

Avis
Drehbahn 15–25,
Tel. 34 16 51
Flughafen, Tel. 50 83 14

Car Rent
Heidenkampsweg 54,
Tel. 23 23 73

Europcar-Autovermietung
Spaldingstraße 77–79,
Tel. 24 44 55

Hertz
Amsinckstraße 45,
Tel. 50 83 02
Flughafen, Tel. 50 83 02

InterRent
Rödingsmarkt 14,
Tel. 5 08 28 12

Bankservice

(am Wochenende)
**Deutsche Verkehrs-Kredit-Bank
im Hauptbahnhof**
2 DVKB-Wechselstuben
tägl. 7.30–20.00 bzw. 22.00 Uhr
So. 10.00–18.00 Uhr
Im Flughafen: Deutsche Bank
täglich 6.30–22.30 Uhr
**Deutsche Verkehrs-Kredit-Bank
im Altonaer Bahnhof**
Mo.–Sa. 7.30–13.00 und
13.45–20.00 Uhr,
sonn- und feiertags 10.00–13.00,
13.45–18.00 Uhr

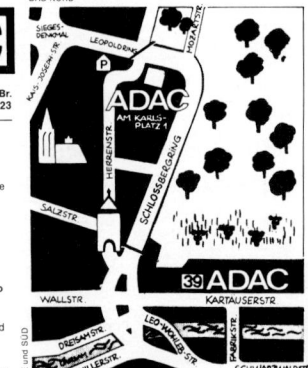

Reisebüro

1

Pauschal package-(prearranged)

ČSSR common abbreviation for "die Tschechoslowakische Sozialistische Republik"; you may also say "die Tschechoslowakei"

HERR JUNG	Guten Morgen. Ich war gerade beim Verkehrsamt. Man hat mir dort gesagt, Sie hätten Auskunft über Pauschalreisen von München nach Österreich.
FRAU EIGER	Ja. An was haben Sie gedacht? Tagesausflüge nach Innsbruck oder Salzburg?
HERR JUNG	Ich dachte zuerst an eine Wochenendreise nach Wien, und vielleicht später eine längere Reise in die ČSSR.
FRAU EIGER	Hier können wir Ihnen vieles anbieten. Interessieren Sie sich für Gruppenreisen?
HERR JUNG	Gruppenreisen? Ja, wenn sie billiger sind und wenn man genug Zeit für sich hat. Ich möchte unabhängig sein.
FRAU EIGER	Ich gebe Ihnen zuerst einige Prospekte. Die können Sie sich mal anschauen. Dann können wir über Ihre Wünsche weitersprechen.

2

Neu!

Fahrradverleih

Neu: Das Entdecker-Fahrrad.
In die Pedale! Und kreuz und quer durch Hamburg. Bei der Fremden-verkehrszentrale können Sie vom 1.4. bis 30.9.85 Fahrräder nach Maß leihen. Für 2,– DM pro Stunde, 8,– DM pro Tag oder 20,– DM für das Wochenende (Freitag bis Sonntag).
Mietzeit: werktags 8–18 Uhr, samstags 8–14.30 Uhr.
Sie buchen am besten im voraus. Direkt bei der Fremdenverkehrs-zentrale, Tel. 040/24 87 00.

FRAU MÖNCH	Der Zwei-Tage-Ausflug nach Lindau interessiert mich sehr. Könnten Sie das alles etwas näher beschreiben?
FRAU GLADBACH	Ja, gern. "Zugreise 2. Klasse Lindau hin und zurück. Zwei Übernachtungen im Europahof, inklusive Frühstück DM 200,-. Abfahrt freitags um 14.30 vom 24.5 bis zum 25.10."
FRAU MÖNCH	Ich reise allein. Ist das der Preis für ein Einzelzimmer?
FRAU GLADBACH	Nein, das ist der Preis pro Person in einem Doppelzimmer. Für ein Einzelzimmer gibt es einen Zuschlag von DM 20,-.
FRAU MÖNCH	Nun, das klingt sehr schön, aber ich wollte vielleicht auch einen Tagesausflug in die Schweiz machen.
FRAU GLADBACH	Das können Sie auch. Ich würde folgenden Vorschlag machen: Wenn Sie in Lindau ein Fahrrad mieten, können Sie damit nach Friedrichshafen fahren. Dann fahren Sie mit der Fähre von Friedrichshafen nach Romanshorn in der Schweiz. Dort fahren Sie immer am Bodensee entlang.
FRAU MÖNCH	Und vielleicht einen Tag in Stein am Rhein bleiben, dann mit der Fähre nach Meersburg, ja?
FRAU GLADBACH	Richtig. Da sehen Sie viel und genießen auch die frische Luft. Das lohnt sich wirklich sehr.

3

The speech is long, but note that it is made up of discrete parts. Encourage students to create such ACTFL/ETS Advanced utterances by setting up skeleton notes outlining stages in the description of procedures, events, etc.

FRAU KEULER	Nach Leipzig? Die Reise müßten Sie schon 6 Wochen im voraus buchen, wegen dem Visum.
DR. BOND	Wir sind aber nur noch 2 Wochen in Europa.
FRAU KEULER	Es gäbe eine zweite Möglichkeit. Tagesvisen für Ostberlin erhalten Sie direkt an den Grenzübergängen in der Stadt. Sie reisen einfach nach West-Berlin – per Zug oder Flugzeug. Das Hotel müssen Sie im voraus buchen.
DR. BOND	Muß ich dann jeden Tag über die Grenze, wenn ich länger bleiben möchte?
FRAU KEULER	Nein. Die Verlängerung erhalten Sie im Hotel automatisch. Das können Sie also dort erledigen.

STRUKTUR 2

Virtually anything from previous chapters that uses a past tense is fair game for review and *A.A. §39* then expansion with *noch nicht/ kein.* Student A needs only add *schon* to questions formulated earlier: *Haben Sie X gesehen?* Push for fluency by asking the student who responds with *noch nicht/kein* to follow up the negation with an explanatory sentence (*Nein, den Dom haben wir noch nicht gesehen. Das machen wir morgen.*).

Verbs §11; Nouns §15

Both varieties are extremely difficult for Intermediate-level students to manage, and mistakes caused by English interference will be irritating. In the one case the substitution of English present perfect (progressive) for German *seit* + present tense will convey misinformation (**Ich habe hier für 2 Jahre gelebt.*). In the other, the overuse of *für* in imitation of "for," when the interval is commencing (rather than anticipated), may annoy one for several reasons – exaggerated imitation of English future tense, weakness in the

Verbs §§62,63

The topic tests the limits of even the best students, and is beyond the grasp of those who are struggling with the rest of the material. Especially troubled will be those who seek one-for-one correspondence not only in vocabulary, but also in structure. English simply offers no comparable pattern.

See notes in Instructor's Guide.

1. Negating *schon: noch nicht* and *noch kein-*

The entire action isn't negated – just its timing.

- ● **Noch nicht** negates an <u>entire clause</u>.   not yet

  Ist es **schon** gekommen?   Nein, es ist **noch nicht** gekommen.

- ● **Noch kein** negates a *noun*.   not any/none yet

  Haben Sie schon Kinder, Herr Schanz?
        Nein, wir haben **noch keine** Kinder.

2. Stretch-of-time phrases

● action beginning in the past and continuing

Use the present tense + *seit.*

> Wir **machen** diese Wanderung *seit* 40 Jahren.
> *We've been taking this hike for 40 years now.*

> Ich **mache** meinen Urlaub **seit** Jahren hier.
> *I've been vacationing here for years.*

accusative, etc. We suggest you concentrate on *seit* + present tense, both because the error is more egregious and because the intermediate student will find it easier to talk about what indeed has happened rather than what is anticipated.

● action beginning now and continuing into the future

Use present tense + *noch* + an accusative time phrase.

> Wir bleiben **noch ein halbes Jahr** bei meinen Verwandten.
> *We're staying for another 6 months . . .*

> Wir sind nur **noch 2 Wochen** in Europa.
> *We'll be in Europe for just 2 more weeks.*

3. Past tense forms of some common verbs

In ordinary narration, most verbs appear in the present perfect. But *sein, haben,* the modals, and a few other *very common* verbs are frequently used in the past tense, even side-by-side with other verbs that appear in the present perfect.

> Gestern **war** Montag. Du **hast** den ganzen Tag **geschlafen.**
>   past ↗   ↖   present perfect   ↗

> Wir **wollten** die Burg besichtigen, aber wir **haben** uns **verlaufen.**
>   past ↗   ↖ present perfect ↗

Here German and English differ greatly. Overuse of the German past tense will make you sound extremely stilted.

But do learn the past tense forms of at least these very common verbs.

wissen – *wußte-*	glauben – *glaubte-*	denken – *dachte-*	kommen – *kam-*
fragen – *fragte-*	sagen – *sagte-*	geben – *gab-*	sehen – *sah-*

Stage 1

Set up these exercises either with actual maps and other travel information or else by having the class construct imaginary information in schematic form (*Wie heißt das Hotel in Salzburg?*). By now students should be able to invent such material freely, at least in the sense of elaborating on the basic information provided in the realia.

This is a good opportunity to anticipate the material about East Germany. A wall map of Europe, including the Soviet Union, would be helpful. The verisimilitude of students' suggestions about places to sunbathe in Eastern Europe is

	A	**B**
1	Is interested in package tours of Austria.	Has two available; asks how independent A would like to be.
	Doesn't want to worry about basics, but would like lots of free time.	Suggests a possibility, listing cities.
	Agrees; what are price and length of trip?	Tells both.
	Thinks a shorter trip might just be better – and cheaper.	Suggests other possibilities.
2	(Im Reisebüro der DDR in Berlin.)	
	Wants information about trips to other East bloc countries.	Suggests which cities A could visit.
	Is interested in Prag.	Asks whether A has a visa.
	Has no visa; inquires about application procedures.	Suggests A visit other cities in the DDR first, then venture to other countries.
	Wants to do some serious sunbathing.	Suggests appropriate places in the Warsaw Pact countries.
	Asks what to do on vacation there.	Names activities.

Stage 2

less important than either their increased awareness of such countries or the review of *in*, *nach*, time phrases, weather terms, etc.

***3: per Autostop** hitchhiking*

1

You are in a travel office in Basel. Ask about

a) possibilities for outdoor recreation in nearby cities;
b) the cost of rail and/or air transportation to Wien, Dresden, and Luzern;
c) package tours to the Rheinland.

Be sure to give plausible reasons for wanting to undertake each of these activities.

2

The travel bureau has just called you, wondering whether you want to go ahead with payment on your flight to East Berlin. You have not yet received your visa from the authorities and are clearly in a bind.

a) Try to put off payment until the very last moment, and ask about inspiring the East German authorities to expedite your visa request.
b) Make a suggestion about an alternative plan to visit East Berlin – even without a formal visa.

3

Ein portugiesischer Student in der Jugendherberge fragt Sie, wie man am besten Bayern kennenlernt.

a) Sagen Sie ihm die Vorteile und Nachteile von einer *Gruppenreise*.
b) Vergleichen Sie eine solche Reise mit einer Tour *per Autostop*.
c) Schlagen Sie ihm vor, daß er bei einem Reisebüro Information suchen soll.

4

As you pack for a weekend visit to East Berlin, you notice that your companion is taking along some marijuana. Having learned that it is illegal to drive in East Germany with any trace of alcohol at all in one's blood, you suspect that the drug laws there are quite severe. Say what you think you must.

Versuchen Sie doch

Sie waren letztes Jahr einige Wochen lang in München und haben viel gesehen und gemacht. Jetzt planen Sie eine Rückkehr nach der bayrischen Hauptstadt und möchten natürlich etwas Neues machen. Sagen Sie Ihren Freunden, wohin Sie in der Stadt gehen wollen, was Sie in verschiedenen Museen usw. unternehmen möchten und warum Sie sich so sehr dafür interessieren.

219

Chapter 22

BERLIN – DIE GETEILTE STADT/ BERLIN – "HAUPTSTADT DER DDR"

Thäl'mann (tâl'män), Ernst. 1886–1944. German Communist leader; member of the Reichstag (1924); first leader (1925) of newly founded Red Front combat group; arrested and imprisoned during National Socialist revolution (1933).

Checkpoint Charlie.

Songs and poems appropriate to chapter: Berlin songs (M. Dietrich specialty); Morgenstern: *"Palmström"* (note *"ungeschneutzt"* – past participle as adjective) *"Der Werwolf"*; Jürgen Becker: "You are Leaving the American Sector."

FUNKTIONEN – KONTEXTE – STRUKTUREN

Looking ahead

You'll be arriving in Berlin, looking at historical sites in both parts of the city, making arrangements for an extended stay in East Berlin, and exploring the East German outlook on history, society, and personal matters.

You will be using:

- *wollen, daß* . . . and *sagen, daß* . . . to transfer requests
- adjectival nouns (the young and the old)
- past participles as adjectives (The museum is clos<u>ed</u>)
- *wer* in its accusative (*wen*) and dative (*wem*) cases – to who(m), by who(m)

220

Berlin – die geteilte Stadt

1

Warte/Zeit
So steht es That's what it says

The Brandenburger Tor (Brandenburg Gate), at the end of the central boulevard Unter den Linden, symbolizes the division of Germany and Berlin. Built in 1788–93 as a victory monument.

2

zerstört: See note in Instructor's Guide.

der Angriff attack
Haupt chief, main
das Reich empire; Kaiserreich German Empire (1871–1918)

Geschlossen – "Die Deutsche Frage bleibt offen, solange das Brandenburger Tor geschlossen ist." – Bundespräsident Richard von Weiszäcker

3

East German youth organizations; their activities include much political indoctrination.

Feel free to mention that the East German and Soviet soldiers still goose-step.

Hotel Metropol **4**

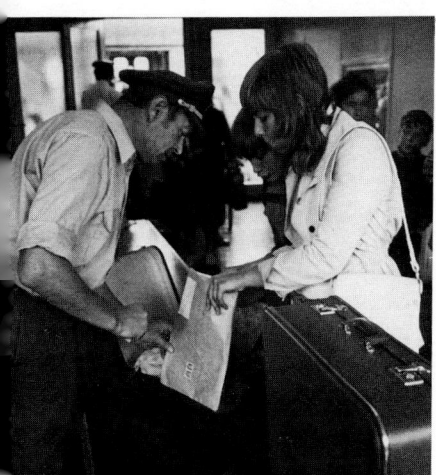

Bebra (DDR) – Zollerklärung.

HERR TÜTSCH	Schade, daß wir an der Grenze so lange warten mußten. Er wollte, daß wir jeden Koffer aufmachen!
FRAU TÜTSCH	Aber lange Wartezeiten sind relativ selten seit 1972 – so steht es im Reiseführer. Und der andere Beamte war ganz nett.
HERR TÜTSCH	Ja, der hat sich sehr für deinen neuen Schach-Computer interessiert.
FRAU WALTHERS	So. Die Mauer. Und drüben Ost-Berlin mit dem Brandenburger Tor.
FRAU FRICK	Das große Gebäude auf dieser Seite muß also der Reichstag sein. Was steht darüber im Reiseführer?
FRAU WALTHERS	"1933 durch Brand zerstört. Bombenangriffe 1945. Renoviert nach dem Krieg. Hauptsymbol des Kaiserreichs wie auch der Nazizeit. . . ."
FRAU FRICK	Also, nicht weit von hier hat sich Hitler erschossen – das war am 30. April 1945.
FRAU WALTHERS	". . . Jetzt Museum mit Ausstellung: 'Fragen an die Deutsche Geschichte.' Samstags geschlossen."
FRÄULEIN HÄNDEL	Was tun die Kleinen da mit den Blumen?
HERR HAHN	Das ist die Ewige Flamme für die Opfer des Faschismus und Militarismus.
FRÄULEIN HÄNDEL	Das sind große Wörter. Was verstehen Kinder davon?
HERR HAHN	Eigentlich lernen sie viel davon in den Schulen – auch bei den Pionieren und der Freien Deutschen Jugend.
FRÄULEIN HÄNDEL	Naja. Höchste Zeit, daß wir draußen gehen. Ich glaube, ich höre Marschmusik.
HERR HAHN	Ja, jetzt kommen die Soldaten. Die aus der DDR marschieren, und die aus Amerika fotografieren.
FRAU SCHUCHARDT	Ja, hier ist Metropol. Bitte, sprechen Sie etwas lauter. Die Verbindung ist schlecht.
MR. ROSENGRANT	Ich hätte gern Auskunft über einen Aufenthalt bei Ihnen. Das wäre für Mitte April. Und ich wollte auch fragen, ob ich mit meiner VISA-Karte zahlen kann.
FRAU SCHUCHARDT	Selbstverständlich. Kreditkarten sind willkommen – mit Zahlung in internationalen Währungen.
MR. ROSENGRANT	Und wo ist der beste Grenzübergang?
FRAU SCHUCHARDT	Für Amerikaner gibt es verschiedene Möglichkeiten – vor allem Checkpoint Charlie für Autos und Fußgänger, und dann auch Friedrichstraße mit der U-Bahn. Das ist etwas näher, aber nur am Tag geöffnet.
MR. ROSENGRANT	Muß ich vorher ein Visum bestellen?
FRAU SCHUCHARDT	Nein. Das Tagesvisum können Sie am Grenzübergang bekommen, und wir verlängern es für Sie im Hotel.

STRUKTUR 1

1. Having someone else do something

- precise way

  Er wollte, daß wir jeden Koffer aufmachen!
  He wanted us to open every suitcase!

  Er sagte uns, daß wir jeden Koffer aufmachen sollten.

  He told us $\left\{ \begin{array}{c} \text{that we should} \\ \text{to} \end{array} \right\}$ open every suitcase.

- easier – but not as precise

  Wir mußten jeden Koffer aufmachen.
  We had to open every suitcase.
     (that is, we assume, because he wanted or told us to do it)

2. Adjectival nouns: obvious noun omitted for the sake of efficiency

The adjective becomes a noun and takes endings as though the noun were there.
     Earlier you learned the patterns

   der   Deutsch**e** – the German (male)   (= der deutsche Mann)

   die   Deutsch**e** – the German (female)   (= die deutsche Frau)

   die   Deutsch**en** – the Germans (all)   (= die deutschen Menschen)

The same system is used with many other adjectives and implied nouns.

   Was tun **die** Klein**en** da mit den Blumen? (= **die** klein**en** Kinder)
   What are the little ones (the little children) doing there with the flowers?

3. The genitive case

- main function: another way to show possession

  Hauptsymbol des **Kaiserreichs** = Hauptsymbol *vom* Kaiserreich
  Main symbol **of the empire** or The **empire's** main symbol

- forms

Masculine and neuter convey a fairly strong signal: de_s_____(e)_s

   Hauptsymbol de_s Kaiserreich_s

The feminine and plural forms are difficult to recognize – they look like the masculine nominative or the feminine dative.

   Mitglieder de_r Freien Deutschen Jugend
   Hauptstädte de_r sozialistischen Länder

4. Past participles as adjectives

ORDINARY ADJECTIVE   PARTICIPLE AS ADJECTIVE
Das Museum ist **groß**.   Das Museum ist samstags **geschlossen**.
ein **frisches** Ei   ein **weichgekochtes** Ei

Stage 1	A	B
1	Says took the subway to East Berlin. Asks how long B had to wait there. Just a few minutes. No hassles.	Says went through Checkpoint Charlie. Quite some time. How about A's wait? Had to leave a copy of Time magazine and two cassettes. Can pick them up upon leaving East Berlin.
	Glad there were no hassles – was carrying a book by a writer who had emigrated from the DDR. A friend wanted A to bring the book to a relative there.	Why? Considers A brave, but foolhardy.

2

See realia for maps of Berlin and descriptions of sights.

Scene: Observation deck of the broadcast tower (130m) in Berlin (West)

A	B
Comments on the height.	Comments on the weather.
Did B bring the map?	Sure. What is A looking for?
What's that straight to the east?	Looks like a tower.
Has to be the East German TV tower.	Verifies with map.

(A and B then use the tower as an orientation point to list a collection of landmarks in both parts of the city. Example:)

Where's the airport?	To the right of the tower and not as far away.

3

Szene: oben auf dem Fernsehturm (365m) in Berlin (Ost)

(Repeat exercise No. 2 above, with comments about West Berlin landmarks, about yesterday's activities, or about plans for the rest of the stay. Here's a start:)

That's the Olympic Stadium.	Is there a soccer game there tomorrow?
Is that the zoo?	Yes. Went there on earlier trip.

Stage 2

1

Tell someone what to expect at the passport and customs check conducted on the train between München and Dresden. Provide also information about train departure/arrival times and ticket costs.

2

Der Terrorismus ist immer ein Problem für Amerikaner in Europa. Die Kontrolle am Flughafen in West-Berlin war viel strenger als am Grenzübergang Checkpoint Charlie bei Ihrer Einreise in die DDR. Erzählen Sie, was Ihnen passiert ist – und warum.

3

Ihre Bekannte spricht sehr wenig Deutsch und hat Angst vorm Telefonieren. Sie möchte, daß Sie das Hotel Newa in Dresden anrufen. Ihre Bekannte braucht folgende Auskunft:

a) Einzelzimmer – Preis? Nächstes Wochenende frei?
b) Zahlung – Reiseschecks (AUS$) OK?
c) Verkehrsverbindung vom Dresdner Bahnhof
d) Welche anderen Hotels in Dresden empfiehlt man?
e) Kontrolle an der Grenze – Kassettenrekorder OK?

VSd: Appropriate realia are provided. Variations: 1) study the information and tell someone what to do; 2) without seeing the information, quiz partner who has the information.

Versuchen Sie doch

The task is indeed challenging, and those better students who attempt it may easily fly off into higher realms of politics. Bring them down to earth by encouraging them to rephrase abstract notions in simpler terms. Thus "There's not much difference between the two ideologies" becomes "*Der Faschist denkt und tut wie der Sozialist.*"

You are beginning to find the historical scenes in Berlin rather depressing, and you've seen enough museums too. Can you use your print resources, or else information from a friendly local, to discuss something more lighthearted to do? How about a sports game, a night out, or a boat ride?

As you watch the East German soldiers on parade at the Monument to the Victims of Fascism and Militarism, you notice that they goose-step – something you have seen only in World War II movies and newsreels. Your dictionary gives the activity as "*im Stechschritt marschieren.*" Discuss the implications of what you have observed.

Schließung des Gebäudes 22.00 Uhr

223

STRATEGIE — KULTUR UND SPRACHE

Cosmopolitan Berlin **Weltstadt Berlin**

A visit to Berlin can be a stunning education in history and modern politics. Perhaps nowhere else on earth can one experience, so intensively and in such a small space, the events that have created our modern world. Berlin is a source and chief symbol of the National Socialism that brought about the Second World War and the Holocaust. There, too, can be seen in the most vivid form the Wall – the confrontation between superpowers and their ideologies that affects every part of our lives. The city's role in the history of Western culture is almost as important. Before 1933 and the Third Reich it was a world center of science and technology, and the rival of New York and Paris as a center of mass entertainment and artistic innovation. Even now the city, tortuously divided and no longer the capital of an empire, offers superb cultural attractions, above all orchestras and museums that are the equal of those in any other city in the world.

Despite the relaxation of tensions that was formalized by diplomatic agreements in the early 1970's, East Berlin and East Germany remain unknown territory to most Westerners and even to many West Germans. The Allied Powers still consider the city's status unresolved, pending a peace treaty that would formally end the Second World War. East Germany considers East Berlin to be its official capital, and emphasizes the point by constantly employing the phrase "Berlin – Hauptstadt der DDR." Personal relationships between East Germans and visitors from the West can be quite cordial, but there are causes of friction. Political opinions – or at least those that are not favorable to the East – cannot be discussed with complete openness. Moreover, East Germans have developed enough commitment to their society and enough pride in their country's economic revival that they resent the condescension of Western visitors.

Major Political Figures Associated with Berlin

Thälmann, Ernst. *Hamburg 1886, †KZ Buchenwald 1944, dt. Politiker; urspr. Transportarbeiter; seit 1903 Sozialdemokrat, 1917 Mitgl. der USPD, 1919 der KPD (seit 1925 deren Vors.); 1924–33 MdR; kandidierte 1925 u. 1932 bei der Reichspräsidentenwahl; 1933 verhaftet, KZ-Haft; erschossen.

See note in Instructor's Guide.

Webster's Biographical Dictionary lists all but Brandt. Mention *Who's Who* and similar resources.

Use your own judgment in bringing up the movie and song about the ship.

We offer here a list of historical figures whose names you might well encounter in Berlin – on monuments or street signs, or perhaps just in casual remarks. Under such circumstances you might find *only* the name, and nothing more. Not knowing more could be mystifying or even embarrassing if everyone else seems to regard such knowledge as commonplace. Biographical information can be found in many reference works, including *Webster's Biographical Dictionary*. You may be pleasantly surprised to discover that you can understand many things in those resources. See what you can do with our list. To sharpen your curiosity we have added some gossipy tidbits.

Friedrich der Große – Wishing to evade the duties of royalty, he sought to flee with a friend. His father – Friedrich Wilhelm, der Große Kurfürst – sentenced both to death. Young Friedrich was forced to witness the execution of his friend and then given a reprieve.
Kaiser Wilhelm II – "Kaiser Bill" habitually tucked his deformed arm into the front of his coat and thus set a fashion in portrait photography.
Otto von Bismarck – His name has been given to the capital of a U.S. state, to a breakfast roll, and to a type of herring.
Paul von Hindenburg – Whoever named the blimp had a sense of humor.
Willy Brandt – An illegitimate child, he left Germany to join anti-Hitler forces in Norway. An espionage scandal toppled the government he led.
Rosa Luxemburg – "Red Rosa" to friends, and to the enemies who murdered her.

East Berlin: currencies, Interhotels, Intershops — and the black market

The East German mark, like the currencies (*Währungen*) of other Communist-bloc countries, is not a freely convertible, commonly accepted international monetary unit of "hard currency." That dry economic statement can be expressed in much more vivid, personal terms. East German citizens live with the upsetting and even corrupting fact that in their own country their own currency is less desired than almost any of the Western currencies. Western currency is needed to purchase valued Western imports. While the government insists on an official exchange rate (*Kurs*) of DM 1 to 1 M, the rate in West German banks is closer to DM 1 = 4 M. One result is a lively black market economy in goods and currency; the black market exchange rate is usually between 5 and 6 East German marks for 1 DM. The attitudes of East German citizens toward obtaining hard currency vary. Some will capitalize on any opportunity. Others, like the few semi-independent craftspeople, need hard currency to purchase scarce ingredients or high-quality raw materials produced in the West. Still others idealistically seek to avoid the habit of dependence on Western currency and goods.

East Germany's rulers live with a similar anxious need, but on larger terms. The country must constantly replenish its stock of "hard" currencies so that it can pay for Western imports. One result is a ceaseless demand that the economy produce more exportable goods, though that demand is necessarily tempered by concessions to the populace, which demands consumer goods and is proud of its living standard, the highest in the Communist bloc. A source of large sums of hard currency in small amounts is the obligatory currency exchange (*der Pflichtumtausch*); visitors to East Germany are required to purchase daily the equivalent of 25 marks at the official exchange rate. Recognizing the strong family ties between many West and East Germans, the government permits reasonably free access from the West; visitors often bring gifts of Western currency. More reprehensible is the acceptance of hard West German currency in exchange for the release of political prisoners or the legal emigration of dissidents.

Far more evident to the ordinary traveler, however, are the *Interhotels* and the related *Intershops*. Foreign visitors who do not have private accommodations must stay, by advance reservation, in one of the several dozen government-operated Interhotels located in larger cities. They charge luxury rates – though no more than their counterparts in the West – and they indeed provide luxury accommodations. Thus both sides get a fair deal, and East Germany can improve its reputation for high-quality products. Moreover, the government increases its hard currency resources, for the Interhotels are "Valuta" institutions; they accept only in Western currencies, above all the Deutsche Mark.

The Intershops, often located in or near Interhotels, do not advertise their presence conspicuously, but everyone knows where they are. They sell Western goods – to anyone, and at a fair price, but only for Western Valuta. They serve not only to attract the funds of Western visitors, but also to get back into government hands Valuta that has found its way into the pockets of private citizens. The Intershops are not particularly large, but they offer an extremely wide range of desirable wares. Luxury, though, is in the eye of the beholder. Some of the items, like fine liqueurs, most Westerners would consider luxuries, though not astronomically expensive. Others, like high-quality textile yardage, household hardware, power tools, and even motorcycles, do not seem extravagant to Westerners; the presence of these goods reveals much about certain chronic shortages in the East German planned economy.

ABOVE: Berlin (DDR) – Alexanderplatz. Can you use your maps to identify the landmarks and to locate where the photograph was taken?
BELOW: Berlin (DDR) – Marx-Engels-Platz mit Dom (l.) und Palast der Republik (r.)

Blick von Berlin (West) nach Berlin (DDR). Can you use your map to identify the landmarks?

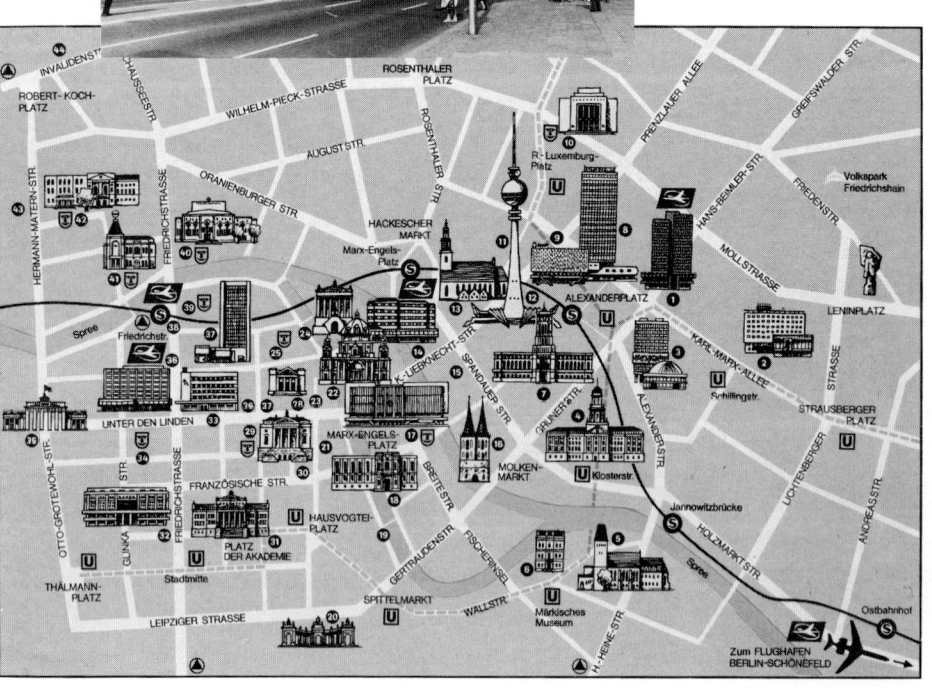

Berlin – Hauptstadt der DDR

INTERFLUG-Stadtbüros
Town Offices

1 Reisebüro der DDR Generaldirektion
2 Interhotel „Berolina" Kino „International"
3 Haus des Lehrers mit Kongreßhalle
4 Sitz des Ministerrates der DDR
5 Märkisches Museum
6 Ermelerhaus
7 Rotes Rathaus
8 Interhotel „Stadt Berlin"
9 Centrum-Warenhaus
10 Volksbühne
11 Fernsehturm
12 Berlin-Information
13 Marienkirche
14 Palasthotel
15 Marx-Engels-Forum
16 Nikolaikirche
17 Palast der Republik mit „Theater im Palast"
18 Sitz des Staatsrates der DDR
19 Jungfernbrücke
20 Spittelkolonnade
21 Ministerium für Auswärtige Angelegenheiten
22 Dom
23 Museum für Deutsche Geschichte
24 Staatliches Museum zu Berlin
National-Galerie
Altes Museum · Pergamon-Museum · Bode-Museum

Berlin – Capital of the GDR

25 Maxim-Gorki-Theater
26 Deutsche Staatsbibliothek
27 Humboldt-Universität
28 Mahnmal für die Opfer des Faschismus und Militarismus
29 Deutsche Staatsoper
30 St.-Hedwigs-Kathedrale
31 Schauspielhaus
32 Haus der Sowjetischen Wissenschaft und Kultur
33 Interhotel „Unter den Linden"
34 Komische Oper
35 Brandenburger Tor
36 Interhotel „Metropol"
37 Handelszentrum
38 INTERFLUG-Stadtbüro Bahnhof Friedrichstraße
39 Metropol-Theater und Distel
40 Friedrichstadtpalast
41 Berliner Ensemble
42 Deutsches Theater und Kammerspiele
43 Charité
44 Naturkundemuseum Grenzübergang

Berlin – "Hauptstadt der DDR"

1

FRAU SCHREIBER	Die Mauer kam 1961. Vorher konnte jeder in den Westen reisen.
ANDREW TALMAN	Und nachher?
FRAU SCHREIBER	Nach der Mauer wußten wir alle, daß nur hier unsere Heimat ist. Und heute ist unser Lebensstandard der höchste in den sozialistischen Ländern.
ANDREW TALMAN	Was würden Sie den Flüchtlingen aus der Zeit vor 1961 sagen, wenn Sie mit ihnen sprechen könnten?
FRAU SCHREIBER	Ich würde ihnen sagen: "Schade, daß ihr weggegangen seid. Schaut nur, was wir geleistet haben."

leisten achieve

2

HERR SONNEMANN	Also der Bebelplatz, vorher der Opernplatz. Da haben die Faschisten im Jahre 1933 Bücher von jüdischen wie auch von allen liberalen Autoren verbrannt.
CAROL BARNES	Bücher von wem, zum Beispiel?
HERR SONNEMANN	Natürlich die Bücher von Marx und Lenin. Es würde wahrscheinlich die Amerikaner in der Gruppe interessieren, daß auch Bücher von Jack London in der Nazizeit verboten waren.

Jack London schrieb The Call
of the Wild *und* Nanook of the
North *und war auch Sozialist.*

3

FRÄULEIN LEOPOLD	Aber was bedeutet Freiheit, wenn man auf der Straße leben muß, so wie in New York?
ANGELA SACCO	Schade, daß Sie nicht nach Amerika reisen dürfen. So viele arme Leute gibt es nicht.
FRÄULEIN LEOPOLD	Aber es gibt sie, und in unserem sozialistischen Staat sieht man keine Armen.
ANGELA SACCO	Und keine Reichen!
FRÄULEIN LEOPOLD	Ja, das meine ich eben – hier sind alle gleich, und der Staat garantiert uns eine Ausbildung und eine Stelle.
ANGELA SACCO	Oh? Verdient der Fabrikarbeiter genausoviel wie der Generalsekretär der Partei?

die Fabrik factory

Source: *East Germany: A Country Study*, ed. Eugene K. Keefe (Washington, D.C.: U.S. Government Printing Office, 1986), p. 132: early 1981, factory worker: M1.000–1.200; East German government publication *Zum Wohle des Volkes* (1985), p. 15: M1.100/month in 1984.

4

HERR SCHWEITZER	Das jährliche Einkommen ist also durchschnittlich 12.000 Mark in der DDR.
ADRIANUS KEIJ	Wieviel kostet denn ein neues Auto?
HERR SCHWEITZER	17 000 Mark. Man muß aber einige Jahre warten. Ich könnte morgen meinen alten Wartburg für 35 000 Mark verkaufen.
ADRIANUS KEIJ	Moment! Ein neues Auto kostet 17 000 Mark, und ein gebrauchtes 35 000?
HERR SCHWEITZER	Ja, doppelt so viel, weil es keine Wartezeit gibt.

5

HERR LIEBKNECHT	Wer hat die Renovierung der Kirche bezahlt, wenn man fragen darf? Nicht der Staat, oder?
FRAU GUSTAV	Der Staat hat einen Teil der Kosten bezahlt, und Christen aus der BRD haben mit der Restauration der Gemälde geholfen.

STRUKTUR 2

Verbs §69

1. More about inseparable-prefix verbs: their participles

no ge-

verbrennen	Da haben die Faschisten Bücher **verbrannt**.
bezahlen	Wer hat die Renovierung **bezahlt**?
erschießen	Hier hat sich Hitler **erschossen**.

Certainly the reading materials offer opportunity to encourage comprehension of the point, but speaking exercises in which students discuss various ideologies will likely go nowhere. You might well use the opportunity to review a construction with which many students will still be having difficulty: the feminine *-in* suffix, and the corresponding masculine and plural forms, in nationalities and related nouns. Check whether your students can point to one or more people and use *Freund, Freunde, Freundin*, and *Freundinnen* accurately – in the nominative, accusative, and dative, and with various possessive pronouns.

2. An important noun-formation pattern

-ismus = English -ism
-ist = English -ist

Many words for ideologies ("-isms") are international. In German they are *der*-nouns. There may be slight differences in spelling.

| der Faschismus | "fascism" | der Militarismus | "militarism" |
| der Feminismus | "feminism" | der Chauvinismus | "superpatriotism," "chauvinism" |

The noun for the person who advocates the ideology ends with the suffix *-ist*.

der Faschist (-en)   der Militarist (-en)   der Kapitalist (-en)

Feminine forms add the suffix *-in*.

die Feminist*in* (singular)   die Feminist*innen* (plural)

Pronouns §21

Set up lower-level exercises in which Student A offers an utterance that establishes a context and case (*"Ich habe deine Schwester gesehen"*), to which Student B responds with a form of *wer* (*"Wen hast du gesehen?"*).

3. More about *wer*

cases: **wer, wen, wem**

von wem?	by whom?	⟨formal English
	by who?	⟨casual English
	who by?	⟨very casual English

Wer, like other pronouns, adheres to the principles of grammatical case. It may help you to remember that its forms are parallel to those of *er* and *der*.

nominative	**wer**	**er**	**der**
accusative	**wen**	**ihn**	**den**
dative	**wem**	**ihm**	**dem**

● placement of preposition – always *before* the pronoun

Von wem?   Mit wem?   Für wen?

Verbs §76

4. Preview of the passive

a form for emphasizing processes

werden: *present tense*
ich werde   wir werden
du *wirst*   ihr werdet
Sie werden   Sie werden
er/sie/es *wird* sie werden
                  past tense
                  ich wurde *etc.*

When past participles are used with *sein*, they indicate that the action described by the verb has reached a *fixed state or condition*. English uses the same pattern, with the verb "to be":

Das Museum *ist* geschlossen.   "The museum *is* closed."

To express an action as a process, rather than as a state, German uses the verb *werden*. English still uses forms of "to be."

Das Museum *wird* jetzt geschlossen.
[The museum isn't closed yet, but the doors are starting to move.]

Chapters 24 and 25 will deal more extensively with the passive.

Stage 1	A	B

1

Scene: East Berlin, foot of Fernsehturm

A	B
(visitor) Has two hours left in East Berlin. What to see?	(Works in DDR tourist office.) Suggests the Soviet War Memorial in Treptow (SE suburb).
Somewhat reluctant – is it far? Is there public transportation? What about walking?	Locates on map and estimates distance. Yes – streetcar. Not recommended: too far, little to see, S-Bahn is cheap
Still reluctant – not particularly interested in Soviet war memorials (but doesn't want to offend). Anything else in that direction?	Boat rides on the river.

Stage 2

See the East German hotel menu on page 95. The key word to convey to *one* partner only: *Kater* = hangover.

1

Your Interhotel breakfast menu lists something called a "*Katerfrühstück*." It looks fishy.

a) Find our something about the kinds of meat it contains.
b) Find out just what a *Katerfrühstück* is.
c) Explain why the breakfast is (or is not) appropriate to your condition.

2

You are staying at the Hotel Metropol in East Berlin. Last night you used the fill-in chart on the hotel room door-hanger card to order breakfast for this morning. No breakfast came, and you complained to the management, after which a nice breakfast was brought compliments of the house. After breakfast you cleaned up a little, which was when you found that the card had fallen down behind your suitcase. Your conscience prods you to go down to the front desk and correct the error.

3

Your bill for two nights at the Hotel Newa in Dresden amounts to DM250. You have a DM100 note to cover some of the bill, but wish to pay the rest in Canadian currency to avoid changing money unnecessarily. Ask whether that is possible, find out the exchange rate, and then complete the transaction. Can you get an extra copy of the bill so that you and your employer can have originals for your tax records?

4

You're waiting in line for a table at a restaurant in East Berlin. The waiter approaches, and you see that he intends to give you preference because you appear to be from the West. Explain to the waiter and the people ahead of you that

a) the people ahead of you were indeed ahead of you;
b) you would not mind sharing a table.

Versuchen Sie doch

Direct the students to the *Stadtchronik* for East Berlin in the *Drucksachen* section of the Study Text: "16 April 1945 Mit 2,5 Millionen Soldaten, 41 600 Geschützen und 7 500 Flugzeugen beginnt die Offensive der Sowjetarmee auf Berlin."

On your tour of East Berlin you have heard and read everywhere about the destruction caused by Anglo-American bombing in the battle over Berlin in World War II. Your tour guide then points out a building and says: "*So, meine Damen und Herren. Die St. Hedwigs-Kathedrale. Ein anglo-amerikanischer Bombenangriff im März 1943 hat sie vollkommen zerstört.*" You're tired of what you consider slanted comments about Anglo-American bombers and Soviet liberators. You think for a while and then speak. Perhaps you speak to the tour guide, perhaps you wait to let off steam until you are talking to a Westerner. In either case, try to adjust your tone to the situation.

You're intrigued by the range of social benefits that East Germans apparently enjoy. The guarantee of education and employment is particularly interesting. How would you follow up that theme, and how – given limited vocabulary – would you ask about other social programs, such as maternity leave and day care?

229

Chapter **23**

GEDENKSTÄTTEN/ RENTNER

Berlin (DDR) – Ehrenmal für die gefallenen sowjetischen Helden.

Berlin (West) – Memorials for persons killed while attempting to cross the wall.

ZUM ANDENKEN
an die am 11. Sept. 1895 durch den
ALTELS--GLETSCHERBRUCH
verunglückten Walliser:
JOSEPH ROTEN vice-Präs.
von Leukerbad,
HYACINTH TSCHOPP,
ALOIS GRICHTING,
KASPAR JEGER v. Turtmann,
ALOIS ROTH von Steg,
PAUL BRENNER von Steg.
Barmherziger Jesus
gieb ihnen die ewige Ruh!
R. J. P.

VON DIESER STELLE AUS
SPRACH DER PRÄSIDENT
DER VEREINIGTEN STAATEN
VON AMERIKA
JOHN F. KENNEDY
AM 23. JUNI 1963 ZU DER
KÖLNER BEVÖLKERUNG

FUNKTIONEN – KONTEXTE – STRUKTUREN

Poems appropriate to chapter:
Lenau: "O Menschenherz, was ist
dein Glück?"; Logau: "Das
menschliche Alter"; Hesse:
"Transzendieren"; Werfel:
"Elternlied"; Hofmannsthal:
"Ballade des äußeren Lebens"
("Und Kinder wachsen auf . . .").

Looking ahead

You'll be talking about human and natural disasters, describing important historical events, and discussing the pleasures and difficulties in the lives of retired people.

You will practice using:

- the passive voice to change the perspective of a sentence (They found him – he was found)
- *ein- von* to identify people and things more closely (My friend – *One of* my friends)
- the subjunctive to hypothesize about the past (if you *had* only *slept* longer . . .) and to report what someone has said about the past.
- expressions for "get" (receive, become, fetch)

230

Gedenkstätten

Many of the topics of Chapter 23, and particularly the Holocaust, will be unpleasant, even emotionally disturbing to some students. Others will be **1** uninterested, and you may even encounter a few followers or emulators of the fringe who mouth the doubts alluded to at the end of Dialog 1. Seek to establish the notion that,

Sozialdemokrat
member of one of the largest left-wing political parties

whatever one's feelings, a serious encounter with German culture will sometimes involve the issues presented **2** here, and one should be prepared – culturally, psychologically, and linguistically – to deal with them. In terms of proficiency concepts, one needs a solid base in the Advanced/ILR 2 skills of narration and description, from which one can venture into higher-level functions like hypothesis, **3** supported opinion, and representing the viewpoints of others.

If there is curiosity, offer the word *Vergangenheitsbewältigung*, both for its cultural value as a major term in German discussions of history and society, and also as an illustration of word formation.

Berlin (DDR) – Museum für Deutsche Geschichte.

HERR DR. SCHULZE	Dachau, wo wir heute hinfahren wollen, war eins von den ersten Konzentrationslagern.
ANDREW GOODMAN	Und da kamen viele Juden schon 1933 hin, nicht?
HERR DR. SCHULZE	Ja, aber eigentlich nicht am Anfang. Die meisten Gefangenen waren politische Gegner Hitlers – Kommunisten, Sozialdemokraten, Journalisten und so.
FRAU DR. SCHULZE	Man wußte nur, der oder der wurde verhaftet, weil er ein "Staatsfeind" war.
ANDREW GOODMAN	Unvorstellbar. Aber einige Menschen glauben immer noch, es hätte gar keine Massenvernichtung gegeben!
FRAU DR. SCHULZE	Das stimmt – 6 Millionen Menschen sind in den KZs gestorben. Und wir haben von all dem gar nichts gewußt, bis der Krieg vorbei war.
ANDREW GOODMAN	Naja, meine Großmutter hat mir gesagt, daß ich nicht nach Deutschland reisen soll. Mein Großvater und meine beiden Tanten wurden dort getötet.
HERR DR. SCHULZE	Vielleicht könnte Ihnen aber der Blick in die Vergangenheit helfen, das alles zu verstehen.
MONIKA WALTHERS	Du, das verstehe ich nicht ganz. Im Ost-Berliner Stadtführer heißt es: "die Stadt wurde durch englische und amerikanische Flugzeuge zerstört."
EBERHART HAYM	Nun? Das stimmt doch. Hast du nicht selber von den Luftangriffen gelesen?
MONIKA WALTHERS	Ja, aber hör mal zu: "die Stadt wurde von den sowjetischen Helden befreit," und ich weiß auch, daß die Sowjets beim Angriff auf Berlin 7 500 Flugzeuge hatten.
EBERHART HAYM	Und du meinst also, keins von diesen Flugzeugen hätte Menschen getötet oder Teile von der Stadt zerstört, ja?
MONIKA WALTHERS	Ja, genau. Wie können die so etwas behaupten?
EBERHART HAYM	Die Russen müssen heute Helden sein, weil die DDR einer von den Ostblockstaaten ist.
HERB BAUSCHINGER	Unglaublich. So viele Tote, so viele Familien zerstört.
FRAU BAUSCHINGER	Ja, stimmt. Aber denk auch mal an die 12 000 000 Flüchtlinge aus den Ostgebieten, die in den Westen fliehen mußten.
HERB BAUSCHINGER	Waren das eigentlich Deutsche?
FRAU BAUSCHINGER	Ja, die meisten schon. Und das ist ganz ironisch – denn eins von Hitlers Lieblingswörtern war "Lebensraum."
HERB BAUSCHINGER	. . . das heißt mehr Raum für sein deutsches Volk.
FRAU BAUSCHINGER	Aber die große Emigration begann erst, nachdem der Krieg zu Ende war. Deswegen wurde im Jahre 1961 die Mauer gebaut – um die Auswanderung zu beenden.

Mechanical transformations of active sentences into passive ones can be useful for illustrating the grammatical

Verbs §§76–77

concept and form, but they do not harmonize with the notion of proficiency as furthered through contextual practice. To promote the latter, you might emphasize that the passive is used when one does not wish to assign (or assume!) responsibility for an action, or at least wants to focus on the process itself. Example of contextual exercise: zoo employee reports about feeding the animals; restaurant employee outlines tasks performed on work shift.

The past passive is presented before the present passive so that the student is not distracted by the irregularities in the conjugation of *werden* in the present tense, and because the

A.A. §9

past passive is prominent in the historical language that is encountered so frequently by the visitor to the culture who has achieved solid intermediate proficiency. Higher in level is the common context of the present passive, which appears often in descriptions of operations or processes taking place (or potentially occurring) in the immediate world (e.g., *"Widerrechtlich geparkte Fahrzeuge werden kostenpflichtig abgeschleppt"*). Note that the preview of the passive in Chapter 22 includes the present tense.

If asked, explain very briefly the distinction between event and process ("aspect").

Conduct "pointing" exercises (*Das ist ein- . . .*); it is a good idea to review noun vocabulary and plural forms; you can expand to include a review of superlatives and even possessives (*Das ist einer von meinen besten Freunden.*).

1. The passive voice: action from another perspective

Until now you have seen the *active voice*, with the *subject acting*, even if the subject was only the indefinite *man*:

> Die Nazis töteten meine beiden Tanten dort.
> **Man** verhaftete den oder den.
> . . . daß **Flugzeuge** die Stadt zerstörten.
> . . . daß **die sowjetischen Helden** die Stadt befreiten.
> Deswegen baute **man** die Mauer im Jahre 1961.
> subjects doing something

The passive voice introduces another perspective. The subject does not act, but is acted upon.

> Meine beiden Tanten **wurden** dort **getötet.** *"were killed"*
> Deswegen **wurde** im Jahre 1961 die Mauer **gebaut.** *"was built"*
> Man wußte nur, daß der oder der **verhaftet wurde.** *"was arrested"*
> . . . daß die Stadt durch . . . Flugzeuge **zerstört wurde.** *"was destroyed"*
> Die Stadt **wurde** durch die sowjetischen Helden **befreit.** *"was liberated"*

- **basic form: subject + a form of *werden* + participle**
- **the past passive:**
  wurde(n) + participle = was (being) [verb]-ed

> Die Stadt **wurde zerstört.** *The city was destroyed.*
> Die Tiere **wurden gefüttert.** *The animals were fed (were being fed).*

2. "One of": *ein-* + *von* + dative or *ein-* + genitive

das Lager – ein̲s von den Lagern (ein̲s der Lager)
Dachau war ein̲s von den ersten Konzentrationslagern.

der Staat – eine̲r von den Staaten (eine̲r der Staaten)
. . . weil die DDR eine̲r von den Ostblockstaaten ist.

die Frau – eine̲ von den Frauen (eine̲ der Frauen)
Eine̲ von den Frauen ist seine Großmutter.

Similarly with *kein-*: "none of"

das Flugzeug – ein̲s von den Flugzeugen (ein̲s der Flugzeuge)
Du meinst, kein̲s von diesen Flugzeugen hätte Menschen getötet.

Im Katastrophen-Winter 1950/51 wurde hier der alte Stall durch eine Lawine bis auf den Grund zerstört. Neu aufgebaut Frühjahr 1951

Dieser Sitz wurde gereinigt und desinfiziert
This seat has been cleaned and disinfected

SITUATIONEN 1 Gedenkstätten

Stage 1	A	B
1	Says didn't really want to see Dachau. Many members of family died there. Would like to see for self where and how everything happened. Says forgetting is impossible.	Asks why A is there. Still wonders why A wanted to see it. Thinks that's probably very hard to do; why not try to forget? Understands; wonders whether dealing with the past ought to be harder for the Germans than for the Jews.
2	Has read that Köln was attacked by 1,000 Allied bombers. Says part of own family was killed then. They had to live with friends for the rest of the war. Mentions the refugees from the east who had to have somewhere to live.	Says it's amazing that the cathedral wasn't destroyed. Asks what the rest of the family did. Talks about the housing shortage – too few places for too many people. Says B's family came from Hungary, had to live with relatives in a one-room basement apartment.
3	Says has heard that students in the DDR don't like to study Russian. Doesn't mean that; wonders about connection between language and politics. Asks why that is so, since the DDR is a Warsaw Pact country. Thinks that's a pretty safe statement.	Says it's required; you never want to study what's required. Admits that Soviets aren't beloved by DDR citizens. Says it probably has something to do with the war. Wonders about West Germans' feelings about American soldiers.

Amazing = unglaublich, unvorstellbar, Ich kann es nicht glauben, etc.

Stage 2

1

You are in Austria on a Rotary International fellowship. Occasionally you visit schools and tell about life in North America. Within the context of a discussion in a history class, you find yourself telling the students what your generation knows about the Nazi atrocities.

2

Sie besuchen eine Familie in Braunschweig – Freunde zu Hause in Nordamerika haben Ihnen ihre Adresse gegeben. Sie möchten so viel wie möglich über die Kriegsjahre lernen, aber Sie haben diese Familie auch noch nie kennengelernt. Seien Sie taktvoll.

Versuchen Sie doch

You are at the Mensa of the Freie Universität in West Berlin, where you have found an interesting group of students to have lunch with. They are shocked when you tell them that there is a small but vocal Nazi party in the United States. Do your best to defend not the Nazi party, but the right of all parties to be represented in a democracy. If relatives of several people you know were victims of the camps in Bergen-Belsen and Auschwitz, would that change your argument?

The Holocaust – could it happen in America? To whom?

233

STRATEGIE – KULTUR UND SPRACHE

German equivalents of American political terms

der Präsident	president
der Premierminister	prime minister
der Senator	senator
der Gouverneur	governor
kandidieren	to run for office
der Vizepräsident	vice-president
der/die Abgeordnete	representative
der Bürgermeister	mayor
wählen	to vote

German political offices

der Bundeskanzler – "Chancellor" or equivalent of prime minister. Highest political office in West Germany.

der Bundespräsident – Ceremonial head of state in West Germany.

The word *Minister* is the equivalent of "Secretary" in the U.S. cabinet.

The common title for the head of the DDR is "Generalsekretär" or, in full, "Generalsekretär des Zentralkomitees der SED." "SED," in turn, stands for "Sozialistische Einheitspartei Deutschlands."

You could introduce better students to Farrell, *German Synonyms*. Beyond the scope of the present discussion are several other senses of "get," as in "Get lost!," "get started," "get going."

Emphasize the interference problem posed by *bekommen/* become.

Point out the dangers of *Ich bin kalt/heiß/warm.*

Expressions for "get"

The English verb "get" performs many different functions, and therefore has several distinct German equivalents.

- "get" in the sense of "receive" – *bekommen*

  Was bekommen Sie, Kaffee oder Tee?

- "get" in the sense of "become" – *werden* by itself

  Es wird kalt.

- "get" in the sense of "to be [verb]ed" or "to be being [verb]ed" – often expressed by the passive voice, consisting of *werden* + past participle

  Der Kaffee wird später gemacht.   The coffee will get made later.

- got or "gotta" in the sense of "have to," "need to" – *müssen*

  Ich muß sie anrufen.   *I've got to call her up.*
  child talk: Ich muß!   *I gotta go (to the bathroom)!*

- "get" in the sense of "be allowed to" – *dürfen*

  Morgen dürfen wir zu Hause bleiben.   *Tomorrow we get to stay home.*

- some specific idioms

to understand	*Oh, I get it!*	Ach, jetzt verstehe ich es!
to fetch things	*I'll get the timetable.*	Ich hole den Fahrplan.
to fetch or pick up people	*I'll come get you at eight*	Ich hole dich um 8 Uhr ab.

But in area measurement: for 10m² read zehn Quadratmeter.

Large numbers and mathematical symbols

ein Tausend (Tausend) – *thousand*		4^2	Say *"vier hoch zwei"*
eine Million (Millionen) – *million*		4×4	Say *"vier mal vier"*
eine Milliarde (Milliarden) – *billion*		$=$	Say *"gleich"* or *"ist"*/*"sind"*
eine Billion (Billionen) – *trillion*		$\div$	Say *"geteilt durch"*

Ask students to compare the ratios of deaths to total population of the various countries, maybe using percentages and common fractions alternately (10%/ein Zehntel). Most will be surprised at the relatively low U.S. (and even British) overall casualty rates, and shocked at the high civilian casualty rates of, for instance, Yugoslavia. An appraisal of the Soviet casualties can lead to discussion of Soviet attitudes toward border security, peace proposals, and relative credit for victory in WW II. Further WW II statistics: Japanese deaths – 2 million (1.3 million combatants, 672,000 civilians); Chinese deaths – 2.2 million combatants, civilian deaths uncertain but perhaps as many as 22 million. Combat deaths in other U.S. wars (good chance to teach the German terms) Revolutionskrieg – 6.000; Sezessionskrieg – 140.414 (dazu 224.097 an Krankheiten Gestorbene); 1. Weltkrieg – 53.000; Korea – 33.629; Vietnam – 47.321.

Zahl der Toten im zweiten Weltkrieg

LAND	BEVÖLKERUNG (1930) in Millionen (Mio)	TOTE Soldaten	Zivilisten	davon Juden
UdSSR	127,5	11 Mio	7 Mio	1,4 Mio
Polen	32	800 000	5 Mio	3,2 Mio
Deutschland	65	3,5 Mio	780 000	125 000
Jugoslawien	13,9	305 000	1,2 Mio	60 000
Italien	40,5	242 000	153 000	7 500
Großbritannien	49	264 000	93 000	–
Frankreich	41,8	213 000	350 000	83 000
USA	123,6	292 000	6 000	–

Gesamtzahl der Toten in allen Ländern: 35 – 60 Millionen
Gesamtzahl der jüdischen Toten: ca. 6 Millionen

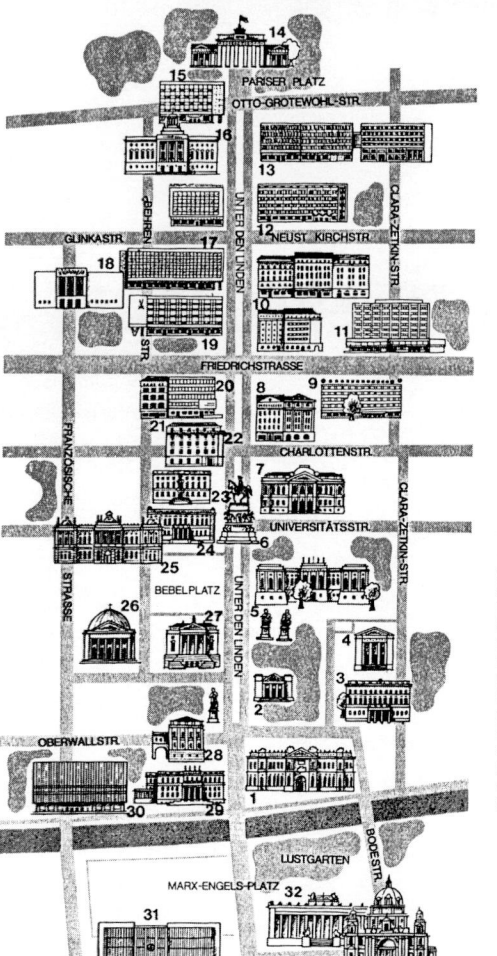

1 Museum für Deutsche Geschichte
2 Mahnmal für die Opfer des Faschismus und Militarismus
3 Zentrales Haus der Deutsch-Sowjetischen Freundschaft
4 Maxim Gorki Theater
5 Humboldt-Universität
6 Denkmal Friedrich II.
7 Deutsche Staatsbibliothek
8 Zentralleitung des Komitees der Antifaschistischen Widerstandskämpfer in der DDR/Bulgarisches Kulturzentrum
9 Interhotel „Unter den Linden"
10 Sitz des Zentralrates der Freien Deutschen Jugend und der Zentralleitung der Pionierorganisation „Ernst Thälmann"
11 Interhotel „Metropol"
12 Ministerium für Außenhandel
13 Botschaften der Volksrepublik Polen und der Ungarischen Volksrepublik
14 Brandenburger Tor
15 Ministerium für Volksbildung
16 Botschaft der UdSSR
17 Funktionsgebäude der Komischen Oper
18 Komische Oper
19 Appartementhaus
20 Gaststätte „Lindencorso"
21 Buchhandlung „Das sowjetische Buch"
22 Haus der Gewerkschaften
23 Ehemaliges Gouverneurshaus
24 Altes Palais
25 Alte Bibliothek
26 St.-Hedwigs-Kathedrale
27 Deutsche Staatsoper
28 Operncafé
29 Palais Unter den Linden
30 Ministerium für Auswärtige Angelegenheiten
31 Palast der Republik
32 Altes Museum
33 Dom

Schweizer Bauern.

WOHNEN IM ALTER ✿

Im Parkstift St. Ulrich finden Sie ein umsorgtes Zuhause – einen Ort, an dem Sie noch einmal Heimat finden können. Dazu gehört, daß niemand Sie bevormundet, keiner Sie nach dem Woher und Wohin fragt. Dazu gehört auch, daß Sie in Ihren eigenen Möbeln wohnen. Vor allem aber, daß Sie sich sicher fühlen können! (Wer pflegebedürftig wird, kann bei uns bleiben.) Und schließlich gehört zum Zuhausesein, daß man am Leben teilhaben kann, gesellschaftlich wie kulturell. Ja, Sie werden bei uns eine Heimat finden.

Parkstift St. Ulrich

Hebelstraße 18,
7812 Bad Krozingen,
Tel. (07633) 4031

SPD = *Sozialdemokratische Partei Deutschlands – Why might a passerby chuckle at the two signs?*

Ranzigen Speck verwendungsfähig machen

Der Salzspeck wird vom gröbsten Salz und der Schwarte befreit, in kaltem Wasser gut ausgewaschen, dann in nicht zuviel kochendes, reines Wasser gelegt und 5—6 Minuten geprellt, also scharf überkocht. Danach wird der Speck vom Sud gehoben, auskühlen gelassen und kleinwürflig geschnitten. Den geschnittenen Speck gibt man in eine Kasserolle mit bodenbedeckt Essig, und zwar kann es auch selbstgemachter oder Obstessig sein. Mengenmäßig ist das so zu verstehen, daß man auf 20 Dekagramm geschnittenen Speck 2 Eßlöffel Essig in das Geschirr gibt. Den Speck läßt man nun auskochen und schmelzen, bis die Grammeln goldbraun geworden sind. Durch die Prozedur verschwindet der ranzige Geschmack von Fett und Grammeln meist vollständig. Der Kochsud, in dem der Speck überkocht wurde, kann zum Aufgießen von Suppen oder eingebrannten Erdäpfeln verwendet werden.

How to make rancid bacon usable – a recipe from a cookbook distributed in Austria shortly after the Second World War.

GESPRÄCHE 2

Rentner

1   FRAU SENSENBRENNER   Ja, mein Mann mußte schon 1939 zur Wehrmacht. Er kam erst 1951 aus Rußland zurück.

WILLIAM LINGLE   Erst 1951? Wie ist denn das möglich? Der Krieg war ja schon 1945 zu Ende.

FRAU SENSENBRENNER   Ja, aber viele kamen erst viel später nach Hause.

WILLIAM LINGLE   Und in der Zeit haben Sie ihn auch nie gesehen?

FRAU SENSENBRENNER   Doch, einmal – als er im Spital war. Aber die Kinder waren schon groß, als sie den Vater wiedersahen.

2   FRAU EBERHARD   Also es ging einfach nicht mehr bei uns zu Hause. Ich mußte meine Mutter in ein Altersheim bringen.

FRAU STAMMLER   So – wegen deiner Arbeit? Oder wegen der Pflege?

FRAU EBERHARD   Ja, eigentlich beides.

FRAU STAMMLER   Aber du hast gesagt, das Altersheim ist wirklich gut.

FRAU EBERHARD   Ja, ich bin sehr zufrieden damit.

FRAU STAMMLER   Und wahrscheinlich hättest du es nicht mehr lange ausgehalten, so mit der Pflege.

3   FRAU STEIERT   Wissen Sie, viele sagen, wir hätten nicht gegen den Hitler gekämpft und wären deswegen auch schuld an der ganzen Nazikatastrophe.

HERR STEIERT   Aber so einfach war das nicht. Viel wurde uns versprochen, und es waren schwere Zeiten nach dem ersten Weltkrieg.

EMILY SANDERSON   Ja, ich weiß – Armut, Inflation, Arbeitslosigkeit.

FRAU STEIERT   Aber heute geht's wirklich gut. Wir haben unsere Wohnung und unsere Rente vom Staat.

HERR STEIERT   Und der kleine Garten sorgt für vieles – nicht nur für Gemüse, sondern auch für Ruhe und Entspannung.

EMILY SANDERSON   Es freut mich sehr, daß es Ihnen beiden gut geht.

4   HERR TSCHARNER   Für uns Schweizer war die Kriegszeit auch schwer. Man meint, wir hätten einfach zu Hause gesessen.

RETO CATHOMAS   Also, das glaube ich nicht. Sie und mein Opa waren ja bei der Grenzwache zusammen, soweit ich weiß.

HERR TSCHARNER   Ja, wir sollten aufpassen, daß nichts passiert.

RETO CATHOMAS   Aber wie war das mit der Neutralität? Da durfte niemand die Schweiz angreifen, oder?

HERR TSCHARNER   Ja, mein Lieber, was heißt denn "durfte"? Der Hitler hatte einfach Angst, daß er bei uns zu viele Soldaten verlieren würde. Sonst hätte er auch uns angegriffen.

RETO CATHOMAS   Nein, ich meine – die Schweiz war neutral, oder?

HERR TSCHARNER   Naja, "neutral" – natürlich, aber sagen wir neutral auf der Seite von den Alliierten.

STRUKTUR 2

Verbs §59

1. The past subjunctive: *hätte-* + participle

● hypothesizing about the past

Wahrscheinlich **hättest** du es nicht mehr **ausgehalten**.

*You probably **wouldn't have stood** it any longer.*

Sonst **hätte** er auch uns **angegriffen**.

*Otherwise he **would have attacked** us too.*

● retelling something someone said

Viele sagen, wir hätten nicht gegen den Hitler gekämpft.

Lots of people say that we didn't fight against Hitler.

2. More about word formation

Complex English words are often composed of Greek, Latin, or French roots whose meanings are not always comprehensible. An example:

un•em•ploy•ment

from Latin *in* ("in") ↗   ↖ from Latin *plicare* ("to fold") (= "fold in"→"involve"→"give work")

Thus to talk in one word about "lacking work" or a "lack of work," English speakers must shift from the common word "work" to words that are quite different. The multiplicity of word origins does contribute to the richness of the language; thus we can talk about "workers," "laborers," or "employees."

Many complex German words are created from native root words and are therefore readily understandable to almost everyone, even the very young and those who have no higher education. Thus from the everyday German word for "work," *Arbeit*, are formed

arbeitslos *unemployed*   die Arbeitslosigkeit *unemployment*

● other examples

glauben *believe*   unglaublich *unbelievable* or *incredible*

nicht *not*
    die Vernichtung *annihilation* (Latin *ad* = to + *nihil* = nothing)

wandern *wander, hike, migrate*   die Wanderung *hike* or *migration*
    auswandern *emigrate*   einwandern *immigrate*

Learn to spot the root in the midst of a long word and then to think what the prefixes and suffixes mean. Here are two more examples:

denken *think*   undenkbar *unthinkable* or *inconceivable*
    die Undenkbarkeit *inconceivability*

das Ende *end*   endlich *finally, finite*   unendlich *infinite(ly)*
    beenden *finish, end,*   die Unendlichkeit *endlessness* or *infinitude*
    terminate

Long German nouns are likely to be feminine in gender, since most of the noun-forming suffixes are feminine: *-heit, -keit, -schaft, -ion, -ung*. Thus when the language gets very abstract or technical, you can expect to encounter many feminine nouns. And thus the plural forms become easier, since the common pattern for the plurals of feminine nouns is *-en*.

238 CHAPTER 23

Don't expect wonders in the management of German word formation – in either comprehension or, much less, in production. Point out examples in the realia, and perhaps mention that German does use some technical words next to German-root words.

Illustrate the difference by pointing out that paragraph two contains the native-root formation "understandable," where the previous one uses "comprehensible." Point out other words with the same opaque root: "apprehend," "prehensile" (*prehendere* = to seize). To illustrate the "transparency" of German compound nouns: types of doctors (*Kinder-, Frauen-, Tier- + Arzt/Ärztin*); *Kreis + Lauf =* circulation; *Herz + Lunge* in medical compounds = cardiopulmonary.

Answer any gripes about how these are just fancy words by pointing out that "annihilate" can be used, with full confidence in comprehension, at any football pep rally ("2, 4, 6, 8 – Who we gonna 'nihilate?") or by anyone on a TV wrestling program.

Remark the tricky sound/ spelling difference between *im-* and *e-*, and the likelihood that few will understand the meanings of the syllables themselves; contrast to the very evident distinction in sound, spelling, and meaning between *aus* and *ein* (= in).

See note in Instructor's Guide.

SITUATIONEN 2 Rentner

Stage 1	A	B
1 Keeping body and soul together – *müssen* or *wollen* + *leben, essen,* and similar verbs. You might mention several other idioms and ask the class to rephrase them in straightforward German: wolf at the door, poor as a church mouse, hard times, tough luck. Such linguistic triumphs can lighten what are sure to be some sad moments. Remind students that the subjects presented here do indeed come up frequently in actual encounters.	Asks when the prisoners came back after the war. Asks about the delay. Is amazed; asks what B did all that time. Asks what kind of work B did. Asks whether that was enough.	Says it was three years later. Says that was relatively short – some didn't come back for another four years. Cared for the children, tried to keep body and soul together. Worked cleaning up in a store. Says they had to get by on that.
2	Says her husband's war wounds drove him to an early grave. Says they had to grow up in separate homes there wasn't enough in her house for them all. In three different cities; now they're still separated. Says they're very faithful, talks about the last visit from the son in Hannover.	Is terribly sorry to hear that; asks about the three children. Makes guesses about where and with whom the children grew up. Asks whether they ever come to visit her in the retirement home. Finds out more about son.
3 Push review of material from early chapters. Perhaps allow longer than usual preparation time for the last exchange in the conversation. For German versions of Stage 2 situations, see Instructor's Guide.	Talks about the advantages of the retirement home. Says insurance takes care of everything. Says there's no insurance for the past. He would have done much more if the Nazis hadn't begun the war. Gives details.	Wonders about medical problems. Praises Austrian insurance system. Asks for explanation. Asks what A means.

You or your students may be ready for a change of theme.

Stage 2

The structural targets of Chapter 23 can be exercised and elicited with situations that require similar functions but draw upon different content. Important are solid past narration and efforts at the past subjunctive. Setups: 1) talk about old people in one's own family; 2) talk about some high or low point in one's own life and explore the consequence of a change of events.

1
You are talking to an old man. Find out what he did during the Second World War and how his life might have been different had the war not intervened.

2
You are talking with a Swiss retiree about the status of Switzerland during the war. Be sure to find out all you can about Swiss neutrality and about the effect of Swiss neutrality on the country's current prosperity.

3
You have been visiting a retired couple, old friends of your parents from their student days in Tübingen. Engage them in conversation about
a) their relationship to your parents during those years;
b) their relationship to their own children since that time;
c) their lives as retirees in a youth-oriented consumer society.

Versuchen Sie doch

Note that while the situation is phrased in grandiose historical terms, the actual focus is on the personal sphere, in accordance with the target proficiency level (Advanced or Advanced-plus). If you have reasonable success, ask for at least the start of a repetition of the situation, altered to describe not the speaker's hypothetical life, but rather that of someone else.

Tell about your own grandparents' lives – earlier and now.

What important turning points have there been in your life? Speculate how things might be now if you had taken a different path.

Assume that the Allied invasion of Normandy had been repelled; that Hitler's air offensive had indeed crushed Britain; that the Russian winter had not been so severe as to cripple the German armies at Stalingrad; and that your grandparents, who in reality came to America a few years after the German defeat, had instead stayed in their home town of Memmingen and raised your father in Hitler's "Thousand-Year Empire" (*tausendjähriges Reich*). Speculate about the direction your life would have taken.

239

Chapter 24
DIE ALTE HEIMAT – DAMALS/
DIE ALTE HEIMAT – JETZT

Niedersächsischer Bauernhof bei Walsrode.

1908

FUNKTIONEN – KONTEXTE – STRUKTUREN

Songs and poems appropriate to this chapter: *"Kein schöner Land"*; *"Hab mei Wage"*; *"Die Gedanken sind frei"*; Goethe: *"Amerika, du hast es besser"*; Eichendorff: *"Heimweh"*; Hölderlin: *"Die Heimat"*; Heine: *"Ich hatte einst ein schönes Vaterland"*; Miegel: *"Wagen an Wagen"*; Konrad Krez (b. 1828 Landau, d. 1897 Milwaukee): *"Da waren Deutsche auch dabei."*

Looking ahead

You'll be tracing roots, talking about kinship, narrating personal history, comparing cultures, advancing opinions, and speculating more about what might have been.

You will be using:

- the formal past tense for systematic narration
- relative pronouns – pronouns that let you introduce peripheral information
- various ways to express "before"
- the past subjunctive with verbs that require *sein* (We would have gone if that had happened)
- fractions and multiples (one-half, double)

Die alte Heimat – damals

CHRISTIANE PRIER	Wir schließen das Archiv in einer halben Stunde. Ich wollte gerade aufräumen, bevor wir zumachen.
KEVIN SMITH	Ich suche Dokumente über meine Verwandten. Ich heiße Smith, aber vorher war der Name anders. Mein Urgroßvater hieß Friedrich Wilhelm Schmidt.
CHRISTIANE PRIER	Und wann ist er nach Amerika ausgewandert?
KEVIN SMITH	Im Jahre 1885 – so steht es in der großen deutschen Bibel zu Hause. Wir haben auch einige Briefe.
CHRISTIANE PRIER	Es wäre besser, wenn Sie morgen früh noch einmal vorbeikommen könnten.
KEVIN SMITH	Gibt es auch solche Dokumente in der Kirche?
CHRISTIANE PRIER	Ja, besonders Geburtsdaten. Das ist wichtig, denn das Rathaus wurde im Krieg zerstört.

MAGDA SEIFERT	Wir sind ziemlich eng miteinander verwandt.
SUSAN WERNER	Ja. Habe ich das richtig? Sie sind also die Enkelin von der ältesten Schwester meines Urgroßvaters.
MAGDA SEIFERT	Ja, so ist es. Ich zeige Ihnen noch ein Foto.
SUSAN WERNER	Der junge Mann, der die Uniform trägt – ist das auch mein Urgroßvater?
MAGDA SEIFERT	Nein. Das ist sein jüngerer Bruder, kurz vor seinem Tod. Er ist 1916 in Frankreich gefallen.
SUSAN WERNER	Und die Frau, die die zwei Kinder in den Armen hält?

SHAWN HINES	Und was ist denn den anderen Kindern passiert?
INGEBORG SAILER	Gerhardt – das ist also der zweitälteste Vetter von deiner Großmutter – studierte Jura an der Universität Leipzig. So hieß damals die Karl-Marx-Universität. Er wurde Anwalt und heiratete ein Mädchen aus . . .

ELISABETH BÜTOW	Erzähl mal, wie deine Großeltern einander kennengelernt haben. War das nach dem Krieg?
ELIZABETH BUETOW	Nein, schon vorher. Mein Großvater hatte ein Schreibwarengeschäft in der Stadtmitte. Eines Tages kam meine Großmutter in das Geschäft und . . .

ADAM SNYDER	Damals mußte mein Vater viel reisen.
JOHANNA SCHNEIDER	Und deswegen die Scheidung?
ADAM SNYDER	Vielleicht. Aber das wäre auch passiert, wenn er öfter zu Hause gewesen wäre.
JOHANNA SCHNEIDER	Na, sprechen wir von anderen Sachen. Du bist also in Süd-Karolinien in die Schule gegangen?
ADAM SNYDER	Als ich 4 Jahre alt war, kamen wir nach Winnebago County. Dort habe ich die Grundschule besucht, von 1973 bis 1979. Dann drei Jahre Mittelschule und drei Jahre Oberschule. Zwischen 1985 und 1987 studierte ich an der Staatsuniversität Michigan. Ich bin seit August 1987 in der Armee . . .

Point out that one says either "im Jahre 19___" or just "19___" – but that "in 19___" is impossible.

Have students write out a graphic horizontal account of their lives:

A	B	C	D	E
1970	73	75	85	88

Events:
A In Keokuk geboren
B Familie nach Detroit
C Schulanfang
D Familienferien in Österreich
E Universität

Students use *im Jahre, vor,* and *vorher* to describe their life histories.

STRUKTUR 1

Verbs §§64–67

Written exercise to demonstrate the difference between the two past tenses: Lengthy quotes from two witnesses to an accident must be combined in a written police report. Each witness saw something the other did not, and there is a significant time overlap in their testimony. Witnesses' statements are in the present perfect; the written summary is in the simple past.

Note that *wollen* and *sollen* show no vowel change in the simple past.

Pronouns §15

Use students in class as props: Student A: *Wer ist Marie?* B: *Marie? Die sitzt neben John.* C: *Das ist die Studentin, die neben John/am Fenster sitzt/schläft.* D: *Das ist die Studentin, die heute einen roten Pullover trägt.*

Most students will not readily produce utterances with any sort of relative pronoun, much less relative clauses showing correct gender, case, and number. Still, you might offer an overall point: where English *can* use a relative pronoun, German *must.*

W.O. §13
Preps. §28

See note in Instructor's Guide.

1. The formal past tense system: summary
`basic patterns`

- for regular verbs like *sagen*

The tense signal is "*-t-*" and there is no change in the stem vowel.
`-t-`

> *sagen: ich sagte, du sagtest, er/sie/es sagte*

- for irregular verbs like *kommen*
`vowel change`

The main signal is a stem-vowel change. Also, there is no "*-t-*".

> *kommen: ich kam, du kamst, er/sie/es kam*

- for a few important verbs like *wissen, kennen,* and the modals
`-t- and vowel change`

The tense signal is "*-t-*" *and* there is usually a vowel change.

> *wissen: ich wußte, du wußtest, er/sie/es wußte*

2. Relative pronouns
`the XX who/that/which`

- main function: insertion of explanatory information
- basic form: NOUN, d __ ...... verb

The relative pronouns look like the demonstrative pronouns you learned earlier. Their gender and number must match those of the nouns they refer to.

> **Der** junge Mann? **Der** trägt die Uniform.   (demonstrative)
> **Der** junge Mann, **der** die Uniform trägt.   (relative)

- German has just one basic pattern. English has several.

d __ Noun, d _____
the (noun for persons) who
the (noun for persons or things) that
the (noun for things) that or which
the (noun) [no signal]

der Mann, der die Uniform trägt, . . .
the man who is wearing the uniform
the man that is wearing the uniform

the man wearing the uniform

3. Expressing "before"

before + subject and verb = **Bevor** + subject and verb   (conjunction)
Before we close, . . .   Bevor wir zumachen, ...

before + noun or pronoun = **vor** + noun or pronoun   (preposition)
before the war   vor dem Krieg

before as a single word for a point in time = **vorher**   (adverb)
After the war? No, before.   Nach dem Krieg? Nein, vorher.

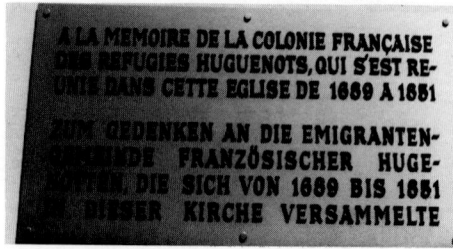

Stage 1

(Szene: Rathaus) 1

Direct equivalents, if you want to supply them: *Geburts-, Heirats-, Todesurkunden;* approximations: *wichtige Information(en), Daten;* functional equivalents (though here the speaker would not need to circumlocute): *Ich möchte wissen, wann der Bruder von meiner Großmutter gestorben ist,* etc.

Mädchenname is the specific term, but the concept can be expressed with *bevor sie heiratete* or *Der (Familien) Name (von ihren Eltern) war,* illustrating important grammatical features of the chapter.

Sehr schnell – but by now a good student should be able to convey the meaning in several ways. "Tells the new things this one can do" – use the occasion to review modal verbs not only in the present but in the past as well, with attention to time indicators (including equivalents of "before").

1
(Looking for genealogical documents)
Greets. Asks about closing time.
Describes self – why in Europe, etc.

Doesn't know much – just a few names and birthdates.

Asks directions, opening time, etc.

(Works in city hall)
5 P.M. (17.00!). Offers to help.
Sounds interested. Asks more about the information A is looking for.
Recommendation: go to the other city hall, where vital statistics are kept. This one is now a museum, but they don't have any documents.
Helps. Wishes A a pleasant stay.

2
(Suspects she is related to B)
Gives name of ancestor, Hermann Scholz.

Born 1862, died 1931 (Midwest).

(Suspects he is related to A)
Interested. Also had an ancestor whose maiden name was Scholz. Checks spelling of name. Asks for details.
Guesses the ancestors were siblings.

A and B then try to figure out how they are related.

3
(Wants to know all about B's family)
Who's that sitting second to left?
Makes nice remarks about the baby.

Remarks that kids grow like weeds.

(Has some recent family pictures)
That's the newest addition to the family.
Explains child's resemblance to various relatives – has mother's eyes, etc.
Indeed. Tells the new things this one can do.

A and B compare the child to other children – including themselves when young.

Stage 2

1
In a church archive you've found some genealogical documents important to you. You'd like to get photographs or photocopies of them. The documents are very fragile. The person in charge of them is concerned about their safety, but is generally friendly. Can you propose some kind of arrangement that will get you what you want? If you yourself may not take the documents to be photo-copied, can you suggest an alternate arrangement and offer to pay for it?

2
Give a thumbnail biography and portrait of a member of your immediate family. Cover at least the following topics: age, size, appearance, education, hobbies.

3
Tell what you know about the earlier years of an older family member.

4
Meeting long-lost relatives can be tiring, and most of us need some privacy. Can you deal with the following circum-stances?

a) The relatives have generously offered to put you up in their home, but you really do want to stay in a hotel room. Explain your wishes – tactfully.
b) The relatives have invited you to stay for dinner, but you've had a long trip. You're not really hungry, and fa-tigue is causing your German to dete-riorate. Perhaps you could suggest something special to do tomorrow.

Yet another review of third person forms; quite likely they are still troublesome, especially

Versuchen Sie doch
when the verb is in a subordinate clause and when the conversation includes second person *Sie* as well as third person singular or plural *sie.*

In the dialogs for *"Die alte Heimat – damals"* you rehearsed inquiries about your own roots. Quite possibly you are not German-American. So try the situation this way: you are traveling in a German-speaking country with someone of German ancestry who does not speak German as well as you. Can you serve as an informal interpreter in your companion's search for genealogical information? Can you describe your companion's kinship relations to various ancestors and living relatives?

STRATEGIE – KULTUR UND SPRACHE

German-Americans: a nonethnic ethnic group

People who can claim to be of German ancestry comprise the largest single ethnic group in the United States – about one-sixth of the population. Nevertheless, for several reasons the German-American minority does not assert its identity strongly; nor does the rest of the population pay it much heed. Once a target of strident advocates of "America for Americans," German immigrants have assimilated rapidly into the "White Anglo-Saxon Protestant" background, though Germans are not "Anglo-Saxon" and many are not Protestant. Still somewhat evident, despite the assimilation, are certain elements that mark the once considerable effect of German culture on American culture and on the evolution of a distinctively American version of the English language. Some German family names have survived, as have naturalized loan words and the things to which they refer. A few examples are kindergarten (and the word "kinder" in the names of businesses and products catering to children), hamburger, frankfurter, schuss, lox and bagels, flak, U-boat, sauerkraut, eiderdown, schnapps, dachshund, delicatessen, gesundheit, and poltergeist.

The term "German-American" is misleading, since it is often applied to Americans of Swiss or Austrian descent, and since the borders of Germany – when it existed as a single nation – have changed greatly through history. The issue is complicated even further by the ambiguous position of Jews within the German-American community and within the parent culture itself. Lastly, the stigma of perpetrating the Holocaust and animosities generated by Germany's role as an enemy in the two world wars have stricken German-American confidence and fostered a public image of Germans that would be considered unacceptably biased if its features were ascribed to other groups. More positive but still superficial is another notion of things German: superior automotive technology, "old world" beer brewing, American soldiers on leave in Heidelberg, and the idea that a certain rollicking romanticism or *Gemütlichkeit* can be suggested by using the words "haus" or "fest" to adorn just about any place or event that is supposed to involve "good times."

Landmark dates and events in German-American relations.

1683   First German immigrants settle in America. They were recruited by William Penn, founder of Pennsylvania, from religious dissenters in the city of Krefeld. Later other exiles also settled in Pennsylvania. Many place-names testify to their presence – Germantown, King of Prussia, Nuremberg, Strasburg. Subsequent immigration produced thriving German communities in Ohio, Texas, and the Middle West.

Revolutionary War   American troops are trained by Friedrich Wilhelm Ludolf Gerhard Augustin "Baron" von Steuben. The British army, especially the force Washington defeated at Trenton after he crossed the Delaware, included Hessians – German troops from the province of Hesse. Many were recruited by coercion and then in effect were sold to the British; more than a few chose to remain in America.

1848   Failure of the liberal-national rebellions in many German-speaking lands causes the emigration of a small but very influential collection of "Forty-Eighters." Among them are the popular St. Louis politician Franz Sigel (1824–1902), who in the Civil War was made a Northern general to keep Missouri loyal to the Union, and Karl Schürz (1829–1906), who as Carl Schurz became Senator from Missouri and Secretary of the Interior.

Sidenotes:

Mention St. Louis park signs in the nineteenth century: No dogs or Germans; Ku Klux Klan persecution of foreigners; general opposition to Catholics and beer gardens.

flak: From *Fliegerabwehrkanone.*

Maybe mention General Peter Osterhaus, who pardoned a poaching soldier when he learned that the soldier had sent some meat to the general's kitchen.

244   CHAPTER 24

Still other German-Americans to mention: Sutter, Levi Straus, John Dillinger, Babe Ruth, Lou Gehrig, Gertrude Ederle, Steinway, Roebling, Studebaker, Haldemann and Ehrlichmann, Otto Preminger, Johnny Weissmuller, Mari Sandoz, the Anheuser-Busch families, Weyerhaeuser, the Hammersteins, Albers (cereal), Kissinger, Joe Theismann, Mike Schmidt, Roger Staubach, Walter Cronkite, Dr. Seuss, Thomas Nast, Erma Bombeck.

Your students might find it surprising and amusing how many show-business personalities began life with German-sounding names. Among them are John Denver (Henry John Deutschendorf, Jr.), Woody Allen (Allen Konigsberg), Fred Astaire (Frederick Austerlitz), Doris Day (Doris von Kappelhoff), James Garner (James Baumgardner), Harry Houdini (Ehrich Weiss).

Late Nineteenth Century   Massive German emigration to America, including many Jews. Germany achieves world-power status in science, the arts, and diplomacy, with a corresponding effect on the culture of the United States, particularly after the Franco-Prussian War (1870–1871). German universities serve as models for new American universities, German classics dominate the musical scene, and in both dress and organization the American military takes on a sober and authoritarian Prussian tinge.

1917   American entry into World War I produces a backlash against things German in the United States. Many families americanize their German names and give up the use of the German language, and some schools cancel German language instruction. While "sauerkraut" is temporarily renamed "victory cabbage," victorious American forces are led by German-American Gen. John J. ("Black Jack") Pershing.

1933   Nazi accession to power in Germany forces the emigration, to America and elsewhere, of hundreds of thousands of refugees. Prominent among them are Albert Einstein and the writers Thomas Mann and Bertolt Brecht.

Second World War   Prominent German-American military figures include Dwight David Eisenhower, commander-in-chief of Allied forces in Western Europe and later U.S. President; Admiral Chester Nimitz (b. Fredericksburg, Tex.), commander-in-chief of the U.S. Pacific fleet; General Carl Spaatz, chief of the U.S. bombing force in Germany and Japan.

Sidelights, curiosities, and popular misconceptions

Yiddish (*jüdisch*, "Jewish") is a close linguistic relative of modern German, but one with a sociological rather than a geographical definition. The language began to emerge in the late Middle Ages (ca. 1100), when the German-speaking area produced a rich Jewish subculture. Yiddish is unmistakably German in grammar and vocabulary but usually written with Hebrew characters. It was once spoken by Jews throughout Europe, and thus also by many Jews in America. It has given American English not only "bagel" and "lox" but also several widely understood slang words, such as "spiel" (elaborate excuse, sales talk or "pitch"), "shtick" (from *Stück* – "thing," "act," "specialty"), "schmaltz" (from *Schmalz* – melted fat), and "schmuck" (vulgar term for an unlikable man).

One occasionally encounters a myth whose common form is that, but for a single vote in the early years of the Republic, America would now be a German-speaking country. No such vote was ever taken. The myth is probably a combination of the Founding Fathers' revolutionary determination to reject undue British influence, and their strategic desire to cultivate the support of the large German community in the middle Atlantic states, particularly near Philadelphia. Thus it is not surprising that the Declaration of Independence was immediately published in German as well as in English.

The Pennsylvania "Dutch" are not Dutch, but rather of German ("Deutsch") and Swiss origin. Many still speak a dialect of German that "fossilizes" the language as it was spoken chiefly in the southwestern German-speaking area hundreds of years ago.

The word "Stein" or "Bierstein" for "beer-mug," particularly of the kitschy beer-hall type, is not used by speakers of German, unless they pick it up from Americans. The common native word is *das Seidel*. The American word "stein" may be a short form of a German word *der Steinkrug* (earthenware jug) brought to America by early immigrants.

Evangelifches

Gefangbuch.

Herausgegeben

von der

Deutfchen Evangelifchen Synode
von Nord-Amerika.

Revidierte Ausgabe.

EDEN PUBLISHING HOUSE,
ST. LOUIS.   CHICAGO.

"Also Henry – Heinrich – war der älteste Sohn von meiner Ur-ur-großmutter . . ."

The child-care facilities at all levels do not burden the family budget since crèches and kindergartens which provide full-day care for children up to the age of six are free. Parents only pay a nominal fee for hot meals and milk and, later, for school meals. All these facilities are financed by extensive subsidies from the state budget.

As a matter of fact, schooling, vocational training and university education are free. Most enterprises run their own holiday camps for the children of their staff. A three-week holiday costs the parents a mere 12 marks. Equally cheap are school holiday camps. Although vacations in a resort run by the trade union holiday service or by an enterprise are inexpensive anyway, families have to pay for their children only 30 marks for a fortnight.

Various forms of financial support are provided for large families with three and more children, as for instance rent allowances, free laundry service, grants for the purchase of children's wear and furniture, etc. Family allowances for the third and any further child amount to 100 marks per month. It should be mentioned that children's wear is inexpensive and heavily subsidized.

From an East German government publication.

Die überall vorhandenen Einrichtungen für Kinder sind keine Belastung des Familienbudgets. Denn die ganztägige Betreuung in der Kinderkrippe und im Kindergarten für Kinder bis zum 6. Lebensjahr sind völlig kostenlos. Nur für das warme Essen und die Milch zahlen die Eltern, ebenso wie für das Essen in der Schule, einen äußerst geringen Betrag. Finanziert werden alle diese Einrichtungen durch bedeutende Zuschüsse des Staates.

Selbstverständlich ist, daß weder Schulgeld gezahlt wird noch Lehrausbildung oder Studium etwas kosten. Drei Wochen im Kinderferienlager (von den meisten Betrieben eingerichtet) kosten nur 12 Mark; die Teilnahme an einer Schulferiengestaltung ist ebenfalls äußerst billig. Auch der ohnehin preiswerte Familienurlaub in einem Heim der Gewerkschaft oder des Betriebes ist für Kinder einheitlich festgelegt und besonders verbilligt (30 Mark für 13 Tage).

Verschiedene finanzielle Unterstützungen gibt es für kinderreiche Familien (drei und mehr Kinder), zum Beispiel Mietzuschüsse, kostenloses Waschen der Haushaltswäsche, Zuschüsse für den Kauf von Bekleidung oder Kindermöbeln; das Kindergeld ab drittem Kind beträgt 100 Mark monatlich. Erwähnt werden soll noch, daß Kinderbekleidung billig ist, da sie in erheblichem Maße staatlich subventioniert wird.

Die alte Heimat – jetzt

Wetterstein: See the Zugbegleiter in the Study Text realia.

Students describe differences between cities or regions known to them: Boston–Los Angeles, Pacific coast–Gulf of Mexico, etc.

Give students a number of English things to explain in German – Student A: *Du sagtest, deine Schwester fährt gern diesen "pickup truck," diesen kleinen LKW. B: Ja, aber auch unseren . . . off-road vehicle. Was ist das? Auch ein LKW? B: Nein, das ist wie ein Motorrad,* etc. Suggestions: cotton candy, anaesthesiologist, recliner (chair), scarecrow, quilting frame, electronic bug zapper, daddy longlegs, possum.

1

HEINZ STRAUCH	Es wäre besser gewesen, wenn du mit dem "Wetterstein" gefahren wärest. Der fährt direkt nach Murnau.
BARBARA FIELD	Ja, das wußte ich schon. Ich wollte aber Nürnberg sehen.

2

CHAD SKAGGS	Was ist der Unterschied zwischen Bayern und Preußen?
HERTA FRANKE	So wie Texas und New York. Wie Sie wissen, Bayern liegt im Süden und ist das größte Land der Bundesrepublik. Preußen ist – oder war – im Norden. Als Staat existiert Preußen nicht mehr.
CHAD SKAGGS	Sind die Leute anders?
HERTA FRANKE	Die Dialekte sind sehr verschieden – und die kulturellen Unterschiede sind auch sehr groß.

3

KARL JÄGER	Deine Tante Rosa ist eine Pink Lady? Was ist das?
CARLA YEAGER	Eine Frau, die in einem Krankenhaus arbeitet und . . .
KARL JÄGER	Das ist bei uns eine Krankenschwester.
CARLA YEAGER	Nein. Sie hilft nur, weil sie das will – ohne Gehalt.

4

GEORG WEIGAND	Ihr bezahlt also 60 Pfennig für ein Liter Benzin, wir aber doppelt soviel.
RICK PETERSON	Aber die geographischen Unterschiede sind sehr groß. Du wohnst z.B. in Bonn, dein Vater aber in Augsburg.
GEORG WEIGAND	Ja. Das sind 529 Kilometer, 5 Stunden mit dem Zug.
RICK PETERSON	Meine Schwiegermutter lebt in New Jersey. Wir wohnen in Sacramento. Das sind fast 3000 Meilen, sagen wir 4800 Kilometer.
GEORG WEIGAND	Und deine Eltern, wo wohnen die?
RICK PETERSON	Nicht weit von uns – in Anaheim. Das sind nur 350 Meilen, also 500 bis 600 Kilometer.
GEORG WEIGAND	Du meinst, das ist nicht weit?

5

KATE MUELLER	Ja, und das kostet eine Menge Geld – $400 im Monat.
TRINA MÜLLER	$400!! Also ein Drittel von ihrem ganzen Einkommen – vor den Steuern – gibt sie für den Kindergarten aus.
KATE MUELLER	Aber die Eltern wollen beide einen Beruf haben. Meine Schwester mußte bald wieder arbeiten.
TRINA MÜLLER	Da gibt es einen großen Unterschied zwischen unseren Systemen. In der DDR bekommt die Mutter 6 Monate frei, mit Gehalt. Der Kindergarten kostet nichts.
KATE MUELLER	Ja, aber das kann man nicht so direkt vergleichen.

6

HOWIE BAKER	Und wenn Großvater nicht nach Amerika ausgewandert wäre? Was wäre dann passiert?
ERNA SCHNEIDER	Wahrscheinlich wäre er Bäcker geblieben.
HOWIE BAKER	Und dann hätte er meine Großmutter nicht kennengelernt.
ERNA SCHNEIDER	Ja, alles wäre anders gewesen. Du wärest nicht hier!

STRUKTUR 2

Verbs §59

1. Past subjunctive of verbs that require *sein*

Students ask each other what
would have happened if
something had not happened
(refer to horizontal life accounts
done above).

- form: *wäre-* + participle

    Was wäre dann passiert? Wahrscheinlich wäre er Bäcker geblieben.

- English equivalents

(If) + had + participle	would have + participle
Wenn er nicht nach Amerika ausgewandert wäre?	Wahrscheinlich wäre er Bäcker geblieben.
If he hadn't emigrated to America?	Probably he would have remained a baker.

Willkommen in der Stadt in der wir zu Hause sind.

Privatbrauerei **GANTER**

Pronouns §15

2. More about relative pronouns

- placement of verb at end of relative clause

This is a further signal that the main idea is being interrupted so that subordinate information can be given.

Main fact	Der Mann ist nicht dein Großvater.
Amplification – which man?	Der Mann, *der die Uniform trägt...*
Main fact with amplification	Der Mann, *der die Uniform trägt,* ist nicht dein Großvater.

Don't forget to fit the verb ending to the subject of the relative clause.

   Eine Pink Lady ist eine Frau, die in einem Krankenhaus arbeitet.
      (Die Frau arbeitet in einem Krankenhaus.)
   "Pink Ladies" sind Frauen, die in Krankenhäusern arbeiten.

Relative constructions are very useful when you lack vocabulary. Put the idea in a larger category and then tell how it is special:

   Eine "Pink Lady" ist eine Frau, die in einem Krankenhaus arbeitet.
                                 category   distinguishing trait

Work with "Categories/
Kategorien" in the
"Bildwörterbuch," pp. 308–9.

3. Fractions and multiples

-tel, -mal

- fractions as nouns

    das/ein Drittel, Viertel, Fünftel, Sechstel, Siebtel, Achtel
    but: **die** Hälfte
    common compound nouns: eine Viertelstunde, ein Halbliter

- **halb** often appears as an adjective, with appropriate endings.

    Wir brauchen eine *halbe* Stunde.
    Sie kommen in einer *halben* Stunde.

- multiples – the reverse of fractions

    zweimal (or *doppelt*) so viel
    dreimal, viermal, fünfmal, . . .

SITUATIONEN 2 Die alte Heimat – jetzt

Stage 1

1: Sie beginnen ein Gespräch mit den "neuen" Verwandten.

a) Beschreiben Sie, was Sie bis jetzt in den zwei Wochen Ihres Europa-Aufenthalts gesehen und gemacht haben.

b) Skizzieren Sie, was Sie in den nächsten Wochen vorhaben.

c) Fragen Sie Ihre Verwandten nach ihren Reisen im In- und Ausland.

3: Erzählen Sie, wie Ihre Familie den Sonntag oder den Sabbat verbringt.

4: Vergleichen Sie europäische und nordamerikan- **Stage 2** ische Entfernungen. Themen:

a) die Wohnsitze Ihrer Verwandten;

b) Ihr Staat oder Ihre Gegend – Städte, Flüsse usw.

1: Diskutieren Sie Gehälter, Steuern und Nebenleistungen – Ihre eigenen, falls Sie berufstä- tig sind, sonst die einer anderen Person. Fangen Sie mit den Tat- sachen an. Zeigen Sie, wie das System der Nebenleistungen funktioniert, indem Sie sich mögliche Fälle vorstellen oder Ereignisse aus der Vergangen- heit beschreiben. Was sollte geändert werden? Was gefällt Ihnen an Ihrem System?

Versuchen Sie doch

2: Perhaps you regret some- thing that happened in your own life or that of someone else. Express the regret and briefly explore what might have been or might now be under other circumstances.

See how well you can use your Bildwörterbuch here.

1

You're having an initial chat with newly located relatives.

a) Tell them about the places you've been and the things you've seen and done in the two weeks you've been in Europe.

b) Outline the rest of your itinerary; fo- cus on your return trip.

c) Ask about their own travels.

3

Tell how your family spends a typical Sunday or Sabbath.

1

Discuss earnings, taxes, and fringe ben- efits – your own, if you are employed, otherwise someone else's. Present the facts first. Illustrate how the benefit sys- tem works by posing hypothetical cases or describing past events. What would you like to see changed in the system? What do you like about it?

2

Vielleicht bereuen Sie etwas, was in Ihrem eigenen Leben oder im Leben eines Angehörigen passiert ist. Drücken

2

Erklären Sie die Unterschiede zwischen Texas und New York. Bei geogra- phischen Sachen können Sie ziemlich genau sein, seien Sie aber vorsichtig, daß Sie bei den Menschenbeschreibungen nicht zu sehr verallgemeinern.

4

Compare European and North American distances. Topics:

a) location of your relatives;

b) your state or region – cities, rivers, etc.

Sie Ihre Reue aus und sagen Sie kurz, was früher anders gewesen wäre oder was jetzt unter anderen Umständen anders wäre.

3

You and your family have had some lucky breaks. Describe them, and then speculate about the alternate course of events.

Sie und Ihre Familie haben in mancher Hinsicht Schwein gehabt. Beschreiben Sie die glücklichen Ereignisse und fragen Sie sich, wie es vielleicht hätte anders werden können.

Your dictionary does not contain every word you will need. Often missing are words for certain everyday items, brand-name products, Americanisms, and "popular culture" things that dictionary makers might consider too trivial. In such cases your choice is to cease communication, use an English word that may not be comprehensible, or attempt to explain what you mean. Think about the strategic advice you have been given through- out *Wie, bitte?*, and then try to express these things in German: manila envelope; cheer- leader; white-water rafting; pickup truck with four-wheel drive.

The people you are visiting have treated you royally, and now you'd like to do something for them to show your appreciation. Come up with an idea – a gift, a festive visit to the *Konditorei*, etc. – and then plan what you will say. Remember that *usually* "it's the thought that counts." Consider two situations. What can you do to express your gratitude to people who have more than you do? On the other hand, your hosts may not be well off, though they will still have their pride. The latter situation is frequently encountered by Westerners visiting East Germany. Gifts of hard currency are not unheard of, and certainly Western consumer items are prized, whether the traveler brings them in from the West or purchases them at the local Intershop.

VSd 2: After students have tried this as a speaking exercise, encourage them to write the note that accompanies the gift.

Chapter 25

WÄSCHEREI/ FOTOENTWICKLUNG

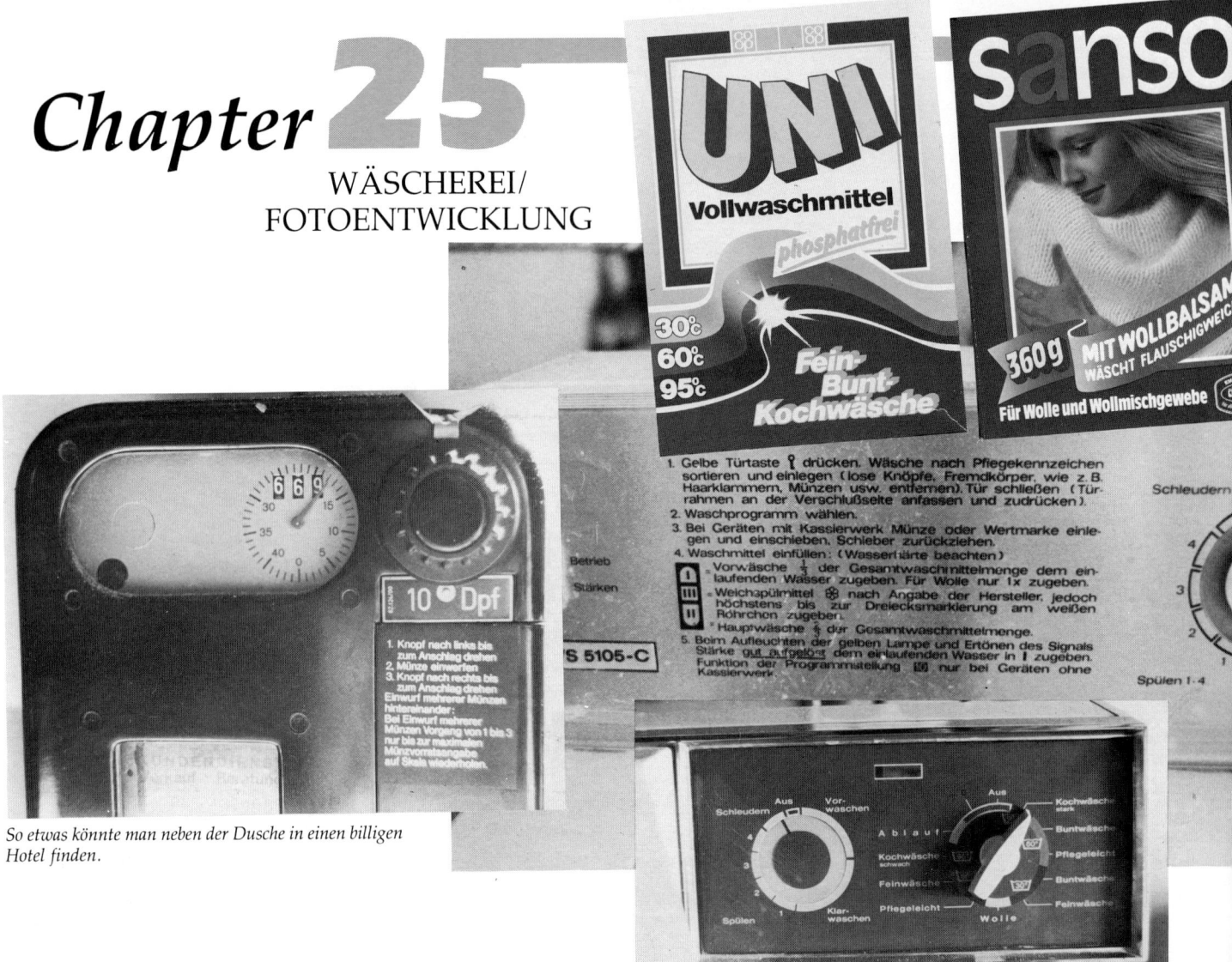

So etwas könnte man neben der Dusche in einen billigen Hotel finden.

FUNKTIONEN – KONTEXTE – STRUKTUREN

Looking ahead

You'll be taking your clothes to a laundromat, learning how the machines work, and arranging for film processing in a photography store.

You will be using:

- the passive voice with modal verbs (*Can* that *be done*?)
- the word *selber* to emphasize "self" (I'll do it *myself.*)
- the passive voice in the present tense (That *is* not *done* here.)
- different ways to give instructions for operating something
- simple words to form compounds (*groß-vergrößern*)

Song: Brahms's "Lullaby"; note the passive: "Morgen früh, wenn Gott will, wirst du wieder geweckt."

250

Wäscherei

Point out 1) *kochen* means "to boil" as well as "to cook," which suggests something about traditional German ways of preparing food; 2) wash-water temperature is often very high.

1

See *Bildwörterbuch* display, "Körperteile – Gesundheit – Kleidung," pp. 294–295.
    This chapter focuses less on washing clothes and developing film than on the idea of describing a *process*. Supplementary exercises added by the teacher could therefore emphasize any process well known to students. Depending on the part of the country, discussion of process can include heavy industry (the manufacture of autos, steel,

2

Selbst/Bedienung self-service

tires, etc.), light industry (electronics, clothing manufacture, food production, etc.), specialized regional

3

Pflege/Wäsche delicates

industry (fishing, logging, mining), or the operation of a business ranging from banking to shoe sales. Most students will have at least passing familiarity with one of these and can be asked to assemble the vocabulary necessary to describe the process. The *Bildwörterbuch* contains several useful displays that illustrate objects and actions. See note in Instructor's Guide.

4

Gebrauchs/Anweisungen operation instructions

HERR LANDAU	So. Eine ganze Menge haben Sie da. Mal sehen, wieviel das wiegt. . . . So, 7 Kilo. Das können wir in einer Maschine machen.
HERR NIKOLAISEN	Wunderbar. Wann kann ich die Wäsche abholen?
HERR LANDAU	Heute schon, wenn Sie vor 18 Uhr vorbeikommen.
HERR NIKOLAISEN	Schön. Darf ich den Koffer hier lassen?
HERR LANDAU	Natürlich. Wir packen dann alles für Sie ein.
HERR NIKOLAISEN	Oh, noch etwas: Bitte kochen Sie die Wäsche nicht.
FRAU KRÜGER	Ich weiß nicht, ob wir das alles in einer Maschine waschen können.
FRAU BALZ	Vielleicht sollte man das in zwei Maschinen waschen. Die Hemden auch mit der Feinwäsche.
FRAU KRÜGER	Ja, die dürfen allerdings nicht gekocht werden.
FRAU BALZ	Es wäre auch besser, wenn Sie die neuen Blue Jeans nicht kochen würden. Sonst gehen sie zuviel ein.
FRAU KRÜGER	Wie Sie meinen. Wir brauchen dann zwei Maschinen.
FRAU BALZ	Oder vielleicht sollte ich die Blue Jeans selber waschen.
FRAU KRÜGER	Wie Sie wollen – aber hier ist keine Selbstbedienung.
CLAUDIA MARGNELLI	Wissen Sie, wie man diese Maschine bedient?
RALPH BAKER	Ja, die Anweisungen sind nicht so leicht zu verstehen, wenn man Ausländer ist. Haben Sie die Kochwäsche und Pflegewäsche schon getrennt?
CLAUDIA MARGNELLI	Ja, denn die meisten Sachen sollen nicht gekocht werden.
RALPH BAKER	Dann stellt man die beiden Maschinen auf Buntwäsche ein. Dann wird nichts gekocht.
CLAUDIA MARGNELLI	Aber werden auch die Blue Jeans sauber?
RALPH BAKER	Sicher. Deutsche Technik.
CHRISTINE HESELMANN	Wollen Sie, daß ich das für Sie mache?
MR. HAWTHORNE	Ach, nein, danke – wenn Sie mir nur zeigen würden, wie das funktioniert, kann ich es selber machen.
CHRISTINE HESELMANN	Tue ich gerne. Aber was für Wäsche haben Sie?
MR. HAWTHORNE	Ja, ich weiß die deutschen Wörter nicht so gut. Hemden und Socken, Jeans und Unterwäsche.
CHRISTINE HESELMANN	Also Hemden sind Pflegewäsche, die sollten Sie in einer Maschine waschen. Und die Jeans und Socken sind Buntwäsche – das wäre noch eine Maschine.
MR. HAWTHORNE	Und die anderen Sachen sind Weißwäsche, ja? Also drei Maschinen.
CHRISTINE HESELMANN	Richtig. Und die Gebrauchsanweisungen sehen Sie hier oben an der Tafel. Geht es so?

Verbs §79

1. The passive with modals

Combine a modal form with the *passive infinitive* – in both English and German.

passive infinitive =
past participle + **werden**

	passive sign			passive sign
Kann das	*gemacht werden?*	*Can* that	*be*	*done?*
modal	participle	modal		participle

Ja, die Hemden **dürfen** nicht **gekocht werden.**
Die normalen Sachen **sollen** auch nicht **gekocht werden.**
Hugo, deine Unterwäsche **muß** einfach **gewaschen werden.**

Exercise in context by having students assume the role of manager and employee in, for example, a new McDonald's restaurant (e.g., *Die Tische müssen alle 20 Minuten geputzt werden.*). Point out how the passive will be used by someone who does not care who gets the job done, or else does not want to tell someone to do it outright.

Remember that the *passive* gives you an opportunity to say things from *another perspective*. These three sentences can be expressed another way but with different implications:

Ja, **man darf** die Hemden nicht **kochen.**
Man soll die normalen Sachen auch nicht **kochen.**
Hugo, **du mußt** einfach deine Unterwäsche **waschen.**

Note: Where no agent is apparent – as in the first two sentences – the *active voice* uses **man.** The passive requires no such equivalent – the agent is simply unstated.

The reference grammar demonstrates the use of *von* with a personal agent. A nonpersonal agent is often part of a *durch* phrase: *Der Wolf wurde durch einen Schuß getötet.*

Ja, **man** darf die Hemden nicht kochen.	(agent: **man**)
Right – **you** can't wash the shirts on ''hot.''	(agent: **you**)

Ja, die Hemden **dürfen** nicht **gekocht werden.**	(no agent)
Right – the shirts **can't be washed** on ''hot.''	(no agent)

Pronouns §22

2. *Selber* – "self" rather than somebody else

- ### *Selber* places special emphasis on the subject.

Oder vielleicht sollte *ich* die Blue Jeans einfach **selber** waschen.
Or maybe *I* should just wash the blue jeans **myself.**
Wenn Sie's mir nur zeigen würden, kann *ich* es schon **selber** machen.
If you'd just show me, *I* can do it **myself.**

Student A nicely offers to do something for Student B (*Ich hole dir eine Flasche Mineralwasser, Soll ich . . .*); B either accedes or counters with a statement including *selber*. Note the opportunity to review the *wollen, daß* feature from Chapter 22.

If asked, explain that *selbst* is an alternate form of *selber*. Don't discuss *selbst* = "even."

- ### *Selber* does not change its form.

Wir wollen **selber** gehen.
We want to go **ourselves.**
Sie möchte es **selber** probieren.
She'd like to try it **herself.**

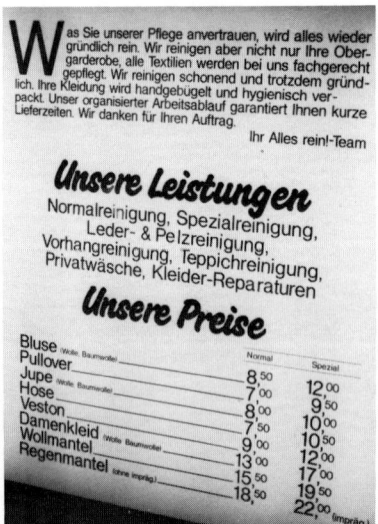

Stage 1

	A	B
1	Asks how much B's laundry weighs. Wonders if it will fit into one machine. Agrees; tells B when it will be ready and what else they will do for B.	Doesn't know – says it's a lot. Says two will be necessary, says why. Is grateful; asks for special treatment for one article.
2	Mentions types of laundry to be done. Wants B to be sure to keep various items separate: colored fabrics from whites, synthetics from naturals. Asks about closing hours, arranges to come back later in the day. Reacts, says it's a must.	Is confident that they can do the job well and quickly. Tells A how long the laundry has been in business, says there's nothing to worry about. Says today will be impossible. Will do their best.
3	Wants to wash two different kinds of clothes, but doesn't understand how the machine works. Lists different articles of clothing, is worried about these machines. Asks how much soap, where to put it into machine, where to insert coins. Is grateful for B's help – is in a hurry.	Is glad to help out. Says the machines are very good; lists clothing to go into each of two loads. Explains everything. Says A needn't worry about time – machines are fast and efficient.

Note the chance to review *seit*.

Unser Service:

- Vollreinigung
- Fleckentfernung
- Appretur
- Perfekte Bügelqualität
- Sachkundige Beratung
- Wäschedienst

Stage 2

1: Sie sind in einer Wäscherei mit einem Koffer voll schmutziger Wäsche. Fragen Sie den Bedienten wie man a) die Maschine betätigt; b) die richtige Seife wählt (Sie müssen sagen, was für Wäsche Sie haben); c) die Wäsche trocknet (Sie haben ein paar Sachen, die Sie lieber im Zimmer aufhängen möchten).

3: Sie unterhalten sich in der Wäscherei mit einer anderen Person über die Vor- und Nachteile, eine Waschmaschine zu besitzen. Führen Sie das Gespräch mit der Voraussetzung, Sie sind: a) Student, b) ein Stadtbewohner mit einer kleinen Wohnung, c) ein Bauer, d) der

1

You are in a laundromat with a suitcase full of dirty laundry. Consult the attendant about how to: a) operate the machine, b) choose the right soap – you'll have to tell what kind of laundry you have, c) dry the laundry – there are a couple of items you would rather take back to your room and hang up to dry.

2

Ein türkisches Ehepaar mit mehreren Kindern erbittet Ihre Hilfe, die Bedienungsanweisungen an einer Waschmaschine zu verstehen.

a) Erklären Sie, wo man was macht, wieviel es kostet und wie man den

Maschinen die verschiedenen Wäschesorten zuteilt.

b) Die Kinder wollen die Babywindeln in einer eigenen Maschine waschen. Erklären Sie ihnen einfach und klar, wie man dies macht.

3

You are talking with another person in the laundromat about the advantages and disadvantages of owning a washing machine. Carry on the conversation, assuming you are one of the following: a) a college student, b) a city dweller in a tiny apartment, c) a farmer, d) the son or daughter of an appliance dealer

Versuchen Sie doch

Sohn oder die Tochter eines Waschmaschinenhändlers.

For translations of **2** and **VSd** see Instructor's Guide.

You've picked up your suit from the cleaners and returned to the hotel, where you intend to change for an important job interview. But when you put on the jacket you noticed a large stain on the pocket. Now you're back at the cleaners and are understandably upset. You just have to have the jacket back before the interview, which is supposed to begin in an hour. Convince the employees to correct the mistake.

Das Fachgeschäft

Abbreviation for *der/die Auszubildende*, "trainee."

In Chapter 19 Fräulein Hardt received advice to buy a bathing suit in a *Fachgeschäft*, a sporting goods specialty store, as opposed to a chain or department store. The notion of a specialty shop is important in Europe. The personnel can be expected to have detailed knowledge of a product or service, knowledge that derives from the apprenticeship (*die Ausbildungszeit, die Lehre*), and probably years of experience as well. The apprentice (*der Lehrling, der/die Azubi*) typically begins work in an area of special interest on a part-time basis during the mid- to late teen years. At the same time there are about eight hours of regular classes per week in a trade school (*die Berufsschule*) that supplement the practical experience with a theoretical background. In a photography apprenticeship, for example, the school training would include work in the chemistry of photo developing and printing; additional classes would include basic business practices, sociology, German, religion, physical education, and a foreign language. The work in a photo store would be compensated, but the wages of an apprentice are typically low – average pay in all apprenticeships is around DM 600 per month. Most apprentices live at home while they are training.

At the end of the apprenticeship the student must pass a *Gesellenprüfung* to become a journeyman (*der Geselle*). After some years of practical experience, and in some fields additional school training, the person may take the *Meisterprüfung* to qualify as a "master" (*der Meister*) – master photographer, master bricklayer, master machinist – who is then entitled to train students in turn. Pride in this long training is understandable, and the expertise that a consumer can count on in a *Fachgeschäft* is welcome.

Deutsche Technik – Made in Germany

● products

The industrial products of the German-speaking countries, especially West Germany and Switzerland, are famed for quality – and sometimes price. *Mercedes* and *Porsche* are household words in North America. Those moderately interested in automotive technology will recognize as well the brands *Blaupunkt* (car stereos) and *Bosch* (replacement parts). The name *Zeiss* will be familiar to anyone seriously involved with photography or optics. Two other companies, well known by their abbreviations, may not be recognized as German: BASF (*Bayerische Anilin- und Sodafabrik*) and BMW (*Bayerische Motorenwerke*). Completing the trio of Bavarian-born technical products known to virtually every American is the "Bayer" of "Bayer aspirin."

● technology

There is no longer a single Germany of world-power rank, and German, Swiss, and Austrian firms have lost their preeminence in certain fields, like optics and clockmaking. Nevertheless, the German-speaking countries remain prominent industrial powers and sources of technological innovation. In gross national product West Germany ranks fourth in the world, behind the United States, Japan, and the USSR. East Germany is also a leading industrial producer. Combined, the gross national products of the two Germanies (population 78 million) would rank ahead of that of the Soviet Union (population 278 million).

Before 1945 Germany was a world power in both scientific research and technological development. Fields of particular strength were chemistry, physics, metallurgy, and electrical engineering. Indeed, many scientists (and other academics) from the United States received their advanced training at German universities; not until 1861 was the first doctoral degree awarded by an American university (Yale). Graduate programs in this country are modeled on those of German universities. Here Johns Hopkins was the pioneer.

● people

German-speaking scientists and technologists have given their names to scientific phenomena or industrial processes generally familiar to American students. Chemistry students encounter the burner invented by Robert Wilhelm Bunsen (1811–1889), and the glass flask originated by Emil Erlenmeyer (1825–1909). Physics courses teach about the shifting of sound and light waves, an effect named for the Austrian Christian Johann Doppler (1803–1853). Our everyday temperature scale was devised by Gabriel Daniel Fahrenheit (1686–1736). Gregor Mendel (1822–1884) founded the science of genetics. Spectrographic analysis features the landmark lines first observed by Joseph von Fraunhofer (1787–1826). The naturalist, traveler, and statesman Alexander von Humboldt (1769–1859) is remembered in the names of an ocean current, a species of penguin, a county and university in California, and the longest river in Nevada. The scale of supersonic flight speeds (Mach 1, 2, 3) is named for the Austrian physicist Ernst Mach (1838–1916). The "hertz," the basic unit of electronic frequency and an everyday word in broadcasting, is named for the physicist Heinrich Rudolph Hertz (1857–1894). And finally, simply mentioning the name of Albert Einstein (1879–1955) suffices to make the point that Germans figure prominently in the history of science and technology.

● standards: "DIN"

In the "*Fotoentwicklung*" dialog, and in one of the Chapter 10 dialogs, people describe film speed by its "DIN" number. The abbreviation stands for "*Deutsche Industrie Norm*" or – in a neat pun – "*Das ist Norm.*" The *Deutsche Industrie Normen* are an elaborate code of technical specifications created over the years since 1917 through a cooperative effort involving industry, trade, research institutions, and government. Even film sold in North America may carry the DIN number. Similarly, the paper-size specification "A4" found on photocopying machines and some computer printer settings refers to the DIN description of a standard paper size.

Film ist nicht belichtet
Film ist vor der Abgabe naß
geworden / am Schutzpapier
angeklebt.

Ihr Fotolabor

GESPRÄCHE 2
Fotoentwicklung

1

FRÄULEIN SCHRANZ
: Interessant. Wo haben Sie die Aufnahmen gemacht, wenn ich fragen darf?

HERR BEINECKE
: In Ost-Berlin. Wir waren 7 Tage dort.

2

HERR HUMMEL
: Ich möchte eine Vergrößerung von diesem Farbfoto.

FRÄULEIN SCHMITTEN
: Oh, das ist sehr schön. Ist das Ost-Berlin?

HERR HUMMEL
: Nein, Dresden. Das ist unsere Studentengruppe. Die Vergrößerung ist ein Geschenk für meine Freundin.

3

FRÄULEIN FONTANE
: Guten Tag. Ich möchte diese Filme zum Entwickeln abgeben.

FRÄULEIN BRUNN
: Schön. Normale Größe, ja? Und matt oder glanz?

FRÄULEIN FONTANE
: Matt. Sie sagten, "normale Größe." Was ist die normale Größe?

FRÄULEIN BRUNN
: Normal ist 9 × 13cm. Die nächste Größe wäre 13 × 18.

FRÄULEIN FONTANE
: Hm. Was ist der Preisunterschied?

FRÄULEIN BRUNN
: Eigentlich minimal. Für 13 × 18 haben wir diese Woche einen Sonderpreis. Mal sehen: 24 Aufnahmen . . . das wäre 31,00DM statt 39,00DM, und Sie bekommen einen Film kostenlos.

FRÄULEIN FONTANE
: Gut. Und wann kann ich meine Fotos abholen?

FRÄULEIN BRUNN
: Schon morgen um diese Zeit. Wir entwickeln hier alles selber.

4

MR. FLYNN
: Wie lange dauert das? Wir fahren morgen weg.

HERR NÄFF
: Mal sehen. 100 ASA – das ist ein amerikanischer Film.

MR. FLYNN
: Ja, den habe ich nach Österreich mitgebracht.

HERR NÄFF
: Kein Problem. Das ist 21 DIN. Können wir machen – also keine Sonderentwicklung.

MR. FLYNN
: Werden die Filme hier entwickelt?

HERR NÄFF
: Nein, in unserem Zentrallabor.

MR. FLYNN
: Aber das braucht viel Zeit, oder?

HERR NÄFF
: Eigentlich nicht viel. Es ist erst 14 Uhr. Sie können Ihre Filme hier lassen. Sie werden noch heute abgeholt und dann in 24 Stunden zurückgebracht.

5

HERR JÜRGENS
: Ich möchte bitte Fotos von diesen Dias.

FRAU KLETT
: Ja, das dauert einige Tage. Haben Sie es eilig?

HERR JÜRGENS
: Nein. Ich bin noch zwei Wochen hier. Aber ist es teuer?

FRAU KLETT
: Nein. Wir haben sogar ein Sonderangebot für alle Größen: 10 × 15, 15 × 25, 20 × 30.

HERR JÜRGENS
: Ich hätte gerne diese 3 in 20 × 30, aber sind die Dias scharf genug?

FRAU KLETT
: Mal sehen. . . . Die zwei Aufnahmen von der Wanderung, ja. Die andere kann aber nicht so groß gemacht werden. Sie hatten zu wenig Licht.

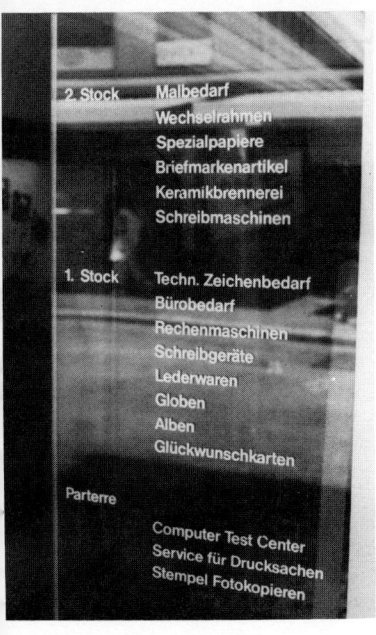

257

1. The passive in the present tense

● **already seen: the past tense**

Die Kirche *wurde* im Krieg *zerstört*
↖ past tense of **werden**

● **the present tense**

Die Filme *werden* hier *entwickelt.*
↖ present tense of **werden**

Der Film *wird* um 2 Uhr *abgeholt.*
↖ present tense of **werden**

2. Operating instructions – context, tone, perspective

a) machine directions

Waschmittel wählen	*Select soap*
Münzen einwerfen	*Insert coins*
Knopf drücken	*Press button*

b) general instruction

Man wählt das Waschmittel.	*You select the soap.*
Dann wirft man die Münzen ein.	*Then you insert the coins.*
Dann drückt man den Knopf.	*Then you press the button.*

c) personal instruction

Wählen Sie zuerst das Waschmittel.	*First choose your soap.*
Dann werfen Sie die Münzen ein.	*Then put in your money.*
Dann drücken Sie den Knopf.	*Then press the button.*

d) process description

Das Waschmittel wird gewählt.	*The soap is chosen.*
Die Münzen werden eingeworfen.	*The coins are inserted.*
Der Knopf wird gedrückt.	*The button is pushed.*

CONTEXT	STRUCTURE
a) – The directions on an apparatus made for public use	**infinitive**
b) – How "one" does it, how it's done in general	***man***
c) – How "you" do it (with personal illustration)	**imperative**
d) – Impersonal; emphasizes process, not person	**passive**

3. More about word formation: nouns

● **nouns and verbs made from adjectives**

groß → die Größe
größer → vergrößern → <u>die</u> Vergrößer<u>ung</u>

● **nouns made from verbs – two patterns**

entwickeln → <u>die</u> Entwick<u>lung</u>; die Sonderentwicklung
schenken → <u>das</u> Ge<u>schenk</u>
packen → <u>das</u> Ge<u>päck</u>

Widerrechtlich geparkte Fahrzeuge werden kostenpflichtig abgeschleppt.

Bitte beachten

▶ Glaspackungen nach Farben getrennt einwerfen

▶ Glasfremdes Material vorher entfernen und im Abfallbehälter deponieren

▶ Metallverschlüsse und -manschetten, Keramik, Porzellan und Umhüllungen gehören nicht in den Container

Ask for equivalents of *groß >* *Vergrößerung* with other adjectives: *klein, lang,* etc. Additional *Ge-* forms: *schreien: das Geschrei, heulen: das Geheul, beten: das Gebet, dichten: das Gedicht, fühlen: das Gefühl, sprechen: das Gespräch, trinken: das Getränk, rauschen: das Geräusch.* You may wish to talk about the collective *das-* nouns that begin with *Ge-*: e.g., *der Busch > das Gebüsch, der Berg > das Gebirge, der Flügel > das Geflügel, das Land > das Gelände, das Wetter > das Gewitter.*

SITUATIONEN 2 Fotoentwicklung

	A	**B**
Stage 1		

1

If students falter, ask them what basic qualities are involved: clarity, promptness, etc.

Don't expect *den genausten Maßstäben gemäß* or *den höchsten beruflichen Anforderungen entsprechend.* "*Wie im besten Fotolabor*" should suffice.

A	**B**
Wants to be sure developing will be done in a professional manner.	Is startled; asks why A would doubt their competence.
Apologizes; says the pictures are of loved ones who are very special.	Says developing is done on the premises according to highest standards.
Is satisfied; needs pictures right away.	Pictures will be finished in a day.

2

Unser Bestes is not necessary. *So schnell und gut wie möglich* is fine.

A	**B**
Has various slides and prints; wants enlargements of prints, copies of slides.	Asks A to specify which ones and how large.
Asks whether prints can be made from slides as well as from negatives.	Says the photo shop can do almost anything.
Asks whether posters can be made from two of the negatives.	It's possible, but will take a good deal longer.
Asks that it be done as soon as possible – it's a gift for a family member.	Says they'll do their best.

3

Use *klar* and *unklar* or *scharf* and *unscharf* for "vivid" and "blurry," or tell what can't be seen.

A	**B**	**C**
Picked up pictures the day before; not satisfied with the quality.		Asks what's wrong.
Says colors aren't vivid; images are blurry.	Says developing cost too much anyway.	Is apologetic, asks to see pictures.
Gives pictures to C.	Notices that A's glasses are very dirty.	Says pictures look fine.
Takes off glasses; confirms what B said.	Says A's glasses just have to be cleaned.	
Says they were cleaned last week.		Asks what was wrong with price.
	Realizes that a 1 has been mistaken for a 7.	Says Americans are often confused about that.
Apologizes for mistaken comment.	Apologizes for comment about price.	Graciously accepts apologies.

Stage 2

For German version of **1** and English of **2** see Instructor's Guide.

1

Your plane is leaving in three hours, but you are worried about the security X-ray equipment and would like to have your pictures developed before going to the airport. You have seen a shop sign: "*Sofortentwicklung.*" You enter the store and carry out the transaction. Make sure the clerk understands the urgency of the job.

2

Sie sind gerade von Berlin zurückgekehrt, wo sie viele Menschen und Dinge fotografiert haben. Erklären Sie der interessierten Fotogeschäftinhaberin, warum Ihre fünf Lieblingsbilder so besonders sind. Erzählen Sie ihr auch von den Umständen, unter denen Sie die Fotos gemacht haben.

Versuchen Sie doch

For German version see Instructor's Guide.

You are about to do some very important photography: As the only person in your family who has the wherewithal to journey to the ancestral homeland, you have been entrusted with making photos of family archives in the churches and town halls in the countryside outside of Leipzig. Your starting point is East Berlin, where you inquire about the equipment necessary for making high-quality pictures under sometimes adverse lighting circumstances. Explain what your technical needs will be and also solicit advice about taking pictures of documents that you assume might be considered sensitive, such as records of military service.

Chapter 26

UNHÖFLICHKEIT – HÖFLICHKEIT/
WILLKOMMEN UND ABSCHIED

Am 4. November 1987 ist unsere liebe Mutter, Großmutter, Urgroßmutter,
Tante und Schwiegermutter

Katharina Brand

geb. Ries

kurz vor Vollendung ihres 96. Lebensjahres nach einem glücklichen und er-
füllten Leben in Gottes Frieden heimgegangen.
Wir werden sie am Freitag, dem 6. November 1987, um 12.30 Uhr, an der Seite
unseres unvergessenen Vaters, ihrer Eltern und Geschwister auf dem Friedhof Mannheim-Friedrichsfeld zur letzten Ruhe betten.
Im Anschluß an die Beisetzung feiern wir eine Heilige Messe in der Pfarrkir-
che St. Bonifatius, Mannheim-Friedrichsfeld.

In Trauer:
Elisabeth Berrang geb. Brand
und die ganze Familie
Fritz Hügel und Frau Marga geb. Brand
und die ganze Familie

Mannheim, den 4. November 1987

Flughafen Frankfurt am Main.

Feel free to introduce Goethe's poem, *"Willkommen und Abschied."* Other cultural enrichment: Schubert, "Gute Nacht" (from *Die Winterreise*); final section of P.D.Q. Bach, "Black Forest Pilgrim."

FUNKTIONEN – KONTEXTE – STRUKTUREN

Looking ahead

You'll be dealing with unpleasant people, maintaining your opinions, talking your way out of awkward situations, asking for favors, preparing for a longer stay, learning about hospitality, and politely taking your leave.

You will be using:

- constructions that offer alternatives and present consequences (otherwise, what happens if)
- more polite and therefore more effective formulations of expressions you learned earlier
- qualifying expressions (not as simple, not for everyone, it seems)
- modal verbs in the past subjunctive (could have visited, should have gone)

Unhöflichkeit – Höflichkeit

1 *Being hassled*

a) Hören Sie doch auf!
b) Lassen Sie mich in Ruhe! Sonst ruf' ich um Hilfe!
c) Wenn Sie nicht sofort aufhören, ruf' ich den Schaffner.
d) Sonst hau' ich dir eins in die Fresse!
e) Das war doch unverschämt!

2 *Too much noise*

a) Ruhe, bitte!
b) Darf ich um Ruhe bitten?
c) Dürfte ich Sie um Ruhe bitten?
d) Ich bitte zum letzen Mal um Ruhe. Sonst gehe ich zu den Herbergseltern.
e) Halt's Maul!

3 *Political arguments*

HERR HENNING	Die Amerikaner wollen immer mehr Atomwaffen in Europa. Warum wählen Sie immer solche Präsidenten?
LINDA MARKS	a) Vielleicht haben Sie recht. Ich weiß nicht.

b) Naja, Politik finde ich nicht so interessant.
c) Na, die Sache ist nicht so einfach, wie Sie meinen.
d) Nun, erstens: Ich bin nicht der Präsident. Und zweitens: Der spricht nicht für alle Amerikaner.
e) Glauben Sie, daß alle Deutschen so denken?
f) Aber es scheint, die Russen wollen auch immer mehr Waffen in Europa haben.
g) Und wenn es in der Bundesrepublik keine Atomwaffen und keine amerikanischen Soldaten mehr gibt?
h) Und hat man hier immer die besten Politiker gewählt?

4 *Apologizing*

ERNST BOHRER HUGO FRIEDRICH	Warum haben Sie das gesagt? Das meinen Sie sicher nicht!
	a) Ich glaube, Sie haben mich falsch verstanden.

b) Das war nicht ernst gemeint.
c) Es tut mir leid, daß Sie es so verstanden haben.

5 *Gripes*

KLAUS WENDT ANNA KOHL	Das hättest du einfach nicht tun sollen!
	a) Ja, das stimmt. Das war wirklich dumm von mir.

b) Ich glaube nicht, daß das *so* schlimm war.

6 *Invitations*

HERR BRACHER FRAU KÖNIG	Könnten Sie Samstag abend zu uns kommen?
	a) Leider nicht. Das ist sehr nett von Ihnen, aber ich habe schon etwas vor.

b) Vielen Dank für die Einladung. Aber leider müssen wir uns entschuldigen. Wir haben schon etwas geplant.
c) Gerne. Das wäre schön. Wann sollen wir da sein?

7 *Doing favors*

FRAU TIEMENS	Entschuldigung. Können Sie mir einen Gefallen tun?
FRAU BERGMANN	Ja, gerne. Wie kann ich Ihnen helfen?

Struktur 1 covers the grammar points of Gespräche 2, so that Struktur 2 can be devoted to the general "farewell" statement about grammar. Nevertheless, the past subjunctive of modals, which is presented intensively in Gespräche 2, is represented in Gespräche 1 as well.

Exercises: Introduce statements with "Ich hoffe, . . . ," expressing wishes that something may happen. Students introduce an alternative with a *sonst* clause. Example: Teacher: "*Ich hoffe, es regnet heute nicht.*" Student: "*Sonst müssen wir zu Hause bleiben.*" T: "*Ich hoffe, Klaus bringt unser Mittagessen.*" S: "*Sonst müssen wir etwas kaufen./ Sonst muß er uns ein gutes Essen kaufen.*"

See note in Instructor's Guide.

Better students will be troubled by *hätten . . . gehen sollen*, etc., since they have worked so hard to understand the use of *sein* with some verbs. Many will not well understand how the modal determines the choice of auxiliary.

Illustrate the difference in English with an example that no normal native speaker will fail to grasp: "If my great-great-great-grandparents could move to California . . . "

1. Offering alternatives and presenting consequences

sonst – "or else"

Sonst – in one word – accomplishes functions that might otherwise require two sentences connected by *oder*, or else a long and perhaps clumsy utterance involving *wenn*, a subject + verb combination, and quite likely a negation. Because it permits efficient expression, *sonst* is very useful when one must issue a warning or threat:

> Du hörst auf, oder ich hau' dir eins in die Fresse!
> Wenn du nicht aufhörst, hau' ich dir eins in die Fresse!
> Hör doch auf. **Sonst** hau' ich dir eins in die Fresse!

> Wenn ihr nicht aufhört, gehe ich zu den Herbergseltern.
> Wenn ihr weiter soviel Lärm macht, gehe ich zu den Herbergseltern.
> Ich bitte zum letzten Mal um Ruhe. **Sonst** gehe ich zu den Herbergseltern.

2. The past subjunctive with modal verbs

• forms

Use *hätte-* as a helping verb, then <u>infinitive</u> + <u>modal</u>.

Das **hättest** du einfach nicht **tun sollen!**   *You just shouldn't have done that!*

WARNING: Here German differs significantly from English, which begins with the modal and then continues with *have* + the participle of the main verb.

> *You just **shouldn't have done** that!*

If you begin with the modal, you will end up with something resembling the *present* subjunctive.

• word order

Both the modal and its verb complement stand at the *end* of the clause.

Sie **hätten** nach Leipzig **reisen können.**   *You **could have traveled** to Leipzig.*
*You **would have been able to travel** to Leipzig.*

NOTE: In the past subjunctive, where English may use *would*, German does <u>not</u> use *würde*.

Stage 1	A	B
See note in Instructor's Guide.	(Hat 2 Flaschen Wein getrunken) Fragt, ob B tanzen und singen möchte. Egal. Stellt dieselbe Frage, lauter. Hört nicht zu. Möchte B küssen. Versucht, B zu küssen.	(Hat 2 Glas Wein getrunken) Tanzt nicht gern; singt nicht gut. Antwortet diplomatisch. Antwortet mit sehr einfachen Worten. Scharfe Antwort.

Remind students: 1) drunks can turn belligerent – choose words carefully; 2) in such situations it is not intrinsically impolite to ask a stranger to dance or join in other fun.

2 Scene: at a concert, during and shortly after intermission.

A	B
(Has unconsciously sung along with the performance) Offers apology.	Hesitantly asks A to stop; doesn't want to spoil all the fun, though. Accepts; smoothes over the conflict by making small talk about concert.

(Music starts up again)

A	B
Gets carried away; sings again. Apologizes very politely; assures A that it really was just a bad habit.	Repeats request for appropriate behavior, this time more sternly. Wants to get back to listening.

Stage 2

See notes in Instructor's Guide.

1 Two other people have been disputing who was in line first. The clerk turns to you for your opinion. You've been there all the time and think you know who's right, but you weren't paying close attention every moment.

2 Im Supermarkt kommen Sie zum Einkaufswagen zurück, wo Sie sehen, daß ein anderer Kunde, der Ihren Wagen mit seinem verwechselt hat, gerade einen großen Sack Kartoffeln hineingelegt hat. Jetzt sieht er, daß Sie den Fehler gesehen haben. Er ist verlegen, aber Sie meinen nicht, daß man sich darüber aufregen soll. Versichern Sie ihm, daß es unwichtig ist und bitten Sie vielleicht sogar um ein neues Kochrezept.

3 An acquaintance invited you out for the evening some time ago, and you had a grand time. Now you'd like to reciprocate. Recall all the fun you had, and then issue your own invitation. Detail your suggestions, but remember that you don't know all of your acquaintance's likes and dislikes; you may want to leave some options.

4 An Ihrem ersten Tag im Büro sehen Sie plötzlich ein, daß Ihnen die Bedienung Ihres Computers nicht mehr so klar ist. Bitten Sie eine(n) Ihrer Mitarbeiter um Hilfe und laden Sie sie/ihn dann als Zeichen Ihrer Dankbarkeit zu einem Getränk während der Mittagspause ein.

Versuchen Sie doch

VSd: First item – see note in Instructor's Guide.

Lesen Sie die Diskussion von deutschen und amerikanischen Fahrgewohnheiten. Dann a) vergleichen Sie Ihre eigene Fahrweise mit der eines typischen Autofahrers in Ihrer Gegend; b) beschreiben Sie die Fahrgewohnheiten in den Nachbarstaaten; c) vergleichen Sie die örtliche Fahrweise mit den amerikanischen Fahrgewohnheiten, die im Artikel beschrieben werden.

Check a major newspaper for stories about the United States and West Germany. You should be able to find something almost every day. Now imagine that a West German not particularly friendly to Americans or their foreign policy has read the item and commented about it to you. The comment was of the tone, *"Na, so sind ja die Amerikaner . . . "* Agree or disagree; can you pursue the discussion for an entire minute?

Read the discussion of American and German driving habits on page 165. Then

a) compare your own driving style with that of the typical driver in your area;
b) describe the driving practices of people in nearby states;
c) compare the local driving style with the American driving style described in the article. Several of the *Drucksachen* have to do with vehicular travel, as does the *Bildwörterbuch* display on *Transportation/Verkehr*, pp. 292–293. You may find it helpful to consult them for specialized vocabulary.

Culture, language, and behavior

The casual tourist visiting one of the German-speaking countries may perceive only the most distorted stereotypes, such as beer-swilling, brass-band Bavarian "Gemütlichkeit" or chilling uniformed "Prussian" officialism. Of course the reasonably intelligent visitor will realize, intellectually at least, what those intimately familiar with German culture and language understand more emotionally: East Germans, West Germans, Austrians, and Swiss are fundamentally like all other human beings. They experience the same feelings, think the same thoughts, and share the universal concerns about family, health, work, money, possessions, and pleasure.

During a visit of a few weeks or more in a German-speaking country, a reasonably perceptive outsider with a knowledge of German comparable to that offered in *Wie, bitte?* might gather – with amusement, annoyance, or just fascination – a collection of observations like the following:

- Flowers are exchanged frequently and with some formality – one often sees people carrying neatly wrapped bouquets.
- Poorly maintained cars ("junkers") are virtually nonexistent. Automobile license plates do not carry commercial or touristic slogans ("Idaho – famous potatoes"), and there are no customized "status" plates with their puns, clever spelling, and boasting. Cute names for car models ("Rabbit") are unheard of.
- Newspapers carry elaborate death notices signed by family and co-workers.
- Dogs – at least small ones – are very common. Despite a general emphasis on cleanliness, they are allowed in many restaurants and hotels, where they are expected to behave well – and indeed do. Dogs must wear muzzles (*der Maulkorb*) on some public transit systems. Virtually unheard of are dogs running loose, much less attacking humans. "Pooper-scooper" vending machines help owners comply with cleanliness ordinances.
- People contemplating purchasing goods or services, such as vacation accommodations, inquire carefully about what will be provided, and advertisements describe such *Leistungen* in detail. Failure to provide what was promised will occasion stern protests and demands for remedies. Customers will not accept a frivolous "Oops, sorry about that." Even menus list the size of beverage servings precisely.

Outsiders differ in their response to such observations. Some consider the emphasis on formality and responsible public behavior to be excessive – the sign of an overly authoritarian society and, in personal terms, an obstacle to self-expression and creativity. Others may find in the insistence on high standards of behavior an appealing forthrightness, and may feel that it offers a sense of security among strangers. They might also consider the scrupulous observation of such events as namedays, promotions, engagements, and deaths to be elegant, emotionally touching, and a sign of familial cohesion and social stability.

In short, everyday social interaction in the German-speaking countries emphasizes responsibility and obligation. People make a point of conducting themselves capably, and they expect others to do so. While all groups of people have rules of behavior, underlying the whole system of behavior described here is the assumption that acceptable conduct can be defined and that such standards are (or should be) universal within the society. That is, in selecting and evaluating behavior people can refer to a *common* code of proper conduct – not merely

UMWELT-SCHUTZ MITMACHEN!

Mention the formal *Mittagspause*.

See note in Instructor's Guide.

See notes in Instructor's Guide.

snooty rules of "etiquette," but rather overall principles of action. Those who violate the common code – wittingly or unwittingly – risk being reminded of it, and generally bystanders will support the offended party.

It is worth speculating about the nature and probable causes of the notion of responsible behavior. The German-speaking countries, like most of Europe, are densely populated, and for centuries people have had to live at close quarters. Over the ages, it would appear, such societies have evolved standards of behavior that make it possible for people to avoid stepping on each other's toes. Stern dog-control codes, then, should not be all too surprising, nor should strict noise laws. Thus unwarranted excessive noise will likely occasion objections that may well refer briefly but pithily, as though a reminder should be unnecessary, to *"die allgemeine Ruhestunde,"* the legally mandated hours of quiet between 10 P.M and 7 A.M. It is conceivable, then, that as our own countries become more crowded, we will find it advantageous to find similar ways to lessen personal friction and will develop a commonly accepted code of conduct to reinforce ordinances and laws.

However the need for a common code of conduct is explained, it is even more significant that the code does exist and is indeed *common*. It may well be that the universality of the code depends on the homogeneousness of German culture. Certainly the German-speaking societies, despite regional differences and the effects of some minority populations, are far more uniform than the United States or even Canada. It is inconceivable that in our own society the values or notions of "responsible" conduct held by any single ethnic or social group could become dominant enough to be virtually beyond question as standards for the behavior of everyone. Moreover, Germans do not move around in their countries nearly as much as Americans do in theirs, and of course their immediate ancestors did not migrate from one continent to another, as did most of ours. Thus individuals feel themselves bound more closely to their families and to the larger local community.

The differences in everyday behavior discussed here may reflect more profound differences in attitudes toward the individual and society. Prominent in the popular notion of English common law and of English and American political history is the expansion of personal rights. Certainly that image was amplified by the settlement of the frontier, and it remains current in a culture whose immense and often sparsely populated territory makes it possible for determined people to live pretty much beyond the law, or at least beyond the obligation to consider the rights and needs of others. Our language provides us with proverbial expressions of such attitudes. We declare that "A man's home is his castle," we refer readily to the Bill of Rights, the Constitution, and the Declaration of Independence, and when pressed we may just simply assert, "It's a free country." The readiness of Germans to speak their minds is rooted not in a jealously guarded assumption of personal *rights,* but rather in notions of *individual competence* and *mutual obligation.* Social behavior is based on a notion of conscious if not explicitly formulated contracts.

Cultural differences and their reflection in language can be fascinating. You will notice them even more as you learn more German. But don't lose sight of the common humanity that links all cultures. Most often, in ordinary situations the same behavior that is proper and effective in our own society will be considered within the normal range in Switzerland, Austria, and the two Germanies, even though the underlying thought processes may differ considerably.

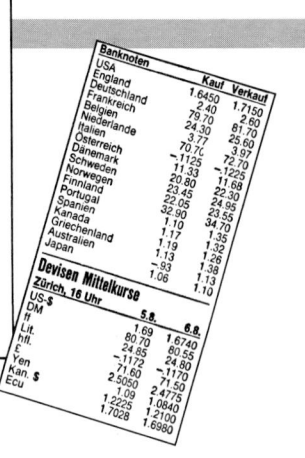

Flughafen Frankfurt am Main.

Willkommen und Abschied

Professional introductions

1 JOHN ALLEN — Ich habe ein Fulbright-Stipendium bekommen, um hier politische Wissenschaft zu studieren.

2

Praktikum on-the-job training

HERR STROBEL — So. Darf ich vorstellen? Das ist Herr Anderson aus Chicago. Er macht bei uns ein Praktikum in internationaler Wirtschaft. Da links ist Frau Mager von der Auslandsabteilung.

ROY ANDERSON — Freut mich sehr, Frau Mager.

HERR STROBEL — Und neben ihr sitzt Fräulein Alpers von der Verkaufsabteilung.

ROY ANDERSON — Angenehm, Fräulein Alpers.

Flowers and hospitality **3**

BENNO KEHL — Es freut mich sehr, daß Sie bei uns bleiben. Bitte, machen Sie's sich bequem.

JUDY ATTERHOLT — Besten Dank. Ich fühle mich schon wie zu Hause.

4

JIM STEPHENS — Guten Tag. Ich möchte bitte Blumen für eine Kollegin, die mich zum Abendessen eingeladen hat.

FRAU BREMER — Schön. Haben Sie an eine gewisse Blumenart gedacht?

JIM STEPHENS — Haben Sie rote Rosen?

FRAU BREMER — Ja, aber in Deutschland bedeuten rote Rosen nur Liebe.

JIM STEPHENS — Das wußte ich nicht. Tja, ich kenne die verschiedenen Blumenarten nicht. Könnten Sie mir etwas empfehlen?

FRAU BREMER — Sie wollen wahrscheinlich einen bunten Strauß. Natürlich muß ich wissen, wieviel Sie ausgeben wollten.

JIM STEPHENS — Oh, so zwischen 20 und 30 Mark.

FRAU BREMER — Da bekommen Sie einen schönen Strauß. Wenn Sie sich nicht entscheiden können, können Sie auch etwas in unserem Schaufenster aussuchen.

Thanks and goodbye **5**

ANN BLACKLER — Wir danken Ihnen sehr, daß Sie uns Ihre Stadt gezeigt haben. Hoffentlich können Sie uns einmal besuchen.

HERR LUDWIG — Hoffentlich hat Ihnen die Reise auch Spaß gemacht. Ich weiß, Sie hatten mit Geschäftssachen die Hände voll zu tun.

PETE HEROLD — Naja, wir hatten genug Zeit, eine kurze Reise nach Berlin zu machen. Ich wollte, wir hätten auch Dresden besuchen können.

HERR LUDWIG — Ja, und Sie hätten auch nach Leipzig reisen sollen. Aber vielleicht nächstes Mal.

6

TOM JEFFERS — Höchste Zeit, daß wir gehen. Vielen Dank für alles!

FRAU BACHMANN — Es hat uns auch gefreut. Also, gute Reise! Und Grüße an die Familie! Kommt gut nach Hause!

267

STRUKTUR 2

See appendix to Reference Grammar in Study Text.

Checklist of Common Errors

- confusion of sounds or spelling; capitalization
- wrong vocabulary choice
- failure to consider gender of nouns
- failure to conjugate verbs according to both subject and tense
- incorrect verb placement
- imitation of the English progressive form of verbs
- incorrect formation of the past tense
- wrong verb tense
- use of *haben* where *sein* is required in the present perfect
- neglect of differences among grammatical cases
- confusion of *du* and *Sie*
- confusion of pronouns, especially Sie/sie
- incorrect negation (*nicht/kein-/nichts;* placement of *nicht*)
- incorrect choice of *wann, wenn, als, ob*

Our final advice

Pay attention to these likely weak spots, but while you are doing that, don't scare yourself into silence. Do practice precisely in those areas where you are weak, but don't sacrifice genuine communication to obsession with perfection. Above all, don't lose your ability to find other ways to express your meaning. Simple words capably combined in simple patterns can also be effective, and there are often several ways to do the same thing.

The greatest error is silence.

Stage 1

1: Ein Gast, den Sie zum Abendessen eingeladen haben, hat Ihnen besonders schöne Blumen gebracht – in der Meinung, es sei Ihr Geburtstag. Drücken Sie Ihren herzlichen Dank aus, seien Sie aber ehrlich und verbessern Sie den Fehler, ohne seine Gefühle zu verletzen.

4: Sie wollen eine schüchterne Person von Ihrem *"Deutsch für Ausländer"*-Kurs zu sich einladen. Es soll eine informelle Zusammenkunft mit Freunden sein, doch glauben Sie, daß diese Person es wohl vermeiden könnte, Unbekannte kennenzulernen. Gestalten Sie die Einladung so, daß die Person einfach kommen muß.

1

Someone coming to supper has brought you especially beautiful flowers, thinking that it's your birthday. Express your thanks in a heartfelt manner, but also be honest and correct the mistake without engendering any hard feelings.

3

Ihr Flug nach Hause startet bald, und Sie haben bis diesen Moment die schwere Aufgabe hinausgeschoben, Ihren Gastgebern zu sagen, wieviel Sie durch ihre Freundschaft und Hilfsbereitschaft während des Aufenthalts bei ihnen profitiert haben. Weil Sie jetzt viel Erfahrung damit haben, das Unsagbare auszudrücken: Sagen Sie ihnen, was Sie im Herzen fühlen.

2

Ein Ehepaar, das Ihnen nicht besonders gut gefällt, hat Sie zu einer Fete eingeladen. Sie hatten schon daran gedacht, an dem Abend etwas anderes zu tun, jedoch waren Ihre Pläne vor der Einladung noch nicht ganz fest geworden. Entschuldigen Sie sich und geben Sie gute Gründe für Ihre Unfähigkeit, zur Fete zu kommen.

4

You want to invite a shy person from your *Deutsch für Ausländer* course over to your apartment for an informal get-together with friends, but you believe that this person might try to avoid meeting strangers. Make the invitation so enticing that the person simply can't refuse.

Stage 2

1: Im Laufe Ihres Europaaufenthalts haben Sie auf die *du/Sie*-Regeln gut aufgepaßt. Nun haben Sie aber in der letzten Woche des Besuchs jemand kennengelernt, mit dem Sie gerne ein tieferes Verhältnis hätten – jemand, den Sie noch nicht mit *du* anreden würden, wenn Sie tatsächlich länger bleiben könnten und mehr Zeit hätten, die Freundschaft zu vertiefen. Trotzdem sollen Sie vorschlagen, daß Sie und die andere Person sich duzen. Dabei müssen Sie vorsichtig vorgehen, damit die Person sich nicht beleidigt fühlt. Vielleicht wollen Sie vorschlagen, daß Sie beide nach Ihrer Abreise in enger Verbindung bleiben und (dies hängt von der Antwort ab) daß die Person einmal zu Ihnen in Ihre Heimat reist.
2: German version in Instructor's Guide.

1

Throughout your stay in Europe you have been careful to obey the rules about using *Sie* and *du*. But now, in the last week of your time abroad, you have met someone with whom you want to have a closer relationship – someone you would not call *du* yet if you were staying longer and had more time to let the relationship mature. Go ahead and suggest that you say *du* to each other, but be very careful how you go about it so the person will be flattered and not insulted. You may want to suggest that the two of you keep in close touch after you leave, and – depending on the response – that the person visit you in your country sometime.

3

Sie haben das ganze Jahr als Mitglied eines Junior-Year-Programms verbracht. Verabschieden Sie sich von einer Person, die Sie verehren: der Direktorin des Programms, einem Professor, Ihrer Mietfrau, vielleicht sogar dem Inhaber vom kleinen Imbiß, wo sie so viele glückliche Stunden verbracht haben.

2

Your landlady has refused to apply your excess monthly heating deposit to the last month's rent, thinking that you, as a foreigner, will not notice or will not consider summoning the proper authorities this close to your departure date. You have already seen a lawyer, however, and have left what you consider to be an equitable last month's rent in escrow. Now, having withheld that rent, you are leaving for the airport. Bid the astonished landlady farewell at the front gate, being polite but firm in justifying what you have done.

4

Durch gemeinsame Freunde haben Sie vereinbart, daß ein mexikanischer Student Ihre Wohnung in Bonn übernimmt. Sie sind jetzt bereit wegzufahren, und der Student will in die Wohnung einziehen. Nehmen Sie sich jetzt etwas Zeit, um ihn über die Einzelheiten dieser Wohnung zu informieren. Fügen Sie dann auch einige Ratschläge hinzu über Gewohnheiten und Benehmen, mit denen dieser Mitbürger aus Amerika vielleicht nicht vertraut ist.

Versuchen Sie doch

Nehmen Sie Abschied von der/dem Geliebten. Vergessen Sie dabei die gewöhnlichen Versprechen und Verzichtleistungen nicht.
   Music: "Gute Nacht" from Schubert's *Winterreise*

When you arrived in Europe you issued an invitation for your landlord's children to visit you and your family in Atlanta sometime. Now, on the eve of your departure, the landlord remembers your invitation. Be polite but firm in your refusal to entertain his little hellions.

Take leave of your beloved, a) including or b) avoiding the usual promises and disclaimers.

269

Afterword

NOCH ETWAS?/SOMETHING MORE?

How much German do you know?

The first year of language study can be a time of immense and very evident progress. If you have done reasonably well with *Wie, bitte?*, you can probably

The profile is based on the ACTFL *Guidelines*, as follows: speaking and writing – intermediate-mid; listening and reading – intermediate-high. The best students in the class, even those with no previous German, may well perform at a level higher.

- speak well enough to satisfy most routine travel and survival needs and limited social demands, such as questions and comments about your personal background or current activities;
- listen well enough to understand short conversations about everyday matters, get the gist of some longer conversations or clear radio broadcasts, and even follow simple discussions of certain specialized topics, such as travel or your academic or occupational activities;
- read well enough to handle with confidence ordinary public signs and simple correspondence, get the gist of many kinds of longer but nonspecialized articles, and extract essential information from travel publications;
- write well enough to meet survival needs and some limited social demands, in particular those tasks encountered by the tourist visiting the culture more than casually, or by the student, businessperson, or other traveler intending to engage in a variety of activities during an extended stay.

The kinds and levels of competence described here should be sufficient for you to perform capably in a German-speaking country under ordinary circumstances. Very likely you can deal with some unexpected complications or challenges. By now you can probably feel when you are getting beyond your depth, and you may even know why. Lack of specialized vocabulary may hinder you, or you may sense gaps in your command of structures – weakness in the past tense, for example, or trouble with time phrases or word order – the sort of things mentioned on page 268.

Thus, in a speaking situation you may find that the hotel room price and facilities are right, but you want something less noisy. Or perhaps the person with whom you are chatting idly about leisure activities turns out to share the same hobby and wants to discuss your common interest at length.

But don't underestimate your capabilities. You can hope to have acquired a working command of basic grammatical structures and a fairly extensive vocabulary. Still more important has been the effort to develop confidence and stamina – the conviction that you can indeed express yourself.

How much is there left to learn? How long might it take?

A lot, but remember that you have already taken the big step of acquiring working fluency under ordinary circumstances. Even very advanced speakers of German, including superbly capable native speakers, spend a good deal of their time communicating about everyday matters. As for other levels of communication, let's start with the specialized highest forms and work down toward those that are more readily accessible and yet represent significant advances.

This is the equivalent of the top range of ACTFL/ETS "Superior," or 4+/5 on the older ILR scale.

- Being truly bilingual means that one can do anything equally well in both languages, from soothing a child to consulting with a lawyer – or a plumber. Such well-educated native speakers of two languages are as rare as hen's teeth, and are likely to be the products of special circumstances, such as members of bicultural families who spend considerable time in both cultures.

This is the equivalent of the middle range of ACTFL/ETS "Superior," or ILR 4.

- Acquiring what might be regarded as native fluency in all nonspecialized circumstances, and also in an occupational specialty, might take many years of study and actual residence in the culture.

This is the equivalent of the low range of ACTFL/ETS "Superior," or ILR 3.

- Performing with full confidence under most conditions, with solid command of grammar and vocabulary, might come after several years of study, including residence in countries where German is spoken. An outstanding German major, someone who took advantage of all that a year abroad might offer, could attain such fluency. So could someone who mastered the grammar, vocabulary, and communicative strategies presented in *Wie, bitte?*

This is the equivalent of the ACTFL/ETS "Advanced" or ILR 2.

- The ability to handle effectively most of the range of ordinary human activity, including some occupational responsibilities, could be attained within another year or so by someone who had done reasonably well with *Wie, bitte?* Such a person could claim the ability to use German vocationally or as a foundation for advanced academic study.

What to work on

The *"Struktur 2"* page of Chapter 26 lists major *grammatical* weaknesses that often plague intermediate students of German. One way you can increase your proficiency is to become more conscious of those structural problems. But it is practice, not knowledge, that makes perfect; proficiency means the ability to *use* the language. While review is important, expansion of vocabulary and structural skills is vital. *You should practice using the language at a level that is steadily challenging but not overwhelming.* Here is an outline.

functions   Work on maintaining, over several sentences, the ability to express facts, give instructions, describe common objects or ideas, and narrate current, past, and future activities; attempt to add detail, to support your opinions ("because . . . "), and to include conditions ("If . . . ")

context   Concentrate on concrete topics (your background, family, personal interests, work or study, travel, and events taking place in your immediate surroundings), but expand your attention to larger social topics, opinions, and the details and issues involved in your special fields of competence. ("In my job we use a lot of machinery, because it saves money, but some of it is dangerous.")

accuracy   Aim to be understandable to tolerant native speakers who are not used to dealing with foreigners; accept that you will sometimes miscommunicate information, and then learn to check whether you are being understood; focus on accuracy in verb-tense formation, use of correct gender and case, and maintenance of word order beyond the simplest subject-verb level; learn the vocabulary of your special interests.

how to practice   As you practice speaking or writing, whether by yourself or with someone who can correct and encourage you, concentrate on *deepening* and *broadening* your language production. You will not expand your linguistic "muscles" – though you will keep them limber – by doing simply more of what you can already do. You probably won't learn much by answering questions that ask for yes/no answers, or initial information about *"Was?," "Wer?,"* or *"Wann?"* Instead, push yourself – or have someone push you – by asking *"Warum?," "Wie?,"* or *"Und dann?,"* and then seek to say more than a single short sentence in reply.

The German major

If you continue your study of German, at some time you may want to consider majoring in the language. Traditionally, majors in foreign languages have concentrated on two overlapping pursuits: teacher training and literary study, with attention to related subjects like history and the arts. At some institutions, however, the scope of the major is being redefined to focus more – though not exclusively – on language ability as a primary professional skill or an important adjunct to other professional training or occupations, such as international business or government service.

Advanced study in foreign languages and literatures, whether pursued as a major, a formal minor, or an informal minor, can be an attractive program. Certainly it contributes to a broader education, whatever one's ultimate field of interest. Foreign language competence can also be that one additional skill that provides the edge in employment and promotion. Lastly, foreign language classes, especially beyond the first year, are likely to be small, even at large institutions; the students in them can expect more individual attention to their needs as students and as human beings.

Other programs and opportunities for study, travel, and employment

● study and travel grants

Many agencies – public and private, American and foreign – offer scholarships and other support for students who study languages. This support is by no means restricted to foreign language majors. For example, the U.S. Fulbright program encourages students in many fields to apply, and the grants cover transportation and living expenses for a year. An interesting statistic: in 1987–88 there were only 27 such grants available nationally for study in Great Britain, and 452 people applied for them (odds for acceptance: 1 chance in 17); the same year there were 179 grants available for study in West Germany, with only 534 applicants (odds: 1 chance in 3).

The several German-speaking countries support similar programs with their own funds. One such is the *Deutscher Akademischer Austauschdienst/German Academic Exchange Service.* Fulbright and DAAD grants often include supplemental support for short-term advanced language training.

● undergraduate internships in government, law, journalism, social science, and the arts

These are offered by several institutions, such as Clark University in Worcester, Mass., the City University of New York, and Antioch College in Yellow Springs, Ohio. Students from other institutions may apply.

● advanced vocational training and employment in languages and international studies

Such instruction is available in several types of programs. The U.S. government operates its own language-training facilities to staff both civilian and military positions. Because competent linguists are in short supply, the Army, for example, offers substantial fringe benefits and cash bonuses upon recruitment and reenlistment. For information, inquire at federal offices or your college or university career counseling service.

Some universities offer advanced-level vocational (rather than academic) training. The University of South Carolina, for example, conducts a master's program in International Business Studies (MIBS); graduate study in business is integrated with accelerated language training and a six-month overseas internship. There are also programs in professional translating, such as the ones at Georgia State University, Georgetown University, or the Monterey Institute of International Studies.

Master's degrees are also offered by a few specialized training institutions, such as the American Graduate School of International Management in Arizona ("Thunderbird").

● some useful addresses

Council for Educational Exchange between the United States of America and the Federal Republic of Germany
D–5300 Bonn 2
Postfach 200–208
Theaterplatz 1a

Fulbright Scholarships:
Institute of International Education (IIE)
809 United Nations Plaza
New York, NY 10017

Goethe-Institut
Lenbachplatz 3
Postfach 201009
D-8000 München

German Academic Exchange Service (DAAD)
Deutscher Akademischer Austauschdienst
535 Fifth Avenue, Suite 1107
New York, NY 10007

U.S. Congress – FRG Bundestag
Youth Exchange Office
3501 Newark St., N.W.
Washington, DC 20016

Liga für Völkerfreundschaft der DDR
Thälmannplatz 8/9
DDR-1080 Berlin

Embassy of Switzerland
2900 Cathedral Ave., N.W.
Washington, D.C. 20008

Austrian Institute
11 E. 52nd St.
New York, N.Y. 10022

Zentralstelle für Arbeitsvermittlung
Feuerbachstraße 42
D-6000 Frankfurt am Main

Books of interest to students of German

CRAIG, GORDON. *The Germans.* New York: Putnam, 1982.
――――. *Germany, 1866–1945.* New York: Oxford University Press, 1978.
DEMETZ, PETER. *After the Fires: Recent Writing in the Germanies, Austria, and Switzerland.* San Diego: Harcourt Brace Jovanovich, 1986.
FLÜELER, NIKLAUS, ed. *Knaurs Kulturführer in Farbe: Schweiz.* München: Knaur, 1982.
KEEFE, EUGENE K., ed. *East Germany, A Country Study.* Washington, D.C.: U.S. Government Printing Office, 1982.
Knaurs Kulturführer in Farbe: Deutschland. München: Knaur, 1976.
LEHNE, INGE, and LONNIE JOHNSON. *Vienna, the Past in the Present.* Wien: Österreichischer Bundesverlag, 1985.
LURIE, JOSEPH, ed. *The Young American's Scholarship Guide to Travel and Learning Abroad.* New York: Intravco Press, 1986.
MCPHEE, JOHN. *La Place de la Concorde Suisse.* New York: Farrar Straus Giroux, 1983. A portrait of the Swiss character from the perspective of an American author accompanying army reserves on maneuvers. In English, despite the title.
MEHLING, FRANZ N., ed. *Knaurs Kulturführer in Farbe: Österreich.* München: Knaur, 1977.

Ein gutes Buch, der beste Freund.

Feste und Feiertage

In the song, *"Hoch soll er leben,"* the words are adjusted to fit the guest(s) of honor: *"Hoch soll sie leben"* (for one person, female) or *"Hoch sollen sie leben"* (for two or more people).

Looking ahead

In this special chapter you'll learn when, why, and how holidays in German-speaking countries are celebrated. You'll also learn what to say on special occasions like birthdays and anniversaries. In addition, you will see how to use German to describe holidays in your own country.

274

Was feiert man?

- **allgemeine Feiertage**/general holidays

USA/CDN:	D/DDR/A/CH:
Halloween	Allerheiligen
Thanksgiving	Erntedankfest
Christmas	Weihnachten
New Year's	Neujahr
Easter	Ostern

- **persönliche Feiertage**/personal holidays

USA/CDN:	D/DDR/A/CH:
birthday	der Geburtstag
baptism	die Taufe
confirmation	die Konfirmation
engagement	die Verlobung
wedding	die Hochzeit
anniversary	der Hochzeitstag
name day	der Namenstag

Wann feiert man?

- **im Herbst**

Rosh ha-Shanah	1. Tishri (Ende September)
Yom Kippur	10. Tishri (Ende September – Anfang Oktober)
Erntedankfest*	erste Oktoberwoche
Allerheiligen*	1. November
Buß- und Bettag*	Mittwoch vor dem Advent
Advent	vom Sonntag um den 30. November bis zum 25. Dezember

- **im Winter**

Chanukah	Um die Wintersonnen-wende
erster, zweiter Weihnachtstag	25. und 26. Dezember
Neujahr	1. Januar
Heilige Drei Könige	6. Januar
Fastnacht/Fasching	bis zum 2. Mittwoch im Februar
Aschermittwoch	2. Mittwoch im Februar

- **im Frühling**

Passah	14. Nisan (März/April)
Gründonnerstag*	Donnerstag vor Ostern
Karfreitag	Freitag vor Ostern
Ostern	22. März – 25. April
Christi Himmelfahrt	6. Donnerstag nach Ostern
Pfingsten	7. Sonntag und Montag nach Ostern
Fronleichnam*	2. Donnerstag nach Pfingsten

*Nicht überall/not celebrated everywhere.

Fasching (Waldkirsch im Schwarzwald)

Was sagt man an Feiertagen?

The most common formula is "**Alles Gute!**" ("Best wishes!").

- **Weihnachten**

Fröhliche Weihnachten!
Schöne Weihnachtsferien!
Ich wünsche dir/euch/Ihnen ein frohes Weihnachtsfest.
. . . und frohe Weihnachten, gel?

Mention the meaning of *weih-* "holy" and of *-nachten* as an old plural form in formulaic use.

- **Neujahr**

Schönes Neujahr!
Alles Gute im Neuen Jahr!

Mention *Silversterabend*, from St. Sylvester, fourth-century pope whose feast is on December 31.

- **Ostern**

Frohe Ostern!
Schöne Osterferien!
Schöne Ostertage!

Mention the probable derivation from IE *awes "to shine," *aus-os "goddess of the dawn." Cf. Roman goddess Aurora.

- **Geburtstag**

Herzlichen Glückwunsch!
Herzliche Glückwünsche zum Geburtstag!
Herzliche Glückwünsche – und alles Gute!
Wir wünschen Dir einen schönen Geburtstag und weiterhin alles, alles
    Gute!

- **Hochzeit/Verlobung**

Herzlichen Glückwunsch (zur Hochzeit)!
Wir gratulieren (recht herzlich) zur Verlobung!
Herzliche Glückwünsche zum zehnten Hochzeitstag!
Ich gratuliere zur silbernen Hochzeit!

- **Ferien/Urlaub**

Schöne Ferien! Gute Ferien!
Schönen Urlaub!

Urlaub-individual vacation; *Ferien*-general vacation such as *Schulferien.*

The holidays are described here on three linguistic levels, intended to be accessible at any time during the school year. Novice-level students can memorize part or all of the a) section. Intermediate-level students can model their speech on the b) and c) sections.

Israelitischer
Gemeindefriedhof
täglich geöffnet
außer Sabbat (samstag)
sowie an den jüd. Hauptfeiertagen

Wie beschreibt man nordamerikanische Feiertage?

● Halloween

a) Das ist für Kinder. Sie tragen komische Kleider und gehen von Haus zu Haus. Dort bekommen sie Obst und Plätzchen und Bonbons.

> That's for children. They wear funny clothes and go from door to door. There they get fruit and cookies and candy.

b) Allerheiligen ist bei uns eigentlich nur für Kinder. Sie sehen aus wie Hexen und Gespenster und wandern in der Stadt herum. Sie verlangen Leckerbissen von den Leuten und wollen sie erschrecken.

> For us Halloween is really just for children. They look like witches and ghosts and wander around the town. They ask for goodies from people and want to scare them.

c) Allerheiligen ist bei uns kein kirchliches Fest mehr. Man weiß wirklich nicht, was das mit der Kirche zu tun hat. An diesem Abend verkleiden sich die Kinder als Dämonen und Hexen und ziehen von Haus zu Haus, um Leckerbissen zu erbetteln. Manchmal spielen die Kinder auch Streiche, die nicht immer harmlos sind.

> We don't celebrate Halloween as a religious holiday anymore. People don't really know what it has to do with religion. On Halloween the children dress up as demons and witches and go from door to door begging for goodies. Also, they often play tricks on people – tricks that aren't always harmless.

● Thanksgiving

a) Das Erntedankfest ist der letzte Donnerstag im November. Familien sind dann zusammen und essen immer sehr viel.

> Thanksgiving is the last Thursday in November. Families are together then and always eat a lot.

b) Zum Erntedankfest kommen amerikanische Familien fast immer zusammen. Wir sind dann dankbar für alles und essen zu viel. Das lange Wochenende ist immer schulfrei, und das ist schön für die Kinder.

> American families almost always get together at Thanksgiving. That's when we're thankful for everything and eat too much. There's a long weekend of vacation from school, which is nice for the children.

c) Im 17. Jahrhundert trafen die ersten Pilger mit Indianern im Nordosten zusammen. Sie wollten Gott für die Ernte danken und die Freundschaft mit den Indianern sichern. Heutzutage kommen Familien Ende November zusammen, um das große Fest mit Truthahn, Brotfüllung und Kürbiskuchen zu feiern. Einige feiern das Erntedankfest in der Kirche – und andere schauen amerikanischen Fußballspielen im Fernsehen zu. Aber im allgemeinen frißt man sich einfach voll.

> In the 17th century the first pilgrims came together with Indians in the Northeast. They wanted to thank God for the harvest and solidify their friendship with the Indians. These days families get together at the end of November in order to celebrate the holiday with turkey, stuffing, and pumpkin pie. Some people celebrate Thanksgiving in church – and others watch football games on TV. But in general people just make pigs of themselves.

Christmas

a) Zu Weihnachten singen wir schöne Weihnachtslieder in der Kirche und bekommen viele Geschenke zu Hause.

At Christmas we sing pretty Christmas songs in church and get lots of presents at home.

b) Am Weihnachtstag stehen wir früh auf. Wir frühstücken zusammen und gehen dann ins Wohnzimmer zum Weihnachtsbaum. Mein Bruder macht immer ein schönes Feuer im Kamin. Dann öffnen wir die Geschenke.

On Christmas morning we get up early. We eat breakfast together and then go into the living room to see the Christmas tree. My brother always makes a nice fire in the fireplace. Then we open the presents.

c) Die Weihnachtszeit macht uns allen viel Freude. Wir fällen einen Christbaum im Wald hinter unserem Haus und schmücken ihn dann zusammen im Familienzimmer. In Amerika darf man keine Kerzen am Baum haben, also gibt's bei uns kleine Lichter, die schön funkeln. Natürlich hängen die Kinder Strümpfe an den Kamin für den Weihnachtsmann. Nachdem wir die Geschenke aufgemacht haben, gibt's ein wunderschönes Essen. Und am Abend gehen wir alle in die Kirche – oder schon zur Mitternachtsmesse am Heiligen Abend.

We all have lots of fun at Christmas time. We cut a Christmas tree in the woods behind our house and then decorate it together in the family room. In America you're not allowed to put candles on the tree, so we have little lights that sparkle. Of course, the children hang stockings on the chimmney for Santa Claus. After we've opened the presents there's a marvelous meal. And in the evening we all go to church – or we go to midnight Mass on Christmas Eve.

Easter

a) Zu Ostern suchen die Kinder Ostereier. Sie bekommen auch Hasen aus Schokolade. Viele Leute gehen in die Kirche.

On Easter the children look for Easter eggs. They get chocolate rabbits, too. Lots of people go to church.

b) Am Ostersonntag geht man in die Kirche – auch wenn man nicht normalerweise in die Kirche geht. Und vor oder nach der Kirche gibt's die große Suche nach Ostereiern.

On Easter Sunday people go to church – even if they usually aren't church–goers. And before or after church there's the big Easter egg hunt.

c) Ostern – für die Kinder ist das die größte Freude. Die Eltern färben Eier am Abend vor Ostern und verstecken sie am nächsten Morgen drinnen im Haus oder draußen ums Haus. Dann nimmt jedes Kind einen Korb und versucht möglichst viele Eier zu finden. Die Suche macht allen viel Spaß, nicht nur den Kindern. Natürlich geht man in die Kirche am Ostersonntag, oft mit neuen Kleidern, die man gerne den Freunden und Freundinnen zeigen will.

Easter – that's the most fun for children. On the evening before Easter the parents dye Easter eggs, and the next morning they hide them inside or outside the house. Then every child takes a basket and tries to find as many eggs as possible. The hunt is lots of fun for everyone, not just the children. Of course, everyone goes to church on Easter Sunday, often with new clothes to show to friends.

Mention that fireworks are used extensively in other countries to celebrate New Year's Eve, *Silvester* in the German-speaking countries.

Tag 5: Katerfrühstück im Hotel, Matinee im Festspielhaus, zur freien Verfügung, Abreise.

Leistungen:
3 oder 4 Übernachtungen mit Frühstück, Begrüßung mit „Bodenseewasser", Abendessen Weinstube, Busausflug mit Kässpätzle-Essen, Eintritt „Casino am See", Geführter Stadtrundgang Bregenz, Abendessen in Restaurant/Hotel, Ausflug Lindau, Stadtführung, Weißwurstessen, Eintritt Silvesterball Festspiel und Kongreßhaus, Bregenz-Informationsmappe und ein persönliches Geschenk sowie ein Bregenzplakat
Das Programm kann auch nur für vier Tage gebucht werden. Es entfällt dann den Tag 2. Der Casinobesuch kann an einem beliebigen Tag durchgeführt werden.

Arrangementpreis:
Pro Person im Doppelzimmer bei Vier-Tage-Aufenthalt
ab öS 3075.— DM 453.— sFr. 385.—
Pro Person im Doppelzimmer bei Fünf-Tage-Aufenthalt
ab öS 3495.— DM 514.— sFr. 437.—

Preis- und Programmänderungen sowie Kursschwankungen vorbehalten.
Das Fremdenverkehrsamt Bregenz tritt als Vermittler auf. Gruppenangebot: Jede 21. Person kann kostenfrei buchen. Auf Wunsch können andere Programmvorschläge erarbeitet werden.
Gesamtbeträge wie auch zusätzliche Programmpunkt-Kosten können mit dem Fremdenverkehrsamt abgerechnet werden.
Zusatztag: Jedes Arrangement kann verlängert werden. Kosten auf Anfrage.
Einzelzimmer: Kosten Einzelzimmerzuschlag auf Anfrage.

FREMDENVERKEHRSAMT BREGENZ
Inselstraße 15, A-6900 Bregenz
Telefon (05574) 2 33 91, Telex 057 707

Fourth of July

a) Der 4. (vierte) Juli ist der Feiertag für die USA. Wir haben immer eine Parade – und Feuerwerk am Abend.

The Fourth of July is the U.S. holiday. We always have a parade – and fireworks in the evening.

b) Der 4. Juli ist der Nationalfeiertag. In jeder Stadt gibt es eine große Parade mit Marschmusik und Soldaten, und die Kinder haben immer eine große Freude am Feuerwerk.

The Fourth of July is the national holiday. In every city there's a big parade with march music and soldiers, and the children always really enjoy the fireworks.

c) Am vierten Juli kommt unser Nationalfeiertag. Wir feiern die Unabhängigkeit von England – eigentlich die Unabhängigkeitserklärung, die im Jahre 1776 geschrieben wurde. Es gibt überall viele Paraden mit patriotischer Musik – Marschmusik, natürlich – und lange Reden über Freiheit und Demokratie. Viele Familien machen einen Picknickausflug, oft irgendwo am Wasser zum Schwimmen. Abends kommt dann Feuerwerk, entweder zu Hause oder auf einem Platz in der Gemeinde. Wir freuen uns immer, die Raketen und Luftgranaten zu hören. Aber 1776 hatte man Krieg.

Our national holiday falls on July fourth. We celebrate independence from England – actually the Declaration of Independence, which was written in 1776. There are lots of parades everywhere with patriotic music – marches, of course – and long speeches about freedom and democracy. Lots of families go on picnics, often someplace where they can swim. In the evening there are fireworks, either at home or in a large clear area in town. We always enjoy hearing the rockets and bombs. But there was war in 1776.

Birthdays

a) Zum Geburtstag haben wir immer eine Party mit Eis und einer Torte. Und mit Geschenken, natürlich.

On a birthday we always have a party with ice cream and a cake. And with presents, of course.

b) Zu meinem Geburtstag hatte ich als Kind immer ein paar Freunde im Haus, und wir haben immer gespielt. Da war auch jedes Jahr ein Kuchen mit Kerzen und Eiskrem.

When I was little I always had a couple of friends over to play for my birthday. Also, every year there was a cake with candles and ice cream.

c) Zum Geburtstag gehört immer ein Kuchen oder eine Torte mit Kerzen darauf. Man zündet die Kerzen an, und das "Geburtstagskind" muß sie alle auf einmal ausblasen. Dann wird sein Wunsch für den Tag erfüllt – oder so sagt man wenigstens. Und Geschenke bekommt man natürlich von allen Familienmitgliedern. Bei uns sind die Geburtstage aber eher für junge Leute; die Eltern wollen nicht alt werden.

A cake with candles is always part of a birthday. You light the candles, and the one having the birthday has to blow them all out with one puff. Then he gets his wish for the day – or at least that's what people say. And of course you get presents from everyone in the family. But at our house birthdays are really more for youngsters; the parents don't want to get old.

Was singt man an Feiertagen?

Weihnachten

Stille Nacht, heilige Nacht

Text: Joseph Mohr, 1818   Melodie: Franz Gruber, 1818

1. Stil - le Nacht, hei - li - ge Nacht! Al - les schläft, ein - sam wacht
nur das trau - te hoch - hei - lige Paar. Hol - der Kna - be im lok - kigen Haar,
schlaf in himm - li - scher Ruh! Schlaf in himm - li - scher Ruh!

2. Stille Nacht, heilige Nacht!
Hirten erst kund gemacht!
Durch der Engel Hallelujah
tönt es laut von fern und nah:
|| Christ der Retter ist da! ||

3. Stille Nacht, heilige Nacht!
Gottes Sohn, o wie lacht
Lieb aus deinem göttlichen Mund,
da uns schlägt die rettende Stund,
|| Christ, in deiner Geburt! ||

*Local costume = die Tracht (related
to* tragen *"to wear").*

O Tannenbaum, o Tannenbaum

Text: Ernst Anschütz, um 1824   Volksweise, 1799

1. O Tannenbaum, o Tannenbaum, Wie treu sind dei - ne Blätter! Du
grünst nicht nur zur Sommerzeit, nein, auch im Win - ter wenn es schneit. O
Tan - nen - baum, o Tan - nen - baum, wie treu sind dei - ne Blätter!

2. || O Tannenbaum, o Tannenbaum,
du kannst mir sehr gefallen. ||
Wie oft hat nicht zur Weihnachtszeit
ein Baum von dir mich hoch erfreut.
O Tannenbaum, o Tannenbaum,
du kannst mir sehr gefallen.

3. || O Tannenbaum, o Tannenbaum,
dein Kleid soll mich was lehren: ||
Die Hoffnung und Beständigkeit
gibt Trost und Kraft zu jeder Zeit.
O Tannenbaum, o Tannenbaum,
dein Kleid soll mich was lehren.

Geburtstag – und so weiter

Ein Prosit der Gemütlichkeit

Ein Pro - sit, ein Pro - sit der Ge - müt - lich - keit, ein
Pro - sit, ein Pro - sit der Ge - müt - lich - keit!

After WWII the Federal Republic (BRD) adopted as its national anthem the "Deutschlandlied," but on official occasions only the verse beginning "Einigkeit und Recht und Freiheit" is sung. Before the war the anthem had been sung with the verse beginning "Deutschland über alles," which many considered too aggressive.

Mention that German nationalism was a cause espoused by many German liberals in the 19th century. Von Fallersleben's own progressive views got him into trouble with the Prussian government.

Deutschlandlied

Text: Hoffmann von Fallersleben, 1841

Melodie: Joseph Haydn, 1797

1. Deutschland, Deutschland, ü – ber al – les, ü – ber al – les in der Welt, wenn es stets zum Schutz und Trut – ze brüder- lich zu- sammen hält, von der Maas bis an die Me – mel, von der Etsch bis an den Belt. Deutsch- land, Deutsch – land ü – ber al – les, ü – ber al – les in der Welt!

2. Deutsche Frauen, deutsche Treue, deutscher Wein und deutscher Sang
   sollen in der Welt behalten ihren alten schönen Klang,
   uns zu edler Tat begeistern unser ganzes Leben lang.
   Deutsche Frauen, deutsche Treue, deutscher Wein und deutscher Sang!

3. Einigkeit und Recht und Freiheit für das deutsche Vaterland!
   Danach laßt uns alle streben brüderlich mit Herz und Hand!
   Einigkeit und Recht und Freiheit sind des Glückes Unterpfand.
   Blüh im Glanze dieses Glückes, blühe, deutsches Vaterland!

Erntedankfest

The composer was not <u>the</u> Karl Marx.

Herbstlied

Hermann Claudius

Karl Marx

Zeit der Rei- fe, Zeit der Ru- he, die du nun zu uns ge- komm- en;

Schluß

sieh wir stehn vor dei- ner vol- len Tru- he. Mö- ge es uns from- men.

1. 2. 3.

Al- les Gut muß wan- dern, wan-dern. Ei- ner ern- tet für den an-dern.

Warum feiert man?

Although most holidays celebrated in Europe have obvious parallels in North America, a number of European holidays have no popular equivalent on this side of the Atlantic. Similarly, two obviously American holidays – the Fourth of July and Thanksgiving – are not celebrated in other countries, although certainly observing the date of a country's political birth, or of an autumn harvest festival, is not unique to the United States.

Most of our holidays (literally "holy days") are religious in origin, in Europe as well as North America. But this was not always so – at least not "religious" in terms of affiliation with one modern creed or another. In pre-Christian Europe there were two high points to the year. The winter solstice in late December (*die Wintersonnenwende*), the day when the sun reached its lowest point on the southern horizon, signaled the gradual lengthening of the days and pointed toward the quickening of life in springtime. The coming of spring fulfilled the promise made on that early winter day: the softening of the earth, the emergence of young plants and animals, the renewing of life itself.

Both of these times evoked a human response involving festivals of light and warmth. In northern Europe the yule log on the hearth drove away the chill and gave light in the early winter, while sprigs of fir, spruce, and pine ("ever-green" trees) symbolized the continuity of green and life in the otherwise lifeless winter landscape. In springtime came ancient rituals still practiced in the Alpine countries: the clanging of bells to frighten away the winter, and the burning of great human figures made of straw to accelerate the coming of warmth to the high pastures.

Each of these festival times corresponds to the most important feasts of the Christian church: Christmas and Easter. At the time of Christmas pre-Christian cultures honored the dead and marked the winter solstice. To these ancient observances was then added that of the birth of Christ. Actually, it was not until the mid-fourth century that the Christian church changed the festival honoring Christ's birth from Epiphany (January 6) to December 25, the day of the Roman celebration of the winter solstice, thus using the well-established heathen festival for its own purposes. The custom of gift-giving, too, is understood today to echo the gifts of the Magi to the Christ child, and yet gift-giving was already a new-year tradition in pre-Christian Roman culture. In much of German-speaking Europe, the giving of gifts to children takes place on December 6, the name day of St. Nicholas (*Sankt Nikolaus, Sammi Klaus*). This leaves December 25 and 26, the first and second days of Christmas (*der erste und zweite Weihnachtstag*), for religious celebration. In the DDR, which actively discourages religious practices, the Christmas holidays are known as *Ferien zum Jahreswechsel*, "holidays at the changing of the year."

As seen above, Epiphany (*Heilige Drei Könige*) is technically a more important holiday than Christmas. It commemorates the baptism of Jesus, the visit of the wise men to Bethlehem (the Adoration of the Magi), and the miracle at Cana (the demonstration of Jesus' ability to work miracles). The eve of Epiphany is known in English as Twelfth Night, the twelfth night after Christmas and the official end of the Christmas season.

Celebrations having to do with Easter (*Ostern*) often begin long before Lent. In German-speaking countries the word *Fastnacht* ("fasting night") and its variants *Fasnet* and *Fasching* are reminiscent of *Carneval* ("farewell to meat") or *mardi gras* ("fat Tuesday") in other cultures. (In Köln the holiday is also celebrated as

Perhaps remark how the German term is much simpler to analyze than the Latin-based "sol-stice."

Köln-Karneval

Mention *Chanukah*, the Jewish Festival of Lights, no longer widely celebrated in the German-speaking countries.

"Um 11 Uhr 11 am 11.11."

Mention *Passah* (Passover), the celebration of the deliverance of the Jews from Egyptian bondage; and North German *Paasche(n)*, "Easter." The time of the Christian festival is calculated from *Passah*.

You might want to mention the former custom of celebrating the birthdays of important leaders – the Kaiser (with a change of celebration depending on the reigning Kaiser's birthdate) and Hitler being prominent examples. In England, of course, the Queen's birthday is an important day.

Karneval.) These terms all denote the custom of fasting during the Lenten season before Easter. Pre-Lenten celebrations are especially extravagant in Bayern, where they begin as soon as Christmas celebrations are over on January 6, and in the Rheinland, where they begin already on November 11. Because *Karneval* is associated primarily with strongly Catholic cultures, it is no surprise that Bayern and the Rheinland, both predominantly Catholic, should be centers of pre-Lenten merrymaking. As with the accommodation of pre-Christian rituals to the Christian celebrations of Christmas and Epiphany, the church turned ancient springtime fertility rites to its own purposes in establishing *Fastnacht/Fasching*.

The Easter season begins on *Gründonnerstag*, Maundy Thursday, the day before *Karfreitag*, Good Friday, the anniversary of the Crucifixion, and culminates in *Ostern*, the celebration of the Resurrection and the high point of the Christian year. Other holidays celebrated in conjunction with Easter – and not widely celebrated in North America – are *Christi Himmelfahrt* (Ascension Day), the sixth Thursday after Easter, and *Pfingsten* (Pentecost), which comes fifty days after Easter and marks the end of the Easter season. *Fronleichnam* (Corpus Christi, "body of Christ"), which comes just after *Pfingsten*, commemorates the founding of the sacrament of the eucharist in the 13th century. School children in areas outside Österreich, Bayern, and the Rheinland envy their comrades in heavily Catholic states, where these celebrations are school holidays.

Politische Feiertage/Political Holidays

Just as July 4th is a festive day in the United States, other days of the year are important political anniversaries in the German-speaking countries.

Der Tag der deutschen Einheit, on June 17, an important holiday in West Germany, commemorates a 1953 strike of workers in East Berlin, who protested an increase in work quotas. The strike quickly grew into a general political uprising in East Berlin and East Germany, and was crushed by Soviet forces. *Die Straße des 17. Juni* in West Berlin stands as a memorial to the workers who were killed in the rebellion. The holiday is not celebrated – at least not openly – in East Germany. June 17 is a much more important West German national holiday than the date of the founding of the Federal Republic in 1949, but it is still not celebrated with the fervor that attaches to July 4 in the United States.

The East German state was founded on October 7, 1949, celebrated annually with speeches and parades as *Gründungstag*.

In 1889 the Second Socialist International declared May 1 a day to honor the labor movement, and this *Tag der Arbeit* has become an important holiday worldwide, and – especially in Eastern Europe – an occasion for speeches and demonstrations nominally on behalf of workers. The American Labor Day was set in September to dissociate it from socialism.

The Austrian *Bundesfeiertag* on October 26 marks the 1955 ratification of a treaty re-establishing that nation's sovereignty and declaring its permanent neutrality. The day is generally not celebrated with the fervor typical of political festivities elsewhere, but many Austrians recall that the agreement signaled the withdrawal of occupation forces, especially those of the U.S.S.R.

In midsummer the Swiss celebrate their *Bundesgründung*. In 1291 three of the later cantons (Uri, Schwyz, and Unterwalden) formed a political alliance that has been commemorated on August 1 for nearly 700 years as the foundation of the Swiss Confederation (Latin: <u>c</u>onfoederatio <u>h</u>elvetica, thus the CH country abbreviation). The day is celebrated with fireworks and spectacular bonfires on the highest mountain peaks.

Bildwörterbuch

1 das Restaurant, -s
2 die Garderobe, -n
3 der Mantel, ⸚
4 der Herrenhut, ⸚e
5 der Gast, ⸚e
6 das Personal
7 der Ober, -
— der Kellner, -
8 die Serviererin, -nen
9 der Koch, ⸚e
(die Köchin, -nen)
10 die Kochmütze, -n
11 die Küche, -n
12 der Anrichtetisch, -e
13 die Weinkaraffe, -n
14 der Weinkellner, -
15 die Schleife, -n
— die Fliege, -n
16 der Frack, ⸚e
17 die Weinflasche, -n
18 das Etikett, -e
19 der Flaschenkork, -e
20 der Korkenzieher, -
21 das Tuch, ⸚er
22 der Eßtisch, -e
23 die Krawatte, -n
24 der Stuhl, ⸚e
25 die Theke, -n
26 die Kasse, -n
27 der Zahnstocher, -
28 die Speisekarte, -n
— die Tageskarte, -n

1 das Gedeck, -e
2 die Tischdecke, -n
3 das Besteck, -e
4 der Teller, -
5 die Gabel, -n
6 das Messer, -
7 der (Eß)Löffel, -
8 der Suppenteller, -
9 der Salatteller, -
10 die (Kaffee)Tasse, -n
11 die Untertasse, -n
12 der Eierbecher, -
13 das Ei, -er
14 das Salz und
der Pfeffer
15 die Weinkarte, -n
16 die Vase, -n
17 die Blume, -n
18 der Aschenbecher, -
19 das Weinglas, ⸚er
20 die Serviette, -n
21 der Bierdeckel, -
22 der Bierkrug, ⸚e
23 der Brotkorb, ⸚e
24 das Brötchen, -
— die Semmel, -n

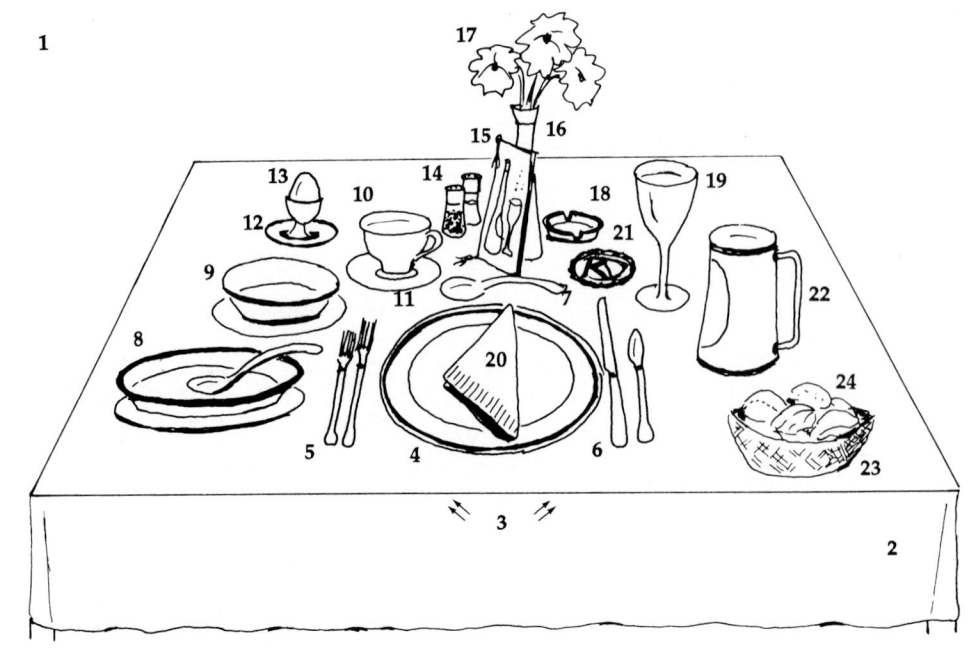

Essen – Trinken Food – Drink

Fleisch • Meat

Geflügel • Poultry

das Brathuhn, ¨er
- das Brathendl, -

Rindfleisch • Beef

das Filet, -s
das Rind, -er

Schweinefleisch • Pork, Ham

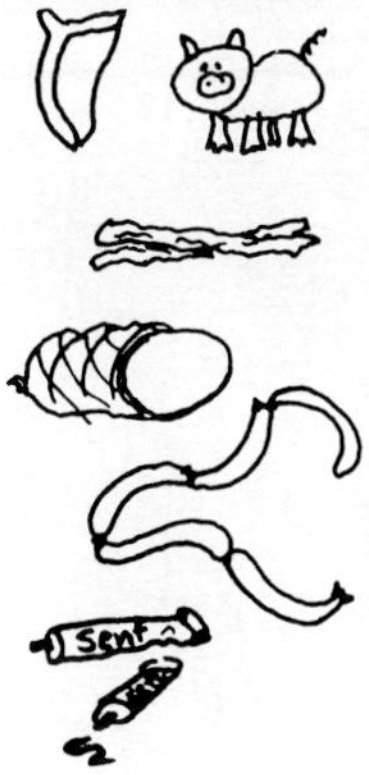

das Schweinekotelett, -s

das Schwein, -e

der Speck,

der Schinken

die Wurst, ¨e

der Senf
- der Mostrich

Meeresfrüchte • Seafood

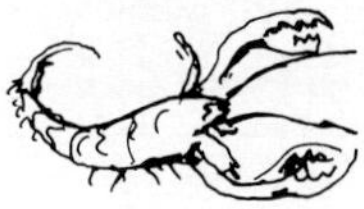

der Hummer, -

die Krabbe, -n

die Zange, -n

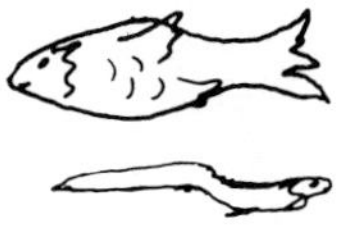

der Fisch, -e

der Aal, -e

Milchprodukte • Dairy Products

das Ei, -er
die Eierschale, -n

der Käse

die Milch
die Butter

Obst • Fruit

der Apfel, ¨
die Apfelsine, -n
- die Orange, -n

die Birne, -n

die Banane, -n

die Ananas, -

die Traube, -n
- die Weinbeere, -n

die Zitrone, -n

die Kirsche, -n

die Erdbeere, -n

die Wassermelone, -n

Gemüse • Vegetables

die Karotte, -n
- die Mohrrübe, -n
- die Möhre, -n 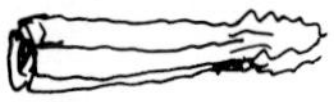
der Sellerie, -

die Tomate, -n

die Gurke, -n

der (Rot)Kohl, -e
- das Kraut, ¨er

der Mais

die Erbse, -n

der Blumenkohl, -e

die Zwiebel, -n

die Kartoffel, -n

der Pilz, -e
- der Pfifferling, -e
- der Champignon, -s

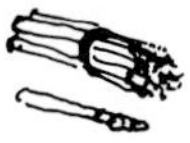

der Spargel

Gebäck • Baked Goods

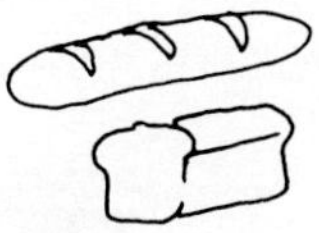

das Brot, -e
(das Weißbrot)
(das Roggenbrot)
(das Vollkornbrot)

die Brezel, -n

das Brötchen, -
- die Semmel, -n

der Kuchen,

der Keks, -e
- das Plätzchen, -

Nachtisch • Dessert

das Eis, Eissorten

der Pudding, -e

die Tafel Schokolade

Getränke • Drinks

das Kännchen, -
- die Teekanne, -n
der Tee
der Teebeutel, -

der Kaffee
der Zucker
die Sahne
- der Rahm

das Faß, Fässer

die Krone, -n
das Bier, -e
der Maßkrug, ¨e
(die Maß, -)

der Wein, -e

die Cola, -s
der Saft, ¨e

der Kakao

Stadt – Straße – Haus City – Street – Building

1 die Mauer, -n
2 die Kirche, -n
3 der Kirchturm, ¨e
4 das Kreuz, -e
5 das Kirchenfenster, -
6 das Dach, ¨er
7 die Parkuhr, -en
8 der Baum, ¨e
9 der Baumstamm, ¨e
10 der Spielplatz, ¨e
11 der Sandkasten, -
12 die Schaukel, -n
13 die Rutschbahn, -en
14 der Zaun, ¨e
15 der Taxistand, ¨e
16 der Junge, -n
17 das Mädchen, -
18 die Hecke, -n
19 der Eingang, ¨e
20 der Kirchhof, ¨e
21 der Springbrunnen, -
22 die Statue, -n
23 die Blume, -n
24 das Geschäft, -e
25 das Fenster, -
26 der Fensterladen, ¨
27 das Straßenschild, -er
28 das Ladenschild, -er
29 das Schaufenster, -
30 die Schaufensterpuppe, -en
31 die Markise, -n
32 die Haltestelle, -n
33 die Straßenlampe, -n
— die Laterne, -n
34 die Verkehrsampel, -n
35 die Straße, -n
36 die Kreuzung, -en
37 der Zebrastreifen, -
38 der Gully, -s
39 der Rinnstein, -e
40 die Litfaßsäule, -n
41 das Plakat, -e
— das Werbeplakat, -e
42 der Fußgänger, -
— der Passant, -en
43 die Fußgängerzone -n
44 der Bürgersteig, -e
— das Trottoir, -s
— der Gehweg, -e
45 die Bordsteinkante, -n
46 das Tor, -e
47 der Bogen, ¨

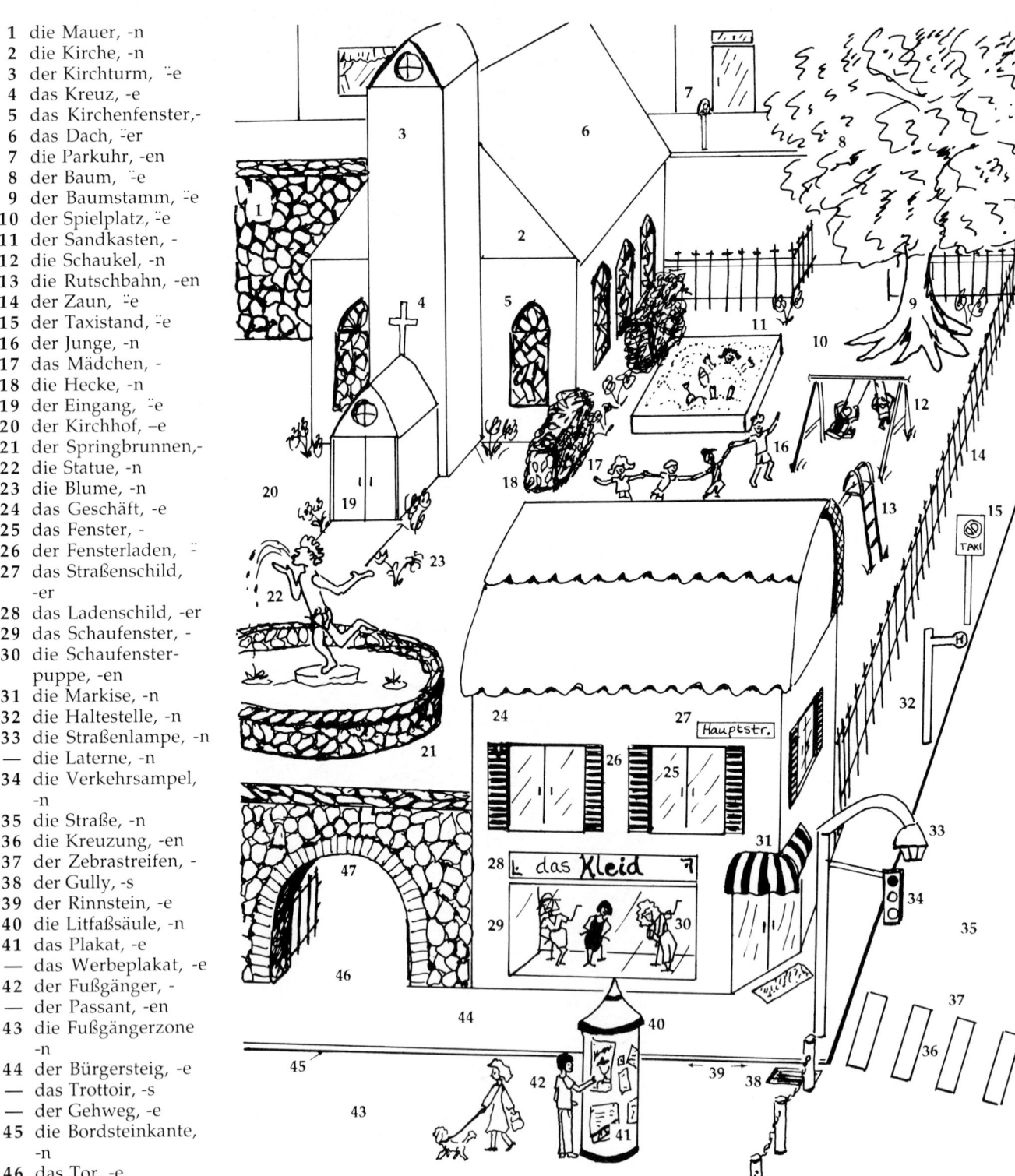

1 der Stadtplan, ⸚e
2 der Stadtteil, -e
3 die Stadtmitte, -n
4 die Ringstraße, -n
5 die Gasse, -n
6 der Bahnhof, ⸚e
7 der Platz, ⸚e
8 die Bahnlinie, -n
9 die Brücke, -n
10 der Fluß, Flüsse
11 das Ufer, -
12 die Autobahn, -en
13 die Spur, -en
14 die Ausfahrt, -en
15 die Einfahrt, -en
16 das Grundstück, -e
17 das Fahrrad, ⸚er
18 der Radler, -s
19 der Busch, ⸚e
20 die Straße, -n
21 die Einfahrt, -en
22 der Hof, ⸚e
23 der Hinterhof, ⸚e
24 das Dach, ⸚er
25 der Schornstein, -e
26 der Rauch
27 der Zaun, ⸚e
28 die Pforte, -n
29 die Wäsche
30 der Garten, ⸚
31 das Gartengerät, -e
32 die Pflanze, -n
33 das Obstgarten, ⸚
34 der Rasen, -
35 die Wiese, -n
36 der Bach, ⸚e
37 der Steg, -e

1 das Gebäude, -
2 der Stock, ⸚e
— die Etage, -n
3 das Erdgeschoß,
   Erdgeschösse
4 das Untergeschoß,
   Untergeschösse
5 der Empfang, ⸚e
6 der Empfangschef, -s
7 die Rolltreppe, -n
8 der Aufzug, ⸚e
9 der Portier, -s
10 der Hauseingang, ⸚e
11 die Haustür, -en
12 das Guckloch, ⸚er
13 die Türklinke, -n
14 das Schlüsselloch,
   ⸚er
15 die Klingel, -n
16 die Sprechanlage, -n
17 die Hausnummer, -n
18 die Laterne, -n
19 der Blumenkasten, -
20 das Geländer, -
21 die Schwelle, -n
22 die Treppe, -n

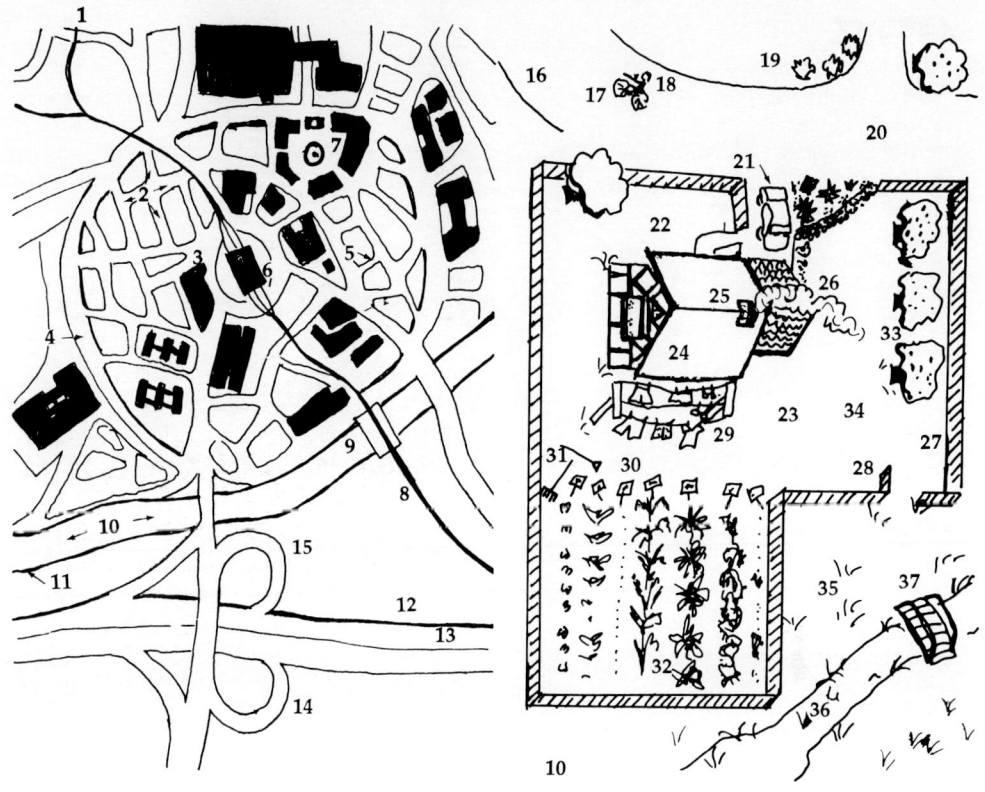

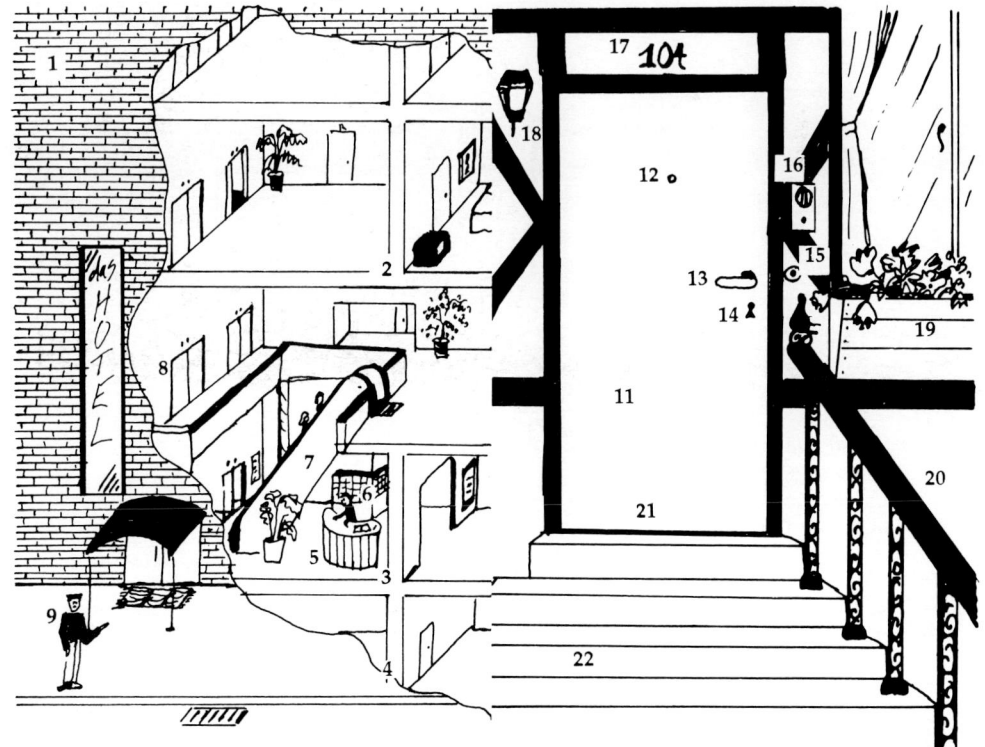

Zimmer Rooms

1 das Wohnzimmer, -
2 die Pflanze, -n
3 die Schrankwand, ⏜e
4 die Stereoanlage, -n
5 der Plattenspieler, -
6 der Fernseher, -
7 die Schublade, -n
8 das Bücherregal, -e
9 die Stehlampe, -n
10 die Schnur, ⏜e
— das Kabel, -
11 der Lampenschirm, -e
12 die Wand, ⏜e
13 die Gardine, -n
14 das Bild, -er
15 der Bildrahmen, -
16 die Tischlampe, -n
17 das Foto, -s
18 der Brief, -e
19 der Sessel, -
20 das Sofa, -s
— die Couch, -es
21 das Kissen, -
22 der Couchtisch, -e
23 die Zeitschrift, -en
24 die Zeitung, -en
25 der Teppichboden, ⏜
26 der Zeitungsständer,

1 das Badezimmer, -
2 der Medizinschrank, ⏜e
3 der Spiegel, -
4 die Zahnpasta
5 die Zahnbürste, -n
6 das Waschbecken, -
7 der Wasserhahn, ⏜e
8 die Seife
9 das Handtuch, ⏜er
10 die Toilette, -n
11 das Toilettenpapier
12 der Abfallkorb, ⏜e
13 die Bürste, -n
14 die Badewanne, -n
15 die Dusche, -n
— die Brause, -n
16 das Schampoo
17 der Waschlappen, -
18 der Haken, -
19 der Schwamm, ⏜e
20 der Heizkörper, -
21 die Türklinke, -n
22 der Boden, ⏜
23 die Kachel, -n
24 die Bademmatte, -n
— der Vorleger, -

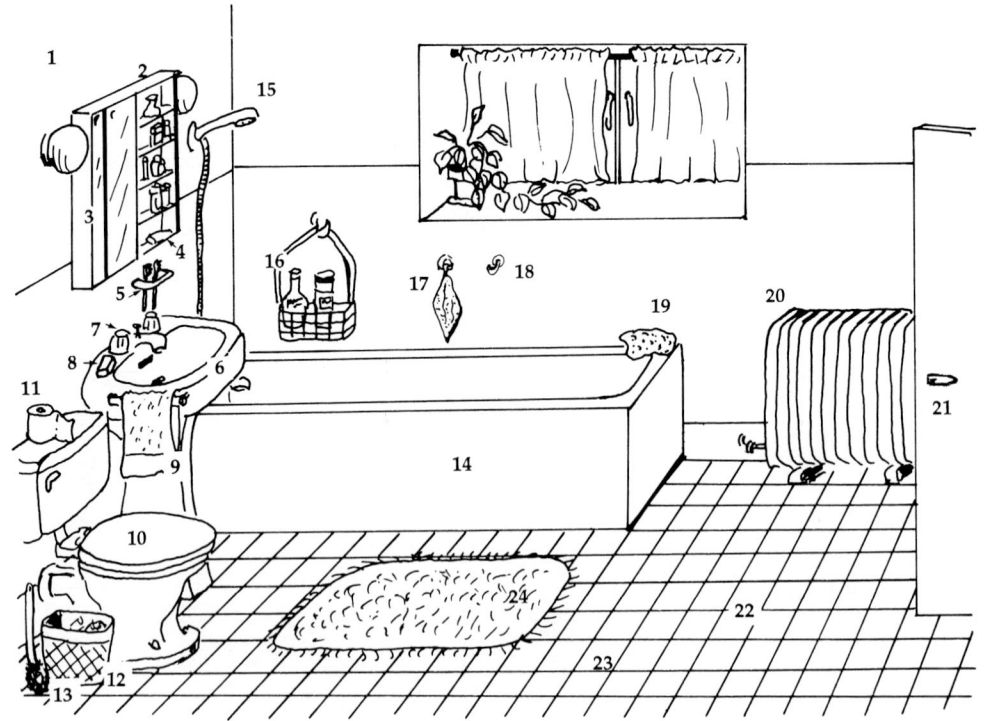

1 das Schlafzimmer, -
2 der Lichtschalter, -
3 der Teppich, -e
4 das Bett, -en
5 die Decke, -n
6 das Kopfkissen, -
7 der Nachttisch, -e
8 das Radio, -s
9 die Lampe, -n
10 das Poster, -
11 der Morgenrock, ⁻e
— der Bademantel, ⁻e
12 der Pullover, -
13 der Gürtel, -
14 die Shorts
15 die Socke, -n
16 die Unterhose, -n
17 die Schuhe (pl.)
18 das Unterhemd, -en
19 der Kleiderbügel, -
20 die Bluse, -n
21 die Garderobe, -n
22 der Kalender, -
23 die Kommode, -n
24 der Spiegel, -
25 die Bürste, -n
26 der Kamm, ⁻e
27 die Truhe, -n

1 die Küche, -n
2 der Schrank, ⁻e
3 das Spülbecken, -
4 das Geschirr
5 der Geschirrspüler, -
6 die Steckdose, -n
7 der Toaster, -
8 die Butter
9 die Besteck-
   schublade, -n
10 die Küchen-
   maschine, -n
11 die Haube, -n
12 der Herd, -e
13 die Kochplatte, -n
14 der Ofen, ⁻
15 der Topflappen, -
16 der Topf, ⁻e
17 das Weingestell, -e
18 der Kühlschrank, ⁻e
19 der Tiefkühlschrank,
   ⁻e
20 der Küchentisch, -e
21 das Gedeck, -e
22 das Glas, ⁻er
23 die Salz- und
   Pfefferstreuer (pl.)
24 die Obstschale, -n
25 der Krug, ⁻e
26 die Hängelampe, -n
27 die Glühbirne, -n

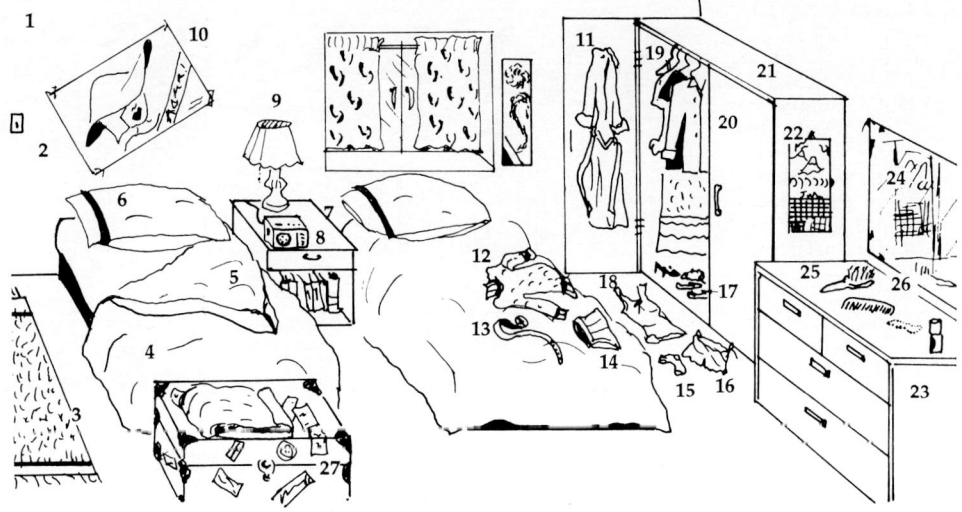

Geld und Geschäft Money and Store

1 **das Geschäft**, -e
— der Laden, ¨
— die ___handlung, -en
   (ex.: Buchhandlung)
2 die Kundin, -nen
3 der Kunde, -n
4 der Verkäufer, -
5 die Verkäuferin, -nen
6 die Preistafel, -n
7 das Sonderangebot
8 die Auslage, -n
9 der Gang, ¨e
10 das Regal, -e
11 der Kassenstand, ¨e
12 die Kasse, -n
13 der Kassierer, -
14 der Einkaufswagen, -
15 die Einkaufstasche, -n
16 die Tüte, -n
17 die Dose, -n
18 der Karton, -s
19 der Sack, ¨e
20 die Waage, -n
21 die Milchprodukte
22 die Obst- und
   Gemüseabteilung
Other Departments:
 baked goods • Backwaren
 frozen foods • Gefriergut
 meats • Fleischwaren
 pet food • Tiernahrung

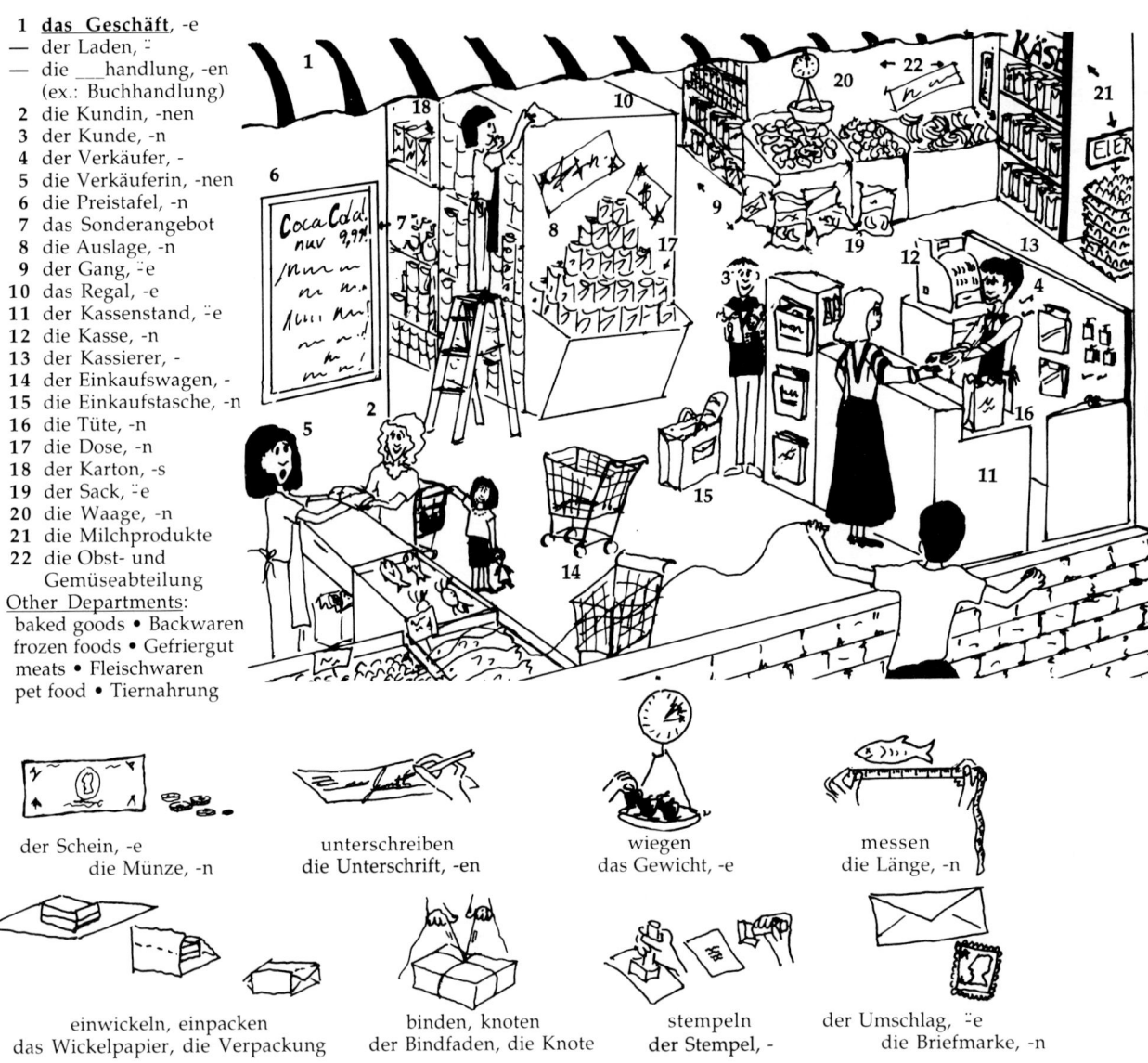

der Schein, -e
die Münze, -n

unterschreiben
die Unterschrift, -en

wiegen
das Gewicht, -e

messen
die Länge, -n

einwickeln, einpacken
das Wickelpapier, die Verpackung

binden, knoten
der Bindfaden, die Knote

stempeln
der Stempel, -

der Umschlag, ¨e
die Briefmarke, -n

Leute / Personen
chairman • der/die Vorsitzende, -n
executive • der Manager, -s
manager • der Geschäftsführer, -
boss • der Chef(in), -s
supervisor • der/die Vorgesetzte, -n
employee • der/die Angestellte, -n
worker • der Arbeiter, -
secretary • der Sekretär(in), -en
staff • das Personal
official • der Beamte, -n; Beamtin
landlord/lady • der Hauswirt(in), -e
banker • der Bankier, -s
teller • der Kassierer, -
MBA • der Diplomkaufmann, ¨er
stockbroker • der Börsenmakler
realtor • der Grundstücksmakler
lawyer • der Anwalt, ¨e

Firma + Arbeit
income • das Einkommen
salary • das Gehalt, ¨er
wages • der Lohn, ¨e
workplace • der Arbeitsplatz, ¨e
tax • die Steuer, -n
share (stock) • die Aktie, -n
stock market • die Börse
insurance • die Versicherung, -en
profession • der Beruf, -e
job • der Job; die Stelle, -n
branch office • die Zweigstelle, -n
department • die Abteilung, -en

Waren
product, goods • die Ware, -n
brand • die Marke, -n
type, variety • die Sorte, -n
kind • die Art, -en

Finanz
bank • die Bank, -en
   savings ~ • die Sparkasse, -n
account • das Konto, -en
   checking ~ • das Girokonto
   savings ~ • das Sparkonto
check • der Scheck, -s
deposit • die Einzahlung, -en
withdrawal • das Abheben
fee • die Gebühr, -en
loan • die Anleihe, -n
mortgage • die Hypothek, -en
interest • der Zins, -en

Eigenschaften
broken • kaputt
fragile • zerbrechlich
repaired • repariert
used • gebraucht

Verben
borrow • borgen
lend • leihen
save • sparen
deposit • einzahlen
cash (check) • einlösen
insure • versichern
register • anmelden
rent, lease • mieten
rent out • vermieten
sublet • untermieten
fire • feuern
hire • anstellen
repair • reparieren
mend • flicken
send, ship • schicken
return • zurückbringen
exchange • umtauschen

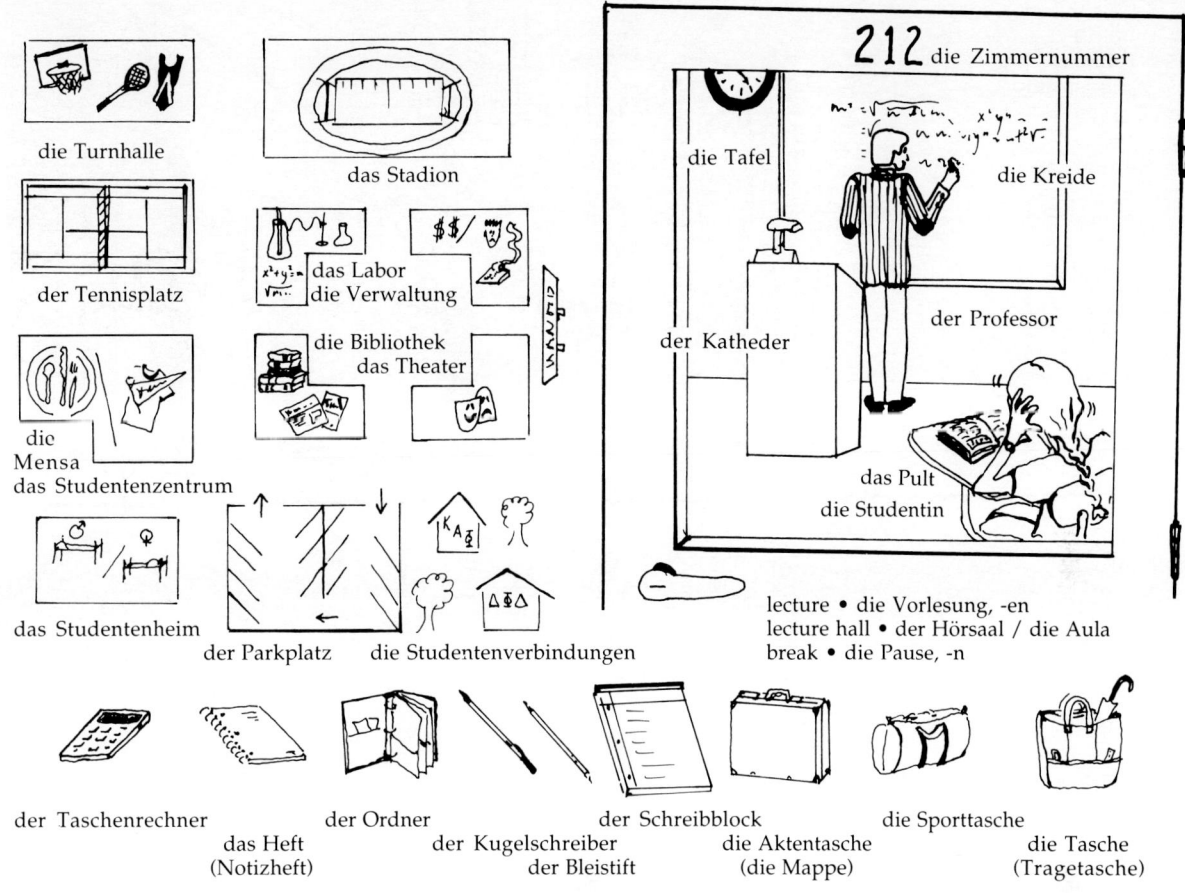

die Turnhalle

das Stadion

der Tennisplatz

das Labor
die Verwaltung

die Bibliothek
das Theater

die Mensa
das Studentenzentrum

212 die Zimmernummer

die Tafel

die Kreide

der Katheder

der Professor

das Pult
die Studentin

das Studentenheim

der Parkplatz

die Studentenverbindungen

lecture • die Vorlesung, -en
lecture hall • der Hörsaal / die Aula
break • die Pause, -n

der Taschenrechner

das Heft
(Notizheft)

der Ordner

der Kugelschreiber
der Bleistift

der Schreibblock

die Aktentasche
(die Mappe)

die Sporttasche

die Tasche
(Tragetasche)

die Wissenschaften

Geisteswissenschaften
Amerikanistik
Anglistik
Dramatik
Englisch als Fremdsprache
Englische Literatur
Fremdsprachen
Germanistik
Kunst
Logik
Musik
Philosophie
Religion
Theologie
———
Feministische Studien
Landwirtschaft
Sport

Naturwissenschaften
Astronomie
Biologie
Botanik
Chemie
Computerwissenschaft
Elektrotechnik
Erdkunde (Geographie)
Geologie
Maschinenbau
Mathematik
Meteorologie
Paläontologie
Physik
Tierkunde (Zoologie)
Medizin
   Krankenpflege
   Naturheilkunde
   Psychiatrie
   Tierheilkunde
   Zahnheilkunde

Sozialwissenschaften
Anthropologie
Archäologie
Ethnologie
Geschichte
Journalismus
Jura
Linguistik
Pädagogik
Politische Wissenschaft
Psychologie
Rhetorik
Soziologie

Wirtschaft (Ökonomie)
Betriebsverwaltung
Betriebswirtschaft
Buchhaltung
Handelswirtschaft
Publizistik
Werbung

die Note, -n		
1	A	sehr gut
2	B	gut
3	C	befriedigend
4	D	ausreichend
5	E	mangelhaft
6	F	ungenügend

register (university) • immatrikulieren
register (class) • einschreiben
attend (class) • besuchen
drop (class) • fallen lassen
homework • die Hausaufgabe, -n
term paper • die Semesterarbeit
report • das Referat, -e
exam • die Prüfung, -en
pass (test) • bestehen
fail • durchfallen
cheat • mogeln
finals • die Abschlußprüfungen
graduate (from) • absolvieren

For unlisted subjects, try these suffix changes: -y > -ie;   -logy > -logie;   -ics or -y > -ik
XYZ science/engineering > XYZtechnik;   XYZ engineering/construction > XYZbau

1 der Bahnsteig, -e
2 die Tafel, -n
— das Schild, -er
3 das Stationsschild
4 die Uhr, -en
5 der Zeiger, -
6 der Fahrkarten-
   schalter, -
7 der/die Reisende, -n
8 die Handtasche, -n
9 die Unterführung,
   -en
10 die Überführung,
   -en
11 der Personenwagen,-
12 der Einstieg, -e
13 das Trittbrett, -er
14 die Schwelle, -n
15 die Schiene, -n
16 der Schaffner, -
17 die Mütze,
18 die Bank, ¨e
19 der Kofferkuli, -s
20 das Gepäck
21 das Schließfach, ¨er
22 die Bedienungs-
   anweisungen
23 der Damenhut, ¨e

1 das Abteil, -e
2 die Notbremse, -n
3 das Abteilfenster, -
4 die Landschaft, -en
5 der Vorhang, ¨e
6 der Klapptisch, -e
7 der Fahrplan, ¨e
8 der Aschenbecher, -
9 die Zigarette, -n
10 der Rauch
11 das Nummernschild,
   -er
12 der Abfallbehälter, -
13 der Abfall, ¨e
14 die Heizung
15 die Heizungs-
   regulierung, -en
16 der Eckplatz, ¨e
— der Fensterplatz, ¨e
17 die Armlehne, -n
18 die Kopflehne, -n
19 der Auszieh-
   polstersitz, -e
20 die Gepäckablage, -n
21 der Koffer, -
22 der Kleiderhaken, -
23 der Klappsitz, -e
24 die Fußstütze, -n
25 der Fußboden, ¨

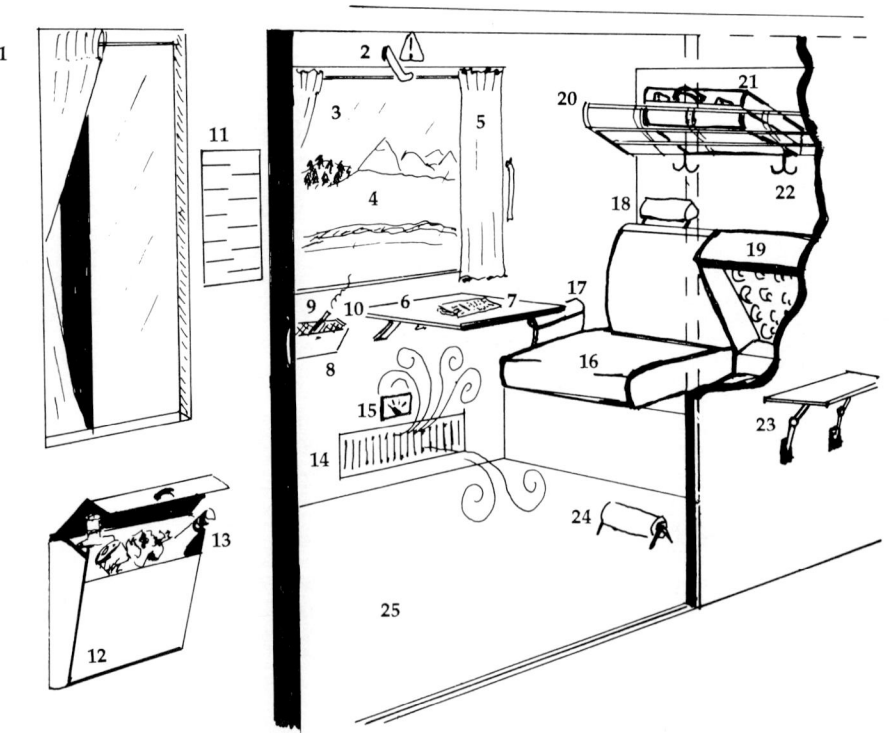

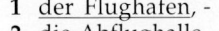

1 <u>der Flughafen</u>, -
2 die Abflughalle, -n
3 der Kontrollturm, ⁻e
4 die Antenne, -n
5 der Bus, -se
6 der Busfahrer, -
7 der Gepäck-
   bandwagen, -
8 der Passagier, -e
— der Fluggast, ⁻e
9 der Spion, -e
   (die Spionin, -nen)
10 der Trenchcoat, -s
11 die Aktentasche, -n
12 das Flugpersonal
13 der Steward, -s
14 die Stewardess, -en
15 der Pilot, -en
   (die Pilotin, -nen)
16 das Flugzeug, -e
17 der Propeller, -
18 der Motor, -en
19 der Flügel, -
20 die Landepiste, -n
21 die Landung, -en
22 der Abflug, ⁻e
— der Start, -s

1 <u>das Verkehrsmittel</u>, -
2 der Reifen, -
3 der Lenker, -
4 der Sitz, -e
5 die Kette, -n
6 das Pedal, -e
7 die Luftpumpe, -n
8 das Schloß, ⁻(ss)er
9 die Windschutz-
   scheibe, -n
10 der Benzintank, -e
11 der Auspuff, -e
12 das Abgas, -e
13 der Schutzhelm, -e
14 der Ersatzreifen, -
15 die Tanksäule, -n
16 die Motorhaube, -n
17 die Stoßstange, -n
18 das Kennzeichen, -
— das Nummernschild,
   -er
19 der Scheinwerfer, -
20 der Kotflügel, -
21 das Lenkrad, ⁻er
— das Steuerrad, ⁻er
22 der Scheiben-
   wischer, -
23 der Rückspiegel, -
24 das Schiebedach, ⁻er
25 der Sicherheitsgurt,
   -e
26 der Kofferraum, ⁻e
27 der Fahrer, -
   (die Fahrerin, -nen)

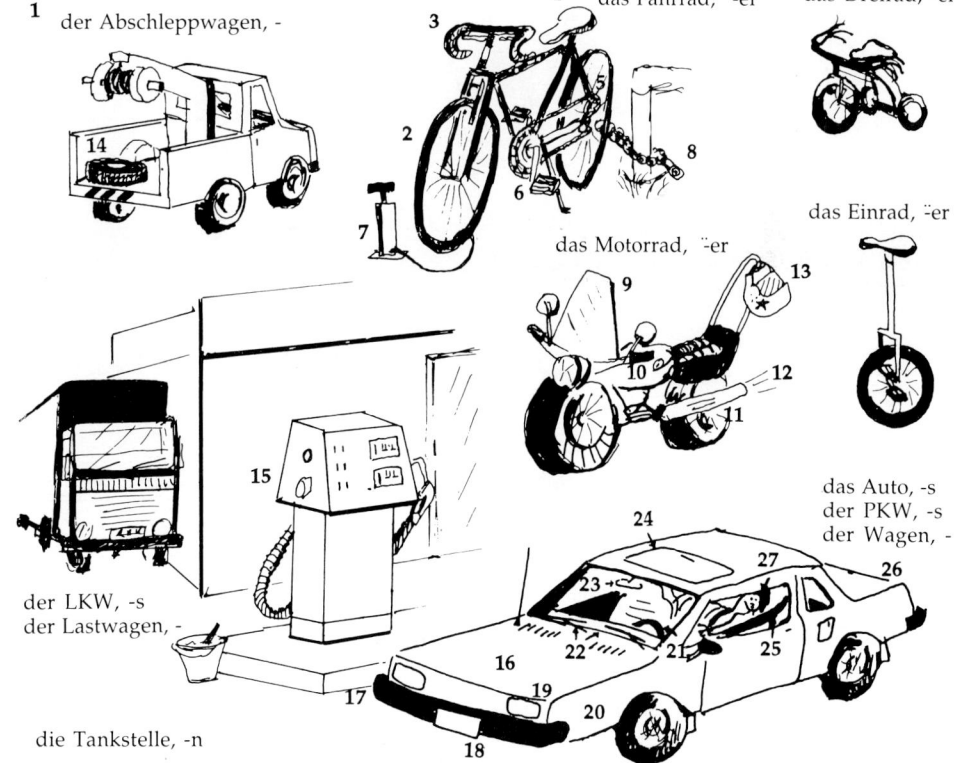

der Abschleppwagen, -

das Fahrrad, ⁻er

das Dreirad, ⁻er

das Motorrad, ⁻er

das Einrad, ⁻er

das Auto, -s
der PKW, -s
der Wagen, -

der LKW, -s
der Lastwagen, -

die Tankstelle, -n

1 der Kopf, ⁻e
2 die Schulter, -n
3 der Arm, -e
4 der Ell(en)bogen, -
5 das Handgelenk, -e
6 die Hand, ⁻e
7 der Daumen, -
8 der Finger, -
9 der Zeigefinger, -
10 die Brust, ⁻e
11 die Achselhöhle, -n
12 der Bauch, ⁻e
13 der Nabel, -
14 die Taille, -n
15 die Hüfte, -n
16 das Bein, -e
17 der Schenkel, -
18 das Knie, -
19 das Fußgelenk, -e
20 der Fuß, ⁻e
21 die Ferse, -n
22 der Zeh, -e

23 das Haar, -e
24 die Stirn, -e
25 die Augenbraue, -n
26 das Auge, -n
27 das Ohr, -en
28 die Wange, -n
— die Backe, -n
29 das Kinn, -e
30 der Hals, ⁻e
31 der Mund, ⁻er
32 die Nase, -n
33 die Lippe, -n
34 der Schnurrbart, ⁻e
35 der Bart, ⁻e

1 sich (acc) waschen
— sich (acc) duschen
2 sich (acc) baden
3 sich (dat) die Hände
    waschen
4 sich (dat) die Zähne
    putzen
5 die Zahnpasta

6 sich (dat) die Haare
    bürsten
7 die Bürste, -n
8 sich (dat) die Haare
    kämmen
9 der Kamm, ⁻e

10 sich (acc) schminken
11 der Schminktisch, -e
12 der Lippenstift, -e
13 das Parfüm, -s
14 die Schere, -n
15 das Armband, ⁻er
16 der Ring, -e
17 die Spraydose, -n

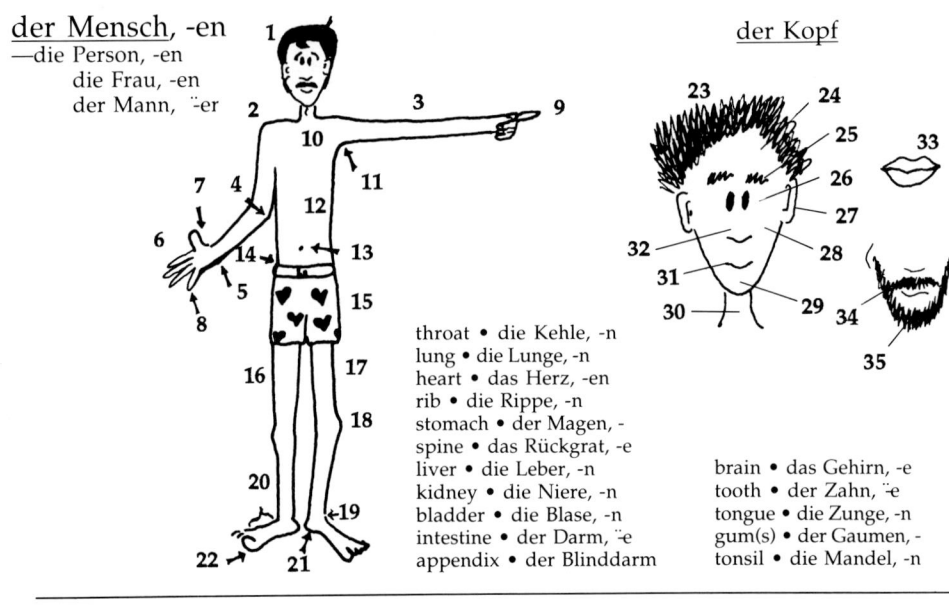

der Mensch, -en
—die Person, -en
die Frau, -en
der Mann, ⁻er

der Kopf

throat • die Kehle, -n
lung • die Lunge, -n
heart • das Herz, -en
rib • die Rippe, -n
stomach • der Magen, -
spine • das Rückgrat, -e
liver • die Leber, -n
kidney • die Niere, -n
bladder • die Blase, -n
intestine • der Darm, ⁻e
appendix • der Blinddarm

brain • das Gehirn, -e
tooth • der Zahn, ⁻e
tongue • die Zunge, -n
gum(s) • der Gaumen, -
tonsil • die Mandel, -n

1 die Jacke, -n
2 das Ärmel, -
3 die Manschette, -n
4 der Mantel, ¨
— der Regenmantel, ¨
5 der Hut, ¨e
6 die Strickjacke, -n
7 der Regenschirm, -e
8 der Schirmständer, -
9 der Anzug, ¨e
10 das Revers, -
11 die Hose, -n
12 die Krawatte, -
— der Schlips, -e
13 der Preiszettel, -
14 das Preisschild, -er
15 die Modepuppe, -n
16 die Mütze, -n
— die Kappe, -n
17 die Jeans (pl.)
18 der Tennisschuh, -e
   (der Sportschuh)

19 der Kleiderbügel, -
20 das Kleid, -er
21 die Baskenmütze, -n
22 der Gürtel, -
23 die Handtasche, -n
24 die Kundin, -nen
   (der Kunde, -n)
25 der Badeanzug, ¨e
26 der Schuh, -e
27 der Strumpf, ¨e
— die Socke, -n
28 der BH , -s
— der Büstenhalter, -
29 der Slip, -s
— das Höschen, -
30 die Shorts, -
31 das Abendkleid, -er
32 die Bluse, -n
33 das Haarband, ¨er
34 der Pullover, -
— der Pulli, -s
35 der Bikini, -s
36 die Verkäuferin,-nen
   (der Verkäufer, -)

1 die Armbanduhr, -en
2 der Reißverschluß,
   -schlüsse
3 der Rock, ¨e
4 der Unterrock, ¨e
5 die Strumpfhose, -n
6 die Sohle, -n
7 der Absatz, ¨e
8 die Haarspange, -n
9 die Brille, -n
10 die Frisur, -en
11 der Ohrring, -e
12 der Kragen, -
13 die Halskette, -n
14 der Knopf, ¨e
15 die Tasche, -n

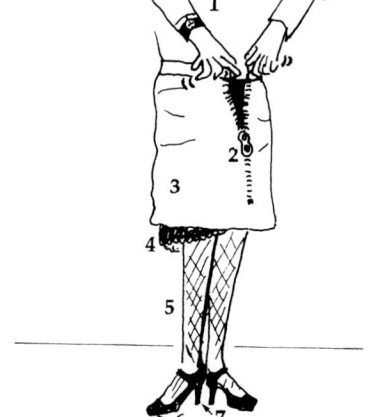

Leute People

The Family Tree • der Stammbaum

single • ledig, nicht verheiratet
in love • verliebt
engaged • verlobt
fiance(e) • der/die Verlobte
engagement • die Verlobung
wedding • die Hochzeit, die Ehe
couple • das Ehepaar, -e
wife • die Ehefrau
husband • der Ehemann
pregnant • schwanger
birth • die Geburt, -en
child • das Kind, -er
divorce • die Scheidung
divorced • geschieden
widowed • verwitwet

meine Großeltern

My X's Y = d_ Y von mein_ X
X-in-law = d_ SchwiegerX (usu.)
StepX = d_ StiefX

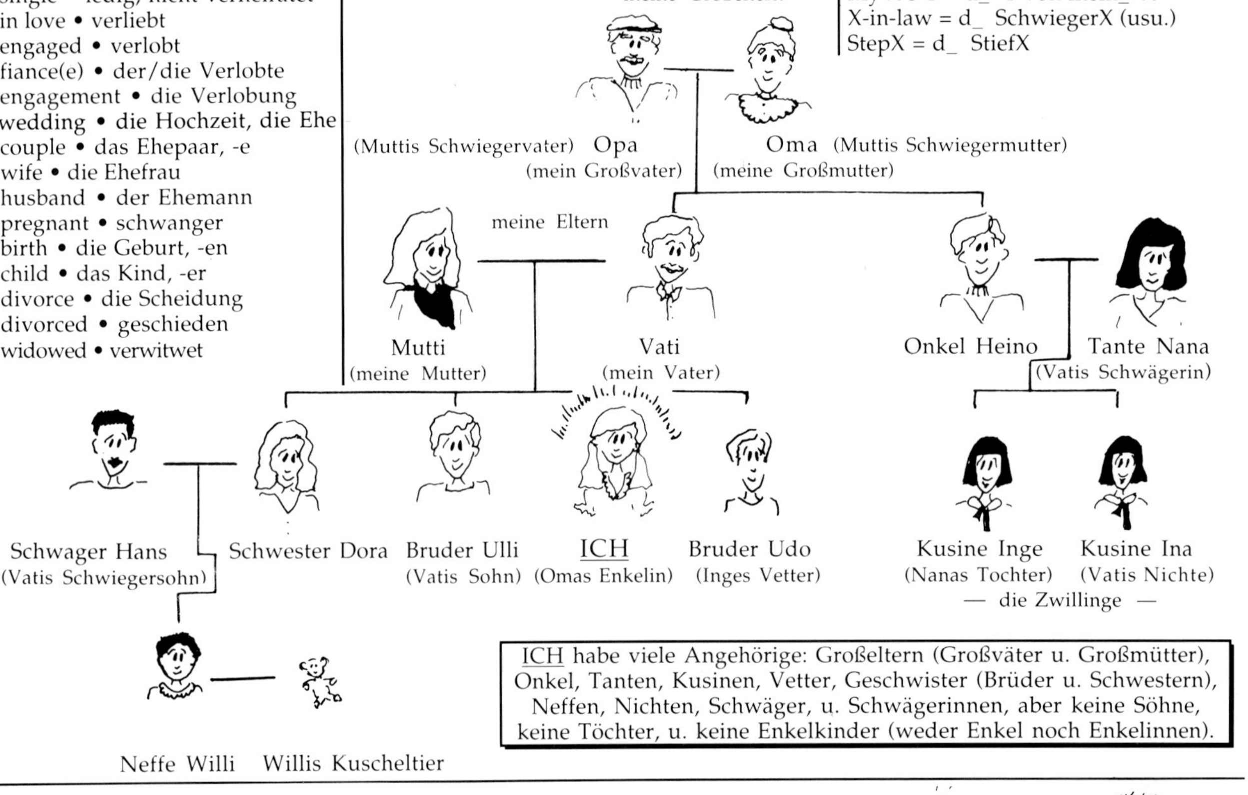

(Muttis Schwiegervater) Opa
(mein Großvater)

Oma (Muttis Schwiegermutter)
(meine Großmutter)

meine Eltern

Mutti
(meine Mutter)

Vati
(mein Vater)

Onkel Heino

Tante Nana
(Vatis Schwägerin)

Schwager Hans
(Vatis Schwiegersohn)

Schwester Dora

Bruder Ulli
(Vatis Sohn)

ICH
(Omas Enkelin)

Bruder Udo
(Inges Vetter)

Kusine Inge
(Nanas Tochter)

Kusine Ina
(Vatis Nichte)

— die Zwillinge —

> ICH habe viele Angehörige: Großeltern (Großväter u. Großmütter),
> Onkel, Tanten, Kusinen, Vetter, Geschwister (Brüder u. Schwestern),
> Neffen, Nichten, Schwäger, u. Schwägerinnen, aber keine Söhne,
> keine Töchter, u. keine Enkelkinder (weder Enkel noch Enkelinnen).

Neffe Willi   Willis Kuscheltier

froh
glücklich

traurig
deprimiert

böse
sauer

überrascht
erstaunt

frustriert
ratlos

ängstlich
erschrocken

der (Büro)Angestellte, -n
printer • der Drucker, -
computer • der Computer, -s
printer paper • das Endlospapier

die Sekretärin, -nen
typewriter • die Schreibmaschine, -n
swivel chair • der Drehstuhl, ‑e
steno pad • der Stenoblock

der (Fabrik)Arbeiter, -
shift • die Schicht, -en
factory • die Fabrik, -en
assembly line • das Fließband

die Bäuerin / der Bauer
pitchfork • die Mistgabel, -n
farm • der Bauernhof, ‑e
grow, cultivate • bauen

das Reinigungspersonal
custodian • der Hausmeister
cleaning lady • die Putzfrau
clean (up) • putzen, saubermachen

der Zimmerer
or. Tischler, Schreiner
toolbox • der Werkzeugkasten
hammer/saw • hämmern/sägen

der Klempner
pipe • das Rohr, -e
leak • das Leck, -s
fix • reparieren

die Blumenhändlerin
bouquet • der Strauß
die Rose, -n / die Tulpe, -n
carnation • die Nelke, -n

die Schneiderin
style, cut • der Schnitt, -e
material • der Stoff
tailormade ___ • Maß___

der Friseur / die Friseuse
beauty parlor • der Schönheitssalon
hairstyle • die Frisur
have (hair) cut • schneiden lassen

der Künstler
model • das Modell, -e
artwork • das Kunstwerk, -e
painting • das Gemälde, -

der Ingenieur
drafting table • der Zeichentisch
drawing • die Zeichnung
blueprint • die Blaupause, -n

der Anwalt
judge • der Richter
witness • der/die Zeuge, -n
courtroom • der Gerichtssaal

der Zahnarzt
patient • die Patientin
drill • bohren
fill • plombieren

die Ärztin
orderly • der Krankenpfleger
diagnosis • die Diagnose, -n
treat • behandeln

der Politiker
party • die Partei, -en
campaign • der Wahlkampf
vote • wählen

Kultur Culture

1 die Oper, -n
2 der Lautsprecher, -
3 der Vorhang, ⁻e
4 die Bühne, -n
5 das Rampenlicht, -er
6 der/die Sänger(in),
    -(nen)
7 das Mikrophon, -e
8 der Zuschauerraum,
    ⁻e
9 das Parkett, -e
10 die Reihe, -n
11 der Platz, ⁻e
12 der Rang
13 die Loge, -n
14 der Eingang, ⁻e
— der Ausgang, ⁻e
15 der Zuschauer, -
16 der Platzanweiser, -
17 die Karte, -n
18 der Stehplatz, ⁻e
19 der Gang, ⁻e
20 der Beifall
— Beifall klatschen
21 der Dirigent, -en
22 das Orchester, -

1 das Museum,
    Museen
2 der Raum, ⁻e
3 die Statue, -n
4 der Wandbehang, ⁻e
5 das Gemälde, -
— das Bild, -er
6 das Porträt, -s
7 der Preis, -e
8 der Titel, -
9 das Mobile, -s
10 die Skulptur, -en
11 der Museum-
    besucher, -

major • Dur
minor • Moll
scale • die Tonleiter
interval • die Tonstufe
octave • die Oktave
score • die Partitur
rehearsal • die Probe
grace note • die Verzierung
trill • der Triller
song • das Lied
choir, chorus • der Chor
quartet • das Quartett
voice • die Stimme
to tune • stimmen
to accompany • begleiten
Classical • klassisch
Romantic • romantisch
Baroque • barock

der Komponist, -en
komponieren
die Melodie, -n
die Harmonie, -n
der Rhythmus,
    Rhythmen
die Sonate, -n
das Konzert, -e
die Symphonie, -n

die Saiteninstrumente

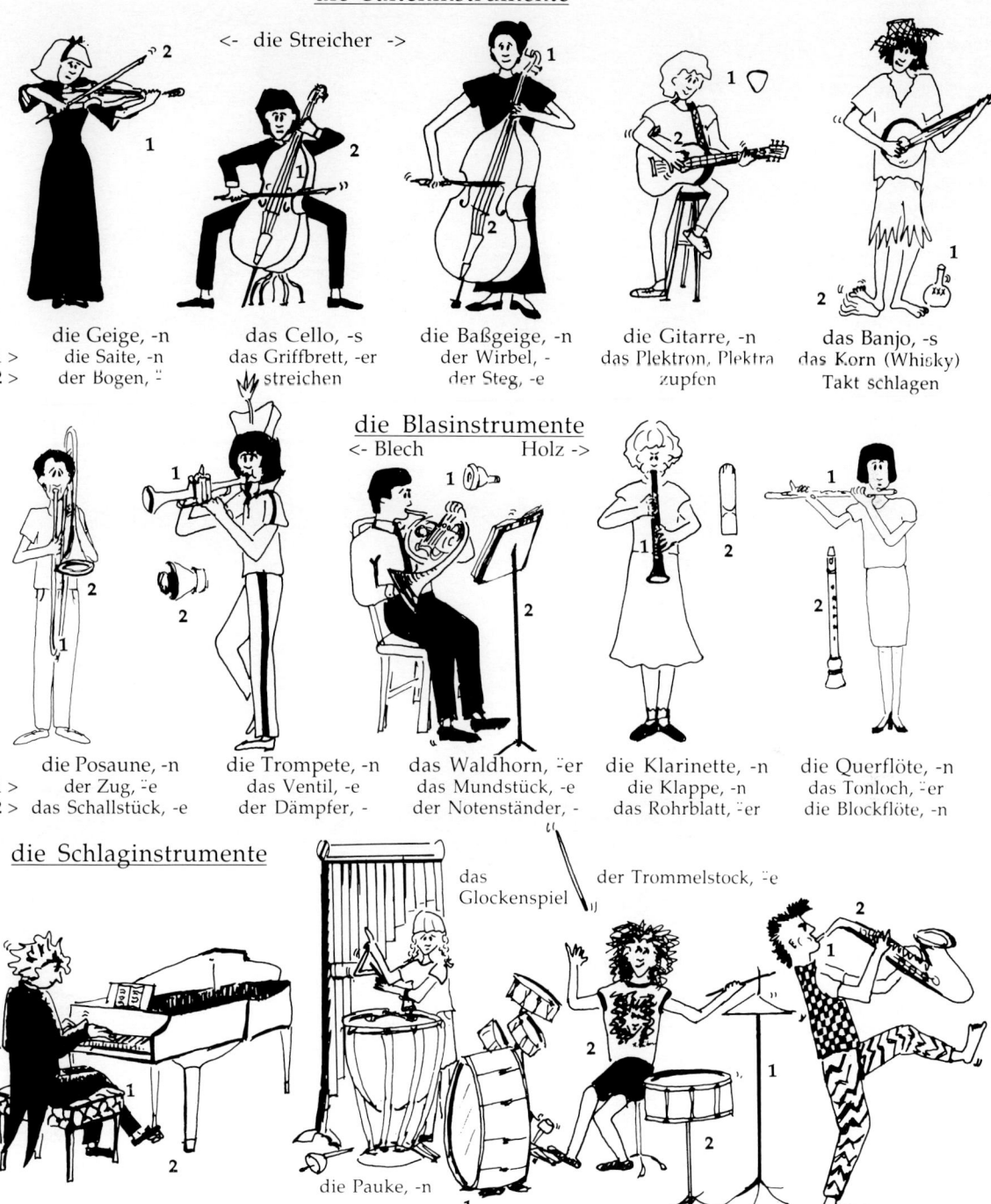

<- die Streicher ->

die Geige, -n	das Cello, -s	die Baßgeige, -n	die Gitarre, -n	das Banjo, -s
1 > die Saite, -n	das Griffbrett, -er	der Wirbel, -	das Plektron, Plektra	das Korn (Whisky)
2 > der Bogen, ⏜	streichen	der Steg, -e	zupfen	Takt schlagen

die Blasinstrumente

<- Blech   Holz ->

die Posaune, -n	die Trompete, -n	das Waldhorn, ⏜er	die Klarinette, -n	die Querflöte, -n
1 > der Zug, ⏜e	das Ventil, -e	das Mundstück, -e	die Klappe, -n	das Tonloch, ⏜er
2 > das Schallstück, -e	der Dämpfer, -	der Notenständer, -	das Rohrblatt, ⏜er	die Blockflöte, -n

die Schlaginstrumente

das Glockenspiel   der Trommelstock, ⏜e

die Pauke, -n

— der P i a n i s t / das K l a v i e r , -e —
1 > die Klaviatur   (grand piano • der Flügel)
2 > das Pedal, -e   (harpsichord • das Cembalo)

— d a s   S c h l a g z e u g , -e —
die große Trommel, -n   das Becken, -
der Trommler, -   die kleine Trommel, -n

das Saxophon, -e
die Mundstellung
das Ansatzrohr, ⏜e

Natur Nature

1 das All
2 der Himmel, -
3 der Engel, -
4 die Sonne, -n
5 der S(onnens)trahl, -en
6 die Erde
7 der Kontinent, -e
8 der Ozean, -e
9 der Schatten, -
10 der Mond, -en
11 die Mondsichel
12 der Stern, -e
13 die Milchstraße
14 der Planet, -en
15 der Satellit, -en
— der Trabant, -en
16 das Raumschiff, -e
17 die Rakete, -n
18 der Fallschirm, -e
19 die Raumkapsel, -n
20 die Flugbahn, -en

1 die Himmels-richtung, -en
2 der Kompaß, Kompasse
3 der Norden; nördlich
4 der Süden; südlich
5 der Osten; östlich
6 der Westen; westlich
7 der Längengrad, -e
8 der Breitengrad, -e
9 der Äquator
10 der Pol, -e
11 die A(nta)rktis
12 die Tropen (pl.)

1 die Natur
2 der Berg, -e
3 der Gipfel, -
— die Bergkuppe, -n
4 der Hügel, -
5 der Wald, ⁻er
6 der Nadelbaum, ⁻e
7 der Fluß, Flüsse
8 der Wasserfall, ⁻e
9 der Stein, -e
10 das Ufer, -
11 die Mündung, -en
12 das Meer, -e
13 die Welle, -n
14 der Strand, ⁻e
15 der Sand, -e
16 der Sonnenaufgang, ⁻e
— der Sonnen-untergang, ⁻e
17 das Ferienhaus, ⁻er
18 der See, -n
19 das Boot, -e
20 der Rettungsring, -e

1 <u>die Jahreszeit</u>, -en
2 der <u>Winter</u>, -
3 der Schnee
4 die Schneeflocke, -n
5 der Schneemann, ¨er
6 der Eiszapfen, -
7 die Schaufel, -n
8 der <u>Frühling</u>, -e
9 das Gewitter, -
10 die Wolke, -n
11 der Blitz, -e
12 der Regen(tropfen)
13 der Regenschirm, -e
14 die Pfütze, -n
15 der <u>Sommer</u>, -
16 der Sonnenschirm, -e
17 das Segelbrett, -er
18 die Insel, -n
19 der <u>Herbst</u>, -e
20 das Blatt, ¨er

1 <u>das Thermometer</u>, -
2 der Siedepunkt
3 die Körper-
temperatur
4 der Gefrierpunkt
— der Schmelzpunkt
5 der Grad

1 <u>die Landschaft</u>, -en
2 die Katze, -n
3 das Nest, -er
4 der Ast, ¨e
5 der Zweig, -e
6 das Spinngewebe, -n
7 die Spinne, -n
8 die Fliege, -n
9 die Weide, -n
10 die Ziege, -n
11 der Traktor, -en
12 der Bauer, -n
13 das Feld, -er
14 das Pferd, -e
15 das Schaf, -e
16 die Kuh, ¨e
17 die Scheune, -n
18 das Schwein, -e
19 der Bauernhof, ¨e
20 der Hahn, ¨e
21 die Maus, ¨e
22 die Ratte, -n
23 das Heu
24 die Mistgabel, -n
25 das Gras, ¨er
26 der Vogel, ¨
27 der Wurm, ¨er
28 der Frosch, ¨e
29 die Ente, -n
30 der Fisch, -e
31 der Teich, -e
32 der Schmetterling, -e
33 das Huhn, ¨er
34 der Hund, -e
35 die Gans, ¨e

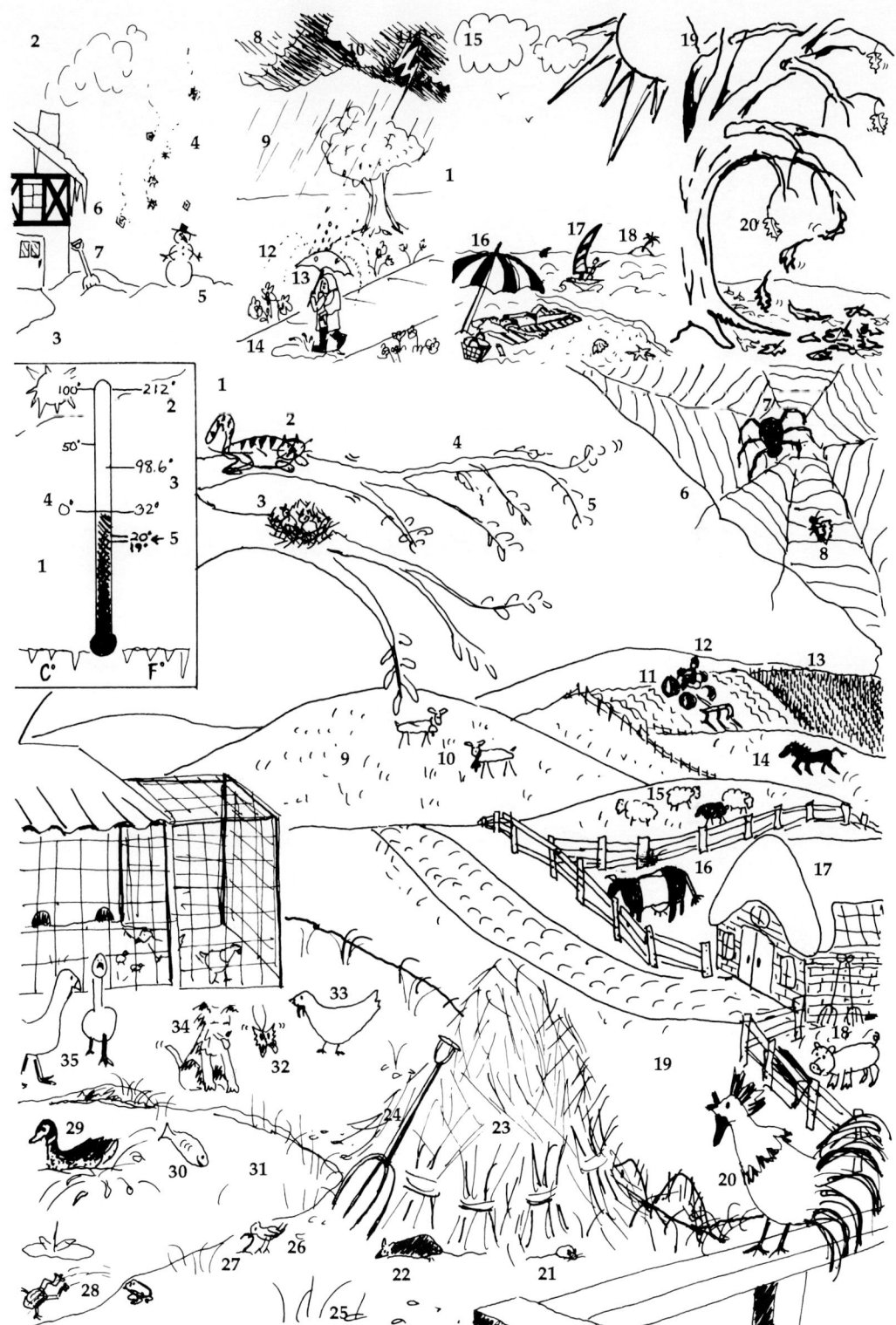

essen
meal • das Essen
Tiere fressen

trinken
alkoholfrei
drunk • betrunken

gehen
zu Fuß gehen
bummeln

sehen
schauen
look, seem • aussehen

hören
listen (to) • zuhören
be quiet • schweigen

beißen
chew • kauen
swallow • schlucken

einschenken
pour • gießen
flow • fließen

laufen
'run' or 'walk'
jogger • der Läufer

lesen
(un)lesbar
lecture • die Vorlesung

sagen
narrate • erzählen
sprechen, reden

rauchen
lighter • das Feuerzeug
Haben Sie Feuer?

probieren
smell • riechen
Das schmeckt!

fahren
travel • reisen
traffic • der Verkehr

schreiben
paint • malen
draw • zeichnen

grüßen
introduce • vorstellen
die Hände schütteln

kaufen
shop • einkaufen
look • sich umschauen

zahlen
count • zählen
calculate • rechnen

fliegen
der Flughafen
starten / landen

zeigen
point • deuten
erklären, beschreiben

rufen
shout • schreien
jodeln, singen

geben
gift • das Geschenk
give a gift • schenken

bekommen
keep • behalten
borrow • leihen

fallen
climb • steigen
drop • fallen lassen

fernsehen
der Fernseher
program • die Sendung

anrufen
telefonieren mit __
phone call • der Anruf

schlafen
dream • träumen
zu Bett gehen

liegen
lie down • s. hinlegen
rest • sich ausruhen

denken
believe • glauben
consider • überlegen

arbeiten
position • die Stelle
occupation • der Beruf

lieben
hate • hassen
kiss • küssen, der Kuß

aufstehen
aufwachen
der Wecker

sitzen
sit down • s. hinsetzen
place, set • setzen

suchen
finden
lose • verlieren

bauen
building • das Gebäude
bldg. site • die Baustelle

heiraten
married • verheiratet
divorced • geschieden

sich anziehen
sich umziehen
sich ausziehen

stehen
warten
stay • bleiben

öffnen
Ich mache die Tür auf.
zumachen, schließen

ziehen
press • drücken
shove • schieben

lachen / lächeln
amusing • lustig
odd • komisch

tragen
mitnehmen
lug, drag • schleppen

springen
tanzen
limp • hinken

antasten
grab • (an)fassen
let go • loslassen

schlagen
quarrel • streiten
quarrel • der Streit

weinen
sad • traurig
angry • böse

schneiden
separate • trennen
divide, share • teilen

werfen
catch • fangen
(in der Hand) halten

aufheben
fetch • abholen
pick up • aufräumen

brechen
fix • reparieren
maintain • pflegen

wachsen
leben / sterben
der/die Erwachsene

Hobbys, Sport, Sonderinteressen Hobbies, Sports, Special Interests

das Hobby, Hobbys
der Sport, Sportarten
der Athlet, -en
der Sportler, -
die Sportlerin, -nen
der Baseball
der amerikanische Fußball
der Volleyball
das Karate

<u>male/female patterns</u>

der ___er, -
   die ___erin, -nen
der ___spieler, -
   die ___spielerin, -nen
der ___sportler, -
   die ___sportlerin, -nen
der Liebhaber • amateur
   die Liebhaberin
der Hobby+activity(er)
   die Hobby+activity(er)+in
der Profi, -s • the pro
   die Profi, -s

I go ___ing •
   ich gehe <verb infinitive>
I do, pursue ___ •
   ich treibe <name of sport>

der Fußball
goal • das Tor, -e
goalie • der Torhüter, Torwart
kick • schießen

das (Eis)Hockey
stick • der Stock, ⸚e
puck • der Puck, -s
sideline • die Seitenlinie, -n

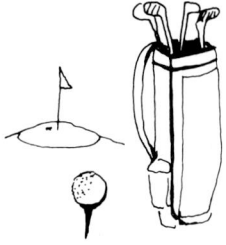

das Golf
club • der (Golf)schläger, -
tee • der Aufsatz, ⸚e
putt • putten

Kegeln
alley • die Kegelbahn, -en
pin • der Kegel, -
bowler • der Kegler, -

Stemmen
weight • das Gewicht, -e
pump iron • Gewichte heben
muscle • der Muskel, -n

Turnen
gym • die Turnhalle, -n
gymnast • der Turner, -
Barren, Ringe, Sprungpferd

die Gartenarbeit
der Hobbygärtner, -
seed • der Samen, -
tool(s) • das Gartengerät, -e

Sammeln
stamp • die Briefmarke, -n
coin • die Münze, -n
das Album, Alben

Karten spielen
shuffle • mischen
deal • geben, austeilen
ace of spades • das Pikas

der Schach
chessboard • das Schachbrett, -er
move • der Zug, ⸚e
checkmate • das Schachmatt

Holzschnitzen
chisel • der Meißel, -
shavings • der Span, ⸚e
carving • die Schnitzerei

Basteln
do-it-yourself • selber machen
kit • der Baukasten, -
model ___ • d_ Modell___

Keramik / töpfen
clay • der Ton
potter's wheel • die Drehscheibe, -n
earthenware • die Tonwaren

die Handarbeit
knit • stricken
crochet • häkeln
sew • nähen

der (Tisch)Tennis
racket, paddle • der Schläger, -
serve • aufschlagen
love • null

die Leichtathletik
track • die Rennbahn, -en
pole vault • der Stabsprung
hurdle • die Hürde, -n

Schilaufen
ski • der Schi, -er
pole • der Schistock, ¨e
run • die Piste / lift • der Lift

stadium • das Stadion, Stadien
athletic field • der Sportplatz, ¨e
-court, -field • -platz
game • das Spiel, -e
referee • der Schiedsrichter
point • der Punkt, ¨e
score • die Punktzahl
(1-0 • eins zu null, eins-null)
versus • gegen
win • gewinnen, siegen
defeat • besiegen
lose • verlieren
ball • der Ball, ¨e
net • das Netz, -e
finish line • das Ziel, -e
goal • das Tor, -e
record • der Rekord, -e
record-holder • der Rekordler
world championship •
   die Weltmeisterschaft, -en
prize • der Preis, -e
cup • der Pokal, -e
exercise • trainieren
practice • üben
team • die Mannschaft, -en
equipment • die Ausstattung
race • das Rennen
bout, contest • der Wettkampf

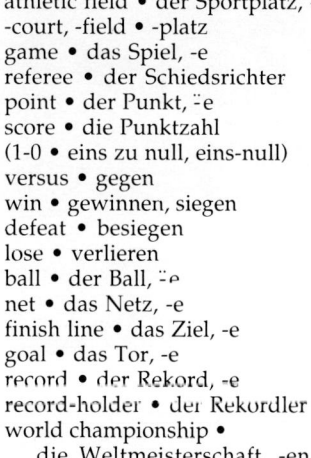

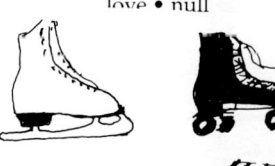

Rollschuhlaufen
Schlittschuhlaufen
Skateboardfahren

Radfahren
gear • der Gang, ¨e
brake • die Bremse, -n
handlebar • die Lenkstange, -n

Reiten
horse • das Pferd, -e
saddle • der Sattel, ¨
reins • der Zügel, -

Surfen
wave • die Welle, -n
sailboard • der Windsurfer
surfboard • das Surfbrett, -er

Schwimmen / Springen
swimming pool • das Schwimmbad, ¨er
diving board • das Sprungbrett, -er
lifeguard • der Bademeister

Segeln
sail • das Segel, -
rudder • das Ruder, -
sailboat • das Segelboot, -e

Wasserschilaufen
life jacket • die Schwimmweste, -n
towrope • das Schleppseil, -e
handle • die Hantel, -n

Camping / Wandern
campground • der Campingplatz
tent • das Zelt, -e
campfire • das Lagerfeuer

Bergsteigen
rock (cliff) • der Fels, -en
rock (stone) • der Stein, -e
(rock) climbing • Klettern

Angeln
pole • die (Angel)Rute, -e
hook • der Haken, -
bait, lure • der Köder, -

Jagen / die Jagd
hunter • der Jäger, -
firearm • das Gewehr, -e
game • das Wild

Alltagssachen Common Objects

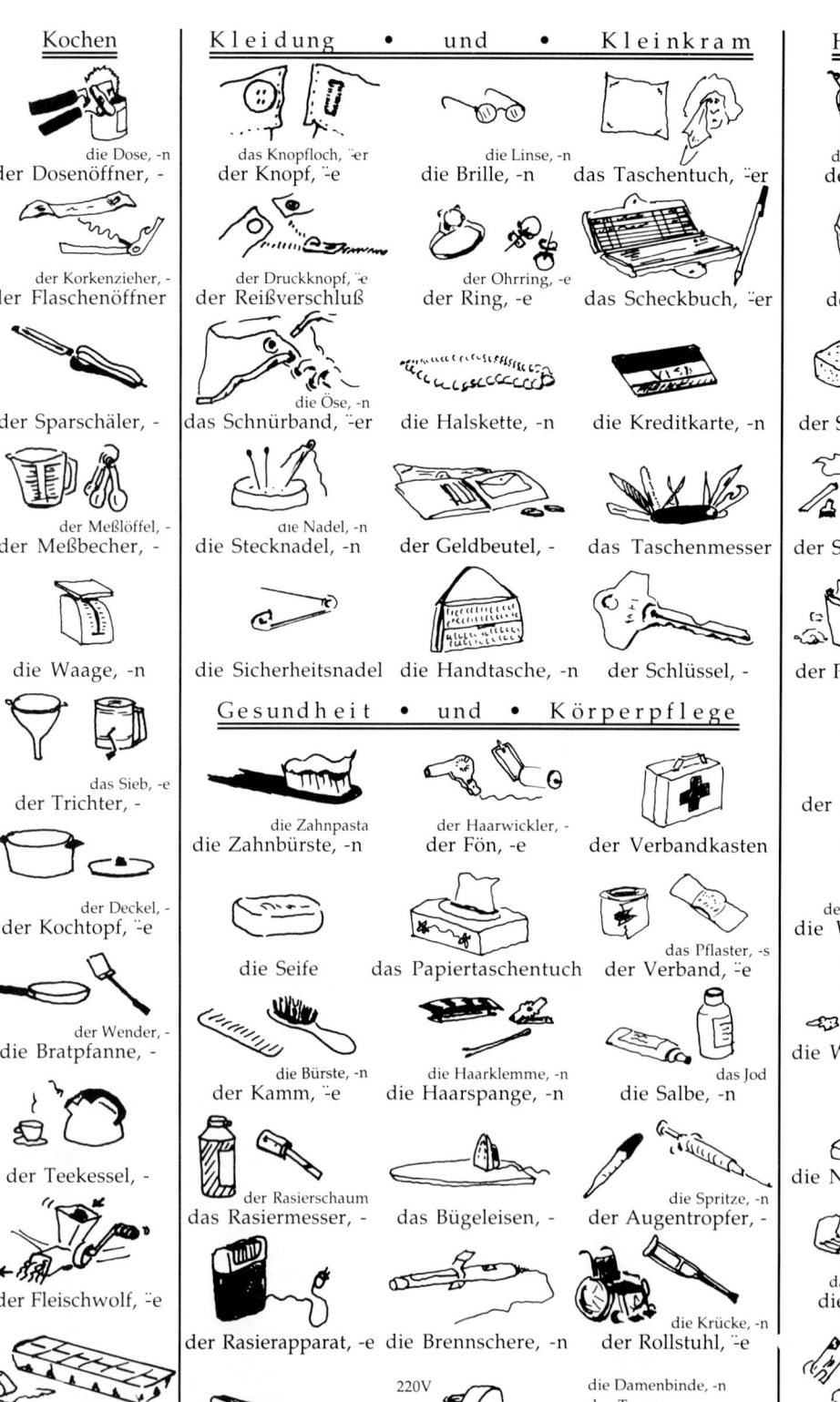

Kochen

die Dose, -n
der Dosenöffner, -

der Korkenzieher, -
der Flaschenöffner

der Sparschäler, -

der Meßlöffel, -
der Meßbecher, -

die Waage, -n

das Sieb, -e
der Trichter, -

der Deckel, -
der Kochtopf, ⸚e

der Wender, -
die Bratpfanne, -

der Teekessel, -

der Fleischwolf, ⸚e

die Eiswürfelschale, -n

Kleidung • und • Kleinkram

das Knopfloch, ⸚er
der Knopf, ⸚e

der Druckknopf, ⸚e
der Reißverschluß

die Öse, -n
das Schnürband, ⸚er

die Nadel, -n
die Stecknadel, -n

die Sicherheitsnadel

die Linse, -n
die Brille, -n

der Ohrring, -e
der Ring, -e

die Halskette, -n

der Geldbeutel, -

die Handtasche, -n

das Taschentuch, ⸚er

das Scheckbuch, ⸚er

die Kreditkarte, -n

das Taschenmesser

der Schlüssel, -

Gesundheit • und • Körperpflege

die Zahnpasta
die Zahnbürste, -n

die Seife

der Kamm, ⸚e

der Rasierschaum
das Rasiermesser, -

der Rasierapparat, -e

die Pinzette (pl.)

der Haarwickler, -
der Fön, -e

das Papiertaschentuch

die Haarklemme, -n
die Haarspange, -n

das Bügeleisen, -

die Brennschere, -n

220V
110V
der Adapter, -

der Verbandkasten

das Pflaster, -s
der Verband, ⸚e

das Jod
die Salbe, -n

die Spritze, -n
der Augentropfer, -

die Krücke, -n
der Rollstuhl, ⸚e

die Damenbinde, -n
das Tampon, -s
das kontrazeptive Mittel
das Condom, -e
die Antibabypille, -n

Haushalt

die Kehrschaufel, -n
der Besen, -

der Eimer, -

die Bürste, -n
der Schwamm, ⸚e

der Staubsauger, -

der Abfall, ⸚e
der Papierkorb, ⸚e

der Mülleimer, -

der Wäschetrockner, -
die Waschmaschine

die Wäschetruhe, -n

die Nähmaschine, -n

das Streichholz, ⸚er
die Kerze, -n

der Briefkasten, ⸚

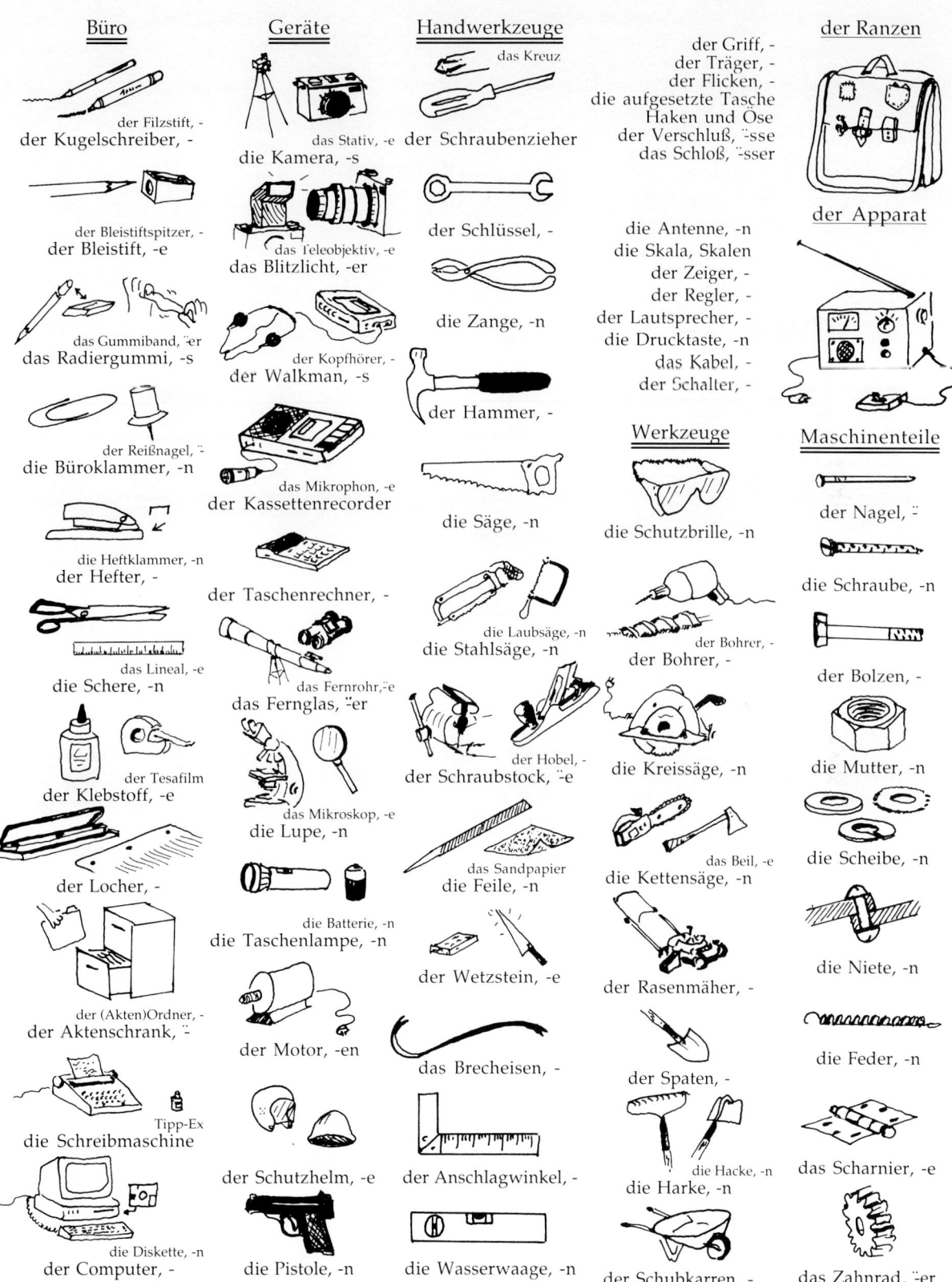

Büro

der Filzstift, -
der Kugelschreiber, -

der Bleistiftspitzer, -
der Bleistift, -e

das Gummiband, ¨er
das Radiergummi, -s

der Reißnagel, ¨
die Büroklammer, -n

die Heftklammer, -n
der Hefter, -

das Lineal, -e
die Schere, -n

der Tesafilm
der Klebstoff, -e

der Locher, -

der (Akten)Ordner, -
der Aktenschrank, ¨-

Tipp-Ex
die Schreibmaschine

die Diskette, -n
der Computer, -

Geräte

das Stativ, -e
die Kamera, -s

das Teleobjektiv, -e
das Blitzlicht, -er

der Kopfhörer, -
der Walkman, -s

das Mikrophon, -e
der Kassettenrecorder

der Taschenrechner, -

das Fernrohr, ¨e
das Fernglas, ¨er

das Mikroskop, -e
die Lupe, -n

die Batterie, -n
die Taschenlampe, -n

der Motor, -en

der Schutzhelm, -e

die Pistole, -n

Handwerkzeuge

das Kreuz
der Schraubenzieher

der Schlüssel, -

die Zange, -n

der Hammer, -

die Säge, -n

die Laubsäge, -n
die Stahlsäge, -n

der Hobel, -
der Schraubstock, ¨-e

das Sandpapier
die Feile, -n

der Wetzstein, -e

das Brecheisen, -

der Anschlagwinkel, -

die Wasserwaage, -n

der Griff, -
der Träger, -
der Flicken, -
die aufgesetzte Tasche
Haken und Öse
der Verschluß, ¨sse
das Schloß, ¨sser

die Antenne, -n
die Skala, Skalen
der Zeiger, -
der Regler, -
der Lautsprecher, -
die Drucktaste, -n
das Kabel, -
der Schalter, -

Werkzeuge

die Schutzbrille, -n

der Bohrer, -
der Bohrer, -

die Kreissäge, -n

das Beil, -e
die Kettensäge, -n

der Rasenmäher, -

der Spaten, -

die Hacke, -n
die Harke, -n

der Schubkarren, -

der Ranzen

der Apparat

Maschinenteile

der Nagel, ¨

die Schraube, -n

der Bolzen, -

die Mutter, -n

die Scheibe, -n

die Niete, -n

die Feder, -n

das Scharnier, -e

das Zahnrad, ¨er

Kategorien: wieviel, wie, was und was nicht
Categories: quantities and qualities, parts and shapes, antonyms

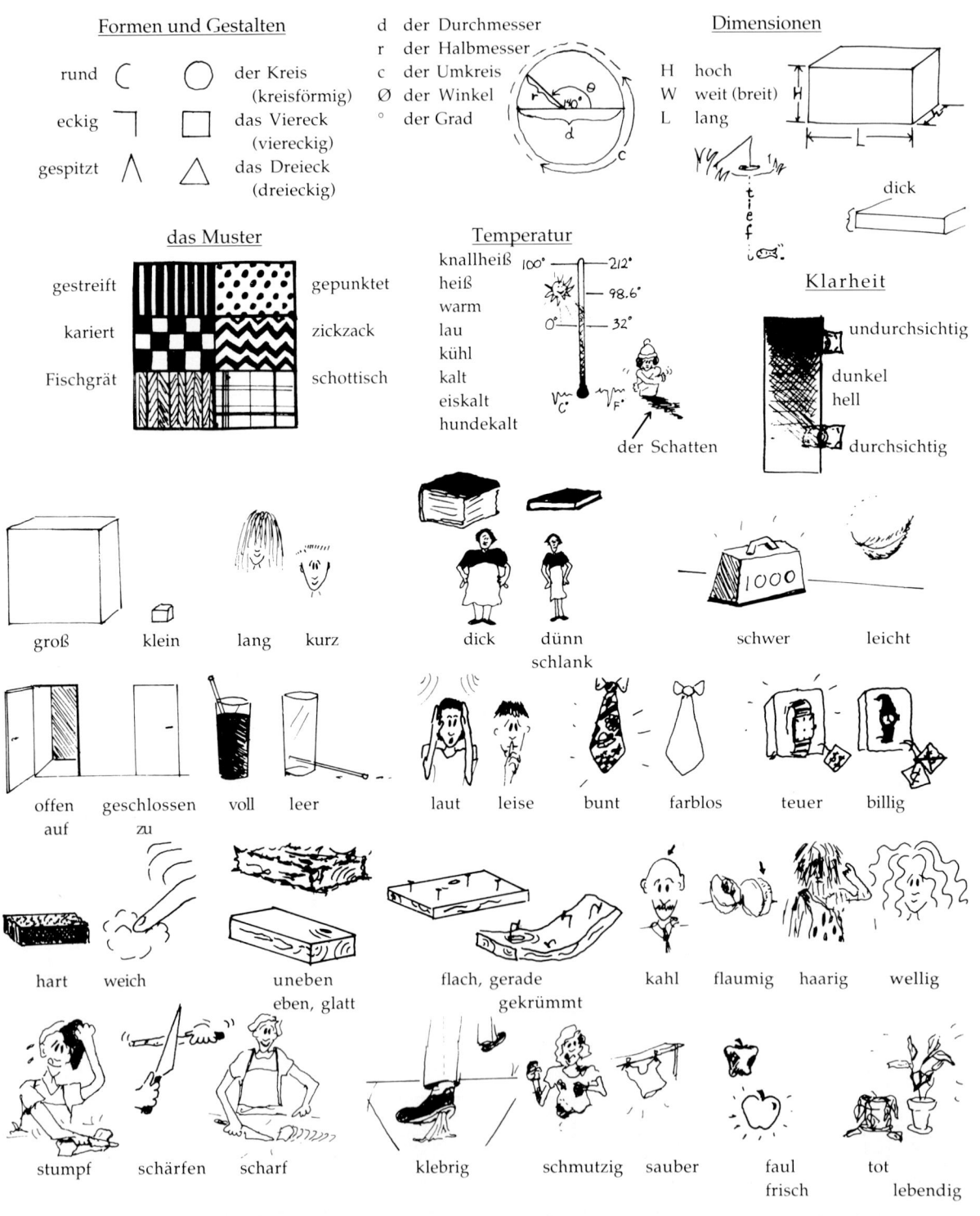

Formen und Gestalten

rund
eckig
gespitzt

der Kreis
(kreisförmig)
das Viereck
(viereckig)
das Dreieck
(dreieckig)

d der Durchmesser
r der Halbmesser
c der Umkreis
Ø der Winkel
° der Grad

Dimensionen

H hoch
W weit (breit)
L lang

dick

das Muster

gestreift
kariert
Fischgrät

gepunktet
zickzack
schottisch

Temperatur

knallheiß 100° 212°
heiß 98.6°
warm
lau 0° 32°
kühl
kalt
eiskalt
hundekalt

der Schatten

Klarheit

undurchsichtig
dunkel
hell
durchsichtig

groß klein lang kurz   dick dünn schlank   schwer leicht

offen geschlossen voll leer   laut leise bunt farblos teuer billig
auf zu

hart weich uneben flach, gerade kahl flaumig haarig wellig
eben, glatt gekrümmt

stumpf schärfen scharf klebrig schmutzig sauber faul tot
frisch lebendig

beschreiben erklären • wie Wenn... Zum Beispiel • (nicht) sehr __ • __er als so __ wie • ein bißchen

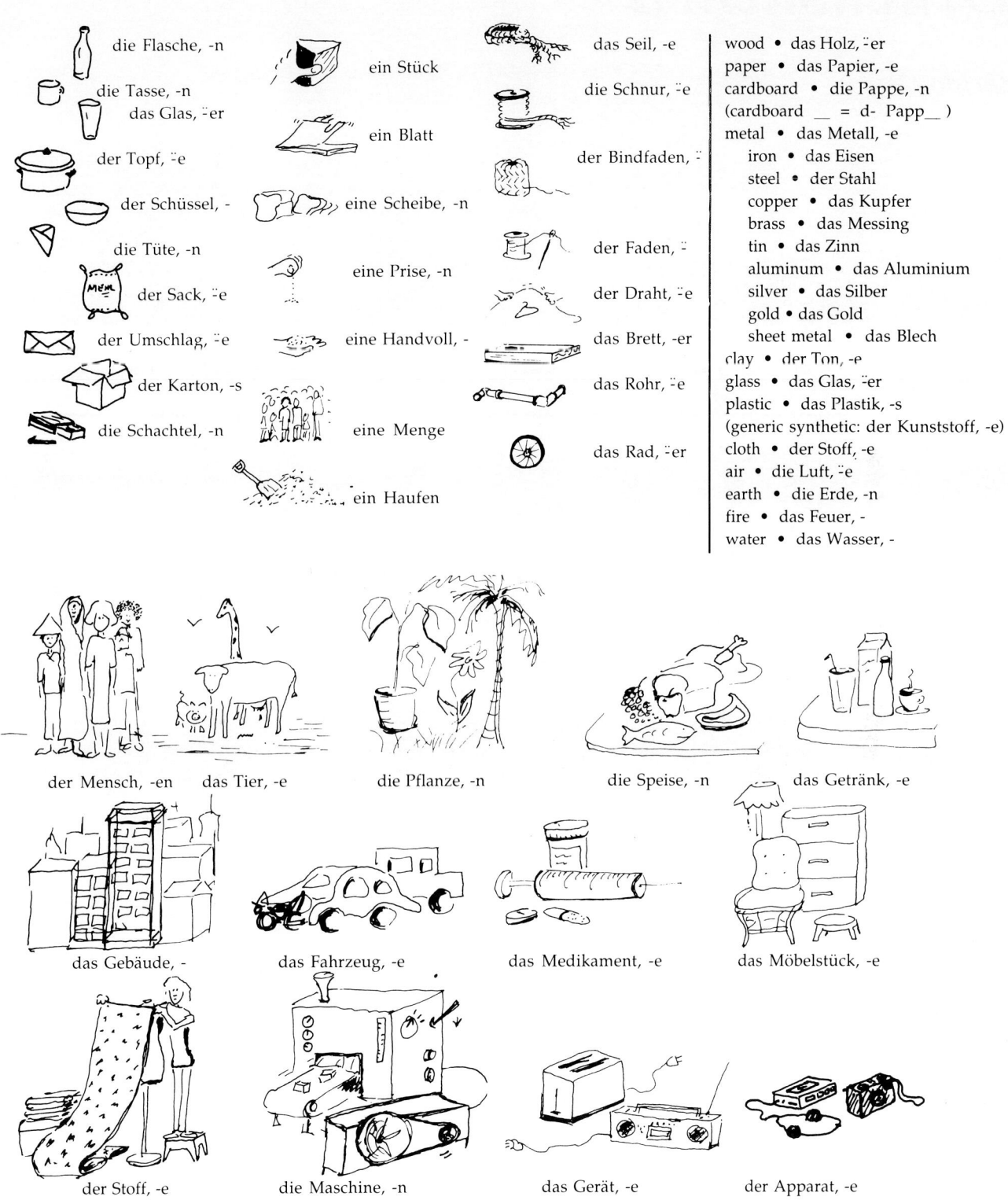

die Flasche, -n

die Tasse, -n

das Glas, ⸚er

der Topf, ⸚e

der Schüssel, -

die Tüte, -n

der Sack, ⸚e

der Umschlag, ⸚e

der Karton, -s

die Schachtel, -n

ein Stück

ein Blatt

eine Scheibe, -n

eine Prise, -n

eine Handvoll, -

eine Menge

ein Haufen

das Seil, -e

die Schnur, ⸚e

der Bindfaden, ⸚

der Faden, ⸚

der Draht, ⸚e

das Brett, -er

das Rohr, ⸚e

das Rad, ⸚er

wood • das Holz, ⸚er
paper • das Papier, -e
cardboard • die Pappe, -n
(cardboard __ = d- Papp__)
metal • das Metall, -e
    iron • das Eisen
    steel • der Stahl
    copper • das Kupfer
    brass • das Messing
    tin • das Zinn
    aluminum • das Aluminium
    silver • das Silber
    gold • das Gold
    sheet metal • das Blech
clay • der Ton, -e
glass • das Glas, ⸚er
plastic • das Plastik, -s
(generic synthetic: der Kunststoff, -e)
cloth • der Stoff, -e
air • die Luft, ⸚e
earth • die Erde, -n
fire • das Feuer, -
water • das Wasser, -

der Mensch, -en   das Tier, -e

die Pflanze, -n

die Speise, -n

das Getränk, -e

das Gebäude, -

das Fahrzeug, -e

das Medikament, -e

das Möbelstück, -e

der Stoff, -e

die Maschine, -n

das Gerät, -e

der Apparat, -e

anders   der Unterschied (zwischen) • ein- X mit/ohne Y   ein- X, aber ...   ein- X, d-__...<verb>

Drucksachen

Karten Maps

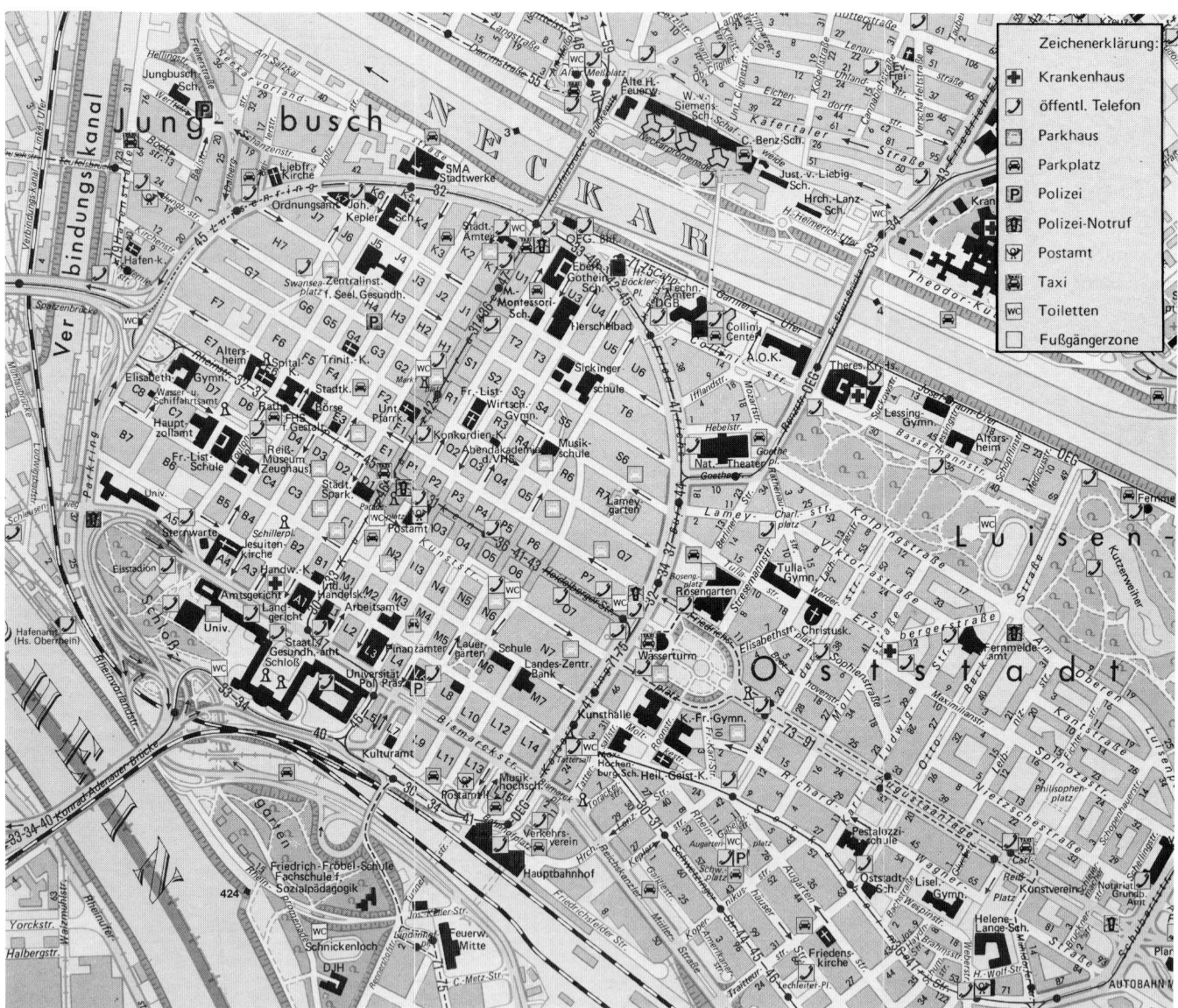

MANNHEIM

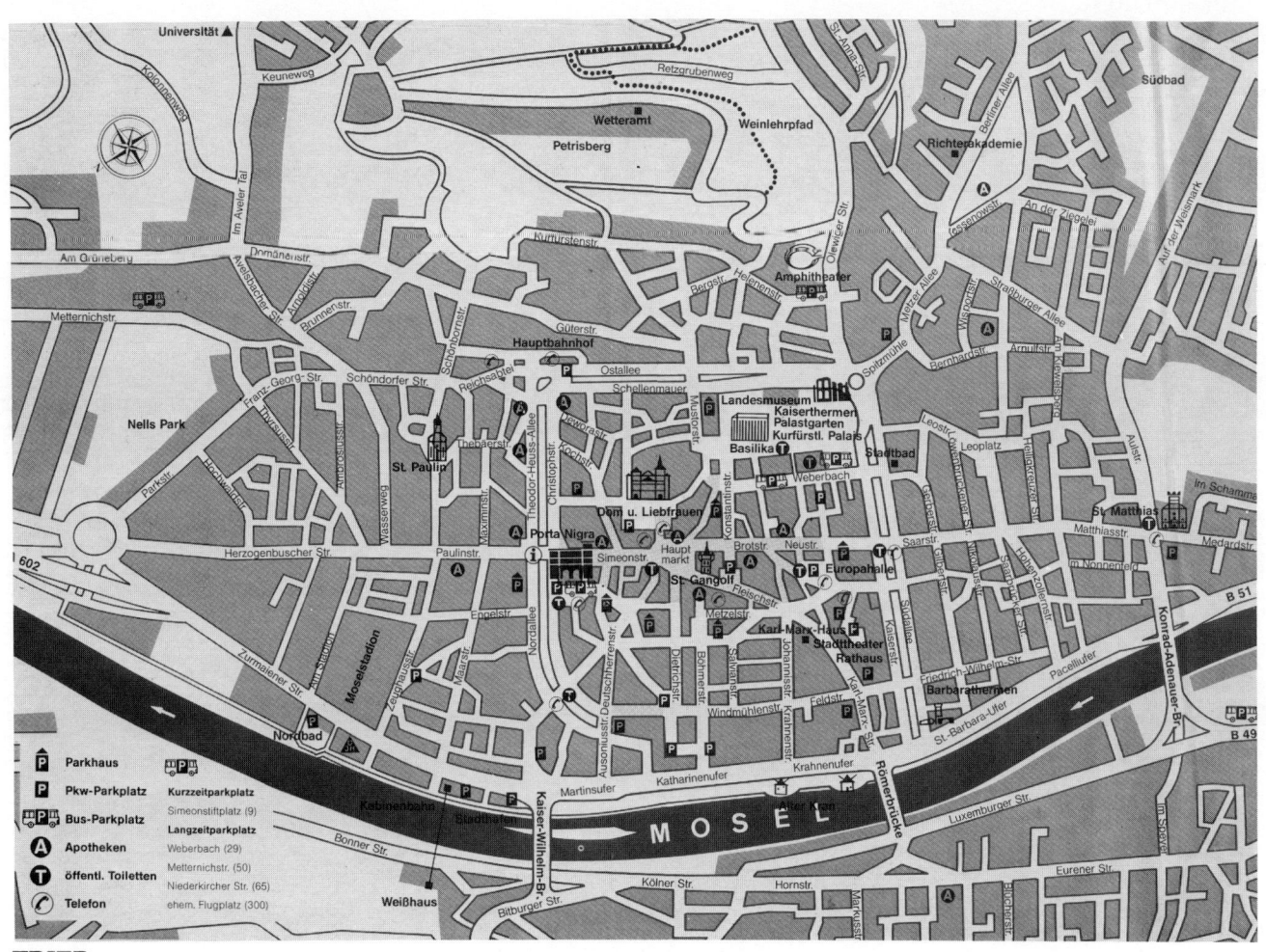

TRIER

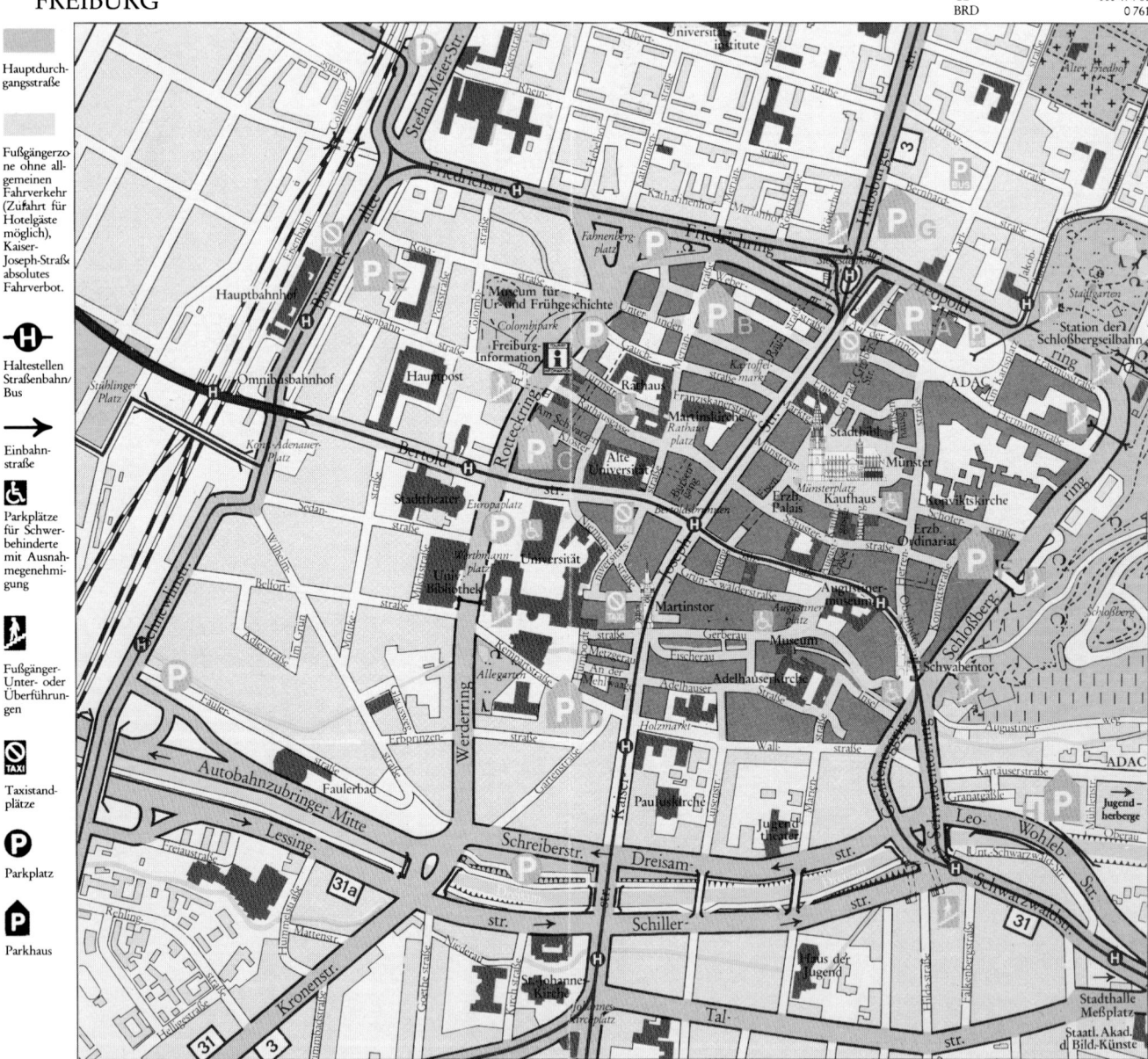

Ihr Partner in allen Freiburg-Fragen: die Freiburg-Information.

Verkehrsamt der Stadt Freiburg
Rotteckring 14, Postfach 1549, D-7800 Freiburg im Breisgau.

Öffnungszeiten:			☎-Landeskennzahlen	BRD/Freiburg
Montag bis Mittwoch	9-18	Uhr	Schweiz	00 49 761
Donnerstag und Freitag	9-21.30	Uhr	Österreich	00 60 761
Samstag	9-18	Uhr	Frankreich	19 49 761
Sonn- und Feiertag	10-12	Uhr	Holland	09 49 761
Telefon-Kontaktzeit:	9-16	Uhr	Belgien	00 49 761
			Luxemburg	0 50 761
			GB	010 49 761
			BRD	0 761

FREIBURG

Hauptdurchgangsstraße

Fußgängerzone ohne allgemeinen Fahrverkehr (Zufahrt für Hotelgäste möglich), Kaiser-Joseph-Straße absolutes Fahrverbot.

H Haltestellen Straßenbahn/ Bus

→ Einbahnstraße

Parkplätze für Schwerbehinderte mit Ausnahmegenehmigung

Fußgänger-Unter- oder Überführungen

TAXI Taxistandplätze

P Parkplatz

P Parkhaus

A **Parkhaus am Karlsplatz,**
Tag und Nacht durchgehend

B **Schwarzwald-City, Schiffstraße,**
Mo.-Sa. 7.00-22.00 h,
Sonn- und Feiertag geschl.

C **Rotteckgarage am Rotteckring,**
Öffnungszeiten von 7.30-1.00 h,
Sonn- und Feiertag geschl.

D **Parkhaus in der Rempartstraße,**
Mo.-Fr. 7.00-19.00 h,
Sa. 7.00-15.00 h,
langer Sa. 7.00-19.00 h,
Sonn- und Feiertag geschl.

E **Parkhaus in der Volksbank, Bismarckallee,**
Mo.-Fr. 7.00-19.00 h,
Sa. 8.30-15.00 h,
langer Sa. 8.30-19.00 h,
Sonn- und Feiertag geschl.

F **Schloßberggarage, Schloßbergring,**
täglich 8.00-1.00 h

G **Parkhaus Zähringer Tor, Bernhardstr.,**
Mo.-Fr. 7.00-19.00 h,
Sa. 7.00-14.30 h,

langer Sa. 7.00-18.30 h,
Sonn- und Feiertag geschl.

H **Parkhaus Schwabentorgarage**
Mo.-Fr. 7.30-19.30 h,
Sa. 7.30-14.30 h,
langer Sa. 7.30-19.30 h,
Sonn- und Feiertag geschl.

Kurzer Rundgang durch die Freiburger Altstadt

(Dauer etwa eine Stunde)

Ausgangspunkt: *Verkehrsamt der Stadt* **(33)** Rotteckring 14. Gegenüber der *Colombipark* mit dem Colombischlößle, heute Museum für Ur- und Frühgeschichte **(32).** Durch die enge Rathausgasse zum *Rathausplatz* **(19).** "Neues" Rathaus **(20),** aus zwei Bürgerhäusern des 16. Jahrhunderts entstanden, geschmückt mit schönen Renaissancegiebeln und reichen Erkern (im Sommer Freilichtaufführungen). Südlicher Erker mit Einhornrelief aus dem Jahre 1545. Täglich 12 Uhr Glockenspiel. Berthold-Schwarz-Denkmal. *Franziskanerkirche* **(17)** aus dem 13. Jahrhundert mit spitzbogigem Kreuzgang, der abends beleuchtet ist. Durch die Franziskanerstraße zum *"Haus zum Walfisch"* **(11),** 1516 als Altensitz für Kaiser Maximilian erbaut, historischer Bau mit einem der schönsten Erker der deutschen Spätgotik. Heute Städt. Sparkasse. Auf der Kaiser-Joseph-Straße der *"Basler Hof"* **(8),** ehemaliger Sitz des Basler Domkapitels, welches nach der Reformation der Stadt Basel 150 Jahre in Freiburg residierte. Die Figurengruppe an der Fassade stellt die Madonna mit den Basler Stadtteilen Kaiser Heinrich II. und Bischof Pantalus dar. Durch die Münsterstraße zum Münsterplatz mit dem gotischen *Münster* **(1).** Feingegliederter, 116 m hoher Turm mit der kühn durchbrochenen Steinpyramide. Großartiger Skulpturenschmuck der Münstervorhalle und einzelner Portale. "Dämonisches Volk der Wasserspeier". Prächtige Glasmalereien in den Seitenschiffen. Großer Flügelaltar im Hochchor von Hans Baldung Grien. Alter Glockenstuhl mit einer der ältesten Glocken Deutschlands, der 100 Zentner schweren "Hosanna". Münsterführung empfohlen. – An der Südseite das *Kaufhaus* **(2)** mit gewölbter Arkadenvorhalle und schönen Erkern. Standbilder von vier habsburgerischen Herrschern (Maximilian I., Philipp von Burgund, Karl V., Ferdinand I.). Links das *Wenzingerhaus* **(3),** das "zum Allerfeinsten" der bürgerlichen Baukunst des 18. Jahrhunderts gehört, ein Werk des Malers, Bildhauers und Architekten Christian Wenzinger. Hier wird zur Zeit das Museum für Stadtgeschichte eingerichtet. – Am Barockbau der ehemaligen *Hauptwache* **(10)** und an der *Münsterbauhütte* **(14)** (fränkisches Fachwerk) vorbei, kommen wir über die Herrenstraße zu einem echten Stück Alt-Freiburg, nach *"Oberlinden"* mit dem Schwabentor **(26),** dem Marienbrunnen unter der Linde und dem *"Bären",* dem urkundlich nachgewiesenen ältesten Gasthof Deutschlands. Durch die Salzstraße weiter zum *Augustinermuseum* **(25),** dem ehemaligen Kloster, mit einer Fülle kostbarer Arbeiten oberrheinischer Herkunft. Werke oberrheini-

scher Meister des Mittelalters, Bildteppiche des 14. und 15. Jahrhunderts, hervorragende Goldschmiedearbeiten des frühen Mittelalters bis zum 16. Jahrhundert. Original-Glasgemälde des Münsters und anderer Kirchen und Klöster Freiburgs. Durch die Salzstraße zur Kaiser-Joseph-Straße (Stadtmitte), dem

Standort des Bertoldsbrunnens **(12),** wo im Wiederaufbau der heitere Charakter der alten Zähringer Bürgerstadt gewahrt wurde. Durch das Martinstor **(23),** und die Rempartstraße zur *Neuen Universität* **(37)** und Universitätsbibliothek **(39)** mit sehr reichhaltigen Buchbeständen. In der Nachbarschaft das

1949 wiederausgebaute Große Haus der *Städtischen Bühnen* **(36),** ein Zeugnis für die Kulturpflege der Stadt. In der nahen Bertoldstraße der restaurierte Bau der *Alten Universität* **(21)** mit der Jesuitenkirche **(22).** Bei der Freiburg-Information beenden wir den Rundgang durch die Altstadt.   *Peter Kalchthaler*

152

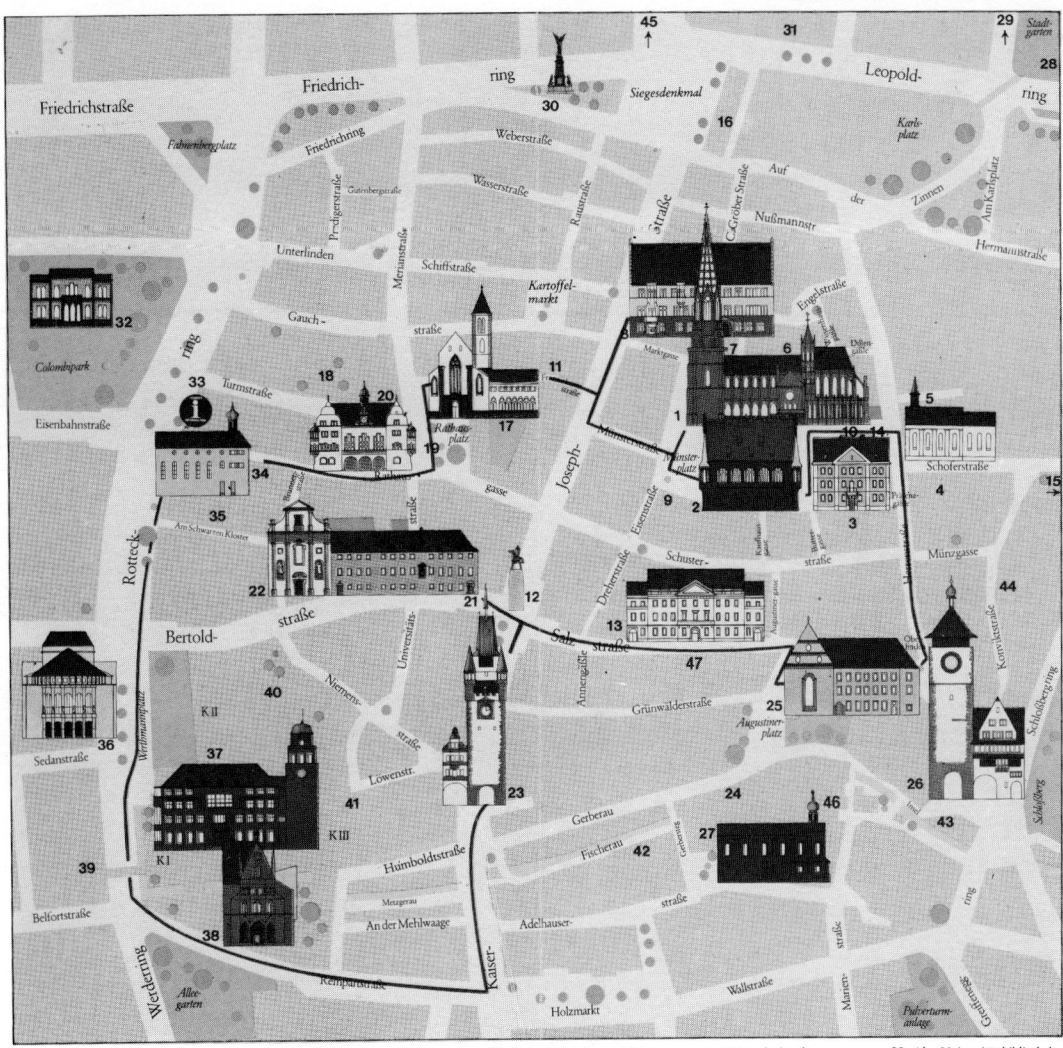

1 Münster	
2 Kaufhaus	
3 Wenzingerhaus „Haus zum schönen Eck" Museum für Stadtgeschichte	
4 Erzbischöfliches Ordinariat	
5 Konviktskirche	
6 Stadtbibliothek	
7 Kornhaus	
8 Basler Hof – Regierungspräsidium	
9 Erzbischöfliches Palais	

10 Alte Stadtwache
11 Haus zum Walfisch
12 Bertoldsbrunnen
13 Sickingen-Palais
14 Münsterbauhütte
15 Münstermuseum (nicht öffentlich)
16 Ehem. Karlskaserne
17 Martinskirche
18 Ehem. Gerichtslaube
19 Rathausplatz

20 Rathaus – Altes und Neues
21 Alte Universität
22 Universitätskirche
23 Martinstor
24 Natur- und Völkerkundemuseum
25 Augustinermuseum
26 Schwabentor
27 Adelhauserkirche u. eh. Kloster
28 Stadtgarten – Schloßbergseilbahn
29 Alter Friedhof

30 Siegesdenkmal
31 Landeszentralbank
32 Colombi-Schlößle Museum für Ur- und Frühgeschichte
33 Verkehrsamt
34 St.-Ursula-Kirche
35 Schwarzes Kloster
36 Stadttheater
37 Universität, KG I/II/III/IV

38 Alte Universitätsbibliothek
39 Neue Universitätsbibliothek
40 Peterhof
41 „Haus zur lieben Hand"
42 Fischerau
43 Insel
44 Konviktstraße
45 48. Breitengrad
46 Museum für Neue Kunst
47 Deutschordenskommende

D Zeichen-
erklärung

•—— Lage des Hotels

123 — Nummer im
Hotelverzeichnis

97 ↓ Hotels außerhalb des
Planes, in Richtung →

S S-Bahn-Station, bzw.
U-Bahn-Station

U jeweils mit dem Namen
der Haltestelle

O–12–• Straßenbahnlinie (12–29)
O–31–• Buslinie (Nr. 31–198)
jeweils mit dem Namen
der Haltestelle

12–31 Endstation Straßen-
bahn- oder Buslinie

Bundesautobahn

»Altstadtring« bzw.
»Mittlerer Ring«

Maßstab dieses Plans
0   300m

MÜNCHEN-INNENSTADT

5   6   7   8

IC 125 Erasmus

Amsterdam · Utrecht · Emmerich · Düsseldorf · Köln · Bonn · Wiesbaden · Frankfurt (Main) · Würzburg · Nürnberg · Augsburg · München · Kufstein (Ex 215) · Innsbruck

— ab München vom 1. bis 8. I., und ab 18. III. sowie ⑤ und ⑥ vom 14. I. bis 19. III. —

✗ Amsterdam—München/Innsbruck
✗ Emmerich—München/Rosenheim

Erasmus — Desiderius, genannt Erasmus von Rotterdam, geb. um 1466 in Rotterdam, gest. 1536 in Basel. Theologe, bedeutendster Geist des deutschen Humanismus. Als Vorläufer der Reformation wandte er sich später gegen Luther.

„Ihr Zug-Begleiter" // "Your guide in the train"

Erläuterungen: // Explanations:

unterrichtet Sie über Fahrplan und wichtige Anschlüsse dieses Zuges. Zugführer und Zugchaffiner nennen Ihnen gerne die Abfahrtgleise für Anschlußzüge von größeren Bahnhöfen und stehen Ihnen auch für weitere Auskünfte zur Verfügung. // Provides information about the schedule of this train and important connections. The train crew will inform you about the track number for connections at important stations.

Die Bahnhöfe, auf denen der Zug seine Fahrtrichtung ändert, sind unterstrichen. // Names of stations where the train changes direction are underlined.
Die in der km-Spalte angegebenen Entfernungen zwischen den Haltebahnhöfen stimmen nicht immer mit den Entfernungen überein, nach denen die Fahrpreise berechnet sind. // The distances between the stops shown in the km-column are not always the same as distances used for the calculation of fares.
Zur Benutzung der angegebenen Anschlüsse ist in manchen Fällen eine Umwegkarte erforderlich. // For some connecting trains a ticket by an indirect route is necessary.
Die in Schrägschrift angegebenen Orte werden vom Anschlußzug bzw. Kurswagen nicht berührt. Nach diesen Orten muß nochmals umgestiegen werden. // Places shown in italics are not served directly by the connecting train or through coach. Passengers to these destinations must change trains once more.
Bei den Anschlußzügen ist nicht immer der Endbahnhof der Züge angegeben. // In the connection column the station shown is not always the destination station of the train concerned.
Eine Gewähr für die Richtigkeit der Fahrplanangaben kann nicht übernommen werden. // No guarantee can be given for the exactness of the timetables.

Zeichenerklärung: // Explanation of Signs:

TEE	= **Trans-Europ-Express,** nur 1. Klasse (TEE-Zuschlag erforderlich, Platzreservierung unentgeltlich) // 1st class only, (TEE-supplementary charge, seat reservation free)
IC	= **Intercity-Zug // Intercity-Train,** 1. und 2. Klasse (IC-Zuschlag erforderlich, Platzreservierung unentgeltlich) // 1st and 2nd class; (supplementary charge, seat reservation free)
D	= **Schnellzug** (zu Fahrausweisen bis 50 km sowie zu Streckenzeitkarten ist Schnellzugzuschlag erforderlich) // Express Train (supplementary charge for distances up to 50 km for seasonticket-holders)
E	= Eilzug // Semi Fast Train
S	= DB-Schnellbahnzug // DB-Urban railway

Ohne Buchstaben = Zug des Nahverkehrs //
Without any letter = Local Train
✝ = an Sonn- und allgemeinen Feiertagen // runs on Sundays and Public Holidays only
✗ = an Werktagen // runs on weekdays
Ⓜ = Montag // Monday
② = Dienstag // Tuesday
③ = Mittwoch // Wednesday
④ = Donnerstag // Thursday
⑤ = Freitag // Friday
⑥ = Samstag (Sonnabend) // Saturday
⑦ = Sonntag // Sunday
✗ außer ⑥ on ✗ (weekdays) except Saturdays

Ⓑ = täglich außer ⑥ // Daily except Saturdays
Ⓒ = ⑥ und ✝ // Saturdays and ✝ (Sundays and Holidays)
🚌 = Kurswagen // Through coach
🛏 = Schlafwagen // Sleeping Car
🛋 = Liegewagen // Couchettes
🍴 = Zugrestaurant // Restaurant Car
🍴✗ = Quick-Pick-Zugrestaurant // Quick-Pick-Restaurant Car
▽ = Speisen und Getränke im Zug erhältlich // Light refreshments available on the train
☎ = Münz-Zugtelefon // Self-service telephone on the train
⊞ = Grenzbahnhof mit Paß und Zoll // Frontier station with Passport and Customs Paß und Zoll im fahrenden Zug // Passport and Customs at the running train
🚌 = Omnibuslinie // Bus service
♦ = Umsteigen // Change of trains
Zug wartet nicht bei Verspätung // Connection does not wait for delayed trains

MEZ = Mitteleuropäische Zeit // Central European Time
OEZ = Osteuropäische Zeit (1 Stunde vor gegenüber MEZ) // Eastern European Time (one hour **ahead** of MEZ)
(200) = Streckennummer im Kursbuch // Table number of timetable

Weitere Zeichen siehe Fußnoten // For the explanation of other symbols see foot notes in the connections column

Left table

Ankunft	km	Abfahrt	Anschlüsse	
		6.57	**Amsterdam CS**	
		→		
	39			
7.25		**Utrecht CS 7.28**		
	58			
8.00		**Arnhem ⊞ 8.03**		
	37			
		→		
8.22		**⊞ Emmerich 8.33**		
	61	x	8.53 Wesel 9.12 Dinslaken 9.21	(310)
			8.56 in Richtung Oberhausen Hbf	(310)
9.02		**Oberhausen Hbf 9.03** ⊞		
		→ E 9.18	Essen-Altenessen 9.24 Gelsenkirchen Hbf 9.30	(300)
			Wanne-Eickel Hbf 9.36 Herne 9.41	
	8		Castrop-Rauxel Hbf 9.48 Dortmund-Mengede 9.53	
			Dortmund Hbf 10.01	
		s	S-Bahnanschlüsse bestehen in Richtung:	
			Mülheim (Ruhr) Hbf—Essen Hbf—Hattingen (Ruhr)	
9.10		**Duisburg Hbf 9.19**		
		IE 9.15	„Lötschberg"	
			Bonn Hbf 10.15 Koblenz Hbf 10.49 Mainz Hbf 11.41	(300)
	24		**Mannheim Hbf 12.24 Karlsruhe Hbf 12.58**	
			Baden-Baden 13.14 Freiburg (Brsg) Hbf 14.01	
			Basel Bad Bf 14.39 Basel SBB 14.46 Bern 16.09	
			Brig 18.00	
		→ E 9.19	Rheinhausen 9.24 Krefeld-Uerdingen 9.31	(465)
			Krefeld-Oppum 9.34 Krefeld Hbf 9.38 Viersen 9.50	
			Mönchengladbach Hbf 10.00	
		E 9.30	Moers 9.51 Xanten 10.21 Kleve 10.47	(475)
			(hält auf allen Bahnhöfen außer Appeldorn (Rhl))	
		s	S-Bahnanschlüsse bestehen in Richtung:	
			Angermund—Düsseldorf Hbf	
9.32		**Düsseldorf Hbf 9.35**		
		→ s 9.53	in Richtung Ratingen Ost—Kettwig	(396)
		E 9.56	Wuppertal-Vohwinkel 10.10 Wuppertal-Elberfeld 10.16	(400)
	40		Wuppertal-Barmen 10.23 Wuppertal-Oberbarmen 10.25	
			Schwelm 10.31 Ennepetal (Gevelsberg) 10.36	
			Hagen Hbf 10.45	
		E 9.58	Düsseldorf-Benrath 10.05 Leverkusen-Mitte 10.15	(300)
			Köln-Deutz 10.24	
		s	S-Bahnanschlüsse bestehen in Richtung:	
			Düsseldorf-Garath—Langenfeld (Rhl)	
			Düsseldorf Flughafen	
			Hilden—Solingen-Ohligs	

Right table

Ankunft	km	Abfahrt	Anschlüsse	
9.59		**Köln Hbf 10.03**		
		→ E 10.09	Köln-Mülheim 10.17 Opladen 10.25	(400)
			Solingen-Ohligs 10.32	
	34	E 10.12	Köln-Deutz 10.15 Porz (Rhein) 10.22 Troisdorf 10.29	(420)
			Siegburg 10.37 Hennef (Sieg) 10.42 Eitorf 10.51	
			Herchen 10.57 Schladern (Sieg) 11.03 Au (Sieg) 11.09	
			Wissen (Sieg) 11.17 Betzdorf (Sieg) 11.26	
			Kirchen 11.34 Niederscheiden 11.45 Siegen 11.52	
		10.15	in Richtung Solingen-Ohligs	(400)
		10.19	in Richtung Bonn Hbf	(600)
		s 10.19	Köln Chorweiler Nord 10.33	(491)
		10.20	Overath 11.02	(491)
		s 10.32	Berg sch Gladbach 10.51	(415)
		▄ 10.33	Overath 11.27 Dieringhausen 12.13	(491)
			Gummersbach 12.28 (über Bensberg)	(415)
			▲ = ab Bahnhofsvorplatz	
10.21		**Bonn Hbf 10.23**		
		→ x E 10.39	in Richtung Euskirchen	(433)
	59	E 10.48	Bonn-Bad Godesberg 10.53 Oberwinter 10.59	(600)
			Remagen 11.03 Sinzig (Rhein) 11.07 Bad Breisig 11.11	
			Brohl 11.14 Andernach 11.20	
10.55		**Koblenz Hbf 10.57**		
		→ E 11.07	Boppard 11.19 Bad Salzig 11.23 St Goar 11.31	(600)
			Oberwesel 11.37 Bacharach 11.42 Bingerbruck 11.50	
	97		Bingen (Rhein) 11.53 Gau Algesheim 12.01	
			Ingelheim 12.04 Mainz Hbf 12.17	
		▯ Ⓐ 11.07	Cochem (Mosel) 12.01 Bullay (DB) 12.14	(620)
			Wittgeroh 12.32 Trier Hbf 13.09	
		x E 11.12	Niederlahnstein 11.17 Bad Ems 11.30	(540)
			Nassau (Lahn) 11.38 Diez 11.59 Limburg (Lahn) 12.03	
			Weilburg 12.34 Braunfels (Lahn) 12.45 Wetzlar 12.54	
			Gießen 13.06	
		Ⓐ 11.34	Braubach 11.52 St Goarshausen 12.19	(610)
			Abmannshausen 12.42 Eltville 13.12 weiter in	
			Richtung Wiesbaden Hbf	
		D 11.38	Rüdesheim (Rhein) 12.21	(610)
			▯ = nicht 1. I.	
11.54		**Wiesbaden Hbf 12.00**		
		→ S x 12.16	Mainz Hbf 12.26 Rüsselsheim 12.43	(594)
			Frankfurt (Main) Flughafen 12.58 weiter in Richtung	
			Frankfurt (Main) Hbf	
	42	E 12.25	Mainz Süd 12.41 Mainz-Bischofsheim 12.45	(552)
			Croß Gerau 12.59 Darmstadt Hbf 13.12	
		Ⓐ 12.42	Niedernhausen (Taunus) 13.04 Idstein (Taunus) 13.14	(542)
			Bad Camberg 13.23 Niederselters 13.28	
		Ⓒ 12.49	Niedernhausen (Taunus) 13.10	(542)
			weiter in Richtung Limburg (Lahn)	

Frankfurt (Main) Hbf 12.32 — Ankunft 12.26

Ankunft	km	Abfahrt	Anschlüsse	
		E 12.35	Frankfurt (Main) Süd 12 40 Offenbach (Main) Hbf 12 46 Hanau Hbf 12.55 Kahl (Main) 13.02	(300)
	136		Aschaffenburg Hbf 13.14 Obernburg-Elsenfeld 13.36 Miltenberg Hbf 13.51 Stadtprozelten 14.11 Wertheim 14.24 Tauberbischofsheim 14.50 Lauda 14.57	
			Bad Mergentheim 15.12	
		E 12.40	Seligenstadt (Hess) 13.09 Babenhausen (Hess) 13.17 Groß Umstadt 13.27 Wiebelsbach-Heubach 13.31	(588)
			Höchst (Odenw) 13.42 Bad König 13.48 Michelstadt 13.55 Erbach (Odenw) 13.59 Hetzbach 14.05 Eberbach 14.25	
		E 12.40	Darmstadt Hbf 12.55 Bensheim 13.08	(550)
			Heppenheim (Bergstr) 13 13 Weinheim (Bergstr) 13.19 Mannheim-Friedrichsfeld 13.26 Heidelberg Hbf 13.34	
		E 12.44	Gelnhausen 13.17 Wächtersbach 13.25	(500)
			Bad Soden-Salmünster 13.32 Steinau (Straße) 13.38 Schlüchtern 13.44 Flieden 13.52	
			Neuhof (Kr Fulda) 13.56 Kerzell 14.00 Fulda 14.08	
Ⓐ		12.44	in Richtung Hanau Hbf (über Hochstadt Dornigheim)	(800)
		E 12.45	Walldorf (Hess) 12.58 Mörfelden 13.01	(551)
			Groß Gerau-Dornberg 13.07 Goddelau-Erfelden 13.14 Gernsheim 13.22 Groß Rohrheim 13.26 Biblis 13.28	
			Bürstadt 13.33 Lampertheim 13.40	
			Mannheim-Waldhof 13.46	
Ⓒ		12.52	in Richtung Hanau Hbf (über Hochstadt Dornigheim)	(800)
		12.55	in Richtung Hanau Hbf (über Mühlheim (Main))	(800)
s			S Bahnanschlüsse bestehen in Richtung: Niedernhausen (Taunus) Kronberg (Taunus) Bad Soden (Taunus) Bad Homburg—Friedrichsdorf (Taunus) Bad Vilbel—Friedberg (Hess) Mainz-Kastel—Wiesbaden Hbf	

Würzburg Hbf 13.59 — Ankunft 13.53

Ankunft	km	Abfahrt	Anschlüsse	
		13.58	„Ernst Barlach" München Hbf 16.25	(920)
	102	Ⓧ 14.09	Würzburg Süd 14 12 Winterhausen 14.24 Ochsenfurt 14.31 Marktbreit 14.35	(920)
		D 14.29	Kitzingen 14.44 Neustadt (Aisch) 15.05 Fürth (Bay) Hbf 15.27	(800)
		E 14.32	Schweinfurt Hbf 14.59 Schweinfurt Stadt 15.06 Haßfurt 15.17 Zeil 15.24 Ebelsbach-Eltmann 15.29 Oberhaid 15.38 Bamberg 15.46 Lichtenfels 16.12 Hochstadt-Marktzeuln 16.20 Burgkunstadt 16.26 Kulmbach 16.36 Neuenmarkt-Wirsberg 16.48 Münchberg 17.16 Schwarzenbach (Saale) 17.29 Oberkotzau 17.33 Hof Hbf 17.41 Bad Kissingen 15.38 Selbitz 18.19 Bad Steben 18.41	(810)

🚂 = nicht 6. I.

Nürnberg Hbf 15.02 — Ankunft 14.56

Ankunft	km	Abfahrt	Anschlüsse	
		E 15.04	Lauf (r Pegnitz) 15.17 Hersbruck (r Pegnitz) 15.24 Neuhaus (Pegnitz) 15.41 Pegnitz 15.53 Schnabelwaid 16.00 Creußen (Oberfr) 16.07 Bayreuth Hbf 16.17	(840)
	137		in Richtung Neuhaus (Pegnitz)— Bayreuth Hbf	(840)
			in Richtung Roth	(880)
		D	Ansbach 15.49 Crailsheim 16.19 Schwäbisch Hall 16.45 Öhringen 17.05 Heilbronn Hbf 17.24	(785)
		E 15.04	Fürth (Bay) Hbf 15.10 Erlangen 15.22 Forchheim (Oberfr) 15.33	(820)
		E 15.12	Schwabach 15.22 Roth 15.31 Georgensgmünd 15.37 Pleinfeld 15.44 Weißenburg (Bay) 15.51 Treuchtlingen 16.00 Eichstätt Bf 16.20 Ingolstadt Nord 16.35 Ingolstadt Hbf 16.38 Wolnzach Bf 16.53 Pfaffenhofen (Ilm) 17.02 Dachau Bf 17.21	(880)
		15.25	Nürnberg-Mögeldorf 15.30 Röthenbach (Pegnitz) 15.43 Hartmannshof 16.12 Lauf (l Pegnitz) 15.50 Hersbruck (l Pegnitz) 16.02 Neukirchen (b Sulzbach-Rosenberg) 16.21 in Richtung Ansbach	(785)
		15.28	Feucht 15.41 Altdorf (b Nürnberg) 16.00	(890)
Ⓐ		15.28	Neumarkt (Oberpf) 16.01 Regensburg Hbf 16.42	(870)
		E 15.40	Straubing 17.07 Plattling 17.23 Osterhofen (Niederbay) 17.38 Vilshofen (Niederbay) 17.48 Passau Hbf 18.05 🚂 Bayerisch Eisenstein 19.06 🚂 Pfarrkirchen 19.42	

🚂 = nicht 6. I.
🚂 = täglich außer Ⓐ, nicht 1., 5. I., 3. IV., 22. V.
🚂 = ab Neuhaus (Pegnitz) täglich außer Ⓐ, auch 1. I.

Augsburg Hbf 16.12 — Ankunft 16.10

Ankunft	km	Abfahrt	Anschlüsse	
		16.16	Bobingen 16.29 Schwabmünchen 16.38	(970)
Ⓐ		16.17	in Richtung Günzburg	(900)
Ⓐ	62	16.20	in Richtung Günzburg	(913)
Ⓐ		16.31	Welden 17.04	(900)
		16.31	Maisach 17.10	(900)
		D 16.33	Günzburg 17.06 Ulm Hbf 17.23	(900)

🚂 = nicht 6. I.

IZB erscheint monatlich in Zusammenarbeit mit der Deutschen Bundesbahn zur Auslage in den Zügen. Bezugsbedingungen: 0,20 DM je Einzelexemplar und 2 DM Versandkosten, 30 DM alle TEE- und IC-IZB. 20 DM alle D-IZB, 50 DM alle IZB und 4 DM Versandkosten. Herausgeber- und Anzeigenverwaltung: Deutsche Eisenbahn-Reklame GmbH, Am Hauptbahnhof, 3500 Kassel 1, Telefon (0561) 16781, Telex 0992298, Bank: Deutsche Verkehrs-Kredit-Bank AG, Kassel, Nr. 6173 BLZ 520 103 00. Druck: Rosenberger Druckerei GmbH, Im Teelbruch 63, 4300 Essen 18. Printed in Germany · Imprimé en Allemagne.

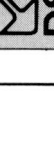

Darauf haben Eisenbahnliebhaber lange gewartet:

BETRIEBSBÜCHER

beliebter Dampf- und E-Lokomotiven

bis 31.1.1983 zum ermäßigten Subskriptionspreis

Zu jeder Lokomotive gehört, gewissermaßen als ständig fortgeschriebener Lebenslauf, ein Betriebsbuch. Es wird angelegt, wenn die Lokomotive fertiggestellt ist und enthält alle wesentlichen technischen Daten, an die sich dann die regelmäßigen betrieblichen Eintragungen über die erreichten Kilometerleistungen, über Ausbesserungen, Untersuchungen und Stationierungen anschließen. Betriebsbücher von Lokomotiven gehören heute zu beliebten Sammlerobjekten. Hier bieten wir Ihnen im Nachdruck gleich 3 Leckerbissen an:

Betriebsbuch der Dampflok 05002

Die Weltrekord-Dampflokomotive 05002, die am 11. Mai 1936 zwischen Hamburg und Berlin 200,4 km/h erreichte. 2. Auflage, 165 Seiten DIN A5 mit Fotos, einfarbig schwarz/weiß
ISBN 3-921 200-08-2
Subskriptionspreis

bis 31. 1. 1983	DM 18,00
späterer Preis	DM 20,00
+ Porto und Verpackung	DM 2,50

Betriebsbuch der Dampflok 18451

Die bayerische S 3/6 Pacifik-Lokomotive — ein Star unter den Dampflokomotiven, erreichte ihren Titel nicht zuletzt durch ihre „Beförderung" zur „Rheingold"-Lokomotive — die 18451 hat diesen Luxuszug gefahren. Nachdruck in Originalgröße DIN A4, ca. 200 Seiten, mit Fotos schwarz/weiß
ISBN 3-921 200-09-0
Subskriptionspreis

bis 31. 1. 1983	DM 20,00
späterer Preis	DM 24,00
+ Porto und Verpackung	DM 2,50

Betriebsbuch der Lokomotive 194577

Aus der Reihe der deutschen „Krokodile". Eine der wichtigsten deutschen Entwicklungen im Elektrolokomotivbau. Nachdruck in Originalgröße DIN A 4, ca. 200 Seiten, mit Fotos schwarz/weiß
ISBN 3-921 200-10-5
Subskriptionspreis

bis 31. 1. 1983	DM 20,00
späterer Preis	DM 24,00
+ Porto und Verpackung	DM 2,50

3 Leckerbissen für Freunde der Eisenbahn zu Weihnachten!

Bis zum 31. 1. 1983 können Sie noch zum ermäßigten Subskriptionspreis bestellen. Wenn Ihre Bestellung und Ihre Vorauszahlung bei uns eingeht, erhalten Sie postwendend einen Gutschein über die von Ihnen bestellte Ausgabe zugesandt. Nach Fertigstellung der Druckwerke (etwa bis Ende Jan. 1983) geht Ihnen ein umgehend Ihr Exemplar zu. Bestellen Sie bitte bei:

VERKEHRSWISSENSCHAFTLICHE LEHRMITTELGESELLSCHAFT MBH
3500 Kassel, Bürgermeister-Brunner-Straße 2
Deutsche Verkehrs-Kredit-Bank, Kassel, Kto.-Nr. 6 169 (BLZ 520 103 00)
Postscheck Frankfurt/M. Kto-Nr. 98851-603

TIROLER WANDERSOMMER 1987

HOTEL	HOTELANGEBOT	PREISE*	AKTIVITÄTEN	FAMILIENANGEBOT

ACHENKIRCH — Karwendelgebirge und Achensee

| WANDER · HOTEL · RESTAURANT ACHENTALERHOF Familie Waldhart A-6215 Achenkirch 115 a Tel.: 0 52 46/63 91 | Komfortzimmer mit Bad/WC, Telefon und Balkon, geheiztes Freibad, großer Garten mit Sauna, Stockbahn; Panoramaterrasse, Grillecke. Frühstücksbuffet, Menüwahl, Unterhaltungsprogramm | öS 380,- bis öS 440,- VP + öS 100,- EZ + öS 50,- bis öS 80,- | 16. 5. — 13. 6.: Bergfrühling 13. 6. — 11. 7.: Enzianblüte mit Fotosafaris 5. 9. — 26. 9.: Wadelwochen mit Almabtrieb 26. 9. — 31. 10.: Goldener Herbst Steinölkuren im nahegelegenen Therapiezentrum! | Im Garten Sandkästen, Rutsche, Schach, Billard, Schwimmbad und Stockbahn. Eigenes Kinderspielzimmer, Video-, Billard- und Tischtennisraum im Haus; bis 6 Jahre gratis, bis 12 Jahre im Elternzimmer 50 % Ermäßigung |

THIERSEE — Thierseetal und Kaisergebirge

| Hotel Charlotte •••• Ihr Wander- und Erlebnishotel Familie Knörnschild A-6335 Kufstein/Thiersee Tel. 0 53 76/55 00 | Komfortable Einzel-, Doppel- und Dreibettzimmer mit Dusche/WC oder Bad/WC, preiswerte Jugendzimmer, alle mit Radio, Telefon, Haarfön, Bademantel, teils Balkon und TV-Anschluß. Hallenbad, Sauna, Solarium, große Liegewiese, Sonnenterrasse, Frühstücksbuffet, freie Menüwahl, absolut ruhige Lage am See | öS 480,- bis öS 680,- Jugendzimmer ohne Dusche/WC ab öS 410,- | Täglich Ferienaktivitäten, jeder kann mitmachen, nichts ist verpflichtend, Sonnenaufgangswanderung, Bogenschießen, Tennis im Ort, Reitstall (7 km), Badesee vor der Haustüre, Surfen, Bootfahren, Möglichkeit zum Fischen, Passionsspiele Thiersee | Kinderermäßigung: bis 6 Jahre kostenlos, bis 12 Jahre 50 % im Elternzimmer, Kinderbetreuung, Kinderolympiade im Juni und Juli, Kinderfeste, Kindertisch, eigener Wald am Haus |

KITZBÜHEL — Kitzbüheler Alpen

| FAMILIEN Erika •••• Familie Schorer A-6370 Kitzbühel/Tirol Tel.: 0 53 56/48 85 Telex 051/264 | Komfortzimmer mit Bad/WC, Telefon, Radio, Safe, Balkon, großes Frühstücksbuffet, täglich Salatbuffet, täglich 4gängiges Abendmenü, kostenlose Hallenbad- (28° C) und Saunabenützung, großer Parkplatz am Haus, Gratisliegestühle für Sonnenanbeter, täglich umfangreiches „Erika"-Freizeitprogramm. Preiswerte Extras: Massagen, Solarium, Maniküre und Pediküre | 27. 6. — 29. 8. öS 530,- übrige Zeit öS 490,- | Gratisbegrüßungstrunk, Stadtführung mit Familie Schorer, gemütliche Weinkost, sportlicher Schießwettbewerb, kaltes Buffet bei Kerzenlicht, Grillfest im Garten, Radwanderung mit allen Gästen, Kutschenfahrt zum Bauernhausmuseum, lustige Wettspiele im großen Garten, Golfausflug | Familiengerechte Zimmer, tägl. Unterhaltungsprogramm für Erwachsene und Kinder, Familienwanderungen, großer Kinderspielplatz im Garten, Kinderbetreuung möglich, Familienradwandern, Basteln und Malen . . . Kinderermäßigung im Zimmer der Eltern: bis 6 Jahre 50 %, 6 bis 12 Jahre 30 % |

OBERNDORF — Kaisergebirge und Kitzbüheler Alpen

| Kitzbühler HOTEL RESTAURANT Horn Ihr Wander- und Erlebnishotel Familie Heim A-6372 Oberndorf Tel.: 0 53 52/28 83 | Komfortzimmer und Appartements mit Dusche/Bad/WC, Radio, Telefon, Balkon. Whirlpool, Sauna, Restaurant „Barbarastubn", große Liegewiese, Frühstücksbuffet, Unterhaltungsabend, Festmenüs | öS 395,- | Fahrradtouren und Fahrradverleih, Grillen auf der Alm, geselliges Unterhaltungs- und Sportprogramm | Kinderspielzimmer, Kinderspielplatz, wöchentlich Kinderfest. Kinderermäßigung: bis 6 Jahre GRATIS, 7 bis 12 Jahre 50 % Ermäßigung (im Zimmer der Eltern schlafend) |

EHENBICHL/REUTTE — Lechtaler und Allgäuer Alpen

| HOTEL Maximilian Familie Edwin Koch A-6600 Ehenbichl/Reutte Tel.: 0 56 72/25 85 | Komfortzimmer mit Bad oder Dusche/WC, Telefon, teilweise Balkon, Hauslift, Kinderspielzimmer, TV- und Musikraum, Hotelbar, Frühstücksbuffet, Wahlmenü | von öS 330,- bis öS 390,- | „Frühlingserwachen", Fahrradverleih im Haus, Hotelausflugsdienst, Fischen am Plansee (7 km entfernt), Schlauchbootfahren auf der Lech, „Mit Musik durch den Sommer" | Kinderspielzimmer, Spielplatz, Familientretmobile, Kinderermäßigung: bis 3 Jahre gratis, bis 6 Jahre 50 % und bis 12 Jahre 25 % Ermäßigung im Elternzimmer |

OBERGURGL — Ötztaler Alpen

| Hotel Gasthof Mühle Das Familienhaus für Ihre SOMMERFRISCHE Familie Gstrein A-6456 Obergurgl am Königsrain Tel.: 0 52 56/230, 351 | Komfortzimmer und Appartements mit Bad oder Dusche, WC, Selbstwähltelefon, größtenteils TV-Anschluß und Balkon. HALLENBAD, Sauna, Solarium, Hobby-, Tischtennis-, TV-Raum. Liegewiese, Hausbücherei, Riesenschach, Frühstücksbuffet, 4-Gang-Abendmenü, Grillparty im Freien | von öS 340,- bis öS 430,- im EZ öS 400,- bis öS 470,- | Wanderauftakt: vom 17. — 21. 6. 1987 Alpenrosenblüte: von Ende Juni bis Ende Juli Gletscherflohmarsch: von Gurgl nach Vent, Ende Juli Schmuggelwanderungen: nach Südtirol, Italien Alpenländischer Trödelmarkt: 1 Woche Mitte August | Eigenes Kinderspielzimmer, Kinderspielplatz im Freien, Kinderfest einmal wöchentlich, Kinderbetreuung. Kinderermäßigung im Elternzimmer: bis 5 Jahre gratis, 6—11 Jahre 50 % Ermäßigung |

MIEMING — Mieminger Kette und Wetterstein

| Hotel-Gasthof Schwarz Das Wander- und Erlebnishotel am Mieminger Plateau Familie Pirktl A-6414 Mieming Tel.: 0 52 64/52 12 Telex 054186 | Komfortzimmer und Appartements mit DU/BAD/WC, Telefon, Radio, Balkon, Sitzecke; Hallenbad, Sauna, Whirlpool, Massage, 2 Tennisplätze (Sand), große Liegewiese, „Obergartl", Frühstücksbuffet, 4gängiges Wahlmenü, Salat-, Dessertbuffets, Stimmungsabende, sportliches, geselliges Wochenprogramm | ein Zimmer öS 530,- bis öS 580,- m. HP ein Appartement ab öS 600,- bis öS 700,- | Geführte Radwanderungen, Gipfelwanderungen und Bergwandersafari, Wildererwaldfeste, Bergleabend, Mieminger Kulturwochen und Kirchweih, Tenniskurse. Fordern Sie unser Sommerjournal an! | Spiel und Spaß im ROBINSON-Miniclub, Kinderbetreuung, Kinderspielplatz, „Märchenwald". Kinderermäßigung: Im Elternzimmer schlafend, bis 6 Jahre 70 %, von 6 bis 14 Jahre 50 % Ermäßigung |

ST. ANTON — Arlberg und Verwallgruppe

| HOTEL St. Antoner Hof ••••• Familie Raffl A-6580 St. Anton am Arlberg Tel.: 0 54 46/29 10 Telex 58-17528 ahof | Komfortzimmer mit Bad/WC, Appartements und Maisonetten mit Kachelofen, Bad und Dusche, teilweise Whirlbad, TV — 12 Programme, Telefon, Radio, Minibar, Balkon oder Terrasse; Hallenbad/Sauna/Hot-Whirlpool, Sport- und Fitneßcenter, Spielraum; Frühstücksbuffet, 4gängiges Wahlmenü mit Salatbuffet, 1x wöchentlich Fondueabend und Tiroler Spezialitätenabend | ab öS 550,- | Fahrradtouren, Schlauchbootfahren auf dem Inn, Gewehr- und Pistolenschießen, Bergund Videovorführungen, Picknick + Grillen im Grünen, Fischen im Ferienpark, Tischtennisturniere, Wasserballschlachten, Tennishalle mit 3 Hallen- und 5 Freiplätzen vis-à-vis vom Hotel, Waldfeste | Im Zimmer der Eltern: bis 5 Jahre gratis, ab 6 Jahre 40 % Ermäßigung |

ZELL AM ZILLER — Zillertaler und Tuxer Alpen

Wir vermitteln:

- Eintrittskarten für kulturelle und sportliche Veranstaltungen
- Fahr-, Platz- und Flugkarten
- Informationen über Freizeitgestaltung in der Stadt und im Bezirk Karl-Marx-Stadt anhand von Tagesprogrammen
- Blumenbestellungen
- Tischreservierungen im Hotel und in ausgewählten Gaststätten der Stadt
- Friseurleistungen und kosmetische Behandlung
- Botengänge zur Erledigung von Paß- und Visaangelegenheiten
- Gepäckaufbewahrung
- Aufbewahrung von Wertgegenständen im Hotelsafe
- Taxi- und Mietwagenbestellungen
- Hotelbetten in den Hotels der DDR
- Übersetzungs- und Dolmetscherdienste
- Leistungen außerhalb des Hotels
  Chemische Reinigung
  Reparaturen an Schuhen, Täschnerwaren, Uhren, Brillen, Schirmen u. a.

Wir leihen aus:

- Fernsehapparate
- Schreibmaschinen (deutsch, kyrillisch)
- elektrische Rasierapparate
- Heißluftduschen
- Regenschirme
- Schach- und Brettspiele
- Spielkarten
- Blumenvasen
- Tischventilatoren
- Krawatten
- Tonbandgeräte
- Plattenspieler

Telefon/Telex
durchgehend geöffnet

Entgegennahme von Weckaufträgen

Sie können Ihre Gespräche sowohl in der Hotelhalle als auch von Ihrem Zimmer aus führen.

Bevor Sie wählen!

0 = Direktwahl für Stadtgespräche
9 = Vermittlung von Ferngesprächen

Bank-Service
in der Hotelhalle an der Reception
durchgehend geöffnet
- Ankauf und Umtausch von Geldbeträgen
- Einlösung von Schecks und Reiseschecks für Hotelleistungen

Fitness-Center
Eingang in der 25. Etage
Auskünfte über Öffnungs- und Aufenthaltszeiten für Damen und Herren sowie Voranmeldung über die Mitarbeiter der Reception
- Sauna
- Solarium
- Sportraum

Parken
Bitte benutzen Sie die Parkmöglichkeiten an der Auffahrt zum Hotel und in der Tiefgarage.
Das Parken vor dem Hotelportal ist grundsätzlich untersagt. Über weitere Parkmöglichkeiten informieren Sie die Mitarbeiter der Reception.

Souvenir-Shop
in der Hotelhalle

Montag bis Freitag	7.00 bis 19.00 Uhr
Sonnabend und Sonntag	8.00 bis 16.00 Uhr

Außerhalb der Öffnungszeiten erhalten Sie Reiseartikel für den täglichen Bedarf an der Reception.

Intershop
Eingang Karl-Marx-Allee

Montag bis Freitag	8.00 bis 19.00 Uhr
Sonnabend und Sonntag	8.00 bis 15.00 Uhr

Hotelwäscherei
Vermittlung über Rufnummer −9
oder über die Zimmerfrau
- Waschen und Bügeln von Gästewäsche
  (Benutzen Sie bitte die ausliegenden Wäschebeutel und Leistungsaufträge; vergessen Sie nicht, Ihren Namen, Zimmernummer, Abreisedatum sowie Art und Anzahl der Wäschestücke einzutragen)
- Wäscheschnelldienst erledigen wir nach Art der Kleidungsstücke in 3 bis 5 Stunden
- Reparaturen an Oberbekleidung

Sanitätsstelle
Erste Hilfe erhalten Sie durch die Sanitätsstelle des Hotels
Vermittlung über die Rufnummer −9
oder über die Reception
Ärztliche Betreuung erfolgt durch Vermittlung der Reception

Um allen Gästen unseres Hotels einen angenehmen und erholsamen Aufenthalt zu ermöglichen, bitten wir Sie, nachstehende Festlegungen unserer Hotelordnung zu berücksichtigen:

- Das Hotelzimmer steht nur dem polizeilich gemeldeten Hotelgast zur Verfügung. Bitte empfangen Sie Ihren Besuch in einer unserer gastronomischen Einrichtungen oder in der Hotelhalle.

- Um Lärmstörungen zu vermeiden, bitten wir alle Gäste, die Radio- und Fernsehgeräte auf Zimmerlautstärke zu stellen.

- Bitte schließen Sie Ihr Zimmer stets ab und geben Sie den Schlüssel beim Verlassen des Hotels am Empfang ab.

- Bei Feueralarm ertönt ein unterbrochenes akustisches Signal.

- Aus Gründen der Sicherheit ist das Benutzen von elektrischen Geräten im Hotelzimmer grundsätzlich nicht gestattet.
  Ausnahmen bilden Rasierapparate und Heißluftduschen.
  Aus dem gleichen Grunde bitten wir Sie, im Bett nicht zu rauchen.

- Das Kochen in den Hotelzimmern ist nicht gestattet. Besuchen Sie bitte unsere gastronomischen Einrichtungen.

- Wir gewähren Ihnen eine kostenlose Aufbewahrung Ihrer Wertsachen und Ihres Geldes im Hotelsafe.
  Für Wertsachen und Geld, das sich im Hotelzimmer befindet, übernehmen wir keine Haftung.

- Am Abreisetag geben Sie bitte das Zimmer bis spätestens 11.00 Uhr frei. Sollten Sie eine Verlängerung wünschen, stimmen Sie das bitte rechtzeitig mit der Reception ab.

Verehrter Gast!

Wir begrüßen Sie recht herzlich im Hotel Kongreß und wünschen Ihnen einen angenehmen Aufenthalt in Karl-Marx-Stadt

Bitte nutzen Sie unser umfangreiches Serviceangebot und Möglichkeit der Erholung und Entspannung in unseren gastronomischen Einrichtungen sowie dem Fitness-Center in der 25. Etage.

Unser SERVICE umfaßt alle international üblichen Leistungen, ein breites Angebot an Ausleih- und Vermittlungsdiensten und steht Ihnen jederzeit mit Auskünften und Informationen zur Verfügung.

Alle Mitarbeiter und Geschäftspartner des Hotels bemühen sich ständig, Ihre Aufträge pünktlich und zuverlässig zu erfüllen.

Bei Inanspruchnahme der aufgeführten Serviceleistungen bitten wir Sie, sich mit unserem

Hotelservice

erreichbar in der Hotelhalle an der Reception in Verbindung zu setzen.

Rufnummer −9

Hotel Kongreß
9010 Karl-Marx-Stadt
Karl-Marx-Allee
PSF 632
Telefon 68 30
Telex 7-108

Gaststättenverzeichnis Restaurant List

Hotel- und Gaststättenverzeichnis

Mannheim
Restaurants,
Gaststätten

Name Tel. Vorwahl: 06 21	Ausstattung des Hauses	Empfehlungen des Hauses	Öffnungszeiten Ruhetag	Lage Umgebung
„Savarin" Restaurant im Rosengarten Joachim Mayer Friedrichplatz 7 a Tel. 44 30 07 / 09	☒ 140 P. Weinzimmer 16 P.	DIÄT Französische Spezialitäten, Internationale Spezialitäten, Spezialitäten der Region, Weinprobe nach Voranmeldung	Öffnungszeiten: Jederzeit nach Bedarf. Voranmeldung für geschlossene Gesellschaften	Innenstadt, Nähe Fußgängerzone „Planken, Shopping, Kunsthalle, Nationaltheater, Friedrichplatz, Wasserturm
Schloß-Klause Hans Zickgraf M 4, 1 Tel. 1 28 36	☒ 65 P. Ⓝ 50 P.	Bürgerliche Küche, Spezialitäten	Öffnungszeit: 9.00 – 24.00 Uhr Ruhetag: Sonntag	Innenstadt, Nähe Fußgängerzone „Planken", Schloß
Schwarzwaldstube im Weber-Hotel Hans Danner Frankenthaler Straße 85 Mannheim-Sandhofen Tel. 77 22 00	☒ 80 P.	Grillspezialitäten, Internationale Spezialitäten, Spezialitäten der Region	Öffnungszeit: 11.00 – 24.00 Uhr Ruhetag: Samstag	Randlage Nord, Autobahn Mannheim-Nord
„Skyline" Drehrestaurant im Fernmeldeturm Mayer-Gastro GmbH Tel. 44 30 07	☒ 154 P	Internationale und regionale Spezialitäten	Öffnungszeiten: 11.30 – 17.00 Uhr 18.30 – 23.00 Uhr Ruhetag: –	Innenstadt Ost, Am Neckar, Rundblick über MA bis zur Bergstraße und zur Haardt, Luisenpark
Speiserestaurant Georg Martin Lange Rötterstraße 53 Tel. 33 38 14	☒ 70 P. Ⓝ 30 P. ⊙ 70 P.	Regionale und Internationale Spezialitäten, Täglich Frisch-Fisch Angebot	Öffnungszeit: 11.00 – 23.00 Uhr Ruhetag: Mittwoch	Nähe Alte Feuerwache, B 38 und Herzogenried-Park
Stattmüller Hotel-Restaurant Hubert Stattmüller Neckarhauser Straße 60 Mannheim-Friedrichsfeld Tel. 47 30 11	☒ 70 P. Ⓣ 120 P. Ⓝ 18 P.	Internationale Spezialitäten	Öffnungszeiten: 11.00 – 14.00 Uhr 17.00 – 24.00 Uhr Sa ab 17.00 Uhr Ruhetag: Freitag	Randlage Ost, zwischen MA und HD, BAB-Ausfahrt MA-Seckenheim
„Stern" Henriette Oroboni Hauptstraße 130 Mannheim-Seckenheim Tel. 47 14 88	☒ 40 P. Ⓝ 40 P.	–	Öffnungszeiten: 11.30 – 14.00 Uhr 17.30 – 24.00 Uhr Ruhetag: Samstag	Randlage Ost, Hallenbad Seckenheim
Wartburg Hotel-Restaurant Michael A. Rauser F 4, 4-11 Tel. 2 89 91	☒ 150 P. Saal 400 P. ▓	DIÄT Grillspezialitäten Internationale Spezialitäten, Typische Spezialitäten der Region	Öffnungszeit: 6.30 – 24.00 Uhr	Innenstadt, Shopping, Reiß-Museum, Marktplatz, Wochenmarkt, Altes Rathaus, Untere Pfarrkirche
„Zur Rose" Karlheinz Walter Mosbacher Straße 36 Mannheim-Wallstadt 51 Tel. 70 93 13	☒ 40 P. Ⓝ 50 P. Biergarten mit Grill	Grill- und Wildspezialitäten	Öffnungszeiten: 10.30 – 14.30 Uhr 18.00 – 24.00 Uhr Ruhetag: Montag	Randlage Ost

Hotel- und Gaststättenverzeichnis

Mannheim
Ausländische
Spezialitäten-Restaurants

Ausländische Spezialitäten-Restaurants

Name Tel. Vorwahl: 06 21	Ausstattung des Hauses	Empfehlungen des Hauses	Öffnungszeiten Ruhetag	Lage Umgebung
„Akropolis" D. Chazinikolau K 4, 11 Tel. 2 13 25	☒ 60 P. Ⓝ 20 P.	Grillspezialitäten, Griechische Spezialitäten	Öffnungszeit: 18.00 – 6.00 Uhr Ruhetag: Montag	Innenstadt, Nähe OEG-Bahnhof, Schiffsanlegestelle, Neckarpromenade, Nähe Fußgängerzone „Breite Straße", Shopping
„Buffalo" Argentinisches Steakhaus GmbH Friedrichplatz 1 Tel. 1 34 91	☒ 100 P.	Argentinische Grillspezialitäten	Öffnungszeit: 11.30 – 24.00 Uhr Ruhetag: –	Innenstadt, Nähe Fußgängerzone „Planken", Shopping, Kongreßzentrum Rosengarten, Friedrichplatz, Wasserturm
Da Gianni Ristorante G. Julito R 7, 34 Tel. 2 03 26	☒ 85 P.	Italienische Spezialitäten, Fischspezialitäten	Öffnungszeiten: 12.00 – 14.30 Uhr 18.00 – 22.30 Uhr Ruhetag: Montag	Innenstadt, Nähe Fußgängerzone „Planken", Shopping, Kongreßzentrum Rosengarten, Nationaltheater, Friedrichplatz, Wasserturm
„Dionysos" Georg Hatzikripreou O 7, 16 Tel. 2 30 48	☒ 80 P. Ⓝ 20 P. Ⓣ 250 P.	Grillspezialitäten vom Holzkohlengrill, Griechische Spezialitäten	Öffnungszeit: 11.00 – 3.00 Uhr Ruhetag: –	Innenstadt, Fußgängerzone „Planken", Shopping, Kongreßzentrum Rosengarten, Kunsthalle, Friedrichplatz, Wasserturm
„Garda" Ristorante Mario und Franco Pezzaiuoli P 6, 12–13 Tel. 1 40 61/62	☒ 65 P. Ⓝ 30 P. Pizzeria 45 P.	Italienische Spezialitäten	Öffnungszeiten: 12.00 – 15.00 Uhr 18.00 – 24.00 Uhr Ruhetag: –	Innenstadt, „Freßgasse", Nähe Fußgängerzone, „Planken", Shopping
Goldener Drache Fuh-Tzana Wu U 3, 18 Tel. 2 31 84	☒ 45 P.	Chinesische Spezialitäten	Öffnungszeiten: 11.30 – 14.30 Uhr 17.30 – 24.00 Uhr Ruhetag: –	Innenstadt

Benutzerhinweis

Verzeichnis der Hotels und Gaststätten: Es sind nur Betriebe aufgeführt, die Mitglied des Verkehrsvereins Mannheim sind.

Reihenfolge der Betriebe: Die Reihenfolge des Hotels richtet sich nach dem Höchstpreis der Einzelzimmer, bei gleichem Preis nach dem Alphabet. Der Gaststättenteil ist alphabetisch geordnet.

Zimmerpraise: Die Preise wurden vom jeweiligen Betrieb mitgeteilt, Stand 1. 12. 1985.

Reservoirung leicht gemacht: Sie können ihre Reservierung am einfachsten über den Verkehrsverein vornehmen. Bedienen Sie sich dazu der Zimmerbestellkarten oder teile Sie uns ihre Wünsche schriftlich mit. Wir werden alles tun, sie zu erfüllen. Die Reservierungsbestätigung geht ihnen unverzüglich zu. Für die Vermittlung berechnen wir eine Gebühr von 2 DM, die mit der Hotelrechnung erhoben wird. Der Verkehrsverein ist nur als Vermittler tätig; eine Haftung wird nicht übernommen.

Gute Reise & guten Appetit

Essen und Trinken im Abteil.

Sie können sich aus diesem Angebot eine Erfrischung gönnen oder eine richtige Zwischenmahlzeit zusammenstellen. In Zügen mit Restaurantwagen bekommen Sie Appetitliches direkt aus dem Zugrestaurant ins Abteil serviert. Oder Sie können – falls Sie auf den Abteilservice nicht warten möchten – natürlich auch selbst in den Restaurantwagen gehen und sich dort etwas ins Abteil mitnehmen. In Zügen ohne Restaurantwagen rollt unser minibar-Service direkt zu Ihnen ans Abteil.

Welche Möglichkeiten es in Ihrem Zug gibt, unser Angebot zu nutzen, finden Sie im Faltblatt „Ihr Zugbegleiter" in Ihrem Abteil.

✕ steht für Züge mit Zugrestaurant.

♈ steht für Züge mit minibar-Service.

Daneben finden Sie eine Erläuterung, auf welchen Strecken Sie welche Art von Service in Anspruch nehmen können. **Gute Reise & guten Appetit!**

Je nach Vorrat		(D) in Deutschland DM	(B) in Belgien FB	(F) in Frankreich FF	(A) in Österreich ÖS	(NL) in den Niederld. hfl	(CH) in der Schweiz Sfrs.
Imbiß							
1 Bockwurst, 1 Scheibe Brot, Senf		3,35	72,–	9,90	24,–	3,75	3,–
3 Döschen Streichwurst, 2 Scheiben Brot, 1 Portion Butter		5,30	113,–	15,60	38,–	5,90	4,70
1 Portion Käse 50 g, 2 Scheiben Brot, 1 Portion Butter		5,30	113,–	15,60	38,–	5,90	4,70
1 Stück Cabanossi 100 g ●		3,70	8,–	10,90	26,–	4,10	3,30
1 Portionspackung Brot		–,45	10,–	1,30	3,–	–,50	–,40
Warme Getränke							
1 Kännchen Kaffee		3,90	83,–	11,50	28,–	4,40	3,40
1 Kännchen Tee (1 Kännchen-Portionsbeutel)		3,90	83,–	11,50	28,–	4,40	3,40
1 Kännchen entcoffeinierter Kaffee (HAG)		3,90	83,–	11,50	28,–	4,40	3,40
Verschiedenes							
1 Tafel Schokolade 100 g *		1,80	38,–	5,30	13,–	2,–	1,60
1 Packung Ritter-Sport-Täfelchen (150 g) *		2,70	58,–	8,–	19,–	3,–	2,40
Leibniz-Keks 100 g		1,80	38,–	5,30	13,–	2,–	1,60
Marmorkuchen 100 g		2,65	57,–	7,80	19,–	3,–	2,30
Schoko-Kokos-Makrone 75 g		1,60	34,–	4,70	11,–	1,80	1,40
Mandelhörnchen 50 g		1,60	34,–	4,70	11,–	1,80	1,40
Zigaretten (Automat.-Packg.) *		4,60	–	–	–	–	–
Kalte Getränke							
1 Dose Exportbier / 1 Dose Pilsbier	einschl. 0,33 l / Trinkb. 0,33 l	2,60	56,–	7,70	19,–	2,90	2,30
1 Fl. Selters Mineralwasser	0,33 l	2,60	56,–	7,70	19,–	2,90	2,30
1 Dose Pepsi-Cola	0,33 l	2,60	56,–	7,70	19,–	2,90	2,30
1 Dose Fanta	0,33 l	2,60	56,–	7,70	19,–	2,90	2,30
1 Dose Florida Boy Orange (Ohne Kohlensäure)	0,33 l	2,60	56,–	7,70	19,–	2,90	2,30
Spirituosen							
Jägermeister	2 cl	3,10	–	–	–	–	–
Doornkaat	2 cl	2,80	–	–	–	–	–
Weinbrand Dujardin „Imperial"	2 cl	2,90	–	–	–	–	–

Warme Getränke DM

Kaffee	Tasse	2,30
	Kännchen	4,50
Mocca	Kännchen	5,00
Kaffee Melange	Tasse	2,30
Kaffee Hag	Tasse	2,30
	Kännchen	4,50
Idee-Kaffee	Tasse	2,30
	Kännchen	4,50
Tee mit Sahne oder Zitrone	Glas	2,30
	Kännchen	4,50
Tee mit Rum	Glas	4,80
Schokolade mit Sahne	Tasse	2,50
Schokolade	Kännchen	4,80
Schokolade mit Rum	Tasse	5,00
Grog von Rum	Glas	4,50
Glühwein	Glas	4,50

Alle Preise sind einschließlich Bedienung und MwSt!

Torten und Gebäck je Stück DM

Buttercreme-Torte	3,00 - 3,30
Sahne-Torte	3,00 - 3,30
Spezialtorte	3,00 3,40
Eis-Splitter-Torte	3,30
Käsekuchen	3,20
Diverse feste Kuchen	3,20
Obsttorten nach Wahl	3,00 - 3,40
Plunderteilchen	2,60
Blätterteig-Teile	2,20 - 2,60
Diverse Buttercreme oder Sahneteilchen	2,80 - 3,00
Sahne-Baiser	3,20
Florentiner	3,00
Nußknacker	3,00
Mandelhörnchen	3,20
Ananastörtchen	3,20
Baumkuchen, Portion	3,30
Butter-Hefe-Kranz	3,10
Portion Sahne	0,90

Alle Preise sind einschließlich Bedienung und MwSt!

Bestellungsannahme Telefon 21 33 15

Eis-Karte während der warmen Jahreszeit DM

Portion gemischtes Eis	3,20
Portion Eis mit Sahne	4,10
X Fürst-Pückler-Eis mit Sahne	6,00
X Vanille-Eis mit warmer Schokoladen-Tunke	7,50
Eis mit Früchten, Spezialität	7,50
Pfirsich-Melba mit Sahne	7,50
Ananas-Melba mit Sahne	7,50
Eis-Baiser mit Sahne	7,50
Eis-Kaffee mit Sahne	6,50
Eis-Schokolade mit Sahne	6,50
Eisbecher-Hawaii	7,50
Eisbecher-Krokant	7,50
Eis-Sorbet	7,50
Eis-Creme mit Burgunder	7,50
Birne „Helene"	7,50
Schwarzwald-Becher	9,50
X Haus-Becher	7,50

X auch während der Winter-Saison

Alle Preise sind einschließlich Bedienung und MwSt!

Aus eigener Konditorei empfehlen wir Ihnen

Pralinen
feinste Qualität, reichh. Mischung

Teegebäck
etwas für den Feinschmecker

Baumkuchen
etwas für den Kenner

Torten und Dessertteile
in großer Auswahl

Für Diabetiker bieten wir täglich eine Auswahl frischer Backwaren!

Bestellungsannahme Telefon 21 33 15

Frühstück nur bis 13 Uhr	DM
1 Tasse Kaffee, Tee oder Schokolade mit 2 Brötchen, Butter und Konfitüre	5,50
1 Kännchen Kaffee, Tee oder Schokolade mit 2 Brötchen, Butter und Konfitüre	7,50
1 Tasse Kaffee, Tee oder Schokolade mit 2 Brötchen, Butter, Konfitüre, 1 gekochtes Ei	6,50
1 Kännchen Kaffee, Tee oder Schokolade mit 2 Brötchen, Butter, Konfitüre, 1 gekochtes Ei	8,50
Tasse Kaffee, Tee oder Schokolade mit " Brötchen, Butter und Aufschnitt	7,50
1 Kännchen Kaffee, Tee oder Schokolade mit 2 Brötchen, Butter und Aufschnitt	9,50
1 Brötchen	0,40
1 Portïon Butter	0,80
1 gekochtes Ei	1,00
1 Portion Aufschnitt	5,50

Alle Preise sind einschließlich Bedienung und MwSt!

Küche (ganztägig außer 15–18 Uhr)	DM
Schweizer Käse-Toast mit Schinken und Ei	8,50
Königin-Pastetchen	8,50
Ragout fin, überbacken	7,50
Omelette mit feinem Ragout	9,00
Omelette mit Champignons	8,50
Omelette Konfitüre	8,00
2 Eier im Glas mit Brötchen und Butter	5,00
2 Spiegeleier mit Brot und Butter	5,50
Schnittchen Schinken mit Remoulade	6,50
Schnittchen Käse oder Wurst	6,00
Schnittchen Schinken mit Ei	6,50
3 Sandwiches	7,00
3/2 gefüllte Eier mit Remoulade	5,50
Champignons auf Toast, überbacken	7,50
Ochsenschwanzsuppe mit Brot	3,50
Champignon-Cremesuppe	3,50

Alle Preise sind einschließlich Bedienung und MwSt!

Erfrischungen		DM
Coca-Cola mit Zitrone		2,20
Presta Orange		2,20
Apollinaris		2,00
Apfelsaft	Flasche	2,20
Donath-Kirschsaft	Flasche	3,80
Donath-Sanddorn Orange	Flasche	3,80
Donath Schwarzer Johannisbeersaft	Flasche	3,80
Donath Traubensaft, rot	Flasche	3,80
Zitrone, naturell		3,20
Orangensaft - frisch gepreßt		4,20
Joghurt-Cocktail mit frischer Orange und Cognac		5,80
Joghurt-Cocktail mit frischer Orange und reinem Bienenhonig		5,80
König Pils	Flasche	3,00
HITCHCOCK TOMATENSAFT Naturrein 0,2-l-Fl		3,20

Alle Preise sind einschließlich Bedienung und MwSt!

Spirituosen		DM
Dujardin Fine 8 Jahre alt		3,00
Jacobi 1880		2,80
Asbach Uralt		2,80
Napoléon		4,50
VAT 69 Finest Scotch Whisky		4,50
VAT 69 Finest Scotch Whisky mit Soda		6,00
Pott Rum		2,80
Pott Golf	4 cl	5,50
Orig. Schladerer Schwarzwälder Kirschwasser		4,50
Orig. Schladerer Schwarzwälder Himbeergeist		5,00
Jägermeister		2,50
Steinhäger Urquell		2,50
Underberg - Magenbitter		3,00
NAYIF SLIVOVITZ Orig. serbisch		3,50
Campari mit Soda		6,00
PERNOD		6,00

Alle Preise sind einschließlich Bedienung und MwSt!

Weine und Südweine		DM
Cinzano Rosso		3,50
Cinzano Bianco		3,50
Cinzano Extra Dry		3,50
Cinzano mit Himbeergeist		7,00
Cinzano mit Soda		5,00
TAYLOR'S PORT Ruby		3,50
Sherry DRY SACK		3,50
Moselwein	Glas	3,80
Rheinwein	Glas	3,80

Liköre	DM
Curacita - Triple Sec	3,00
Bols Mocca	3,00
Bols Curaçao	3,00
Schlehenfeuer	3,00
Liqueur BÉNÉDICTINE D.O.M	4,00
Cusenier Orange	4,00
Cusenier Apricot-Brandy	4,00

Alle Preise sind einschließlich Bedienung und MwSt!

Sekt	DM
0,2-l-Flasche	
DEINHARD CABINET _Trocken_	7,00
0,375-l-Flasche	
Deinhard Lila Imperial Riesling Dry	16,00
0,75-l-Flasche	
DEINHARD CABINET _Trocken_	25,00
Deinhard Lila Brut Riesling · Jahrgangs-Cuvée	30,00

Besonders zu empfehlen:

„ UNSER HAUSBECHER "

eine köstliche Eis-Erfrischung.

Alle Preise sind einschl. Bedienung, Sekt- und MwSt!

MOTEL-CENTER
KIRCHHEIM
Deutschlands größtes Motel

D-6437 Kirchheim/Hessen · Tel.: (0 66 25) 6 31 · Tx 04–93 337

Steaks vom Grill

Saftige Steaks vom Grill – je ca. 160 g – mit Kräuterbutter,
uberbackenen Rahmkartoffeln und Grilltomate

Dazu empfehlen wir unseren
16 **Steaksalat 4,80**
aus gartenfrischen Salaten mit French-Dressing

17 **Puterbruststeak 16,80**
18 **Rumpsteak 22,50**
19 **Schweinerückensteak 15,90**

Beilagen
55 **Erbsen oder Möhren 1,80**
51 **Pommes frites 1,80**
52 **Kartoffelpüree 1,80**
53 **Patna-Reis 1,80**
54 **Sc. Bèarnaise 3,50**

Steak-Spezialität

20 **Chef's Special,** ca. 200 g **17,40**

Mariniertes und pikant gewürztes
Schweinekammsteak mit
Kräuterbutter und Grilltomate,
überbackene Rahmkartoffeln

Bestellen Sie dazu einen
Steaksalat
aus gartenfrischen Salaten

Salate
bunt und gartenfrisch

Unsere Salatsaucen werden mit
leicht verdaulichem Pflanzenöl zubereitet

16 **Steaksalat 4,80**
Frènch-Dressing
– Empfehlen wir auch als Appetitanreger
vor odèr zu Ihrem Hauptgericht –

21 **Salatplatte** (2) mit Ei **10,80**

22 **Chef-Salat 16,50**
Knackiger Eisbergsalat
mit Hühnerbrustfleisch,
Mandarinen und Ananas (2),
1000-Island-Dressing

Kuchen &
Torten

– auch zum Mitnehmen – am Kuchenbüffet

Suppen hausgemacht, mit Brot

01 **Kartoffelsuppe**   4,40
mit vielen Gemüsen

02 **Rinderbouillon**   3,90
mit Reiseinlage

03 **Gulaschsuppe**   6,80
große Portion

Kaltes

04 **Restaurationsteller**   10,90
Braten, Wurst, Ei und Käse,
Kartoffelsalat und Bauernbrot (1, 2, 6)

Belegtes Brot mit
05 **gekochtem Schinken**   7,50
06 **rohem Schinken**   8,50

09 **Wurst-Käse-Salat**   9,40
in pikanter Marinade (1, 2),
Bauernbrot

Herzhaftes

10 **Spießbraten**   13,50
Möhren und Pommes frites

11 **Fischfilet**   10,60
Merlan gebacken mit Remouladensauce (1, 2)
und Kartoffelsalat

12 **Hausmacher Würste**   9,30
auf Sauerkraut, Kartoffelpüree

13 **Saftgulasch**   12,80
vom Rind und Schwein,
grüne Nudeln

14 **Wiener Schnitzel**   14,80
vom Schwein,
Möhren und Pommes frites

15 **Frankfurter Rippchen**   16,60
ca. 300 g Frischgewicht,
Kartoffelsalat (1, 2, 6)

Leichtes

23 **Tomaten-Spaghetti**   8,90
Spaghetti mit frischem würzigen Tomatengemüse
überzogen und viel Parmesankäse

24 **Curry-Rahmgeschnetzeltes**   13,70
mit Früchten im Reisrand

25 **Rührei-Schinken**   9,40
Erbsen und Kartoffelpüree

Wiener Würstchen   7,50
26 mit Kartoffelsalat (1, 2, 6)
27 oder Pommes frites

Süßes

69 **Frankfurter Pudding**   3,80
mit Brombeersauce

70 **Gekühlter Weinschaum**   4,70
mit Masalatrauben

74 **Eisbecher BANANA-SPLIT**   7,20
Mövenpick Vanille –
Traumeis, Bananen,
Schokoladensauce, Sahne

71 **Frischer Fruchsalat**   6,50
72 mit Schlagsahne   7,50

73 **Traum-Eiskrem**
– je Kugel Mövenpickeis – **1,70**
Etwas ganz Besonderes.
Kombinieren Sie Ihren Eistraum
aus Chocolate-Chip, Vanille,
Erdbeer, Pistazie, Rumrosine
und Zitrone.

**Beachten Sie auch bitte
die Sondereiskarte.**

Käse

mit Brotauswahl und Butter wahlweise:

31 **Edamer**   7,70
32 **Camembert**   6,50
33 **Harzer,** Griebenschmalz   5,50
34 **Käseteller**   9,80
Edamer, Camembert,
Edelpilz, Le Tartare, Harzer

Heute
Bitte beachten Sie
auch das Angebot auf unserer
HEUTE-TAFEL

Kinderecke

Nur für unsere kleinen Gäste bis zu 12 Jahren

28 **Saftgulasch**   7,20
vom Rind und Schwein,
Spaghetti

29 **Milchreis**   3,90
mit Früchten

30 **Brühwurstscheiben**   4,80
in Ketchupsauce und Pommes frites (6)

Getränke

Schoppenweine 0,2 L

Mosel – halbtrocken	4,60
Spätburgunder Weißherbst – süffig	5,80
Blauer Portugieser (Rotwein) – zart	4,80
Riesling d'Alsace – trocken	6,60
Bordeaux (Rotwein) – kräftig	5,50

Bier vom Faß 0,3 L

König-Pilsener	3,30

Flaschenbiere 0,33 L

Alkoholfreies Bier	3,30
Malzbier	2,70
Berliner Weiße mit Schuß	3,50
Kristallweizenbier 0,5 L	3,50
Alsterwasser	2,90

Alkoholfreie Getränke 0,2 L

Coca-Cola oder Sprite oder Fanta	2,30
Roter Traubensaft	3,40
Orangensaft	3,40
Schwarzer Johannisbeer-Nektar	4,40
Apfelsaft	2,50
Tomatensaft	3,40
Mineralwasser SELTERS	2,40
Staatl. Fachingen 0,33 L	3,30
Tonic Water oder Bitter Lemon	3,00
Trinkmilch 0,25 L	2,20

Spirituosen 2 cl

Schlitzer Doppelkorn 38 %	2,00
Malteserkreuz Aquavit	2,60
Aalborg Jubiläums Akvavit	3,00
Schladerer Kirschwasser	4,50
Gordon's Dry Gin	3,00
Moskowskaja Wodka	3,00
Weinbrand Dujardin Imperial	2,80
Kümmerling	2,30
Pott Rum 54 %	3,00
Fernet Branca	3,20

Drinks – Sekt

Campari-Soda (5) 4 cl	6,50
Martini weiß/rot/dry 5 cl	3,50
Sherry Tio Pepe 5 cl	4,30
Scotch Whisky 4 cl	5,80
Fürst von Metternich – trocken 1/4 Fl.	11,00

Heiße Getränke Portion

Kaffee DARBOVEN oder Kaffee HAG	4,20
Espresso, Tasse	2,50
Trinkschokolade oder Ceylon-Tee	4,20
Mokka	6,00
Rum Grog 4 cl	6,00
Glühwein 0,2 L	6,00

TRIER
Deutschlands
älteste Stadt

PROGRAMM

Angeln
Mosel von der Sauermündung bis Staustufe Detzem. Auskunft über Angelscheine durch Tourist-Information-Trier.

Baby-Wickelstation
für die kleinsten Gäste im Kiosk Palastgarten (20 m von der Aula Palatina entfernt); Mai bis Oktober.

Gottesdienste
siehe Gottesdienstordnung im Veranstaltungskalender „Der fröhliche Steuermann."

Hotels
Rund 2600 Gästebetten in Hotels, Gasthäusern und Pensionen. Aktuelle Preise im jährlich erscheinenden „Hotelführer Trier".

Jugendunterkunft
Marineschiff „Uranus", am Oberstau der Mosel (Estricherhof) Anmeldung: Telefon (0 65 02) 5 88 07. Das Schiff ist geöffnet vom 1. 4. – 31. 10. (33 Betten).

Jugendzeltplatz Trier
Luxemburger Straße 81, Telefon 06 51/8 69 21. Aufnahmekapazität: 250 Personen.

TOURISTISCHE INFORMATIONEN VON A BIS Z

Auskunft
Prospekte, Hotelvermittlung, Führungsdienst, Ausflugsberatung, Weinproben bei:

Tourist-Information,
5500 Trier, An der Porta Nigra (B 3), Tel. (06 51) 7 54 40 u. 4 80 71. Parkplätze und Parkhäuser in unmittelbarer Nähe.

Ausflugsfahrten
In den Sommermonaten finden mehrmals wöchentlich Gesellschaftsfahrten in das Trierer Land und nach Luxemburg statt. Bahn, Bus und Mosel-Schiffahrt (siehe unten) ermöglichen ebenso wie der eigene Wagen vielfältige individuelle Ausflüge.

Bäder
Stadtbad (Hallenbad), Südallee (D 2); Nordbad (beheizt), Zurmaiener Str. (A 4); Südbad (beheizt), An der Härenwies (E 1).

Camping
Im Schloßpark Monaise (E 3). Siehe auch: Trier-Hotelführer. City-Campingplatz.

Devisenumtausch
Bei allen Banken und Sparkassen und im Hauptbahnhof.

Domführungen
mit Domkreuzgang und Liebfrauenkirche ab Sakristei-Eingang, 1 Std., Sonderführungen nach Absprache mit Dombüro (Tel. 7 58 01).

Einkaufszentrum
Der Hauptmarkt mit den von ihm in nördlicher und südlicher Richtung ausgehenden Straßenzügen. Verkehrsfreie Innenstadt.

Fundbüro
Hindenburgstr. 2 (C 3), Tel. 7 18–23 24

Gärten und Parks
Palastgarten (C 2), Nells Park (A 2), Mattheiser Weiher (E 2).

Hotels, Gasthöfe, Gaststätten
Siehe Trier-Hotelführer.

Jugendherberge
Maarstr./Zurlaubener Ufer (B 4), Tel. 4 10 92.

Kabinenseilbahn
Von Zurlauben zum Weißhaus (B 4 nach A 5).

Kulturveranstaltungen
Oper, Operette, Schauspiel im Stadttheater, Am Augustinerhof (C/D 3); Konzerte des Städtischen Orchesters und der Musikvereinigungen, Kirchenkonzerte, Gastkonzerte;

Vorträge der wissenschaftlichen Gesellschaften, der Universität, Kunstausstellungen. Programme und Termine im Trierer Veranstaltungskalender „Der fröhliche Steuermann" und im Kulturtertial.

Literatur über Trier
In den Buchhandlungen und bei „Tourist-Information".

Moselschiffahrt
In den Sommermonaten Ausflugs- und Linienverkehr ab Stadthafen Zurlauben (B 4, Bus Nr. 2.):

nach den luxemburgischen Moselgemeinden,

nach dem Stadtteil Pfalzel.

Bootshafen für Sportboote, Jachten usw. oberhalb der Moselstaustufe bei Schloß Monaise (E 3, linkes Ufer).

Auskunft: Tourist-Information, Faltblatt: Sommerprogramm.

Notrufe
Überfall und Verkehrsunfall Tel. 1 10.
Feuerwehr Tel. 1 12.
Nachtdienst der Ärzte und Apotheken Tel. 11 50.

Öffnungszeiten
der Baudenkmäler und Museen im Trierer Veranstaltungskalender „Der fröhliche Steuermann".

Parkhäuser/Tiefgaragen
Kaufhof-Parkhaus, am Simeonstiftplatz/Margareteng. (B 3), Tiefgarage Konstantin (C 2), Tiefgarage Porta Nigra, Engelstr. (B 3), City-Parkhaus, Metzelstr. (C 3), Parkhaus Walramsneustr. (B 3) und Mustorstr. (C 2).

Pauschalangebote
Arrangements: „Trierer Amorette". „Auf den Spuren der Römer" und Wochenend-Weinseminare, Wetterkundeseminare.
Spezialprospekte durch: „Tourist-Information".

Post
Postamt, Am Kornmarkt (C 3); Hauptpostamt, Bahnhofsvorplatz (B 1).

Reisebüros
Reinemann, Bahnhofsplatz 4 (B 1) und Kornmarkt 8 (C 3); Reisebüro im Kaufhof, Simeonstr. 53 (B 3); City-Reisebüro, Fleischstr. (C 3); Reisebüro Dahm & Erl, Saarstr. 12 (D 3).

Stadtbesichtigung
Siehe Innenseiten.

Sport und Hobby
Sportplätze für Leichtathletik, Fußball, Tennis usw.: Moselstadion, Zeughausstr. (A 3), und Bezirkssportanlagen;
Kanu-, Ruder-, Segel- und Wasserskisport auf der Mosel; Regattastrecke u. Sportboothafen bei Schloß Monaise (E 3);
Motorfliegen: Flugplatz Föhren (Entf. 17 km);
Reiten: Trimmelter Hof, Trier-Olewig (über D 1); Freizeitanlage Diedenhofener Str.: Tennis, Squash, Eissport (E 4);
Kleingolf: Südbad (E 1).

Angeln in der Mosel und ihren Nebenflüssen.

Stadtrundgang (im Sommerhalbjahr)
Werktäglich um 10.30 u. 15 Uhr, Anmeldung Tourist-Information.

Stadtrundfahrten (ab 1. 6.)
Werktäglich 10 Uhr u. 14.30 Uhr.
Auf Bestellung während des ganzen Jahres. Auskunft und Anmeldung bei Tourist-Information.

Taxiruf
Trierer Taxi-Vereinigung:
Tel. 7 25 25, 4 50 50, 7 41 41.
Taxi-Funk-Service: Tel. 3 30 30.

Touristen-Tages-Netzkarte
Für einen Tag für alle Busse in der Kernzone. Auskunft und Verkauf: Tourist-Information.

Urlaub im Trierer Land
Auskunft durch „Tourist-Information".

Veranstaltungen
Siehe die Veranstaltungskalender: „Der fröhliche Steuermann" (erscheint monatlich), „Trierer Sommertreff" (erscheint jährlich) und „Trierer Gäste-Programm Sommer-Stunden-Plan" (erscheint jährlich). Jährlich wiederkehrende Großveranstaltungen: Karneval (Jan./Feb.), Moselfest, Weinfest, Altstadtfest, Blumentage.

Weinlehrpfad
Täglich geöffnet (ausgenommen zur Lesezeit). Spezialführer durch Tourist-Information.

Weinproben
Täglich von 10 bis 18 Uhr.
Auskunft: Tourist-Information.

Weinstuben
Siehe Trier-Hotelführer.

Zoo
Kein Zoologischer Garten, aber ein Wildfreigehege im Weißhauswald (A 5).

Änderungen sind vorbehalten. Ausführliche Auskünfte bei Tourist-Information-Trier.

Herausgeber: Verkehrsamt der Stadt Trier. Druck: Paulinus-Druckerei, Trier. Printed in Germany: Imprimé en Allemagne, 100 · 3 ·

EIN BESUCH IN OSTBERLIN

Alte Bauten
Ein Spaziergang unter den Linden

„Unter den Linden" – wer kennt sie nicht, die Traumstraße von einst, oft beschrieben und besungen. Nach dem Krieg hat sie durch den Bau der Mauer, die unmittelbar am Brandenburger Tor verläuft, ihre alte Bedeutung als Teil einer Verkehrsachse verloren. Im westlichen Teil sind viele Neubauten entstanden, während im östlichen Teil, durch Restaurierung und Wiederaufbau nach historischen Vorbildern, die Straße ihr historisches Aussehen erhielt.

Nehmen Sie sich einen Tag Zeit und durchwandern Sie deutsche Geschichte im anderen Teil Berlins. Östlich der Friedrichstraße finden Sie das wiederaufgebaute Alte Palais von Langhans.

Einst lebte hier Kaiser Wilhelm bis zu seinem Tod (1888). Heute studieren in dem alten Bau die Pädagogik-Studenten der Humboldt-Universität.

Ein neues Gesicht zeigt der Alexanderplatz. Er ist zur Fußgängerzone umgestaltet worden, umgeben vom Hotel Stadt Berlin, dem Centrum-Warenhaus, dem Haus des Lehrers und einer Kongreßhalle.

Der Ostberliner Fernsehturm am Alexanderplatz überragt die Stadt mit einer Höhe von 361,5 Meter. Die Turmkugel mit dem Télécafé dreht sich jede Stunde einmal um ihre eigene Achse.

Das beeindruckende Pergamon-Museum, auf der Museumsinsel gelegen, sollte in jedem Fall besichtigt werden. Es ist eines der wenigen anerkannten Museen der Antiken Kunst in der ganzen Welt.

Vom Pergamon-Altar bis zur Skulpturensammlungen der griechischen und römischen Antike sind hier bedeutende Zeugnisse vergangener Hochkulturen ausgestellt.

Rund um den ehemaligen Opernplatz – heute Bebelplatz – stehen eine Reihe sehenswürdiger Bauten, die Ihnen einen Eindruck von der Schönheit des „alten Berlin" vermitteln. Zwischen der alten Königlichen Bibliothek, der St. Hedwigs-Kathedrale und der Deutschen Staatsoper sehen Sie den alten Stadtteil von Berlin. Von hier aus kann man schnell über die Behren- und Wilhelm-Külz-Straße (früher Markgrafenstraße) den Platz der Akademie – ehemals Gendarmenmarkt – erreichen, wo der Deutsche und der Französische Dom stehen. Im Jahr 1817/18 entstand die Neue Wache, heute ein Mahnmal.

Dahinter liegt das Haus der Sing-Akademie – jetzt Maxim-Gorki-Theater. Hier hielt Alexander von Humboldt seine Kosmos-Vorlesungen, führte Felix Mendelssohn-Bartholdy 1829 Bachs wiederentdeckte Matthäus-Passion auf, hier musizierten so berühmte Künstler wie Paganini, Liszt und Clara Schumann.

Den Abschluß der Straße bildet das Museum für Deutsche Geschichte (Zeughaus), das mit seiner 90 Meter langen barocken Straßenfront einen markanten Akzent setzt. Jenseits der Marx-Engels-Brücke, der alten Schloßparkbrücke, steht der 1893-1905 erbaute Dom, der zur Zeit wieder aufgebaut wird. In seiner Krypta sind die Särge vom Großen Kurfürsten, Friedrich I. und Sophie Charlotte.

Die Theater

Ostberlin verfügt über eine Reihe von guten Theatern. Das Berliner Ensemble hat sich auf modernes Schauspiel und Stücke von Brecht spezialisiert.
Adresse:
Am Bertolt-Brecht-Platz, 104 Berlin.

Die Deutsche Staatsoper widmet sich mehr den klassischen Programmen (Oper, Ballett, Konzert). Adresse: Unter den Linden 7, 108 Berlin.

Als scharfzüngiges Kabarett ist die »Distel« bekannt:
Friedrichstraße 101, 108 Berlin.

Die Museen

Wer als Besucher von Berlin (West) nach Ostberlin fährt, sollte auf jeden Fall einen Kulturbummel durch die reichhaltige Museenlandschaft machen. Empfehlenswert ist vor allem das Pergamon-Museum (Eingang Kupfergraben). Das Pergamon-Museum gilt als das berühmteste Architektur-Museum der Welt. Es enthält unter anderem die Antiken-Sammlung (darunter der Pergamon-Altar, der schon in der Antike zu den Weltwundern gerechnet wurde, das römische Markttor von Milet und weltberühmte Werke der griechischen Skulpturen).

ÜBERGÄNGE, RUNDFAHRTEN

Ausländische Gäste und Besucher aus dem Bundesgebiet bekommen gegen Gebühr eine Tagesaufenthaltsgenehmigung, die bis 24 Uhr gültig ist. Sie müssen nur ihren Reisepaß mitbringen. Bei einem Besuch Ostberlins ist ein Pflichtumtausch zu entrichten. Ausländische Autofahrer brauchen außerdem zum Kraftfahrzeugschein (Zulassung) noch die Internationale grüne Versicherungskarte.

Für Besucher aus dem Bundesgebiet: Die Übergänge Bornholmer Straße und Heinrich-Heine-Straße (Moritzplatz) können von Fußgängern und Autofahrern benutzt werden. Der Übergang auf dem Bahnhof Friedrichstraße ist nur mit der U-Bahn oder der S-Bahn zu erreichen. Die Übergänge nach Ostberlin sind für die Einreise von 7 bis 20 Uhr geöffnet, für die Ausreise bis 24 Uhr.

Für ausländische Besucher: Ausländische Besucher passieren den internationalen Übergang Friedrichstraße (Checkpoint Charlie). Dieser Übergang ist Tag und Nacht geöffnet. Außerdem können Ausländer mit der U-Bahn oder der S-Bahn zum Bahnhof Friedrichstraße fahren und den dortigen Übergang benutzen. Er ist von 7 bis 24 Uhr geöffnet.

Für Besucher aus dem Bundesgebiet und dem Ausland: Stadtrundfahrten von Berlin (West) nach Ostberlin bieten drei Berliner Stadtrund-

fahrt-Unternehmen an: Berliner Bärenstadtrundfahrt, Berolina und Severin+Kühn. Alle privaten und selbst organisierten Omnibus-Stadtrundfahrten durch Ostberlin müssen vorher in Ostberlin beim Reisebüro der DDR, Berlin Information, Berolinastraße 7, DDR 102 Berlin angemeldet werden.

DM-Beträge und Beträge in Währungen der westlichen Länder können in unbegrenzter Höhe mitgenommen werden. Die Ein- und Ausfuhr von Mark der DDR sowie osteuropäischen Währungen ist verboten.

Die drei Berliner Stadtrundfahrt-Unternehmen bieten eine große Auswahl von Sightseeing-Touren durch Berlin (West) und Ostberlin an. Allen Nachtschwärmern sei eine Fahrt durch das Berliner Nachtleben empfohlen.

Berliner Bärenstadtrundfahrt (BBS) (Telefon 883 60 02): täglich Abfahrten am Kurfürstendamm und an der Gedächtniskirche/Ecke Rankestraße.

Berolina Stadtrundfahrt (Telefon 881 68 57): täglich Kurfürstendamm/Ecke Meinekestraße.

Severin+Kühn (Telefon 883 10 15): täglich ab Kurfürstendamm 215/216.

Für alle Stadtrundfahrten durch Ostberlin muß der Reisepaß mitgebracht werden.

LOS →

SHOPPING		Hanse-Viertel	Gerhof-Passage	Gänsemarkt
Einzelhandelsgeschäfte, Warenhäuser und Einkaufszentren sind in der Regel von 9 bis 18.30 Uhr (montags bis freitags) bzw. 9 bis 14 Uhr (samstags) geöffnet. An jedem 1. Samstag im Monat bleiben die Geschäfte bis 18 Uhr geöffnet.				**Neuer Gänsemarkt**

Gewonnen

Hamburg ist immer ein Gewinn! Kaufleute kommen hier auf ihre Kosten: Shopping, Börse, Spielbank, Fischmarkt… Sie haben noch nicht genug? Dann noch mal los bei LOS!

Große Elbstraße
Ⓤ Königstraße

Fischmarkt
← zwischen →

St.-Pauli-Landungs-brücken
Ⓤ Landungsbrücken

Gemein-schaftsfeld ?

❶ Shopping

Bummeln, schauen, kaufen…
Rund um die Binnenalster pulsiert das Leben. Die Stadt der Kaufleute zeigt sich von ihrer faszinierenden Seite. Ob auf der Mönckebergstraße mit den großen Kaufhäusern und renommierten Spezialgeschäften, auf dem Jungfernstieg, dem Pracht- und Bummelboulevard direkt an der Binnenalster, oder in den Fußgängerzonen Spitalerstraße, Gerhart-Hauptmann-Platz und Colonnaden – hier finden Sie alles, was das Herz begehrt. Und: Hamburg ist die heimliche Hauptstadt der Einkaufspassagen, die Stadt mit den meisten über-dachten Laden-Straßen auf dem Kontinent.
Das engmaschige Netz dieser Einkaufsparadiese ist nicht nur ein Schlaraffenland für Kauf- und Seh-Leute, sondern auch eine architektonische Wunderwelt aus Marmor, Backstein, Stahl und Glas. Insgesamt 250 Boutiquen, Fachgeschäfte, Restaurants, Galerien und Cafés bilden eine raffinierte Mischung aus Boulevard und Salon. Sie bieten Köstliches und Kostbares, Exklusives und Erlesenes, Antikes und Modisches. Hamburg hat Kauf-Leuten viel zu bieten – auch die »Qual der Wahl«.

❹ Fischmarkt

Immer wieder sonntags, so ab sechs Uhr morgens. Eigentlich eine unmögliche Zeit für Trödel und Fischbrötchen – oder vielleicht doch nicht!? Jedenfalls drängen sich an manchen Sonntagen mehr als 100 000 Fischmarktbummler zwischen den bunten Ständen, an denen so ziemlich alles verkauft wird, was sich zu Geld machen läßt: vom lebenden Hammel bis zum original Orient-Teppich (noch mit echtem Wüsten-sand!), von Elvis-Platten bis zu Opas Gehrock. Der Fischmarkt ist einmalig auf der Welt.
Seine Tradition reicht bis in das Jahr 1703, als eine »Magistratusverordnung« es den Fischern erlaubte, auch sonntags frischen Fisch zu verkaufen, damit die Ware nicht verderbe. Heute dreht es sich nicht mehr hauptsächlich um Fisch – der wird zwar auch noch verkauft und sogar frisch vom Kutter –, heute geht es nur um den Spaß. Auf dem Fischmarkt trifft man die verrücktesten Typen: Marktschreier und Hamburger Originale, Nachtbummler und Tagträumer.
Und wenn um zehn Uhr die letzten Bananen unters Volk geworfen sind, dann füllen sich die umliegenden Kneipen…

❷ Spielbank

»Rien ne va plus.« Und: »Wer nicht wagt, der nicht gewinnt…«
Neulinge werden natürlich beraten, wenn sie sich unter die rund 800 Gäste wagen, die täglich in der Zeit von 15 bis 3 Uhr in der Hamburger Spielbank ihr Glück auf die Probe stellen. Überraschend: Jeder dritte Gast ist eine Frau. Die elf Roulettetische üben eine starke Anziehungskraft aus – die Jetons »kleben« manchmal förmlich an den Tischen. C'est la vie!
Steigender Beliebtheit erfreuen sich auch Black-Jack und Baccara. Und die komfortable Bar kann sogar eingefleischte Nicht-Spieler verlocken. Denn Hamburgs Spielbank liegt hoch über den Dächern der Stadt,

Hauptbahnhof

Kleines Spiel
Mini-Roulette, Slot-Machines, Steindamm 1, Hamburg 1, Nähe Hauptbahnhof

Spielbank
Fontenay 10 (Hotel Intercontinental), Hamburg 13, täglich geöffnet von 15 bis 3 Uhr
Ⓤ Dammtor

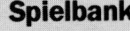

Ankerplatz Hamburg

Hamburg liegt dort, wo das Leben Spaß macht: am Wasser und zwischen den Meeren. Hier weht eine frische Brise. Würzig, wohltuend und belebend. Genau das richtige Flair für unternehmungslustige Leute.

Gehen Sie an Land und erleben Sie Hamburg. Ganz nach Ihrem Geschmack: Als »Bergsteiger« erklimmen Sie den Michel, als »Gourmet« pulen Sie Ihre erste Krabbe, als »Verliebte« schippern Sie (und sie) über die Alster.
Hamburg breitet sich hier vor Ihnen aus. ● Punkt für ● Punkt und mit ● jeder Menge ● Tips.
Blättern Sie sich einfach durch diese Viel-Seitigkeit und entdecken Sie »Ihr« Hamburg.
48 Vorschläge für Ziele in und um Hamburg. Landgänge für ein paar Stunden oder einen ganzen Tag; mit allen wichtigen Informationen über Adressen, Anfahrtswege, Öffnungszeiten…

Wie wär's? Der Ankerplatz Hamburg wartet auf Sie!

Jungfernstieg	Spitaler-straße	Mönckeberg-straße Landesbank-Galerie	Kaufmanns-haus	

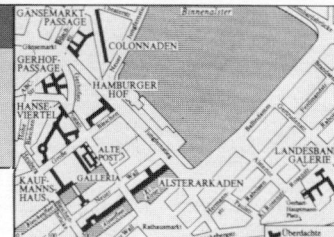

LANDGANG FÜR KAUF-LEUTE

Alte Post

Galleria

Börse

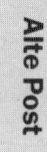

❷ Börse

Ein Spaziergang mit Börsenbesuch? Zugegeben, ein etwas ungewöhnlicher Vorschlag. Aber wann und wo hat man denn schon mal die Gelegenheit, das Börsengeschehen »live« mitzuerleben und es auch noch sachkundig erklärt zu bekommen?

Die Hanseatische Wertpapierbörse veranstaltet regelmäßig von montags bis freitags (jeweils um 11.15 Uhr) ein etwa einstündiges Informationsprogramm, zu dem jeder Zutritt hat. Ein akademischer Leckerbissen für Kaufleute.

In einem kurzen einführenden Film werden die Bedeutung Hamburgs und seiner Börse für den internationalen Handel und die Funktion der Wertpapiere im Wirtschaftskreislauf erläutert. Anschließend können die Besucher dann von der Galerie aus das hektische und lautstarke Treiben der Börsianer fast hautnah miterleben.

Zur Hamburger Börse, übrigens die älteste Deutschlands (von 1558!), gehören die Hanseatische Wertpapierbörse, der Devisenhandel, die Versicherungs-, die Getreide- und die Allgemeine Börse.

im neunten Stock des Hotels Intercontinental, mit einem herrlichen Blick auf Alster und City. Schon überzeugt? Dann vergessen Sie bitte nicht Ihre »Eintrittskarte«, sprich: Personalausweis. Auch gepflegte Kleidung (Krawatte) ist vorgeschrieben. Jugendliche unter 18 Jahre haben keinen Zutritt.
Das »Kleingeld« spielt erst an den Tischen eine gewisse Rolle...
»Faites vos jeux!«

❾ ❿ Jungfernstieg
Eingang:
Adolphsplatz

Für Besucher geöffnet (montags bis freitags) von 11.30 bis 13.30 Uhr, Führungen mit Film jeweils 11.15 Uhr. Voranmeldung für Gruppen: 36 74 44.

Gehen Sie

ins Casino

Hamburg

HAMBURG

Ausstellungen

29. 6. – 31. 8. »Orthodoxe Juden in Berlin 1869–1942«; Landesarchiv Berlin, Telefon 783 85 86

Bis 6. 7. Nino Langobardi – Neue Arbeiten; Nationalgalerie im Kunstforum der Grundkreditbank, Telefon 250 01 01

Bis 17. 8. Alf Lechner – Neue Eisenskulpturen; Nationalgalerie, Telefon 2 66–26 62

Bis 31. 8. Xingú – »Unter Indianern Zentralasiens«; Museum für Völkerkunde, Sonderausstellungshalle, 83 01–1

Bis 31. 8. Die Griechenlandreise des romantischen Zeichners Haller von Hallenstein; Antikenmuseum, Tel. 32 01–2 16

Bis 31. 8. Bauhaus: Architektur, Werkstätten, Design, Unterricht; Bauhaus-Archiv, Telefon 261 16 18

Bis 31. 8. Graphik '80–'85 im Berliner Kupferstichkabinett; Kupferstichkabinett, 83 01–2 28

Bis 31. 8. Trachten und Stickereien aus Siebenbürgen; Galerie im Deutschlandhaus, Telefon 261 10 46

14. 9. – 30. 12. Große Ostpreußen; Galerie im Deutschlandhaus, Tel. 261 10 46

Bis 7. 9. Schauspiel und Tanz im japanischen Holzschnitt; Museum für ostasiatische Kunst, 83 01–3 82

Bis 12. 10., sonntags, von 10.00 bis 13.00 Uhr Führungen durch das Museumsdorf Düppel, Telefon 802 66 71

Bis Mitte Oktober, sonntags, 10.00 Uhr Kostenlose Führungen im Botanischen Garten; Treffpunkt Eingang Königin-Luise-Straße, Telefon 831 40 41

Bis 30. 10. Troja – Heinrich Schliemanns Ausgrabungen und Funde; Museum für Vor- und Frühgeschichte, Telefon 32 01–1

Bis 15. 12. »325 Jahre Staatsbibliothek«; Telefon 2 66–1

Bis 26. 7. Königliche Bücher – Bucheinbände des Hauses Hohenzollern; Staatsbibliothek, Telefon 2 66–1

18. 8. – 4. 10. Spaniens Sprache und Literatur in Deutschland; Staatsbibliothek, Telefon 2 66–1

Bis 26. 4. 1987 Bunzlauer Geschirr; Museum für Deutsche Volkskunde, Telefon 83 20 31

18. 7. Rudolf Schwarzkogler; Nationalgalerie im Kunstforum der Grundkreditbank, Tel. 250 01 01

7. 8 – 28. 9. »Zündapp – Aufstieg und Fall einer Weltmarke«; Museum für Verkehr und Technik, Telefon 2 54 84–0

9. – 17. 8. Dendriten-Ausstellung; Alte Dorfschule Lübars, 415 41 50

September bis November »Napoleon«; Zitadelle Spandau, Telefon 33 03–24 03

6. 9. – 19. 10. Majolika und Fayence des 16. bis 18. Jahrhunderts; Kunstgewerbemuseum, 266 29 02

9. 9. – 30. 11. Gewandausstellungen im japanischen Holzschnitt; Museum für ostasiatische Kunst, 83 01–3 82

11. – 28. 9. »Orangerie '86« – Deutscher Kunsthandel; Schloß Charlottenburg, Telefon 32 01–1

12. 9. – 2. 11. Christian Attersee; Nationalgalerie im Kunstforum der Grundkreditbank, Tel. 250 01 01

19. 9. 1986 bis 4. 1. 1987 »Zwischen Tradition und Aufklärung« – Deutsche Zeichnungen des 18. Jahrhunderts; Kupferstichkabinett, 83 01–2 28

24. 9. – 9. 11. Plakate aus Israel; Kunstbibliothek, Sonderausstellungshalle, 83 01–1

Theater

Bis 5. 7. und ab 25. 8. »Master Harold … und die Boys« (Fugard), »Wenn Du geredet hättest, Desdemona« (Brückner), »Es war die Lerche« (Kishon), »Drei alte Männer« (Benn), »Kaspar« (Handke); Vaganten Bühne Berlin, Telefon 312 45 29

Bis 6. 7. und ab 22. 8. »Eine linke Geschichte« (ab 16), »Voll auf der Rolle« (ab 14), »Jule, was ist los?« (ab 5), »Linie 1 – ein Musical« (ab 15); Grips Theater, Telefon 391 40 04

Bis 10. 7. und ab 20. 9. »Elvis – Stationen einer Karriere« (Regina Leßner); Berliner Kammerspiele, Telefon 391 55 43

Bis 11. 7. und ab 3. 9. »Nathan der Weise« (Lessing), »Die schmutzigen Hände« (Sartre), »Unverhofftes Wiedersehen« (Fischer), »Der Tod des Handlungsreisenden« (Miller), »Der Diener zweier Herren« (Goldoni), »Savannah Bay« (Duras), »Das weite Land« (Schnitzler), »Einfach kompliziert« (Bernhard), »Vom Teufel geholt« (Hamsun); Schiller-Theater, Telefon 319 52 36

Bis 11. 7. und ab 3. 9. »Der Talisman« (Nestroy), »Alberta und Alice« (Svevo), »Extremeties« (Mastrosimone), »Der Unbestechliche« (von Hoffmannsthal), »Wer hat Angst vor Virginia Woolf« (Albee), »Die Marquise von Arcis« (Sternheim), »Das große ABC oder Monsieur Topas« (Paniol); Schloßpark-Theater, Tel. 791 12 13

Bis 12. 7. und ab 13. 9. »Peter und der Wolf« (ab 3), »Geschichten von Oskar Nili« (ab 4), »Komm spiel mit mir« (ab 4), »Das ungeheuerliche Spiel« (ab 4), »Der kleine Prinz« (ab 5), Dr. Dolittle« (ab 4); Klecks-Theater, 693 77 31

Bis 13. 7. und ab 25. 8. »Leonardo hat's gewußt« (Topor), »Das Leben ist Traum« (Calderon); Freie Volksbühne, Telefon 881 37 42

Bis 31. 8. »Das Küssen macht so gut wie kein Geräusch«; Kleines Theater, Telefon 821 20 21

Bis Anfang September »Halb auf dem Baum« mit Heinz Drache; Theater am Kurfürstendamm, Telefon 882 37 89

Bis 13. 9. »Frühling im September« mit Anaid Iplicijan, Thomas Fritsch; Komödie, Telefon 882 78 93

Juli bis September »Ich bin's nicht, Adolf Hitler ist es gewesen«; Freie Theateranstalt Berlin, Telefon 321 58 89

1. – 6. 7. »Die schlesische Nachtigall«; Theatermanufaktur am Halleschen Ufer, Tel. 251 09 41

3. – 27. 7. »Offene Zweierbeziehung« (Rame/Fo); Renaissance-Theater, 312 42 02

11. – 26. 7. und ab 2. 9. »Ich denke oft an Piroschka«; Hansa-Theater, Telefon 391 44 60

12. – 27. 7. »Berliner ZauberZauber – Magie, Zauberei und Illusion; Theater des Westens, 852 20 58

Ab 20. 8. »Das Fenster zum Flur«, »Strahlende Zeiten«, »Die Flüchtungsgespräche«; Tribüne, Telefon 341 26 00

Ab Ende August »Ein heißes Herz« (Ostrowski); Schaubühne am Lehniner Platz, Tel. 89 00 23

Ab 4. 9. »California Suite« mit Harald Juhnke; Theater am Kurfürstendamm, Tel. 882 37 89

Ab 13. 9. »Nekrassow« (Sartre), »Brennende Geduld« (Skarmeta); Theatermanufaktur am Halleschen Ufer, Telefon 251 09 41

Ab 18. 9. »Hochzeitsreise« mit Anaid Iplicijan, Günther Ungeheuer; Komödie, 882 78 93

Festivals

Juni bis August »Berliner Sommernachtstraum«; Info: Verkehrsamt Berlin, Tel. 21 23–4

Bis 6. 7. »Ex Libris« – Berliner Bücherforum; Akademie der Künste, Telefon 391 10 31

4. und 5. 7. Drehorgelfest; In der City, Tel. 815 41 28

8. – 13. 7. »Bachtage Berlin 1986« – Friedrich II und Johann Sebastian Bach; Info: VDMK Berlin, Telefon 312 36 77

25. 7. – 3. 8. »Gauklerfest der Phantasie«; Los-Angeles-Platt, Info: Hotel Steigenberger, 2 10 80

14. – 17. 8. »Berlin goes Country« – Ein Festival, präsentiert von Nancy Wood und Band; Info: Hospes, Hotel Berlin KG,

Hardenbergstraße 29, 1000 Berlin 12, Telefon 2 60 08–0

21. – 24. 8. »Berlin-Musikfestival« – für Amateur-Blaskapellen; Kurfürstendamm, Infos: Ibis-Reisen München, Telefon 089/53 96 25

1. – 28. 9. »36. Berliner Festwochen«; Info: Berliner Festspiele, Telefon 25 48 90

Deutsche Oper Berlin
Telefon 34 38–1

1. und 2. 7. Ballettabend
1. 7. »Untergang der Titanic«; Foyer
3. und 6. 7. »Rigoletto«
4. und 5. 7. »Die Fledermaus«
26. und 30. 8. »Montezuma«
27. und 28. 8. »Orpheus in der Unterwelt«
29. 8. Ballettabend
31. 8. »Das Rheingold«
1., 9. und 18. 9. Ballettabend
2., 13. und 16. 9. Liederabend: Dietrich Fischer-Dieskau
3. 9. »Die Walküre«
4. und 6. 9. »Don Giovanni«
7. 9. »Siegfried«
8. und 22. 9. »Montezuma«
11. 9. »Zar und Zimmermann«
12., 15. und 17. 9. »Falstaff«
14. 9. »Götterdämmerung«
19. und 26. 9. »Die Meistersinger von Nürnberg«
20. 9. »Die Zauberflöte«
21. 9., vormittags »Zauber(flöten)reich Theater«
21. und 25. 9. »Aida«
24. 9. »25 Jahre Deutsche Oper Berlin« – Gala-Abend
27. und 29. 9. »La Bohème«
28. 9. Konzertante Aufführung »Die Bassariden«
30. 9. »Die lustigen Weiber von Windsor«

Operette und Musical
Theater des Westens, 312 10 22

Bis 6. 7. »Wiener Blut«
Ab 8. 8. »La cage aux folles«

Konzerte

Jeden Samstag, 18.00 Uhr Bach-Kantate oder Orgelvesper; Kaiser-Wilhelm-Gedächtniskirche,
Juli und August, jeden Sonntag, 17.00 Uhr »Sonntagsmusik«; Kaiser-Friedrich-Gedächtniskirche im Hansaviertel, Telefon 302 35 88
Juli und August, jeden Samstag, 20.00 Uhr und jeden Sonntag, 18.00 Uhr Sommerkonzerte: Eosander-Kapelle des Schlosses Charlottenburg, Telefon 817 33 64
4. 7. »Jazz in the garden«; Skulpturengalerie an der Nationalgalerie, 313 70 07 (Laur)

4. 7., 20.00 Uhr, 27. 7. und 31. 8. 11.00 Uhr Sommerkonzerte mit jungen deutschen Künstlern; Musikinstrumentenmuseum, Telefon 2 54 81–1 78

5., 12. und 19. 7., 20.30 Uhr Glienicker Schloßkonzerte; Telefon 792 75 27 (Sabine Wüsthoff-Oppelt)

5. und 6. 7. Radio-Symphonie-Orchester, Dirigent: Riccardo Chailly (Strawinsky, Bartók, Brahms); Großer Sendesaal des SFB, Telefon 302 72 42

6. und 13. 7., 18.00 Uhr Bläser-Serenaden; Hof des Jagdschlosses Grunewald, Telefon 817 33 64 (concertino)

6., 13. und 20. 7., jeweils 11.00 Uhr und 25. 7., 19.30 Uhr Konzert; Parkhaus im Englischen Garten, Telefon 39 05–22 34

16. 8. Sonderkonzert aus Anlaß des 200. Todestages Friedrich II – Sebon-Quantz-Ensemble; Schloßpark Glienicke, 2 54 89–0

23. 8. Sinfoniekonzert aus Anlaß des 200. Todestages Friedrich II – Chamber Orchestra of Europe, Dirigent: Claudio Abbado; Philharmonie, Telefon 2 54 89–0

26. 8. Sonderkonzert – Soirée Friedrich II; Musikinstrumentenmuseum, Telefon 2 54 89–0

27. 8., 20.00 Uhr Klavierabend – Daniel Barenboim; Waldbühne, Tel. 852 40 80 (concert concept)

3. 9., 15.00 Uhr Kurkonzert des Polizeiorchesters Berlin; Greenwichpromenade Tegel

16. 9. Utah Sinfonieorchester – Joseph Silverstein; Philharmonie, Telefon 825 63 33 (Adler)

21. 9. Kammerkonzert – Solisten des Radio-Symphonie-Orchesters Berlin; Staatsbibliothek, 302 72 42

27. 9. Berliner Barock-Orchester (Mozart); Hochschule der Künste, Telefon 805 14 18

Cabaret

Bis 30. 9., sonntags bis freitags 20.00 Uhr, samstags 20.00, 22.00 und 24.00 Uhr La vie en rose »Revue de Luxe«; Telefon 323 60 06

Bis 30. 9., mittwochs 22.00 Uhr La vie en rose »Brasilian night«; Telefon 323 60 06

Bis 30. 9., sonntags bis donnerstags 20.30 Uhr, Freitags und samstags 20.30 und 23.30 Uhr Prinz Georg Cabaret »Reise um die Welt«; Telefon 784 69 53

Ab 19. 8., 20.00 Uhr Kabarett Klimperkasten »Das hat uns gerade noch gefehlt«; Telefon 313 70 07 (Laur)

Ab 20. 8., mittwochs 20.00 Uhr Kabarett Klimperkasten »Sie wissen zwar nicht, was Sie

wollen – aber das mit Telefon 313 70 07 (Lau

Messen

30. und 31. 8. »8. Berliner Mode-Tage«; Info: Tel. 211 70 25 (Berliner Mode-Messe-GmbH)

31. 8. »Avantgarde-Schau«; Info: Telefon 211 70 25

3. – 7. 9. 24. Übersee-Import-Messe »Partner des Fortschritts«; Messegelände, 30 38–1 (AMK)

Unterhaltung

Bis 14. 7. »Deutsch-Französisches Volksfest«; Kurt-Schumacher-Damm, Reinickendorf, Telefon 313 83 60

Juli und August, sonnabends und sonntags 11.00 Uhr »Entdecken Sie die Kunst der Gärten« – Kombinierte Stadt-/ Schiffsrundfahrt mit Parkführung; Abfahrt: Meinekestraße Telefon 810 00 40/803 87 50 (Stern und Kreisschiffahrt)

Juli bis September, freitags und sonnabends ab 21.00 Uhr »Abendliche Rundgänge« des Spandauer Nachtwächters; Telefon 33 03 24 03 (BA Spandau)

5. 7., 19.00 Uhr »Sommernachts-Party« – Formationsfahrt der Fahrgastschiffe und Feuerwerk bei Musik und Tanz; Abfahrt: Wannsee/Bahnhof, Telefon 810 00 40/803 87 50 (Stern und Kreisschiffahrt)

5. und 6. 7., 16.00 bis 22.00 Uhr »Mit Rock in die Ferien 1986«; Freilichtbühne am Juliusturm, Telefon 33 03 24 03 (BA Spandau)

13. 7., 11.00 bis 12.00 Uhr »Sommer-Konzert« mit der Britischen Militärkapelle; An der Rehwiese in Nikolassee, Telefon 807 23 02 (BA Zehlendorf)

22. 7. – 3. 8., 22.00 Uhr, täglich außer 28. 7. »The Vicious Boys«; Tempodrom, Telefon 394 40 45

27. 7., 16.00 Uhr »Die große Revue« – frech, erotisch, kabarettistisch – »Das Kommödianten-Theater«; Freilichtbühne am Juliusturm, Telefon 33 03 24 03 (BA Spandau)

30. 7. – 17. 8. »Deutsch-Amerikanisches Volksfest«; Hüttenweg, Zehlendorf, Telefon 313 83 60

1. – 17. 8., 21.00 Uhr, außer montags »Le Quartuor/Paris« – ein Streichquartett besonderer Art (von Vivaldi bis Beatles); Tempodrom, Telefon 394 40 45

9. – 14. 8. Kinderzirkus Santelli; Tempodrom, Telefon 394 40 45

17. 8., 16.00 Uhr »Zurück aus den Ferien« – Ein bunter Nachmittag für Kinder und Erwachsene;

Freilichtbühne am Juliusturm, Telefon 33 03 24 03 (BA Spandau)

22. 8. »ARD-Wunschkonzert«; Halle 1, Jafféstraße, 30 31–0 (SFB)

23. 8. – 7. 9. »Kreuzberger festliche Tage; Katzbachstraße, Viktoriapark, Telefon 313 83 60

29. 8. – 7. 9. »Freie Scholle«; Waidmannsluster Damm, 313 83 60 (Schaustellerverband)

30. 8., 10.00 bis 18.00 Uhr »Spandauer Land- und Bauernmarkt«; Marktplatz, Spandauer Altstadt, Telefon 33 03 24 03 (BA Spandau)

31. 8., 11.00 bis 12.00 Uhr »Sommer-Konzert« mit dem Polizeiorchester Berlin; Im Schwarzen Grund, Dahlem, Telefon 807 23 02 (BA Zehlendorf)

3. – 13. 9., montags bis donnerstags 21.00 Uhr, freitags und samstags 22.00 Uhr Gordi Hutter – Kabarettistin und Clownin in ihrer One-Woman-Show; Tempodrom, Telefon 394 40 45

7. 9. »Film-, Musical- und Operettenmelodien« – Tanzorchester Spandau; Freilichtbühne am Juliusturm, Telefon 33 03 24 03 (BA Spandau)

7. 9. »Polizei-Musikschau 1986«; Deutschlandhalle, 30 38–1 (AMK)

13. und 14. 9., ab 13.00 Uhr »Mittelalterliches Burgfest auf der Zitadelle Spandau«; Telefon 33 03 24 03 (BA Spandau)

19. 9. – 19. 10. »Berliner Oktoberfest«; Jafféstraße, Charlottenburg, Telefon 313 83 60

20. 9., 20.00 Uhr »Skyline-Party« im Blauen Satellit; Kurfürstendamm-Karree, Telefon 313 70 07 (Laur)

25. 9., 20.00 Uhr Clown Dmitri – Urania, Telefon 313 70 07 (Laur)

24. – 28. 9. »Cirque de Barbarie« – Der einzige Frauenzirkus der Welt; Tempodrom, Tel. 394 40 45

25. 9. – 2. 10. »British Berlin Tattoo 1986«; Deutschlandhalle, 30 38–1 (AMK)

27. 9., 19.30 Uhr »Wannsee in Flammen« – Formationsfahrt der Fahrgastschiffe mit Feuerwerk; Abfahrt: Wannsee/Bahnhof, Telefon 810 00 40/803 87 50 (Stern und Kreisschiffahrt)

29. 9. Mireille Mathieu; Philharmonie, Telefon 852 40 80 (concert casse)

Sport

3. – 6. 7. Polo: »Internationales Poloturnier«; Maifeld, 304 55 51 (Landesverband der Reit- und Fahrvereine Berlin e.V.)

11. – 13. 7. Leichtathletik: »Deutsche Meisterschaften – Männer/Frauen«; Tel. 305 72 50

24. – 27. 7. Schwimmen: »Jugend-Europameisterschaften im Schwimmen, Springen, Kunstschwimmen und Wasserball«; Telefon 784 20 37

26. und 27. 7. Motorsport: »Internationales ADAC-Motorbootrennen; Greenwichpromenade, Tegel, Telefon 86 86–2 84 (ADAC-Berlin)

28. 7. – 1. 8. Segeln: »Internationale Deutsche Jugendmeisterschaft; Tegel, Telefon 861 61 51

5. – 10. 8. Tauchen: »4. Weltmeisterschaft im Flossenschwimmen und Strockontauchen; Telefon 603 45 33 (Herr Morzuch)

9. – 17. 8. Schach: 4. Internationales Schachturnier »Berliner Sommer '86«; Hotel Palace im Europa-Center, Telefon 775 45 38 (Berliner Schachverband e.V.)

15. 8. Leichtathletik: »ISTAF '86«; Olympiastadion, Telefon 784 47 04 (OSC Berlin)

30. und 31. 8. Kanu: »Internationaler Spree-Havel-Cup«; Regattastrecke Gatow, 433 60 21 (Landes-Kanu-Verband)

11. 9. Radsport: Internationales Profi-Radrennen »City Night Berlin«; Start und Ziel: Europa-Center, Telefon 334 40 31

13. 9. Radsport: »Internationale Berliner Rundstreckenmeisterschaft«; Telefon 784 54 53 (Berliner Radsport-Verband)

13. und 14. 9. Motorsport: »Internationales ADAC-Avus-Rennen für Motorräder«; Telefon 868 62 84 (ADAC-Berlin)

14. 9. Radsport: »35. Rund um Berlin« – Internationales Straßenrennen; Telefon 784 57 53 (Berliner Radsport-Verband)

23. – 28. 9. Bundeswettbewerb der Schulen »Jugend trainiert für Olympia« Telefon 305 30 20 (Senator für Schulwesen, Berufsausbildung und Sport)

27. und 28. 9. Kanu: »Internationaler Herbstslalom«; Zitadelle Spandau, Tel. 433 60 21

28. 9. Leichtathletik: »Berlin-Marathon«; Telefon 882 64 05 (SCC Berlin)

ZIRKUS · SHOW · MUSIK

Tempodrom:

Kinder, was für ein Zirkus

Ab 18. Juni gibt's wieder den Kinderzirkus im Tempodrom. Mit Clowns, Jongleuren, Zauberern und Artisten und den Tieren vom Tempodrom: Ziege Elsa, Walter der Esel, das Schwein Monika und der Berliner Mischlingshund Scotti. Dazu Musik der Tempodrom-»Hausmusikanten«.

Und in der Pause geht der Zirkus richtig los: 60 Kinder aus dem Publikum werden zu echten Zirkusleuten. Umziehen, Schminken, etwas einüben, noch die Clownnase aufgesetzt und dann raus in die Manege. Jetzt machen die Kinder ihr eigenes Programm!

Bis zum 3. Juli Montag, Dienstag, Donnerstag und Freitag um 10.30 Uhr, Mittwoch und Sonntag 15.00 Uhr.

Und noch etwas: Vom 9. bis 14. August gastiert der Kinderzirkus »Santelli« im Tempodrom, mit 20 Kindern aus der holländischen Zirkusschule.

Tempodrom. In den Zelten (Nähe Kongreßhalle). Telefon 030/394 40 45. Busse 69 und 83.

Travestie:

La Grande Revue

Voilà, die Milords aus Paris sind da! Fünf feine Herren in noch feineren Damenkleidern steigen in den Keller der »Stachelschweine« hinunter, um den Berlinern ein kabarettistisches wie musikalisches Bühnenbonbon zu präsentieren.

Ihre Show »Paris – Paris« ist atemberaubend, temporeich, witzig mit einem guten Schuß Ironie. Die Parodien, Pointen und Gags der Milords sitzen.

Eine tolle Show, die den Untertitel »Grande Revue« verdient. Der Zuschauer staunt, lacht und gluckst vor Vergnügen.

Berlin erlebt wieder tolles Travestie-Theater, vom 1. 7. bis 30. 8., Mo. bis Fr.: 19.30 Uhr, Sa.: 19.00 und 22.00 Uhr.

Die Stachelschweine, Europa-Center, Infos: Telefon 030/261 47 95.

Auch im bekanntesten Berliner Travestie-Theater, dem »La vie en rose«, geht jeden Abend eine farbige wie freche Show über die Bühne. »Revue de Luxe« und »Brasilian Night« heißen die neuen Programme.

Das Theater liegt ganz in der Nähe der »Stachelschweine«, im Untergeschoß des Europa-Centers.

Vorstellungsbeginn »Revue de Luxe« Sonntag bis Freitag 20.00 Uhr, Samstag 20.00, 22.00 und 24.00 Uhr; »Brasilian Night« Mittwoch 22.00 Uhr.

La vie en rose, Telefon 030/323 60 06. Europa-Center. U-Bahn Kurfürstendamm. Busse 9, 19, 29, 54, 60, 69, 73, 85, 90 und 94.

Tattoo:

Die Tower Bridge unter'm Funkturm

Auf dem traditionellen Tattoo zeigen die Briten in Berlin einen eindrucksvollen Ausschnitt aus der Geschichte und der Leistungsfähigkeit ihrer Royal Army.

In diesem Jahr inszenieren sie ihre musikalische Militärschau vor der Kulisse des viktorianischen Londons in der Deutschlandhalle.

Mit Glitter und Glanz ziehen Truppen Ihrer Majestät in die Arena ein, zum Beispiel die »Pearly Kings und Queens«, deren Uniformen über und über mit Perlen und Knöpfen besetzt sind.

Gefolgt von der Kavallerie des Hofstaates und den bekannten Gardisten im roten Waffenrock mit Fellmütze. In Massenszenen wird eine historische Schlacht nachgestellt, bei der sogar Elefanten mit spielen.

400 Musiker, darunter Jagdhornbläser und Dudelsackpfeifer, liefern die passende Musik für dieses glitzernde Spektakel.

Vom 25. September bis 2. Oktober jeweils 15.00 und 20.00 Uhr. Eintritt: 12,00 bis 40,00 DM. Deutschlandhalle. U-Bahn Theodor-Heuss-Platz und Kaiserdamm, S-Bahnhof Westkreuz. Busse 4, 10, 65, 69 und 94.

Dampferfahrten:

Leinen los!

Sommerzeit ist Dampferzeit in Berlin. Zwar stehen die weißen Fahrgastschiffe auf Spree und Havel schon lange nicht mehr unter Dampf, doch immer noch hat eine Reise durch die märkischen Seen-Landschaften etwas Romantisches.

250 Kilometer Wasserwege ziehen sich durch Berlin/West. Sie führen durch Wälder, Parks und Wiesen, aber auch mitten durch die Stadt.

Anlegestellen finden sich überall, von der Pfaueninsel bis zur Greenwichpromenade, von Kreuzberg bis Wannsee.

Neben den üblichen Rundfahrten bietet die Stern und Kreisschiffart bis 30. 8. eine Fahrt »Unter den Brücken von Berlin« an, vorbei an vielen Sehenswürdigkeiten der Innenstadt, die ein Kunsthistoriker näher erklärt. Abfahrt täglich 10.00 Uhr ab Schloßbrücke Charlottenburg.

Eine Schiffsreise durch die Geschichte Berlins veranstaltet die Geschichtswerkstatt e.V. Infos und Abfahrtszeiten unter Telefon 030/215 44 50 (mittwochs und freitags).

Informationen anderer Routen geben folgende Reedereien bzw. Veranstalter:
Riedel, Telefon 030/691 37 82,
Winkler, Telefon 030/391 46 93,
Dannenberg,
Telefon 030/431 30 91
(»Heiligenseer Sause«),
Laur, Telefon 030/313 70 07
(Mondscheinfahrten)
und viele andere (siehe Branchentelefonbuch unter »Personenschiffahrt«).

Musik:

Live is Live

Berlins Musik-Szene ist »still alive«! Ob Superstars auf der großen Bühne in der Deutschlandhalle oder Avantgarde-Jazzer im kleinen Keller des »Flöz« (Nassauische Straße 37), irgendwo in der Stadt ist immer Live-Musik angesagt. Hier ein paar Tips:

Fast täglich spielen bekannte Rock-Bands im »Quartier Latin« (Potsdamer Straße 96). Auch »Joe am Ku'damm« und »Joe's Bierhaus« am Theodor-Heuss-Platz bieten die ganze Woche über ein internationales Pop-Programm.

Im »Quasimodo« (Kantstraße 12a) gibt's jeden Tag guten Jazz, Funk oder Blues. Und in der »Eierschale« an der Podbielskiallee spielen meist Dixieland- und Oldie-Gruppen auf.

Absolut auf der Höhe ist das Musik-Programm in Berlins »Rock-Zirkus«, dem »Tempodrom«, In den Zelten (Nähe Kongreßhalle).

Wer auf Country steht, sollte im »Nashville« am Breitenbachplatz vorbeischauen, und den Blues bekommt man im »Blues-Café« (Körnerstraße 11). Südamerikanisch geht's im »Salsa« (Wielandstraße 13) zu, allerdings nur am Wochenende.

Etwas ab vom Schuß: die UFA- Fabrik in Tempelhof. Aber der Weg in die Viktoriastraße 13 lohnt sich. Fast täglich spielt hier eine Gruppe.

Auch in Deutschlands größter Diskothek, dem »Metropol«, treten in unregelmäßigen Abständen internationale Rockgruppen auf. Die weniger bekannten Avantgarde-Bands spielen eine Etage tiefer im »Loft«, beides Nollendorfplatz 5.

Weitere Live-Plätze sind: Ballhaus-Tiergarten (Rock), Perleberger Straße 62. KOB (Rock, Funk, Avantgarde), Potsdamer Straße 157. DaCapo (Diverse), Hauptstraße 150. Go in (Folklore), Bleibtreustraße 17.

Also dann, Ohren auf und reingehört!

Museen: Übersicht

Karlsruhe Programm Ständige Ausstellungen

Badisches Landesmuseum
Schloß, Telefon 135 65 14 / 65 42

Bodenfunde der Ur- und Frühgeschichte. Kunstwerke von der Antike bis zur Gegenwart. Skulpturen, Kunstgewerbe, Türkische Trophäensammlung, Volkskunst, Münzkabinett, Wechselausstellungen, Sonderveranstaltungen.
Geöffnet täglich (außer Montag) von 10-17.30 Uhr. Donnerstag durchgehend von 10-21 Uhr. Eintritt frei.

Staatliche Kunsthalle und Orangerie
Hans-Thoma-Straße 2 und 6
Telefon 135 33 55 / 33 70
Gemäldegalerie europäischer Meisterwerke vom 14. bis 20. Jahrhundert.
Im Hauptgebäude: Grünewald, Grien, Dürer, Cranach, Rubens, Rembrandt, Lorrain, Poussin, Chardin, Maulbertsch, C. D. Friedrich, Spitzweg, Feuerbach, Menzel, Mareès, Leibl, Thoma, Trübner.
In der Orangerie: Monet, Manet, Cézanne, Gauguin, Bonnard, Delaunay, Léger, Heckel, Kirchner, Kandinsky, Nolde, Klee, Moholy-Nagy, Ernst Tanguy, Miró, Dix, Fautrier, Dubuffet, Beckmann, Schultze, Wols, Antes, zeitgenössische deutsche Künstler.
Kindermuseum, Wechselausstellungen, Malstube.
Geöffnet täglich (außer Montag) von 10-17 Uhr, an Samstagen, Sonn- und Feiertagen auch bis 18 Uhr geöffnet. Hauptgebäude von 13-14 Uhr geschlossen. Eintritt frei.

Museum am Friedrichsplatz
(Naturkundemuseum und Vivarium)
Telefon 17 51 11
Schausammlungen mit Versteinerungen und Mineralien, Tiere der Vorzeit; Säugetiere und Vögel in Lebensgruppen, Insekten, Vivarium mit Kriechtieren, Lurchen, Fischen und niederen Tieren.
Geöffnet Montag und Mittwoch bis Freitag von 10-16 Uhr, Dienstag 10-20 Uhr, Samstag geschlossen, Sonntag 10-17 Uhr. Eintritt frei.

Pfinzgaumuseum Durlach und
Karpatendeutsches Museum
Karlsburg (Prinzessinnenbau)
Telefon 133 20 14
Durlacher Fayencen; Gemälde von Karl Weysser, Revolution 1848 bis 1849. Kulturgut der Deutschen aus der Slowakei.
Geöffnet Samstag von 14-17 Uhr, Sonntag von 10-12 und 14-17 Uhr. Eintritt frei.

Badischer Kunstverein
Waldstraße 3, Telefon 2 82 26
Wechselausstellungen zeitgenössischer Kunst, Jazzkonzerte, Diskussionen, ständige Ausstellung der Jahresgaben u.a.
Geöffnet Dienstag bis Sonntag 10-13 und 14-18 Uhr, Donnerstag auch 19-21 Uhr, Montag geschlossen. Eintrittspreise: Erwachsene DM 3,-, Schüler, Studenten DM 1,-, Mitglieder frei.

Prinz-Max-Palais
Karlstraße 10, Telefon 133 36 70/71
Stadtgeschichte. Ständige Ausstellung: Stadtgeschichte als Baugeschichte, Politik, Theatergeschichte, bürgerliche Kultur. Wechselaustellungen.

Städtische Galerie. Ständige Ausstellung: Badische Kunst seit Gründung der Akademie (1854) und Deutsche Kunst nach 1945. Mal- und Bastelraum, Wechselausstellungen, Vorträge, Diskussionen etc.
Geöffnet Dienstag bis Sonntag 10-13 und 14-18 Uhr, Mittwoch auch 19-21 Uhr. Führungen nach tel. Vereinbarung. Eintritt frei.

Oberrheinisches Dichtermuseum
Röntgenstraße 6, Telefon 84 38 18
Bilder, Handschriften und Bücher aus einem Jahrtausend dichterischen Schaffens am Oberrhein.
Geöffnet Montag bis Freitag 9-12 Uhr und 14-17 Uhr. Eintritt frei.

Rechtshistorisches Museum
Stephanienstraße 19, Telefon 84 25 25
4000 Jahre Rechtsgeschichte von Babylon bis Karlsruhe.
Geöffnet Samstag von 12.30-17 Uhr. Gruppenbesuche auch an anderen Tagen — nach telefon. Vereinbarung.

Freilichtmuseum ,,Diedelsheimer Mühle''
An der Pfinz, Karlsruhe-Grötzingen, Telefon 4 85 18
Ständig geöffnet, Eintritt frei.

Heimatmuseum Leopoldshafen
im ehem. Rathaus, Ortsteil Leopoldshafen, Telefon 7 08 50
Geöffnet Sonntag 10.30-12 Uhr und 14-16 Uhr. Eintritt frei.

Fahrzeugmuseum Marxzell
18 km von Karlsruhe, zwischen Ettlingen und Bad Herrenalb
Telefon (07 21) 4 28 17 oder 0 72 48 / 62 62
Ca. 200 historische Fahrzeuge und Modelle aller Art — sehenswerte Sammlungen vieler landwirtschaftlicher und technischer Geräte — u.a. Telephone, Grammophone, Radios, Photoapparate, Bildwerfer, Lampen usw. — Vorführung technisch-historischer Filme und Dias.
Geöffnet täglich von 10-18 Uhr oder nach Vereinbarung.

Landesgewerbeamt
Karl-Friedrich-Straße 17, Telefon 135 40 33
Ausstellungen, Führungen, Vorträge.
Geöffnet Montag bis Freitag 10-17 Uhr, Samstag 10-13 Uhr.

Galerie Hardy Schneider-Sato
Karlsruhe-Durlach, Zunftstraße 9, Telefon 4 25 74
Ständige Ausstellung: Künstler des 20. Jahrhunderts.
Geöffnet Dienstag bis Donnerstag von 16.30-18.30 Uhr, Freitag von 16.30-20.30 Uhr.

Verkehrsmuseum
Werderstraße 63, Telefon 37 44 35
(Lehrschau der Verkehrs- und Fahrzeugtechnik)
Geöffnet Mittwoch von 15-20 Uhr und Sonntag von 10-13 Uhr. Eintrittspreise: Erwachsene DM 3,-, Kinder DM 1,-. Gruppenbesuche nach Vereinbarung unter Telefon 56 26 22.

Mausoleum, Großherzogliche Grabkapelle
Hardtwald, nordöstliches Ende des Fasanengartens,
Telefon 2 49 51
Sarkophagen u.a. Großherzogs Friedrich I.
Geöffnet Mittwoch 15-17 Uhr, Sonntag und Feiertag 10-12 Uhr oder nach Vereinbarung. Eintritt: Erwachsene DM 0,50, Kinder DM 0,25.

Staatliche Majolika-Manufaktur Karlsruhe AG
Ahaweg 6-8 (hinter dem Schloß), Telefon 2 70 11
Verkaufsausstellung im Hause.
Geöffnet Montag bis Freitag 8-16.30 Uhr, Donnerstag auch bis 18 Uhr. Am 1. Samstag eines Monats von 9-13 Uhr.

MUSEEN IN ZÜRICH

Wohnmuseum Bärengasse

Bärengasse 22 (Eingang Seite Basteiplatz), 8001 Zürich, T 01/211 17 16, Postadresse: c/o Schweiz. Landesmuseum, Postfach, 8023 Zürich, Tram 2, 6, 7, 8, 9, 11, 13 bis Paradeplatz

Öffnungszeiten
Di-Fr, So 10-12, 14-17, Sa 10-12, 14-16 (Mo geschlossen). Mitte Juni bis Mitte Sept. über Mittag geöffnet

Eintritt frei

Dienstleistungen
Führungen, auch ausserhalb der Öffnungszeiten, nach Vereinbarung mit dem Landesmuseum, T 01/221 10 10 (80 Fr., Schulen gratis)

Übersicht
Die im 16. und 17. Jh. erbauten Wohnhäuser «Zum Schanzenhof» und «Zur Weltkugel» wurden, vom

Abbruch bedroht, 1972 um 60 m an den heutigen Standort verschoben und zum Museum umgestaltet. Das Ausstellungsgut stammt zum grössten Teil aus den Beständen des Landesmuseums. Das Wohnmuseum vermittelt anhand verschiedenster Interieurs einen Eindruck zürcherischer Wohnkultur von der Spätrenaissance bis in die Zeit des Biedermeiers (etwa 1650 bis etwa 1840). Im Untergeschoss Puppenmuseum Sasha Morgenthaler. Regelmässig Sonderausstellungen.

Wohnstube und Herrenzimmer 1. Hälfte 18. Jh

Zoologisches Museum

der Universität Zürich Winterthurerstr. 190, 8057 Zürich, T 01/257 49 11/13, Tram 9, 10 bis Irchel

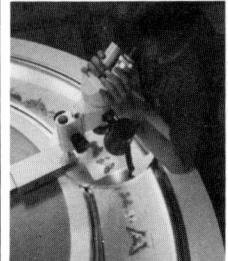

Öffnungszeiten
Di-Fr 9-17, Sa u. So 10-16 (Mo geschlossen)

Eintritt frei

Dienstleistungen
Führungen von Gruppen nach Vereinbarung, auch ausserhalb der Öffnungszeiten.

[1] Geöffnet Di-Fr

Übersicht
Wirbellose und Wirbeltiere der Schweiz. Seltene und ausgestorbene Vögel und Säugetiere der Welt. Embryonalentwicklung des Menschen. Möglichkeit, präparierte Insekten und lebende Wassertierchen mit Stereolupen zu betrachten. Vogel- und Amphibienstimmen ab Tonband. Diaprojektionsanlagen mit Bildwahl durch Besucher. Ständiges Tonbildschauprogramm mit wechselnden Serien. Filmvorführungen um 11 und 15 h. Informations- und Bücherecke, Sonderausstellungen.

Jacobs Suchard Museum

Sammlung zur Kulturgeschichte des Kaffees Seefeldquai 17/Ecke Feldeggstr., 8034 Zürich, T 01/385 12 83, Tram 2, 4 bis Feldeggstrasse

Gruppe mit Dame, Mohr und Kaffeetischchen. Modell von J. J. Kandler, Meissen, um 1740

Öffnungszeiten
Fr 15-18, Sa 10-16 (geschlossen an Sa vor Ostern und Pfingsten sowie zwischen Weihnachten und Neujahr)

Eintritt frei

Dienstleistungen
Führungen für Gruppen nach Vereinbarung. Benutzung der Bibliothek auf Anfrage.

Übersicht
Einziges Museum seiner Art: Es zeigt den Einfluss des Kaffees auf das kulturelle und gesellschaftliche Leben anhand der Sammlungsgebiete. Bibliothek: Quellen- und Sachliteratur zum Kaffee seit dem 16. Jh., ca. 2000 Titel. Porzellan, Silber, Graphik und Gemälde. Sonderausstellungen zu kulturellen, sozialen und wirtschaftsgeschichtlichen Aspekten des Kaffees.

Museum der Zeitmessung Beyer

Bahnhofstr. 31, Ecke Bärengasse, 8001 Zürich, T 01/221 10 80

Öffnungszeiten
Mo-Fr 10-12, 14-16, Sa 10-12

Eintritt frei

Dienstleistungen

Übersicht
Zeitmessinstrumente seit vorchristlichen Epochen: Schattenstäbe,

Sonnen-, Öl-, Sand- und Wasseruhren. Kuriose Zeitmessung: Eisenuhren. Schweizer Holzräderuhren 1550-1750. Uhren aus der Zeit Ludwigs XIV. bis zum Empire. Vollständige Reihe von Neuenburger Pendulen 1700-1850. Süddeutsche Renaissance-Uhren. Taschen-, Reise- und Emailuhren. Automaten. Uhren aus dem Fernen Osten. Marine-Uhren und Navigationsinstrumente.

Medizin-historisches Museum

der Universität Zürich
Rämistrasse 71 (Eingang Künstlergasse 16, Hauptgebäude der Universität, 4. Stock, Lift), 8006 Zürich, T 01/257 23 77 oder 257 22 98, Tram 6, 9, 10 bis ETH-Zentrum

Öffnungszeiten
Mi u. Do 14-17, Sa 10-12, Bibliothek (6. Stock): Mo-Fr 8-12, 13.30-17

Eintritt frei

Dienstleistungen
Führungen nach Vereinbarung, auch ausserhalb der Öffnungszeiten.

Übersicht
Ausstellung zur Entwicklung der Medizin und ihrer Spezialgebiete: Geräte, Illustrationen und Dokumente vom ausgehenden Mittelalter bis heute. Bedeutende Studiensammlungen. Wechselausstellungen.

¹) Etage E (Rondell)
²) Eingang rechts neben Haupteingang, Rämistrasse 71

Schwangerschaftskalender auf Schnupftabakdose, 1826
Ø 10.7 cm

27

Schweizerisches Landesmuseum

Museumstr. 2 (beim Hauptbahnhof), 8001 Zürich, T 01/221 10 10, Postadresse: Postfach, 8023 Zürich, Tram 4, 11, 13, 14 bis Bahnhofquai

Öffnungszeiten
Di-Fr, So 10-12, 14-17, Sa 10-12, 14-16 (Mo geschlossen). Mitte Juni bis Mitte Sept. über Mittag geöffnet. Lesesaal der Präsenzbibliothek Mo-Fr 8-12, 14-17

13

Eintritt frei
(Kinder unter 6 Jahren nur in Begleitung Erwachsener)

Dienstleistungen
Kostenlose öffentliche Führungen jeweils Di- und Do-Abend um 18 Uhr. Dauer etwa 1 Stunde. Sonderführungen für Gruppen ab 8 Personen, auch ausserhalb der Öffnungszeiten, nach Vereinbarung (80 Fr., Schulen gratis).

¹) Mit Stativ bewilligungspflichtig
²) Lift für bestimmte Abteilungen

Übersicht
Das Landesmuseum als schweizerisches Nationalmuseum zeigt die kulturelle Vielfalt unseres Landes mit Objekten teils internationaler Bedeutung von der Altsteinzeit bis zur letzten Jahrhundertwende. Hauptabteilungen: Ur- und Frühgeschichte/Waffen, Fahnen, Uniformen/Gold- und Silberschmiedearbeiten/Buntmetall, Zinn/Keramik, Glas/Textilien, Kostüme, Schmuck/Münzen, Medaillen/Siegel/Glasmalerei/Plastik/Malerei, Graphik/Möbel, Interieurs/Uhren/Musikinstrumente/bäuerliche Sachgüter, handwerkliche und gewerbliche Altertümer. In der Waffenhalle berühmtes monumentales Fresko «Rückzug der Eidgenossen bei Marignano» von Ferdinand Hodler 1899/1900. Reichhaltige Studien- und Spezialsammlungen, Kataloge und Fotosammlung auf Voranmeldung zugänglich. Präsenzbibliothek mit beschränkten Ausleihmöglichkeiten. Mehrere Sonderausstellungen während des Jahres.
Das in einem eigens von Gustav Gull errichteten historisierenden Repräsentationsbau untergebrachte Museum wurde 1898 eröffnet und gehört der Eidgenossenschaft.

Öffnungszeiten über Festtage

	1. Januar	2. Januar	Sechseläuten	Karfreitag	Ostersonntag	Ostermontag	1. Mai	Auffahrt	Pfingstsonntag	Pfingstmontag	1. August	Knabenschiessen	Bettag	24. Dezember	25. Dezember	26. Dezember
Kunsthaus	×	●	×	×	●	●	×	●	●	●	×	×	●	●	×	●
Rietberg, Wesendonck	×	●	×	×	●	●	×	●	●	●	×	×	●	●	×	●
Rietberg, Kiel	×	●	×	×	●	●	×	●	●	●	×	×	●	●	×	●
Sammlung Bührle	×	×	×	×	×	×	×	×	×	×	×	×	×	×	×	×
Strauhof	×	×	×	×	×	×	×	×	×	×	×	×	×	×	×	×
Graphiksammlung ETH	×	×	◖	×	×	○	×	○	×	○	×	◖	×	×	×	×
Museum für Gestaltung	×	○	×	×	○	×	×	○	×	○	×	×	◖	×	×	○
Museum Bellerive	×	●	×	×	●	●	×	●	●	●	×	×	●	●	×	●
Zinnfigurenmuseum	×	●	●	×	●	●	×	●	●	●	×	●	●	●	×	●
Spielzeugmuseum	×	×	×	×	×	×	×	×	×	×	×	×	×	×	×	×
Zunfthaus zur Meisen	×	●	×	×	●	●	×	●	●	●	×	×	●	●	×	●
Wohnmuseum Bärengasse	×	●	×	×	●	●	×	●	●	●	×	×	●	●	×	●
Landesmuseum	×	●	×	×	●	●	×	●	●	●	×	×	●	●	×	●
Archäologische Sammlung	×	×	×	×	×	×	×	×	×	×	×	×	×	×	×	×
Haus zum Rech	×	×	×	×	×	×	×	×	×	×	×	×	×	×	×	×
Staatsarchiv	×	×	◖	×	×	×	×	×	×	×	◖	◖	×	◖	×	×
Zentralbibliothek	×	×	◖	×	×	×	×	×	×	×	×	◖	×	◖	×	×
Thomas-Mann-Archiv	×	×	◖	×	×	×	×	×	×	×	◖	×	×	◖	×	×
Stadthaus	×	×	×	×	×	×	×	×	×	×	◖	×	×	×	×	×
Helmhaus	×	○	×	×	×	×	×	○	×	○	○	×	○	×	×	○
Jacobs Suchard Museum	×	×	×	×	×	×	×	×	×	×	×	×	×	×	×	×
Mus. der Zeitmess. Beyer	×	×	◖	×	×	×	×	×	×	×	◖	×	×	◖	×	×
Völkerkundemuseum	×	×	×	×	●	×	●	×	●	×	×	×	●	×	×	×
Indianermuseum	×	×	×	×	×	×	×	×	×	×	●	×	×	×	×	×
Mühlerama	×	×	×	×	×	●	●	×	×	×	×	×	×	×	×	×
Geol.-mineral. Sammlung	×	×	◖	×	×	×	×	×	×	×	◖	×	×	◖	×	×
Medizinhist. Museum	×	×	×	×	×	×	×	×	×	×	×	×	×	×	×	×
Paläontologisches Museum	×	×	×	×	×	×	×	×	×	×	×	×	×	×	×	×
Kulturama	×	×	×	×	×	×	×	×	×	×	×	×	×	×	×	×
Anthropolog. Museum	×	×	×	×	×	×	×	×	×	×	×	×	×	×	×	×
Zoologisches Museum	×	●	×	×	●	×	●	×	●	×	×	◖	×	●	×	×
Zoologischer Garten	●	●	●	●	●	●	●	●	●	●	●	●	●	●	●	●
Botanischer Garten	●	●	●	●	●	●	●	●	●	●	●	●	●	●	●	●
Stadtgärtnerei	●	●	●	●	●	●	●	●	●	●	●	●	●	●	●	●
Sukkulentensammlung	●	●	●	●	●	●	●	●	●	●	●	●	●	●	●	●

Alle Angaben ohne Gewähr.
Vergewissern Sie sich telefonisch bei den einzelnen Museen

● geöffnet
× geschlossen
◖ vormittags geöffnet
○ nur bei Ausstellungen geöffnet

Standesscheibe von Zürich, Arbeit des Lukas Zeiner, Zürich, 1501

13

Freiburg kennenlernen

Das Freiburger Ausflugs-Programm.

Hinweis: Der Treffpunkt für alle Rundfahrten, Führungen und Wanderungen ist die Freiburg-Information, Rotteckring 14. Der Veranstalter behält sich vor, bei ungünstiger Witterung oder zu geringer Teilnehmerzahl die Fahrt bis zu 24 Std. vorher abzusagen.

 = Gästeführer spricht deutsch

 = Gästeführer spricht englisch

Ⓕ = Gästeführer spricht französisch

Touren in und um Freiburg

Unser Angebot beschränkt sich nicht nur auf Freiburg: z.B. Colmar, Basel oder Straßburg, Schwarzwald, Vogesen und Alpen stehen zur Auswahl. Ob Kunstfahrt, Feinschmeckertour, Vergnügungsreise oder alles zusammen: Bei unseren Touren und Führungen sind Sie bestens aufgehoben.

Gästeführungen	DM
Gäßle, Bächle und das Münster	
Erwachsene	4,50
Kinder	2,50
Kunsthistorische Stadt-, Münster- oder Münsterbauhütten-Führung	8,—
Freiburg zum Kennenlernen, Busfahrt rund um die Stadt	
Erwachsene	10,—
Kinder	8,—
Stadt- und Münsterführung oder Führung in der Münsterbauhütte (diese Führung ist nur dienstags von 15.00-17.00 Uhr und donnerstags von 10.00-12.00 Uhr möglich) zu Fuß von 1,5-2 Stunden	
Dauer an allen Tagen	59,—
Fremdsprachen	68,—
Kunsthistorische Stadt- und Münsterführung zu Fuß täglich, Dauer 3 Stunden	
D:	78,—
GB, F:	90,—
Die Gruppenstärke sollte 25-30 Personen nicht überschreiten	
1/2 Tag Reiseleitung in Freiburg oder Umgebung an allen Tagen	94,—
Fremdsprachen	114,—
1 Tag Reiseleitung in Freiburg oder Umgebung an allen Tagen	152,—
Fremdsprachen	171,—
1 Tag Reiseleitung für Kunstfahrten	
D:	180,—

Land und Leute kennenlernen

Hier das Programm der „Freiburger Woche". Alle Fahrten werden in erstklassigen Bussen (Güte – 3-Stern) durchgeführt; von sach- und sprachkundigen Führern begleitet. Führungen im Fahrpreis inbegriffen! Eintrittsgelder nicht inbegriffen! Kinderermäßigung möglich. Passport! Bitte Reisepaß oder Personalausweis mitführen. In allen Orten, die fettgedruckt sind, ist ein Aufenthalt vorgesehen.

Montag
Gäßle, Bächle und das Münster

  Ⓕ

Ein gemütlicher Rundgang durch Freiburgs Altstadt mit Münsterbesichtigung.
Wir bieten einen Rollstuhlservice für Schwerbehinderte, ein Helfer des Malteserhilfsdienstes sowie ein Rollstuhl können auf Anfrage gestellt werden.
Erwachsene DM 4,50, Kinder DM 2,50
31.3. – 27.10.86, 10.00 Uhr
Dauer: 1 1/2 – 2 Stunden.

Schwarzwald von St. Peter zum Titisee

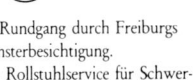

Freiburg — Gottertal — **St. Peter** (Besichtigung der von Peter Thumb 1724/57 erbauten Klosteranlage) — St. Märgen — Hinterzarten — **Titisee** (bekannter Kurort am Ufer des Gletschersees) — Höllental — Freiburg.
Erwachsene DM 21,—
Kinder DM 15,—
14.4. – 6.10.86
Abfahrt: 14.00 Uhr
Rückkehr: 18.30/19.00 Uhr

Führung in der Münsterbauhütte für Einzelreisende

Original Skulpturen vom Freiburger Münster und mittelalterliche Werkzeuge vermitteln einen Einblick in jahrhundertealte Handwerkstradition.
Termin:
Ganzjährig dienstags ab 7.1.86 in 14tägigem Wechsel in den Wochen 2, 4, 6, 8,... 50, 52, 10.00 – 12.00 Uhr,
maximal 25 Personen, keine Fremdsprachen.
Preis:
D: Erwachsene DM 8,—, Kinder DM 4,—

Kaiserstuhl – Land des Weines

Freiburg — Bötzingen — Vogelsangpaß — Oberbergen —Kiechlinsbergen — **Burkheim** (romantisches Städtchen mit Schloßruine) —Oberrotweil — Bickensohl — Achkarren — **Breisach** (Besichtigung des St.-Stephans-Münsters, bedeutender spätgotischer Schnitzaltar, Fresken von Martin Schongauer) — Ihringen — Freiburg.
Erwachsene DM 21,—, Kinder DM 15,—
1.4. – 27.5.86
Abfahrt: 14.00 Uhr
Rückkehr: 18.30/19.00 Uhr

Ins Land der Uhrmacher

  + Eintritt

Freiburg — Simonswäldertal — Hornberg — **Gutach** (Schwarzwälder Bauernhausmuseum am Vogtsbauernhof) — Landwassereck — Elzach — Freiburg.
Erwachsene DM 21,—, Kinder DM 15,—
3.6. – 21.10.86
Abfahrt: 13.00 Uhr
Rückkehr: 18.30/19.00 Uhr

Das Freiburger Münster (Kunsthistorische Führung)

Das Münster und der Münsterplatz als Spiegel des mittelalterlichen Lebens-, Kunst- und Kulturgeschichte Freiburgs, rund um das Münster.
Unserer Lieben Frau.
Ganzjährig ab 14.1.86 in 14tägigem Wechsel in den Wochen 2, 4, 6, 8 ... 50, 52,
10.00 – 12.00 Uhr,
maximal 25 Personen
Erwachsene DM 8,—, Kinder DM 4,—

Mittwoch
Gäßle, Bächle und das Münster

Ein gemütlicher Rundgang durch Freiburgs Altstadt mit Münsterbesichtigung.
Wir bieten einen Rollstuhlservice für Schwerbehinderte; ein Helfer des Malteserhilfsdienstes sowie ein Rollstuhl können auf Anfrage gestellt werden.
Erwachsene DM 4,50, Kinder DM 2,50
2.4. – 29.10.86, 14.30 Uhr
Dauer: 1^1/$_2$ – 2 Stunden.

Nachbarland Elsaß

  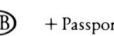 + Passport!

Freiburg — Kaiserstuhl, Vogelsangpaß — Sasbach — **Straßburg** (Münsterführung — Rundgang in der Altstadt — Kleine Rundfahrt: Universität — Europaparlament — Stadtgraben — „Schanz") — über die Elsässische Weinstraße — **Reichenweier** (mittelalterliches Weinstädtchen) — Breisach — Freiburg.
Erwachsene DM 33,—, Kinder DM 22,—
30.4. – 4.6.86
Abfahrt: 8.00 Uhr
Rückkehr: ca. 19.00 Uhr

Vom Schwarzwald zu den Alpen

  + Passport!

Freiburg — Basel — **Luzern** (Kaffeepause) — Sarner See — Brüningpaß — Brienzer See — Interlaken — **Grindelwald** (Aufenthalt am Fuß von Eiger, Mönch und Jungfrau) — Thuner See — **Bern** (Bundeshauptstadt der Schweiz — kleiner Rundgang) — Basel — Freiburg.
Erwachsene DM 40,— Kinder DM 26,—
11.6. — 24.9.86
Abfahrt: 7.00 Uhr
Rückkehr: ca. 19.30 Uhr

Donnerstag
Freiburg zum Kennenlernen

Busfahrt rund um die Stadt.
Erwachsene DM 10,— Kinder DM 8,—
1.5. — 2.10.86, 10.00 Uhr
Dauer: 1½ — 2 Stunden.

Nachbarland Elsaß

  + Passport!

Freiburg — Kaiserstuhl, Vogelsangpaß —Sasbach — **Straßburg** (Münsterführung — Rundgang in der Altstadt — Kleine Rundfahrt: Universität — Europaparlament — Stadtgraben — „Schanz") — über die Elsässische Weinstraße — **Reichenweier** (mittelalterliches Weinstädtchen) — Breisach — Freiburg.
Erwachsene DM 33,—, Kinder 22,—
12.6. — 23.10.86
Abfahrt: 8.00 Uhr
Rückkehr: ca. 19.00 Uhr

Markgräflerland zwischen Schwarzwald und Rhein

Freiburg — Hexental — Staufen (Fauststadt) — Münstertal — Haldenhof — Sirnitzpaß — **Badenweiler** (römische Badeanlage im Kurpark, Kurhaus zu Füßen der Burgruine) — Britzingen — **Sulzburg** (Besichtigung der ottonischen Klosterkirche St. Cyriak) — Bad Krozingen — Freiburg.
Erwachsene DM 21,—, Kinder DM 15,—
8.5. — 25.9.86, 14tägig
Abfahrt: 13.00 Uhr
Rückkehr: 18.30/19.00 Uhr

Malerischer Südschwarzwald

  + Eintritt

Freiburg — Schauinsland (ADAC-Bergrennstrecke) — Todtnau — **Bernau** (Gelegenheit zur Besichtigung des Hans-Thoma-Museums im Rathaus) — **St. Blasien** (bedeutendes Benediktinerkloster — eindrucksvolle Kuppelkirche des späten 18. Jh.) — Schluchsee — Titisee — Höllental — Freiburg.
Erwachsene DM 21,—, Kinder DM 15,—
1.5. — 2.10.86, 14tägig
Abfahrt: 14.00 Uhr
Rückkehr: 18.30/19.00 Uhr

Freitag
Gäßle, Bächle und das Münster

Ein gemütlicher Rundgang durch Freiburgs Altstadt mit Münsterbesichtigung.
Wir bieten einen Rollstuhlservice für Schwerbehinderte; ein Helfer des Malteserhilfsdienstes sowie ein Rollstuhl können auf Anfrage gestellt werden.
28.3. — 24.10.86, 10.00 Uhr und 14.30 Uhr
Dauer:1½ — 2 Stunden.

Mainau, Blumeninsel im Bodensee

 + Eintritt, Passport!

Freiburg — Höllental — Hüfingen — Überlingen — Wallfahrtskirche **Neu-Birnau** (Barockjuwel am Bodensee) Rundgang — **Meersburg** (alte Stadt am Bodensee) — Überfahrt mit der Bodensee-Fähre nach Konstanz Petershausen — **Insel Mainau** (herrliche Parkanlagen mit altem Baumbestand — barockes Schloß) — Konstanz — **Stein am Rhein** (eindrucksvolles Stadtbild mit bemalten Hausfassaden, kleiner Rundgang) — **Rheinfall bei Schaffhausen** (Europas mächtigster Wasserfall) — Bonndorf — Lenzkirch — Titisee — Freiburg.
Erwachsene DM 35,—, Kinder DM 24,—
2.5. — 3.10.86
Abfahrt: 8.00 Uhr
Rückkehr: ca. 19.30 Uhr

Nachmittag auf dem Schauinsland

Kombinierte Bus- und Seilbahnfahrt auf den Freiburger Hausberg (1284 m), Kaffee und Kuchen, Gelegenheit zur Rundwanderung, Blick vom Aussichtsturm auf dem Gipfel.
Erwachsene DM 18,—, Kinder DM 12,—
11.4. — 28.9.86
Abfahrt: 13.00 Uhr
Rückkehr: ca. 17.00 Uhr

Weinproben in der Münsterstube, Münsterplatz 15

Kommentierte Weinprobe für Einzelpersonen mit 6 Freiburger Weinen der Stiftungskellerei.
pro Person DM 9,50 (mit Bauernbrot)
Maximal 35 Personen.
16.5. — 10.10.86, jeweils Freitag 17.00 Uhr
Dauer: ca. 1 Std.

Samstag
Gäßle, Bächle und das Münster

Ein gemütlicher Rundgang durch Freiburgs Altstadt mit Münsterbesichtigung.
Wir bieten einen Rollstuhlservice für Schwerbehinderte; ein Helfer des Malteserhilfsdienstes sowie ein Rollstuhl können auf Anfrage gestellt werden.
Erwachsene DM 4,50, Kinder DM 2,50
ganzjährig, 10.00 Uhr
Dauer: 1½ — 2 Stunden.

Ein Nachmittag im Elsaß

 + Eintritt, Passport!

Freiburg — Breisach — **Colmar** (Führung durch das Unterlindenmuseum mit dem weltberühmten Isenheimer Altar und Rundgang durch die malerische Altstadt) — **Kaysersberg** (Geburtsort von Albert Schweitzer) — Breisach — Freiburg.
Erwachsene DM 21,—, Kinder DM 15,— ganzjährig.
Abfahrt: 13.00 Uhr
Rückkehr: 18.30 — 19.00 Uhr

Kunstspaziergänge

Ausgewählte Themen zur Kunst- und Kulturgeschichte Freiburgs
— Alter Friedhof
— Freiburger Brunnen
— Glasfenster des Münsters
— Kunst der Gegenwart
u. a. m.
Erwachsene DM 8,—, Kinder DM 4,—
Jeden 2. Samstag des Monats 10.00 Uhr
ab 18.1.86

Sonntag
Gäßle, Bächle und das Münster

Ein gemütlicher Rundgang durch Freiburgs Altstadt mit Münsterbesichtigung.
Wir bieten einen Rollstuhlservice für Schwerbehinderte; ein Helfer des Malteserhilfsdienstes sowie ein Rollstuhl können auf Anfrage gestellt werden.
Erwachsene DM 4,50, Kinder DM 2,50
1.5. — 2.10.86, 10.00 Uhr
Dauer: 1½ — 2 Stunden.

Auf Freiburgs Wanderwegen

Lassen Sie sich auf Freiburgs Wanderwegen die Schönheiten unserer Heimat zeigen. Es ist keine spezielle Wanderausrüstung, aber wetterfeste Kleidung und gutes Schuhwerk erforderlich.
Die Wanderroute wird je nach Jahreszeit und Witterung kurzfristig für Sie ausgesucht.
Erwachsene DM 5,—, Kinder DM 3,50 incl.
Führung durch einen unserer erfahrenen Gästeführer.
Jeden Sonntag in der Zeit vom 1.6. —28.9.86
Beginn: 11.00 Uhr
Rückkehr: ca. 17.00 Uhr

Freiburg ist Mitglied:

Hotel Zum Roten Bären

Selber kochen im ältesten Gasthof Deutschlands

Erbaut um 1120, ist das Haus „Zum Roten Bären", das seine Gastwirte seit 1311 lückenlos nachweisen kann, Deutschlands ältester Gasthof.

An einigen Wochenenden (Freitagabend bis Montagmorgen) wartet hier auf maximal 4–5 Hobbyköche ein ganz besonderes Erlebnis: Unter Anleitung des erfahrenen Küchenchefs dieses Hauses können Sie Ihre Kunst beweisen, dem Meister über die Schulter schauen.

Ihre Familie, Ihre Freunde sollten schon einmal im Restaurant Platz nehmen – serviert wird Ihr Menü! Natürlich bleibt neben dem „Dienst" in der Küche genügend Zeit, die Stadt kennenzulernen.

Ferien in der Altstadt
ist ein weiteres Angebot desselben Hauses, das direkt in der Freiburger Altstadt (Innenstadt ohne Autoverkehr) liegt. Auskünfte und Prospekte über die Freiburg-Information.

Leistungen:
3 Übernachtungen/Frühstück (Zimmer mit Bad/Dusche/WC)
1 Abendessen „Alemannisch angerichtet"
1 Abendessen „Aus der Jahreszeit"
1 Abendessen „Selbstgekocht"; unter Anleitung kaufen Sie die Zutaten für „Ihr Menü" selbst auf dem Wochenmarkt des Münsterplatzes.
Preis:
Pro Teilnehmer
575,– DM.   Code 1021
Für Begleitperson im Doppelzimmer inkl. aller Abendessen
300,– DM.   Code 1022

Termine:
17., 24. + 31.1.1986
14. + 21.2.1986
14., 21. + 28.11.1986
5.12.1986
16., 23. + 30.1.1987

Hotel Markgräfler Hof

Alles über badische Weine

Leistungen:
2 Übernachtungen mit Frühstück (Zimmer mit Dusche/WC).

Vorstellung des badischen Weinbaugebietes, Einführung in das deutsche Weinrecht und seine Bezeichnungen, Darstellung der Rebsorten mit Weinprobe, Fahrt ins Markgräflerland mit Kellereibesichtigung und Weinprobe bei deftigem Winzervesper, Überraschungsmenü in sieben Gängen, dazu große Weinprobe; gemütlicher Ausklang bei badischen „Wässerle" (still – aber tief …). Außerdem Stadtführung in Freiburg.
Preis:
Pro Teilnehmer
650,– DM.   Code 1023

Unter Weinkennern und Freunden guter Küche ist das kleine Hotel in der Altstadt keine unbekannte Adresse. Der Chef des Hauses, Hans Leo Kempchen, zählt zu „den" Weinkennern. Bei einer Mindestbeteiligung von neun, maximal aber 15 Personen führt er an den Wochenenden im März, Mai und Juli individuell gehaltene Weinseminare durch, die Liebhaber zu Experten machen. In Theorie und Praxis. Ein unbedingt Freiburg-typisches Gaumen-Erlebnis.

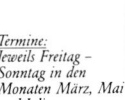

Termine:
Jeweils Freitag – Sonntag in den Monaten März, Mai und Juli.

PLANETARIUM
MANNHEIM

PLANETARIUM
MANNHEIM

KRAFTWERK
SONNE

vom 16. Juli – 21. September

KRAFTWERK SONNE

Text, Regie und Gestaltung: Planetarium Mannheim
Sprecher: Karin Schroeder und Peter Rühring
Die Sonne ist die unerschöpflich scheinende Quelle, die alles Leben auf der Erde mit Energie versorgt, ein gewaltiges Kraftwerk im All. Als scheinbar ruhig leuchtende weiß-gelbe Scheibe steht sie am Himmel. Doch der Schein trügt: gigantische Energieausbrüche toben an ihrer Oberfläche und schleudern unvorstellbare Mengen heißer Gase in den Weltraum.
Was wir heute über die Sonne wissen, verdanken wir nicht nur den Beobachtungen von der Erde aus. Die Röntgenaufnahmen, die von Weltraumsatelliten aus gemacht wurden, lassen ein ganz anderes Gesicht erkennen.
Die flammenden Polarlichter, die Störungen des Kurzwellenfunks, das Wetter, ja vielleicht sogar die Entstehung der Eiszeiten auf der Erde sind eine Folge der Sonnenaktivität, die sich in einem geheimnisvollen Zyklus verändert, der an den Sonnenflecken abzulesen ist. Wie dieses Kraftwerk seine Energie erzeugt und wie lange seine Vorräte noch reichen, erfahren Sie in unserem neuen Programm.
Sie erleben auch den Ablauf einer Sommernacht und lernen die wichtigsten Sternbilder dieser Jahreszeit kennen. Die Stellungen des Mondes und der Planeten werden gezeigt und erläutert. Sie erfahren, warum unser Nachbarplanet Venus – jetzt noch am Abendhimmel sichtbar – zum Jahresende vor Sonnenaufgang als heller Morgenstern erscheinen wird.

Dienstag, 5. August   19.30 Uhr

DER STERNENHIMMEL IM AUGUST

Referent: Dr. Wolfgang Wacker

Dienstag, 2. September   19.30 Uhr

DER STERNENHIMMEL IM SEPTEMBER

Luisenpark Mannheim
eine der schönsten Parkanlagen Europas.

HINWEISE FÜR UNSERE BESUCHER:

WIE ERREICHE ICH DAS PLANETARIUM?

Das Planetarium liegt genau an der Autobahnausfahrt Mannheim-Mitte (BAB A 656). Parkplätze: Gottlieb-Daimler-Str. (gegenüber ÖVA) oder Friedensplatz (Nähe Novotel bzw. ADAC). Straßenbahnlinien 36 und 47 bis Haltestelle „Planetarium" oder „Landesmuseum".

KARTENRESERVIERUNGEN

(0621) 402086 nur zu folgenden Zeiten:

Dienstag bis Freitag 10 bis 12.00 Uhr und 14 bis 16.00 Uhr. Samstag, Sonntag und an Feiertagen 13.30 bis 18.00 Uhr.

Rufen Sie bitte nur während der angegebenen Zeiten an. Wegen der Vielzahl der Anrufe ist unsere Telefonzentrale häufig überlastet. Bitte haben Sie Verständnis dafür, wenn Sie nicht sofort einen Anschluß bekommen.

Reservierte Karten können nur bis 30 Minuten vor Beginn der Vorführung zurückgelegt werden.

SCHULVORFÜHRUNGEN

Das Planetarium führt auch spezielle Vorführungen für Schulklassen der allgemein- und berufsbildenden öffentlichen Schulen durch. Diese Veranstaltungen finden vormittags statt. Der Eintrittspreis beträgt DM 2,- pro Schüler. Für die Astronomie-Grundkurse der Gymnasien findet in unregelmäßigen Abständen eine besondere Vorführung nachmittags statt. Für alle Klassenbesuche ist rechtzeitige Anmeldung unbedingt erforderlich. Nähere Auskünfte erteilt das Sekretariat.

SONDERVORFÜHRUNGEN

Für Gruppen ab 120 Personen sind Sondervorführungen außerhalb der üblichen Vorführungszeiten möglich. Auskünfte hierüber erteilt das Sekretariat.

SONSTIGES

Die Vorführungen beginnen pünktlich zur angegebenen Zeit, dauern ca. 50 Minuten bis 1 Stunde und finden bei jedem Wetter im vollklimatisierten Kuppelsaal statt. Nach Beginn der Vorführung ist kein Einlaß mehr möglich. Die Kasse öffnet jeweils eine Stunde vor Beginn der Vorführung.

PLANETARIUM MANNHEIM

Wilhelm-Varnholt-Platz 1 (Autobahnoval)
6800 Mannheim 1 · Telefon (0621) 402086
Direktor: Dr. Wolfgang Wacker
Sekretariat: Frau Veronika Johnson,
Frau Edith Otto-Lechler
Dienstag bis Freitag 10.00 bis 12.00 und 14.00 bis 16.00 Uhr

Öffentliche Vorführungen im Planetarium:

Dienstag	10.00 Uhr	15.00 Uhr		
Mittwoch		15.00 Uhr		20.00 Uhr
Donnerstag		15.00 Uhr		
Freitag		15.00 Uhr		20.00 Uhr
Samstag		15.00 Uhr	17.00 Uhr	19.00 Uhr
Sonntag		15.00 Uhr	17.00 Uhr	19.00 Uhr

Die Vorführungen beginnen pünktlich und dauern etwa 50 Minuten. Nach Vorführungsbeginn ist kein Einlaß mehr möglich. Die Kasse öffnet 1 Stunde vor Beginn der Vorführungen. Reservierte Karten werden nur bis 30 Minuten vor der Vorstellung zurückgehalten.

Eintrittspreise:

Erwachsene	DM 6,–
Auszubildende, Schüler, Studenten, Rentner	DM 4,–
Erwachsenen-Gruppe ab 15 Personen (pro Person)	DM 5,–

Für Gruppen ist rechtzeitige Terminvereinbarung (drei Wochen vor dem gewünschten Termin) unbedingt erforderlich. Für Kinder unter 6 Jahren sind die Vorführungen nicht geeignet.

SONDERREGELUNGEN

Während der Schulferien in Baden-Württemberg finden keine speziellen Vorführungen für Schulklassen statt. Dafür wird jeweils an folgenden Donnerstagen das öffentliche Programm gezeigt:

17. 7.   7. 8.
24. 7.   14. 8.
31. 7.   21. 8.

An den folgenden Tagen finden keine Vorführungen statt: Regelmäßig montags
Dienstag, 23. September (Programmwechsel)

ALTE AARE
Im Kanu durch den Urwald

Ein Urwald mitten in der Schweiz? Das klingt überraschend – aber fahren Sie einmal mit dem Kanu auf der Alten Aare und Sie werden staunen! Der Fluss ist hier nur wenige Meter breit und windet sich mit rascher Strömung durch ein dichtgrünes Baum- und Buschwerk. Gelegentlich versperren umgestürzte Bäume die Weiterfahrt – aber das Umtragen ist mit den leichten Booten kein Problem. Auf lautloser Fahrt werden Sie sich fühlen wie die Pioniere in den Wäldern Kanadas oder des Amazonas – hinter jeder Flussbiegung offenbart die reiche Pflanzen- und Vogelwelt neue Höhepunkte.
Für diesen Ferientag in der freien Natur brauchen Sie keine Ausrüstung und keine Vorkenntnisse. Im EUROTREK-Kanuzentrum in Aarberg stehen erstklassige Boote für Sie bereit. Ein erfahrener Instruktor wird Sie auf ruhendem Gewässer in die Paddeltechnik einführen, bevor Sie zu zweit oder zu dritt im Boot die Fahrt durch den Urwald antreten. Und am Ziel in Büren können Sie die ganze Ausrüstung wieder abgeben und per Bahn unbelastet die Heimreise antreten.

Ihr Programm
Täglich ab 09.30 bis 11.30 Uhr:

Treffpunkt beim Schwimmbad Aarberg. Von unserem Kanuinstruktor werden Sie mit Boot, Paddel, Schwimmweste und Helm ausgerüstet.
Anschliessend 50 Minuten Kanukurs auf ruhendem Gewässer (gestaute Aare): Einführung in die Grundtechnik des Kanufahrens. Dann starten Sie beim Schwimmbad Aarberg zu Ihrer Kanufahrt auf der Alten Aare nach Büren. Die reine Fahrzeit beträgt 3–4 Stunden, es bleibt Ihnen also genügend Zeit für Verschnaufpausen und ein gemütliches Picknick.
Von 16.00 bis 18.00 Uhr erwartet Sie unser Kanuinstruktor in Büren a.A., wo Sie Boot und Ausrüstung wieder deponieren können. Ein Tip für die Heimreise: Sie können in Büren die Flussfahrt fortsetzen und mit einem Motorschiff der Aareschiffahrt nach Solothurn oder Biel gelangen. Von dort gute Schnellzugsverbindungen in alle Richtungen.

Unsere Kanus
Die von uns verwendeten, aufblasbaren Kanadier-Wanderboote der Marke METZELER Indio bieten Platz für 2–3 Erwachsene bzw. 2 Erwachsene und 1–2 Kinder ab 9 Jahren. Seen und Flüsse, auch mit starker Strömung, sind sein Revier. Hart und fest aufgeblasen, bietet das Boot viel Raum, Bewegungsfreiheit und Bequemlichkeit beim Sitzen, Knien und Paddeln: Die elastische Bootshaut macht das Boot bruchsicher und unsinkbar selbst bei totaler Flutung. Dank diesen Sicherheiten ist das Indio ein ideales Freizeit- und Erlebnisboot für Sportler, Naturfreunde und Familien mit Sinn für nichtalltägliche Erholung.

Alle Teilnehmer werden mit Schwimmweste, Paddel und Kanuhelm (gegen tiefhängende Äste) ausgerüstet. Bei kühler Witterung können beim Kanuinstruktor Surfanzüge aus Neopren gemietet werden (Fr. 10.–/Tag).

Ihre persönliche Ausrüstung
Siehe Seite 2 in diesem Prospekt.

Saison 1987
Unsere Kanufahrten auf der Alten Aare werden täglich vom 9. Mai bis zum 18. Oktober durchgeführt.

Information und Reservation
Reservieren Sie sich Ihr Boot bitte frühzeitig, spätestens aber bis am Vortag um 17 Uhr. Adresse und Telefonnummer Ihrer Buchungsstelle finden Sie auf der letzten Seite in diesem Prospekt.

Ein neues Angebot von Eurotrek in Zusammenarbeit mit der
↔ SBB-Fitnessbahn

Treffpunkt und Abfahrtszeiten
In Aarberg beim Schwimmbad: Täglich von 09.30 bis 11.30 Uhr. Der Einführungskurs mit unserem Instruktor beginnt um 10, 11, 12 Uhr.

Hinreise
Am besten per Bahn über Bern–Lyss (umsteigen) nach Aarberg oder ab Bern HB mit Postauto nach Aarberg.

Rückreise
Ab Büren a.A. per Bahn oder Weiterfahrt mit Passagierschiff nach Solothurn oder Biel.

Preis pro Boot
Mietpreis **pro Boot** (für 2–3 Erwachsene oder 2 Erwachsene und 1–2 Kinder): Fr. 70.–

Inbegriffen:
Miete Kanu und Ausrüstung (Schwimmweste, Paddel, Kanuhelm), Einführungslektion durch Kanuinstruktor (50 Minuten), Kleidertransport zum Ziel in Büren a.A., Rücktransport der Boote und Ausrüstung.

Freiburgs Stadtgeschichte leicht gemacht

1120 Herzog Konrad II. von Zähringen siegelt die Gründungsurkunde der Stadt Freiburg noch während der Regierungszeit seines Bruders, Herzog Bertold III.

1146 Der hl. Bernhard von Clairvaux predigt in der Freiburger Kirche. Er wirbt für den Kreuzzug. An Stelle dieser Kirche wird später das Münster errichtet.

1200 Beginn des Münsterbaus.

1218 Der letzte Zähringer Herzog, Bertolt V., der Bern gründete, stirbt kinderlos. Er wird im romanischen, schon fertiggestellten Teil des Münsters beigesetzt.

Bertolds Neffe, Graf Egino von Urach, erbt die Herrschaft Freiburg und nennt sich Graf von Freiburg.

1248 Freiburg erhält eine neue Stadtverfassung.

1250 Beginn des gotischen Münsterbaus.

1258 Freiburg erhält aus den Silberbergwerken am Schauinsland und im Münstertal Silber für die Münze.

Die „Hosanna", die älteste Glocke, wird auf den Münsterturm gebracht, der bereits bis zum Glockenstuhl gebaut ist. Diese Glocke gehört heute noch zum Münstergeläute.

1303 Erste Erwähnung eines Rathauses, der heutigen „Gerichtslaube".

1349 Der Pest erliegt ein großer Teil der Bevölkerung.

1368 Freiburg zahlt dem ungeliebten Herrscher Graf Egino III., dessen Burg sie zerstört hatten, 15 000 Mark Silber, wird so den Grafen los und begibt sich in den Schutz des Hauses Habsburg.

1378 Das historische Kaufhaus auf dem Münsterplatz wird erwähnt. Die Stadt erhält ein weiteres Marktrecht.

1386 In der Schlacht bei Sempach gegen die Eidgenossen, an der die Freiburger unter den Habsburgern teilnehmen mußten, fallen Ritter Martin Malterer und der größte Teil des Freiburger Adels.

1415 Der vom Konstanzer Konzil abgesetzte Papst Johannes XXIII. findet im Predigerkloster ehrenvolle Aufnahme. Er

wird später bei der Weiterreise in Breisach gefangengenommen.

1457 Herzog Albrecht VI. stiftet die Freiburger Universität. Erste österreichische Universitätsgründung.

1473 Kaiser Friedrich III. und sein 14jähriger Sohn Maximilian, der später Kaiser wurde, besuchen die Stadt. In einer Edelsteinschleiferei wird Maximilian der Schnabelschuh von einer Poliermaschine abgerissen.

1490 Maximilian besucht als König Freiburg. Er ordnet das Finanz- und Verwaltungswesen neu. Eisen- und Salzhandel kommen in die Regie der Stadt.

1498 Reichstag zu Freiburg. Maximilian I., sein Sohn Philipp der Schöne, die Reichsfürsten und viel Gesinde weilen in der Stadt. Das Kornhaus ist vollendet, es dient Tanz und festlichen Veranstaltungen. In der Gerichtslaube wird der Reichstag eröffnet. Maximilian und seine Gemahlin, Maria Bianka Sforza, wohnen im Predigerkloster.

Holzschnitt 1504

1507 Der Freiburger Cosmograph Martin Waldseemüller und der Elsässer Humanist Mathias Ringmann widmen Kaiser Maximilian ein neues Kartenwerk, auf dem erstmals der neue Weltteil mit dem Namen „America" bezeichnet wird.

1513 Der Turm und der Chor des Münsters sind vollendet. Das Freiburger Münster ist damit

der einzige Sakralbau am Oberrhein, der noch in der gotischen Epoche vollendet wurde.

1516 Hans Baldung Grien vollendet das Gemälde für den Hochaltar des Münsters.

1529 Das Basler Domkapitel flüchtet der Reformation wegen aus Basel und findet in Freiburg Asyl. Es wird ihm das Stürtzelsche Haus zugewiesen, das seitdem „Baslerhof" genannt wird. Auch der Humanist Erasmus von Rotterdam kommt von Basel her nach Freiburg und wohnt im „Haus zum Walfisch", heute Sparkasse.

1532 Das Kaufhaus auf dem Münsterplatz wird vollendet.

1564 An der Pest sterben etwa 2000 Einwohner. Der Hexenwahn nimmt seinen Anfang.

1620 Die Jesuiten übernehmen die Universität.

1632 Dreißigjähriger Krieg, die Schweden ziehen in Freiburg ein. Freiburg hat nur noch 2000 Einwohner. Die Stadt wird bis 1648 fünfmal belagert und umkämpft.

1677 Französische Truppen nehmen Freiburg ein. Die Stadt wird unter Ludwig XIV. französisch. Festungsbaumeister Vauban läßt die Mauern der Zähringer Stadt schleifen, legt Vororte nieder und baut Freiburg zur Festung um. Es ist die größte Zerstörung und Veränderung der Stadt in ihrer ganzen Geschichte. Das Schloß wird in die Festung einbezogen, in den neuen Bauten am Schloßberg sind bis zu 5000 Soldaten kaserniert.

1681 Ludwig XIV. besucht mit dem Dauphin und dem ganzen Hofstaat die Stadt und wohnt im Basler Hof. Die Universität wird nach französischem Muster eingerichtet.

1698 Freiburg wird wieder österreichisch.

1754 Die Stadt ist in größter Armut. Nur noch 3000 Menschen leben hier, meist Frauer. In den Kriegen der letzten 50 Jahre wird Freiburg mehrmals von den Franzosen besetzt, die Festungswerke der Stadt und auf dem Schloßberg werden geschleift.

1770 Die Tochter Kaiserin Maria Theresias, Maria Antonia, kommt auf ihrem Brautzug nach Freiburg. Die Friedhofsmauer um das Münster wird abgerissen, alle Häuser müssen weiß getüncht werden. Antonia heiratet den Dauphin von Frankreich und wird später als Königin Maria Antoinette mit Ludwig XVI. bei der französischen Revolution hingerichtet.

1777 Kaiser Joseph II. wohnt im Gasthaus „Zum Storchen", das später „Römischer Kaiser" hieß. Die Straße wurde in „Kaiserstraße" umbenannt, heute „Kaiser-Joseph-Straße".

1797 Napoleon steigt im Gasthaus „Zum Mohren" ab.

1798 Freiburg kommt in den Besitz des Herzogs Herkules III. von Modena, die Franzosen besetzen 1800 die Stadt erneut.

1803 Freiburg wird Sitz einer „Breisgauisch-Ortenauischen Regierung" unter den Herren von Modena. „Regierungspräsident" wird Hermann von Greiffenegg.

1805 Freiburg wird mit dem Breisgau Teil des von Napoleon geschaffenen Großherzogtums Baden.

1813/14 Im Zuge der Befreiungskriege marschieren die Heere der Verbündeten, vor allem Russen, durch die Stadt. Zar Alexander I., Kaiser Franz II., König Friedrich Wilhelm von Preußen weilen in der Stadt. Die Truppen ernähren sich aus den Beständen der Stadt, des Landes, der Bürger, Teuerung und Not sind die Folgen.

1818 Baden erhält eine Verfassung. Freiburg verbleibt beim Großherzogtum.

1821 Freiburg wird Sitz des Bistums, das bisher in Konstanz war. Es wurde auch Sitz der neuen Oberrheinischen Kirchenprovinz.

1823 Das Theater wird vom Kornhaus in das Augustinerkloster verlegt.

1845 Der Bahnhof ist fertig. Die Linie Freiburg–Offenburg wird in Betrieb genommen.

1848/49 Badische Revolution. Preußische Truppen besetzen

die Stadt und erschießen Max Dortu und zwei seiner Anhänger.

1850 Die erste Gasfabrik wird eröffnet, die freiwillige Feuerwehr wird gegründet.

1866 Freiburg wird Garnisonsstadt. Das Predigertor wird abgebrochen, die Karlskaserne dort gebaut.

1876 Das Siegesdenkmal, das an den deutsch-französischen Krieg 1870/71 erinnert, wird im Beisein von Kaiser Wilhelm I. eingeweiht.

1887 Die Höllentalbahn zwischen Freiburg und Neustadt wird eröffnet.

1901 Das Martinstor und Schwabentor erhalten hohe Aufbauten.

1914 Weltkrieg. Feindliche Luftschiffe und Flugzeuge werfen bis 1918 immer wieder Bomben über Freiburg ab, die Todesopfer fordern.

1918 Auf dem Karlsplatz wird zur Revolution aufgerufen. Baden wird Republik.

1920 Der Freiburger Rechtsanwalt Konstantin Fehrenbach wird Reichskanzler.

1921 Dr. Joseph Wirth, Freiburger, wird Reichskanzler.

1925 Erstes Bergrennen durch den ADAC am Schauinsland.

1926 Der Freiburger Sender beginnt sein Programm.

1934 Der Bahnhof Wiehre wird eröffnet.

1940 Am 10. Mai wird Freiburg von deutschen Flugzeugen irrtümlich bombardiert. 57 Tote.

1943 Die seit 1784 bestehende „Freiburger Zeitung" muß ihr Erscheinen einstellen.

1944 Luftangriff am 27. November. Etwa 3000 Tote, die Altstadt und andere Gebiete werden zerstört.

1945 Am 21. April besetzen die Franzosen die Stadt. Am 5. September erscheint wieder eine Zeitung.

1946 In Freiburg wird eine Regierung und Verwaltung für das Land Baden eingerichtet, das im Territorium der französisch besetzten Zone Badens gegründet wird.

1948 Erzbischof Dr. Conrad Gröber stirbt am 14. Februar; Nachfolger wird Dr. Wendelin Rauch.

1952 Land Baden-Württemberg. Die Badische Landesregierung in Freiburg wird aufgehoben.

1956 Oberbürgermeister Dr. Wolfgang Hoffmann stirbt. Nachfolger wird Dr. Joseph Brandel.

1957 500-Jahr-Feier der Albert-Ludwig-Universität. Sie ist die älteste österreichische Universität.

1959 König Ibn Saud weilt mit seinem Hofstaat in Freiburg.

1962 Oberbürgermeister Dr. Brandel stirbt. Nachfolger wird Dr. Eugen Keidel.

1965 Der neue Bertoldsbrunnen wird aufgestellt.

1970 850-Jahr-Jubiläum der Stadt in Anwesenheit von Bundespräsident Dr. Heinemann.
Dr. Eugen Keidel wird mit 78,1% aller Stimmen erneut zum Oberbürgermeister gewählt.

1974 Die Gebietsreform ist abgeschlossen. Die Gemeinden Lehen, Hochdorf, Munzingen, Tiengen, Opfingen, Waltershofen, Ebnet und Kappel werden Freiburger Stadtteile.

1978 85. Deutscher Katholikentag in Freiburg.

1982 Oberbürgermeister Dr. Keidel tritt nach 20jähriger Amtszeit in den Ruhestand. Zum Nachfolger wählen die Freiburger Dr. Rolf Böhme.

1983 Die Stadtbahn, das leistungsfähige öffentliche Verkehrsmittel, das westliche Stadtteile mit dem Stadtkern verbindet, wird eröffnet.

1984 Freiburg führt als erste deutsche Stadt eine Umweltschutzkarte mit verbilligtem Tarif bei Benutzung der öffentlichen städtischen Verkehrsmittel ein.

1985 Ministerpräsident Lothar Späth sagt der Freiburger Regio-Gesellschaft, der deutschen Partnerin der Regio-Institutionen im Elsaß und der Nordwestschweiz, die Unterstützung des Landes zu.

DIE SCHWEIZ IM SPIEGEL IHRER MARKEN

Wappen von Schwyz — Schweizerische Landesausstellung 1939 — Dunant, Gründer des Roten Kreuzes — Auslandschweizerorganisation

Das Hoheitszeichen

Das weisse Schweizerkreuz im roten Feld geht auf die Notwendigkeit zurück, in kriegerischen Auseinandersetzungen über ein gemeinsames Kennzeichen zu verfügen. So begannen die Einzelkrieger weisse Leinenkreuze über ihren sonst verschiedenen Rüstungen zu tragen und auf die Feldzeichen wurden weisse Kreuze geheftet. Erst 1815 setzte die Tagsatzung, das «Parlament» der alten Schweiz, rechtskräftig ein schweizerisches Hoheitszeichen und Staatssiegel fest: das freischwebende weisse Kreuz im roten Feld, umrahmt von 22 kantonalen Wappen als Ausdruck des Ausgleichs zwischen der angestrebten zentralistischen Staatsform und dem geschichtlich gewachsenen Föderalismus. Vom Stand Schwyz ist im 14. Jahrhundert der Name «Schwyzer», Schriftdeutsch «Schweizer», auf die übrigen Bundesgenossen übertragen worden. Die 1864 beschworene Genfer Konvention zum Schutze der Kriegsverwundeten und -gefangenen wählte das Schweizer Wappen in umgekehrter Farbengebung: das rote Kreuz im weissen Feld.

Die Geschichte

Der schweizerische Staat ist im Laufe des 15. Jahrhunderts aus verschiedenen Bündnissystemen von Reichsstädten und Reichsländern entstanden. Den Kern bildeten die drei Waldstätte Uri, Schwyz und Unterwalden, deren Bündnis zur Wahrung gemeinsamer Interessen 1291 fassbar ist. Städte und Länder bauten ihre politische Selbständigkeit aus in vielen kriegerischen Auseinandersetzungen mit den Fürstenstaaten Habsburg-Oesterreich, Mailand und Savoyen. 1515 zwang eine Niederlage in den Italienkriegen zu Marignano und kurz darauf die Reformation die «Eidgenossen» zur Besinnung: es galt, im Lande den innern Frieden zu erhalten und die Neutralität nach aussen zu fördern. Das 17. Jahrhundert brachte in den Städten den Gewerbefleiss und eine frühe Industrie zur Blüte. Nach dem Wienerkongress von 1815 wurde der Staatenbund der Eidgenossen endgültig zum Bund von 22 selbständigen Kantonen. In der Bundesverfassung von 1848 festigte sich dieser zum heutigen zentralistischen Bundesstaat.

Kreuzberge — Silsersee — Walliser Dorf — Das geistige Leben, dargestellt durch eine symbolische Gruppe

Land und Leute

Das Binnenland Schweiz liegt in der Mitte Westeuropas. Die grossen Flüsse Rhone und Rhein entspringen am Gotthardmassiv. Die Bodenfläche der Schweiz beträgt rund 42 000 km2. Beinahe ein Viertel des Landes ist nicht kultivierbarer Boden. Das Klima ist allen europäischen Einflüssen ausgesetzt. Die Vegetation ist vielfältig und reich, von Mittelmeerpflanzen bis zu arktischen Arten. In der Schweiz leben über 6 Millionen Menschen in sprachlich-kultureller, konfessioneller und politischer Vielfalt. Die Hauptstadt, meist Bundesstadt genannt, heisst Bern und zählt 160 000 Einwohner. Arm an Raum, arm an weltpolitischer Macht und arm an Urprodukten ist der einzige Reichtum der Schweiz Arbeit, Leistung und Qualität. Erst gegen Ende des 19. Jahrhunderts hat das Land einen wachsenden Wohlstand erworben. Wie in andern Ländern ist im Gefolge dieses Strebens nach «Fortschritt» auch in der Schweiz die Nutzung des Bodens und die Erhaltung der Naturreichtümer zu einem Problem angewachsen.

Vier Sprachen

Die Landessprachen verteilen sich wie folgt: deutsch 64,9%, französisch 18,1%, italienisch 11,9%, rätoromanisch 0,8% und andere 4,3%. Bis ins 19. Jahrhundert stellte die Viersprachigkeit keine besonderen Probleme, einmal weil kein Einheitsstaat vorhanden war und weil die sprachlichen Verschiedenheiten auch in den Untertanengebieten respektiert wurden. Erst die stärkere Zusammenfassung des Staatenbundes in der Bundesverfassung von 1848 führte zur Notwendigkeit der Schaffung eines eidgenössischen Sprachenrechts: Die Gleichberechtigung der drei verbreitetsten Sprachen wurde anerkannt. So setzte sich in allen gemeineidgenössischen Beziehungen der Respekt vor den sprachlichen Minderheiten durch. Etwaige Schwierigkeiten konnten in der Regel durch gegenseitige Toleranz gelöst werden. Immer ist ja das friedliche Zusammenleben von Gemeinschaften gewährleistet, wenn es sich an den Entfaltungsmöglichkeiten des Einzelnen orientiert und von möglichst vielen getragen wird.

»Freibrief« für Hamburg

Hafengeburtstag am 7. Mai

Ihrem Hafen verdanken die Hamburger viel, wenn nicht alles. Ohne diesen Hafen, der das Gesicht der Stadt prägt, wäre Hamburg nie zu dem geworden, was es heute ist: eine internationale und weltoffene Wirtschafts-, Handels- und Kulturmetropole im Herzen Europas.

Der Hamburger Hafen gehört zur Spitzengruppe der europäischen Umschlagplätze und zu den zwölf bedeutendsten Container-Häfen der Welt. Rund 15.000 Seeschiffe löschen und laden hier jährlich rund 60 Mio. Tonnen Güter – darunter viele Waren des täglichen Bedarfs: Kaffee aus Kolumbien, Hifi-Anlagen aus Japan, Obst aus Neuseeland, Fleisch aus Argentinien, Spielzeug aus Hongkong, Orangen aus Marokko u.v.m.

Dennoch basiert Hamburgs wirtschaftliche Potenz heute nicht mehr allein auf seiner Funktion als Seehafen. Andere Branchen – Banken und Versicherungen, Flugzeugbau und Elektrotechnik, Presse, Funk und Fernsehen – sind hinzugekommen. Aus der Hafenstadt Hamburg wurde eine Weltstadt mit Hafen. Trotzdem

gilt: Auch in Zukunft bleibt der Hafen, der direkt und indirekt etwa 140.000 Arbeitsplätze sichert, eine tragende Säule der Hamburger Wirtschaft.

Daß die Hamburger wissen, was sie ihrem Hafen schuldig sind, demonstrieren sie alljährlich mit viel Elan und fröhlicher Ausgelassenheit. Die dreitägigen Feiern zum Hafengeburtstag um den 7. Mai erinnern an das Jahr 1189, als Kaiser Friedrich Barbarossa den Hamburgern die später in einem »Freibrief« dokumentierten Zoll- und Abgabenfreiheit auf der Unterelbe einräumte. Und spätestens mit diesem Datum begann der wirtschaftliche Aufstieg des Hafens und der Stadt.

Der Freihafen

Milliardenwerte hinter dem Zollzaun

Reichskanzler Otto v. Bismarck gab sich gönnerhaft: Er wolle, so verkündete er 1881, nicht derjenige sein, der »die erste Handelsstadt Deutschlands schädigt«. Allerdings: Gerade Bismarck war es, der den »preußischen Zollring« um die Freihandelsstadt Hamburg immer enger zog und sie konsequent zum Beitritt in den Deutschen Zollverein drängte. Einzige Konzession: Die Stadt Hamburg erhielt durch den Zollanschlußvertrag mit dem Deutschen Reich (25. Mai 1881) einen Freihafen.

Die notwendigen Bauarbeiten dauerten sechs Jahre. Am 15. Oktober 1888 war es soweit: Der Hamburger Freihafen wurde seiner Bestimmung übergeben. Die anfangs in der Hansestadt verbreiteten Befürchtungen, der Wandel von der »Freihafenstadt« zur »Stadt mit einem Freihafen« könne sich nachteilig für den Handel auswirken, bewahrheiteten sich jedoch nicht. Im Gegenteil: Hamburg entwickelte sich zeitweise zum drittgrößten Hafen der Welt.

Der Freihafen hat bis heute nichts an seiner Attraktivität eingebüßt. Das Geschäft floriert, denn der Güterumschlag ist frei von jeder zollrechtlichen Beschränkung. Ohne Formalitäten und Abgaben können

innerhalb des 16 qkm großen Freihafengebietes alle Waren ungehindert gelagert, gehandelt, transportiert, bemustert oder einer besonderen und fachgerechten Behandlung unterzogen werden.

Außerdem ist im »alten Freihafen« – durch einen Seitenarm der Elbe vom 1910 neu hinzugekommenen Teil »Waltershof« getrennt – die Be- und Verarbeitung von Waren erlaubt. So werden z. B. Tee, Tabak und Kaffee in Hamburg erst »genießbar« gemacht – genauer gesagt: einem veredelnden Reifeprozeß unterzogen.

Im Freihafen lagert heute alles, was international gehandelt wird – vom Rohkaffee aus Brasilien bis zum Computer, vom Motorrad aus Japan bis zur echten Orientbrücke. Im Teppichgeschäft gilt Hamburg als bedeutendster Lager- und Umschlagplatz der Welt. Geschätzter Wert der gelagerten Teppiche: mehr als eine Milliarde Mark.

Namhafte internationale Unternehmen verfügen über riesige Auslieferungslager im Freihafen. Vorteil bei Bestellungen: Die gewünschte Ware muß nicht erst aus Übersee herangeschafft werden.

Erst wenn Waren den Freihafen verlassen, werden Zölle erhoben. Zur Sicherung der Zollinteressen des Bundes ist das gesamte Freihafengelände von einem 3 Meter hohen Zaun umgeben. An der fast 30 km langen Freihafengrenze gibt es 39 Zolldurchlässe – davon 16 an Land, 12 zu Wasser und 11 auf der Schiene.

Der Container

Eine Transportidee hat sich durchgesetzt

Ohne Container geht kaum etwas. Ganz gleich, ob nun ein Rennwagen nach Australien oder ein kompletter Operationssaal nach Nigeria verschifft werden soll. Die universelle Box schluckt einfach alles und prägt heute das Bild der Häfen in der ganzen Welt.

Schottischer Whisky reist im Tank-Container, amerikanisches Fleisch im Kühl-Container, marokkanisches Obst im isolierten Container, selbst vor Kaffee macht der Kisten-Boom nicht halt: In speziellen Ventilations-Containern mit Lüftungskanälen halten sich die Bohnen sogar besser als in den traditionellen Säcken! Sperrige Güter werden »oben ohne« verschifft: in Open-Top-Containern. Inzwischen gibt es sogar Container ohne Wände – für Güter, die viel Luft brauchen.

Eine Transportidee hat sich durchgesetzt – im Eiltempo, sozusagen. Denn die Blitzkarriere der genormten 20-Fuß-Kiste (ein Fuß = 30,5 cm) mit einer Breite und Höhe von jeweils 2,44 m, einer Länge von 6,10 m und einem maximalen Beladungsgewicht von 20 Tonnen begann in Hamburg 1967. Damals wurden im Hafen insgesamt 15.189 Metall-Behälter umgeschlagen. Inzwischen liegt der Container-Umschlag bei mehr als einer Million TEU (**T**wenty **F**oot **E**quivalent **U**nit = 20-Fuß-Basis; 40-Fuß-Container werden doppelt gezählt) und einem Gewicht von rund zehn Millionen Tonnen. Hamburg festigte damit seinen Platz in der Weltrangliste unter den zwölf wichtigsten Container-Umschlagplätzen.

Bewegt werden die bunten Boxen zwischen Kai und Schiff von sogenannten Containerbrücken. Das Hochstapeln an Land übernehmen allradgelenkte Portal-Hubstapler oder spezielle Stapelbrücken (Constacker). Transportiert werden die regen- und spritzwasserfesten Metall-Kisten entweder von Semi-

Container-Schiffen (semi = halb) – sie befördern nebenbei noch konventionelles Stückgut – oder von Voll-Containerschiffen. Die schwimmenden Giganten (ca. 300 m lang,

30 m breit) fassen in ihren Luken und an Deck bis zu 3000 Container.

Gelöscht und geladen wird überall im Hafen. Bedeutendster Mehrzweckterminal ist das Containerzentrum Waltershof. Auch hier wird unter anderem nach der sogenannten Ro/Ro-Praxis (Roll-on/Roll-off) gearbeitet. Wie bei den Autofähren rollen alle Güter vom Kai ins Schiff und umgekehrt.

NEUES DEUTSCHLAND

Proletarier aller Länder, vereinigt euch!

Montag,
31. März 1986
41. Jahrgang / Nr. 75

B-Ausgabe
Einzelpreis 15 Pf

Redaktion und Verlag 1017 Berlin,
Franz-Mehring-Platz 1, Telefon: 58 50
(Sammelnummer). Abonnementspreis
monatlich 3,50 Mark. ISSN 0323-4940

ORGAN DES ZENTRALKOMITEES DER SOZIALISTISCHEN EINHEITSPARTEI DEUTSCHLANDS

Michail Gorbatschow im sowjetischen Fernsehen:

UdSSR auch weiterhin zu Verzicht auf nukleare Explosionen bereit

Voraussetzung: USA müssen ebenso handeln / Unverzüglich Verhandlungen über vollständiges Testverbot, einschließlich der Fragen der Kontrolle, aufnehmen

Stopp der Nukleartests ist der realste Weg zu einer Beendigung des Wettrüstens

Zu baldigem Treffen mit Präsident Reagan in europäischer Hauptstadt bereit

Moskau (ADN). Der Generalsekretär des ZK der KPdSU, Michail Gorbatschow, hielt am Sonnabend im sowjetischen Fernsehen folgende Rede.

Bei unserer heutigen Begegnung möchte ich auf die Situation eingehen, die um das Moratorium der Sowjetunion für die nuklearen Explosionen entstanden ist.

Vor einigen Tagen haben die Vereinigten Staaten eine weitere Kernexplosion gezündet. Es liegt für uns alle klar auf der Hand, daß der Zeitpunkt dafür nicht zufällig gewählt worden ist. Die Explosion wurde kurz vor dem Ablaufen des von der Sowjetunion einseitig verkündeten Moratoriums durchgeführt. Gestern ist bekannt geworden, daß die USA demnächst einen weiteren nuklearen Sprengsatz zu zünden beabsichtigen.

Die sowjetischen Menschen sind wie alle Menschen guten Willens in allen Ländern über dieses Vorgehen der USA empört. Sie schreiben darüber in ihren Briefen an das Zentralkomitee der Partei und bitten um eine Einschätzung der entstandenen Situation. Sie fragen: Wie ist das alles zu verstehen? Was ist daraus zu folgern? Warum haben die USA diesen Schritt unternommen? Was der ... angesichts dessen die Füh... res Landes zu tun?

... es als unsere ... Fragen zu beant... eigentlich der ... heute an

und Festigung des Friedens abgehen, der auch vom XXVII. Parteitag der KPdSU mit allem ... wurde. Der

... gefallen ist. Wenn ... bedurfte es zu die ... wohl des Verstän ... Verantwortung, ... gierungen, ... ruht, als auch der ... politischen Wil ... sowjetische Füh ... anders handelt ... Mandat ihres ... Preis des Frie ... richtig nach Erf ... gung des Fried ... zusammenarbeit ... strebt.

Als wir so ... von der W ...

Michail Gorbatschow

Im Wettbewerb zum XI. Parteitag der SED

Jugendforscherkollektive sichern großen Zeit- und Qualitätsgewinn

Mit Bürocomputer den Projektierungsaufwand im Tiefbau um 30 Prozent gesenkt

Neue mikroelektronisch gesteuerte Schmelzanlage spart 160 000 Kilowattstunden

Von unseren Bezirkskorrespondenten

Berlin. Zwei Wochen vor dem ursprünglich geplanten Termin schließt in diesen Tagen ein Jugendforscherkollektiv der FDJ aus dem Berliner Tiefbaukombinat die Projektierung der ersten Trasse des Entwässerungsnetzes für das Wohngebiet Hohenschönhausen IV ab. Mit dem dabei erstmals eingesetzten Bürocomputer wird eine Senkung des Projektierungsaufwandes von 30 Prozent und des Bauaufwandes von ... Prozent erreicht.

XI. PARTEITAG

... wand um 160 000 Kilowattstunden.

... burg. Der Einsatz

chender Rechnerprogramme mitgewirkt. Die elf jungen Leute stellten wichtige Teillösungen bereits fertig beziehungsweise erproben sie gegenwärtig.

Leipzig. Einen Warenproduktionszuwachs von 4,7 Millionen Mark jährlich ermöglicht die schnelle Überführung der Ergebnisse eines Jugendforscherkollektivs aus dem Flachglaskombinat Torgau. Ende dieses Jahres soll die von den Jugendlichen entwickelte, mit einer hauchdünnen Metalloxidschicht bedampfte Herdscheibe in Serienproduktion gehen. Die Wärmestrahlen reflektierende ...rd in Elektroherden ... verhindert die Back- ... n Beschichtungsvor- ... übernimmt ein von ... l Forschern program- ... lustrieroboter.

Festliche Jugendweihen in allen Bezirken der DDR

Über 30 000 Mädchen und Jungen legten das Gelöbnis ab

Berlin (ADN). Am Osterwochenende erhielten rund 30 900 Mädchen und Jungen der DDR die Jugendweihe. Auf über 1000 Feiern legten sie im Beisein ihrer Eltern und Lehrer das Gelöbnis ab, sich mit ihrem Wissen und Können für ihr sozialistisches Vaterland und die Sicherung des Friedens einzusetzen. Persönlichkeiten des gesellschaftlichen Lebens, Wissenschaftler und Künstler hielten Festreden. So sprachen in Güstrow der Abteilungsleiter des ZK der SED Dr. Klaus Sorgenicht, Mitglied des Staatsrates, in Gardelegen Siegfried Grünwald, Vorsitzender des Rates des Bezirkes Magdeburg, in Neubukow Heinz Hanns, Mitglied des Präsidiums des Bundesvorstandes und Vorsitzender des Bezirksvorstandes Rostock des FDGB, und in Berlin Hans-Peter Reinecke,

Schauspieler am Berliner Ensemble.

Die Festredner appellierten an die vierzehnjährigen FDJler, stets Partei für die menschlichste Sache der Welt, für den Sozialismus, zu ergreifen und Spezialisten ihres Fachs zu werden. Jedem werde in der DDR eine fundierte Berufsausbildung und ein sicherer Arbeitsplatz garantiert.

Während der Vorbereitung auf die Jugendweihe hatten sich die Schüler auch mit den revolutionären Traditionen der deutschen Arbeiterklasse vertraut gemacht. Mädchen und Jungen der Goethe-Oberschule Gardelegen gedachten im Stadtmuseum der 1016 Antifaschisten, die im April 1945 von SS-Schergen nahe der altmärkischen Kreisstadt ermordet worden waren.

Tips für Ihren Bahnurlaub

Urlaub in Deutschland – Urlaub mit der Bahn

Deutschland ist ein Urlaubsland, das viele Abwechslungen zu bieten hat. Im Norden die rauhe, herbe Schönheit der Nordseeküste mit den Ost- und Nordfriesischen Inseln. Dann die Ostsee mit ihren vielverzweigten, romantischen Buchten. Der Küste schließt sich weites Flachland an. Hier wechselt das saftige Grün der Weiden mit schattigen Wäldern. Verträumte Flußtäler bilden das Herzstück dieses Urlaubslandes. Hier gedeiht auch ein guter Wein. Nach Süden hin ziehen sich bewaldete Hügel, bis schließlich die schroffen Felsenregionen der Alpen die Grenze des Urlaubslandes Deutschland bilden.
Genauso abwechslungsreich und vielfältig wie die Landschaft sind Kultur, Historie und die Menschen selbst. Zwei Dinge jedoch sind überall gleich: die Gastfreundschaft der Bewohner und ein fast perfektes Verkehrsmittel. Beide garantieren dafür, daß Ihr Urlaub in Deutschland angenehm und abwechslungsreich wird.
Auf der Rückseite dieses Prospektes stellt sich Ihnen eine von 16 deutschen Landschaften vor. Auf dieser Seite präsentiert sich die Bahn. Nahverkehrs- und Eilzüge befördern die Reisenden im Regionalverkehr. Innerhalb vieler Verkehrsverbünde in den Ballungszentren können Sie mit der gleichen Fahrkarte auch U-, S-Bahnen und Busse benutzen. Auf weiten Strecken bringen Sie D-Züge weiter. Für Ihren Urlaub empfehlen wir besonders die Fern-Express-Züge, mit denen Sie aus den Räumen Ruhrgebiet und Hamburg die schönsten Ziele in Süddeutschland, vielfach ohne Umsteigen, erreichen. Das Inter-City-System verbindet im Stundentakt die großen Städte miteinander. Ein ganz besonderes Reiseerlebnis hat Ihnen das „Flaggschiff" der Bahn, der „TEE Rheingold" zu bieten. Aber auch auf dem Wasser ist die Bahn anzutreffen. Bei vielen Schiffen auf dem Bodensee, bei der Überfahrt nach Wangerooge und auf den Fähren der Vogelfluglinie steht ein Bundesbahn-Kapitän am Steuer. Kapitäne der Straße stehen ebenfalls im Dienst der Bahn. Omnibusse bringen Sie in viele reizvolle Orte, die nicht in das Schienennetz der Bundesbahn eingebunden sind.
Nachfolgend wollen wir Ihnen die Leistungsangebote der Bahn näher vorstellen.

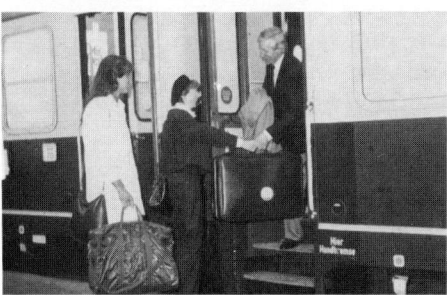

IC-Züge
Bequem und schnell verbindet dieses Zugsystem viele Städte, 36 davon im Direktanschluß miteinander. Bei Umsteigeverbindungen wartet der Anschlußzug am gleichen Bahnsteig auf dem Gleis gegenüber oder läuft in den nächsten Minuten dort ein. Zwischen der 1. und 2. Wagenklasse ist das Zugrestaurant, in dem Sie vom DSG-Team gerne erwartet werden.

Preiswert in jeder Verbindung

Natürlich wollen Sie auch wissen, was eine Reise mit der Bahn kostet und welche Fahrpreisangebote von Ihnen genutzt werden können. Deshalb ist es für uns selbstverständlich, Ihnen die Angebote der Bahn übersichtlich vorzustellen.

Vorzugskarte

Mit der Vorzugskarte (Ermäßigte Fernrückfahrkarte) sparen Sie ca. 20% des normalen Fahrpreises. Kinder von 4–11 Jahre zahlen sogar nur den halben ermäßigten Fahrpreis. Die Vorzugskarte (Ermäßigte Fernrückfahrkarte) ist unser Angebot für alle, die zu ihrem Urlaubsort über 200 km anreisen und frühestens am Sonntag nach dem 1. Geltungstag zurückfahren. Wenn Sie jedoch an einem Sonntag anreisen, können Sie am gleichen Tag auch zurück. Die Rückreise muß allerdings vor 3 Uhr des folgenden Tages beendet sein. In unserer Preistabelle haben wir für Entfernungen über 200 km gleich die Preise der Vorzugskarte (Ermäßigte Fernrückfahrkarte) angegeben.

Tourenkarte, die Entdecker-Karte für Ihr Urlaubsgebiet

Mit der Tourenkarte können Sie rund um den Urlaubsort, zu dem Sie, wie bei der Vorzugskarte (Ermäßigte Fernrückfahrkarte), über 200 km angereist sind, auf einem Streckennetz von ca. 1000 km 10 Tage lang beliebig oft fahren. Selbstverständlich bekommen Sie diese Karte auch, wenn Sie die Ermäßigungen des Familien-, Senioren- bzw. Junior-Passes in Anspruch genommen haben oder wenn Sie mit einer Mini-Gruppe oder in einer Gesellschaftsfahrt angereist sind. Einzige Bedingung: Das Reiseziel muß über 200 km entfernt sein, und Sie müssen mit der Bahn hin- und zurückfahren. Auch wer mit einem Reiseveranstalter (Ameropa, Hummel, Touropa) oder dem Angebot „Städtetouren – Kurzurlaub" anreist, kann die Tourenkarte am Zielort lösen. Hierbei spielt die Anreiseentfernung keine Rolle. Die Tourenkarte kostet für 1 Person 46,– DM, für 2 Personen 62,– DM, und für 77,– DM kann die ganze Familie einschließlich aller unverheirateten Kinder unter 18 Jahren 10 Tage lang auf dem gewählten Streckennetz fahren; es kann auch noch für den gleichen Zeitraum das Nachbarnetz sein, wenn Ihr Zielbahnhof im Geltungsbereich beider Gebiete liegt. Für die 1. Wagenklasse benötigen Sie eine Übergangskarte. TEE- und IC-Zuschläge müssen besonders gelöst werden. FD/D-Zuschläge sind bereits eingerechnet.

Nähere Auskünfte, besonders über die Ausdehnung der verschiedenen Bezirke, finden Sie in dem Prospekt „Bezirkskarte, Bezirkswochenkarte, Tourenkarte".

Tramper-Monats-Ticket
Einen Monat lang auf dem gesamten Schienennetz der DB für 245,– DM (Junior-Paß-Inhaber zahlen nur 212,– DM).
Dieses Angebot gilt für junge Leute unter 23 Jahren, für Schüler und Studierende unter 27 Jahren. Das Tramper-Monats-Ticket wird mit einem Lichtbild versehen und gilt in allen Zügen der DB in der 2. Klasse und auf den Omnibuslinien der Bahn. IC-Zuschlag ist eingeschlossen. Für Reisen in der 1. Klasse benötigen Sie eine Übergangskarte.

Glossary

See notes in Instructor's Guide.

The Glossary is based on the Class Text and aims to provide a vocabulary of everyday German. For two reasons the list does not include every word you may encounter in your study. First, such a list – covering every word in the authentic listening and reading materials – would be very long, containing perhaps five times as many words as the nearly 2000 listed here. Second, the desire to understand language by mechanically translating it, word by tedious word, is an obstacle to the attainment of proficiency, which is the ability to use the language under realistic conditions.

The best way to use the Glossary is to learn how to avoid using it. In real communication there is often simply no time to thumb a dictionary. When you speak and write, try to do the best you can with what you already have. Learn to express complex or specialized concepts with simpler language. Within the Class Text itself is the *Bildwörterbuch*, the pictorial dictionary that provides words in natural contexts rather than artificial alphabetical lists. When you listen and read, work on the skills of tolerating words you don't understand, recognizing those you do, and thereby puzzling out meaning, with the aid of common sense and your knowledge of the world. Other resources include the dialog translations and chapter vocabularies in the Study Text.

The Glossary is organized to encourage you to learn as you look up a word. Decide first whether it is a *noun* – a word that names a person, place or thing. That decision is easier to make in German than in English or most other languages, since in printed German *nouns are capitalized*.

If the word is not a noun, look for it under the category "OTHER." If the word is a noun, look in the "NOUNS" section under its gender heading *der*, *die*, or *das*. The noun lists are organized that way because gender is a basic feature of German. Failure to learn the gender of commonly used words will cause you severe problems in managing other structures. You should also acquire the ability to guess gender by the "shape" of the word and by anything you can derive from the context in which the word is used. So you may have to guess the gender of the noun you are looking up. But the Glossary pages are organized so that you will not have to look very far.

Plurals: Like English, German has several major patterns of pluralization that a speaker learns to apply by reflex. Truly irregular plural forms and patterns of lesser frequency are learned as exceptions. In the Glossary, the two common regular patterns of plural formation are not indicated; instead, you are expected to supply them. The two general principles are:

If the word ends in **-e,** add **-n**	die Fahrkarte, pl. **Fahrkarten**
If the word does not end in **-e,** add **-e**	der Tag, pl. **Tage**

350

In all other cases the plural is indicated, or else the abbreviation *"no pl"* will tell you that the plural form either does not exist or is uncommon.

The indication of umlaut in the pluralization symbols needs explanation.

¨ = umlaut the stem vowel and then add any other indicated letters:
der Mann, ¨er   pl. = Männer

The umlaut applies to the last word in a compound noun:
der Sommermantel, ¨   pl. = Sommermäntel
(not *Sömmermantel*)

The double vowel *au* is umlauted to **äu:**
das Haus, ¨er   pl. = Häuser

The treatment of verbs also emphasizes major structural patterns unless an exception is indicated. If the bold-type listing of the verb contains no other information, you can be sure that its subject-forms and tenses follow regular patterns (example: **leben** – past tenses are formed with **-t-: lebte, hat gelebt**). If there is *any* irregularity in formation, it is spelled out, in the following form:

infinitive (*er/sie/es* present tense, past tense, present perfect)
sehen (sieht, sah, gesehen)

If the verb forms its common past (= present perfect) with **sein,** that information is given.
reisen (ist gereist)

Separable prefixes are indicated by a dot between prefix and stem:
an•rufen

Abbreviations

acc	accusative
adj	adjective
adv	adverb
conj	conjunction
dat	dative
fem	feminine
masc	masculine
neut	neuter
no pl	plural nonexistent or not common
pl	plural
P1, P2	preliminary chapters
prep	preposition
pron	pronoun
refl	reflexive
sing	singular
w/	with
»	see

To provide a change of pace, the leftover space in the Glossary has been filled with other alphabetical material. The *Grabstätten berühmter Deutscher* is a list of where famous figures in German culture are buried.

A

NOUNS

plural only

Alliierten the WWII Allies (US, USSR, GB, F) 23

Alpen the Alps

der

Abend evening (including "night" before sleeping time) »**Guten Abend** P2

Abschied *no pl* farewell, leave-taking **Abschied nehmen** take one's leave 26

Abstieg descent, way down 19

Affe ape, primate 11

Altar, ⁻e altar 8

Amerikaner, - American (male); The adjective is **amerikanisch** P1

Anfang, ⁻e beginning, start 23

Angehörige relative

Angriff attack, raid 22

Anruf telephone call 12

Anwalt, ⁻e lawyer (male); **Anwältin** (female) 24

Anzug, ⁻e suit 18

Apfel, ⁻ apple 6

Apparat apparatus, appliance 19

Appetit *no pl* appetite »**Guten Appetit** 2

April *no pl* April 8

Arbeiter, - worker, laborer 22

Arm arm 13

Arme (the) poor (one, person) 22

Artikel, - article, item 10

Arzt, ⁻e doctor (male); **Ärztin** (female) 13

Aufenthalt stay, visit, stopover 16

Aufenthaltsraum, ⁻e lounge, waiting room 13

Aufstieg climb, ascent 19

Augenarzt, ⁻e eye doctor 13

August *no pl* August 8

Ausflug, ⁻e excursion, outing, sidetrip 21

Ausgang, ⁻e exit 15

Ausländer, - foreigner 25

Austauschstudent, -en exchange student

Ausweis ID card 1

Automat, -en vending machine 6

Autor, -en author; **Autorin** (female) 22

die

Abendfahrt, -en evening trip 8

Abfahrt, -en departure 11

Abteilung, -en department 10

Adresse address (street) 4

Altstadt, ⁻e Old Town 8

Amerikanerin, -nen American (female) P1

Amerikanistin, -nen (female) specialist in American studies 17

Angst, ⁻e worry, anxiety, fear **Angst haben** (**vor** *dat*) be afraid (of) 13

Ansichtskarte (picture) postcard 7

Anweisung, -en instruction(s) 25

Arbeit, -en work, labor, task; job, position **der Job, die Stelle** 23

Arbeitslosigkeit *no pl* unemployment 23

Armee army 17

Armut *no pl* poverty 23

Art, -en kind (of), sort, type; variety »**Blumenart**

Atomwaffe atomic weapon 26

Aufführung, -en performance, staging 20

Aufgabe task, job; exercise, homework

Aufnahme photo, exposure 10

Ausbildung *no pl* training, instruction, practical education 22

Auskunft, ⁻e information; details 4

Auslandsabteilung, -en foreign department, export-import department 26

Auslese select vintage 11

Aussicht, -en view, prospect 10

Ausstellung, -en exhibit(ion), show 22

Auster, -n oyster 17

Auswahl *no pl* selection, range, choice 10

Auswanderung, -en emigration 23

Autobahn, -en freeway, expressway 21

das

Abendessen, - dinner, supper 9

Abitur *no pl* high-school exit/univ. entrance exam 17

Abteil (train) compartment 3

Affenhaus, ⁻er monkey house 11

Alter *no pl* age; old age 18

Altersheim retirement home 23

Amerikahaus, ⁻er U.S. cultural facility 9

Archiv record office; archives 24

Ausland *no pl* abroad; foreign countries 10

Austauschprogramm exchange program 17

Auto, -s automobile, car 8

Adenauer, Konrad (°1876, †1967), Politiker — Bad Honnef, Waldfriedhof Rhöndorf

Anno (°um 1010, †1075), Erzbischof von Köln, Heiliger — Siegburg, Klosterkirche

Arnim, Achim von (°1781, †1831), Dichter — Bonn, Alter Friedhof

---

OTHER

ab *dat & sep pref* away, down, off 7; after, from (a certain time) on 13

aber but, however 3

ab·fahren (fährt ab, fuhr ab, ist abgefahren) leave, depart 7

ab·geben (gibt ab, gab ab, abgegeben) check, deposit, turn in 14

ab·holen pick up, fetch 7

ab·legen take off, remove (coat, etc.) 21

ab·schließen (schließt ab, schloß ab, abgeschlossen) close, lock up 13

ach! oh! 1

all *adj* all, every **alle X Minuten** every X minutes 5

alle *pron* everyone 17

allein alone; only 21

allerdings of course, however 25

alles everything 3

als than 10; when 14

also so, therefore, well, oh, OK P1

alt old P1

am (= an dem) at the, by the, on the 5

amerikanisch *adj* American (the noun is **Amerikaner/in**) 17

an *acc/dat* at, on 5

an·bieten (bietet an, bot an, angeboten) offer 20

ander other, different *adj* 12

anderes else, different; **etwas anderes** something else 10

ändern (sich) change 17

anders different *adv* 15

an·fangen (fängt an, fing an, angefangen) begin 7

an·greifen (greift an, griff an, angegriffen) attack 23

ängstlich worried 13

an·hören listen (to) **sich** *dat* **etwas anhören** listen to something 19

an·kommen (kommt an, kam an, ist angekommen) arrive 16; **es kommt darauf an** it all depends 11

an·nehmen (nimmt an, nahm an, angenommen) assume, presume, accept 20

an·probieren try on (clothing) 18

an·rufen (ruft an, rief an, angerufen) call up (telephone) 7

an·schauen look at 12

antworten *dat* **(antwortet, antwortete, geantwortet)** answer, reply

an·ziehen (sich) (zieht an, zog an, angezogen) put on (clothes), get dressed 14

April *no pl* April 8

arbeiten (arbeitet, arbeitete, gearbeitet) work 4

arm poor; **der/die Arme, -n** poor person 22

atheistisch atheist(ic) 10

Au(a)! ouch! 13

auch also, too, even 2

auch wenn even if, even though 13

auf *acc/dat* on, upon, until 7

auf einmal suddenly; all at once 13

Auf Wiederhören! Good-bye! (on the phone), Talk to you later! 15 »wiederhören

Auf Wiedersehen! Good-bye! P1 »wiedersehen

auf·hören quit, stop doing (something) 26

auf·machen open (up); 22

auf·passen watch out, pay attention, look sharp 9

auf·räumen clean up, pick up, tidy up 15

auf·regen excite, upset; **sich aufregen** get excited, get upset

auf·stehen (steht auf, stand auf, ist aufgestanden) get up, stand up, rise, arise 11

aus *dat* from, out of P1

aus·bleiben (bleibt aus, blieb aus, ist ausgeblieben) stay out 13

aus·drücken express

aus·füllen fill out 12

aus·geben (gibt aus, gab aus, ausgegeben) spend (money), pay 9

aus·gehen (geht aus, ging aus, ist ausgegangen) go out 13

ausgezeichnet excellent 11

aus·halten (hält aus, hielt aus, ausgehalten) bear, endure, stand 23

ausländisch foreign 14

aus·packen unpack 15

aus·ruhen (sich) rest (up) 21

aus·sehen (sieht aus, sah aus, ausgesehen) look (appear, seem) 8

außerdem besides, in addition (to that) 17

aus·steigen (steigt aus, stieg aus, ist ausgestiegen) get out (of bus, etc.) 5

aus·suchen pick out, look for 26

ausverkauft sold out 8

aus·wandern (ist ausgewandert) emigrate 19

aus·weisen (sich) (weist aus, wies aus, ausgewiesen) identify (___self) 18

aus·ziehen (sich) (zieht aus, zog aus, ausgezogen) take off (one's clothes), undress 20

automatisch automatic 21

B

NOUNS

der

Babysitter, - baby sitter 7
Bäcker, - baker 24
Badeanzug, ¨e swimsuit 19

Bahnhof, ¨e train station 4
Bär, -en bear 11
Baum, ¨e tree 14

Beamte (male) official, civil servant
Becher, - cup (for ice cream) 7
Bekannte acquaintance (male) 10

B

NOUNS

der (cont'd.)

Berater, - advisor
Berg mountain 14
Beruf profession 24
Bescheid *no pl* information; notification; decision; **Bescheid wissen** know how, be informed 16; **Bescheid sagen** inform 19
Betrieb business, enterprise; factory, works; **außer Betrieb** out of order; **in Betrieb** working, in working order 19
Blick glance, look; view 23
Blitz flash (photo, lightning) 7
Bodensee *no pl* Lake Constance 21
Bohnensalat bean salad 2
Bombenangriff bombing raid 22
Brand, ⁻e fire, blaze 22
Brief letter (mail) 12
Bruder, ⁻ brother 4
Bundeskanzler, - Federal Chancellor (of BRD, etc.; = Prime Minister) 23
Bus, -se bus 5

die

Babywindel, -n diaper
Bahn, -en railway, cableway 14
Bahnhofsnähe *no pl* vicinity of the railway station 15
Banane banana 6
Bank, -en bank (financial) 4
Beamtin, -nen (female) official; civil servant
Bedienung *no pl* operation; service (personnel)
Beere berry, grape 21
Beerensoße berry sauce 21 »**Soße**
Bekannte acquaintance (female) 10
Bergstation, -en station at top end of cable railway; **Station** station, stop 14
Bettwäsche *no pl* bed linens 13
Bevölkerung, -en population, populace 23
Bibel, -n Bible 24
Birne pear; lightbulb (**Glühbirne**) 15
Blume flower 22
Blumenart, -en kind of flower 26
Bluse blouse 14
Bombe bomb 22
Bratwurst, ⁻e type of (grilled) sausage »**Wurst** 1
BRD (Bundesrepublik Deutschland) *no pl* West Germany (FRG: the Federal Republic of Germany) P2
Breite width, breadth 18
Briefmarke postage stamp 10
Brücke bridge 10
Bühne stage; platform 20
Bundesrepublik Deutschland (BRD) *no pl* the Federal Republic of Germany (FRG); West Germany P2
Buntwäsche *no pl* colored wash 25
Burg, -en castle 21
Buslinie bus line 16

das

Bad, ⁻er bath(-tub, -room) 2
Badezimmer, - bathroom 15
Bayern *no pl* Bavaria 13
Becken, - basin, bowl, sink 15
Beispiel example, instance; **zum Beispiel (z.B.)** for example 18
Benehmen *no pl* conduct, behavior
Benzin *no pl* gasoline 24
Bett, -en bed 13
Bier, - *or* -e beer (note: **2 Bier** 2 beers; **Biere** kinds of beer) 1
Bild, -er picture 10
Bilderbuch, ⁻er picturebook 10
Bildwörterbuch pictorial dictionary
Brathuhn, ⁻er roast(ing) chicken 17
Brötchen, - breakfast roll 1
Buch, ⁻er book 10
Büfett buffet, snack counter 12
Büro -s office 18

OTHER

baden (sich) bathe, swim 5
bald soon 11
bar (in) cash 6
basteln tinker, build, put together (as a kit) 19
bauen build 14
bay(e)risch Bavarian
bedeuten mean, signify 22
bedienen operate 25
beeilen (sich) hurry 18
beenden finish, complete, end 23
befreien liberate, (set) free, release 23
beginnen (beginnt, begann, begonnen) begin, start 7
behaupten (behauptet, behauptete, behauptet) claim, assert, maintain 23
behindert handicapped 16
bei *dat* at, by, near, with, while, during; **bei Ihnen (zu Hause)** where you live, in your country; **bei mir** on/with me

beide both 2
beides both (things) 23
beißen (beißt, biß, gebissen) bite 11
bekommen (bekommt, bekam, bekommen) get, receive; (become = **werden**) 5
belegt occupied, taken 15
bemerken remark, observe, comment 21
bequem comfortable; **es sich** *dat* **bequem machen** make oneself comfortable 18
bereuen regret, rue
berühmt famous, well-known 11
beschreiben (beschreibt, beschrieb, beschrieben) describe 12
besetzt occupied, busy 4
besichtigen see, view 8
besonders especially 10
besprechen (bespricht, besprach, besprochen) discuss

besser better 4
best best *adj*; **am besten** best *adv* 13
besteigen (besteigt, bestieg, bestiegen) climb, ascend 9
bestellen order, reserve 11
bestimmt certain(ly), particular(ly), definite(ly) 7
besuchen visit, attend, go to 11
bevor before *conj*; »**vor** *prep* and **vorher** *adv* 14
bezahlen pay (needs a direct object) 12
billig cheap 6
bis *acc & conj* until, up to, by; **bis zu** *dat* up to, as far as, until the 4
bißchen (a) little (of something) **ein bißchen** 2
bitte please; here you go; you're welcome P1
bitte schön/sehr you're welcome; there you go; yes? can I help you? 1

bitten (bittet, bat, gebeten) ask, request (ask, inquire = **fragen**) 15
blau blue (color, not emotion); tipsy (from drink) 5
bleiben (bleibt, blieb, ist geblieben) stay (remain) 2
böse angry; **mir böse** angry with, me 14
botanisch botanical 16
braten (brät, briet, gebraten) roast; bake; fry, grill gebraten 17
brauchen need, require; use 2
braun brown 5
breit wide, broad 18
bringen (bringt, brachte, gebracht) bring, fetch, take 2
buchen book, reserve 21
bummeln (ist gebummelt) stroll, wander 8
bunt colorful, many-colored 18

C

NOUNS

der

Christ, -en Christian (person) 22
Club, -s club; also spelled **Klub** 13

Computer, - computer 7

Curry *no pl* curry (powder) 17

die

Currywurst, ⁻e curried sausage; two orders of currywurst **zwei Stück, zweimal Currywurst** 1

Bach, Johann Sebastian (°1685, †1750), Komponist — Leipzig, Thomaskirche

Beethoven, Ludwig van (°1770, †1827), Komponist — Wien, Zentralfriedhof

Benn, Gottfried (°1886, †1956), Schriftsteller — Berlin (West), Waldfriedhof Dahlem

Benz, Karl (°1844, †1929), Erfinder — Ladenburg am Neckar

das

Café, -s café 10

D

NOUNS

der

Dank *no pl* thanks »**vielen Dank, schönen Dank** 3
Deutsche German (male) 17
Dezember *no pl* December 8
Diafilm slide film 10
Dialekt dialect 24

Dienstag Tuesday P2
Doktor, -en doctor (title of address – includes Ph.D., etc.) 4
Dolmetscher, - interpreter, translator 17

Dom cathedral 4
Domplatz, ⁻e cathedral square 7
Donnerstag Thursday P2

Bismarck, Otto Fürst von (°1815, †1898), Politiker — Friedrichsruh (Kreis Herzogtum Lauenburg)

D

NOUNS (cont'd.)

die

D-Mark, - West German mark 6
Dame lady, woman 2
Damentoilette women's restroom 3
Dankbarkeit *no pl* thankfulness, gratitude

DDR (Deutsche Demokratische Republik) *no pl* East Germany (GDR: German Democratic Republic) P2
Decke blanket, comforter 13
Deutsche German (female) 17

Deutsche Demokratische Republik (DDR) *no pl* German Democratic Republic (GDR); East Germany P2
Droge drug 13
Dusche shower (bath) 2

das

Datum, Daten (calendar) date 6
Deutsch *no pl* German (language) 5; **auf deutsch** in German
Deutschland *no pl* Germany P2
Dia(positiv), Dias, Diapositive slide (film) 10

DIN (Deutsche Industrie Norm) *no pl* set of German industrial standards 10
Ding thing (usually concrete) 18
Dokument document 24

Doppelzimmer, - double room in hotel 2
Dorf, ¨er village 16
Drittel, - third (the ordinal is »**dritt-**) 24

OTHER

da there, here P2
dabei along, there; meanwhile, while (doing something) 13
dafür for that, in favor of that 20
dagegen against, opposed to that 20
daher thus, from that, hence 14
dahin to there, that way 5
dahin·kommen (kommt dahin, kam dahin, ist dahingekommen) get to there 9
damit so that *conj* 14; with that/those 21
dankbar grateful, thankful 18
danke thanks P1
danke schön/sehr thanks a lot 1
danke vielmals thanks a lot 3
danken *dat* thank 26
dann then 3
daran about that, at that, on that 20
darauf on that, to that 11
darauf (ankommen) depend (up)on; **es kommt darauf an** it all depends 11

darüber about that, over that 20
das that; the (*neuter gender sign*) P1
das heißt that is, means »**heißen** 6
daß *conj* that 12
dauern last, take (time) 17
davon about that, of that, from that 22
denken (denkt, dachte, gedacht) think 11
denn then, anyway, indeed (expresses interest or impatience) 6
deswegen therefore, thus, consequently 23
deutsch German *adj* 4 »**der/die Deutsche**
dienen *dat* serve 18
dies *adj and pron* this 4
dieselbe the same
diesmal this time 11
direkt direct(ly) 5
diskutieren discuss 13

doch sure(ly), indeed, by all means, but, however, nevertheless 2
doppelt double, twice (as much) 22
dort (over) there 4
draußen outside 11
drin (= darin) inside, in it, in that 16
drinnen inside (a room, building, etc.) 11
dritt third (the fraction is »**Drittel**) 8
drüben over there 11
drücken press 16
du you (familiar) 11
dumm dumb, stupid 26
dunkel dark; **dunkelgrün** dark green 18
durch *acc* through, by means of 4
durchschnittlich (on the) average 22
dürfen (darf, durfte) may, be allowed/permitted 7
duschen (take a) shower 5

Brahms, Johannes (°1833, †1897), Komponist — Wien, Zentralfriedhof

Brecht, Bertolt (°1898, †1956), Schriftsteller — Berlin (Ost), Dorotheenstädtischer Friedhof

Busch, Wilhelm (°1832, †1908), Maler, Grafiker und Schriftsteller — Mechtshausen (Kreis Hildesheim-Marienburg)

Clausewitz, Carl von (°1780, †1831), Kriegstheoretiker — Burg bei Magdeburg, Ostfriedhof

Cranach, Lucas d.Ä. (°1472, †1553), Maler — Weimar, St. Jakobus-Friedhof

E

NOUNS

plural only
Eltern parents 10

der
Eingang, ¨e (building) entrance 7
Einkaufswagen, - shopping cart
Eintritt entry, admission (price) 14

Eisbär, -en Polar bear 11
Elefant, -en elephant 11
Enkel, - grandson 24

Erwachsene adult (male); **die Erwachsene** (female) 11

die
Ecke corner 3
Einheit, -en unit (of measure) 12
Einladung, -en invitation 26
Einreise entry (into a country, at a border-crossing)
Einzelheit, -en detail, particular
Emigration, -en emigration, exile 23

Endstation, -en end of the line, terminus 16
Enkelin, -nen granddaughter 24
Ente duck 11
Entschuldigung, -en Excuse me!; pardon; apology P2
Entspannung, -en relaxation 23

Entwicklung, -en development; evolution; production 25
Erfahrung, -en experience (acquired knowledge)
Ermäßigung, -en reduction, discount 12
Ernte harvest(ing) 20

das
Ehepaar (married) couple 17
Ei, -er egg 9
Einkommen, - income 22
Einzelzimmer, - single room in hotel 2
Eis, -sorten ice cream, ice 7

Ende end, outcome; **zu Ende** finished, over 23
Enkelkind, -er grandchild
Entwickeln *no pl* development, developing 25

Ereignis, -se event, occurrence
Essen *no pl* food, meal 7
Europa *no pl* Europe 15

OTHER

eben exact(ly), precisely 22
echt genuine, real; honest, honorable
egal all the same; **das ist mir egal** I don't care 9
eigen own *adj* 13
eigentlich actually, really 13
eilig in a hurry, hurriedly; **ich habe es eilig** I'm in a hurry 25
ein bißchen a little »**bißchen** 2
ein paar a couple (of), a few (not necessarily a pair) »**paar** 4
einander each other 24
einfach one-way 3; easy, easily, simple, simply 5
ein·gehen (geht ein, ging ein, ist eingegangen) shrink 25
eingerichtet furnished, arranged 17
einige some, a few 12

ein·kaufen shop, make purchases 7
ein·laden (lädt ein, lud ein, eingeladen) invite 20
einmal one (order of) 3; once 18; **auf einmal** suddenly 13
einmalig unique 10
ein·packen pack (up), wrap (up) 10
ein·schenken pour (wine, etc. into a glass) 20
ein·steigen (steigt ein, stieg ein, ist eingestiegen) get in, board (bus, etc.) 16
ein·stellen set 25
ein·werfen (wirft ein, warf ein, eingeworfen) insert (money into slot) 16
ein·ziehen (zieht ein, zog ein, ist eingezogen) move in, come in
empfehlen (empfiehlt, empfahl, empfohlen) recommend 9

endlich finally 16
eng tight(ly), close(ly) 24
englisch English 17
entlang along 21
entscheiden (sich) (entscheidet, entschied, entschieden) decide 20
entschuldigen (sich) excuse 10; excuse oneself, take a raincheck 26
entwickeln develop 25
erbitten (erbitten, erbat, erbeten) request, ask
erhalten (erhält, erhielt, erhalten) get, receive 21
erinnern remind **sich erinnern an** *acc* remember 18
erkältet sein have a cold 13
erklären explain 12
erledigen accomplish, do, finish up 20

E

OTHER (cont'd.)

ernst serious(ly) 13
ernten (erntet, erntete, geerntet harvest, earn 20
erreichen reach, get to, attain 21
erschießen (erschießt, erschoß, erschossen) shoot (dead); **sich erschießen** shoot oneself 22
erst first 5; not until, only *adv* 16
erstens first of all, in the first place 26

erzählen tell (a tale); tell (command) **sagen**
Es freut mich (sehr) (Very) glad/pleased to meet you 10 »**freuen**
es gibt there is, there are + *acc* 3 »**geben**
essen (ißt, aß, gegessen) eat 1
etwa about, approximately, roughly 9

etwas something 2; somewhat 11
etwas anderes something else 10
europäisch European *adj* 17
evangelisch Protestant *adj* 10
ewig eternal(ly), forever 22
existieren exist 24
exotisch exotic 17
extra extra, additional(ly) 5

F

NOUNS

plural only

Ferien vacation (general) 13 »**Urlaub**

Dürer, Albrecht (°1471, †1528), Maler — Nürnberg, St. Johannisfriedhof

der

Fabrikarbeiter, - factory worker (male) 22
Fahkartenautomat, -en ticket vending machine 6
Fahrkartenschalter, - ticket counter, window 3
Fahrplan, ⁻e schedule (transportation) 11
Fahrschein transit ticket 16
Familienname last name, family name P1

Faschismus *no pl* fascism 22
Faschist, -en fascist 22
Februar *no pl* February 8
Fehler, - mistake, error
Feiertag holiday FF
Film film (camera or movie) 10
Fisch fish 2
Flüchtling refugee 22
Flug, ⁻e flight (airplane)
Flur entrance hall, hallway 15
Fluß, Flüsse river 7

Franken, - Swiss Franc 1
Freitag Friday P2
Freund friend (male), boyfriend 4
Frühling spring (season) 4
Führer, - guidebook, guide, leader 16
Fünfziger, - fifty (banknote or stamp) 6
Fuß, ⁻e foot 14 »**zu Fuß**
Fußgänger, - pedestrian 8

die

Fabrik, -en factory 22
Fähre ferryboat 9
Fahrkarte ticket (train, etc.) 1
Fahrt, -en trip (vehicular) 7
Familie family (singular!) 4
Farbe color 17
Feinwäsche *no pl* delicate laundry 25
Fete party
Flamme flame 11

Flasche bottle 1
Fotoentwicklung, -en film developing 25
Frage question 10
Frau, -en Mrs., Ms. P1; woman 3; wife 4
Freiheit, -en freedom 22
Freizeit *no pl* free time, leisure time 19

Fresse trap, mug, "kisser" 26
Freundin, -nen friend (female), girlfriend 25
Freundschaft, -en friendship
Funktion, -en function 1
Fußgängerzone pedestrian zone(s) 8
Fütterung, -en feeding (animals) 11

Ebert, Friedrich (°1871, †1925), Politiker — Heidelberg, Bergfriedhof

Einstein, Albert (°1879, †1955), Physiker — Urne in einem Fluß bei Trenton, N.J. (USA), versenkt

Engels, Friedrich (°1820, †1895), Sozialtheoretiker und Politiker — Asche bei Eastbourne (England) ins Meer gestreut

das

Fachgeschäft specialty shop 19
Fahrrad, -er bicycle 21
Farbdia, -s color slide(s) 10
Farbfoto, -s color photo 25
Faß, Fässer barrel, vat 20
Fenster, - window 7
Ferngespräch long-distance call 12
Fest festival FF
Fieber *no pl* fever (98.6°F = 37.1°C) 13

OTHER

fahren (fährt, fuhr, ist gefahren) travel, drive 4; **radfahren** ride a bicycle 13
fallen (fällt, fiel, ist gefallen) fall; die in battle 24
fällig due 15
falsch wrong, incorrect (of things) 16 (you're wrong = **Sie haben unrecht**)
fangen (fängt, fing, gefangen) catch 11
fantastisch fantastic, great 2
fast almost 10
faul lazy; rotten (fruit) 11
feiern celebrate 11
fein fine 17
fern far, distant, tele- 10
fern·sehen (sieht fern, sah fern, ferngesehen) watch TV 10
fertig finished, ready 12

Fleisch *no pl* meat, flesh 17
Flugzeug airplane 19
Formular form, blank 12
Foto, -s photograph 10
Fotogeschäft camera store 10
Fräulein, - Miss, Ms.; waitress! P1
Freibad, -er open-air swimming pool 19
Freilichttheater, - open-air theater 20

fest firm, solid
finanzieren finance 17
finden (findet, fand, gefunden) find 3
fliegen (fliegt, flog, ist geflogen) fly
fliehen (flieht, floh, ist geflohen) flee, escape 23
folgend following, subsequent 21
fotografieren photograph, take pictures 7
fragen ask (inquire) 3; ask (request) = **bitten**
französisch French *adj* 17 (Frenchman = **der Franzose**, Frenchwoman = **die Französin**)
frei free 4
frei·halten (hält frei, hielt frei, freigehalten) hold, keep open, keep clear 15

Friesland *no pl* Frisia (northwest German coastal regions & islands) 17
Frühstück breakfast 2
Fundbüro, -s lost and found office 18

> Friedrich I. Barbarossa (°1122, †1190), Kaiser — im Saleph (heute Göksu, Türkei) ertrunken; Eingeweide in Tarsus beigesetzt

freitags on Fridays 21
fremd strange, foreign **fremd sein** be a stranger 16
fressen (frißt, fraß, gefressen) eat (animal activity), feed 11
freuen please, make happy 11; **freut mich sehr**: pleased to meet you 17; **sich freuen auf** + *acc* look forward to 19
frisch fresh (foods) 11
früh early 7 »**morgen früh**
fühlen feel, sense; **sich fühlen: Ich fühle mich besser** I feel better
führen lead 8
funktionieren work, function, operate, run 5
für *acc* for; in favor of 2
furchtbar horrible 8

G   (S)

NOUNS

der

Garten, - garden 16
Gast, -e guest, customer 5
Gastgeber, - host
Geburtstag birthday 18
Gefallen, - favor 26
Gefangene prisoner (male) 23
Gegner, - opponent 23
Geldbeutel, - wallet, pocketbook 18
Geldwechsel *no pl* currency exchange 6

Generalsekretär General Secretary 22
Gepäckkarren, - baggage cart 18
Gipfel, - peak, summit (mountain) 14
Glanz *no pl* glossy finish; gleam, shine 25
Gott, -er God 16
Gottesdienst religious service 7
Grad, - degree (temperature) 11

Grenzübergang, -e border crossing point 21
Groschen, - Austrian coin 1
Großvater, - grandfather 23
Grund, -e reason, basis
Grünewald German painter 14
Gruß, -e greeting 19

> Friedrich II. der Große (°1712, †1786), König von Preußen — Burg Hohenzollern bei Hechingen

NOUNS (cont'd.)

die

Gabel, -n fork 9
Garage garage 15
Garderobe tall, free-standing wardrobe closet; hat & coat check at restaurants, etc. 8
Gebrauchsanweisung, -en operating instructions, manual 25
Gedenkstätte memorial, monument 23
Gefangene prisoner (female) 23

Gegend, -en area, vicinity; neighborhood; region 19
Geisteswissenschaft, -en humanities (academic subjects) 17
Geldstrafe fine, penalty 16
Geschäftssache business matter 26
Geschichte history 17
Gewohnheit, -en habit, custom
Grenze border, boundary; limit 19

Grenzwache border guard 23
Größe size (of clothes, etc.); extent 10
Großmutter, ⁻ grandmother 23
Grundschule elementary school 24
Gruppe group; combo 19
Gruppenreise group excursion 21
Güte *no pl* goodness, kindness; **meine Güte!** my goodness! 16

das

Gasthaus, ⁻er inn, restaurant 21
Gebäude, - building, edifice; structure 22
Gebiet region, area 23
Geburtsdatum, -daten birthdate 24
Gehalt, ⁻er salary 24
Geld *no pl* money, currency 6
Gemälde, - painting 22
Gemüse *no pl* vegetable(s) 17
Gepäck *no pl* baggage, luggage 1

Geschäft shop, store; business 10
Geschenk gift, present 10
Geschirr *no pl* utensils, knives & forks; "dishes" 13
Geschirrspülen *no pl* washing of dishes 13
Gespräch conversation, talk P1
Getränk drink
Glas, - *or* ⁻er glass 1 (note: **zwei Glas Wein** two glasses of wine; **Weingläser** wineglasses)

Gleis track (railroad) 3
Gramm, - gram (1 lb. = approx. 500g) 3
Gymnasium, Gymnasien high school (college prep track) 17; (American high school = **Oberschule**)

Friedrich, Caspar David (°1774, †1840), Maler — Dresden, Trinitatis-Friedhof

OTHER

ganz quite, complete(ly) 5
gar quite; **gar nicht** not at all 9
garantieren guarantee 22
ge- past participle prefix (look under main verb & on flyleaf)
geben (gibt, gab, gegeben) give 5 »**es gibt**
geboren born 8
gebraten roasted; baked; fried, grilled 17 »**braten**
gebraucht, used, second-hand; **Gebraucht___** used ___ 22
gefährlich dangerous 10
gefallen *dat* **(gefällt, gefiel, gefallen)** please; **das gefällt mir** I like that 14
gegen *acc* against 14
gegenüber *adv* opposite, across the way 15
gegessen eaten 12 »**essen**
gehen (geht, ging, ist gegangen) go; walk; run, function 3
gehören *dat* belong (to X) **es gehört mir** it belongs to me 14

gekocht boiled; cooked 17 »**kochen**
gelb yellow 5
gemeinsam in common
genau exact(ly) 5
genausoviel just as much 22
genießen (genießt, genoß, genossen) enjoy 21
genug enough 3
geöffnet open(ed) »**öffnen** 19
geographisch geographical(ly) 24
gerade just now, recently; straight 11
geradeaus straight ahead 4
germanisch Germanic 14
gern(e) gladly, with pleasure; "Sure! Glad to!" 2; **gern geschehen** glad to help 18; **ich singe gern** I like to sing
geschehen (geschieht, geschah, ist geschehen) happen; **gern geschehen** glad to do it 18
geschlossen closed, shut 3 »**schließen**

gesessen sat 23 »**sitzen**
gestern yesterday P2
gestorben dead 23 »**sterben**
gesucht wanted (newspaper ad) 17 »**suchen**
geteilt divided, split 22 »**teilen**
gewesen been *past participle* 24 »**sein**
gewiß certain, specific 26
gewöhnlich usual(ly) 13
gibt es Is there . . . ? *acc* 7
glauben believe, think 2
gleich (time) right away, directly 4
gleichfalls The same to you! 9
gotisch Gothic (art & architecture style) 8
grau gray 5
griechisch Greek 17
groß big, large; tall 10
großartig wonderful, superb, splendid 19
größer bigger, larger 11
grün green 5

Grüß Gott! Hello! Good morning, etc. 16
gucken look (casual or child talk) 11
gültig valid 16

gut good; well 1
Guten Abend! hello; good evening P1
Guten Appetit! Enjoy your meal! 2

Guten Morgen! hello; good morning P1
Guten Tag! Hello (late a.m. to early p.m.) P1

H

NOUNS

plural only

Herbergseltern youth hostel supervisors 13

Herrschaften ladies and gentlemen; gentlemen; everyone, one & all 2

> Gluck, Christoph Willibald von (°1714, †1787), Komponist — Wien, Zentralfriedhof
>
> Goethe, Johann Wolfgang von (°1749, †1832), Dichter — Weimar, Fürstengruft

der

Hamburger, - hamburger 17
Hauptbahnhof, ⁀e central train station 4
Held, -en hero 23
Herbst fall (autumn) 4
Herd stove, range 15

Herr, -en Mr.; gentleman P1
Hirsch deer, stag 21
Hochzeitstag wedding day 21
Hof, ⁀e yard, courtyard; farm; royal court; hotel, inn 16
Hofgarten, ⁀ courtyard garden 16

Hohenfels High Rock (castle) 21
Hotelschlüssel, - hotel key 15
Hunger *no pl* hunger; **Hunger haben** be hungry 14
Hut, ⁀e hat 11

die

Hälfte half (of something) 14
Haltestelle stop (transit) 5
Hand, ⁀e hand 11
Hauptstadt, ⁀e capital city 22
Hausordnung, -en house rules 13
Heimat, -en homeland, native land 22
Heizung, -en heating (system) 15
Herrenabteilung, -en men's department 10

Hilfe *no pl* help, assistance, aid 18
Hilfsbereitschaft *no pl* helpfulness, readiness to help
Hinsicht, -en respect, regard, instance
Hintertür, -en back door 15
Hochschule college, university 17
Höflichkeit, -en politeness, courtesy 26

Höhe height, elevation 18
Hohenzollernbrücke the Hohenzollern Bridge in Köln 10
Hotelrechnung, -en hotel bill 15
Hüfte hip 13
Hütte (mountain) cabin, hut 14

> Grimm, Jacob (°1785, †1863), Sprachwissenschaftler — Berlin (West), Friedhof der St. Matthäi-Gemeinde

das

Hackfleisch *no pl* ground meat (usually beef) 17
Handtuch, ⁀er towel 5
Hauptfach, ⁀er major (academic) 17
Hauptsymbol primary symbol 22
Haus, ⁀er house 13; **zu Hause** at home (location) 9; **nach Hause**

home (direction) 23; **Krankenhaus** hospital 19
Hemd, -en shirt 18
Herz, -en heart 13
Himbeereis *no pl* raspberry ice cream 7
Hirschfilet, -s venison filet 21

Hobby *no pl* hobby 10
Hochhaus, ⁀er high-rise building 17
Hotel, -s hotel 2
Hotelrestaurant, -s hotel restaurant 15
Hotelzimmer, - hotel room 8

OTHER

haben (hat, hatte, gehabt) have 1
halb half *adj*; **halb drei** 2:30, half past two 9
halten (hält, hielt, gehalten) hold; stop (transportation) 24

hätte would have; **hätte gern** would like to have 9 »**haben**
hatte had 9 »**haben**
hätte gern would like to have 9
hauen (haut, haute, gehauen) punch, hit, sock 26

hauptsächlich primarily, mainly, mostly 19
heiraten (heiratet, heiratete, geheiratet) marry, get married 24; **verheiratet** married
heiß hot 5

H   ⌐

OTHER (cont'd.)

heißen (heißt, hieß, geheißen) be named, be called **ich heiße** my name is P2; **das heißt** mean 6

helfen *dat* **(hilft, half, geholfen)** help 13 **hilf mir!** help me!

hell light, clear, bright 18; **hellbraun** light brown

Herr Ober! waiter! 2

herrlich wonderful, glorious 9

herzlich heartily, cordially 19

heute today P2; **heute abend** this evening 1

hier here P2

hierher over here (motion) 18

hin there, toward there; **hin und zurück** there and back, round trip 3

hinauf up(ward) 8

hinauf·steigen (steigt hinauf, stieg hinauf, ist hinaufgestiegen) climb (up) 21

hinaus out (inside to outside) 15

hinaus·schieben (schiebt hinaus, schob hinaus, hinausgeschoben) postpone; push out

hinaus·tragen (trägt hinaus, trug hinaus, hinausgetragen) carry out 15

hinein·gehen (geht hinein, ging hinein, ist hineingegangen) enter, go in 14

hin·fahren (fährt hin, fuhr hin, ist hingefahren) go, travel (away) 15

hin·kommen (kommt hin, kam hin, ist hingekommen) get there, arrive 23

hin·setzen (sich) set down; sit down (seat oneself) 14

hinten behind, to the rear 7

hinter *acc/dat* behind, in back of 8

hinüber over (toward)

hinunter down 8

hinunter·fallen (fällt hinunter, fiel hinunter, ist hinuntergefallen) fall down 14

hinzu·fügen add (to what has been said)

hoch up, high, upstairs; **eine Treppe hoch** one flight up 5; with endings: **hoh-**

höchst highest; **höchste Zeit** (it's) high time, about time 21

hoffen hope 14

hoffentlich (subject) hopes that; hopefully 26

hoh- high; without endings: **hoch**; **höher** higher 8

höher higher (see **hoch**) 10

holen get, fetch 4

hören hear, listen 9

hübsch pretty; handsome 10

hungrig hungry 8

I   ⌐

NOUNS

der

Imbiß, Imbisse fast food place, snack bar 1

Indianer, - Indian (North American) 14

Inhaber, - owner, proprietor; **Inhaberin** (female)

Inhalt content(s), ingredients 18

> Gutenberg, Johannes (°um 1397, †1468), Erfinder — Mainz, ehemalige Franziskanerkirche; 1742 abgerissen

die

Idee idea, thought 8

Inflation, -en inflation ($) 23

Information, -en information 19

das

Instrument instrument; tool, implement 19

> Händel, Georg Friedrich (°1685, †1759), Komponist — London, Westminster Abbey

> Hegel, Georg Wilhelm Friedrich (°1770, †1831), Philosoph — Berlin (Ost), Dorotheenstädtischer Friedhof

OTHER

ich I P1

Ich weiß nicht I don't know P2

im (= in dem) in the 2

immer always, ever 4

in *acc/dat* in P2

in Ordnung OK, all right, check! 1

indisch Indian 17

inklusive including, included 15

ins (= in das) into the 13

interessant interesting 4

interessieren to interest 17; **sich interessieren für**/*acc* be interested in 19

international international 22

inzwischen in the meantime, meanwhile 13

irgendetwas something (or other) 18

irgendwo somewhere 13

ironisch ironic 23

ist is P1 »**sein**

Ist gut OK, all right, sure 1

Ist recht OK, all right, fine 2

italienisch Italian 17

J

NOUNS

der

Jahrgang, ¨e vintage 20
Januar *no pl* January 8
Jazz *no pl* jazz 19
Johannisberger, - a Riesling wine 20

die

Jacke jacket, coat 11
Jugend *no pl* youth (time of life) 22
Jugendherberge youth hostel 4

das

Jahr year; **im Jahre 1989** in 1989 10

OTHER

ja yes; of course, after all P1
jährlich yearly, annual(ly) 22
jed- each, every 11

Journalist, -en journalist 23
Jude Jewish person (male) 23; **Jüdin** (female)

Jura *no pl* law (academic subject) 24; law, ordinance = **das Gesetz**

Jahrhundert century 8

jedoch however
jemand someone 17
jetzt (right) now 4

Juli *no pl* July 8
Junge boy, fellow 13
Juni *no pl* June 8

Heine, Heinrich (°1797, †1856), Schriftsteller — Paris, Montmartre-Friedhof

Hertz, Heinrich (°1857, †1894), Physiker — Hamburg, Ohlsdorfer Friedhof

Hesse, Hermann (°1877, †1962), Schriftsteller — S. Abbondio bei Lugano (Schweiz)

jüdisch Jewish 10
jung young 10

K

NOUNS

plural only

Kopfschmerzen headache 13

Hindemith, Paul (°1895, †1963), Komponist — La Chiésaz (Kanton Waadt, Schweiz)

Hindenburg, Paul von (°1847, †1934), Heerführer und Politiker — Marburg, Elisabethkirche

Holbein, Hans der Jüngere (°1497/98, †1543), Maler — London, Begräbnisort unbekannt

Humboldt, Alexander von (°1769, †1859), Naturforscher — Berlin (West), Schloßpark Tegel

der

Kabinett *no pl* Cabinet (wine quality designation) 11
Kaffee *no pl* coffee; two coffees, please **zweimal Kaffee, bitte** 1
Kanadier, - (male) Canadian P1; **Kanadierin** (female)
Karren, - cart 18
Kartoffelsalat potato salad 1
Käse, -sorten cheese 3
Kassettenrekorder, - cassette recorder 19

Keller, - cellar, basement 15
Kindergarten, ¨ kindergarten 24
Kinderwagen, - stroller 14
Kiosk kiosk, newsstand 6
Kleine the little one (child) 22
Klub, -s club (organization) 19
Knopf, ¨e button 16
Koffer, - suitcase 15
Kommunist, -en communist 23
Komponist, -en composer 20

Kontext context 1
Kopfhörer, - headphone 19
Krankenwagen, - ambulance 13
Krieg war 8
Küchentisch kitchen table 14
Kühlschrank, ¨e refrigerator 15
Kunde customer, client
Kurs exchange rate 6; university course 17

die

Kabine booth 12
Kamera, -s camera 13
Kapelle band (music) 11
Karte ticket; map; card; menu 3
Kasse cashier's station; ticket office 8

Kassette (audio) cassette 10
Kellnerin, -nen waitress (waiter = **der Ober, Kellner**)
Kirche church 7
Kiste box, case, crate, chest 20
Klasse (school) class; sort, kind 13

Klinik, -en private hospital; clinic 13
Kneipe pub, bar, saloon, dive 19
Kochnische kitchenette 15
Kochwäsche *no pl* hot-water laundry 25

K

NOUNS

die (cont'd.)

Kollegin, -nen colleague, co-worker (female); **Kollege** (male) 26
Konditorei, -en pastry shop 4
Kontrolle control (post); check, inspection 1
Kosmetik *no pl* cosmetic(s) 18

Krankenschwester, -n nurse 24; **Krankenpfleger** (male nurse)
Krankheit, -en illness, ailment 13
Kreditkarte credit card 22
Kriegszeit, -en wartime 23

Krone crown 4
Küche kitchen 13
Kultur, -en culture; civilization 17
Kunst, ˝e art 14
Kusine cousin (female) 16 »**Vetter**

das

Kaiserreich empire 22
Kanada Canada P1
Kännchen, - small pot (of coffee, etc.) 7
Kaufhaus, ˝er department store 18
Kilo(gramm), -s(-) kilogram (2.2 lb) 12
Kind, -er child 4
Kinderbuch, ˝er children's book 10

Kino, -s movie theater 8
Kissen, - pillow 13
Knie, - knee 13
Kochrezept recipe
Konzentrationslager (KZ), - concentration camp 23
Konzert concert; concerto 7
Kotelett, -s (meat) chop, cutlet 2

Krankenhaus, ˝er hospital 5
Kriegsjahr war year
Krokodil crocodile 11
Kunsthaus, ˝er art museum 16
Kunstmuseum, -museen art museum 14
KZ (= Konzentrationslager), -s concentration camp 23

OTHER

kalt cold (temperature) 5
kämpfen fight 23
kanadisch Canadian 6
kann can (I/he/she/it) 5 »**können**
kaputt broken, out of order 6
katholisch Catholic 10
kaufen buy 8
kein no, none, not any 2
keine mehr no (not any) more 8
kennen (kennt, kannte, gekannt) know, be acquainted with 9
kennen·lernen meet, get acquainted 13
kilometerlang kilometers long 8; **kilometerweit** kilometers away 14

klasse! great, terrific! 19
klassisch classic(al) 19
klein small, little 6
klingen (klingt, klang, geklungen) sound, ring 11
knapp scarce, in short supply; barely (almost not) 19
kochen cook, boil 13 »**gekocht**
Kölner *adj* from Köln 10
komisch funny (odd) 15
kommen (kommt, kam, ist gekommen) come 4
kompliziert complicated 19
können (kann, konnte) can, be able to 6

konnte was able to, could 9 »**können**
könnte could, might be able to 10 »**können**
konservativ conservative 10
kosten (kostet, kostete, gekostet) cost; taste with enjoyment P2
kostenlos free 25
krank sick 13
kühl cool 11
kulturell cultural 24
kurz short, for a short time 14
küssen kiss

L

NOUNS

plural only

Leute people 7

Jaspers, Karl (°1883, †1969), Philosoph — Basel, Hörnlifriedhof

Kafka, Franz (°1883, †1924), Schriftsteller — Prag, Neuer jüdischer Friedhof

der

Laden, ˝ shop, store 19
Langlaufschi, -er cross-country ski 19

Lärm *no pl* noise 12
Lebensraum *no pl* room to live (for a population) 23

Lebensstandard, -s standard of living 22
Lehrling apprentice 25

Lenin Russian revolutionary leader 22

Liebhaber, - enthusiast, fan, lover (of __) 19

die

Lampe lamp 15
Länge length 18
Liebe love 26
Lieblingsfarbe favorite color 18
Linguistik *no pl* linguistics 17

das

Labor, -s laboratory, lab 25
Lamm, ¨er lamb 15
Land, ¨er country, land, nation; province; countryside 14

OTHER

lang long 10
lange for a long time 2 »**wie lange**
lassen (läßt, ließ, gelassen) let, leave, allow; (cause to) have done 13
laufen (läuft, lief, ist gelaufen) run, walk 13
laut loud(ly) 11
leben live, be alive 19
leer empty 20
legen lay, set, or put; **sich hinlegen** lie down 15

Lift (ski) lift; elevator 19
Löffel, - spoon 9
Löwe lion »**Seelöwe**

Linie line; bus or streetcar line 4
Literatur literature 17
Loreley famous Rhine rock 11
Luft, ¨e air, atmosphere 19

Leben, - life 13
Leder *no pl* leather 18 »**Wildleder**
Licht, -er light 25

leicht easy, easily; light 4
leider unfortunately 6
leisten (leistet, leistete, geleistet) do, accomplish, achieve 22
lernen learn 15 »**kennenlernen**
lesen (liest, las, gelesen) read 8
letzt last 13
liberal liberal 10
lieben love; like (something) a lot 3
lieber rather (used with verb); prefer, like __-ing more 11

Luftangriff air raid 23
Luftpostaufkleber, - airmail sticker 12

Luftpost *no pl* airmail 12
Lust, ¨e pleasure, joy; desire; **Lust haben zu** like, be interested in __-ing, want to __ 17

Lieblingswort, ¨er favorite word 23

> Kant, Immanuel (°1724, †1804), Philosoph — Königsberg (Kaliningrad), Dom

liegen (liegt, lag, gelegen) lie (be prone), be situated 13
lila purple 18
links *adv* (to the) left 3; left *adj* **link-**
lohnen (sich) es lohnt sich it's worth it (the effort, doing) 20
los loose; wrong; free; away; Let's go! 13
los·gehen (geht los, ging los, ist losgegangen) get going, start up 13
lustig jolly, merry; fun 21

M ——————————————— 𝔐

NOUNS

der

Magen, - stomach (internal organ) 20; **Magenschmerzen** stomach ache 13
Mai *no pl* May 8
Main the Main River P1
Mann, ¨er man (male person); husband 5
Mantel, ¨ coat; cloak 14
Marienplatz main square in München 16
Marktplatz, ¨e market place 5
März *no pl* March 8

Meister, - master; expert 25
Mensch, -en human being, person 11; **Mensch!** Man! Wow! 10
Militarismus *no pl* militarism 22
Mitarbeiter, - coworker
Mitbürger, - fellow citizen
Mittag noon **zu Mittag essen** eat lunch
Mittwoch Wednesday P2
Moment moment; Wait a moment! 1

Monat month 16
Montag Monday P2
Morgen, - morning P1
Moselwein Moselle wine 20
Müll *no pl* garbage, refuse, trash 15
Münzensammler, - coin collector, numismatist 19
Museumsbesucher, - museum visitor 14

> Karl der Große (°742, †814), König der Franken und römischer Kaiser

NOUNS (cont'd.)

die

Mahlzeit, -en meal (time) 17
Mark, - BRD and DDR currency unit P2
Marke brand, make (of product) 10
Marmelade jam, marmalade 9
Marschmusik *no pl* march music 22
Maschine machine; engine 25
Massenvernichtung, -en mass annihilation 23
Mathematik *no pl* mathematics P1
Mauer, -n wall (external) 8
Meile mile 24
Menge bunch, a lot; amount, quantity; crowd 14

Mensa, Mensen university cafeteria 17
Messe mass (religious service and musical piece) 20; trade fair
Miete rent (payment) 15
Mietfrau, -en landlady
Minute minute 4
Mitte center, middle; **Mitte April** in the middle of April 22
Mittelklassenmahlzeit, -en middle-class meal 17

Mittelschule junior high school 24
Mode fashion(s) 18
Möglichkeit, -en possibility; chance; opportunity 15
Monatskarte monthly pass (for public transit, e.g.) 16
Münze coin 16
Musik *no pl* music 19
Mutter, ⁻ mother 4
Mutti, -s Mom(my) 11

das

Mädchen, - girl 24
Mal time (occurrence, occasion) 11
Maul, ⁻er (animal) mouth, trap; **halt's Maul!** shut up! 26
Messer, - knife 2
Meter, - meter (= 1.1 yard) 3

Mexiko Mexico 17
Mineralwasser *no pl* mineral water 1
Mitglied, -er member (of a group) 19
Mittagessen *no pl* lunch 7

Mittelalter *no pl* Middle Ages 8
Monatsende end of the month 16
Monatsprogramm program for the month (concerts, e.g.) 16
Museum, Museen museum 4
Musical, -s musical show 19

OTHER

Mach schnell! Hurry up! 11
machen do, make; **das macht X** that totals X; **das macht nichts** that's OK 2
Mahlzeit! mealtime greeting 17
mal once, just; **Xmal** Xtime(s): **viermal** four times 3
man one, a person, people, they 7
manch *adj* many (a)
manchmal often 20
marschieren (ist marschiert) march, trot 18
matt matte finish (photo) 25
mehr more 3
mehrere several
meinen mean (intend, imply) 5
meinetwegen OK with me 20
meist most 23; **meistens** mostly 17
melden report officially; declare 18
mich me (*acc, dir, obj*) 7

mieten (mietet, mietete, gemietet) rent 11
mindestens at (the) least, no less than 20
minimal minimal(ly) 25
mißverstehen (mißversteht, mißverstand, mißverstanden) misunderstand 21
mit *dat* with 1; along 6
mit·bringen (bringt mit, brachte mit, mitgebracht) bring, take along 19
miteinander together, with each other 20
mit·fahren (fährt mit, fuhr mit, ist mitgefahren) go along (by vehicle), travel along (with) 18
mit·kommen (kommt mit, kam mit, ist mitgekommen) come along, with

mit·machen participate, take part; go along, have to do with, be associated with 17
mit·nehmen (nimmt mit, nahm mit, mitgenommen) take along, with 11
Mittel- middle ___, central ___; **das Mittelalter** Middle Ages 8
möbliert furnished 17
möchten *present tense only* would like (to) 1
modern modern 8
möglich possible 17
moll minor (musical key) 20
morgen tomorrow »**morgen früh** P2
morgen früh tomorrow morning
müde tired 8
Münchner *adj* from München 13
müssen (muß, mußte) must, have to 5

Kepler, Johannes (°1571, †1630), Astronom — Regensburg, St. Peter-Friedhof; während des 30jährigen Krieges zerstört

Kollwitz, Käthe (°1867, †1945), Grafikerin — Berlin (Ost), Zentralfriedhof Friedrichsfelde

Kopernikus, Nikolaus (°1473, †1543), Astronom — Frauenburg (Dom)

N

NOUNS

der

Nachmittag afternoon; **heute nachmittag** this afternoon 7
Nachteil disadvantage

die

Nacht, ⁻e night 2
Nähe neighborhood, vicinity; nearness **in der Nähe** nearby 8
Natur, -en nature 19
Naturkunde *no pl* natural history

das

Nashorn, ⁻er rhinoceros 11
Nationalmuseum, -museen National Museum 16

Name (last) name P1
Nebel, - fog, mist 9
Nichtraucher, - non-smoker 12

Naturwissenschaft, -en science 17
Nazikatastrophe the Nazi catastrophe 23
Nazizeit *no pl* the Nazi era 22
Neutralität -en neutrality 23

Nichtraucherabteil non-smoking compartment 12

Nord(en) *no pl* (the) north 14
November *no pl* November 8

Nummer, -n number; 2 size (of clothing, shoes, etc.)
Nuß, Nüsse nut 3
Nußtorte nut cake 7

Leibniz, Gottfried Wilhelm von (°1646, †1716), Philosoph — Hannover, Neustädter Kirche

OTHER

na well . . . 6
nach *dat* to, toward, after 3
nachdem *conj* after 23
nachher afterwards 22
nach·schauen check, look up, take a look, have a look 11
nach·sehen (sieht nach, sah nach, nachgesehen) look, check 7
nächst next 3
nachts at night 19
näher closer, nearer 15
naja well now . . . 6
nämlich of course, as you know; you see 17
naß wet 10
natürlich sure, of course, certainly; natural 2
neben *acc/dat* next to 7

nebenan right nearby; next door; in the next room 6
nebeneinander next to each other 20
nehmen (nimmt, nahm, genommen) take 3; **nehmen Sie Platz** sit down, take a seat 4
nein no P1
nett nice, neat; friendly 15
neu new 8
neutral neutral 23
nicht not P2; **noch nicht** not yet 21
nicht (wahr)? *invites agreement* right? Doesn't it? etc. 11
nichts nothing 1
nichts + *adj*-es nothing that is + adj: **nichts Gutes**, etc. 18
nie never 13

nieder down; (in place names) Lower 14
niemand no one 17
noch still, yet 2
noch etwas something else, more 3
noch kein still no 5
noch nicht not yet 8
nördlich northern, (to the) north 14
nordöstlich northeast(ern), (to the) northeast 16
normal normal 25
normalerweise normally, ordinarily 16
Not- emergency (as part of compound) 16
nun now, now then, well 8
nur only, merely; except (that) 2
nur noch just __ (left, remaining) 8

O

NOUNS

der

Ober, - waiter; (direct address) **Herr Ober!** 2
Oktober *no pl* October 8
Onkel, - uncle 11

Opa, -s grandpa 23
Opernkenner, - opera fan 20
Ort place, location; town 16

Ost(en) *no pl* (the) east 14
Ostblockstaat, -en eastern bloc nation 23

O

NOUNS (cont'd.)

die

Oberschule high school 24
Oper, -n opera 8
Opernkasse opera ticket office 8

Orange orange 3
Ordnung *no pl* order; routine; rules
»**in Ordnung** 1

Ostseite East side 10

das

Oberbayern upper Bavaria
(between München and the Alps)
13

Obst *no pl* fruit 6
Opfer, - victim 22
Orgelkonzert organ concert 9

Ostberlin East Berlin 21
Österreich Austria P2
Ostgebiet eastern region(s) 23

OTHER

ob whether, if 16
oben up there, upstairs, above 5
Ober- upper, chief (as part of noun
compounds) 14

oder or 2
öffnen (öffnet, öffnete, geöffnet)
open, unlock 19

oft often; **öfter** more often 17
ohne *acc* without 2
östlich (to the) east 14

P

NOUNS

plural only

Pommes frites French fries 1

> Liebknecht, Karl (°1871, †1919),
> Politiker — Berlin (Ost),
> Zentralfriedhof Friedrichsfelde

> Luther, Martin (°1483, †1546),
> Reformator — Wittenberg,
> Schloßkirche

der

Paprika, -s paprika; pepper
(vegetable) 17
Park, -s park 8
Paß, Pässe passport 1
Paßbeamte passport official (male);
Paßbeamtin (female) 1
Personalausweis ID card 18
Pfennig, - & -e 1/100th of a mark 1
Photoapparat camera (not movie)
14; often spelled **Foto-**

Pionier pioneer 22
Plastikschaum *no pl* styrofoam 12
Platz, ⸚e seat 4; (market) square;
place
Präsident, -en president 26
Preis price 21; prize
Preisunterschied difference in
price 25

Professor, -en professor 6
Prospekt brochure, pamphlet,
leaflet, catalog 14
Proviant *no pl* provisions, supplies
(of food) 3
Pulli (Pullover), Pullis (Pullover)
sweater, pullover 11

die

Partei, -en political party 22
Paßhöhe elevation of a pass 21
Paßkontrolle passport check 1
Pauschalreise package tour 21
Pause intermission, break; rest 20
Person, -en person, human being 3
Pflanze plant 21
Pflege *no pl* care; nursing; attention;
maintenance 23

Pflegewäsche *no pl* delicates,
special-attention laundry 25
Physik *no pl* physics 4
Plastiktasche plastic carrying bag
10
Platte record (music) 10; from **die
Schallplatte**
Politik *no pl* politics 26
Polizei *no pl* police (force) 18

Post *no pl* post office; mail; postal
system 4
Postkarte post card 12
Postleitzahl, -en zip code 12
Postverpackung, -en postal
packing 14
Preislage price range 15
Promenade promenade 8

das

Päckchen, - pack, packet; parcel,
small package 3
Paket package, carton 12

Parkett *no pl* theater stalls, parquet
20
Parkhaus, ⸚er parking structure 16

Pech *no pl* bad luck; **so ein Pech!**
What lousy luck! 18
Pfand, ⸚er deposit 19

Picknick, -s picnic 14
Plakat poster; placard 10
Plastik *no pl* plastic 10
Postpaket mailing carton 12

Praktikum, Praktika practical training, internship 26
Preußen Prussia 14

Problem problem 13
Programm TV channel, radio station 16; program

OTHER

paar »ein paar a few, a couple, some 4; **das Paar** pair, couple
packen pack
Pardon Excuse me 7
parken park 16
passen *dat* fit; suit; be proper 18
passieren (ist passiert) happen, occur 14

per per Luftpost via air mail 12
perfekt perfect 19
planen plan
plötzlich suddenly
politisch political(ly) 23
portugiesisch Portuguese
praktisch practical(ly); almost 15
preiswert reasonable (price) 15

prima! great! 8
privat private(ly) 15
pro per 2
probieren try, have a look at; taste 15
pünktlich on time, punctual 13
putzen clean, polish 15

Q   𝔔

NOUNS

die
Qualität, -en quality 19
Quantität, -en quantity, amount 19

Quittung, -en receipt 6

> Mann, Thomas (°1875, †1955), Schriftsteller — Kilchberg (Kanton Zürich, Schweiz)
>
> Marx, Karl (°1818, †1883), Philosoph und Politiker — London, Friedhof Highgate

das
Quadratmeter, - square meter 15

R   𝔑

NOUNS

der
Rappen, - Swiss coin (1/100 of a Franken) 1
Ratschlag, ̈e (often in pl) advice; tips, hints
Raum, ̈e room; space 23
Regenschirm umbrella 11
Reiche rich person (male) 22
Reichstag *no pl* upper house of German parliament (1871–1945) 22

Reifen, - tire (car, bicycle) 19
Reis *no pl* rice 17
Reiseführer, - travel guide 11
Reiseproviant *no pl* travel food, snacks 3
Reisescheck, -s traveler's check 6
Rentner, - pensioner, retiree 23; **Rentnerin** (female)
Rhein the River Rhine 7

Rheinpark, -s park on the Rhine 7
Rheinwein Rhine wine 20
Riesling *no pl* Riesling (grape or wine) 11
Rotwein red wine 2
Rucksack, ̈e knapsack, backpack 14
Russe Russian (male) 23; **Russin** (female)

die
Radtour, -en bicycle trip 13
Rechnung, -en bill, check 15
Reihe row (seats) 8; turn (to play): **ich bin an der Reihe** it's my turn 15
Reise trip, journey 4; **auf der Reise** traveling
Renovierung, -en renovation, restoration 19
Rente pension (retirement) 23

Restaurierung, -en restoration, renovation 22
Reue *no pl* regret(s)
Rheinbrücke Rhine bridge 11
Rheinfahrt, -en Rhine river boat excursion 11
Richtung, -en direction (e.g., north) 19
Ringstraße beltway, circumferential street 15

Rolltreppe escalator 10
Rose rose (flower) 20
Rosine raisin 6
Rückkehr *no pl* return (from journey)
Ruhe *no pl* rest; (peace &) quiet, peacefulness 13
Ruhestunde quiet hour(s) 13
Rundfahrt, -en tour, excursion 7

R

ᔆ NOUNS (cont'd.)

das

Rathaus, ⸚er city hall 8
Reich empire 22
Reisebüro, -s travel bureau, agency 18

Restaurant, -s restaurant 2
Rheinschiff Rhine excursion boat 10
Rußland Russia 23

Mendelssohn-Bartholdy, Felix (°1809, †1847), Komponist — Berlin (West), Friedhöfe am Hallischen Tor

OTHER

rad·fahren (fährt rad, fuhr rad, ist radgefahren) ride a bicycle 13
rauchen smoke 13
recht- right (hand) 15 »**richtig**
recht very, pretty, quite 18; right, good »**ist recht**
recht haben be right (persons); **du hast recht** you're right 13
rechts to the right, on the right-hand side 3
reden (redet, redete, geredet) talk, speak 13

regnen (regnet, regnete, geregnet) rain 5
reich rich 22
reichen pass (food, etc.), hand 9
reif ripe 20; mature »**vollreif**
reisen (ist gereist) travel 4
relativ relative(ly) 22
renovieren renovate, restore 22
reservieren reserve, book 7
reserviert reserved, booked 7
richtig right, correct 4

romanisch Romanesque (art & architecture style) 8
romantisch romantic 11
römisch Roman 8
rosa pink 5
rot red 5
rufen (ruft, rief, gerufen) call (out); shout; **rufen um** call for 13
ruhig können + ruhig + verb = go ahead and + verb 9; calmly, peacefully 13

S

NOUNS

plural only

Spätzle type of southern German noodle 17

Mozart, Wolfgang Amadeus (°1756, †1791), Komponist — Wien, St. Marxer Friedhof

Nietzsche, Friedrich (°1844, †1900), Philosoph — Röcken (Kreis Weißenfels)

der

Sack, ⸚e sack, bag
Salat salad 1
Sammler, - collector 19
Sammlerwert value to a collector 19
Samstag Saturday P2
Schaffner, - conductor 1
Schalter, - counter, ticket window; light switch 3
Schatz *no pl* treasure; sweetheart, darling 21
Schaum, ⸚e foam, froth 12
Schein bill (money), banknote, certificate 6
Schilling, - *or* **-e** Austrian monetary unit 1
Schlaf *no pl* sleep 13
Schlafsack, ⸚e sleeping bag 13
Schlager, - hit (song) 20

Schlüssel, - key 2; clef
Schmerz, -en pain, ache 13
Schnee *no pl* snow
Schrank, ⸚e cabinet, closet, cupboard 15
Schüler, - student (male); **Schülerin** (female) 17
Schwarztee *no pl* straight tea 9
Schweizer, - Swiss (male); **Schweizerin** (female) 23
Schweizerkäse, - Swiss cheese 3
Seehund seal 11
Seelöwe sea lion 11
Sekretär secretary (male) 22; **Sekretärin** (female)
Sekt German sparkling wine; champagne 11
September *no pl* September 8

Siebziger, - 70 (postage stamp) 12; 1970 (vintage) 20
Sohn, ⸚e son 4
Soldat, -en soldier 22
Sommer, - summer 4
Sommeranzug, ⸚e summer suit 18
Sonderkurs special class 17
Sonderpreis special price 25
Sonnenaufgang, ⸚e sunrise, sunup 19
Sonntag Sunday P2
Sowjet, -s Soviet (citizen) 23
Sozialdemokrat, -en Social Democrat (SPD party member) 23
Spaß *no pl* fun 13; **es macht Spaß** it's fun
Spaziergang, ⸚e stroll, walk 16
Speisewagen, - dining car 12

ᔆ **370** GLOSSARY

Spezialist, -en specialist 13
Sport *no pl* sports, physical training 10; kinds of sports = Sportarten
Sportler, - athlete 10
Staat, -en government; state, nation 17
Staatsfeind enemy of the state 23
Stadtführer, - city guide (book) 8

die

S-Bahn, -en streetcar, suburban/urban train 5
Sache thing, item; situation; affair 13
Salzkartoffel, -n boiled (salted) potatoes 2
Sammlung, -en collection 19
Schallplatte phonograph record 19; »Platte
Scheidung, -en divorce 24
Schiffskapelle ship's orchestra 11
Schlange snake; waiting line 11
Schokolade chocolate(s) 3
Schönheit, -en beauty, loveliness 19
Schule school 17
Schulklasse school class 13
Schulzeit, -en time in school 17
Schweiz *no pl* Switzerland P2
Schwester, -n sister 4
Schwiegermutter, ¨ mother-in-law 24
Schwierigkeit, -en difficulty, trouble 19
See sea, ocean 11
Seife soap 5

das

Salz *no pl* salt 2
Saubermachen *no pl* cleaning (up) 15
Schach *no pl* chess 22
Schauinsland *no pl* mountain near Freiburg 14
Schiff ship, boat 10
Schild, -er sign(post) 8; nameplate, number plate
Schlafraum, ¨e (dormitory-style) sleeping area 13
Schließfach, ¨er baggage locker 15
Schloß, Schlösser castle 11; lock
Schokolandeneis *no pl* chocolate ice cream 7
Schreibwarengeschäft stationery store 24

Stadtpark, -s city park 13
Stadtplan, ¨e city map 7
Stadtteil part, district of a city 15
Staubsauger, - vacuum cleaner 15
Stehplatz, ¨e standing room (tickets) 8
Stein rock, stone 14
Stock, ¨e story, floor 5; stick

Seilbahn, -en gondola, overhead cableway 14
Seite page, side 10
Selbstbedienung *no pl* self-service 25
Seltenheit, -en rarity, rareness 19
Situation, -en situation 1
Socke sock (usually man's) 25
Sonderentwicklung, -en special processing (film) 25
Sonderfahrt, -en special excursion 11
Sonne sun 14
Sonnenbrille sunglasses 18
Soße sauce 21
Spätlese late vintage (wine quality designation) 20
Speise food, fare; dish 12
Spielwarenabteilung, -en toy department 10
Sprache language; speech 1
Sprachgeschichte linguistic history 17
Sprachwissenschaft, -en linguistics 17

Schwimmbad, ¨er swimming pool 7
Seelachsfilet, -s salmon filet 2
Semester, - semester, term 17; quarter = das Quartal
Seminar seminar 17
Sofa, -s sofa, couch 15
Sonderangebot special (offer) 25
Spiel game 10
Spielzeugmuseum, -museen toy museum 16; das Spielzeug toy
Spital, ¨er hospital 23
Sportgeschäft sporting goods store 19
Stadtmuseum, -museen city museum 4

Straßenplan, ¨e street map 16
Strauß, ¨e bouquet, bunch of flowers 26
Strom, ¨e current; electricity 15
Student, -en student 14
Studentenausweis student ID 14
Süd(en) *no pl* (the) south 14
Supermarkt, ¨e supermarket 15

Staatsuniversität, -en state university 17
Stadt, ¨e city 4
Stadtgeschichte city history 14
Stadtmitte city center 7
Stadtrundfahrt, -en round-trip city tour 7
Station, -en station, stop 14
Stelle job 22; place, spot, location
Steuer, -n tax 24
Straße street; block 4
Straßenbahn, -en streetcar 6
Strategie strategy 1
Strecke stretch, section, leg (of a trip) 16
Struktur, -en structure 1
Stube small comfortable room 15
Studentengruppe student organization 25
Stunde hour 1
Stundenkarte transit ticket valid for one hour 6
Synagoge synagogue 7

Stativ tripod 7
Stipendium, Stipendien scholarship 26
Stück, - *or* ¨e piece, unit (note: 2 Stück ___ 2 pieces of ___) 3
Studentendorf, ¨er student residence area 17
Studentenheim dormitory 17
Studium, Studien study/studies, program of study 17
Symbol symbol 22
System system 24

OTHER

saftig juicy 17
sagen say, tell 3
sammeln collect, gather 19
samstags on Saturdays 22
Sankt Saint 8
sauber clean 13
schade too bad, a shame 4
schaffen manage; do 19
scharf sharp, spicy 17
schauen look 10
scheinen (scheint, schien, geschienen) seem; shine 6
schicken send 12
schi·laufen (läuft schi, lief schi, ist schigelaufen) ski, go skiing 19
schlafen (schläft, schlief, geschlafen) sleep 4
schlagen (schlägt, schlug, geschlagen) hit, strike 14
schlau clever, sneaky, wily 16
schlecht bad, poor 9
schließen (schließt, schloß, geschlossen) close, shut 13
schlimm bad, serious; unfortunate 13
schmal narrow 18
schmecken taste (food) 2
schmerzen hurt, ache 13
schnell quick(ly) 7
schnell·machen hurry up 11
schön fine, great, beautiful 2
schon already; really; **schon mal** before 2
schönen Dank thank you (very much) »Dank
schreiben (schreibt, schrieb, geschrieben) write 6
schuld guilty; **schuld sein an**/*dat* be guilty of 23
schwarz black 1
schwarz·fahren (fährt schwarz, fuhr schwarz, ist schwarzgefahren) ride without a valid ticket 16

schwedisch Swedish 17
Schwein haben be lucky, get off easy
schwer heavy 12; hard, difficult
schwimmen (schwimmt, schwamm, ist/hat geschwommen) swim 7
sehen (sieht, sah, gesehen) see 4; understand
sehr very 2
sein (ist, war, ist gewesen) be P1
sein his, its 5
seit *dat* since, for (time span) 13
selber *intensifier* (by) myself, yourself, etc. 11
selbstverständlich obviously, of course, certainly 9
selten seldom, rarely 19
servieren serve (dining) 20
setzen (sich) set, put, place, sit; **setz dich, setzen Sie sich** sit down 14
sich oneself (reflexive) – *dat* and *acc* 16
sicher certain(ly), sure(ly) 10
sind are P2 »**sein**
singen (singt, sang, gesungen) sing 12
sitzen (sitzt, saß, gesessen) sit 7
so OK, now then, that's it, well then; thus(ly); so 1
so . . . wie as . . . as 5
sofort right away, at once, immediately 2
sogar even, in fact
solch such, like that/these etc. 18
sollen (soll, sollte) be supposed to, should really 5
sondern but rather 17
sonnig sunny 10
sonst sonst noch (et)was anything else; **sonst nichts** nothing else 3; or else, otherwise 26
sorgen sorgen für take care of 23
soviel so much 14

soweit so far; as far as 23
sowieso anyway, anyhow 8
sowjetisch Soviet 23
sozialistisch socialist 22
Spaß machen be fun, enjoyable **es macht mir Spaß** I enjoy it; **es macht Spaß** It's fun 13
spät late P2
spätestens at the latest, no later than 19
spielen play 11
sprechen (spricht, sprach, gesprochen) speak, talk 6
springen (springt, sprang, ist gesprungen) jump 11
spülen wash, rinse 13
stammen (aus) date from; arise from, originate in 10
stark strong(ly); severe(ly); heavy, heavily 5
statt instead of 9
statt·finden (findet statt, fand statt, stattgefunden) take place 20
stehen (steht, stand, gestanden) stand 12
stehlen (stiehlt, stahl, gestohlen) steal
steigen (steigt, stieg, ist gestiegen) climb 14
steil steep 21
stellen put, place, position 18; **eine Frage stellen** ask a question
sterben (stirbt, starb, ist gestorben) die 23
stimmen be right, make sense 8; tune (musical instruments)
stören disturb, annoy, bother 7
streng strict, severe 10
studieren study; major in P1
suchen look for, seek 4
südlich southern, southerly 15
süß sweet 11

Ohm, Georg Simon (°1787, †1854), Physiker — München, Südlicher Friedhof

Piscator, Erwin (°1893, †1966), Regisseur — Berlin (West), Waldfriedhof

Planck, Max (°1858, †1947), Physiker — Göttingen, Sadtfriedhof

Porsche, Ferdinand (°1875, †1951), Ingenieur — Zell am See

T

NOUNS

der

Tag day 8 »**Guten Tag**
Tagesausflug, ⸚e day trip, excursion 21
Tee, -sorten tea 1
Teil part, section; share 22
Text text; lyrics 20

Tisch table 7
Tod *no pl* death 24
Tote dead person (male) 23; **die Tote** (female)
Touring-Club, -s travel club 13
Tourist, -en tourist 20

Touristenartikel, - tourist item; souvenir 10
Träger, - baggage carrier 18
Traubensaft, ⸚e grape juice 17
Turm, ⸚e tower 9

die

Tablette pill, tablet 13
Tafel, -n bar (of chocolate, soap) 3; board, display, sign, plaque 10
Tageskarte menu of the day 17
Tagesspezialität, -en today's special 2
Tanne fir tree 14
Tante aunt 23
Tasche satchel, purse, pocket 10
Tasse cup 7

Technik *no pl* technology; engineering 25
Theke counter, bar 15
Tochter, ⸚ daughter 4
Toilette restroom, toilet, bathroom 3
Tour, -en tour, trip, outing 19
Tragetasche tote bag, carrying bag 14

Traube grape 20
Treppe stairs, stairway 5
Turmbesteigung, -en tower climb, ascent 9
Tüte cone (ice cream) 7; small sack, paper bag

Ranke, Leopold von (°1795, †1886), Historiker — Berlin (Ost), Alter Sophienkirchhof

das

T-shirt, -s T-shirt 10
Tagesvisum, -visen 24-hour visa 22
Tal, ⸚er valley 21
Taxi, -s taxi 2

Telefon telephone 5
Theater, - theater 8
Ticket, -s ticket (transportation) 1
Tier animal 11

Tierchen, - little animal 17
Toilettenpapier *no pl* toilet paper 5
Tor gate, gateway; archway 22

OTHER

täglich daily 16
taktvoll tactful(ly)
tanzen dance 7
tatsächlich really, actually; indeed 21
tauschen exchange, swap 20
teilen divide, split
teil·nehmen (nimmt teil, nahm teil, teilgenommen) participate, take part; + **an**/*dat* take part in 19
telefonisch by telephone 20

teuer expensive 2
tief deep 13
Tja Oh well, Gee, Hmm 18
toll fantastic, great, "crazy" 12
tot dead 11
töten (tötet, tötete, getötet) kill 23
totmüde dead tired 13
tragen (trägt, trug, getragen) wear; carry, bear 18
treffen (sich) (trifft, traf, getroffen) meet (by

arrangement) 7; **wir treffen uns später** we'll meet later
trennen separate, divide 25
trinken (trinkt, trank, getrunken) drink 1
trocken dry 11
tun (tut, tat, getan) do, make 25; **(es) tut mir leid** I'm sorry
türkisch Turkish
tut mir leid I'm sorry P2

Rilke, Rainer Maria (°1876, †1926), Schriftsteller — Raron (Kanton Wallis, Schweiz)

Rommel, Erwin (°1892, †1944), Heerführer — Herrlingen (Kr. Ulm)

Röntgen, Wilhelm (°1845, †1923), Physiker — Gießen, Alter Friedhof

Rudolf von Habsburg (°1218, †1291), deutscher König — Speyer, Dom.

Schiller, Friedrich von (°1759, †1805), Schriftsteller — Weimar, Fürstengruft

Schumann, Robert (°1810, †1856), Komponist — Bonn, Alter Friedhof

U

NOUNS

der

Umstand, ⸚e fact, circumstance; trouble

Untermieter, - subletter, subleaser 17

Unterschied difference 24

Urgroßvater, ⸚ great-grandfather 24

Urlaub vacation (from work), holiday 18 »**Ferien**

die

Übernachtung, -en overnight stay 21

Übersee *no pl* overseas 12

Übersetzung, -en translation 20

Übersichtskarte general map

Uhr, -en clock, watch; o'clock P2

Unfähigkeit, -en inability

Unhöflichkeit, -en impoliteness, rudeness 26

Uni, -s university, college 17

Uniform, -en uniform 24

Universität, -en university 17

Unterschrift, -en signature 6

Unterwäsche *no pl* underwear 25

das

Untergeschoß, -geschosse basement, cellar 10

> Schütz, Heinrich (°1585, †1672), Komponist — Dresden, Alte Frauenkirche (um 1725 abgerissen)

> Strauss, Richard (°1864, †1949), Komponist — Garmisch-Partenkirchen, Villa Strauss

OTHER

üben practice, exercise 19

über *acc/dat* over, above, beyond; about, concerning 17

überall everywhere, all over 10

überhaupt at all, of any kind 11

überlegen (sich) consider, reflect (on); **das muß ich mir überlegen** I'll have to think about that 18

übermorgen day after tomorrow 7

übernehmen (übernimmt, übernahm, übernommen) take over, assume

übrigens by the way, incidentally 9

um *acc* around 3; about, concerning

um __ Uhr at __ o'clock 1

um . . . zu in order to . . . 20

um·schauen (sich) look around, browse 18

um·steigen (steigt um, stieg um, ist umgestiegen) transfer (transit) 5

um·ziehen (sich) (zieht um, zog um, umgezogen) change (one's clothes) 20

un- un- 16

unabhängig independent 21

unbedingt certainly, without fail; absolutely 9

und and P1

und so weiter (usw.) and so forth (etc.) 4

unglaublich unbelievable, incredible 23

ungültig invalid, no good 16

unmöglich impossible 17

unnatürlich unnatural 17

unrecht haben be (in the) wrong (of people) 21

unsagbar unspeakable, unutterable

unten down below, downstairs 5

unter *acc/dat* under 15; (in place names) Lower 14

unternehmen (unternimmt, unternahm, unternommen) undertake, do 16

unterschreiben (unterschreibt, unterschrieb, unterschrieben) sign 6

unterwegs on the way, on the road, en route 13

unverschämt shameless, socially unacceptable 26

unverständlich incomprehensible 18

unvorstellbar inconceivable 23

unwichtig unimportant 14

ur- *prefix* first, original, prime(val) »**Urgroßvater**

usw. (und so weiter) etc. (and so forth) 17

V

NOUNS

der

Vater, ⸚ father 4

Verkehr *no pl* traffic; trade, business; dealings 7

Verwandte relative (male); **die Verwandte** (female) 24

Vetter, - cousin (male) 24 »**Kusine**

Vogel, ⸚ bird 11

Vorname first name, given name P1

Vorschlag, ⸚e suggestion, proposal 16

Vorteil advantage

die

Verbindung, -en connection 22
Vergangenheit *no pl* the past 23
Vergrößerung, -en enlargement (photographic), magnification 25
Verkaufsabteilung, -en sales department 26
Verkehrsverbindung, -en connection (transportation)

Verlängerung, -en extension, renewal 21
Verspätung, -en delay 12
Verzeihung *no pl* pardon; **Verzeihung!** pardon me! 12
Viertelstunde quarter-hour 11

Völkerkunde *no pl* ethnology
Volksmusik *no pl* folk music 10
Vorlesung, -en lecture; course 17
Vorstellung, -en performance; idea, notion 8
Vorwahl, -en area code 12

das

Verkehrsamt, ¨er tourist (information) office 9
Verkehrsbüro, -s chamber of commerce; tourist information office 4

Videospiel video game 10
Vierminutenei, -er softboiled egg, 4-minute egg 9
Viertel, - quarter, district; (one) fourth; **Viertel vor drei** 2:45 4

Visum, Visen visa 1
Volk, ¨er people; nation 23
Voralpenland *no pl* Alpine foothills 13

OTHER

verabschieden (sich) say goodbye, take one's leave
verallgemeinern generalize
verboten forbidden, prohibited 22
verbrannt burnt (up) 22 »**verbrennen**
verbrennen (verbrennt, verbrannte, verbrannt) burn (up) 22
verbringen (verbringt, verbrachte, verbracht) spend (time) 19 »**ausgeben**
verdienen earn (money), deserve 22
vereinbaren agree, arrange
verfehlen miss (destination) 21
vergessen (vergißt, vergaß, vergessen) forget 3
vergleichen (vergleicht, verglich, verglichen) compare 20
verhaften (put under) arrest; **verhaftet** under arrest 23
verkaufen sell 14
verlängern lengthen, extend; renew 22
verlassen (verläßt, verließ, verlassen) leave; abandon
verlaufen (sich) (verläuft, verlief, verlaufen) lose one's way (walking) 21

verlegen embarrassed
verlieren (verliert, verlor, verloren) lose 18
verloren lost 18 »**verlieren**
vermieten rent (out) 15; »**mieten**
verpacken pack, wrap up 14
verschieden varied, various; different 20
versichern assure, insure, make sure
versprechen (verspricht, versprach, versprochen) promise; **ich verspreche es dir** I promise you 23
verstehen (versteht, verstand, verstanden) understand 3
versuchen try, attempt 1
vertraut familiar, close, intimate
verwandt related 24
verwechseln mix up, confuse
viel many 3; much 7
vielen Dank thanks a lot, many thanks 3 »**Dank**
vieles much 21
vielleicht maybe, perhaps 6
vielmals a lot, often 3
viermal four times 16

voll full 15
vollreif fully ripe; mature 20; »**reif**
vom (= von dem) of the; from the 7
von *dat* from, of, belonging to 4
vor *acc/dat* before, in front of 4
vor allem above all 19
voraus im voraus in advance 21
vorbei past, gone 23
vorbei·kommen (kommt vorbei, kam vorbei, ist vorbeigekommen) come by (visit) 24
vor·haben (hat vor, hatte vor, vorgehabt) plan (to do something) 19
vorher before, previously 22
vorn(e) in front 7
vor·schlagen (schlägt vor, schlug vor, vorgeschlagen) suggest, propose 14
vorsichtig careful, cautious, circumspect
vor·stellen (sich) introduce 11; **sich** *acc* **vorstellen** introduce oneself 17

Telemann, Georg Philipp (°1681, †1767), Komponist — Hamburg, Grab verschollen

Ulbricht, Walter (°1893, †1973), Politiker — Berlin (Ost), Zentralfriedhof Friedrichsfelde

Valentin, Karl (°1882, †1948), Komiker — Planegg (Kreis München)

Wagner, Richard (°1813, †1883), Komponist — Bayreuth, Park der Villa Wahnfried

Weber, Carl Maria von (°1786, †1826), Komponist — Dresden, Alter katholischer Friedhof

Wilhelm II (°1859, †1941), Kaiser — Doorn (Niederlande)

W

NOUNS

der

Wagen, - car (auto or train) 12
Wald, ⸚er forest, woods 14
Wander-Klub, -s hiking club 19
Wanderweg (hiking) path 14
Wartburg *no pl* kind of automobile 22

Weg way; path 21
Wein wine 2
Weißwein white wine 2
Weltkrieg World War 8
Wert worth, value 19
West(en) *no pl* (the) west 14

Wiener, - wiener (sausage) 17; Viennese 17
Wind wind (weather) 14
Winter, - winter 4
Wunsch, ⸚e wish, desire 9
Wurstsalat sausage salad 2

die

Waffe weapon 26
Währung, -en national currency 22
Wand, ⸚e wall (interior) 18
Wanderung, -en hike, walk 13
Wartezeit, -en wait, waiting period 22
Wäsche *no pl* laundry (clothes) 25
Wäscherei, -en laundry (establishment) 25
Wäschesorte kind of laundry
Wehrmacht *no pl* German imperial army 23

Weinprobe wine-tasting 20
Weißwäsche *no pl* light or white laundry 25
Weltstadt, ⸚e cosmopolitan city 22
Wildspezialität, -en wild game special dish 21
Wirtschaft *no pl* economics; business 26
Wissenschaft, -en academics, science (not just physical sciences) 17

Woche week 8
Wochenendreise weekend trip 21
Wochenkarte weekly ticket (bus, etc.) 16
Wohngemeinschaft, -en apartment collective, commune 17
Wohnung, -en apartment, home, dwelling 15
Wolke cloud 14
Wurst, ⸚e sausage 1; »Bratwurst

das

Wasser *no pl* water »Mineralwasser
Weinfest wine festival 20
Weinglas, ⸚er wine glass 10
Wetter *no pl* weather 9

Wildleder *no pl* deerhide, suede 18 »Leder
Wochenende weekend 19

Wort word (in context); plural ⸚er in the sense of individual unrelated words 13

OTHER

wählen dial 12; choose; elect 26
wahr true 11
während while, during 20
wahrscheinlich probably 8
wandern (ist gewandert) hike, walk 7
wann when (in questions) 1
war was P2 »sein
wär- would be 12
warm warm 14
warten (wartet, wartete, gewartet) wait 5 **warten auf** *acc* wait for
warum why 2
was what P1; **(et)was** something
was für what kind of 14
waschen (wäscht, wusch, gewaschen) wash 25
wechseln (ex)change 6
weg away, off, gone 7

wegen because of, due to 20
weg·fahren (fährt weg, fuhr weg, ist weggefahren) leave, go away (vehicular) 7
weg·gehen (geht weg, ging weg, ist weggegangen) go away 22
weh tun *dat* **(tut weh, tat weh, wehgetan)** ache, hurt 13
weichgekocht softboiled 9
weil because, since 13
weiß (I) know, (he/she) knows P2 »wissen
weiß white 5
weit far 4
weiter furthermore; farther 3
weiter- ___ further, continue to ___ 21
welch which 10
wem *dat* (to, for) whom 22

wen *acc* whom 22
wenig little; few *pl*; **ein wenig** a little 13
weniger less, fewer 15
wenn if; when, whenever 5
wer who, whoever P1
werden (wird, wurde, ist geworden) become 13
werfen (wirft, warf, geworfen) throw 11
westlich west(ern) 14
wichtig important 19
wie how P1; like, as
Wie heißen Sie? What is your name? P1
Wie ist der Name? What is your name? P1
wie lange how long 2
wie viele how many 7

wieder again; back 4

wieder·geben (gibt wieder, gab wieder, wiedergegeben) give back, return 12

wieder·hören short form of »**Auf Wiederhören** 15

wieder·sehen (sieht wieder, sah wieder, wiedergesehen) see again 23

wiegen (wiegt, wog, gewogen) weigh 12

wieso why, how come 14

wieviel how much P2

Wieviel Uhr ist es? What time is it? P2

willkommen welcome 19

wird present tense of »**werden**

wirklich really 8

wissen (weiß, wußte, gewußt) know (facts) 4

wissenschaftlich scholarly, scientific, academic 17

wo where P2

woher where from, whence »**wohin**

wohin where to, whither 3

wohl well, good; probably, likely 2

wohnen live (reside) 24

wollen (will, wollte) want (to) 6

womit with what 18

wunderbar great, fine, wonderful 2

wunderschön beautiful 13

wünschen wish 16

würde would (conditional, not habitual) 15 »**werden**

wurde past tense of **werden** 23

Z _____ ᛜ

NOUNS

der _____

Zahn, ⸚e tooth 11

Zettel, - slip of paper; note 15

Zimmerschlüssel, - room key (hotel) 11

Zirkus, -se circus 7

Zivildienst *no pl* alternate service 17

Zivilist, -en civilian 23

Zoll, ⸚e customs, duty 20

Zoo, -s zoo 4

Zug, ⸚e train 3

Zuschlag, ⸚e surcharge, extra charge 21

Zwanziger, - 20 (banknote or stamp) 12

die _____

Zahl, -en number, count (of objects); figure; numeral »**Postleitzahl**

Zahlung, -en payment 22

Zeit, -en time 7

Zeitschrift, -en magazine, journal 6

Zeitung, -en newspaper 6

Zigarette cigarette 20

Zimmervermittlung, -en room-finding service 15

Zone zone 8

Zugreise train trip 21

das _____

Zeichen, - sign, symbol

Zentrallabor, -s central laboratory 25

Zeug *no pl* stuff, gear, things; clothes 18

Zimmer, - room 2

> Zeiss, Carl (°1816, †1888), Optiker — Jena, Alter Friedhof
>
> Zeppelin, Ferdinand Graf von (°1838, †1917), Erfinder — Stuttgart — Pragfriedhof

OTHER

z.B. (= zum Beispiel) for example 18

zahlen pay 2

zeigen show, indicate 15

zerstören destroy 24

zerstört destroyed 8

ziemlich rather, quite 11

zirka circa, about 19

zu *dat* to, at; too; shut, closed 1

zu Fuß on foot 4

zuerst first *adv*; first of all; at first 7

zufrieden contented, satisfied 23

zu·hören listen to 23

Zum Wohl Cheers! Here's mud in your eye! 2

zum (= zu dem) to; to (the) 2

zu·machen shut (door, etc.) 19

zur (= zu der) to the 8

zurück back, change (money) 1

zurück·bringen (bringt zurück, brachte zurück, zurückgebracht) bring back, return 25

zurück·fahren (fährt zurück, fuhr zurück, ist zurückgefahren) return, go back 14

zurück·kehren (ist zurückgekehrt) return, come back

zurück·kommen (kommt zurück, kam zurück, ist zurückgekommen) return, come back 12

zusammen together 2

zu·teilen allocate, allot

zuviel too much 3

zweimal two (of something), twice, two orders of __ 2

zweit- second 5

zweitens secondly, in the second place 26

zwischen *acc/dat* between 15

Photo Credits

Chapter Twenty

p. 200: (top left and bottom right) Keystone/The Image Works, (top right) Beryl Goldberg; p. 206: (center right) Fritz Henle/ Photo Researchers, (top left and bottom right) German Information Center.

Chapter Twenty-One

p. 210: (top left) Ulrike Welsch/Stock, Boston, (top right) René Burri/Magnum Photos, (bottom left) Keystone/The Image Works, (bottom right) Peter Menzel; p. 216: (top) Christa Armstrong/Photo Researchers, (center left) German Information Center, (center right) Beryl Goldberg, (bottom right) Uta Hoffmann; p. 219: Christa Armstrong/Photo Researchers.

Chapter Twenty-Two

p. 220: (top) Ulrike Welsch, (center) Beryl Goldberg, (bottom) German Information Center; p. 221: German Information Center; p. 226: (top left) Keystone/The Image Works, (top right) Ulrike Welsch/Stock, Boston, (center) Beryl Goldberg.

Chapter Twenty-Three

p. 230: (top left) Beryl Goldberg, (top right) Ulrike Welsch; p. 231: Uta Hoffmann; p. 234: From Meyers Großes Personenlexikon Mannheim: Bibliographisches Institut,

1968; p. 236: (top) Martine Franck/Magnum Photos, (bottom right) German Information Center.

Chapter Twenty-Four

p. 240: Keystone/The Image Works; p. 246: (top right) Ulrike Welsch, (bottom) Peter Menzel.

Chapter Twenty-Five

p. 255: (top) Jan Lukas/Photo Researchers, (bottom left and right) Beryl Goldberg; p. 256: Beryl Goldberg.

Chapter Twenty-Six

p. 260: (top right) Christa Armstrong/Photo Researchers, (bottom right) Ulrike Welsch; p. 266: (top) Ulrike Welsch, (center) Katrina Thomas/Photo Researchers; p. 272: Uta Hoffmann; p. 273: Beryl Goldberg.

Feste und Feiertage

p. 274: Ulrike Welsch; p. 275: (bottom) Owen Franken/Stock, Boston; p. 277: (center) Owen Franken/Stock, Boston; p. 281: (left) Ulrike Welsch; p. 282: Martine Franck/Magnum Photos.

All other photos and authentic materials provided by the authors.

Index

*BW = Bildwörterbuch

Participles of Common Irregular Verbs

note verbs that take *sein*

bleiben	ich bin geblieben
bringen	ich habe gebracht
denken	ich habe gedacht
essen	ich habe gegessen
fahren	ich bin gefahren
finden	ich habe gefunden
fliegen	ich bin geflogen
geben	ich habe gegeben
gehen	ich bin gegangen
helfen	ich habe geholfen
kennen	ich habe gekannt
kommen	ich bin gekommen
lesen	ich habe gelesen
nehmen	ich habe genommen
schlafen	ich habe geschlafen
schreiben	ich habe geschrieben
sehen	ich habe gesehen
sein	ich bin gewesen
sprechen	ich habe gesprochen
trinken	ich habe getrunken
tun	ich habe getan
verstehen	ich habe verstanden
werden	ich bin geworden
wissen	ich habe gewußt

Past Tenses of Common Verbs

sein	war
haben	hatte-
können	konnte-
müssen	mußte-
sollen	sollte-
wollen	wollte-
dürfen	durfte-
sagen	sagte-
glauben	glaubte-
wissen	wußte-
hören	hörte-
denken	dachte-
fragen	fragte-
kommen	kam
gehen	ging
sehen	sah
nehmen	nahm
werden	wurde

Verb-Last (Subordinating) Conjunctions and Word Order

"Verb-Last" Conjunctions

daß

weil

wenn *means "if," "when," "whenever"*
   in questions: When? – Wann?

als   *"when" for one-time-only events in the past*
   Als ich 4 Jahre alt war . . .

bevor

the verb that takes *endings* comes *last*

single verb   wenn du den Dom <u>siehst</u>
modal + verb   wenn du den Dom sehen <u>mußt</u>
present perfect   wenn du den Dom gesehen <u>hast</u>

Sentences beginning with a subordinate clause still follow the basic principle: the conjugated verb of the main clause appears in <u>second</u> position.

Wenn du den Dom gesehen hast, (dann) <u>können</u> wir gehen.

_____ _____/
                    1   2

Past Tense Forms of Regular and Irregular Verbs

	singular			plural	
	present	past		present	past
ich	sage	sagte	wir	sagen	sagten
du	sagst	sagtest	ihr	sagt	sagtet
Sie	sagen	sagten	Sie	sagen	sagten
er/sie/es	sagt	sagte	sie	sagen	sagten
ich	komme	kam	wir	kommen	kamen
du	kommst	kamst	ihr	kommt	kamt
Sie	kommen	kamen	Sie	kommen	kamen
er/sie/es	kommt	kam	sie	kommen	kamen

Common Verbs Used with *sein*

aufstehen
aussteigen
bleiben
einsteigen
fahren
fliegen
gehen
reisen
sein
sterben
umsteigen
werden

Subjunctives

Present tense – *ich* forms

	sein	haben	können	müssen	wollen	sollen
fact	bin	habe	kann	muß	will	soll
unreal/polite	**wäre**	**hätte**	**könnte**	**müßte**	**wollte**	**sollte**

general pattern: würde- + infinitive

Wenn Sie . . . sagen würden
{
If you would say/be saying
If you said
If you did say
If you were to say
If you were (to be) saying
}

Past tense – the pattern must include either *hätte* or *wäre*

hätte- {
gesagt *had said, would have said*
had been saying, would have been saying
sagen sollen *should have said/been saying*
}

wäre- {
gewesen *had been, would have been*
gegangen *had gone, would have gone/been going*
}

Passive – forms of *werden* + participle

Die Filme <u>werden</u> **entwickelt**.
   The films are (being) developed.
   The films will/are going to be developed.
Die Filme <u>wurden</u> **entwickelt**.
   The films were (being) developed.
Sie <u>müssen</u> **entwickelt** <u>werden</u>.
   They (will) have to be developed.
Sie <u>mußten</u> **entwickelt** <u>werden</u>.
   They had to be developed.
Sie <u>müßten</u> **entwickelt** <u>werden</u>.
   They would have to be developed.
Sie <u>hätten</u> **entwickelt** <u>werden müssen</u>.
   They would have had to be developed.
Sie <u>hätten</u> **entwickelt** <u>werden sollen</u>.
   They should have been developed.